Legal Aid Handbook

The Legal Action Group is a national, independent charity which campaigns for equal access to justice for all members of society. Legal Action Group:
- Strengthens the voice of people and communities denied access to justice
- Supports frontline charities, lawyers and advisers to deliver access to justice
- Influences law and policy to improve access to justice and create a fair legal system for all.

Legal Aid Handbook 2024/25

The 2024 Standard Civil Contract and the 2025 Standard Crime Contract

Edited by Vicky Ling, Sue James and Simon Mullings

LAG
the access to
justice charity

This edition published in Great Britain 2025
by LAG Education and Service Trust Limited
Gatehouse Chambers, 1 Lady Hale Gate, London WC1X 8BS

www.lag.org.uk

© Legal Action Group 2025

While every effort has been made to ensure that the details in this text are correct, readers must be aware that the law changes and that the accuracy of the material cannot be guaranteed, and the author and the publisher accept no responsibility for any loss or damage sustained.

The rights of the authors to be identified as author of this work has been asserted by them in accordance with the Copyright, Designs and Patents Act 1988.

All rights reserved. No part of this publication may be reproduced, stored in a retrieval system or transmitted in any form or by any means, without permission from the publisher.

British Library Cataloguing in Publication Data
A CIP catalogue record for this book is available from the British Library.

Crown copyright material is produced with the permission of the Controller of HMSO and the King's Printer for Scotland.

This book has been produced using Forest Stewardship Council (FSC) certified paper. The wood used to produce FSC certified products with a 'Mixed Sources' label comes from FSC certified well-managed forests, controlled sources and/or recycled material.

print 978-1-913648-68-8
ebook 978-1-913648-69-5
bundle (print and ebook) 978-1-913648-70-1

Typeset by Refinecatch Limited, Bungay, Suffolk
Printed in Great Britain by Hobbs the Printers, Totton, Hampshire

This book is dedicated to the memory of Andrew Wilson (1953–2001) and of Simon Mullings (1967–2024). Both were fine lawyers who believed passionately in justice for all, fought tenaciously for their clients, and inspired all who worked with them.

Preface

Legal aid matters. It is a public service critical to ensuring the fairness of the justice system – but it is currently not sustainable. The Handbook grows in size as the legal aid scheme becomes more complicated, yet the funding for civil legal aid has not increased since 1996. We can think of no other public service where rates of pay have actually reduced (with a 10% cut with the enactment of LASPO). Inadequate increases have been made to some crime fees but the Ministry of Justice has still not responded to the Law Society's successful judicial review for failure to increase them across the board by 15% as recommended by the Independent Review of Criminal Legal Aid in December 2021. It has now reached crisis point. Immediate investment is needed in both the civil and criminal legal aid schemes.

We said in the last two editions that legal aid lawyers do a difficult job in difficult circumstances – but we know it continues to get harder. Recruitment is increasingly challenging and large areas of England and Wales are struggling to find legal aid practitioners, leaving deserts and droughts of provision. The justice system in England and Wales cannot function effectively without a sustainable legal aid profession. Something has to change.

That said, we would like to acknowledge the commitment and resourcefulness of the legal aid practitioners still working in these difficult circumstances. We hope this Handbook will continue to be a tool you use time and time again to ensure your clients can seek redress and you also get paid for the work you do.

In this edition, we are pleased to be joined by Carita Thomas, Jamila Duncan-Bosu and Jonathan Wilson as new contributors, as well as retaining the expertise of our excellent regular contributors. Your breadth of knowledge is inspiring. Thank you all for being part of the Handbook team.

We are also joined by LAG's new publisher, Helen Vaux, who has brilliantly steered this Handbook to publication with her usual calmness and good humour. Thank you, Helen!

Our new co-editor, Simon Mullings, brought his incredible legal aid knowledge and practice to this edition. We were thrilled that he agreed to join us. His commitment and dedication to legal aid work was exceptional. He will be greatly missed.

We would like to express our huge thanks to Matt Howgate who not only stepped in at the last minute to ensure the accuracy of the HLPAS section in Chapter 11 but did so with kindness and sensitivity. Matt's support and thoughtfulness is a perfect example of the compassionate community that pervades the legal aid sector.

We have endeavoured to give as complete an account of the legal aid scheme as at 1 September 2024 (when the new civil contract commenced) as we can. Any errors or omissions are, of course, our responsibility.

Comments and contributions are always welcome. We want the *Legal Aid Handbook* to be practical and relevant. Readers can contact us via Legal Action Group at lag@lag.org.uk. Without legal aid there is no access to justice.

Vicky Ling and Sue James

November 2024

Contributors

Vicky Ling is a Chartered Quality Professional and management consultant. Vicky worked for the Legal Aid Board in the early 1990s at the inception of 'franchising', has experience of managing organisations with legal aid contracts and has written and lectured extensively on legal aid practice management. Vicky is a founder member of the Law Consultancy Network, an international team of highly experienced law firm management consultants and is a consultant with Infolegal, providing compliance and practice advice. She has advised hundreds of firms of solicitors and not for profit organisations on all aspects of legal aid contracts and quality standards.

Sue James is chief executive of Legal Action Group. She was formerly director and solicitor at Hammersmith and Fulham Law Centre and a specialist in housing law. In 2017 she won the Legal Aid Lawyer of the Year Outstanding Achievement Award. She is a founding trustee of Ealing Law Centre and North Wales Community Law and chair of the Renters Reform Coalition. Sue is co-author of *Housing Possession Duty Desk: a practical guide*, co-editor of the *Legal Aid Handbook, Justice Matters* and *Legal Aid Matters* and a contributor to *Access to Justice in Rural Communities – Global Perspectives*. Sue is currently a PhD candidate at Cardiff University and writes and campaigns on housing, legal aid and access to justice issues.

Simon Mullings was housing team leader at Hammersmith and Fulham Law Centre and former co-chair of the Housing Law Practitioners' Association. His work included homelessness challenges, possession proceedings, including extensive court duty desk experience, unlawful eviction, and housing-related public law and Equality Act cases. In 2021 he won the Legal Aid Lawyer of the Year Award for social welfare law. Simon served as a trustee at Newham Rights Centre, Waltham Forest Citizens Advice and Ealing Law Centre where he was among the founders. He was co-author of *Housing Possession Duty Desk: a practical guide*, co-editor of *Justice Matters* and *Legal Aid Matters*. Simon was a passionate advocate, campaigner and speaker on housing law, legal aid and access to justice issues and wrote regularly for Legal Action Group.

Itpal Dhillon is a criminal solicitor with over 20 years' experience. She is a Senior Crime Supervisor at Bindmans LLP. Prior to this, she was Partner and Head of the Criminal Department at ITN Solicitors. She specialises in defending the most serious and complex criminal cases, including terrorism, murder, drug trafficking and firearms-related offences. She also has extensive experience in dealing with business frauds, money laundering and complex confiscation. She has been listed in the Legal 500 on numerous occasions and has been described as 'very impressive and a notable terrorism specialist'.

Jamila Duncan-Bosu is an employment solicitor, specialising in obtaining compensation for victims of trafficking and modern slavery. She has a particular interest in ensuring access to justice, bringing a number of challenges to the legal aid scheme to ensure those suffering labour abuse and exploitation have access to public funding. Jamila is a founding member of the Anti Trafficking and Labour Exploitation Unit (ATLEU), the only UK charity providing holistic legal representation to survivors of trafficking and modern slavery.

Daniel Grütters is a civil and public law barrister at One Pump Court Chambers. He specialises in civil claims against public authorities, inquests, housing and immigration. Before moving to the Bar, he was an international law adviser at the British Red Cross.

Hilton von Herbert is an IAAS Accredited Supervisor and Level 3 Advanced Immigration Caseworker. His experience in legal aid immigration practice exceeds 20 years. For a period of 10 years, he was also a trainer in Immigration, Asylum and Nationality law for Citizens Advice Bureaux throughout the Cambridge and Hertfordshire region. In 2013, Hilton was awarded the Legal Aid Lawyer of the Year award in the Immigration category. 2014 saw his appointment as an Independent Funding Adjudicator, followed by his appointment as an Independent Costs Assessor. He is currently the Immigration Supervisor at Ealing Law Centre.

Paul Keeley is a solicitor at South West London Law Centres, a community-based charity that helps local people access justice and uphold their rights. Paul specialises in immigration and asylum. Paul was an Independent Funding Adjudicator and Independent Costs Assessor for the Ministry of Justice between 2016 and 2024. In that role, Paul adjudicated on appeals by legal aid providers against decisions of the Legal Aid Agency. In May 2018, Paul was appointed as an Independent Peer Reviewer, also for the Ministry of Justice, a role in which he assesses the quality of legal advice of immigration legal aid providers. Paul also works as a Legal Contractor, on a freelance basis, for Freedom from Torture, advising doctors on the preparation of medico-legal reports.

Samantha Little is a Consultant at Russell-Cooke Solicitors. She has specialised in Children Law since 1994 and has been a Law Society Children Panel member since 1998. Samantha is a Resolution accredited specialist in public law, private law and adoption. She has Higher Courts (Civil Proceedings) advocacy rights and is an experienced advocate, representing children (directly and through their guardians), parents and family members in court. She advises and represents clients in all aspects of public and private children law. In public law, she has a particular interest in assisting kinship carers. Samantha also advises in all aspects of adoption law, including domestic and international adoption, with a particular interest in Hague Convention adoptions from the UK to the US. She has advised and represented many foster carers and prospective adopters as they navigate adoption applications and support packages. She has experience of family creation, surrogacy (domestic and international) and declaration of parentage cases. Samantha is an active member of Resolution and is a long standing member of their Legal Aid Committee. She has engaged on Resolution's behalf with a number of consultations with the Legal Aid Agency and Ministry of Justice about legal aid issues. She provides training for Resolution. Samantha is also a member of the Association of Lawyers for Children and has co-presented a legal aid update at the ALC conference for a number of years.

Silvia Nicolaou Garcia is an associate solicitor at Bindmans' Public Law and Human Rights team, where she specialises in public law, human rights and community care cases. She has a particular interest in assisting trafficked individuals, unaccompanied minors and vulnerable adults. In 2019, Silvia completed a secondment with the Helen Bamber Foundation, where she was a Specialist Counter-Trafficking Legal Officer. She was appointed as an Independent Funding Adjudicator and Independent Costs Assessor for the Ministry of Justice in

2019. Silvia is a regular contributor to *Legal Action*. In 2017 and 2018, Silvia was nominated for two national awards (Junior Lawyer of the Year at the Law Society Excellence Awards 2017 and Children's Rights Lawyer at the Legal Aid Lawyer of the Year Awards 2018). In 2018, she received the ECPAT UK Children's Champion Award.

Paul Seddon is a regulated costs lawyer and owner of Seddon Costs Law with a wide range of clients, including private law firms and law centres. Paul has practised costs law for over 20 years. He spent many years working in-house at law firms in London where he trained as a law costs draftsman before qualifying as a costs lawyer. Paul has been chair and vice-chair of the Association of Costs Lawyers legal aid group since 2013, representing the group on the LAA's Civil Contract consultative group. He is also a member of the LAPG's advisory committee. He authors and delivers training to solicitors, barristers and fellow costs professionals on key aspects of procedure and caselaw and drafted the Bar Council's guidance *Claiming enhancements for civil (non-family) legal aid work*.

Carita Thomas is an immigration solicitor at the Anti Trafficking and Labour Exploitation Unit (ATLEU). She has worked in legal aid since 2006, training and practising at Howells LLP before moving to ATLEU in 2015. She is an immigration legal aid supervisor and Head of Legal Practice at ATLEU.

Jonathan Wilson is a consultant solicitor at Campbell Law Solicitors and runs Mental Health Law Online (www.mentalhealthlaw.co.uk). He co-authored *Mental Health Tribunals: Law, Policy and Practice* (Law Society, 2013) and writes mental health law update articles for *Legal Action* magazine.

Contents

Preface   vii
Contributors   ix
Table of cases   xix
Table of statutes   xxiii
Table of statutory instruments   xxxi
Table of EU and international legislation   xliii
Abbreviations   xlv
Glossary   li

Part A: Legal aid advice and litigation   1

1 **Legal aid: what you need to know at a glance   3**
   Introduction   5
   How legal aid works   6
   The LAA documentation   10
   Keeping up to date   10
   Civil and family – key documentation   11
   Criminal defence – key documentation   15
   Client and Cost Management System   17
   Training and support   17
   Legal challenges   21
   Logos   23
   Legal aid support on X (formerly Twitter)   23
   Legal Aid Agency's coronavirus responses   23

2 **Taking on civil and family cases   25**
   Introduction   27
   Scope of the scheme   27
   Scope of contracts   36
   Financial eligibility   39
   Reassessment of means   49
   Merits tests   50
   Other restrictions on taking on cases   50
   Permitted work   52

3　Exceptional case funding　55
Introduction　58
When should non-inquest ECF be available: *Gudanaviciene*　60
The operation of the non-inquest ECF scheme – *IS*　61
The Lord Chancellor's Guidance: non-inquest ECF　63
Some recent cases　67
Changes ahead　68
Inquest ECF　69
Application process: non-inquest and inquest ECF　72

4　Conducting a civil/family case　81
Introduction　85
Legal Help　86
Disbursements　97
Help at Court　99
Help with Family Mediation　101
Ending a case　101
Legal aid representation certificates　104
CCMS and forms　117
Refusals and appeals　118
Funding　118
Urgent cases　130
Delegated functions　132
Very expensive cases/special case work　134

5　Client and Cost Management System　139
Introduction　141
The logic of CCMS　142
How to use CCMS in your practice　144
Who does what within CCMS?　145
What application should you make?　150
Billing through CCMS　163
Contingency plans if CCMS is not available　165
Technical difficulties　166

6　Conducting a family private law case　167
Introduction　170
Scope of the scheme　171
Private family law – controlled work　180
Help with Family Mediation　188
Certificates – private family law　189

7　Conducting a family public law case　201
Introduction　203
What is public family law?　203

Public family law – controlled work 206
Certificates – public law cases 210

8   Family mediation 217
Introduction 219
Scope of the scheme 219
Contract 220
Financial eligibility 221
Merits test 221
Forms 222
Funding 222

9   Conducting immigration and asylum cases 223
Introduction 227
What immigration work is in scope of legal aid? 228
Definition of an immigration or an asylum matter 240
Who can carry out the work? 242
Structure of immigration work 245
Conducting the case 254
Managing costs 259
Licensed work 260

10   Conducting a mental health case 263
Introduction 265
What is mental health work? 266
Overview 267
Levels of funding 269
Operating under standard fees 273
Escape fee cases 275
Separate matters 276
Disbursements 277
Licensed work 277
Contact with the LAA 278

11   Conducting a housing case 279
Introduction 282
What housing work is in the scope of legal aid? 283
Housing Loss Prevention Advice Service (HLPAS) 302

12   Conducting a community care case 309
Introduction 311
What is community care law? 311
What community care law is within the scope of legal aid? 312
Who can do community care law? 313
Levels of funding for community care work 313
How to conduct a community care case 315

13 Conducting a public law case 323
Introduction 324
Public law and judicial review 325
Overlaps between categories 325
What public law work is within the scope of legal aid? 326
Who can do public law? 331
Levels of funding for public law work 331
Common reasons for refusal of funding in legal aid cases 333
How to conduct a public law case 334

14 Conducting a criminal case 339
Introduction 342
General rules 343
Work in the investigations class 346
Work in the proceedings class 362
Appeals and reviews 386
Prison law work 388
Associated civil work 392
Very High Cost Cases 392

15 Getting paid for civil and family work 393
Introduction 397
Terms of assessment and guidance 400
Exceptional case funding 401
Disbursements 402
Controlled work 406
Legal aid representation certificates 408
Recoupment and limitation 437
Pro bono costs orders 438
Family 440
Immigration and asylum 453

16 Getting paid for criminal work 463
Introduction 466
Remuneration Regulations 467
Investigations class work 469
Payment rates and escape fee cases 473
Proceedings class work 477
Standard fees 478
The claiming process 487
Crown Court – litigator fees 488
Crown Court – advocates' fees 490
Very High Cost Cases 491
Topping up criminal legal aid fees 491

17 Appeals to Independent Funding Adjudicators and Costs Assessors in civil cases 493
Introduction 495
When might you need to appeal? 496
Appeals to Independent Funding Adjudicators 496
Nil assessment appeals in controlled work cases 502
Appeals to Independent Costs Assessors 504
Special casework decisions 506
Family mediation 506
Further challenges 506

Part B: Legal aid advocacy 507

18 Advocacy in civil cases 509
Introduction 511
General principles 511
Help at Court 512
Controlled Legal Representation 515
Representation certificates 515
Payment for advocacy services 516

19 Advocacy in family cases 523
Introduction 524
Merits test 526
Family cases started prior to 9 May 2011 526
Family cases started on or after 9 May 2011 527

20 Advocacy in criminal cases 545
Introduction 546
Funding 547
Advocacy assistance – investigations stage 548
Advocacy assistance – court duty solicitor 550
Advocacy under a representation order 553
Appeals 558
Advocacy assistance – prison law 559

Part C: Managing legal aid work 561

21 Legal aid contracts 563
Introduction 567
Standard Civil Contract 567
Standard Crime Contract 567
Elements of the contracts 568
Applying for civil or family contracts 578
Tenders 580
Applying for crime contracts 581

The Public Defender Service   581
Crime – Very High Cost Case accreditation   581
Community Legal Advice services   582
Other kinds of contract with the LAA   582

22 Quality standards and performance monitoring   583
Introduction   585
Practice management and quality of advice standards   586
Specialist Quality Mark   587
Lexcel   590
Supervisors   591
Peer review   600
Key performance indicators   606
Service standards   609
Covid-19 arrangements – civil and crime   614

23 Financial and contract management   617
Introduction   619
Payment for civil controlled work and crime lower   620
Reconciliation of contracts   621
Payments on account   623
Key performance indicators   625
Service standards   625
Costs audits   625
Contract notices   629

APPENDICES   633

A **Legal Aid, Sentencing and Punishment of Offenders Act 2021 Sch 1**   635

B **Standard Civil Contract 2024 Category Definitions**   669

C **Civil costs: what you can claim for**   683

D **Criminal costs: what you can claim for**   691

E **Standard monthly payment reconciliation process**   697

Index   699

Table of cases

A Local Authority v DS [2012] EWHC 1442 (Fam), [2012]
1 WLR 3098, [2012] 5 WLUK 970, [2013] 1 FLR 1429,
[2012] Fam Law 1078 ..... 15.18
Airey v Ireland (Application No A/32) [1979] 10 WLUK
79, (1979–80) 2 EHRR 305, ECtHR 3.7
Brown v Haringey LBC [2015] EWCA Civ 483, [2017] 1
WLR 542, [2016] 4 All ER 754, [2015] 5 WLUK 357,
[2015] HLR 30 ..... 14.87, 15.65
CH v CT (committal: appeal) [2018] EWHC 1310 (Fam),
[2018] 4 WLR 122, [2018] 5 WLUK 515, [2019] 1 FLR 700 ..... 14.87
Children Act 1989 (taxation of costs), Re [1994] 8 WLUK
116, [1994] 2 FLR 934, [1995] 1 FCR 688, [1995] Fam
Law 126, (1995) 159 LG Rev 809, (1994) *Times*,
October 21, FD 15.69
Crane v Canons Leisure Centre [2007] EWCA Civ 1352,
[2008] 1 WLR 2549, [2008] 2 All ER 931, [2007] 12
WLUK 554, [2008] CP Rep 15, [2008] 1 Costs LR 132,
(2008) 105(1) LSG 23, (2008) 158 NLJ 103, (2008)
Times, January 10 ..... 15.108
Devon CC v Kirk [2016] EWCA Civ 1221, [2017] 4 WLR
36, [2016] 12 WLUK 91 ..... 14.87
Director of Legal Aid Casework v R (Sisangia) [2016] EWCA
Civ 24, [2016] 1 WLR 1373, [2016] 1 WLUK 487 ..... 2.10
Haji-Ioannou v Frangos [2006] EWCA Civ 1663, [2008] 1
WLR 144, [2007] 3 All ER 938, [2006] 12 WLUK 85, [2007]
CP Rep 14, [2007] 2 Costs LR 253, (2006) 156 NLJ 1918 ..... 15.127
Hanlon v Law Society [1981] AC 124, [1980] 2 WLR 756,
[1980] 2 All ER 199, [1980] 5 WLUK 6, (1980) 124 SJ
360, HL 4.161
Harold v Smith (1860) 157 ER 1229, (1860) 5 Hurl & N
381, [1860] 1 WLUK 16, Exch 15.119
IS v Director of Legal Aid Casework and Lord Chancellor
[2016] EWCA Civ 464, [2016] 1 WLR 4733, [2017] 2 All
ER 642, [2016] 5 WLUK 468, [2016] 3 Costs LR 569,
[2016] 2 FLR 392, [2016] Fam Law 959; *Reversing* [2015]
EWHC 1965 (Admin), [2015] 1 WLR 5283, [2015] 7
WLUK 481, [2015] ACD 126 ..... 3.6, 3.16–3.21, 3.69, 6.93

JG v Lord Chancellor [2014] EWCA Civ 656, [2014] 5
    WLUK 742, [2014] 5 Costs LO 708, [2014] 2 FLR 1218,
    [2014] 3 FCR 567, [2014] HRLR 18, [2014] Fam Law
    1097   15.32
KPP v Director of Legal Aid Casework CO/779/2014   3.30
King's Lynn and West Norfolk BC v Bunning [2013]
    EWHC 3390 (QB), [2015] 1 WLR 531, [2014] 2 All ER
    1095, [2013] 11 WLUK 189, [2014] 1 Costs LO 85   14.87
LR v Director of Legal Aid Casework C0/5587/2017   3.30
Legal Services Commission v Henthorn [2011] EWCA Civ
    1415, [2012] 1 WLR 1173, [2012] 2 All ER 439, [2011]
    11 WLUK 878, [2012] 1 Costs LR 169, (2011) 155(46)
    SJLB 31, [2011] NPC 123   15.144, 15.145,
                                                          15.146
London Borough of A v M and SF [1994] Costs LR (Core)
    374 *See* Children Act 1989 (taxation of costs), Re—
MG v Cambridgeshire CC (SEN) [2017] UKUT 172
    (AAC), [2017] 4 WLUK 413, [2017] ELR 351   15.124
MS (Pakistan) v Secretary of State for the Home
    Department [2020] UKSC 9, [2020] 1 WLR 1373, [2020]
    3 All ER 733, [2020] 3 WLUK 246, [2020] Imm AR 967,
    [2020] INLR 460, (2020) *Times*, March 24   3.29
Northamptonshire CC v Lord Chancellor [2018] EWHC
    1628 (Fam), [2018] 6 WLUK 31, [2019] 1 FLR 169,
    [2018] 3 FCR 161   4.184
O (committal: legal representation), Re [2019] EWCA Civ
    1721, [2019] 4 WLR 140, [2019] 10 WLUK 246, [2019]
    Costs LR 1559, [2020] 1 FLR 288, [2020] 1 FCR 258   14.87
Parkes v Legal Aid Board [1994] 5 WLUK 157, [1994] 2
    FLR 850, [1994] 3 FCR 234, [1995] Fam Law 18, (1994)
    Times, May 24, FD   4.161
Practice Note (Solicitors: taxation of costs) [1982] 1 WLR
    745, [1982] 2 All ER 683, [1981] 12 WLUK 226   18.26
R (AA (Afghanistan)) v Secretary of State for the Home
    Department [2013] UKSC 49, [2013] 1 WLR 2224,
    [2013] 4 All ER 140, [2013] 7 WLUK 298, [2013] 3
    FCR 515, [2013] HRLR 34, [2014] INLR 51, (2013)
    163(7569) NLJ 15, (2013) *Times*, August 2   13.50
R (AR) v Hammersmith and Fulham LBC [2018] EWHC
    3453 (Admin), [2018] 12 WLUK 312, (2019) 22 CCLR
    56   12.37
R (Ajani) v Secretary of State for the Home Department
    [2018] EWHC 913 (Admin), [2018] 4 WLR 89, [2018] 3
    All ER 79, [2018] 4 WLUK 477   13.50
R (Alhasan) v Director of Legal Aid Casework [2024]
    EWHC 2031 (Admin), [2024] 8 WLUK 161   3.34, 3.35
R (Bahta) v Secretary of State for the Home Department
    [2011] EWCA Civ 895, [2011] 7 WLUK 727, [2011] CP
    Rep 43, [2011] 5 Costs LR 857, [2011] ACD 116   15.119

R (Ben Hoare Bell Solicitors) v Lord Chancellor [2015] EWHC 523 (Admin), [2015] 1 WLR 4175, [2016] 2 All ER 46, [2015] 3 WLUK 66, [2015] ACD 93	13.45, 13.46, 15.74, 15.75
R (Burkett) v Hammersmith and Fulham LBC (costs) [2004] EWCA Civ 1342, [2004] 10 WLUK 429, [2005] CP Rep 11, [2005] 1 Costs LR 104, [2005] JPL 525, [2005] ACD 73, (2004) 101(42) LSG 30, (2004) 148 SJLB 1245, (2004) *Times*, October 20	15.120
R (Duncan Lewis Solicitors) v Lord Chancellor [2015] EWHC 2498 (Admin), [2015] 7 WLUK 753	4.24, 5.48, 17.40–17.45
R (Duncan Lewis Solicitors) v Lord Chancellor CO/1551/2018	13.46
R (FF) v Director of Legal Aid Casework [2020] EWHC 95 (Admin), [2020] 4 WLR 40, [2020] 1 WLUK 146, [2020] ACD 46	13.18
R (Faulkner) v Director of Legal Aid Casework [2016] EWHC 717 (Admin), [2016] 4 WLR 178, [2016] 3 WLUK 239, [2016] 2 Costs LR 237	4.166
R (G) v Southwark LBC [2009] UKHL 26, [2009] 1 WLR 1299, [2009] 3 All ER 189, [2009] PTSR 1080, [2009] 5 WLUK 474, [2009] 2 FLR 380, [2009] 2 FCR 459, [2009] BLGR 673, (2009) 12 CCLR 437, [2009] Fam Law 668, (2009) 159 NLJ 791, (2009) 153(20) SJLB 42, [2009] NPC 73, (2009) *Times*, June 4	12.25
R (GS) v Camden LBC [2016] EWHC 1762 (Admin), [2017] PTSR 140, [2016] 7 WLUK 732, [2016] HLR 43, (2016) 19 CCLR 398	12.37
R (Gudanaviciene and others) v Director of Legal Aid Casework and Lord Chancellor [2014] EWCA Civ 1622, [2015] 1 WLR 2247, [2015] 3 All ER 827, [2014] 12 WLUK 521	3.6, 3.9, 3.10, 3.11, 3.13, 3.14, 3.15, 3.16, 3.17, 3.27, 3.28, 3.32, 3.36, 9.18, 9.39, 9.40, 9.41
R (Humberstone) v Legal Services Commission [2010] EWCA Civ 1479, [2011] 1 WLR 1460, [2010] 12 WLUK 737, [2011] 5 Costs LR 701, [2011] HRLR 12, [2011] UKHRR 8, [2011] Med LR 56, (2011) 118 BMLR 79, [2010] Inquest LR 221, [2011] ACD 51, (2011) *Times*, February 16	3.48
R (Khan) v Director of Legal Aid Casework [2018] EWHC 3198 (Admin), [2018] 11 WLUK 77, [2018] 6 Costs LO 799	14.148
R (Law Centres Federation Ltd (t/a Law Centres Network)) v Lord Chancellor [2018] EWHC 1588 (Admin), [2018] 6 WLUK 452	1.93

R (Letts) v Lord Chancellor [2015] EWHC 402 (Admin),
    [2015] 1 WLR 4497, [2016] 2 All ER 968, [2015] 2
    WLUK 696, [2015] 2 Costs LR 217, [2015] Inquest LR
    15, [2015] ACD 94   3.40, 3.41, 3.42
R (Liberty) v Director of Legal Aid Casework [2019] EWHC
    1532 (Admin), [2019] 1 WLR 5185, [2019] 6 WLUK
    215, [2019] ACD 88   13.13–13.18
R (London Criminal Courts Solicitors' Association, Law
    Society and others) v Lord Chancellor [2015] EWCA
    Civ 230, [2016] 3 All ER 296, [2015] 3 WLUK 747;
    Affirming [2015] EWHC 295 (Admin), [2015] 2 WLUK
    600, [2015] ACD 95   1.91
R (Oji) v Director of Legal Aid Casework [2024] EWHC
    1281 (Admin), [2024] 4 WLR 53, [2024] 5 WLUK 431   3.33
R (Rights of Women) v Lord Chancellor and Secretary of
    State for Justice [2016] EWCA Civ 91, [2016] 1 WLR
    2543, [2016] 3 All ER 473, [2016] 2 WLUK 505, [2017]
    1 FLR 615, [2016] 2 FCR 65, [2016] Fam Law 453;
    Reversing [2015] EWHC 35 (Admin), [2015] 1 WLUK
    464, [2015] 2 FLR 823, [2015] 3 FCR 409, [2015] Fam
    Law 277   1.92
R (SG) v Haringey LBC [2017] EWCA Civ 322, [2017] 5
    WLUK 40   12.37
R (SL) v Westminster City Council [2013] UKSC 27, [2013]
    1 WLR 1445, [2013] 3 All ER 191, [2013] PTSR 691,
    [2013] 5 WLUK 234, [2013] HLR 30, [2013] BLGR 423,
    (2013) 16 CCLR 161   12.37
R (Sanjari) v Birmingham Crown Court [2015] EWHC
    2037 (Admin), [2015] 7 WLUK 453, [2015] 2 Cr App R
    30   14.128
R (Southwark Law Centre) v Legal Services Commission; R
    (Dennis) v Legal Services Commission [2007] EWHC
    1715 (Admin), [2008] 1 WLR 1368, [2007] 4 All ER 754,
    [2007] 7 WLUK 625, [2008] HLR 12, (2007) 157 NLJ
    1119, [2007] NPC 97, (2007) *Times*, August 20   2.55
R (TMX) v LB Croydon LBC [2024] EWHC 129 (Admin),
    [2024] 1 WLUK 342, (2024) 27 CCLR 233, [2024] ACD
    42   12.37
Rantsev v Cyprus (Application No 25965/04) [2010]
    1 WLUK 30, (2010) 51 EHRR 1, 28 BHRC 313,
    CLW/10/24/31, CLW/10/24/30, CLW/10/24/28,
    ECtHR   3.29
Revenue and Customs Prosecution Office v Stokoe
    Partnership [2007] EWHC 1588 (Admin), [2007] 5
    WLUK 654, [2007] ACD 84   14.188
Rrapaj v Director of Legal Aid Casework [2013] EWHC
    1837 (Admin), [2013] 7 WLUK 31   9.55

Table of statutes

Access to Justice Act 1999	1.21, 1.25, 2.2, 4.24, 4.138, 15.32, 19.45, 21.47	Banking (Special Provisions) Act 2008	14.86
		Banking Act 2009	14.86
		British Nationality Act 1981—	
		s40A	9.47
Sch 2	2.4	Care Act 2014	12.4, 12.7, 12.16, 12.34–12.36, 14.96
Adoption and Children Act 2002	6.13, 7.6		
Pt 1 Ch 3 (ss18–65)		preamble	12.34
s21	7.9	Pt 1 (ss1–80)	2.10, 11.29, 12.6, 12.35
s26	7.9		
s36	7.9	s9(3)	11.31
s41	7.9	s19(3)	12.36, 13.30
s46	7.9		
s84	7.9	ss31–33	14.64
Anti-social Behaviour Act 2003—		Carers and Direct Payments Act (Northern Ireland) 2002	14.96
s20	14.86		
s22	14.86		
s26	14.86	s8(1)	14.64
s28	14.86	Children Act 1989	4.217, 4.218, 6.14, 6.96, 7.7, 12.4, 12.18–12.33, 15.32, 17.41
Anti-social Behaviour, Crime and Policing Act 2014	11.5, 11.15, 11.62, 11.64, 11.66, 11.67, 13.14, 15.6, 15.65, 15.66, 16.10		
		s4(2A)	6.19
		s6(7)	6.19
		Pt II (ss8–16A)	6.19, 7.8
		s8	5.13, 6.29, 19.18
Pt 1 (ss1–21)	11.70, 14.86, 16.76, 20.22	ss11A–11G	4.49
s66	13.13, 13.14, 13.15, 13.16, 13.17	s11E	4.49
		s14A	6.12
		s16A	4.49
		Pt III (ss16B–30A)	12.23
s80	14.86, 20.22	s17	4.24, 11.29, 11.31, 12.6, 12.18, 12.22, 12.23, 13.31
s80(5)(a)	14.86		
s82	14.86, 20.22		
s83	14.86, 20.22		
s84	14.86, 20.22		

Children Act 1989 *continued*		Civil Partnership Act 2004—	
s20	11.29, 11.31, 12.6, 12.7, 12.18, 12.24– 12.26, 12.30, 13.30	Sch 5 para 25(2)	4.165
		Sch 5 para 26	4.165
		Coroners Act 1988	3.38
		Crime and Disorder Act 1998—	
		s8	7.9
s20(1)	12.24	s8(1)(b)	14.86
s22A	11.29, 12.6, 12.18	s9(5)	14.86
		s11	7.9
s22B	11.29, 12.6, 12.18	s51	16.66, 20.34
		Crime and Security Act 2010—	
s22C	11.29, 12.6, 12.18	ss24–33	20.22
		s24	6.26
s23	11.29	s26	14.86
ss23A–23CA	12.29	s27	14.86
s23B	11.29, 12.6, 12.18	s29	14.86
		Criminal Finances Act 2017—	
s23C	11.29, 12.6, 12.18	Pt 3 (ss44–52)	22.15
		Criminal Justice and Immigration Act 2008—	
s24	11.29, 12.6, 12.18, 12.32, 12.33	s100	14.86
		s101	14.86
		s103	14.86
s24A	11.29, 12.6, 12.18	s104	14.86
		s106	14.86
s24B	11.29, 12.6, 12.18	Data Protection Act 1998	13.5
ss25–41	7.48	Data Protection Act 2018 (UK GDPR)	15.27
s25	7.4, 7.9		
s27	7.35	Sch 2 para 5(2)	15.27
Pt IV (ss31–42)	7.9, 7.49	Sch 2 para 5(3)	15.27
s31	2.60, 7.4, 7.27, 7.35, 7.46, 7.50, 15.157, 15.159, 15.163, 15.171, 15.174, 15.175, 15.194, 15.200, 15.201, 19.30, 19.40	Domestic Violence, Crime and Victims Act 2004	10.18
		Energy Prices Act 2022—	
		s13	14.64, 14.96
		s15	14.64, 14.96
		Environmental Protection Act 1990—	
		s82	11.54
s38	7.38	Equality Act 2010	1.93, 2.10, 3.66, 4.168, 10.27, 11.9, 11.16, 11.18, 13.5
s41(6)	15.182, 19.14		
Pt V (ss43–52)	7.9, 7.49		
s43	7.4, 7.48	s20	3.66
s44	7.4, 7.35, 7.48	Family Law Act 1986—	
s45	7.4, 7.35, 7.48	s33	6.8, 6.17, 6.19
Sch 2 para 19	7.9	s34	6.8, 6.17, 6.19
Children and Families Act 2014	8.8, 14.96	s37	6.8
		Family Law Act 1996—	
s10	6.81	Pt IV (ss30–63)	4.165, 6.9, 6.110, 11.43
s49(3)	14.64		

Table of statutes   xxv

Family Law Act 1996 *continued*
    s46   6.26
    s62   9.10
    s62(1)   11.43
    s63E   6.26
Female Genital Mutilation
    Act 2003   15.182, 19.14
    Sch 2 para 3   14.86
    Sch 2 para 6   14.86
Football Spectators Act 1989—
    s14B   14.86, 20.22
    s14D   14.86, 20.22
    s14G   14.86, 20.22
    s14H   14.86, 20.22
    s21B   14.86, 20.22
    s21D   14.86, 20.22
Forced Marriage (Civil Protection)
    Act 2007   15.182, 19.14
Freedom of Information
    Act 2000   21.21
Homelessness Reduction Act 2017—
    s1(2)   11.21
Homes (Fitness for Human Habitation)
    Act 2018   11.42
Housing Acts   5.18
Housing (Wales)
    Act 2014   11.21–11.28
    Pt 2 (ss50–100)   11.5, 11.22
    s55(4)   11.21
    s85   11.24
    s85(3)   11.23
    s88   11.22, 11.23
    s89   11.27
    s93   11.23
    s94   11.23
Housing Act 1985—
    s84A   11.70
Housing Act 1988—
    s8   11.10
    s21   11.10, 11.16
    Sch 2 ground 7A   11.70
Housing Act 1996   11.21–11.28
    s153A   11.5
    Pt 6 (ss159–174)   11.5, 11.21, 11.22
    Pt 7 (ss175–218)   4.107, 11.5, 11.21, 13.30
    s175   11.21
    s202   11.24
    s202(1)(f)   11.23

Housing Act 1996 *continued*
    s204   5.18, 11.22, 11.23, 11.27
    s204A   11.27
    s204A(4)(a)   11.27
    s211   11.23
    s212   11.23
Human Fertilisation and Embryology
    Act 2008   15.182, 19.14
Human Rights
    Act 1998   2.10, 2.25, 3.2, 4.180, 4.184, 4.226, 9.38, 12.42, 13.5, 13.21, 13.22
    s7   2.6, 9.4
    s7(1)(a)   13.22
Illegal Migration
    Act 2023   9.3, 9.77, 9.83, 9.127, 15.6, 15.211
    s56   9.56
Immigration Act 1971—
    Sch 2   9.46
    Sch 3   9.6
    Sch 3 para 2(5)   9.6
Immigration Act 2016—
    Sch 10   9.90
Immigration and Asylum Act 1999—
    s4   2.42, 9.88, 9.89, 11.5, 11.32
    s95   2.42, 9.88, 9.89, 11.5, 11.32
    s98   9.90, 11.33
Inheritance (Provision for Family and Dependants)
    Act 1975   4.165, 15.182, 19.14
    s5   4.165
Jobseekers Act 1995   14.64
    s26   14.64
Landlord and Tenant Act 1985—
    ss8–10   11.42
Legal Aid, Sentencing and Punishment of Offenders
    Act 2012   1.21, 1.45, 2.7, 2.9, 2.11, 2.25, 3.1, 3.4, 3.6, 4.5, 4.56, 4.82, 4.87, 4.116, 4.138, 4.163, 4.203,

Legal Aid, Sentencing and Punishment of Offenders Act 2012 *continued*		Legal Aid, Sentencing and Punishment of Offenders Act 2012 *continued*	
	4.213, 4.217, 5.46, 5.76, 6.5, 6.18, 6.32, 6.40, 6.60, 6.68, 7.12, 8.2, 9.20, 9.105, 10.4, 11.50, 15.6, 15.15, 15.32, 15.39, 15.126, 15.179, 15.211, 17.9, 17.13, 17.15, 17.24, 18.16, 21.47, 23.8	Sch 1 Pt 1 para 1A	6.12, 6.15, 7.8
		Sch 1 Pt 1 para 3	9.3, 13.22
		Sch 1 Pt 1 para 3(1)	9.36
		Sch 1 Pt 1 para 5	10.4
		Sch 1 Pt 1 para 6	2.10, 11.29, 12.6, 12.18
		Sch 1 Pt 1 para 6(n)	2.10, 12.35
Pt 1 (ss1–43)	2.25, 3.38, 16.106	Sch 1 Pt 1 para 7	2.10
		Sch 1 Pt 1 para 9	6.7, 7.5, 7.10, 10.4
s8	1.22		
s9	1.24	Sch 1 Pt 1	
s10	1.25, 3.1, 3.11, 3.18, 3.71, 9.3, 9.38	para 10	6.8, 6.17
		Sch 1 Pt 1 para 11	6.9, 6.110
s10(2)	3.32, 3.62	Sch 1 Pt 1	
s10(3)	2.25, 3.2, 3.3, 3.6, 3.32, 3.35, 9.37	para 12	6.17, 6.18, 6.26, 6.110
		Sch 1 Pt 1 para 12(9)	6.18
s10(3)(a)	3.35		
s10(3)(b)	3.35	Sch 1 Pt 1	
s10(4)	3.38, 3.62	para 13	6.19, 6.20, 6.29
s11	1.26		
s13	10.4	Sch 1 Pt 1	
s14(h)	15.65	para 13(3)	6.18
s15	10.4	Sch 1 Pt 1	
s16	10.4	para 14	6.12, 8.5
s17(2)	14.104	Sch 1 Pt 1	
s21	1.26	para 15	6.12
s25	1.26, 4.158, 4.179	Sch 1 Pt 1	
		para 15A	6.12
s25(1)(a)	4.162	Sch 1 Pt 1	
s26	1.26, 4.84, 13.48	para 16	6.12
s28	16.106	Sch 1 Pt 1	
s28(2)	16.106	para 17	6.12
s28(2)(b)	16.108	Sch 1 Pt 1	
Sch 1	1.13, 1.21, 1.24, 2.4, 2.5, 9.56	para 18	7.12
		Sch 1 Pt 1	
Sch 1 Pt 1 (paras 1–46)	1.25, 2.5, 3.2, 6.5, 9.3, 9.83, 13.9, 13.21	para 19	2.8, 3.75, 9.3, 13.9, 13.10, 13.12, 13.19
		Sch 1 Pt 1	
Sch 1 Pt 1 para 1	7.5, 7.9	para 19(1)	9.49, 13.17

Table of statutes xxvii

Legal Aid, Sentencing and Punishment of Offenders Act 2012 continued		Legal Aid, Sentencing and Punishment of Offenders Act 2012 continued	
Sch 1 Pt 1 para 19(2)(a)	2.8, 13.10	Sch 1 Pt 1 para 26	9.58
Sch 1 Pt 1 para 19(3)	9.49, 13.12, 13.12, 13.13, 13.15, 13.16, 13.18	Sch 1 Pt 1 para 26(1)	9.3, 9.6, 9.36
		Sch 1 Pt 1 para 27	9.58
Sch 1 Pt 1 para 19(4)	13.12, 13.13	Sch 1 Pt 1 para 27(1)	9.3, 9.6, 9.36
Sch 1 Pt 1 para 19(5)	9.50	Sch 1 Pt 1 para 27A	9.58
Sch 1 Pt 1 para 19(5)(a)–(c)	13.19	Sch 1 Pt 1 para 27A(1)	9.3
Sch 1 Pt 1 para 19(6)	9.51	Sch 1 Pt 1 paras 28–29	9.46
Sch 1 Pt 1 para 19(7)	9.52, 13.19	Sch 1 Pt 1 para 28	9.3, 9.10, 9.58
Sch 1 Pt 1 para 19(8)	9.53, 13.19	Sch 1 Pt 1 para 28(3)	9.15
Sch 1 Pt 1 para 19(10)	13.11, 13.15	Sch 1 Pt 1 para 28(5)	9.10
Sch 1 Pt 1 para 19(10)(a)	13.13	Sch 1 Pt 1 para 29	9.3, 9.10, 9.58
Sch 1 Pt 1 para 19(10)(b)	14.13	Sch 1 Pt 1 para 29(3)	9.15
Sch 1 Pt 1 para 20	13.9	Sch 1 Pt 1 para 29(4)	9.10
Sch 1 Pt 1 para 20(1)	13.20	Sch 1 Pt 1 para 30	9.58
Sch 1 Pt 1 para 21	4.113, 9.3, 10.4, 13.21, 13.22	Sch 1 Pt 1 para 30(1)	9.3, 9.16
		Sch 1 Pt 1 para 30(1)(b)	9.17
Sch 1 Pt 1 para 21(1)	9.36	Sch 1 Pt 1 para 30(3)	9.19
Sch 1 Pt 1 para 21(4)	2.10	Sch 1 Pt 1 para 31A	9.5
Sch 1 Pt 1 para 22	4.113, 9.3, 10.4, 13.21, 13.22	Sch 1 Pt 1 para 31A(2)(a)	4.95, 4.98
Sch 1 Pt 1 para 22(1)	9.36	Sch 1 Pt 1 para 31C	15.6
Sch 1 Pt 1 para 24	9.58	Sch 1 Pt 1 para 32	9.58
Sch 1 Pt 1 para 24(1)	9.37	Sch 1 Pt 1 paras 32(1)–32A(1)	9.46
Sch 1 Pt 1 para 25	9.58	Sch 1 Pt 1 para 32(1)	9.3, 9.20
Sch 1 Pt 1 para 25(1)	9.3, 9.6, 9.36	Sch 1 Pt 1 para 32(1)(a)	9.21

Legal Aid, Sentencing and
    Punishment of Offenders
    Act 2012 continued
  Sch 1 Pt 1
    para 32(1)(b)   9.21
  Sch 1 Pt 1
    para 32(6)–(8)   9.21
  Sch 1 Pt 1
    para 32A   9.58
  Sch 1 Pt 1
    para 32A(1)   9.3, 9.20
  Sch 1 Pt 1
    para 32A(1)(a)   9.21
  Sch 1 Pt 1
    para 32A(1)(b)   9.21
  Sch 1 Pt 1
    para 32A(6)   9.21
  Sch 1 Pt 1
    para 32A(7)   9.21
  Sch 1 Pt 1
    para 32A(10)   9.21
  Sch 1 Pt 1
    para 33   2.7, 11.10, 11.35
  Sch 1 Pt 1
    para 33(3)   11.13
  Sch 1 Pt 1
    para 33(6)   11.18, 11.55
  Sch 1 Pt 1
    para 33(6)(a)   11.55
  Sch 1 Pt 1
    para 33(7)   11.18, 11.57
  Sch 1 Pt 1
    para 33(9)   11.7
  Sch 1 Pt 1
    para 33(10)   11.8
  Sch 1 Pt 1
    para 33(11)   11.7
  Sch 1 Pt 1
    para 34   13.9
  Sch 1 Pt 1
    para 34(1)   11.23
  Sch 1 Pt 1
    para 35   11.43, 11.54
  Sch 1 Pt 1
    para 35(1)   11.43
  Sch 1 Pt 1
    para 35(2)(b)   11.54
  Sch 1 Pt 1
    para 39   9.3
  Sch 1 Pt 1
    para 39(1)   9.36

Legal Aid, Sentencing and
    Punishment of Offenders
    Act 2012 continued
  Sch 1 Pt 1
    para 40   14.209
  Sch 1 Pt 1
    para 43(3)   2.10
  Sch 1 Pt 1
    para 45   9.3, 9.58
  Sch 1 Pt 2
    (paras 1–18)   2.5, 2.6, 2.7,
                       2.8, 2.9, 2.10,
                       3.37, 9.4, 11.13,
                       11.18, 11.43,
                       11.55, 11.57,
                       13.10, 13.20
  Sch 1 Pt 2
    para 2   11.18
  Sch 1 Pt 2
    para 15   2.7, 2.8
  Sch 1 Pt 3
    (paras 1–25)   2.5, 11.43,
                       11.54, 13.10,
                       13.11, 13.20,
                       18.7
  Sch 1 Pt 3
    paras 1–3   9.48
  Sch 1 Pt 3
    para 4   10.4, 10.5
  Sch 1 Pt 3
    paras 11–13   9.46
  Sch 1 Pt 3
    para 11(a)   9.46
  Sch 1 Pt 3
    para 11(b)   9.46
  Sch 1 Pt 3
    para 12   9.47
  Sch 1 Pt 3
    para 12(b)   9.47
  Sch 1 Pt 3
    para 13   9.46
  Sch 1 Pt 3
    para 15   9.46
  Sch 1 Pt 3
    para 21   9.37
  Sch 1 Pt 4
    (paras 1–8)   2.5
Legal Services Act 2007—
  s194   15.150
  s194(3)   15.150
  s194(8)   15.149

Legal Services Act 2007 *continued*		Nationality and Borders Act 2022 *continued*	
s194(10)	15.150	s12(3)	9.31
s194A	15.150	s67	3.37
s194B	15.150	Nationality, Immigration and Asylum Act 2002—	
s194C	15.149		
Limitation Act 1980	15.147	s17	11.5
Local Authority Social Services Act 1970	7.27	s62	9.6
		s82(1)	9.46
Localism Act 2011—		s94	9.52, 13.19
s1	12.37	s96	9.52, 13.19
Magistrates' Courts Act 1980—		Sch 3	12.37
s22	16.51	Sch 3 para 1	12.37
Matrimonial Causes Act 1973—		Offences against the Person Act 1861—	
s25B	4.165		
s25C	4.165	s18	16.27
Mental Capacity Act 2005	2.10, 10.4, 10.5, 10.11, 10.12, 10.13, 10.35, 10.54, 10.58, 14.70, 22.42	s20	17.27
		Offensive Weapons Act 2019—	
		Pt 2 (ss14–33)	20.22
		Police and Criminal Evidence Act 1984	14.21, 14.30, 14.49, 14.52
s21A	2.60, 10.60	s30CB	14.47
Mental Health Act 1983	2.10, 10.4, 10.11, 10.28, 12.16, 14.114, 22.42	s43	14.44, 20.9
		s44	14.44, 20.9
		s47(1E)	14.47
		s47ZF	14.83, 16.37, 20.22
s1(2)	19.38		
s3	11.29, 12.7, 12.16	s47ZG	14.83, 16.37, 20.22
s37	12.16	Powers of Criminal Courts (Sentencing) Act 2000—	
s45A	12.16		
s48	12.16	s1	16.51
Pt V (ss65–79)	10.49	Proceeds of Crime Act 2002	14.2, 14.206, 14.207, 16.73
s117	11.29, 12.4, 12.6, 12.16, 12.17		
		s41	14.64, 14.96
Modern Slavery Act 2015—		Prosecution of Offences Act 1985—	
s14(1)(b)	14.86		
s14(1)(c)	14.86	s16A	14.173
s15	14.86	s16A(4)(a)	14.172
ss20–22	14.86	s16A(4)(b)	14.176
s23	14.86	Protection from Harassment Act 1997	11.5
ss27–29	14.86		
National Assistance Act 1948—		s3	11.60
s21	13.30	s3A	11.60
National Health Service and Community Care Act 1990—		s5A	14.86, 20.22
		Public Order Act 2023—	
s47(5)	13.30	s21	14.86
Nationality and Borders Act 2022	3.36, 9.3, 9.31	s28	14.86
		s29	14.86
s12(2)	9.31		

Repatriation of Prisoners Act 1984	10.4	Social Security Contributions and Benefits Act 1992—	
Sch para 5(2)	2.10, 10.4	Pt I (ss1–19B)	15.63, 15.64
Road Traffic Act 1988—		Social Services and Well-being (Wales) Act 2014	14.96
s4	14.27		
s5	14.27		
s6	14.27	s15	12.6
s7	14.27	Pt 4 (ss32–58)	12.6
s7A	14.27	s36	13.30
Senior Courts Act 1981—		ss50–53	14.64
s31	13.11	s76	12.6
Sentencing Act 2020 (Sentencing Code)	14.86	s79	12.6
		s80	12.6
s90	14.86	s81	12.6
Ch 2 Pt 11 (ss330–342)	14.86	ss105–116	12.6
		s119	7.9
s330	14.86	s124	7.9
s336(10)	14.86	Stalking Protection Act 2019—	
s338	14.86	s1	14.86
s342H	14.86	s4	14.86
s342I	14.86	s5	14.86
s345	14.86	s7	14.86
s350	14.86	Terrorism Act 2000—	
s353	14.86	s41	16.27
s366	7.9, 14.86	Sch 8 para 29	14.44, 20.9
s369	7.9	Sch 8 para 36	14.44, 20.9
s374	14.86	Terrorism Prevention and Investigation Measures Act 2011—	
Serious Crime Act 2007—			
s19	14.86		
s20	14.86	s2	9.35
s21	14.86	Tribunals, Courts and Enforcement Act 2007—	
s24	14.86		
Sexual Offences Act 2003	14.164	s9	10.40
		s11	10.40
s97	14.86, 20.22	s13	14.86
s100	14.86, 20.22	Trusts of Land and Appointment of Trustees Act 1996	15.182, 19.14
s101	14.86, 20.22		
s103A	14.86		
s103E	14.86		
s103F	14.86	UK Borders Act 2007—	
s103H	14.86	s36	9.6
s122A	14.86, 20.22	Welfare Reform Act 2012—	
s122D	14.86, 20.22	Pt 1 (ss1–43)	14.62
s122E	14.86, 20.22	Pt 4 (ss77–95)	14.64
s122G	14.86, 20.22	Youth Justice and Criminal Evidence Act 1999—	
Social Security (Additional Payments) Act 2022	14.64		
		s28	16.10
		s38	14.83, 20.22

Table of statutory instruments

Civil and Criminal Legal Aid (Amendment) Regulations 2015 SI No 1416	14.86, 15.6, 16.10
Civil and Criminal Legal Aid (Amendment) (No 2) Regulations 2015 SI No 1678	16.10
Civil and Criminal Legal Aid (Remuneration) (Amendment) Regulations 2015 SI No 325	15.6, 15.65, 16.10
Civil Legal Aid (Costs) Regulations 2013 SI No 611	4.84, 4.116
reg 21(3)	15.119
Civil Legal Aid (Financial Resources and Payment for Services) Regulations 2013 SI No 480	1.48, 2.31, 6.52, 23.34
reg 2	2.38
reg 5	2.60, 7.38
reg 5(1)(f)	10.29, 10.32
reg 5(1)(gb)	8.13
reg 5(1)(h)	6.39
reg 6(1)	9.88
reg 12	2.49, 6.14, 6.15, 6.87, 7.7, 7.8
reg 13	4.92
reg 14(2)	4.22
reg 16(2)	2.38
reg 16(3)	2.59
reg 16(4)	2.59
reg 16(5)	4.97
reg 18	2.65
reg 20	2.64
reg 21	2.54
reg 23	2.55
reg 24	2.54
reg 25	2.55
reg 26	2.55
reg 27	2.55
reg 28	2.55
reg 30	2.44
reg 31	2.44, 2.46
reg 32	2.44
reg 33	2.44

Civil Legal Aid (Financial Resources and Payment for
        Services) Regulations 2013 SI No 480 *continued*
    reg 34   2.45
    reg 36   2.45
    reg 37   11.20
    reg 38   2.48
    reg 41   2.50
    reg 44(6)   4.92
Civil Legal Aid (Financial Resources and Payment for
        Services) (Amendment) Regulations 2020 SI
        No 1584   2.46, 11.20
Civil Legal Aid (Financial Resources and Payment for
        Services and Remuneration) (Amendment)
        Regulations 2023 SI No 1177   15.6
Civil Legal Aid (Immigration Interviews) (Exceptions)
        Regulations 2012 SI No 2683   9.19
    reg 2   9.105
    reg 2(b)   9.105
    reg 3   9.105
    reg 4   9.105
Civil Legal Aid (Immigration Interviews) (Exceptions)
        (Amendment) Regulations 2017 SI No 192   9.105
Civil Legal Aid (Immigration Interviews (Exceptions)
        and Remuneration) (Amendment) Regulations
        2022 SI No 1379   15.6
Civil Legal Aid (Merits Criteria) Regulations 2013
        SI No 104   1.48, 3.6, 3.16, 3.18,
                                                    3.19, 4.7, 4.94, 4.108,
                                                    4.113, 6.52, 6.93,
                                                    17.38, 23.34
    reg 2   4.87, 4.107, 4.111,
                                                    6.13, 7.4, 7.6, 9.94,
                                                    11.25, 11.30, 13.9
    reg 3   9.96
    reg 5   4.102, 9.94
    reg 5(1)   6.92
    reg 5(1)(a)   9.96
    reg 5(1)(b)   9.96
    reg 5(1)(c)   9.96
    reg 6   4.104, 9.94
    reg 7   4.51, 4.104, 6.44, 6.98,
                                                    7.17, 9.94
    reg 8   4.104, 9.94
    reg 11(6)   11.56
    reg 18(2)   13.41
    reg 18(3)   13.41
    reg 20   6.11
    reg 32   4.7
    reg 32(b)   4.29, 6.44, 7.17

Civil Legal Aid (Merits Criteria) Regulations 2013
SI No 104 *continued*

reg 33	4.63, 18.12
reg 35	6.52, 7.27, 23.34
reg 37	6.81, 8.18
reg 39	4.87, 4.95, 4.99, 6.90, 13.32
reg 39(c)	4.98
reg 40	12.11, 13.28
reg 41	4.85, 4.109
reg 42	4.105
reg 43	4.103, 11.12, 11.37, 11.60
reg 44	4.106
reg 46	5.44
reg 52(1)	10.59
reg 52(2)	10.59
reg 52(3)	10.5
reg 53	4.111, 13.27
reg 53(b)	4.111
reg 54	13.28
reg 56	4.112, 11.25, 11.30, 12.10
reg 56A	9.133
reg 57	12.11
reg 60(2)–(3)	9.93, 9.132
reg 61	11.12
reg 63	11.37, 11.60
reg 66	6.15, 7.8, 7.41
reg 67	6.111
reg 67(2)	6.11
reg 67(3)	6.11
reg 68	6.98
reg 69	6.104

Civil Legal Aid (Merits Criteria) (Amendment)
　　　Regulations 2013 SI No 772　　　　　4.111
　　reg 2　　　　　　　　　　　　　　　　4.111
Civil Legal Aid (Merits Criteria) (Amendment) (No 3)
　　　Regulations 2013 SI No 3195—
　　reg 2　　　　　　　　　　　　　　　　9.133
Civil Legal Aid (Merits Criteria) (Amendment)
　　　Regulations 2014 SI No 131　　　　　11.12
Civil Legal Aid (Merits Criteria) (Amendment) (No 2)
　　　Regulations 2015 SI No 1571　　　　4.94, 4.113, 12.11
　　reg 2(3)　　　　　　　　　　　　　　4.105
　　reg 2(4)　　　　　　　　　　　　　　4.103
　　reg 2(5)　　　　　　　　　　　　　　4.112

Civil Legal Aid (Merits Criteria) (Amendment) Regulations 2016 SI No 781	4.94, 4.113, 11.25, 11.30, 12.11
reg 2(3)	4.105
reg 2(4)	11.12, 11.37, 11.60
reg 2(5)	4.112
Civil Legal Aid (Procedure) Regulations 2012 SI No 3098	1.48, 2.77, 6.52, 11.19, 23.34
regs 4–10	2.78
reg 5	4.55, 18.9
reg 8	6.68, 6.70
reg 21(2)	6.69
reg 22	2.57
reg 22(2)	4.14
reg 22(3)(a)	4.14
reg 22(3)(b)	4.14
reg 22(4)	4.16, 10.25
reg 23(4)	2.72
reg 28(1)	17.18
reg 30(2)	12.20
reg 30(2)(b)	4.91
reg 31(3)	4.89
reg 31(5)	15.212
reg 35	17.34
reg 35(3)	4.190, 5.49
reg 38	13.42
reg 39(3)(b)	4.208, 6.109
reg 40(1)(a)	7.37
reg 42	4.116, 4.155
reg 42(1)	4.116
reg 42(1)(k)	4.116
reg 42(2)	4.187
reg 42(3)	4.116
reg 42(4)	17.17
reg 43	4.155, 17.14
reg 44	4.125, 17.16
reg 44(1)(a)	17.15
reg 44(1)(b)	17.15
reg 44(1)(c)	17.15
reg 44(1)(d)	17.15
reg 44(1)(e)	17.15
reg 44(4)	4.126
reg 45(1)	17.24
reg 45(2)	17.30
reg 45(3)	17.31
reg 46(1)(a)	17.26
reg 46(1)(b)	17.27

Civil Legal Aid (Procedure) Regulations 2012
　　SI No 3098 *continued*

reg 47(1)	17.26, 17.27
reg 47(2)	17.28
reg 48(1)	17.27
reg 48(4)	17.32
reg 48(5)	17.33
reg 50(3)	17.14
reg 52(1)(b)	6.114
reg 52(2)	6.114
reg 53	4.209, 4.224
reg 53(1)(a)	17.25
Pt 6 (regs 54–59)	15.193, 19.62
reg 54	4.213
reg 54(3)	15.193
regs 58–59	17.54
reg 58	4.226
reg 65	17.55
Pt 8 (regs 66–69)	2.26
reg 68	2.27
reg 68(1)	10.71
reg 69(1)(b)	17.9
reg 69(2)	10.71, 17.10
reg 69(4)	17.12
Sch 1	6.17, 6.21, 6.26
Sch 1 para 22	6.26
Sch 2	6.20, 6.29

Civil Legal Aid (Procedure) (Amendment) Regulations
　　2019 SI No 130　　　　　　　　　　　　17.34
　　reg 2(4)　　　　　　　　　　　　　　　5.50

Civil Legal Aid (Procedure) (Amendment) Regulations
　　2020 SI No 439　　　　　　　　　　　　11.19
　　reg 31(8)　　　　　　　　　　　　　　　9.23

Civil Legal Aid (Procedure, Remuneration and
　　Statutory Charge) (Amendment) Regulations
　　2014 SI No 1824　　　　　　　　　　　15.6

Civil Legal Aid (Procedure, Remuneration and
　　Statutory Charge) (Amendment) Regulations
　　2018 SI No 803　　　　　　　　　　　　9.131, 15.6
　　reg 5　　　　　　　　　　　　　　　　　9.131

Civil Legal Aid (Remuneration) Regulations 2013 SI
　　No 422　　　　　　　　　　　　　　　1.42, 1.48, 4.44,
　　　　　　　　　　　　　　　　　　　　　4.50, 4.139, 4.140,
　　　　　　　　　　　　　　　　　　　　　9.78, 9.116, 15.6,
　　　　　　　　　　　　　　　　　　　　　15.7, 15.10, 15.18,
　　　　　　　　　　　　　　　　　　　　　15.54, 15.157, 15.220,
　　　　　　　　　　　　　　　　　　　　　15.227, 18.29, 18.31,
　　　　　　　　　　　　　　　　　　　　　19.45, 19.46, 21.27
　　reg 5A　　　　　　　　　　　　　　　　13.45, 13.46, 15.76

Civil Legal Aid (Remuneration) Regulations 2013
  SI No 422 *continued*
  reg 6(3)   15.70
  reg 7(3)   18.34
  reg 7(4)   18.33
  reg 7(5)   18.35
  reg 11   18.38
  reg 12   18.41
  Sch 1   6.47, 7.24, 7.37, 7.47,
                                                    15.235
  Sch 1 table 4(a)   15.213
  Sch 1 table 4(c)   15.208
  Sch 1 table 4(ca)   15.208, 15.219
  Sch 1 table 6   11.88
  Sch 1 table 7(d)   15.220
  Sch 2   15.235, 18.30
  Sch 3   19.10
  Sch 5   4.138, 4.140
  Sch 5 para 2   11.47
  Sch 5 para 4   15.23
Civil Legal Aid (Remuneration) (Amendment)
  Regulations 2013 SI No 2877   4.140, 15.6, 15.56
  Sch 1   18.33
  Sch 2   4.138, 4.140, 11.47
Civil Legal Aid (Remuneration) (Amendment)
  Regulations 2014 SI No 7   15.6
Civil Legal Aid (Remuneration) (Amendment) (No 2)
  Regulations 2014 SI No 586   15.6
  reg 2(1)   15.164
Civil Legal Aid (Remuneration) (Amendment) (No 3)
  Regulations 2014 SI No 607   15.72
Civil Legal Aid (Remuneration) (Amendment) (No 4)
  Regulations 2014 SI No 1389   15.6, 19.45
Civil Legal Aid (Remuneration) (Amendment)
  Regulations 2015 SI No 898   13.46, 15.6, 15.76
  reg 2   15.76
Civil Legal Aid (Remuneration) (Amendment)
  Regulations 2023 SI No 1322   15.6
Civil Legal Aid (Remuneration) (Amendment)
  (Coronavirus) Regulations 2020 SI No 515   15.6
Civil Legal Aid (Remuneration) (Amendment) (No 2)
  (Coronavirus) Regulations 2020 SI No 1001   15.6, 15.213
  reg 4   15.210, 15.213
Civil Legal Aid (Remuneration and Statutory Charge)
  (Amendment) Regulations 2016 SI No 983   15.6
Civil Legal Aid (Statutory Charge) Regulations 2013 SI
  No 503   4.158, 4.165, 6.62
  reg 4(1)   4.159
  reg 4(2)   4.160, 6.67

Table of statutory instruments   xxxvii

Civil Legal Aid (Statutory Charge) Regulations 2013
  SI No 503 *continued*
reg 6	4.168
reg 8	6.65
reg 9	4.174
reg 11	4.169
reg 13	4.164, 4.169
reg 15(1)(a)	4.169
reg 15(3)	4.171
reg 22	4.168, 4.175
reg 25	4.176
Civil Procedure Rules 1998 SI No 3132	11.84, 15.10, 15.13, 15.107, 15.108, 15.109, 15.111, 15.112, 15.123, 15.124, 15.130, 15.132
Pt 8	4.184
r21.2	12.20
Pt 36	15.122, 15.130, 15.132
r44.3(2)	15.13
r44.4	15.13
r44.9	15.122
r44.10	15.122
PD 44 paras 2.1–2.11	15.108, 15.125
PD 44 para 9.8	15.124
Pt 45	15.151
r46.7	15.150, 15.151
r46.7(3)	15.154
r46.14	15.126
PD 46 para 4.1	15.151, 15.152
Pt 47	15.107, 15.109, 15.111, 15.123, 15.127
r47.7	15.61
r47.10	15.131
r47.15	15.109, 15.132
r47.18	15.109, 15.132
r47.20	15.130
rr47.21–47.24	15.109, 15.133
PD 47	15.112
PD 47 paras 4.1–4.3	15.112
PD 47 paras 5.1–5.1A	15.125
PD 47 para 5.2	15.127
PD 47 paras 5.7–5.22	15.108, 15.125
PD 47 para 5.19	15.111
PD 47 para 8.2	15.125
PD 47 para 10.7	15.128
PD 47 para 13.12	15.109, 15.132
PD 47 para 14.3	15.132

Civil Procedure Rules 1998 SI No 3132 *continued*
PD 47 para 17.2(2) — 15.109
PD 47 paras 17.6–17.9 — 15.137
PD 47 para 19 — 15.130
PD 47 Schedule of Costs Precedents: Precedent G — 15.125
PD 47 Schedule of Costs Precedents: Precedent H — 15.108
Pt 52 — 15.109, 15.133
r52.21(1) — 15.133
r55.11 — 11.11
Civil Procedure Rules 1998 Practice Directions — 11.84
Civil Procedure Rules 1998 Pre-Action Protocols — 15.211
Civil Procedure Rules 1998 Pre-Action Protocol for Housing Disrepair Cases (Wales) — 11.48
Civil Procedure Rules 1998 Pre-Action Protocol for Housing Disrepair Claims (England) — 11.48
Civil Procedure Rules 1998 Pre-Action Protocol for Judicial Review — 11.30, 11.32, 12.10, 12.17, 12.25, 13.26, 15.81

Civil Proceedings Fees Order 2008 SI No 1053—
Sch 1 para 5.1 — 15.113
Community Legal Service (Funding) Order 2007 SI No 2441 — 19.45
Community Legal Service (Funding) (Amendment No 2) Order 2011 SI No 2066 — 4.138, 15.53
Community Legal Service (Funding) (Amendment) Order 2014 SI No 1818 — 19.45
Community Legal Service (Funding) (Counsel in Family Proceedings) Order 2001 SI No 1077 — 19.7
Criminal and Civil Legal Aid (Amendment) Regulations 2023 SI No 745—
reg 3(2)(c) — 3.62
Criminal Defence Service (General) (No 2) Regulations 2001 SI No 1437—
reg 10(5) — 14.188
Criminal Legal Aid (Amendment) Regulations 2017 SI No 1319 — 14.203, 16.10
Criminal Legal Aid (Contribution Orders) Regulations 2013 SI No 483 — 14.135
reg 16 — 14.140
reg 26 — 14.148
reg 27 — 14.145
reg 28 — 14.145
Criminal Legal Aid (Coronavirus, Remuneration) (Amendment) Regulations 2020 SI No 472 — 16.10
Criminal Legal Aid (Determinations by a Court and Choice of Representative) Regulations 2013 SI No 614 — 14.123
reg 7 — 14.180

Criminal Legal Aid (Determinations by a Court and
    Choice of Representative) Regulations 2013
    SI No 614 *continued*
  reg 8   14.184, 14.188,
                                          14.189, 20.55
  reg 13   14.123
  reg 14   14.127
  reg 16   16.107, 20.30, 20.36,
                                          20.40, 20.43
  reg 17   16.107, 20.43
  reg 18   20.46, 20.48
  reg 18(2)   20.48
  reg 18(3)   20.48
  reg 18(4)   20.48
  reg 18(5)   20.48
  reg 18(6)   20.48
  reg 19   20.48
Criminal Legal Aid (Financial Resources) Regulations
    2013 SI No 471   14.91
  reg 2   14.62, 14.94
  Pt 2 (regs 5–15)   14.19, 14.45, 14.48
  reg 6   14.64
  reg 8   14.61
  reg 9   14.64
  reg 11   14.64
  reg 12   14.64
  reg 13   14.63
  reg 18   14.95, 14.99
  reg 19   14.93
  reg 20   14.96
  Sch 1   14.97
Criminal Legal Aid (General) Regulations 2013 SI No 9   1.59
  Pt 2 (regs 7–8)   14.19
  reg 9   14.86, 14.164, 16.51,
                                          16.103, 20.22
    reg 9(f)   14.86
    reg 9(g)   14.86
    reg 9(v)   14.87
  reg 12   14.203, 14.205
  reg 18   14.132
  reg 21   14.131, 14.180,
                                          14.190
  reg 23   14.106
  reg 24   14.132
  reg 25   14.132
  reg 29   14.108
Criminal Legal Aid (General) (Amendment)   14.86, 14.203, 14.205,
    Regulations 2013 SI No 2790   16.10

xl Legal Aid Handbook 2024/25 / Table of statutory instruments

Criminal Legal Aid (Recovery of Defence Costs Orders) Regulations 2013 SI No 511	14.180
Criminal Legal Aid (Remuneration) Regulations 2013 SI No 435	1.59, 14.111, 15.65, 15.74, 16.10–16.23, 16.24, 16.29, 16.33, 16.39, 16.58, 16.69, 16.76, 16.82, 16.99, 20.13, 20.18, 20.25, 20.31, 20.44, 20.59, 21.27
reg 9	20.54
reg 13	14.162
reg 14	14.163, 16.94
reg 16(2)	14.16
reg 16(3)	14.16
reg 21	16.98
reg 28	16.92
Sch 1	16.100, 20.49, 20.52
Sch 1 para 1(2)–(5)	16.84
Sch 2	16.86
Sch 2 para 1(2)–(5)	16.84
Sch 2 para 20A	16.87
Sch 2 para 20A(2A)	16.88
Sch 2 para 26	16.87
Sch 4	16.38, 20.12
Sch 4 para 3(2)	14.45
Sch 4 para 3(3)	14.45
Sch 4 para 3(4)	14.48
Sch 4 para 3A	14.53
Sch 4 para 5	16.51
Sch 4 para 5(6)	16.67
Sch 4 para 5A	15.65
Sch 4 para 7	14.167, 15.65
Sch 4 para 8	14.186
Sch 4 para 10	20.54
Sch 4 para 11	14.196, 14.197
Sch 4 para 12	15.65
Sch 5	14.13, 14.16
Criminal Legal Aid (Remuneration) (Amendment) Regulations 2013 SI No 2803	16.10
Criminal Legal Aid (Remuneration) (Amendment) Regulations 2014 SI No 415	16.10
Criminal Legal Aid (Remuneration) (Amendment) (No 2) Regulations 2014 SI No 2422	16.10, 16.95
Criminal Legal Aid (Remuneration) (Amendment) Regulations 2015 SI No 882	16.10
Criminal Legal Aid (Remuneration etc) (Amendment) Regulations 2015 SI No 1369	16.10

Table of statutory instruments   xli

Criminal Legal Aid (Remuneration etc) (Amendment) (No 2) Regulations 2015 SI No 2049	16.10
Criminal Legal Aid (Remuneration) (Amendment) Regulations 2016 SI No 313	16.10
Criminal Legal Aid (Remuneration) (Amendment) Regulations 2017 SI No 1019—	
Sch 2 para 20	16.87
Criminal Legal Aid (Remuneration) (Amendment) Regulations 2018 SI No 220	16.10
Criminal Legal Aid (Remuneration) (Amendment) (No 2) Regulations 2018 SI No 1323	16.10
Criminal Legal Aid (Remuneration) (Amendment) Regulations 2020 SI No 903	16.10
Criminal Legal Aid (Remuneration) (Amendment) Regulations 2021 SI No 80	16.10
Criminal Legal Aid (Remuneration) (Amendment) (No 2) Regulations 2021 SI No 497	16.10
Criminal Legal Aid (Remuneration) (Amendment) Regulations 2022 SI No 848	16.10
Criminal Legal Aid (Remuneration) (Amendment) (Amendment) Regulations 2022 SI No 1010	16.10
Criminal Legal Aid (Remuneration) (Amendment) (Amendment) (No 2) Regulations 2022 SI No 1035	16.10
Criminal Legal Aid (Remuneration) (Amendment) (No 2) Regulations 2022 SI No 1267	16.10
Criminal Legal Aid (Remuneration) (Amendment) Regulations 2023 SI No 97	16.10
Criminal Legal Aid (Remuneration) (Amendment) (No 2) Regulations 2023 SI No 366	16.10
Criminal Legal Aid (Remuneration) (Amendment) (No 3) Regulations 2023 SI No 542	16.10
Criminal Legal Aid (Remuneration) (Amendment) (No 4) Regulations 2023 SI No 1140	16.10
Criminal Legal Aid (Standard Crime Contract) (Amendment) Regulations 2017 SI No 311	16.10
Family Procedure Rules 2010 SI No 2955	15.28
PD 3A	6.101
PD 12J: Child Arrangements and Contact Orders: Domestic Abuse and Harm	19.20, 19.27
r16.6	12.20
r25.12(6)	15.32
r27.3	15.28
PD 27A	19.45
PD 27A para 4.2	19.50
PD 27A para 4.3	19.50
r28.1	15.150
PD 28A para 2.8	15.112
PD: Residence and Contact Orders: Domestic Violence and Harm, 14 January 2009	19.20

Family Proceedings Fees Order 2008 SI No 1054—	
Sch 1 para 9.1	15.113
Immigration (European Economic Area) Regulations 2006 SI No 1003	9.46, 9.47
reg 26	9.47
Immigration (European Economic Area) Regulations 2016 SI No 1052	9.10, 9.15, 9.47
Legal Aid, Sentencing and Punishment of Offenders Act 2012 (Legal Aid for Separated Children) (Miscellaneous Amendments) Order 2019 SI No 1396	9.5
Legal Services Act 2007 (Prescribed Charity) Order 2008 SI No 2680	15.149
Mental Health Tribunal for Wales Rules 2008 SI No 2705 (L 17)—	
r13(5)(a)(1)	10.38
Money Laundering, Terrorist Financing and Transfer of Funds (Information on the Payer) Regulations 2017 SI No 692	22.15
Naval, Military and Air Forces Etc (Disablement and Death) Service Pensions Order 2006 SI No 606	14.96
Prison Rules 1999 SI No 728—	
r46	14.192, 14.203
r46A	14.192, 14.203
Public Contracts Regulations 2015 SI No 102	21.21
reg 113	21.21
Retained EU Law (Revocation and Reform) Act 2023 (Consequential Amendment) Regulations 2023 SI No 1424	3.12
Supreme Court Rules 2024 SI No 949—	
Pt 7 (rr52–61)	15.123
UKSC PD 13: Costs	15.123, 15.151
Transfer of Undertakings (Protection of Employment) Regulations 2006 SI No 246	21.21
Tribunal Procedure (First-tier Tribunal) (Health, Education and Social Care Chamber) Rules 2008 SI No 2699	
r11(7)(a)	10.38
Universal Credit (Transitional Provisions) Regulations 2014 SI No 1230—	
reg 17	14.64
Universal Credit (Transitional Provisions) Regulations (Northern Ireland) 2016 SI No 226—	
reg 17	14.64

Table of EU and international legislation

Charters and conventions
Charter of Fundamental Rights of the European Union
   (2000/C 364/01)—
    Art 47   9.39
Council of Europe Convention on Action against
   Trafficking in Human Beings 2005   9.21
European Convention on Human Rights and
   Fundamental Freedoms 1950   2.25, 3.2, 3.7, 3.9,
                                                           3.12, 3.30, 3.33, 3.35,
                                                            3.39, 3.40–3.49, 4.113,
                                                            4.226, 9.4, 9.36, 9.38,
                                                            9.93, 11.25, 11.30,
                                                            12.10, 12.37, 13.21,
                                                            13.22, 13.27, 15.32,
                                                            15.33
    Art 2   3.39, 3.40, 3.43, 3.45,
                                                            3.62, 9.16, 9.56
    Art 3   3.35, 9.16, 9.17, 9.56
    Art 4   3.28–3.30, 13.23
    Art 6   3.7, 3.8, 3.9, 3.11,
                                                            3.23, 3.24–3.26, 3.27,
                                                            3.28, 3.29, 3.30, 3.33
    Art 6(1)   9.39, 14.86, 14.205
    Art 8   3.7, 3.9, 3.11, 3.23,
                                                            3.27, 3.28, 3.29, 3.33,
                                                            3.35, 9.18, 9.39, 9.41,
                                                            13.23
European Convention on Recognition and
   Enforcement of Decisions concerning Custody
   of Children and on Restoration of Custody of
   Children 1980 (ETS No 105)   2.60
Hague Convention on the Civil Aspects of
   International Child Abduction 1980   2.60, 6.39
United Nations Convention relating to the Status of
   Refugees 1951   9.16
    Protocol relating to the Status of Refugees 1967   9.16

EU Regulations

Regulation (EU) No 604/2013 of the European Parliament and of the Council of 26 June 2013 establishing the criteria and mechanisms for determining the Member State responsible for examining an application for international protection lodged in one of the Member States by a third-country national or a stateless person (Dublin III Regulation) 9.133

Regulation (EU) No 2016/679 of the European Parliament and of the Council of 27 April 2016 on the protection of natural persons with regard to the processing of personal data and on the free movement of such data, and repealing Directive 95/46/EC (General Data Protection Regulation, GDPR) 15.27

EU Directives

Council Directive 2001/55/EC of 20 July 2001 on minimum standards for giving temporary protection in the event of a mass influx of displaced persons and on measures promoting a balance of efforts between Member States in receiving such persons and bearing the consequences thereof (Temporary Protection Directive) 9.16

Council Directive 2004/83/EC of 29 April 2004 on minimum standards for the qualification and status of third country nationals or stateless persons as refugees or as persons who otherwise need international protection and the content of the protection granted (Qualification Directive) 9.16

Council Directive 2005/85/EC of 1 December 2005 on minimum standards on procedures in Member States for granting and withdrawing refugee status (Procedures Directive) 9.52

Abbreviations

AAF	Advocates Attendance Form
ABH	actual bodily harm
ABP	advocates' bundle payment
ADR	alternative dispute resolution
AGFS	Advocates' Graduated Fee Scheme
AIT	Asylum and Immigration Tribunal
AJA 1999	Access to Justice Act 1999
APIL	Association of Personal Injury Lawyers
APPG	All Party Parliamentary Group
ASBCPA 2014	Anti-social Behaviour, Crime and Policing Act 2014
ASBI	anti-social behaviour injunction
ASBO	anti-social behaviour order
ASU	Asylum Screening Unit
ATE	after the event
ATP	Agency Transformation Programme
AvMA	Action against Medical Accidents
BACS	Bankers' Automated Clearing Service
BC	Borough Council
BSB	Bar Standards Board
CAFCASS	Children and Family Court Advisory and Support Service
CAPA	claims against public authorities
CBA	Criminal Bar Association
CBAM	Criminal Bills Assessment Manual
CBP	court bundle payment
CCA	contract compliance audit
CCFS	Care Case Fee Scheme
CCG	clinical commissioning group
CCLF	Crown Court Litigator Fee
CCMS	Client and Cost Management System
CCRC	Criminal Cases Review Commission
CCU	Complex Crime Unit; or Criminal Cases Unit
CDS	Criminal Defence Service
CFA	Conditional Fee Agreement
CILEx	Chartered Legal Executive
CJSM	Criminal Justice Secure Mail
CLA	Civil Legal Advice

CLAC	Community Legal Advice Centre
CLAN	Community Legal Advice Network
CLAS	Criminal Litigation Accreditation Scheme
CLR	Controlled Legal Representation
CLS	Community Legal Service
CMRF	Consolidated Matter Report Form
CMRH	case management review hearing
CMS	case management system
CoP	Court of Protection
CPGFS	Care Proceedings Graduated Fees Scheme
CPR	Civil Procedure Rules 1998
CPS	Crown Prosecution Service
CWA	Contracted Work and Administration
DAR	designated accredited representative
DBS	Disclosure and Barring Service
DDVC	Destitution Domestic Violence Concession
DFT	detention fast track
DHSC	Department of Health and Social Care
DLA	disability living allowance
DoL	deprivation of liberty
DPA 2018	Data Protection Act 2018
DSCC	Defence Solicitor Call Centre
DWP	Department for Work and Pensions
ECCT	Exceptional and Complex Case Team
ECF	exceptional case funding
ECF Guidance	Lord Chancellor's Exceptional Funding Guidance (Non-Inquests)
ECHR	European Convention for the Protection of Human Rights and Fundamental Freedoms
EEA	European Economic Area
EPA	Environmental Protection Act 1990
ESA	employment and support allowance
EU	European Union
FAQs	frequently asked questions
FAS	Family Advocacy Scheme
FDR	Financial Dispute Resolution
FGFS	Family Graduated Fees Scheme
FGM	female genital mutilation
FLBA	Family Law Bar Association
FOH	Flexible Operating Hours
FOIA 2000	Freedom of Information Act 2000
FTE	full-time equivalent
FTT	First-tier Tribunal of the Senior Courts of England and Wales
GBH	grievous bodily harm
GDPR	General Data Protection Regulation
GF	graduated fee
GFS	Graduated Fee Scheme
HCCH	Hague Conference on Private International Law

HLPAS	Housing Loss Prevention Advice Service
HMCTS	His Majesty's Courts and Tribunals Service
HMRC	His Majesty's Revenue and Customs
HPCDS	Housing Possession Court Duty Scheme
HR	hourly rates
HRA 1998	Human Rights Act 1998
IAAS	Immigration and Asylum Accreditation Scheme
IAC	Immigration and Asylum Chamber
IALS	Institute of Advanced Legal Studies
ICA	Independent Costs Assessor
ICC	individual case contract
IDPC	Initial Details of Prosecution Case
IFA	Independent Funding Adjudicator
ILR	indefinite leave to remain
Inquest ECF	Lord Chancellor's Exceptional Funding Guidance (Inquests) Guidance
IPCC	Independent Police Complaints Commission
IRC	immigration removal centre
IRH	Issues Resolution Hearing
JSA	jobseeker's allowance
KC	King's Counsel
KPI	key performance indicator
LAA	Legal Aid Agency
LAB	Legal Aid Board
LAPG	Legal Aid Practitioners Group
LASPO	Legal Aid, Sentencing and Punishment of Offenders Act 2012
LAT	Legal Aid Transformation
LBC	London Borough Council
LCN	Law Centres Network
LGFS	Litigators' Graduated Fee Scheme
LIP	litigant in person
LLP	limited liability partnership
LSC	Legal Services Commission
MCA 2005	Mental Capacity Act 2005
MHA 1983	Mental Health Act 1983
MHLA	Mental Health Lawyers Association
MHRT	Mental Health Review Tribunal
MHT	Mental Health Tribunal
MI	management information
MIAM	Mediation Information and Assessment Meeting
MoJ	Ministry of Justice
MOU	memorandum of understanding
MPA	multi-party action
NAA 1948	National Assistance Act 1948
NABA 2022	Nationality and Borders Act 2022
NAM	non-asylum matter
NAO	National Audit Office
NASS	National Asylum Support Service

NCVD	National Centre for Domestic Violence
NfP	not-for-profit
NIAA 2002	Nationality, Immigration and Asylum Act 2002
NRM	National Referral Mechanism
NRPF	no recourse to public funds
OFS	open financial statement
OISC	Office of the Immigration Services Commissioner
PACE	Police and Criminal Evidence Act 1984
PAR	Provider Activity Report
PAS	Prisoners' Advice Service
PAYG	pay as you go
PD	practice direction
PDS	Public Defender Service
PFLRS	Private Family Law Representation Scheme
PIP	personal independence payment
PMS	practice management system
POA	payment on account
POCA 2002	Proceeds of Crime Act 2002
PoD	Point of Dispute
POP	Point of Principle of General Importance
PRFD	Principal Registry of the Family Division
PRN	Priority Removal Notice
PSED	public sector equality duty
PSPO	public spaces protection order
PSQ	Police Station Qualification
PSRAS	Police Station Representative Accreditation Scheme
PTE	part-time equivalent
PTPH	pre-trial preparation hearing
QASA	Quality Assurance Scheme for Advocates
QM	Quality Mark
RDCO	Recovery of Defence Costs Order
RSS	really simple syndication
SAAC	Self-Assessment Audit Checklist
SCA	Single Competent Authority
SCCO	Senior Court Costs Office
SCU	Special Cases Unit
SEN	special educational needs
SGO	special guardianship order
SIAC	Special Immigration Appeals Commission
SMOD	subject matter of the dispute
SMP	standard monthly payment
SQM	Specialist Quality Mark
SRA	Solicitors Regulation Authority
SWL	social welfare law
SWPI	significant wider public interest
TFR	targeted file review
TLS	The Law Society
TPIM	Terrorism Prevention and Investigation Measure
UASC	unaccompanied asylum-seeking child

UFN	unique file number
UKBA	UK Border Agency
UKVI	UK Visas and Immigration
UT	Upper Tribunal of the Senior Courts of England and Wales
VAT	value added tax
VHCC	Very High Cost Case
VMP	variable monthly payment
YLAL	Young Legal Aid Lawyers
YOI	Young Offender Institution

Glossary

Advice and Assistance	Funding for advice short of representation in criminal cases, granted by the provider under contract with the LAA
CCMS	Client and Contract Management System – online portal to submit applications, amendments and claims to the LAA for civil and family licensed work.
CMRF	This used to be an actual paper form (controlled matter report form) used to submit monthly claims for civil and family controlled work and crime lower claims to the Legal Services Commission. The forms have been replaced with the CWA portal; but the expression 'CMRF code' remains in use to describe the codes which are still used. https://www.gov.uk/government/publications/consolidated-matter-reportforms-civil-codes
Community Legal Service	Holistic provision of civil legal advice and representation under the Access to Justice Act 1999. Concept and branding abolished under the LASPO Act 2012.
Contract Compliance Audit	An audit assessing whether, based on a sample of files, an organisation is complying with the requirements of civil or criminal contracts.
Contract Manager	Official of the LAA with responsibility for managing the contractual relationship between the two parties.
Contract Manager Visit	See Financial Stewardship audit.
Controlled Legal Representation	Representation before the Mental Health Review Tribunal, or in the Immigration Appellate Authority, granted by the provider under contract with the LAA.
Contract Liaison Manager	A member of the organisation's staff designated as the person responsible for quality and contract compliance and the main point of contact for the LAA. This role was previously known as the Quality Representative or Franchise Representative.

Controlled Work Administration (CWA)	Online portal used to submit monthly claims for civil and family controlled work and crime lower. Also used by the LAA for e.g. execution of contract documentation.
Corrective Action	Action agreed with an LAA auditor to rectify a breach of a Quality Mark or contract requirement.
Criminal Defence Service	Provision of Criminal defence advice and representation funded under the Access to Justice Act 1999. Concept and branding abolished under the LASPO Act 2012.
Delegated Function	Delegated function (e.g. to grant emergency representation in civil and family matters) by the Lord Chancellor and the LAA's Director of Casework to practitioners. See Devolved Power.
Devolved Power	A power (e.g. to grant a Representation Certificate) that could be exercised on the LAA's behalf by the provider in certain defined circumstances. Known as a 'delegated function' under the LASPO Act 2012.
Escape fee case	Case which would normally be paid by way of fixed fee; but which escapes because the time and item value exceeds a set ratio (the exact ratios differ depending on the scheme).
Exceptional and Complex Cases Unit	Department of the LAA, dealing with individual case contracts in high cost civil cases.
Exceptional case	Previous name under the Access to Justice Act 1999 for an escape fee case. See also below.
Exceptional case funding	Case which would normally be outside the scope of the LASPO Act 2012, but is eligible for funding under Section 10, because failure to do so would breach the client's human rights (or would be likely to do so).
Financial Stewardship audit	Type of audit conducted by a Contract Manager on a provider's premises, focussing on financial issues. Also referred to as 'Contract Manager Visit'.
Franchise Representative	See Contract Liaison Manager.
Funding Code	The criteria by which the LAA decided whether to grant all levels of civil funding under the Access to Justice Act 1999. Preserved only for cases existing as at 31 March 2013.
Help at Court	An adjunct to Legal Help, which allows representation at particular hearings in defined cases

Glossary

Individual Case Contract	A separate contract between the LAA and a provider on a particular case, usually because of high costs.
Inter partes costs	Costs agreed between the parties when cases are settled between them rather than by Court Order. The rates are higher than Legal Aid rates.
Legal Aid	Legal advice and representation funded by the central government through the LAA and the Courts.
Legal Help	Advice short of representation, granted by the provider under contract with the LAA.
Licensed Work	Civil representation certificates – funding granted by the LAA or under delegated functions by providers.
Matter Start	Also known as a 'new matter start' or NMS, a Matter start is a case started under Legal Help, Help with Mediation or Controlled Legal Representation and Family Help Lower (Public Law) where there has been no previous Legal Help.
McKenzie Adviser	A person who is present at a hearing to advise and assist, but not represent, a party.
Miscellaneous work	Work which falls within LASPO sch. 1 but does not fall within one of the defined categories of work. The work included is listed in the 2018 contract category definitions. All contract schedules include at least 5 matter starts which can be used for this work, and more can be requested.
Operational Assurance	Department of the LAA, which carries out data analysis and audits to support Contract Managers. Previously known as Provider Assurance.
Prior Authority	Formal confirmation that the LAA considers a disbursement to be reasonable, and therefore that the costs will be paid at the end of the case. May also allow a payment on account.
Peer review	An assessment of the quality of legal work carried out by independent lawyers working under contract with the LAA.
Pro bono	Free legal advice and/or representation.
Procurement area	Geographical area covered by a contract with the LAA, often based on a top tier local authority area; but increasingly on larger geographical areas.
Provider	Term used by the LAA to describe any type of organisation with which it has a contract to deliver services.

Public Defender Service	Solicitors employed by the LAA to do criminal work, in competition with private practice. 4 offices in England and Wales.
Quality Concern	A failure to meet a requirement of the Specialist Quality Mark.
Critical Concerns	are more serious than General Concerns. The organisation will be required to put corrective action in place, or in particularly serious cases, will be at risk of SQM termination.
Quality Mark	An accreditation scheme regulating conduct and quality of legal services. Providers of legal services must hold a Specialist Quality Mark (awarded by the LAA) or Lexcel (awarded by the Law Society) in order to be eligible to hold a contract. Compliance may be audited by the LAA or their authorised contractor, Recognising Excellence (from April 2017).
Quality Representative	See Contract Liaison Manager.
Regional Office	Historically, an office of the LAA dealing with all funding and local policy matters within its region. Following restructuring, Regional offices act as a base for staff and may have some processing functions.
Representation Certificate	Funding for representation in civil and family cases, granted by the LAA or in emergencies by the provider.
Representation Order	Funding for representation in criminal cases, granted by the Courts.
Schedule payment limit	The total amount payable to an organisation under a contract.
Special Cases Unit	Former name. See Exceptional and Complex Cases Unit.
Specialist Quality Mark	See Quality Mark.
Standard monthly payment	The monthly payment to an organisation under contract usually one twelfth of the schedule payment limit (subject to variation during the year). See also variable monthly payment.
Statutory Charge	A charge held by the LAA over property recovered or preserved in funded civil proceedings, intended to allow the LAA to recover the costs of funding the case.

Transaction Criteria	An audit tool, consisting of checklists used to assess whether a file contained required information from the early days of 'franchising'. Superseded by peer review.
Variable monthly payment	An alternative to the standard monthly payment to an organisation under contract, paid to the value of claims submitted.
Very High Cost Cases Panel	A panel of organisations accredited by the LAA to conduct VHCC crime cases. Only accredited organisations may do these cases.

PART A

Legal aid advice and litigation

CHAPTER 1

Legal aid: what you need to know at a glance

Edited by Sue James and Simon Mullings

1.1	**Introduction**
1.5	**How legal aid works**
1.21	The statutory foundation
1.28	**The LAA documentation**
1.30	**Keeping up to date**
1.37	**Civil and family – key documentation**
1.37	The Standard Civil Contract 2024
	Overview • The Standard Civil Contract Specification
1.44	Guidance
1.47	Eligibility guidance
1.48	Regulations and guidance
1.50	Costs Assessment Guidance
1.52	Fee exemption and remission
1.54	**Criminal defence – key documentation**
1.54	The 2022 and 2025 Standard Crime Contracts
	Overview • The Crime Specification and regulations
1.60	Eligibility guidance
1.63	Criminal Bills Assessment Manual
1.65	**Client and Cost Management System**

continued

1.67	**Training and support**
1.68	Case management roles
1.69	Billing roles
1.70	Office manager
1.71	Making applications and supervision
1.78	Declarations
1.79	Notifications
1.82	Expiry dates
1.83	Assigning counsel
1.84	Payments on account
1.86	Trouble-shooting
1.88	**Legal challenges**
1.96	**Logos**
1.97	**Legal aid support on X (formerly Twitter)**
1.98	**Legal Aid Agency's coronavirus responses**

Introduction

1.1 We know that you may not read this book from beginning to end but will dip into it as needed. However, we suggest you take a few minutes to read this chapter. It provides an overview of the legal aid scheme and an outline of the rules and guidance you will need to be aware of and consult where necessary.

1.2 Legal aid has a history of going back to at least 1948 and is the means by which access to justice is available to some of the poorest people in society. The history has been well documented, including previous editions of this Handbook, Sir Henry Brooke's history[1] written for the Bach Commission and LAG publications, including the pamphlet 'Legal Aid Matters'[2] and the book *Austerity Justice* and *The Justice Gap*.[3]

1.3 Legal aid is very heavily regulated and controlled. If you do not ensure that you are aware of the statutes, regulations, rules and guidance, you may have applications or bills delayed or rejected by the Legal Aid Agency (LAA) for technical errors (and there is a contract key performance indicator[4] (KPI) that limits rejects to five per cent as part of the schedule), or refused because you have not explained your client's case in an appropriate way, or you may have claims for payment disallowed. All these things are important because they may cause your client unnecessary delay, waste your time, and could even threaten the financial viability of your organisation. If you are not sure what to do, look it up and discuss the issue with your supervisor or a colleague. Legal Aid Practitioners Group (LAPG) has a useful online course for people new to civil legal aid.[5]

1.4 In this book we provide at the start of each chapter a list of the key points and resources you need in that particular area of law or practice.

---

1 Bach Commission on Access to Justice, *The History Of Legal Aid 1945–2010*, 2017, Appendix 6, available at: www.fabians.org.uk/wp-content/uploads/2017/09/Bach-Commission-Appendix-6-F-1.pdf.
2 Available as a free download at: www.lag.org.uk/shop/products/209225/legal-aid-matters.
3 S Hynes, *Austerity Justice*, Legal Action Group, 2012; S Hynes and J Robins, *The Justice Gap: Whatever happened to legal aid?*, LAG, 2009.
4 Standard Civil Contract 2024 Specification para 2.67 (available at: www.gov.uk/government/publications/standard-civil-contract-2024).
5 See: https://lapg.co.uk/courses.

How legal aid works

1.5 Legal aid is funding, by the state, of individual cases for individual members of the public. It is primarily delivered by lawyers[6] contracted to a government body, the LAA (an agency of the Ministry of Justice). This section looks at the underlying principles necessary to understand how the scheme works in practice.

1.6 Under the current scheme, the government has decided that it is prepared to fund certain types of legal problem. Broadly speaking, these are:

- advice to and representation of people being prosecuted in the criminal courts, though generally not for very minor offences;
- advice to and representation of people seeking to appeal criminal convictions;
- advice to and representation of prisoners in respect of their detention;
- advice to people with certain limited types of civil and family legal problems; and
- representation of claimants and defendants/respondents in certain types of civil and family cases in courts and some tribunals.

1.7 The LAA only directly pays lawyers or the organisations that employ them. However, those payments will cover both the professional charges of the lawyers involved (usually called 'profit costs') and expenses they incur in running the case – both out-of-pocket expenses and the services of other professionals such as expert witnesses (usually called 'disbursements'). Lawyers are paid on the basis of either an hourly rate, a fixed fee per case or a combination of the two, depending on the type of case.

1.8 The first level of separation within the legal aid scheme is between civil and criminal cases.

1.9 **Criminal cases** are those involving police investigations;[7] criminal prosecutions and appeals; and the treatment of prisoners. Funding covers:

- advice to those subject to police investigation, including representation at the police station and in interviews under caution;

---

6 For these purposes, we define lawyers broadly as including not just solicitors, barristers and legal executives and their staff, but also non-qualified advisers working alongside them.
7 Including investigations by other agencies with similar powers – see chapter 14.

- representation in court during investigations for matters such as bail and police applications for extensions of detention time;
- the provision of duty solicitors to advise and represent people at court without their own solicitor – but only for one hearing, not the whole case;
- representation in criminal proceedings and appeals, including:
  - advice on the law and evidence;
  - investigation of defences and interviewing witnesses;
  - commissioning expert witness evidence; and
  - advocacy in the court; and
- advice and representation to prisoners on matters relating to detention and release.

1.10 The main types of funding available in criminal cases are:
- **Advice and assistance** – funding for a solicitor and their staff or agents to give general advice about criminal matters, including in situations where other types of funding are not available.
- **Police station attendance** – funding for a solicitor and their staff or agents to attend a police station to advise and represent someone who is the subject of a police investigation.
- **Advocacy assistance** – funding, generally for a solicitor rather than a barrister, to represent someone in court for something other than a prosecution – for example, a police bail application – or in prison disciplinary hearings.
- **Representation orders** – funding for a solicitor to prepare a defence case where someone is being prosecuted for an offence (or is appealing a conviction), and funding for an advocate (barrister or solicitor) to present the case in court.

1.11 Almost all legal aid funding – civil and criminal – is only available if the applicant for legal aid can show that they pass two tests: the means test and the merits test:
- **The means test** says that legal aid will only be available to people whose income and capital are below prescribed levels.
- **The merits test** in criminal cases says that legal aid will only be available where it is justified, often by the seriousness of the offence and any sentence that might follow. The merits test in civil cases says that legal aid will only be available where it is justified either by the importance of the case or by the chances of it being successful.

1.12 There are exceptions where either the means test, the merits test or both do not apply. These cases are generally only what are perceived to be the most important ones – mainly police station representation in crime, housing possession court duty advice and representation and some early legal advice to those facing possession proceedings, mental health detention, and taking children into care in civil cases.

1.13 As well as the means and merits tests, civil cases must pass a **scope test**. This limits the sorts of civil cases legal aid will fund not by the circumstances of the applicant, but the characteristics of their case. Legal aid is only available if the case is one of those specifically listed in Schedule 1 to the Legal Aid, Sentencing and Punishment of Offenders Act 2012 (LASPO) (see chapter 2 and appendix A for the full list).

1.14 In civil cases, most (but not all) claims about money are not funded, but cases involving loss of the home, abuses by the state, human rights, detention and liberty and freedom from persecution generally are. For a full discussion of what is and is not funded, see chapter 2 and the subject-specific chapters.

1.15 Cases that are outside the scope of legal aid can still sometimes be funded. Chapter 3 describes the exceptional funding scheme – a discretionary scheme where legal aid may be made available, on a case-by-case basis, in situations where it is generally outside the scope of the scheme.

1.16 If a case is in scope, and qualifies on means and merits (where applicable), there are two main types of funding available:

- **Legal Help** – this covers general advice on cases which are not (or are not yet) in court, either because proceedings have not started, or because help is needed to apply for funding to cover proceedings. This type of funding does not cover representation in court (except in very limited cases where one-off hearings can be done under an extension of Legal Help called Help at Court).
- **Legal Representation** – this is only available once court proceedings have been issued (though it is also available to claimants to fund the issuing of proceedings). It allows a solicitor to give advice, prepare the case, commission expert evidence and instruct an advocate, and allows an advocate (either solicitor or barrister) to present the case in court. This type of work is sometimes called certificate or certificated work because the grant of legal aid is signified by the issuing of a legal aid certificate.

1.17 There are some extra types of funding available in certain family cases, immigration cases, housing cases and mental health cases – see chapters 6, 7, 9, 10 and 11.

1.18 For both civil and criminal work, the LAA contracts with organisations (mostly solicitors' firms and not-for-profit advice agencies, but also a few who are regulated by the Bar Standards Board (BSB) and the Office of the Immigration Services Commissioner (OISC)) to provide legal aid to the public. The contracts allow organisations to take on cases and be paid for them.

1.19 The contracts provide for fixed or variable monthly payments to be made to the organisation. These payments cover lower value casework. The monthly payments are set off against individual case fees, with the idea that the two balance out over time. Crown Court representation and Legal Representation are paid separately to the monthly contract payments.

1.20 Barristers who do legal aid work are not paid under a contract with the LAA. In the magistrates' court, they are usually paid by solicitors out of their contract payment. In the Crown Court and civil courts, they are paid direct by the LAA on a case-by-case basis.

The statutory foundation

1.21 Civil legal aid, or as described within the Act, 'civil legal services', is defined by LASPO as only that which is included in Schedule 1 to the Act. In contrast to the Access to Justice Act (AJA) 1999, which provided that work was in scope unless specifically excluded by the Act, LASPO says that only work explicitly *included* in Schedule 1 is in scope.

1.22 LASPO s8 defines what civil legal aid is. It includes providing:
- advice as to how the law applies in particular circumstances;
- advice and assistance in relation to legal proceedings;
- other advice and assistance in relation to the prevention, settlement or other resolution of legal disputes; and
- advice and assistance in relation to the enforcement of decisions in legal proceedings or other decisions by which disputes are resolved.

1.23 Advice and assistance includes both representation and mediation and other forms of dispute resolution.

1.24 LASPO s9 provides that only areas of law expressly listed in Schedule 1 are in scope and can be funded under legal aid. If work is not listed in Schedule 1, it will not be covered by legal aid and you will not be paid for doing it.

1.25 LASPO s10 makes provision for what are known as 'exceptional cases'. Where cases are not covered by the scope rules in Part 1 of

Schedule 1 but certain conditions are satisfied, an application may be made to the Director of Legal Aid Casework to fund the case even though it is otherwise out of scope. See chapter 3 for more on exceptional cases. Note that these cases should not be confused with Legal Help cases where costs exceed three times the fixed fee – such cases were previously known as 'exceptional cases' under the AJA 1999 regime, but are now called 'escape fee' cases.

1.26 LASPO ss11 and 21 provide that legal aid will only be awarded if merits and financial criteria respectively are satisfied. Sections 25 and 26 create the statutory charge and give costs protection.

1.27 It is under these sections that the relevant regulations are made.

The LAA documentation

1.28 Until 2015 the LAA produced a manual which contained all relevant documents such as statute, regulations, rules and guidance. However, the LAA Manual was withdrawn from 31 August 2015.[8] The LAA's view is that all necessary guidance is available on its website.

1.29 In this book, wherever possible, we tell you where you can download a document from the LAA's website. We have given web addresses to help you locate what you need, although these are subject to change.

Keeping up to date

1.30 Legal aid can change quickly, as the LAA changes its approach to issues and as challenges are played out in the courts. Everyone involved with legal aid funding needs to keep up with the latest developments. The LAA relies on you to check what is on its website. So, what is the best way of keeping up to date?

1.31 You can sign up to the LAA's email newsletter, which will provide you with updates, announcements and changes. The updates give you a brief summary of the issue, and a link to further information. They make keeping up much easier. You can subscribe through the LAA website at: https://labulletin.org.uk/p/4P-5T3/sign-up-form.

1.32 The LAA website is part of the gov.uk network and so follows the standard gov.uk layout and contents structure. This means that it can

---

8 See: www.gov.uk/government/news/civilcrime-news-providers-no-longer-need-to-buy-legal-aid-manual.

1.33 One useful feature of the LAA site is the 'Latest from the Legal Aid Agency' section on the front page, which is automatically updated whenever any document or page on the LAA site is added or amended. The 'See all latest documents' link contains an RSS feed which can be added to a feed reader to alert you to any changes or newly published material on the LAA site. It is well worth bookmarking the key pages within the LAA site – such as the forms, contracts and billing pages – so that they are easy to return to.

1.34 The Legal Aid Agency has two X (formerly known as Twitter) accounts that are worth following if you are on X: @LAAHelpTeam, which is the customer service account, and @LegalAidAgency, which is the official channel.

1.35 The civil legal aid regulations, contracts and guidance can be found at: www.gov.uk/guidance/civil-legal-aid-civil-regulations-civil-contracts-and-guidance#statutory-materials. The crime regulations, contracts and guidance can be found at: www.gov.uk/guidance/criminal-legal-aid-crime-regulations-crime-contracts-and-guidance.

1.36 There is also a public information website on legal aid at: www.gov.uk/legal-aid. Other useful public information sites are Advicenow[9] and Citizens Advice.[10]

Civil and family – key documentation

The Standard Civil Contract 2024

Overview

1.37 Most civil legal aid providers operate under the LAA's Standard Civil Contract 2024 and the Civil Legal Advice contracts, which govern the provision of the telephone service.

1.38 The Standard Civil Contract 2024 includes the housing possession duty and early legal advice scheme, called the Housing Loss Prevention Advice Service (HLPAS).

1.39 The contract contains many detailed provisions concerning the way you work with clients, as well as setting out the formal relationship between your organisation and the LAA. You can download the

---

9 At: www.advicenow.org.uk.
10 At: www.citizensadvice.org.uk.

contract from the LAA website at: www.gov.uk/topic/legal-aid-for-providers/contracts.

1.40 Part A of this book sets out where you can find the main provisions in relation to casework; see Part C: 'Managing legal aid work' for more information on the contractual relationship with the LAA.

The Standard Civil Contract Specification

1.41 The section of the contract that you will need to be familiar with is the Standard Civil Contract Specification. The Specification can be downloaded from the website noted above. It is split into general rules and category-specific rules; where the two conflict, the category-specific rules take precedence.[11] The Specification rules are discussed in detail in chapters 2–13 of this book.

1.42 The Specification contains an introduction to the main workings of the various funding schemes:
- Section 1 contains general provisions; for example, it explains how to apply regulations and guidance, what is in your contract schedule and rules concerning additional matter starts.
- Section 2 gives information about service standards, where work can or must be done, supervisor standards, and, crucially, KPIs.
- Section 3 explains the scope of controlled work and rules applying to it.
- Section 4 explains how controlled work is paid for.
- Sections 5 and 6 discuss the scope and main rules applying to licensed work, payment arrangements and the statutory charge.[12]

1.43 The remaining sections are category-specific, and each Specification has its own sections depending on which contract it is part of. Each category-specific section begins with supervisor standards, and then moves on to any additional rules that apply to that category:
- section 7 – family;
- section 8 – immigration;
- section 9 – mental health;
- section 10 – housing and debt;
- section 11 – community care;
- section 12 – welfare benefits;

---

11 See Standard Contract 2024 Specification para 1.2.
12 Although rates of payment are shown in the Civil Legal Aid (Remuneration) Regulations 2013 – see: www.gov.uk/guidance/civil-legal-aid-civil-regulations-civil-contracts-and-guidance#statutory-materials.

- section 13 – claims against public authorities;[13]
- section 14 – public law;
- section 15 – clinical negligence;
- section 16 – education;
- section 17 – discrimination; and
- section 18 – family mediation.

Guidance

1.44 The LAA has created a training and support website, which covers civil and family and also crime and online services.[14] These include many quick guides to LAA processes, including the Client and Cost Management System (CCMS) (see chapter 5 for more information) and a recorded webinar on family high cost cases.

1.45 The Lord Chancellor and the Director of Legal Aid Casework have issued a series of guidance documents using their LASPO statutory powers,[15] including:

- *Lord Chancellor's Guidance under section 4 of the Legal Aid, Sentencing and Punishment of Offenders Act 2012*;
- *Lord Chancellor's Guidance on Exceptional Case Funding* (there are two, one for inquest cases and one for other cases); and
- *Director's Guidance on Evidence Requirements for Private Family Law Matters*.

1.46 There is a series of guides and manuals covering general subjects such as financial eligibility and costs assessment, as well as category-specific matters such as family mediation and housing court duty schemes. There is also guidance for crime practitioners, such as *Crown Court Fee Guidance* and the *Criminal Bills Assessment Manual*.[16]

Eligibility guidance

1.47 The legal aid website has links to guidance materials on eligibility on its training and support website.[17] There is also a means testing tool

---

13 The category formerly known as actions against the police, etc.
14 See: https://legalaidlearning.justice.gov.uk.
15 See: www.gov.uk/guidance/funding-and-costs-assessment-for-civil-and-crime-matters#lord-chancellors-guidance.
16 See: www.gov.uk/guidance/funding-and-costs-assessment-for-civil-and-crime-matters.
17 See: https://legalaidlearning.justice.gov.uk.

on the website to check whether your client qualifies for legal aid.[18] This was up to date at the date of writing (last updated on 15 May 2024) but check the updates list at the bottom of the page. See chapter 2 of this Handbook for more information about eligibility.

Regulations and guidance

1.48 The regulations create a set of rules that govern whether an individual's case can be funded under legal aid. The key regulations are:
- Civil Legal Aid (Merits Criteria) Regulations 2013;
- Civil Legal Aid (Procedure) Regulations 2012;
- Civil Legal Aid (Remuneration) Regulations 2013; and
- Civil Legal Aid (Financial Resources and Payment for Services) Regulations 2013.

If legislation.gov.uk shows that regulations have been amended but not incorporated you should always check the amendment regulations as well as the original ones.

1.49 In addition, the LAA has issued the *Lord Chancellor's Guidance under section 4 of the Legal Aid, Sentencing and Punishment of Offenders Act 2012*[19] on the way the regulations should operate. It is a key reference document, whether you are granting legal aid yourself, as controlled work, or under delegated functions (previously known as devolved powers), or whether you are submitting an application for the LAA to decide.

Costs Assessment Guidance

1.50 Many caseworkers focus so hard on achieving the best possible job for their clients that they lose sight of the financial side of the case. This is not sustainable, so it is important to be aware of the rules that govern what you can and cannot claim for.

1.51 The LAA has guidance on claiming, the Costs Assessment Guidance, which can be downloaded from: www.gov.uk/guidance/funding-and-costs-assessment-for-civil-and-crime-matters. See chapters 15 and 16 of this book for more information about getting paid. There is also a summary of the Costs Assessment Guidance at appendix C.

---

18 See: https://check-your-client-qualifies-for-legal-aid.service.gov.uk.
19 See: www.gov.uk/guidance/funding-and-costs-assessment-for-civil-and-crime-matters#lord-chancellors-guidance.

Fee exemption and remission

1.52 The fee exemption and remission scheme is administered by HM Courts and Tribunals Service (HMCTS) and is not part of legal aid funding. If your client has a representation certificate, court fees are a recoverable disbursement so you do not need to worry about exemption. However, if your client is being assisted under Legal Help or Controlled Legal Representation then the fee is not recoverable as a disbursement. Such clients are not automatically exempt from fees, but they may apply for exemption or remission of fees based on their means where the type of proceedings is covered by fee exemption.

1.53 There is an eligibility checker at: www.gov.uk/get-help-with-court-fees.

Criminal defence – key documentation

The 2022 and 2025 Standard Crime Contracts

Overview

1.54 The 2022 Standard Crime Contract[20] came into effect on 1 October 2022. It is due to come to an end on 30 September 2025. It covers both 'own client' and duty solicitor work.

1.55 In September 2024, the LAA started a tender process for new contracts. In a radical change to past practice, the LAA announced that the contract is intended to run for a maximum of 10 years and new providers will be able to join at any point between the contract start date and the final year.

1.56 Part A of this Handbook sets out where you can find the main provisions in relation to casework; see Part C: 'Managing legal aid work' for more information on the contractual relationship with the LAA.

The Crime Specification and regulations

1.57 The section of the contract that caseworkers will most need to be familiar with is the Specification. The 2022 Contract can be downloaded from: www.gov.uk/government/publications/standard-crime-contract-2022. The 2025 Contract can be downloaded at: www.gov.uk/government/publications/standard-crime-contract-2025.

---

20 Available at: www.gov.uk/government/publications/standard-crime-contract-2022.

1.58 The Specification covers general rules, among other things: definitions, service standards, qualifying criteria, carrying out and claiming for work, as well as specific provisions for very high cost cases, prison law, appeals and associated civil work. It also provides information about claims assessment and review procedures (although this is not the main source document, see below). The Standard Crime Contract Specification 2025 is broken down into 13 sections.

1.59 The crime fees are set out in the Criminal Legal Aid (Remuneration) Regulations 2013 and subsequent amendments (eg in 2022, increasing a range of fees) – see chapter 16. Other rules are set out in the Criminal Legal Aid (General) Regulations 2013 and other regulations. If legislation.gov.uk shows that there are amendments that have not been incorporated, you should always check the amendment regulations as well as the original ones.

Eligibility guidance

1.60 Advice in the police station is not means tested.

1.61 Representation in the magistrates' court is means tested. There is an eligibility calculator on the legal aid website: www.gov.uk/criminal-legal-aid-means-testing. Clients who are not eligible for legal aid in the magistrates' court and pay for their defence privately can apply to reclaim their costs from Central Funds if they are subsequently acquitted.

1.62 Representation in the Crown Court is also means tested. If clients are found not guilty, their contributions will be repaid. Clients who are not eligible for legal aid in the Crown Court and pay for their defence privately can apply to reclaim their costs from Central Funds if they are subsequently acquitted. The rules and forms can be found at: www.gov.uk/claim-back-costs-from-cases-in-the-criminal-courts. In either case, any refund will be paid at legal aid rates – not the full private costs incurred.

Criminal Bills Assessment Manual

1.63 Ensuring that you will be paid is as important in criminal defence work as in civil and family, mentioned above.

1.64 The *Criminal Bills Assessment Manual* (CBAM) elaborates many of the principles in the contract. It can be found at: www.gov.uk/funding-and-costs-assessment-for-civil-and-crime-matters.

Client and Cost Management System

1.65 A detailed guide to the LAA's CCMS is set out in chapter 5. This section provides an introduction for those unfamiliar with it. CCMS is the LAA's system for managing civil cases and dealing with providers.

1.66 CCMS became mandatory for all new civil and family certificate work from April 2016 (February 2016 for Special Children Act cases). The LAA is in the process of replacing the user interface aspect of CCMS with a new digital service called 'Apply'. Details of this are set out in chapter 5.

Training and support

1.67 The LAA has guides to setting up the system and training modules for many common functions: https://legalaidlearning.justice.gov.uk.

Case management roles

1.68 Users need to be allocated case management roles. The key roles are 'Case management' and 'Case Management Supervisor'. Case management allows for cases to be viewed and amendments and applications to be prepared. Only Case Management Supervisors, who must be 'authorised litigators' (ie solicitors, barristers or Chartered Legal Executives authorised to conduct litigation by their regulatory body), can submit applications, amendments and outcome codes. It is essential that staff are allocated the correct role (and not given privileges that would not be compliant with their job role).

Billing roles

1.69 There are two billing roles: 'Bill Preparation' and 'Bill Supervisor'. 'Bill Preparation' allows bills to be drafted but not submitted. Supporting documents can be submitted as 'Bill Preparation'. A Bill Supervisor must be sufficiently qualified to sign bills. External costs draftsmen can be authorised to prepare but not submit bills.

Office manager

1.70 This role has an overview of all cases, notifications and actions within an organisation, but does not allow the user to create or submit applications or bills.

Making applications and supervision

1.71 CCMS has been created in such a way that, to an extent, the questions asked are dependent on answers to other questions and so the electronic screens do not mirror the paper forms which they replaced.

1.72 CCMS has a significant impact on supervision. A printed summary of an application can be given to the supervisor (authorised litigator), but they must then:
- log in;
- navigate to the correct case; and
- submit the case.

1.73 All communication on a case is done through secure online message boards. This means that supervisors need to be proactive to monitor the way cases are developing. As there is no direct way to pass on an action in the system, good communication is essential. Supervisors will not automatically receive details of the notifications and actions sent to a fee earner. However, a 'Case Management Supervisor' can review them by going to 'Your actions/notifications', 'Refine search'.

1.74 It helps to ensure that the LAA reference number (currently a 12-figure number starting with a 3) is always clear on a file and in any communication. This ensures that the case can be easily accessed on CCMS.

1.75 The best process for making submissions and other tasks will depend on the supervisor, support staff and fee earner. A number of practitioners report that it can be more effective and efficient if support staff carry out as much work as possible on CCMS before work is checked and submitted by an appropriately qualified fee-earner.

1.76 The majority of the information submitted on CCMS is not then accessible in the same format again. To ensure that it is clear on the file when work was done, it is essential that contemporaneous records are kept on the organisation's own electronic system or paper file. Sometimes the easiest way to do this will be to take a screenshot. For example, when an application is made, the confirmation screen can be captured with the time and date visible.

1.77 One benefit of CCMS is that there is a direct link to the Department for Work and Pensions (DWP), so that when a client is in receipt of a passporting benefit, this can be confirmed automatically. If there is a problem in obtaining electronic confirmation, paper documentation can be uploaded.

Declarations

1.78 Although no paper is sent to the LAA when using CCMS, there is at least one piece of paper (or PDF of the signed declaration) that must almost always be held on file – a signed declaration. This declaration is generated by the system only after the application is completed as a draft and it must be signed and retained on the file before submission. This requires a device that can connect to the internet plus access to a printer. If this is not possible, a promissory declaration can be used. In pre-Covid-19 times, it was vital that there was always a signed declaration on the file which could be audited by the LAA. It was never submitted to the LAA, but without it the file was not validated for payment. However, the LAA responded to the Covid-19 pandemic to allow some flexibility in relation to signatures during lockdowns and where clients needed to isolate, and allowed alternatives to a wet signature.[21]

Notifications

1.79 Notifications are a key part of the design of CCMS. The system is designed to save LAA caseworkers' time by processing many case management steps through a 'rules engine' incorporated in the software. This means that certain notifications are (or should be) produced automatically. Other types of notification need the consideration of an LAA caseworker.

1.80 For example, when you submit a substantive application, the system will generate a list of evidence requirements that are sent to you. This happens before an LAA caseworker has seen the application. This type of notification is referred to below as an automatic notification. Automatic notifications should never take more than an hour and, if the system is functioning correctly, should arrive in less than 15 minutes.

1.81 CCMS sends an email each day there is a notification. Otherwise, all communication to users in firms is through notifications that are accessed through the CCMS portal itself. It is vital that solicitors and caseworkers check, open and deal with their notifications promptly.

Expiry dates

1.82 Draft applications, bills and amendments that have not been 'submitted' all automatically delete themselves from CCMS after 28 days

---

21 See: www.gov.uk/guidance/coronavirus-covid-19-working-with-clients.

(42 days for bills that are to be assessed by the court). This can undo valuable work. To avoid this, access the un-submitted form within this time limit to 'restart the clock'. If someone is going on holiday, they need to ensure the 28 days will not expire when they are away. See chapter 4 for details on emergency certificates, which will need the substantive application to be submitted within five days, otherwise they will be revoked or nullified.

Assigning counsel

1.83 All advocates who undertake any work on a case must be assigned to the case on CCMS. The easiest way to assign counsel is to use their LAA reference number. The cost limit assigned to advocates limits the total costs they can claim under a certificate. Advocates still need to submit a bill for the work undertaken, which is reviewed by a caseworker and assessed in the traditional way. An advocate cannot submit a claim for work done until they have been assigned to the case.

Payments on account

1.84 Payments on account (POAs) can be submitted for case costs and for disbursements. You enter 100 per cent of the profit costs incurred to date and then the system calculates 80 per cent of the costs (up from 75 per cent from July 2021[22]). Once a POA has been submitted, it will generate a notification allowing supporting documents to be uploaded.

1.85 Some cases, such as high cost case contracts, allow payments on account of 100 per cent of costs as each case stage is reached. CCMS automatically pays 80 per cent of profit costs; to avoid this, these claims should be submitted using the non-expert disbursement claim function rather than the profit costs function, with a full explanation of the costs entitlement included in the narrative section.

Trouble-shooting

1.86 When technical errors occur, it is essential that the LAA's technical team are notified at: online-support@justice.gov.uk. They should be provided with:

---

22 See 'Permanent changes' at: www.gov.uk/guidance/schedule-of-processes-restarting-after-covid-19-contingency.

- a screenshot of the problem;
- context in relation to what has happened, ie what stage of the application you were at or what was clicked on;
- where necessary, the impact of the potential problem so that it can be triaged and prioritised efficiently; and
- LAA caseworkers may also need to be informed if it affects the handling of the case.

1.87 If you are unable to access CCMS due to a technical issue and you need an urgent decision (needed within 48 hours) on an application or amendment, you can submit a paper application. The LAA will expect you to speak to a member of their Online Support Team before doing so and obtain a contingency reference number – without which the LAA will not consider the application outside CCMS. Contingency cover sheets can be obtained from the Online Support Team if it agrees that you can use the process.[23] See chapter 5 for full details.

Legal challenges

1.88 It is important to remember that the Ministry of Justice and the LAA are public bodies carrying out public functions. As such they are susceptible to public law challenges if their decisions about administrating legal aid are contrary to public law principles.

1.89 As will be seen, in practice challenges are mostly brought against the Lord Chancellor as the minister with overall responsibility for legal aid.

1.90 The years since 2012 have seen a series of court cases challenging aspects of the cuts or their implementation.

1.91 A challenge to the reduction in the number of crime contracts lost in both the High Court and Court of Appeal[24] (though the reduction was eventually stopped by Michael Gove as Lord Chancellor), but cases involving civil legal aid have seen more mixed results.

1.92 In the field of family law, a main area of contention has been the domestic violence gateway to private family law funding (see chapter 6).

---

23 See the contingency process at: www.gov.uk/guidance/bringing-civil-legal-aid-processing-online.
24 *R (London Criminal Courts Solicitors' Association and others) v Lord Chancellor* [2015] EWHC 295 (Admin); and *R (London Criminal Courts Solicitors' Association, Law Society and others) v Lord Chancellor* [2015] EWCA Civ 230.

A High Court challenge to the gateway was unsuccessful,[25] but the Court of Appeal found that a requirement that evidence of domestic abuse date from within the 24 months preceding the application, and a failure to cater for other forms of abuse, specifically financial abuse, were unlawful.[26]

1.93 In June 2018 the High Court quashed the LAA's tender for the Housing Possession Court Duty Scheme (HPCDS).[27] The Law Centres Network argued that the decision to reduce the number of contracts available by increasing the size of scheme areas to cover multiple courts was irrational and in breach of the public sector equality duty (PSED) under the Equality Act 2010. Andrews J was heavily critical of the LAA and Ministry of Justice's approach to decision-making, in particular the gathering of evidence. She found that a series of questionable assumptions had been made without data, and the position of the representative bodies misrepresented. Submissions to ministers were 'woefully inadequate' and necessary enquiries had not been carried out. As a result, the minister making the decision was misled and not properly briefed, and consequently reached a decision no minister, properly briefed and in possession of all the facts, could reasonably have reached.

1.94 In June 2024 a judicial review claim was filed by Duncan Lewis Solicitors in an attempt to force the Lord Chancellor to address the low level of remuneration in legal aid fees for immigration and asylum controlled work or to address the provision issues in a timely and effective manner (reported on by the *Guardian* and *The Law Society Gazette*[28]). No decision on the case had been made at the time of writing.

1.95 There has also been a series of challenges to the exceptional funding regime, which are covered in chapter 3.

---

25 *R (Rights of Women) v Lord Chancellor and Secretary of State for Justice* [2015] EWHC 35 (Admin).
26 *R (Rights of Women) v Lord Chancellor and Secretary of State for Justice* [2016] EWCA Civ 91.
27 *R (Law Centres Federation Ltd (t/a Law Centres Network)) v Lord Chancellor* [2018] EWHC 1588 (Admin).
28 See: www.theguardian.com/law/article/2024/jun/16/lawyers-take-lord-chancellor-to-high-court-legal-aid-alex-chalk-duncan-lewis and www.lawgazette.co.uk/news/duncan-lewis-takes-government-to-court-over-legal-aid-fees/5119980.article.

Logos

1.96 The former Community Legal Service and Criminal Defence Service logos were withdrawn in 2013 and organisations are no longer permitted to use them, but you can use the strapline 'Contracted with the Legal Aid Agency'. If you do not have a contract but do hold the Specialist Quality Mark (SQM), you can use the descriptor 'Specialist Quality Mark Holder'.[29]

Legal aid support on X (formerly Twitter)

1.97 Our X feed – @legalaidhbk – automatically tweets all announcements, additions and amendments to the LAA website. The official LAA X account is @LegalAidAgency. The LAA customer service team's account is @LAAHelpTeam. They cannot deal with individual case queries, but can help with general queries about systems and processes. It can be useful to ask for guidance if it is not something your contract manager can help with.

Legal Aid Agency's coronavirus responses

1.98 On 9 March 2020, the LAA issued the first of its responses to the Covid-19 outbreak, to reassure providers and the wider public that the LAA would continue to provide civil and criminal legal aid and advice in England and Wales to help people deal with their legal problems. The LAA has continually updated its responses to allow amendments to legal processes, procedures and contract requirements in the light of the restrictions placed on society during the pandemic. It has also withdrawn some of those arrangements as government guidance and regulations have changed.

1.99 At the time of writing, the LAA's guidance can be found on its main 'Coronavirus (COVID-19): Legal Aid Agency contingency response' webpage[30] and the following sub-pages:
- 'Coronavirus (COVID-19): processing and payments';[31]

---

29 *Specialist Quality Mark Guidance* A2.2: www.gov.uk/guidance/legal-aid-agency-quality-standards.
30 See: www.gov.uk/guidance/coronavirus-covid-19-legal-aid-agency-contingency-response.
31 At: www.gov.uk/guidance/coronavirus-covid-19-processing-and-payments.

- 'Coronavirus (COVID-19): working with clients';[32]
- 'Coronavirus (COVID-19): contract management and assurance'.[33]

1.100 The LAA has also published a 'Schedule of processes restarting after COVID-19 contingency',[34] which is helpful as it records whether a relaxation that was allowed during the pandemic is still in force and, if it is not, records the period when it was allowed. This may be very useful for audits taking place in the future when memories of the acute phase of the pandemic have faded.

---

32 At: www.gov.uk/guidance/coronavirus-covid-19-working-with-clients.
33 At: www.gov.uk/guidance/coronavirus-covid-19-contract-management-and-assurance.
34 At: www.gov.uk/guidance/schedule-of-processes-restarting-after-covid-19-contingency.

CHAPTER 2

Taking on civil and family cases

Edited by Simon Mullings

2.1	Introduction
2.4	**Scope of the scheme**
2.13	**Scope of contracts**
2.23	Covid-19 changes
2.25	Exceptional cases
2.29	**Financial eligibility**
2.40	Passporting benefits
2.44	Assessment of capital
	Overview • Clients over 60 • Contributions from capital • Assessment of income
2.57	Assessment of the means of a child
2.60	Legal aid available without regard to means
2.63	**Reassessment of means**
2.66	**Merits tests**
2.67	**Other restrictions on taking on cases**
2.67	Referral fees
2.68	Client has received previous advice
2.76	**Permitted work**
2.76	Overview
2.78	Definitions of permitted work

Key resources

Statute and regulations

- Legal Aid, Sentencing and Punishment of Offenders Act 2012 – Schedule 1 Part 1
- Civil Legal Aid (Procedure) Regulations 2012
- Civil Legal Aid (Statutory Charge) Regulations 2013
- Civil Legal Aid (Merits Criteria) Regulations 2013

Contracts

- 2024 Standard Civil Contract Standard
- 2024 Standard Civil Contract Specification
- 2024 Standard Civil Contract – Specification (General Provisions)
- 2018 Standard Civil Contract Table of Amendments – from January 2024
- 2024 Standard Civil Contract Category Definitions
- 2018 Standard Civil Contract Specification, Category Specific Rules – see relevant area of law

Lord Chancellor's Guidance

- Lord Chancellor's Exceptional Funding Guidance (non-inquests)
- Lord Chancellor's Guidance under section 4 of the Legal Aid, Sentencing and Punishment of Offenders Act 2012, May 2023
- Lord Chancellors Guidance on Determining Financial Eligibility for Controlled Work & Family Mediation, April 2021
- Lord Chancellor's guidance on determining financial eligibility for certificated work

Key points to note

- Financial eligibility of your client is a key issue in most civil cases. Have the rules, guidance, calculators and key cards to hand when seeing clients.
- Have systems in place to help clients provide you with their evidence of means.
- Means tests can be complicated. Take time to make sure your client qualifies, do not be afraid to do as our authors and editors do – refer to this handbook when you need to.

> - Make sure you understand the scope of cases that are funded and the merits tests that apply in your area of law. You may need to explain to clients why you cannot take on their out of scope and/or unmeritorious case.
> - Other instructions to taking on cases can apply. Consider whether a checklist of questions will help you, for example to remind you to ask about previous advice.

Introduction

2.1 When a client approaches you with a legal problem, there are a number of considerations to bear in mind in deciding whether you can take the case. These include:
- Is the case within the scope of the legal aid scheme?
- Is it covered by your contract?
- If you need to provide advice rather than going straight to court proceedings, do you have sufficient matter starts to be able to take it?
- Is the client financially eligible?
- Does the client's case pass the merits test?
- Is there any other reason why you cannot take the case?

Only if the case passes all these tests can it be taken on.

2.2 Note that if you have a case that started pre-1 April 2013, it continues under the provisions of the Access to Justice Act 1999 – see the 2011/12 edition of this Handbook for the operation of the Access to Justice Act scheme.[1] For cases under the 2013 and 2018 contracts refer to previous versions of the Handbook.

2.3 In this chapter we will refer to the provisions of the Standard Civil Contract 2024,[2] as that is the one that now governs most civil cases.

Scope of the scheme

2.4 Unless Legal Aid, Sentencing and Punishment of Offenders Act 2012 (LASPO) Sch 1 explicitly puts an issue in scope, it is out of scope.[3] See appendix A for the text of Schedule 1.

1 Previous *Legal Aid Handbooks* are available in electronic form from LAG.
2 Available at: www.gov.uk/government/publications/standard-civil-contract-2024.
3 Previously, legal aid was an inclusionary scheme; unless Access to Justice Act 1999 Sch 2 explicitly put an issue out of scope, it was in scope.

2.5 Schedule 1 is not easy to understand and requires a certain amount of cross-referencing and double or even triple negatives to be navigated to understand whether a case is in fact in or out of scope. The Schedule is in four parts: Part 1 lists the types of proceedings that are in scope but is subject to Part 2 (which excludes certain types of action) and Part 3 (which excludes certain courts and tribunals), as well as the definitions in Part 4. So in order to see whether a case is in scope, you need to check that it is included by Part 1 but not excluded by Part 2, and that your venue is included in Part 3 if you wish to provide advocacy.

2.6 The exclusions in Schedule 1 Part 2 are:

- personal injury or death;
- negligence;
- assault, battery or false imprisonment;
- trespass to goods or land;
- damage to property;
- defamation, etc;
- breach of statutory duty;
- conveyancing;
- making wills;
- trust law;
- a claim for damages for breach of human rights under Human Rights Act 1998 s7;
- company and partnership law;
- matters arising out of a business;
- welfare benefits and social security matters below Upper Tribunal level;
- criminal injuries compensation; and
- change of name.

2.7 The Part 2 exclusions always override the Part 1 inclusions unless specifically disapplied. For example, in housing cases, LASPO Sch 1 Part 1 para 33 says that services in relation to loss of a home are in scope, subject to the exclusions in Part 2 but then Part 2 para 15 says services in relation to benefit matters are out of scope. The result of this is that you can advise and represent in respect of possession proceedings but cannot make representations about housing benefit, universal credit or submit a benefits appeal even where benefit problems are the cause of the arrears underlying the proceedings (see chapter 11 for more information about dealing with housing cases under LASPO).

2.8 Or again, Part 1 para 19 says that services in relation to judicial review are in scope, subject to the exclusions in Part 2. Part 2 para 15 excludes any matter related to welfare benefits but Part 1 para 19(2)(a) disapplies that exclusion. Therefore, notwithstanding the general exclusion of welfare benefits work, judicial review of welfare benefit decisions can be in scope. This allows public law challenges, to the law generally and to the exercise of discretion by benefits authorities, but does not allow advice or representation on routine appeals to the Social Entitlement Chamber of the First-tier Tribunal.

2.9 For the purposes of awarding contracts (see more below) the Legal Aid Agency (LAA) divides the work up into categories. The category definitions documents[4] give a reasonable guide to work which is in scope, but for the detail, particularly in borderline or unclear cases or where the Part 2 exclusions may apply (for example, in the case of benefit work within arrears cases, as above), it is always best to refer back to the Act itself. The category definitions can be found on the LAA website.[5]

2.10 The following table gives a summary of the areas of law in scope in each category.

---

4 See appendix B for the 2024 category definitions.
5 See: https://assets.publishing.service.gov.uk/ media/6569c0739462260013c567df/Draft_Category_Definitions_2024_ Dec_2023__.pdf.

Category	Type of work	Comments
Claims against public authorities	Where the defendant is a public authority with the power to detain, imprison or prosecute: • abuse of a child or vulnerable adult • abuse of position or power by a public authority where the alleged abuse was deliberate or dishonest and resulted in foreseeable harm • significant breach of human rights • advice to victims of sexual offences Allegations of deliberate abuse of a person in the care of a public authority or institution Exceptional funding in claims against a public authority with the power to detain, imprison or prosecute Exceptional funding on: • applications for compensation following wrongful conviction • applications for criminal injuries compensation • claims for damages for professional negligence in bringing a claim in this category	In each of these causes of action, the LASPO Sch 1 Part 2 exclusions around personal injury and death, negligence, assault, etc are disapplied. See *Director of Legal Aid Casework v R (Sisangia)* [2016] EWCA Civ 24 for the proper interpretation of LASPO Sch 1 Part 1 para 21(4) (deliberate or dishonest abuse of position or power by a public authority) – something more than an intentional tort is necessary to amount to 'deliberate or dishonest' but whether that threshold is reached in the individual case will be fact specific.
Clinical negligence	Neurological injury to infants causing severe disablement and which happened in the womb, during birth or up to eight weeks after birth Exceptional funding on any matter claiming damages or making a complaint to a professional body alleging breach of duty in the course of clinical or medical services, or claiming damages for professional negligence in the making of such a claim	

Taking on civil and family cases 31

Community care	The provision of community care services and of facilities for disabled persons	LASPO Sch 1 Part 1 paras 6 and 7 contain an exhaustive list of statutes and statutory provisions that are in scope; if it is not on the list, it is not in. Para 6(n) was added to include Care Act 2014 Part 1.
Debt	Mortgage arrears and possession Orders for sale of the home Involuntary bankruptcy where the home is included in the estate Exceptional funding on any matter relating to proceedings for the payment of monies due or enforcement of orders made in such proceedings Exceptional funding for matters arising out of personal insolvency	Providers with housing contracts can also do debt work. See chapter 11. Also see chapter 11 for details of the Housing Loss Prevention Advice Service (HLPAS) scheme, which extends legal aid for those facing the loss of their home.
Discrimination	Contravention of the Equality Act 2010 or a previous discrimination statute (a prescribed list is given at LASPO Sch 1 Part 1 para 43(3)), including (but not limited to) cases alleging discrimination before an employment tribunal	This category is not limited to employment cases and includes any matter where discrimination can be pleaded. If it overlaps with another category – for example, alleging discrimination in the provision of community care, housing or education services – work can be done in each category. From 1 September 2019, discrimination became a face-to-face contract (and was no longer a mandatory gateway category).
Education	Special educational needs Discrimination in education provision	All other education work is out of scope. From 1 September 2019, education became a face-to-face contract (and was no longer a mandatory gateway category).

Family	Public law children work	In general, child protection work and work required by the UK's international obligations is in scope but most private law work is out of scope. It can be brought back where there is domestic or child abuse, but only where particular prescribed evidence is available. See chapter 6 for more details.
	Child care and supervision	
	Secure accommodation orders	
	Adoption, including placement and adoption orders for parents and those with parental responsibility	
	Child abduction and international child abduction	
	Inherent jurisdiction	
	Forced marriage protection and protection from female genital mutilation (FGM)	
	Domestic abuse and protection from harassment arising out of a family relationship	
	Enforcement of international child maintenance	
	Special guardianship orders for those with parental responsibility and prospective guardians	
	Private law children work and financial provision on relationship breakdown, but only where there is domestic abuse or risk of child abuse – see chapter 6	
	Child safety orders and parenting orders following conviction of a child	
Housing	Possession of a rented home (including most counterclaims in possession proceedings even if they would be out of scope as a stand-alone claim)	Damages only unlawful eviction claims may however be caught by the 'suitability' for a conditional fee agreement' test – see para 7.16 of the *Lord Chancellor's Guidance on Civil Legal Aid* and chapter 11 at para 11.35 of this Handbook.
	Unlawful eviction – both injunction and damages	
	Homelessness	See chapter 12 of the Guidance for how applications for funding for disrepair will be dealt with.
	Allocations where the client is or is threatened with homelessness	

	Provision of accommodation by way of community care services to an individual who is homeless or threatened with homelessness (overlap with the community care category)	Also see chapter 11 for details of the HLPAS scheme, which extends legal aid for those facing the loss of their home.
	Disrepair and housing conditions, but only to require carrying out of repairs (damages only claims are out of scope) and only where the disrepair/conditions causes a serious risk of harm	
	Protection from harassment	
	Accommodation and support for asylum-seekers	
Immigration and asylum	Asylum	Most mainstream non-asylum immigration work is out of scope.
	Detention (but only advice on the detention and bail, not on the substantive issue unless independently in scope) and residence restrictions pending deportation	LASPO Sch 1 Part 1 para 19, which brings judicial review into scope, contains a number of specific restrictions limiting the circumstances in which a judicial review can be brought in an immigration case.
	Applications for leave to remain under the domestic violence rule	
	Applications for leave by victims of trafficking, slavery, servitude or forced labour	Separated migrant children citizenship and non-asylum immigration applications and appeals for under 18-year-olds who are not in the care of a parent, guardian or legal authority.
	Separated migrant children	
	Terrorism prevention and investigation measures	
	Proceedings before the Special Immigration Appeals Commission	

	Judicial review, but not: • where the same issue has been the subject of a previous judicial review or appeal within the last year • of removal directions where the substantive decision or appeal was made in the last year • of a negative decision on an asylum application where there is no right of appeal to the tribunal Exceptional funding of any immigration or asylum matter	
Mental health	Services in relation to the Mental Health Act 1983, Mental Capacity Act 2005 and Repatriation of Prisoners Act 1984 Sch para 5(2), inherent jurisdiction of the High Court in relation to vulnerable adults and children (the latter in relation to medical decisions).	This includes claims for breaches of the Human Rights Act 1998 brought within or separate from Court of Protection proceedings. It does not include creation of Lasting Powers of Attorney or making of advance decisions under the Mental Capacity Act 2005.
Miscellaneous[1]	Working with children and vulnerable adults Protection from harassment where not arising from a family or housing relationship Proceeds of crime Environmental pollution Advice to victims of sexual offences Abuse of child or vulnerable adult except where in the actions against the police etc category Damages claims by victims of trafficking Gang-related violence injunctions Anti-social behaviour injunctions	This is work that does not fit into any other category. Since all categories became 'exclusive' in 2013 (ie tolerance work is not allowed), you can only take on miscellaneous cases if specifically authorised to do so by your schedule. Some – but not all – contracts include an allocation of miscellaneous matter starts.

Public law[2]	Human rights and public law challenges	Many cases will also be in another category. For example, judicial review of a housing decision falls within both the public law and housing categories.
Welfare benefits	Welfare benefit appeals – but only Upper Tribunal cases, cases in the Court of Appeal, Supreme Court and judicial review only

Appeals on a point of law relating to council tax reduction schemes to the High Court and above

Exceptional funding on any welfare benefits or council tax reduction scheme matter | Legal Help only for Upper Tribunal cases, and for High Court appeals in council tax reduction scheme cases. Representation including advocacy in all other High Court and above cases.

Also see chapter 11 for details of the HLPAS scheme which extends legal aid for those facing the loss of their home. |

1 See the Standard Contract 2024 Category Definitions for more information.
2 See the Standard Contract 2024 Category Definitions 'overlaps between categories' for more information.

2.11 Every organisation awarded a housing contract also receives a notional four debt matter starts and is therefore also a debt provider (the supervisor standard is a joint one). In practice, any referral for face-to-face advice will be to a housing provider wearing its 'debt hat' rather than a separate contracted debt provider. The effect of the LASPO cuts is that virtually the only debt work in scope is mortgage possession.

2.12 The 2024 Civil Contract commenced on 1 September 2024 and covers all civil work types.

Scope of contracts

2.13 As described above, legal aid cases are divided into categories by the contracts. At the highest level, civil and crime are treated separately, have separate contracts and different funding rules. See chapter 14 for criminal work.

2.14 Until September 2018, there were a number of different contracts for different areas of law:

- The **Standard Civil Contract 2013**: housing and debt; family; immigration and asylum.
- The **Standard Civil Contract (welfare benefits) 2013** from 1 October 2013 – welfare benefits in London and the South East, and the Midlands and the East.
- The **Standard Civil Contract 2014**: from 1 August 2014 – mental health; community care.
- The **Standard Civil Contract 2015**: from 1 November 2015 – actions against the police, etc; clinical negligence; public law.
- The **Standard Civil Contract (welfare benefits) 2016**: from 1 November 2016 – welfare benefits advice in the North, South West and Wales.

See the 2017/18 edition of this Handbook for the operation of those contracts. See also the 2018/19 and subsequent editions for information about the 2018 Contract.[6]

2.15 The **Standard Civil Contract 2024**: With effect from 1 September 2024, this one single civil contract applies to face-to-face work across all categories. This includes the education and discrimination face-

---

6 These are available in electronic form from LAG.

to-face contracts which commenced on 1 September 2019 and HLPAS.

2.16 Within the contract there are general rules and specific rules for each area of work, and it is vitally important that you apply the correct rules to the particular category of work you are operating in.

2.17 The definitions of each category are set out in the category definitions. See appendix B.

2.18 An organisation can only be funded to conduct civil legal aid cases if it has a Standard Civil Contract with the LAA. The contract will specify what cases the organisation can take on.

2.19 Every contract has a schedule, which is the part specific to the organisation. In order to be allowed to take on cases, you must be permitted to work in that category by your schedule. The schedule will specify the number of matter starts of controlled work, and whether licensed work is allowed for each category. Controlled work – Legal Help, Help at Court and Controlled Legal Representation – is funding for advice granted by the organisation; licensed work, also known as legal representation or certificated work, is funding for representation in courts, mainly granted by the LAA.

2.20 The matter starts permitted in your schedule are the maximum number of new controlled work cases in that category of law you are permitted to take on during the life of the schedule (usually one year). You can only take on cases in a category in which you have a supervisor and a contract.

2.21 Licensed work is not restricted by matter starts, so there is no limit on the number of certificate applications you may make in a year, as long as you have a contract in the appropriate category.

2.22 Therefore, provided you have a contract in the relevant category, the matter is in scope and you have sufficient matter starts (where relevant), you can take on the case, if the client is eligible. Under para 1.21 of the 2024 Specification, you can self-grant supplementary matter starts in a category of law up to 50 per cent of your existing allocation, but only with the consent of your contract manager.

Covid-19 changes

2.23 On 9 March 2020, the LAA issued the first of its responses to the Covid-19 outbreak. The LAA updated its responses to allow amendments to legal processes, procedures and contract requirements in light of the restrictions placed on society during the pandemic. It also withdrew some of those arrangements as government guidance and regulations changed. At the date of writing the LAA's guidance can be found on its main coronavirus response page[7] and the following sub-pages:

- 'Coronavirus (COVID-19): processing and payments';[8]
- 'Coronavirus (COVID-19): working with clients';[9]
- 'Coronavirus (COVID-19): contract management and assurance'.[10]

2.24 The LAA has also published a 'Schedule of processes restarting after COVID-19 contingency',[11] which is helpful as it records whether a relaxation that was allowed during the pandemic is still in force and, if it is not, records the period when it was allowed. This may be very useful for audits taking place in the future when memories of the acute phase of the pandemic have faded.

Exceptional cases

2.25 You may, however, take on cases that would otherwise be excluded but fall within the 'exceptional case' provisions in LASPO.[12] All decisions on exceptional cases are made by the LAA. The test is in section 10(3):

(a) that it is necessary to make the services available to the individual under this Part because failure to do so would be a breach of–
   (i) the individual's Convention rights (within the meaning of the Human Rights Act 1998), or
   (ii) any rights of the individual to the provision of legal services that are assimilated enforceable rights, or
(b) that it is appropriate to do so, in the particular circumstances of the case, having regard to any risk that failure to do so would be such a breach.

2.26 Exceptional cases are dealt with in Part 8 of the Civil Legal Aid (Procedure) Regulations 2012. An application should be made to the LAA, which will determine whether funding should be granted. Guidance on making exceptional applications can be found on the LAA website.[13]

---

7 At: www.gov.uk/guidance/coronavirus-covid-19-legal-aid-agency-contingency-response.
8 At: www.gov.uk/guidance/coronavirus-covid-19-processing-and-payments.
9 At: www.gov.uk/guidance/coronavirus-covid-19-working-with-clients.
10 At: www.gov.uk/guidance/coronavirus-covid-19-contract-management-and-assurance.
11 At: www.gov.uk/guidance/schedule-of-processes-restarting-after-covid-19-contingency.
12 LASPO s10(3).
13 At: www.gov.uk/guidance/legal-aid-apply-for-exceptional-case-funding.

2.27 Legal aid can be backdated to cover making the application under Civil Legal Aid (Procedure) Regulations 2012 reg 68, but only if legal aid is granted. You may have to make the application pro bono unless the client can pay privately.

2.28 See chapter 3 for more information about making applications and a review of relevant case-law. There is also very helpful guidance from the Public Law Project at: https://publiclawproject.org.uk/exceptional-case-funding.

Financial eligibility

2.29 There are two significant barriers to taking on cases: the **means test** and the **merits test**. Every client must qualify financially before their case can be taken on (with very limited exceptions in the family and mental health categories: see chapters 7 and 10), and the case must pass the relevant merits test.

2.30 Financial eligibility is assessed on three separate criteria, all of which the client must satisfy by being below the threshold on capital, gross income and disposable income.

2.31 The limits on each of these are set out in the Civil Legal Aid (Financial Resources and Payment for Services) Regulations 2013, which are amended periodically. Up-to-date limits can be found on the LAA website.[14]

2.32 In the case of controlled work, you should ascertain the client's resources and calculate eligibility; the decision on whether the means test is met is delegated to you. For licensed work, however, the decision is made by the LAA.

2.33 The Ministry of Justice has two online calculator resources concerning eligibility for civil legal aid. One is for members of the public and can be found at: https://civil-eligibility-calculator.justice.gov.uk/ – or more directly at: www.gov.uk/check-legal-aid. These links are useful for you to be able to provide to prospective clients and others.

2.34 The other calculator resource is for legal aid providers and is here: https://check-your-client-qualifies-for-legal-aid.service.gov.uk. The website makes clear that it should not be used to *certificate* eligibility where the prospective client or their partner is self-employed. This does not mean the calculator cannot be used for self-employed prospective clients, but you should consider any assessment of eligibility as entirely provisional and only an application to the LAA will

14 At: www.gov.uk/guidance/civil-legal-aid-means-testing.

determine for certain whether a self-employed person or the partner of such a person is eligible.

2.35 The provider calculator will give an assessment of whether any contribution to legal aid will have to be made by the client, and if so how much, but this should be seen as a provisional guide in all cases.

2.36 An example of an outcome from the calculator (based on an entirely fictional assessment for a legal aid certificate) looks like this:

> **Your client is likely to qualify for civil legal aid, for certificated work**
>
> Your client is likely to qualify financially for civil legal aid based on the information you have entered. We estimate they will have to pay towards the costs of their case:
>
> - £39.35 per month from their disposable income – these contributions will continue for the duration of the case, however long it lasts
> - £0.00 lump sum payment from their disposable capital – any capital contribution will not exceed the likely costs of their case and they might pay less than this amount
>
> This is not a guarantee that your client will get civil legal aid if an application is made for them and the contribution figure(s) displayed may change. For a final decision on eligibility and contributions (if any), an application and supporting evidence must be submitted to the Legal Aid Agency (LAA) for assessment. A full assessment supported by evidence may generate a different result.
>
> The LAA will also consider:
>
> - whether your client's case is in scope for legal aid
> - the case merits, for example its likelihood of success and the benefit it would give your client
>
> These calculations were made in line with the latest version of the Lord Chancellor's Guidance on Determining Financial Eligibility for Certificated Work.
>
> Legal aid is not always free.
>
> In some circumstances, your client may be asked to repay the legal costs of their case, for example from money or assets kept or gained as a result of legal aid if the statutory charge arises.

2.37 Further details of the assessment are also available and can be printed or saved as a PDF. The calculator can be very useful for tricky and/or complicated means assessment and a print-out or PDF could be useful as evidence of how you carried out an assessment in disputed cases.

> **Case study**
>
> *Para 3.23 of the 2024 Standard Civil Contract says that satisfactory evidence of the client's means must be provided before we assess eligibility. Our clients rarely bring this evidence with them to the first appointment. Is there anything we can do about this?*
>
> You need to explain clearly to clients what evidence they will need to bring with them to their first appointment. Many organisations now train a member of support staff to understand what is and not acceptable and to ensure that clients bring what is necessary to the first appointment. This can be confirmed in a standard letter, and clients can be sent a text message the day before to remind them of the appointment and what they need to bring with them.
>
> However, if you can justify it to protect your client's position, then you can start work before the client provides evidence, and in very rare cases the LAA may accept that it is not possible for them to provide it at all due to the client's age, mental disability or homelessness make it impracticable (2024 Contract Specification para 3.24). Prior to the Covid-19 pandemic, the LAA was taking an increasingly strict approach to this provision and tending to nil assess if evidence was provided after the first appointment or not at all. However, a point of principle, CLA59, says that a LAA assessor should only overturn an exercise of discretion allowed by the rules if it was manifestly unreasonable. Points of principle could and can no longer be certified under the 2018 and 2024 Contracts; but it may be useful to argue that the LAA should have regard to it (see chapters 15 and 21 for more information).
>
> The LAA's Covid-19 arrangements provide greater flexibility as to evidence of means, allowing photographed or scanned evidence as well as no evidence where agreed with the LAA.[15]

2.38 Where the client has a partner with whom they are living as a couple, you should always aggregate the means of both the client and the partner. 'Partner' means:

---

15 See: www.gov.uk/guidance/coronavirus-covid-19-working-with-clients.

- spouse or civil partner; or
- person with whom the client lives or ordinarily lives as a couple,

but not where they are separated because of a relationship breakdown likely to be permanent.[16]

2.39 However, if only one partner is seeking advice at your office in person, both are not required to sign the application form. The then Legal Services Commission (LSC) issued guidance in 2009 which clarified the requirement for both to sign only applies to postal and telephone applications.[17]

Passporting benefits

2.40 A client in receipt of passporting benefits automatically qualifies for legal aid on income.[18] However, an assessment of capital will still be required, and legal aid must be refused if the capital test is not met, even if the client receives a passporting benefit.

2.41 Current income passporting benefits are:
- income support;
- income-based jobseeker's allowance;
- universal credit;
- guarantee pension credit; and
- income-related employment and support allowance.

2.42 Support under section 4 or 95 of the Immigration and Asylum Act 1999 is similarly passported, but only for Legal Help and Controlled Legal Representation in the immigration category.

---

16 See: www.legislation.gov.uk/uksi/2013/480/contents/made. Civil Legal Aid (Financial Resources and Payment for Services) Regulations 2013 reg 16(2), as amended. See Civil Legal Aid (Financial Resources and Payment for Services) Regulations 2013 reg 2.

17 Guidance issued by the LSC in 2009. This is available at: http://webarchive.nationalarchives.gov.uk/20121207044149/http://www.LEGALSERVICES.gov.uk/docs/forms/CW1_Client_Certification_Guidance_Nov_2009(1).pdf. It is no longer available on the current LAA website; but equally, we are aware of nothing to suggest that this approach has been changed.

18 The last government's means test review – www.gov.uk/government/consultations/legal-aid-means-test-review/legal-aid-means-test-review#chapter-3-civil-income-thresholds-passporting-and-contributions – proposed removing universal credit from the list of passporting benefits and instead incorporating £500 earnings threshold which would trigger a full means assessment. It was then announced in March 2024 that the means test review recommendations were to be delayed until 2026. While the universal credit passporting proposal is controversial, there were also some welcome reforms within the government's proposals and so there has been dismay at the delay.

2.43 For Legal Representation, the evidence requirement for capital is the provision of three months' up-to-date bank statements or similar. For Legal Help, see chapter 4 at para 4.22.

Assessment of capital

Overview

2.44 Capital is 'every resource of a capital nature belonging to [the client] on the date on which the application is made',[19] either as money or as the realisable value of an asset.[20] It includes money owed to the client, whether or not recovered,[21] and also includes life insurance and endowments if their security can be borrowed upon.[22]

2.45 However, the value of household furniture and effects, a car (unless of exceptional value), clothing and tools of trade is excluded,[23] as is (in the case of controlled work) money the client could realise by selling or borrowing on the strength of any business they may own.[24]

2.46 Where the client owns property, the value of that property should be taken into account in the calculation. The value is the client's equity – that is, the current realisable market value.[25] The LAA *Guide to determining financial eligibility for certificated work*,[26] states that a deduction of three per cent should be made from the value, to allow for the cost of selling the property. This does not appear in the equivalent guidance for assessing eligibility for controlled work;[27] but arguably it should as the regulation is the same. From that is taken the value of any outstanding mortgage which, since 28 January 2021,[28] is no longer capped at £100,000.[29]

---

19 Civil Legal Aid (Financial Resources and Payment for Services) Regulations 2013 reg 30.
20 Reg 31.
21 Reg 32.
22 Reg 33.
23 Reg 34.
24 Reg 36.
25 Reg 31.
26 Para 6.4(8): www.gov.uk/civil-legal-aid-means-testing.
27 See: https://assets.publishing.service.gov.uk/government/uploads/system/uploads/attachment_data/file/793459/Guide_to_determining_controlled_work_.pdf.
28 Civil Legal Aid (Financial Resources and Payment for Services) (Amendment) Regulations 2020.
29 See: www.gov.uk/government/news/civil-news-amendments-to-legal-aid-eligibility-criteria.

2.47 Jointly owned property should be taken into account. Where jointly owned with the client's partner, the entire value will be taken into account because of aggregation of means. Where it is jointly owned with someone else, only the client's share or interest will be taken into account. The default position is that the client's share will be assumed to be 50 per cent, unless there is evidence to the contrary.

2.48 Where any property is the subject matter of the dispute (SMOD), the value of that property may be disregarded from the calculation. It is only the value of the client's interest that is disregarded; the value of the opponent's interest is not taken into account at all.[30] The SMOD disregard is applied after the mortgage disregard, but before the equity disregard. For example:

> A client jointly owns a property worth £400,000 with a mortgage of £170,000. The property is the subject of a dispute with her former husband.
>
> The client's share of the equity is presumed to be 50 per cent of £230,000, leaving £115,000 (as the mortgage cap of £1,000,000 no longer applies). The SMOD disregard of £100,000 is then applied, leaving £15,000. Finally, the equity disregard is applied, leaving a value of nil to be taken into account on the capital assessment – and so the client is eligible on capital.

2.49 A client applying for an injunction in domestic abuse or forced marriage protection proceedings is not subject to the capital threshold[31] and there is no limit on eligibility for capital purposes. However, contributions are not waived, so the practical value of this concession is limited in most cases.

> **Case study**
>
> My client instructs me to advise her regarding financial matters. She qualifies for legal aid because of a history of domestic abuse and has evidence in the form of a letter from her GP. She and her husband own (as joint tenants) a flat, which has just been valued at £550,000. She wants the flat to be transferred to her. The outstanding mortgage is £150,000. Is she eligible for a certificate?
>
> The value of the property should be taken as £533,500 – that is, £550,000 minus three per cent costs of sale. Disregard the mortgage, £150,000 – so the equity is £383,500.

---

30 Civil Legal Aid (Financial Resources and Payment for Services) 2013 reg 38.
31 Reg 12.

> The client's share of this is £191,750, half of the equity – although the asset is in dispute, there is a presumption of equal shares for the purposes of assessment, and they are joint tenants.
>
> Apply the SMOD disregard of £100,000, which leaves £91,750. Then, as this is the client's main home, apply the equity disregard of £100,000 – leaving capital of negative £8,250.
>
> As the capital threshold is below £8,000, the client is therefore eligible.

Clients over 60

2.50 Where a client is aged 60 or over, they are entitled to a further disregard on capital. The level of the disregard is on a sliding scale determined by disposable income (see below) up to a maximum of £100,000 of capital.[32]

2.51 The Ministry of Justice has two online calculator resources concerning eligibility for civil legal aid:

1) for members of the public: https://civil-eligibility-calculator.justice.gov.uk/ or more directly here: www.gov.uk/check-legal-aid; and
2) for legal aid providers: https://check-your-client-qualifies-for-legal-aid.service.gov.uk.

Contributions from capital

2.52 There are two limits for capital – a lower and upper limit. Where a client is below the lower limit (currently £3,000), the client is eligible on capital with no need to pay a contribution. Where the client is above the lower limit but below the upper limit (currently £8,000), the client must pay a contribution. Any contribution is payable at the start of the case and is the lower of the amount by which capital exceeds £3,000 or the estimated likely total costs of the case. Where the eventual costs are lower than any contribution paid, the balance will be refunded to the client. Capital contributions can cause problems in cases where the only capital is the value of the client's home as it may be difficult for the client to raise funds to cover the contribution quickly or at all. If the client cannot access capital, the LAA can disregard it.[33]

---

32 Reg 41.
33 See LAA guidance on trapped capital available at: https://legalaidlearning.justice.gov.uk/trapped-capital-practicalities-and-case-studies.

Assessment of income

2.53 Once you have found the client eligible on capital, you should proceed to the next stage, assessment of income. The client must be eligible on both gross and disposable income, and the thresholds are set on the basis of a calendar month. For example, if the client instructs you on 6 March, you should look at all money received since 7 February.

2.54 'Gross income' means total income from all sources (apart from housing benefit or the housing element of universal credit and some benefits and allowances, most commonly disability living allowance/personal independence payment) and universal credit payments on account.[34] It will include salary, benefits, maintenance and any other income.

2.55 You should deduct the following expenses from gross income to arrive at disposable income:

- the amount payable[35] of any rent or mortgage payments, net of any housing benefit – but capped to £545 per month if the client has no dependants;[36]
- tax and National Insurance contributions on any earnings;[37]
- childcare costs, but only to the extent that they are incurred because of work or study outside the home and only where reasonable to make a deduction;[38]
- where working (not self-employment), a fixed cost of employment allowance of £45 (for each of the client and partner if both are working);[39]
- any maintenance being paid in respect of a child or other dependent relative or former partner not a member of the client's household;[40] and

---

34 Civil Legal Aid (Financial Resources and Payment for Services) Regulations 2013 regs 21 and 24, as amended.
35 Note the amount the client is contractually liable to pay, not the amount they are actually paying. This can be important in housing cases where the client is in arrears and not paying rent. See *R (Southwark Law Centre) v Legal Services Commission; R (Dennis) v Legal Services Commission* [2007] EWHC 1715 (Admin). Although decided on the previous regulations, the same wording is used in reg 28.
36 Civil Legal Aid (Financial Resources and Payment for Services) Regulations 2013 reg 28.
37 Reg 23.
38 Reg 27.
39 Reg 27.
40 Reg 26.

- fixed dependants' allowances for the partner and each other dependent relative who is a member of the household. (Note that it is a common misconception that the dependants' allowances can only be claimed in respect of the client's children, an impression not dispelled by the wording of the forms which refer to 'child'. The regulations are quite clear that the allowance is claimable for *any dependent relative* who is a member of the client's household.)[41]

2.56 The Ministry of Justice has two online calculator resources concerning eligibility for civil legal aid:
1) for members of the public: https://civil-eligibility-calculator.justice.gov.uk, or more directly here: www.gov.uk/check-legal-aid; and
2) for legal aid providers: https://check-your-client-qualifies-for-legal-aid.service.gov.uk.

You should make sure you have the up-to-date key card to make sure you have the correct amounts of allowances and caps to apply to the calculations.[42]

Assessment of the means of a child

2.57 You are allowed to accept applications from a child.[43] When deciding on an application for Legal Help, you should assess the means of the child and those of the person(s) who have care and control, or who are liable to maintain the child or who usually contribute substantially to the child's maintenance. So, in effect, you will often be assessing the means of the parents, with the expectation that they should fund the case if they are able to do so.[44]

2.58 However, you should consider whether it is just and equitable to aggregate the child's means with those of the person(s) liable to maintain them, and if it is not just and equitable you should just assess the means of the child. No guidance is given as to what is 'just and equitable', although the contract says that the presumption is that there should be aggregation but that you can take into account all the circumstances, including the age and resources of the child, and that

---

41 Reg 25.
42 Get it here (scroll down) to ensure it is up to date: www.gov.uk/guidance/civil-legal-aid-means-testing.
43 Civil Legal Aid (Procedure) Regulations 2012 reg 22.
44 Standard Civil Contract 2024 Specification para 3.27.

non-aggregation is more likely to be justified where there is a conflict between the child and the liable person.[45] In the absence of detailed guidance, this is a decision for you as the provider assessing eligibility for Legal Help, and you should therefore keep a detailed file note justifying your decision, especially if it is a decision not to aggregate.

2.59 Where a child applies for a funding certificate, it is generally only the child's means that are taken into account, not those of the litigation friend or any other person liable to maintain the child, and therefore you should only include the child's finances.[46] However, in family cases you should consider whether to aggregate in the same way as for Legal Help.

Legal aid available without regard to means

2.60 Legal aid for the following types of case is not means tested:[47]

- Under 18s applying for Legal Representation and Family Help (Higher), including applications for these services under exceptional case funding;
- parents or those with parental responsibility applying for Legal Representation for matters concerning the withdrawal or withholding of life-sustaining treatment in respect of their child;
- Special Children Act cases and related proceedings (see chapter 7);
- Family Help (Lower) in cases where Children Act 1989 s31 proceedings are contemplated and the client is a parent or person with parental responsibility;
- Legal Representation in a parental placement and adoption case;
- Legal Representation in a parental guardianship case;
- Mental Health Tribunal cases (see chapter 10);
- certificates in Mental Capacity Act 2005 s21A cases before the Court of Protection where the client is deprived of their liberty;
- terrorism prevention and investigation measure applications, notices and proceedings;
- Hague Convention and European Convention on Child Custody cases;
- various cases concerning international enforcement of child maintenance, etc under the UK's international treaties and obligations;

---

45 Standard Civil Contract 2024 Specification para 3.27.
46 Civil Legal Aid (Financial Resources and Payment for Services) Regulations 2013 reg 16(3) and (4).
47 Reg 5.

- mediation information and assessment meetings and mediation in Hague Convention cases;
- appeals on behalf of the child/young person to the First Tier Tribunal (Special Education Needs and Disability) or the Education Tribunal for Wales made by a foster carer/approved prospective adopter of a 'looked after' child or a former foster carer of a young person who lacks capacity and resides with the carer in a 'staying put' arrangement; and
- HLPAS In Court Duty Scheme and Early Legal Advice.

2.61 In family cases concerning injunctions for domestic violence and forced marriage the eligibility limits – but not contributions – can be waived. See chapter 6.

2.62 In inquests (where exceptional funding is granted) multi-party actions and cross-border disputes, eligibility limits and contributions can be waived.

Reassessment of means

2.63 The means tests are not one-off tests – if clients' circumstances change during a case, their means should be reassessed. In the case of controlled work, you should reassess means yourself, and if the client is no longer eligible you may need to withdraw the funding. In the case of licensed work, you should report the change of circumstances to the LAA for it to reassess the means. The LAA *Guide to determining financial eligibility for controlled work*[48] says that it may not be appropriate to reassess the client's means unless they have improved 'dramatically', or the matter is likely to run for some time, suggested as three months or more for controlled work. For certificated work, any change in circumstances must be reported to the LAA and will result in a reassessment of means provided the criteria below are met.

2.64 Civil Legal Aid (Financial Resources and Payment for Services) Regulations 2013 reg 20 provides – for all levels of service subject to means assessment – that where:

- disposable income has increased by more than £60 or decreased by more than £25;
- disposable capital has increased by more than £750; or
- the client is no longer in receipt of a passporting benefit,

48 See: www.gov.uk/civil-legal-aid-means-testing.

a reassessment must take place unless it is inappropriate to do so having regard to the period for which legal aid is likely to continue. In the case of controlled work whether it is inappropriate will be a decision for you, applying the guidance set out above. In the case of licensed work for the LAA further contributions from capital may be required. See the Means Assessment Guidance issued by the LAA's legal team for more information.[49]

2.65 It is the client's duty to report any change of circumstances to you,[50] and therefore you must always advise clients of the existence of this duty at the first meeting. It should be confirmed in your standard letter.

Merits tests

2.66 Each case must satisfy, and continue to satisfy, the merits test. There is a number of different tests, depending on the nature of the case and the type of funding sought, and they are dealt with in the relevant sections of chapters 4–13 of this Handbook. You should always bear in mind that each merits test should be passed at the start of the case and should continue to be passed throughout its life. If there is insufficient merit in a particular step in the proceedings, you should not take that step; if there is not, or is no longer, sufficient merit in the case as a whole, you should refuse or withdraw funding (controlled work), or report that to the LAA (licensed work).

Other restrictions on taking on cases

Referral fees

2.67 There is an absolute prohibition on referral fees in legal aid work. Clause 6.8 of the Standard Civil Contract 2024 Standard Terms makes clear that no payment or benefit may be made to or received from any third party.

---

49 See: www.gov.uk/civil-legal-aid-means-testing.
50 Civil Legal Aid (Financial Resources and Payment for Services) Regulations 2013 reg 18.

Client has received previous advice

2.68 The Legal Help form requires the client to certify that they have not previously received advice on the same matter, and where they have done so within the last six months requires you to explain why you took on the case. This is because there are specific rules in the contract to prevent the legal aid fund paying out twice for the same matter, and therefore in order to make a claim the second time you must be able to demonstrate that the case meets one of the exceptions allowing you to do so.

2.69 Some of the exceptions apply if you are the client's original provider looking to re-open a case that has been closed; others apply if you are a second provider looking to take over a case from the original organisation.

2.70 In the case of controlled work, a second matter start can only be opened on the same case if you are the original provider where:
(a) at least six months has elapsed since there was a claim on the first matter; or
(b) there has been a material development or change in the client's instructions and at least three months has elapsed since there was a claim on the first matter.[51]

2.71 Where you are relying on Specification para 3.35(b) (material development or change), you should note that:
- Giving instructions, following a failure to give instructions, is not a change in instructions.
- A decision or response from any third party to any correspondence, application, appeal, review or other request made in the course of the original matter is not a material development.
- A change in the law that was anticipated in the original matter is not a material development.[52]

However, you can instead re-open the original matter and make a further claim (see chapter 4) in some circumstances.

2.72 Where you are the second provider, looking to take over a case, you can only do so where:
(a) there has been a material change in relevant circumstances since the initial decision to grant Legal Help; or
(b) the client has reasonable cause to be dissatisfied with the first provider; or

---

51 Standard Civil Contract 2024 Specification para 3.35.
52 Standard Civil Contract 2024 Specification para 3.36.

(c) the client has moved a distance away from the first provider and effective communication is not practicable; or
(d) the first provider is not making a claim for the work and confirms that in writing.[53]

2.73 The contract[54] requires you to make reasonable enquiries of the client as to whether there was previous advice. Where there is a transfer, you must establish that there is good reason, and record that reason on the file.[55]

2.74 However, it is not sufficient for you to take the client's word as to the reasons for transfer. You must seek the client's authority to obtain the file from the previous provider and must then request the file from the previous provider. You cannot start work on the case until you receive the file. Where the client refuses to give you authority, or where you obtain the file and discover that there is in fact no good reason for transfer, you may not make a claim for the case. The sole exception is where there is urgent work that is absolutely necessary to protect the client's position or meet a court deadline, in which case you can do the urgent work and claim for it, even if it later transpires there was no good reason.[56]

2.75 In the case of certificated work, there is no specific rule or guidance on transfer of solicitor. However, to transfer, the second solicitor would have to make an application to the LAA to amend the certificate, and the LAA will consider whether the application is justified. The second solicitor must include work done by the first solicitor on the bill at the end of the case, and therefore the LAA (or court) will be able to see all work done by both solicitors and may disallow on assessment any unjustified duplication.

Permitted work

Overview

2.76 So, if your client's case is within the scope of the scheme and your contract, and passes the means and merits tests, you will be able to take it on. However, there are restrictions on what work can be done.

---

53 Civil Legal Aid (Procedure) Regulations 2012 reg 23(4).
54 Standard Civil Contract 2024 Specification para 3.40.
55 Standard Civil Contract 2024 Specification para 3.44.
56 Standard Civil Contract 2024 Specification paras 3.42 and 3.43.

2.77 The Civil Legal Aid (Procedure) Regulations 2012 set out limitations on the work that can be done at each level of legal aid. The definitions in the criteria are important, as they set out in full what can and cannot be done at each level of funding. Where the client's case needs work that is out of the scope of the current level, you will need to make an application for funding at the next level.

Definitions of permitted work[57]

2.78 The main types of funding common to all areas are:
- **Legal Help**, which allows the provision of advice, negotiation and attempts at settlement and resolution, but not acting as a mediator, issuing or conducting court proceedings, instruction of an advocate or advocacy;
- **Help at Court**, which authorises help and advocacy for a client at a particular hearing without formally being on the court record as acting for the client; and
- **Legal Representation**, which allows the provision of representation in proceedings or contemplated proceedings, including the conduct of litigation and advocacy.

2.79 **Controlled Legal Representation** is a form of Legal Representation at the controlled work level – that is, which is controlled work rather than licensed work, and therefore granted by the provider rather than the LAA. It allows you to represent clients before tribunals, but only in the mental health and immigration categories.

2.80 **Family Help** is a form of funding only available in the family category, and slots in between Legal Help and Legal Representation. Family Help (Lower) is a form of controlled work, also known as 'level 2 work', and authorises advice and assistance in attempting to resolve a family dispute through negotiation and settlement. It does not include mediation but can include advice in support of mediation. Family Help (Higher) is licensed work covering all litigation up to but not including a final contested hearing. Final hearings can be covered by Legal Representation (see chapter 6).

2.81 **Help with Mediation** was a newer form of funding from 1 April 2013 for legal advice for those who are in, or have participated in, mediation. It is controlled work.

---

57 Civil Legal Aid (Procedure) Regulations 2012 regs 4–10.

2.82 **Help with Family Mediation** was a newer form of funding from 1 April 2013 for legal advice for those who are in, or have participated in, mediation. See chapters 6 and 8.

2.83 **Investigative representation** is a type of licensed work that allows the LAA to issue a certificate that is limited in scope and costs, permitting the solicitor to investigate the strength of a proposed claim but not generally to issue or conduct proceedings.

2.84 More details of the types of work that can be carried out at each funding level can be found in the following chapters.

CHAPTER 3

Exceptional case funding

Edited by Carita Thomas and Jamila Duncan-Bosu[1]

3.1	**Introduction**
3.7	**When should non-inquest ECF be available:** *Gudanaviciene*
3.16	**The operation of the non-inquest ECF scheme – *IS***
3.22	**The Lord Chancellor's Guidance: non-inquest ECF**
3.24	ECHR Article 6
3.27	ECHR Article 8
3.28	ECHR Article 4
3.31	Extent of services provided
3.33	**Some recent cases**
3.36	**Changes ahead**
3.38	**Inquest ECF**
3.40	Required under the ECHR
3.50	Wider public interest determination
3.51	**Application process: non-inquest and inquest ECF**
3.51	Overview

1 With thanks to Polly Brendon who wrote and updated this chapter in previous editions of the Handbook. Thank you also to Philippa Matthews of Howells Solicitors for additional information on inquest work that was very helpful in contributing to the editing of this chapter.

continued

3.56	Forms and the Client and Cost Management System
	Non-inquest ECF • Inquest ECF
3.66	Timescales
3.69	Payment
3.73	Review process
3.77	Help and support for practitioners

Key resources

Scope
- Legal Aid, Sentencing and Punishment of Offenders Act 2012 – section 10

Guidance
- Lord Chancellor's Exceptional Funding Guidance (Non-inquests), July 2023
- Lord Chancellor's Exceptional Funding Guidance (Inquests), September 2023
- Legal Aid Agency (LAA) provider packs: www.gov.uk/guidance/legal-aid-apply-for-exceptional-case-funding

Key points to note

- The term 'assimilated enforceable rights' has replaced 'retained enforceable EU rights' in relation to EU law from 1 January 2024, ie EU rights that are part of domestic law but without the application of the EU law interpretive features that apply to retained EU law.
- The time that the LAA aims to make a decision on a review of refusal of exceptional case funding (ECF) increased in September 2022 from 10 working days to 25 working days.
- From 12 January 2022, ECF for inquests no longer needs to include means assessments. Means testing was removed for new and pending applications for ECF and associated legal help granted with ECF funding from that date, and contributions were no longer required for existing ECF certificates.
- From 4 September 2023, the provision for a waiver of the financial eligibility limits and contributions in inquests was removed.[2] Instead, stand-alone non-means tested legal help could be applied for where the client was not eligible due to their means. The test for granting this form of legal help was made harder

---

2 Re: Civil Legal Aid (Financial Resources and Payment for Services) Regulations 2013 reg 10.

than the previous legal help waiver scheme. The LAA requires a similar level of detail to the ECF application. The client would need to satisfy the Director of Legal Aid Casework that (after considering the available evidence) if the individual was to make an application for representation at the inquest, the application would be reasonably likely to succeed.[3] Although the Lord Chancellor's *Exceptional Funding Guidance (Inquests)* states that the evidential bar is lower for a stand-alone non-means tested legal help application than for a full ECF application, in practice, there is an equal amount of work involved. If clients are not eligible for means tested legal help, it may be better for providers to simply apply for ECF and tick the box for associated legal help whilst applying.

Introduction

3.1 When the Legal Aid, Sentencing and Punishment of Offenders Act 2012 (LASPO) was passed, the government sought to address concerns that it would result in injustice by making provision, in LASPO s10, for 'exceptional case funding' (ECF) to be granted in limited circumstances where a case was otherwise out of scope for legal aid.

3.2 ECF may be available for civil cases that are not included as in scope for legal aid under LASPO Sch 1 Part 1. It is not available to clients whose case is in scope, but who are not eligible for legal aid for some other reason. The test for when non-inquest ECF should be granted, as set out in LASPO s10(3), is:

(a) that it is necessary to make the services available to the individual ... because failure to do so would be a breach of–
 (i) the individual's Convention [European Convention on Human Rights (ECHR)] rights (within the meaning of the Human Rights Act 1998), or
 (ii) any rights of the individual to the provision of legal services that are assimilated enforceable rights (ie EU law that is part of domestic law), or
(b) that it is appropriate to do so, in the particular circumstances of the case, having regard to any risk that failure to do so would be such a breach.

---

3 Criminal and Civil Legal Aid (Amendment) Regulations 2023 reg 3(2)(c).

3.3 To qualify for ECF, in addition to meeting the test in LASPO s10(3), the client must still meet the financial eligibility criteria to be granted legal aid, and the case must meet the relevant merits criteria set by the Legal Aid Agency (LAA).

3.4 During the passage of LASPO, the government estimated that around 6,500 applications for non-inquest ECF Legal Representation would be made each year, with additional applications for ECF Legal Help. However, when LASPO came into force, the Lord Chancellor issued ECF guidance for decision-makers and providers which made clear that he interpreted its scope very narrowly and expected very few grants.

3.5 In the first year of the ECF scheme, there were only 1,315 applications made, with just 16 of them granted – a success rate of less than one per cent. Since then, largely as a result of litigation, the grant rate has risen, but numbers of applications remain lower than anticipated. At the time of writing, the most recent LAA statistics[4] show that in the financial year 2023/24, 3,342 applications were received, with a grant rate of 74 per cent. The majority of applications were immigration law (2,142), for which the grant rate was nearly 90 per cent. Family law had 412 applications, with a grant rate of nearly 44 per cent. Inquest law had 438 applications, with a grant rate of 63 per cent.

3.6 Non-inquest ECF was one of the most litigated areas of post-LASPO legal aid. There were two main strands to the litigation: the lawfulness of the tests applied by the LAA in deciding whether ECF was required; and the lawfulness of the process for making applications. In *R (Gudanaviciene and others) v Director of Legal Aid Casework and Lord Chancellor*,[5] the High Court and the Court of Appeal considered when LASPO s10(3) would require ECF to be granted, and the lawfulness of the *Lord Chancellor's Exceptional Funding Guidance (Non-Inquests)*[6] ('ECF Guidance'). In *IS (by the Official Solicitor as Litigation Friend) v Director of Legal Aid Casework and Lord Chancellor*,[7] one of the original claimants in *Gudanaviciene* continued with a challenge to the LAA's operation of the ECF scheme, as well as challenging the Civil Legal Aid (Merits Criteria) Regulations 2013 and continuing to challenge the lawfulness of the ECF Guidance.

---

4 See: www.gov.uk/government/collections/legal-aid-statistics.
5 [2014] EWCA Civ 1622.
6 Available at: www.gov.uk/government/publications/legal-aid-exceptional-case-funding-form-and-guidance.
7 [2015] EWHC 1965 (Admin).

When should non-inquest ECF be available: *Gudanaviciene*

3.7 Since the decision in *Airey v Ireland*,[8] it has been accepted that some rights under the ECHR may have an associated right to legal aid so that the rights can be practical and effective. In terms of non-inquest ECF, an ECHR right to civil legal aid is most likely to arise under ECHR Article 6, the right to a fair hearing, and ECHR Article 8, the right to respect for private and family life.

3.8 ECHR Article 6 is engaged where there is a civil right and/or obligation to be determined. There is a body of case-law that considers when this will be the case, which will not be set out here. Of note, however, is that ECHR Article 6 will be engaged by most family and housing proceedings, save in relation to homelessness applications. It could also be engaged, for example, in certain welfare benefits or employment tribunal cases.

3.9 In *Gudanaviciene*, the Court of Appeal held that the procedural obligations inherent in some ECHR rights, including ECHR Article 8, can require ECF to be made available. This has been crucial for clients who need ECF for immigration cases, which generally do not engage ECHR Article 6 but will often engage Article 8. The procedural obligations under Article 8 can be engaged at the application stage, not just when a case is before a court or tribunal.

3.10 In *Gudanaviciene*, the Court of Appeal confirmed that, in making an ECF determination, it was necessary to consider all the circumstances of the case. Contrary to what was stated in the ECF Guidance, the court found that 'exceptional' is not a test of itself, nor does it necessarily imply that grants will be rare. The Strasbourg case-law does not require representation in all but the most straightforward of cases; but nor does it only require representation in extreme cases.

3.11 Whether or not ECF should be granted is case-sensitive – it is not possible to say that a particular class of case will definitely obtain ECF. It will depend on the circumstances and capability of an individual applicant, and the proceedings for which funding is required. The Court of Appeal in *Gudanaviciene* held that, in determining whether funding is required under LASPO s10, the 'critical question' is whether an applicant would be 'able to present his case effectively and without obvious unfairness'.[9] This test is essentially the

---

8 (1979–80) 2 EHRR 305, ECtHR.
9 At para 56.

same under ECHR Articles 6 and 8, and for assimilated retained enforceable EU rights.

3.12 Since the end of the Brexit transition period on 31 December 2020, ECF has been available where the failure to provide funding would breach, or risk breaching, assimilated enforceable rights. The term 'assimilated' has replaced 'retained' in relation to EU law from 1 January 2024,[10] ie EU rights that are part of domestic law but without the application of the EU law interpretive features that applied to retained EU law. In practice, most cases that give rise to a right to legal aid due to an assimilated enforceable EU law right will also give rise to a right under the ECHR.

3.13 Relevant to whether ECF is required will be: '(a) the importance of the issues at stake; (b) the complexity of the procedural, legal and evidential issues; and (c) the ability of the individual to represent himself without legal assistance, having regard to his age and mental capacity' (*Gudanaviciene* para 72).

3.14 Of particular relevance in immigration cases are: '(i) there are statutory restrictions on the supply of advice and assistance; (ii) individuals may well have language difficulties; and (iii) the law is complex and rapidly evolving' (*Gudanaviciene* para 72).

3.15 Practitioners making ECF applications for clients will want to consider the Court of Appeal's judgment in *Gudanaviciene* carefully – although the principles are articulated in the context of the individual claimants' immigration cases, they are relevant to applications for non-inquest ECF in all types of civil case. In addition to explaining when a grant of non-inquest ECF will be required, the Court of Appeal found that the ECF Guidance as it was at the time was unlawful.

The operation of the non-inquest ECF scheme – *IS*

3.16 While the Court of Appeal in *Gudanaviciene* clarified the circumstances in which a grant of non-inquest ECF would be required, there continued to be problems with the operation of the scheme. In addition, the Civil Legal Aid (Merits Criteria) Regulations 2013 had been amended in January 2014 to exclude cases assessed as having 'borderline' prospects of success from legal aid. These issues, and

---

10 Retained EU Law (Revocation and Reform) Act 2023 (Consequential Amendment) Regulations 2023. See: www.legislation.gov.uk/uksi/2023/1424/schedule/paragraph/75/made.

the continuing question of the lawfulness of the ECF Guidance, were considered by the High Court and Court of Appeal in the case *IS v Director of Legal Aid Casework and Lord Chancellor*.

3.17 In a detailed judgment in the High Court,[11] Collins J noted a series of problems with the scheme as it has been implemented by the LAA, including:

- Even after *Gudanaviciene*, the success rate for applications was very low (para 29).
- The forms were too complex, for both practitioners and unrepresented applicants, and did not reflect the test in *Gudanaviciene* (paras 43, 54, 55, 56 and 105).
- The system was not meeting needs of unrepresented applicants (paras 43 and 62).
- There was no funding for the initial investigation of whether a potential applicant would be entitled to ECF (para 57).
- The procedure for determining urgent applications for ECF was inadequate (para 78).
- There was no right of appeal to a judicial person against a refusal of ECF; the only remedy was to seek judicial review (para 93).
- An applicant was required to provide an unnecessary amount of detail with an application for ECF (para 65).
- It should not be necessary for an applicant to provide full means information for a grant of ECF to be made in principle, subject to full means information being provided, with a grant of funding made once financial eligibility had been determined (para 63).
- It was incorrect to assume that, because courts and tribunals have experience of dealing with litigants in person, an unrepresented individual will receive a fair hearing; the extent to which it is proper for a judge to assist a party to litigation is limited (para 71).
- The way in which the LAA had assessed the merits of cases had been flawed: 'it is not for the LAA to carry out the exercise which the Court will carry out, in effect prejudging the very issue which will be determined by the Court' (paras 72, 96, 97).
- The hurdle to accessing ECF for those lacking capacity, particularly the evidential requirements, was too high (paras 74, 75, 80).

3.18 As a result, Collins J found that the way the LAA was operating the scheme was unlawful as it was 'not properly providing the safety net which [LASPO] s10 is supposed to provide' (para 80). He also

---

11 *IS v Director of Legal Aid Casework* [2015] EWHC 1965 (Admin).

3.19 The Lord Chancellor appealed, and the case came before the Court of Appeal, with judgment given on 20 May 2016.[12] By a majority of 2:1 (Laws and Burnett LJJ, Briggs LJ dissenting), the court found that while there were flaws in the operation of the ECF scheme, they were not sufficient to render it unlawful. The court unanimously allowed the Lord Chancellor's appeal on the issues of the lawfulness of the Civil Legal Aid (Merits Criteria) Regulations 2013 and ECF Guidance.

declared parts of the Civil Legal Aid (Merits Criteria) Regulations 2013 unlawful, along with parts of the ECF Guidance.

3.20 Giving the lead judgment, Laws LJ observed that 'systematic failure is not to be equated with proof of a series of individual failures' (para 53), and concluded that the ECF scheme was 'not inherently or systematically unfair' (para 55). In Laws LJ's view, Collins J had not shown how individual criticisms of the scheme added up to systemic unfairness; it was his 'impressionistic' judgment that they did not, and the evidence before the court did not show that the scheme was operating in a way that was so unfair as to be unlawful. However, he also accepted that the court had not read all the evidence filed by the respondent. Notwithstanding his finding that the ECF scheme was operating lawfully, and that there had been improvements, he observed that 'the extent of the difficulties is ... troubling' (para 57).

3.21 Dissenting, Briggs LJ found that the ECF scheme was unlawful. This conclusion was founded on two key features: its complexity, which was such that it was essentially inaccessible without legal assistance, and the lack of an economic business model that would encourage providers to make ECF applications. In his view, these were inherent flaws in the scheme that rendered it unlawful.

The Lord Chancellor's Guidance: non-inquest ECF

3.22 When making an application for ECF, you must have regard to the Lord Chancellor's Guidance and the Provider Pack. They can be found here: www.gov.uk/government/publications/legal-aid-exceptional-case-funding-form-and-guidance. They are to be read in conjunction with the case-law discussed in this chapter.

---

12 *IS v Director of Legal Casework and Lord Chancellor* [2016] EWCA Civ 464.

3.23 The current Guidance covers EHCR Articles 6 and 8, retained, ie assimilated, enforceable EU rights in general terms, and then briefly considers specific categories of law in an annex.

ECHR Article 6

3.24 The ECF Guidance sets out a three-stage test that LAA decision-makers must consider when determining whether a grant of ECF is required under ECHR Article 6:
1) Does the case involve the determination of civil rights and obligations?
2) If yes, will withholding legal aid mean the applicant will be unable to present their case effectively, or lead to an obvious unfairness in the proceedings?
3) If yes, what are the minimum services required to meet the legal obligation to provide legal aid?

3.25 Further guidance is provided on factors to be taken into account in deciding whether the applicant can present their case effectively and without obvious unfairness. These include the importance of the issues at stake, the complexity of law, fact and procedure, and the personal characteristics of the applicant. Specific guidance for adults who lack capacity and children is also given.

3.26 In relation to those factors to be taken into account, the ECF Guidance elaborates as follows:
- **The importance of the issues at stake.** Decision-makers are directed to consider:
  - whether the potential consequences for the applicant are so objectively serious as to add weight to the need for public funds;
  - whether the case is 'merely' a claim for money, or if it is about issues of life, liberty, health, welfare, physical safety or protection from abuse, or about adjustments to medical or other care impacting on the applicant's ability to live independently; and
  - if the claim is financial, what sums are at stake.
- **The complexity of the legal factual procedural or evidential issues.** Decision-makers are directed to consider:
  - whether the case turns on issues of fact within the applicant's own knowledge;
  - whether there will be a significant number of witnesses or a large volume of evidence will be required; and

- whether expert evidence is required or must be tested, as well as the extent to which the evidence has already been dealt with in earlier hearings or hearings in lower courts or tribunals.

It will also include the complexity of the relevant law and procedure, including whether the case is before a specialist court or tribunal and the extent to which it can assist the applicant.

- **The extent to which the applicant is capable of presenting their case effectively without the assistance of a lawyer.** Decision-makers are directed to consider:
  - the complexity of the case;
  - whether the individual has previously had assistance from a lawyer;
  - characteristics of the applicant such as their level of education, level of English language skills, any relevant disabilities, their level of emotional involvement in the case, any special caring responsibilities that could present a barrier to the presentation of the case;
  - the degree to which the court or tribunal is used to assisting litigants in person; and
  - the extent of any other assistance available, including a McKenzie friend.

If the applicant is a child, the role of any litigation friend, official solicitor or CAFCASS (Children and Family Court Advisory and Support Service) will be taken into account, as well as the level of the child's maturity and intelligence. Where court rules require a litigation friend and none other than the Official Solicitor is available, this will be 'important (and potentially determinative)'. Similar considerations apply in the case of an adult lacking capacity.

ECHR Article 8

3.27   The current ECF Guidance acknowledges that the rights under ECHR Article 8 can require ECF to be granted. However, the discussion of ECHR Article 8 in the Guidance is very brief. It directs decision-makers to the factors identified by the Court of Appeal at para 72 of the judgment in *Gudanaviciene*, and to the factors set out elsewhere in the Guidance as relevant to whether ECF is required under ECHR Article 6.

ECHR Article 4

3.28 Because the current ECF Guidance makes express reference to ECHR Articles 6 and 8, it is not uncommon for the LAA to refuse ECF, on the basis that Article 6 or 8 is not engaged. But it is important to note that grants of ECF **are not** limited to Article 6 and Article 8, and this is confirmed by *Gudanaviciene*. Practitioners making ECF applications will therefore need to reiterate that the LAA is required to consider breaches of operational requirements under the ECHR as a whole and not solely Article 6.

3.29 Litigation regarding the LAA's attempt to limit ECF to Articles 6 and 8 has arisen particularly in relation to Article 4 ECHR, which prohibits slavery, forced or compulsory labour, and servitude. Human trafficking falls within its scope: *Rantsev v Cyprus and Russia*;[13] see also *MS (Pakistan) v Secretary of State for the Home Department*.[14] Article 4 imposes positive obligations on the state to take steps to protect persons within its jurisdiction from being subjected to the prohibited acts.

3.30 In *KPP v Director of Legal Aid Casework*,[15] the claimant sought ECF for advocacy before the employment tribunal. The LAA asserted that there was no Article 6 breach as the employment tribunal is regularly accessed by litigants in person, and no consideration was given as what obligation arose under Article 4. Similarly, in *LR v Director of Legal Aid Casework*,[16] the claimant was refused ECF to access the Criminal Injuries Compensation Authority on the basis that such applications did not engage Article 6, and no consideration was given to Article 4. In both cases, grants of ECF were made following a concession that ECF should be granted where there is risk of a breach of operational requirements of any ECHR Article.

Extent of services provided

3.31 The ECF Guidance states that where the LAA is satisfied that legal aid is required, it should be limited to the minimum services required to meet the need for funding, through providing only specific levels of service, or through the placing of limitations on certificates. The Guidance requires decision-makers to consider whether full repres-

---

13 Application No 25965/04 (2010) 51 EHRR 1 at paras 279 and 282, ECtHR.
14 [2020] UKSC 9 at para 25.
15 CO/779/2014.
16 CO/5587/2017.

3.32 Paragraph 1.2 of the Guidance specifically reminds decision-makers that the Guidance is not meant to be an exhaustive account of factors they should take into account in deciding applications under LASPO s10(2) and (3). Applications should be assessed on a 'case-by-case basis', and representations in individual cases and any applicable case-law considered. If you feel that the Guidance is too restrictive to accommodate your case, it would be good to emphasise para 1.2 in your application, and cite the relevant paragraphs from *Gudanaviciene* that may assist.

Some recent cases

3.33 In *R (Oji) v Director of Legal Aid Casework*,[17] an applicant applied for ECF to enable her to make her claim to the Windrush Compensation Scheme (WCS). This application was refused, which was confirmed on internal review. The applicant issued a claim for judicial review, arguing that the Director of Legal Aid Casework had wrongly concluded that the compensation process did not engage her rights under Article 6 or 8 ECHR and wrongly failed to consider whether the circumstances were such that ECF should have been granted. HHJ Bird found that WCS claims did not give rise to the type of civil right protected by Article 6. The grant or refusal of WCS compensation would not engage Article 8, and would also not have a sufficiently significant impact on the essence of the claimant's private and family life to engage Article 8. Further, the outcome of the claim did not dictate whether she would continue to enjoy a family or private life. The court also found that there is no general discretion to grant legal aid where there is a risk of breach of a Convention right, and where a decision is made that no Convention right arises, it follows that no discretion arises to grant ECF. Permission to appeal has been sought.[18]

3.34 In *R (Alhasan) v Director of Legal Aid Casework and another*,[19] the High Court dismissed a claim for judicial review where an

---

17 [2024] EWHC 1281 (Admin).
18 For reflections on the judgment, see this article by Shaila Pal, Director of Clinical Legal Education & Supervising Solicitor at King's Legal Clinic: www.kcl.ac.uk/high-court-determines-that-windrush-victims-are-not-entitled-to-legal-aid.
19 [2024] EWHC 2031 (Admin).

application for ECF was made to cover a lawyer attending with their client at a Home Office interview. The client claimed asylum as a child but had turned 18 by the time the interview took place (meaning they fell out of scope of legal aid for a lawyer to attend with them). The lawyer attended at risk, deciding not to defer the interview to best protect the client's interests, but first applied for ECF, on the basis that if this was granted it would be backdated. The interview went ahead with the lawyer present. ECF was later refused and the refusal was maintained on review. Judicial review proceedings were commenced that challenged both the work excluded from the scope of legal aid and also the ECF refusal.

3.35 In a judgment on 21 August 2024, Mr Justice Fordham found the Director of Legal Aid Casework (and Lord Chancellor) had not acted unlawfully. The section of the judgment regarding ECF is at paras 62–77. Drawing on previous case-law, when considering section 10(3) of LASPO, it was common ground to the parties that the first limb (s10(3)(a)) engages an objective correctness standard of review; whereas the second limb (s10(3)(b)) engages a reasonableness standard of review. In relation to section 10(3)(a), the judgment acknowledged the significant role a legal representative can properly play at an asylum interview. The judge said the question is not whether the claimant's position would have been 'improved by representation', which 'will very often be the case' (para 71) but whether the circumstances fell below a line of inability to participate effectively in the administrative asylum proceedings without obvious unfairness, having regard to the process as a whole and all the circumstances. He felt that the Director of Legal Aid Casework had answered the question of breach of Convention rights in the legally correct way. Legal aid for the lawyer to attend was not necessary as a positive Article 3 or Article 8 obligation, to ensure effective participation in the asylum proceedings without obvious unfairness. The judge also found no flaw in relation to section 10(3)(b) of LASPO, regarding the appropriateness of ECF with regard to any risk that failure to grant would be a breach of Convention rights, as he had already considered that the Director's conclusion on breach of rights was legally correct.

Changes ahead

3.36 The Nationality and Borders Act 2022 made provision for ECF in relation to advice on the National Referral Mechanism (NRM). This is not yet in force, but it may assist to refer to the provision when drafting applications for survivors of modern slavery who would like advice before entering the NRM, as it shows the government's recognition that advice can be needed in this situation, contrary to the position in *Gudanaviciene*.[20]

3.37 Section 67 of the Nationality and Borders Act 2022[21] says that ECF can be granted for services related to a referral into the NRM if a survivor of modern slavery has a claim that removing them from the UK would breach their human rights. This covers advice on the NRM or other civil legal services in connection with accessing it but does not include any services falling under Part 2 of Schedule 1 to LASPO, advocacy or attendance at an interview conducted by the attendance at an interview conducted by the decision-makers under the NRM in order to make an initial stage (reasonable grounds) decision. This provision might help people where they do not know whether they want to claim asylum but can say they might have a claim to stay based on their human rights. In practice, because of the timescales involved in obtaining ECF, it is unlikely to assist those who are in the most urgent situations (eg who are homeless or still in exploitation).

Inquest ECF

3.38 While Legal Help for advice, assistance and preparation in inquests is in scope, advocacy at inquests is not, and ECF may be required. LASPO s10(4) provides for ECF to be available where:

(a) the services consist of advocacy in proceedings at an inquest under the Coroners Act 1988 into the death of a member of the individual's family,
(b) the Director has made a wider public interest determination in relation to the individual and the inquest, and
(c) the Director has determined that the individual qualifies for the services in accordance with this Part,
(and neither determination has been withdrawn).

3.39 There is specific Lord Chancellor's Guidance for inquest cases, and a Provider Pack, which can also be accessed at: www.gov.uk/government/publications/legal-aid-exceptional-case-funding-form-and-guidance. The guidance for inquest cases sets out that there are two grounds for granting legal aid for representation at an inquest:

---

20 [2014] EWCA Civ 1622 at para 123(ii).
21 See: www.legislation.gov.uk/ukpga/2022/36/section/67.

1) That it is required under the ECHR. The guidance explains that in almost all cases this will relate to the procedural obligation in Article 2 ECHR, so the guidance is written on that basis.
2) Where the Director makes a 'wider public interest determination' in relation to the individual and the inquest.

Required under the ECHR

3.40 In *R (Letts) v Lord Chancellor*[22] Mr Justice Green considered the lawfulness of a previous version of the *Lord Chancellor's Exceptional Funding Guidance (Inquests)*[23] ('Inquest ECF Guidance'). After considering carefully the content of the guidance in the light of the obligations of the state under ECHR Article 2 (right to life), and reviewing the law relating to Article 2, Green J determined that:

> 94. . . . For the reasons that I have set out above in my judgment this contains a number of errors.
>
> 95. First, the Guidance indicates that there is but one trigger for Article 2, namely evidence of arguable breach by the State: See, eg para [54(iv)] above. This is incorrect in that case law identifies a variety of circumstances and types of case of real public importance and significance where the duty arises independently of the existence of evidence of arguable breach.
>
> 96. Secondly, where the Guidance refers to case types where the test may be modified (for example in the case of death in custody) it persists in articulating the test upon the basis of arguability of breach. Since these case types include cases where the law now makes clear that the duty can arise automatically the reference to the arguability test is wrong in law: See para [54(vii)] above.
>
> 97. Thirdly, and related to the first two errors, is the failure even at a broad level to acknowledge the existence of cases where the test is other than arguability.

3.41 At para 118 of his judgment, Green J concluded that the test for whether the Guidance was lawful was whether it would 'if followed (i) lead to unlawful acts (ii) permit unlawful acts or (iii) encourage such unlawful acts?'. The 'unlawful act' being a refusal of legal aid where it was required, or a failure to consider the right legal basis for determining an application. He concluded that 'for the reasons already given the Guidance would do all of these three things'.

---

22 [2015] EWHC 402 (Admin).
23 Current version available at: www.gov.uk/government/publications/legal-aid-exceptional-case-funding-form-and-guidance.

3.42 This led the Lord Chancellor to issue revised guidance taking account of the judgment in *Letts*.

3.43 The Inquest ECF Guidance says that there is a two-stage test in ECHR Article 2 cases: (1) whether the procedural obligation (to investigate whether the state has breached the right to life) arises; and then (2) whether representation at the inquest is necessary to discharge the obligation. The Guidance was further revised in June 2018 to make it clearer that the procedural obligation will arise in cases of intentional killing by the state, as well as non-natural deaths (including suicide) of persons detained by the state.

3.44 The Inquest ECF Guidance sets out the situations where the Lord Chancellor believes funding should be granted, but also recognises that this is a complex and developing area of the law and says that caseworkers deciding applications should take into account representations in individual cases and applicable case-law.

3.45 Where there is no automatic triggering of the Article 2 procedural obligation, you need to show the state was arguably in breach of one of its substantive duties (ie the operational duty or the systemic duty).

3.46 The operational duty requires the state to take reasonable measures to protect individuals from a particular risk that is in the actual or imputed knowledge of the authorities. This involves a real and immediate risk to life.

3.47 The systemic duty requires the state to provide an effective regulatory framework for the protection of people's lives. This is engaged only in cases of systemic failures of processes and systems to protect life.

3.48 In relation to allegations against hospital authorities, the Lord Chancellor's Guidance refers at para 16 to *R (Humberstone) v Legal Services Commission*,[24] stating 'that there will **not** be a breach of the substantive obligation where a case involves only allegations of ordinary medical negligence, as opposed to where the allegations of negligence are of a systemic nature' and the need for 'care to be taken to ensure that allegations of individual negligence are not dressed up as systemic failures'. [emphasis in original]

3.49 Information from practice indicates that there have been issues with applications being refused by the LAA, particularly in relation to community mental health deaths.

---

24 [2010] EWCA Civ 1479.

Wider public interest determination

3.50 There remains a relatively high threshold to satisfy the second ground for granting legal aid for an inquest, ie the wider public interest. For a determination to be made on this basis, there must be 'significant' benefits to providing legal aid. And an applicant must be able to demonstrate that representation is necessary to obtain any benefits that may arise, not just that the inquest itself may provide benefits.

Application process: non-inquest and inquest ECF

Overview

3.51 Practitioners cannot use delegated functions to grant ECF. All applications must be made to the LAA. The Exceptional Cases Funding and Inquest Funding Provider Packs[25] produced by the LAA contain information about the application process.

3.52 The LAA generally expects that applications will come from practitioners with contracts in the relevant category. If you do not hold a contract in that category, or at all, you can apply for an individual case contract at the same time as making the application for funding, but will need to show why the 'effective administration of justice' test is met. The test requires that the Director be satisfied it is necessary for the particular provider to provide the services, having taken into account:

1) the provider's knowledge of the particular case and expertise in providing the legal services which are the subject of the application;
2) the nature and likely length of the case;
3) the complexity of the issues; and
4) the circumstances of the applicant.

3.53 If the LAA grants exceptional funding but does not consider the effective administration of justice test to be met, and the client's case falls within category definitions, the applicant should be referred to a provider with a contract in the relevant category.

---

25 *Exceptional Cases Funding – Provider Pack*, v4, 2 September 2022, and *Inquest Funding – Provider Pack*, v7 4 September 2023. See: www.gov.uk/government/publications/legal-aid-exceptional-case-funding-form-and-guidance.

Exceptional case funding 73

3.54 If the case falls outside any of the contracted category definitions, the LAA can award an individual case contract, without the need to consider the effective administration of justice test, to providers without any civil contract. A provider that holds a Standard Civil Contract can carry out miscellaneous work[26] under that contract if the subject matter falls outside their contract category(ies) and so an individual case contract will not be necessary.

3.55 In order to be granted an individual case contract in this situation, a provider without any legal aid contract must hold either the Specialist Quality Mark (SQM) or Lexcel Practice Management Standard, as this is a requirement for providing legally aided services.[27]

Forms and the Client and Cost Management System

Non-inquest ECF

3.56 If you have a civil contract, applications for non-inquest ECF should be made using the CIV ECF1 form, which should be submitted with the appropriate controlled work form, for example, a CW1 (if you are applying for Legal Help) or CW2(IMM) (for immigration CLR).

3.57 Applications for non-inquest ECF licensed work should be submitted through the Client and Cost Management System (CCMS). Or if you do not have access to this because you are applying for an individual case contract, you would use the CIV ECF1 form and CIV APP1 (for civil licensed work or special case work) or CIV APP3 (for family licensed work cases) and the relevant means form. The means form must be submitted as exceptional funding will only be granted if the applicant passes the means and merits tests applicable for the type of legal aid sought.

3.58 Non-CCMS applications and supporting documents should be submitted to the Exceptional Cases Funding Team by email to: contactECC@justice.gov.uk.

3.59 The LAA will also consider applications for non-inquest ECF from individuals who do not nominate any provider, 'direct applicants'. The LAA now asks that direct applicants complete the LAA forms when submitting an application for non-inquest ECF. However, this is not mandatory and the LAA website[28] says:

26 Standard Civil Contract 2024, category definitions, paras 7 and 8.
27 *Exceptional Cases Funding – Provider Pack*, p8; *Inquest Funding – Provider Pack*, p14.
28 At: www.gov.uk/guidance/legal-aid-apply-for-exceptional-case-funding.

As a minimum, send the following to us in writing:
1. Background to your case, including all the main facts.
2. What you need legal advice on or what court proceedings you need representation in. Explain why you cannot represent yourself.
3. What outcome you wish to achieve.
4. Information that will support your application e.g. court applications and orders, expert and medical reports, copies of any decisions you wish to challenge.
5. Information on your financial situation.

3.60 Where an individual has been granted ECF as a 'direct applicant', the LAA no longer requires a provider who is subsequently instructed to submit a further ECF application. However, the provider should review the application made by the individual, complete the provider details and certification, and email it to the LAA together with the client's LAA letter to a direct applicant and any relevant additional documents or further information. For licensed work CCMS does not have to be used. The LAA will put the application on CCMS, unless the provider chooses to do this.

3.61 The LAA has created a list of organisations to assist individuals who have been granted ECF by the LAA for an immigration matter and have been able to instruct a provider. If a provider wants to assist these individuals, they need to review the information in the individual's letter from the LAA and, if there is no change of circumstances, complete the provider details and certification on the client's forms and contact the LAA with confirmation that they are willing to act. To be added to the ECF list a provider will be expected to offer the individual an appointment to discuss their case, although they are not required to take the case on. They need to have the willingness and ability to take on new clients remotely and be available to do the full range of contract work as described in the immigration contract. The provider may be contacted by the Customer Services Team in the LAA with the details of individuals who have an ECF immigration grant but have not been able to instruct a provider. For more information, the LAA can be contacted by email at: IRCqueries@justice.gov.uk.

Inquest ECF

3.62 For inquest work, there are three options for initial legal help for an inquest matter:
1) **Means tested legal help** – legal help for advice, assistance and preparation for a family member, including the preparation of

written submissions to the coroner setting out the family's concerns and any questions that the family wishes the coroner to raise with witnesses, is retained within the scope of the legal aid scheme. This will not cover advocacy, but this form of legal help can be used to apply for ECF for advocacy where it is arguable there has been a breach of Article 2 and/or there is a wider public interest in funding being granted.

2) **Stand-alone legal help** – this can be applied for where the client is not eligible due to their means. The test to obtain it is harder than the previous legal help waiver scheme. The Inquest Funding – Provider Pack says: 'a financial assessment is not required in circumstances where the Director of Legal Aid Casework having considered the available evidence decides that if the individual were to make an application under s10(2) or (4) of the Act for representation at the inquest, the application would be reasonably likely to succeed'.[29] (As the LAA requires similar detail to that given in an ECF application, and in practice there can be an equal amount of work to prepare this application as to applying for ECF, providers may find it more effective to just apply for ECF and tick the box for associated legal help as well while applying.) Applications for non-means tested legal help should be made on form CW1 INQ and submitted to the ECF team by email to: ContactECC@justice.gov.uk with 'CW1 Non-Means Legal Help Application' in the heading. The LAA says that it aims to make a decision within five working days.

3) **Associated legal help** – this is also non-means tested. It can be applied for at the same time as making an application for ECF in cases where there is no requirement for a determination of the client's means. Since 4 September 2023, any associated legal help determination can be backdated to the date of application.

3.63 For advocacy, applications for ECF funding should be made on CCMS. From 12 January 2022, no means test is required for this work (and no contributions will apply).[30]

3.64 Form CIV ECF2 (INQ) can be used by those wanting an individual case contract.

3.65 When it comes to funding, it is worth thinking of the statutory charge in relation to inquests. With the potential connection between

---

29 At pp5–6. See also Criminal and Civil Legal Aid (Amendment) Regulations 2023 reg 3(2)(c).
30 See: www.gov.uk/government/news/civil-news-exceptional-case-funding-for-families-at-inquests.

inquest proceedings and any subsequent civil action, the statutory charge could arise if civil damages are recovered in a related case.

Timescales

3.66 The LAA aims to deal with all applications (inquest and non-inquest) within 25 working days. However, the 25-day period is suspended if the LAA asks the provider or applicant for further information. Despite the LAA's stated intention to process applications within 25 working days, it is common for decisions to take significantly longer than this. Practitioners should consider highlighting in the application any disability that brings the client within the Equality Act 2010 and stating expressly that making a timely decision would in the circumstances amount to a reasonable adjustment Equality Act 2010 s20.

3.67 There is now some, limited, provision for the LAA to consider non-inquest ECF applications on an urgent basis. For an application made on CCMS, the provider should contact the LAA on 0300 200 2020. For an application made using forms, details of the urgency must be included on page 5 of the CIV ECF1 form. This will generally be the expiry of a limitation date, an imminent hearing, or some other reason why delay would prejudice or harm the applicant or their case. If the LAA agrees that the situation is urgent, it will prioritise the application above non-urgent ones and aim to deal with it within 10 working days. However, the LAA will not guarantee to determine an application before a specific deadline in the case.

3.68 In inquest cases, the LAA considers it unusual that an application for advocacy will be urgent. But if an application becomes urgent, a provider should contact the LAA on 0300 200 2020 with information about the urgency of the application. The LAA says it is helpful for any information about urgency to be included in the subject heading of any email sent to ContactECC@justice.gov.uk and in the merits assessment section on CCMS (rather than in separate uploaded documents).

Payment

3.69 There is no mechanism for providers to be paid for making an application for non-inquest ECF, unless the application for ECF funding is successful. However, after the judgment of Collins J in *IS v Director of Legal Aid Casework*,[31] the LAA introduced the possibility of funding

---

31 [2015] EWHC 1965 (Admin).

being granted to investigate whether a client could be eligible for ECF for a further substantive application.

3.70 Grants of ECF will generally be backdated and funding will be available from the date it is backdated to, at the usual payment rates for the type of funding granted. For Legal Help/controlled work, provided the application is submitted within two months of the date when the client signs the controlled work form, the LAA will generally backdate any successful ECF application to the date the client signed the CW1 or CW2 form. For Legal Representation, where the application is submitted on CCMS, the certificate will generally be backdated to the date of submission.[32] Practitioners should check the grant closely as it is not uncommon for the LAA to commence funding from the date of decision rather than submission. For paper applications submitted within two months of the date recorded on the CIVAPP1 or CIVAPP3 as that of the client's first attendance/instruction on the matter, the LAA will backdate the certificate to that date.

3.71 In inquest cases, the LAA may specify that a determination about means-free funding takes effect from a date earlier than the date of the application. It will generally backdate the determination to the date the controlled work form was signed and dated by the applicant. Providers should include any representations about the effective date of funding in their application. For advocacy, there is no provision for Emergency Representation under section 10 of LASPO but a determination can be treated as having effect from a date earlier than the date of the determination.[33] The LAA says it will generally exercise its discretion to backdate funding where the application to it was made at the earliest opportunity and usually funding will take effect from the date of the application, but in appropriate cases it may be backdated to a different date. Any representations concerning the effective date of funding should be provided in the application.[34]

3.72 Providers granted an individual case contract who do not have a Standard Civil Contract will need to make individual arrangements with the LAA to receive payment, but using relevant legal aid claim forms where required.

---

32 *Exceptional Cases Funding – Provider Pack*, pp6–7.
33 Civil Legal Aid (Procedure) Regulations 2012 reg 68(1): www.legislation.gov.uk/uksi/2012/3098/regulation/68.
34 *Inquest Funding – Provider Pack*, p.11

Review process

3.73 There is no independent appeals process, but you can submit an application for review of an unfavourable decision within 14 days from receipt.[35] For applications using forms this is done using form APP9E,[36] which should be completed with grounds for review and any supporting documentation and sent to the ECF Team at contactECC@justice.gov.uk. For applications on CCMS, the Legal Appeal Request task should be used. Contact the LAA if you need a document upload facility. Both inquest and non-inquest provider packs state that the LAA aims to process applications for review in 25 working days. If the matter is urgent, explain this on the App9E form and in the subject heading of the email to the LAA; or for CCMS applications, call the LAA to set this out on 0300 200 2020.

3.74 There is no right of appeal or any further review process. The LAA says that the review will ordinarily be considered by a separate caseworker not involved in the original decision. Practitioners should consider stating expressly in the application that the review should be undertaken by a separate caseworker.

3.75 If a refusal is upheld on internal review, there is no further right of appeal. As there is no alternative remedy it may be necessary to resort to judicial review. A judicial review of a refusal of ECF is in scope under LASPO Sch 1 Part 1 para 19. If you have a public law contract, you can, therefore, grant Legal Help and/or apply for investigative or full representation in the usual way to challenge a refusal of ECF by way of judicial review.

3.76 There is no right of appeal against a negative decision on an application to except an individual from the means test in inquest cases, but a fresh application can be made at any time and the ECF team will consider any representations by way of an informal review. There is also the option of judicial review.

Help and support for practitioners

3.77 The Public Law Project has produced guides to applying for ECF in family, welfare benefits, housing and immigration cases, which you can access on its website.[37] These are no longer maintained but they may still be useful to look at.

---

35 Civil Legal Aid (Procedure) Regulations 2012 reg 69(2).
36 Found here: www.gov.uk/government/publications/legal-aid-exceptional-case-funding-form-and-guidance.
37 At: https://publiclawproject.org.uk/exceptional-case-funding.

3.78 The Inquest Lawyer's Group is a group of lawyers who act in the field of inquest law, predominantly for bereaved families, and share the values and objectives of the charity INQUEST. Member benefits include opportunities to discuss issues with peers in meetings and by email. More information is on the INQUEST website (fees apply to join the group).[38]

---

38 At: www.inquest.org.uk/join-inquest-lawyers-group.

CHAPTER 4

Conducting a civil/family case

Edited by Simon Mullings

4.1	Introduction
4.5	**Legal Help**
4.5	Scope
4.7	Other sources of funding
4.8	Forms
	What if the client cannot sign the form? • Applications on behalf of children/protected parties • Applications by post • People resident outside the EU • Applications by fax • Telephone, webcam and email advice
4.22	Financial eligibility
4.29	Merits test
	Overview • Previous advice • Reopening a closed matter
4.36	Opening more than one matter
	Separate and distinct • Different causes or events • Work that does not address the other problem(s) • More than one client
4.44	Funding
	Fixed fees • More than one fixed fee
4.48	**Disbursements**
4.49	Disbursements that may not be claimed under controlled work
4.54	Enhancements of costs

continued

4.55	**Help at Court**
4.55	Scope
4.61	Financial eligibility
4.62	Merits test
	The sufficient benefit test
4.65	Forms
4.67	Funding
4.70	**Help with Family Mediation**
4.71	**Ending a case**
4.71	Overview
4.79	Ending a case – monitoring
	Key performance indicators
4.83	**Legal aid representation certificates**
4.83	Scope
4.85	Investigative representation
4.87	Before you apply for a certificate
4.88	Clients abroad
	Clients abroad – procedures • Clients from abroad – public funds
4.91	Children
4.93	Financial eligibility
4.94	Merits test
	The standard criteria • The various merits tests • The general merits test for full representation • Public law claims • Claims against public authorities • Other cases
4.115	Changes to prospects of success or cost–benefit
4.117	**CCMS and forms**
4.125	**Refusals and appeals**
4.128	**Funding**
4.128	Overview
4.133	Amendments to scope and costs
4.135	Use of counsel and amendments for a KC

Conducting a civil/family case 83

4.137	Disbursements and prior authority
4.140	Experts' fees
4.151	Funding from the client's point of view

Contributions • Changes in circumstances • Statutory charge • Recovery of money • Recovery of property, and preservation cases • Enforcement of the charge – the LAA's powers • Related proceedings • Ending a case

4.189	**Urgent cases**
4.189	Scope
4.192	Financial eligibility
	Revocation
4.196	Merits test
4.198	Forms
4.200	Funding
4.202	**Delegated functions**
4.202	Scope

Overview • Steps for granting an emergency certificate • Amendments under delegated functions • Refusals under delegated functions

4.210	Financial eligibility
4.211	Merits test
4.212	Funding
4.213	**Very expensive cases/special case work**
4.215	Scope
4.220	Family high cost cases – Care Case Fee Scheme
4.222	Family KC and two-counsel cases
4.224	Financial eligibility
4.225	Merits test
4.227	CCMS and forms
4.230	Funding

Key resources

Statute and regulations

- Legal Aid, Sentencing and Punishment of Offenders Act 2012 – Schedule 1 Part 1
- Civil Legal Aid (Procedure) Regulations 2012
- Civil Legal Aid (Statutory Charge) Regulations 2013
- Civil Legal Aid (Merits Criteria) Regulations 2013

Contracts

- 2024 Standard Civil Contract Standard
- 2024 Standard Civil Contract Specification
- 2024 Standard Civil Contract – Specification (General Provisions)
- 2018 Standard Civil Contract Table of Amendments – from January 2024
- 2024 Standard Civil Contract Category Definitions
- 2018 Standard Civil Contract Specification, Category Specific Rules – see relevant area of law

Lord Chancellor's Guidance

- Lord Chancellor's Guidance under section 4 of the Legal Aid, Sentencing and Punishment of Offenders Act 2012, May 2023
- Lord Chancellors Guidance on Determining Financial Eligibility for Controlled Work & Family Mediation
- Lord Chancellor's Guidance on Determining Financial Eligibility for Certificated Work

Other guidance

- High Costs Case Guidance Civil
- High Costs Case Guidance Family

Key points to note

- We have said it before in this Handbook, but it bears repeating – financial eligibility of your client is a key issue in most civil cases. Have the rules, guidance, calculators and key cards to hand when seeing clients.

- Make sure you understand when cases can be started under a funding regime and the right time for the case to close or continue under another funding regime. Just as our authors and editors do, refer to this Handbook when you need to.
- A number of issues are important for the client to know about legal aid (eg statutory charge). Make sure you have covered them in your advice to your client and that you have a clear record of having done so.
- In some areas of law, delegated functions is a critical part of the service to clients. Make sure you understand when you can and cannot use them.
- Remember that restrictions on legal aid, such as means and merits, can apply throughout the case. Make sure you are keeping these under review and can show you have done so.

Introduction

4.1 This chapter deals with the general procedures that apply to most types of civil/family case, where the procedures are very similar. There are separate chapters on family cases (private (chapter 6) and public law (chapter 7)); immigration (chapter 9); and mental health (chapter 10), which cover their own funding schemes and rules; as well as on housing (chapter 11); community care (chapter 12); and public law (chapter 13).

4.2 In chapter 2, we saw that there are three key stages in providing legal aid services: to ensure that (a) the matter is within scope, (b) the client is financially eligible and (c) the case meets the merits test. In addition, you need to ensure that an application is made properly in the Client and Cost Management System (CCMS) (see chapter 5) so that funding is obtained.

4.3 This chapter explains how these steps are taken successfully in respect of most civil work. Most references are to the Standard Civil Contract 2024,[1] because cases started after 1 September 2024 are governed by that contract. For cases started under previous contracts, see earlier editions of this Handbook.

---

1 Available at: www.gov.uk/government/publications/standard-civil-contract-2024.

4.4 See appendix C for a summary of the Legal Aid Agency's (LAA's) Costs Assessment Guidance,[2] in respect of the most common queries raised by caseworkers.

Legal Help

Scope

4.5 At the most basic level, work must be allowed under the Legal Aid, Sentencing and Punishment of Offenders Act 2012 (LASPO) (see chapter 2 for more information).

4.6 Legal Help allows you to provide advice and assistance in relation to a specific matter, but does not cover issuing proceedings, advocacy or instruction of an advocate (although you may obtain counsel's opinion, where justified in a complex case). For information about clients who are outside England and Wales or who are not from England and Wales, see further 'Clients abroad' at para 4.88 below.

Other sources of funding

4.7 The Civil Legal Aid (Merits Criteria) Regulations 2013[3] state that Legal Help may only be provided if it is reasonable to do so, having regard to any other sources of funding available to the client. This means that, for example, you should check whether the client has legal expenses insurance (perhaps as part of home contents cover) or is a member (or the partner of a member) of a trade union where certain legal services may form part of the benefits of membership.

Forms

4.8 The form is the CW1 Legal Help, Help at Court and Family Help (Lower) form.[4]

4.9 The assessment of means and client's details sections must be fully completed, and signed by the client, normally in the presence of someone from your organisation, before you start doing any legal

---

2 *Costs Assessment Guidance: for use with the 2018 Standard Civil Contract*; also *Costs Assessment Guidance: for use with the 2024 Standard Civil Contract*, available at: www.gov.uk/guidance/funding-and-costs-assessment-for-civil-and-crime-matters.
3 Reg 32.
4 Available at: www.gov.uk/government/publications/cw1-financial-eligibility-for-legal-aid-clients.

work.[5] Covid-19 arrangements were implemented to cover circumstances where this is/was not possible. See para 4.12 below.

> **Case study**
>
> *I don't really want to stick a Legal Help form under the client's nose and ask them to sign, even before we've said 'Good morning'. Does that mean I will not be able to charge for all my time during the initial interview?*
>
> You will be covered for the whole interview, as the Standard Contract 2024 Specification para 3.10 confirms that all the time in an interview will be allowed, when a client signs the CW1 form at any point.

4.10 The form must be kept on the file and is not sent to the LAA, unless requested for an assessment.[6]

What if the client cannot sign the form?

4.11 There will be occasions when your client is a child or patient, and you may not be satisfied of their capacity to sign the form and give instructions. Sometimes a client will not be physically able to attend your office. Under the 2013 Standard Civil Contract you were unable to use more than 10 per cent of your matter starts in any schedule period for clients who cannot attend on you personally. Under the 2018 Contract this was increased to 50 per cent of your allocated matter starts and this remains the case under the 2024 Contract.[7]

4.12 Also note that the LAA has allowed some flexibility in its response to the Covid-19 pandemic in relation to signatures during lockdowns and where clients needed to isolate, and allowed alternatives to a wet signature.[8]

4.13 Whenever you grant Legal Help to a client in the circumstances described below, you should make an attendance note justifying what you did and tick the appropriate box on the relevant page of the Legal Help form – currently page 15.

---

5 Standard Civil Contract 2024 Specification para 3.10.
6 Standard Civil Contract 2024 Specification para 3.12.
7 Standard Civil Contract 2024 Specification para 3.17. This restriction does not apply if you have accepted the case this way in order to comply with the Equality Act 2010.
8 See: www.gov.uk/guidance/coronavirus-covid-19-working-with-clients.

Applications on behalf of children/protected parties

4.14 You can accept an application direct from a child, if the child is entitled to bring, prosecute or defend proceedings without a litigation friend or equivalent;[9] or there is good reason why one of the persons listed in Civil Legal Aid (Procedure) Regulations 2012 reg 22(3)(a) and (b) (see para 4.15 below) cannot apply on the client's behalf and the adviser is satisfied that the child understands the nature of the work and is capable of giving instructions.

4.15 An application can be accepted on behalf of a child from:
- a parent, guardian or other person responsible for the child's care;
- a litigation friend or guardian ad litem; or
- if neither of the above are available, any other person (except anyone who works in your organisation), provided that the other person has sufficient knowledge of all the circumstances to act responsibly in the child's interests and to give proper instructions.

4.16 An application can be made on behalf of a protected party by:
- a person acting or proposing to act as the protected party's litigation friend; or
- any other person (who does not work for your organisation) where there is good reason why a litigation friend or proposed litigation friend cannot make the application.[10]

Applications by post

4.17 You may grant Legal Help to a client by post where there is good reason. Standard Civil Contract 2024 Specification para 3.15 says that this applies 'where the Client requests that the application is made in this way and it is not necessary for the interests of the Client or his or her case to attend in person'.

People resident outside the EU

4.18 You may not grant Legal Help by post to a client resident outside the EU if one of the following applies:[11]
- the client could, without serious disadvantage, delay their application until they had returned to the EU;

---

9 Civil Legal Aid (Procedure) Regulations 2012 reg 22(2).
10 Civil Legal Aid (Procedure) Regulations 2012 reg 22(4).
11 Standard Civil Contract 2024 Specification para 3.16.

- someone resident in the EU could apply in relation to the same matter; or
- it would otherwise be unreasonable to accept the application.

4.19 This means that applications by post can be accepted from persons outside the UK in certain circumstances. This facility has been particularly useful in immigration cases where clients have been refused entry to the UK, or have been removed or deported, but have a right of appeal that can be exercised from outside the UK. From April 2013 such cases are less likely to be in scope, but clients abroad can apply for legal aid if the work does remain in scope, for example, judicial reviews.

Applications by fax

4.20 You can also accept applications by fax; as for post, see paras 4.12, 4.17 and 4.19 above.

Telephone, webcam and email advice

4.21 You can give, and claim for, advice over the telephone or by email, webcam, etc if the client cannot attend your office for a 'good reason' as defined in the Standard Civil Contract 2024 Specification para 3.18 (see 'Applications by post' above), provided the client is later found to be eligible for Legal Help and signs the form. If the client subsequently fails to sign the form, you cannot claim payment.[12] This can be combined with a postal application, subject to the rules above, meaning that the client does not need to attend your offices to sign the form.

Financial eligibility

4.22 Clients must be financially eligible on both capital and income. Evidence must relate to the previous calendar month.[13] They must inform you of any change in their means and you may have to stop work if their means change significantly (see chapter 2 for more information). However, there are no contributions to be paid in respect of Legal Help.

4.23 The Standard Civil Contract 2024 Specification para 3.23 states that you must obtain satisfactory evidence of their means before

---

12 Standard Civil Contract 2024 Specification para 3.20.
13 Civil Legal Aid (Financial Resources and Payment for Services) Regulations 2013 reg 14(2).

assessing eligibility. In practical terms, that means, except in exceptional circumstances, you must obtain evidence of a client's means before starting work and retain that evidence on file. Further guidance and a non-exhaustive list of types of satisfactory evidence may be found in section 12 of the *Lord Chancellor's Guidance on Determining Financial Eligibility for Controlled Work and Family Mediation (September 2023)*.[14] Also see the LAA's Covid-19 guidance: *Coronavirus (COVID-19): working with clients*.[15] What is required is satisfactory evidence to show that the client is eligible. Where reasonable to do so, you may accept evidence that falls outside the computation period – for example, a letter showing an award of benefits issued before the period – but you are advised to make a clear note on file of the reasons for accepting such evidence.

4.24 Generally the evidence should show the amounts received. However (in a case based on the previous Access to Justice Act 1999 rules, which were similarly worded), the High Court has ruled that a nil assessment because a local authority letter showing a client as being in receipt of Children Act 1989 s17 support did not contain the amounts, was irrational because it was within the solicitor's knowledge that such support was within eligibility limits. The question that should have been asked was not whether the evidence contained the amounts, but whether it was reasonably sufficient to show eligibility.[16]

4.25 If it is 'not practicable to obtain it before commencing controlled work', you may start without evidence of means, but you need to show that you acted reasonably in assessing eligibility and starting work without evidence. In practice you should record on your initial attendance note:

- **why** it was reasonable to start work without evidence of means (eg because the client needed advice urgently due to the imminent expiry of a time limit); and
- **how** you assessed eligibility (eg by making sure that the Legal Help form is properly completed, using the information the client was able to give you from their account of what they have been living on).

4.26 You must get the evidence as soon as practicable unless the client's circumstances prevent this being done at all at any point in the case,

---

14 Available at: www.gov.uk/guidance/civil-legal-aid-means-testing.
15 At: www.gov.uk/guidance/coronavirus-covid-19-working-with-clients.
16 *R (Duncan Lewis Solicitors) v Lord Chancellor* [2015] EWHC 2498 (Admin).

for example, due to mental disability, age or homelessness.[17] Where a client states that they have no income or capital, you should assess whether this is credible and note your file accordingly. Where a client has, for example, recently fled domestic violence that may well be the case. You should enquire how they are living day-to-day and if, for example, financial or other support is being provided by a friend or relative, that person should provide a letter setting out the nature and extent – and any financial amounts – of that support.[18]

4.27 If you act reasonably in granting Legal Help to a client before obtaining evidence of their means and you do not claim any disbursement or report any time after the point where the LAA decides it would have been practicable to obtain satisfactory evidence of means, you can still claim payment for the work.

4.28 However, if the LAA decides that you could have obtained evidence of means at any stage of the case, costs will be 'nil assessed' at any audit. Having files 'nil assessed' can have very serious consequences, so it is strongly advisable to get valid evidence of means prior to starting work in all but emergency situations.

Merits test

Overview

4.29 The Legal Help merits test is known as the 'sufficient benefit test', and states that help may only be provided where 'there is likely to be sufficient benefit to the individual, having regard to all the circumstances of the case, including the circumstances of the individual, to justify the cost of provision of legal help'.[19] This is not intended to be a high hurdle, at least to initial advice, but will apply to all steps in the case:

> ... it may well be considered worthwhile for an individual to pay for initial advice, including the advice that the case is not worth pursuing further. The more legal help is provided, however, the more that the benefits deriving from the costs incurred will need to be taken into account.[20]

---

17 Standard Civil Contract 2024 Specification para 3.24.
18 *Lord Chancellor's guidance on determining financial eligibility for Controlled Work and Family Mediation (September 2023)*, para 12.2(16), available at: www.gov.uk/guidance/civil-legal-aid-means-testing.
19 Civil Legal Aid (Merits Criteria) Regulations 2013 reg 32(b).
20 *Lord Chancellor's Guidance under Section 4 of the Legal Aid, Sentencing and Punishment of Offenders Act 2012*, May 2023, para 4.2.14.

Previous advice

4.30 Clients are generally only entitled to advice on a matter from one legal aid provider, so you must always ask the client whether they have taken previous advice before starting work.

4.31 The Standard Civil Contract 2024 Specification paras 3.40–3.45 set out what you must do if the client has received previous advice, whether that is from your organisation or somewhere else.

4.32 There is a list of particular circumstances in which a new matter start will not be justified at para 3.46 of the Standard Civil Contract 2024 Specification. However, in housing law cases it is worth noting that you can open a new matter if a client faces enforcement proceedings because they are alleged to have breached the terms of a suspended or postponed order, or the terms on which proceedings were adjourned.[21]

4.33 You generally cannot open a new matter for a client who has received advice on the same matter within the last six months, unless an exception applies. Exceptions are listed at Standard Civil Contract 2024 Specification para 3.35:

- There has been a material development or change in the client's instructions and at least three months have elapsed since the previous claim was submitted, but:
  - note that if the client has simply failed to give instructions, then returns, that cannot be counted as a change in instructions;
  - change in the law that was anticipated in the original matter cannot count as a material development; and
  - a decision, or other response from another party, arising from the first piece of work cannot count as a material development.
- The client has reasonable cause for dissatisfaction with the previous adviser (this must be justified dissatisfaction with the service, not because the client was unhappy about good advice they were given or wants a second opinion).
- The client has moved away and has difficulty communicating with the previous adviser.
- The first adviser is no longer able to act for a good reason relating to professional conduct, for example, conflict of interest.
- The first adviser has confirmed that no claim will be made.

4.34 If the client says that they are dissatisfied, you must obtain consent from the client to request from the previous organisation confirma-

21 Standard Civil Contract 2024 Specification para 3.48.

tion of the reasons for termination of the retainer, and a copy of the file and must request the file from the previous provider. If the client refuses consent, no advice should be given and no claim can be made.[22] No work may be done until the previous file has been received, unless absolutely necessary to protect the client's position or meet a deadline. When you receive the file, if you believe the client was unreasonable in being dissatisfied with the service, you must stop work but can still claim a fixed fee if urgent work was justified before getting the file.[23]

Case study

Can I open a new matter when the client has already received advice on the same problem from my organisation?

Legal Help forms are also known as 'new matter starts' (see chapter 2 for more information about means tests for Legal Help cases).

Matter claimed	Open new matter?
Up to 3 months ago	No
3–6 months	Yes – if there is a material development or change in instructions
6+ months ago	Yes

Reopening a closed matter

4.35   Although you may not be able to open a new matter, you can (and may be obliged to) do more work on the original matter.[24] The disadvantage is that you cannot claim an additional fixed fee; but there are compensations:[25]

- previous work and additional work after the client comes back can be counted together towards the escape fee threshold; and
- further disbursements can be claimed.

---

22 Standard Civil Contract 2024 Specification para 3.42.
23 Standard Civil Contract 2024 Specification para 3.43.
24 Standard Civil Contract 2024 Specification para 3.34.
25 Standard Civil Contract 2024 Specification para 3.37.

> **Case study**
>
> What is the procedure for reporting a revived Legal Help case to the LAA?
>
> The procedure has changed since the last edition of this Handbook, and we have been informed by a current contract manager that the procedure now is to report the matter to (a) PA-Claimamend@justice.gov.uk and (b) your contract manager with your organisation's name and account number in the subject line and with a request to void the first claim explaining why.

Opening more than one matter

Separate and distinct

4.36 If a client has problems that are 'separate and distinct',[26] you can open more than one matter. Opening more than one matter for a client must be carefully justified in every case if you are not to fall foul of LAA audits. If your organisation is found to have opened matters incorrectly, significant amounts of money may need to be repaid to the LAA, so it is extremely important to get this right.

4.37 It is relatively easy to justify more than one case as 'separate and distinct' if they necessarily fall under different categories of law.

4.38 It is more difficult to justify opening more than one matter within one overall category of law. The first thing to remember is that the rules contained in the category-specific sections of the Specification take precedence.[27] So, if you are considering whether to open more than one matter within a category, you should look up the category-specific rules first. See chapters 6–13 for more on the rules for individual categories.

Different causes or events

4.39 If your client's circumstances are not explicitly dealt with, it is worth applying the wording in the general Contract Specification, which states that matters are 'separate and distinct', 'typically because they arise out of different causes or events'. So, it is a good idea to ask yourself whether the causes or events are separate. For example, if your client has a serious housing disrepair problem and a family law

---

26 Standard Civil Contract 2024 Specification para 3.30.
27 Standard Civil Contract 2024 Specification para 1.2.

Conducting a civil/family case 95

problem which is in scope of legal aid, these would be very likely to be separate and distinct.

4.40 It is more difficult if the client has 'more than one separate and distinct legal problem' within a category.[28] You must be able to demonstrate two things:

> (ii) if legal proceedings were started, or other appropriate remedies pursued, for each problem it would be appropriate for such proceedings to be both issued and heard . . . separately.

and:

> (ii) each problem requires substantial legal work which does not address the other problem(s).[29]

'Substantial legal work' is defined as at least 30 minutes' additional preparation or advice, or separate communication with other parties on legal issues.[30]

Work that does not address the other problem(s)

4.41 If you are going to satisfy the LAA that work on one issue does not address another, this has to be clear in your case recording. If you consistently deal with two or more issues together, it will be very difficult to argue that they were really 'separate and distinct'. You will need to open two separate files and keep separate attendance notes and letters relating to each issue. However, more than one problem may be discussed in one interview with a client as this may be more convenient for them. If so, separate attendance notes should be produced for each and time apportioned between the issues.

4.42 If you consider that the test is satisfied, you can ask the client to sign more than one Legal Help form at the initial meeting, or subsequently.[31]

More than one client

4.43 The LAA says that you should only use one new matter even if the problem involves more than one client, unless:[32]

- if proceedings were issued, each client would be a party to those proceedings;

---

28 Standard Civil Contract 2024 Specification para 3.30.
29 Standard Civil Contract 2024 Specification para 3.30(b).
30 Standard Civil Contract 2024 Specification para 3.31.
31 Standard Civil Contract 2024 Specification paras 3.29(c) and 3.32.
32 Standard Civil Contract 2024 Specification para 3.38.

- each client has a separate and distinct legal interest in the problem or issue; **and**
- in considering whether there is sufficient benefit for the second or any subsequent client to receive Legal Help, you take into account the fact that Legal Help that is already being provided in relation to the same general problem.

> **Case study**
>
> *I have a client who has been unlawfully evicted from his rented property. He doesn't want to go back there, but does want to sue the landlord. He also wants to apply to the local authority as homeless. How many Legal Help forms should he sign?*
>
> This is two matter starts. They are two separate causes of action, albeit both within the housing category, and were the cases to go to court they would be separate proceedings.

Funding

Fixed fees

4.44 Legal Help is paid under fixed fees, although cases that reach the escape threshold (three times the fixed fee) can be paid in full at hourly rates. Current fees and hourly rates are found in the Civil Legal Aid (Remuneration) Regulations 2013.

4.45 Paragraph 3.30 of the Standard Civil Contract Specification 2024 states that you must not open more than one matter start for a client unless the client has more than one 'separate and distinct' legal problem – see above.

More than one fixed fee

4.46 In some circumstances, you may be able to justify opening more than one Legal Help file for a client. For more information about this, see para 4.36 onwards above; and comments in relation to individual categories of law, below.

4.47 The position as regards the Housing Loss Prevention Advice Service (HLPAS) In Court Duty Scheme, HLPAS Early Legal Advice, Legal Help and Legal Representation is complicated and we deal with that in chapter11.

Disbursements

4.48 You can claim allowable disbursements in addition to the fixed fee,[33] provided that they meet the criteria set out in the contract:
- it is in the best interests of the client to incur the disbursement;
- it is reasonable to incur the disbursement for the purpose of providing Controlled Work, ie necessary for the purpose of giving advice to the client or progressing the case;
- the amount of the disbursement is reasonable; and
- it is not a disbursement which is specifically prohibited.[34]

See chapter 15 at para 15.18 for more information.

Disbursements that may not be claimed under controlled work

4.49 The Standard Civil Contract 2024 Specification para 4.28 provides a non-exhaustive list of disbursements that may not be incurred in the provision of controlled work. Note that the same disbursements are prohibited for licensed work, save that court fees are an allowable disbursement under a certificate.[35] These disbursements are:
- costs of (or expenses relating to) the residential assessment of a child or treatment, therapy, training or other interventions of an educative or rehabilitative nature unless authorised by the LAA;
- ad valorem stamp duties;
- capital duty;
- clients' travelling and accommodation expenses save in the circumstances prescribed in the Costs Assessment Guidance[36] and unless they relate to treatment, therapy, training or other interventions of an educative or rehabilitative nature or to the residential assessment of a child (in the immigration category you may in limited circumstances pay the client's travel expenses to attend to give instructions);[37]

---

33 Standard Civil Contract 2024 Specification para 4.8.
34 Standard Civil Contract 2024 Specification para 4.24 and subject-specific sections.
35 Standard Civil Contract 2024 Specification para 6.61.
36 *Costs Assessment Guidance: for use with the 2018 Standard Civil Contract*, v10, LAA, December 2023, and *Costs Assessment Guidance: for use with the 2024 Standard Civil Contract*.
37 Standard Civil Contract 2024 Specification Category Specific Rules: Immigration and Asylum para 8.64.

- all fees, charges and costs of child contact centres, including assessments and reports on supervised contact, and of other professional assessments of contact between children and adults;
- court fees unless for a search/photocopies/bailiff service or as part of Controlled Legal Representation or otherwise permitted by category specific rules;
- discharge of debts owed by the client, for example, rent or mortgage arrears;
- fee payable on voluntary petitions in bankruptcy;
- fee payable to implement a pension sharing order;
- fee payable to the Office of the Public Guardian;
- immigration application fees;
- mortgagees' or lessors' legal costs and disbursements;
- passport fees;
- probate fees;
- in the family category of law only, costs of or expenses in relation to the provision of family mediation, conciliation or any other dispute resolution, including family group conferences;
- in the family category of law only, costs or expenses of risk assessments within Children Act 1989 s16A (as amended) and undertaken by CAFCASS (Children and Family Court Advisory and Support Service) officers or Welsh family proceedings officers, including assessments of the risk of harm to a child in connection with domestic abuse to the child or another person;
- in the family category of law only, costs of or expenses relating to any activity to promote contact with a child directed by the court under Children Act 1989 ss11A–11G (as amended) – this includes all programmes, consideration of suitability under section 11E and other work to or with a view to establishing, maintaining or improving contact with a child or, by addressing violent behaviour, to or with a view to enabling or facilitating contact with a child;
- any administration fee charged by an expert including, but not limited to, (a) a fee in respect of office space or provision of a consultation room; (b) a fee in respect of administrative support services, such as typing services; (c) a fee in respect of courier services; and (d) a subsistence fee;
- any cancellation fee charged by an expert, where the notice of cancellation was given to the expert more than 72 hours before the relevant hearing or appointment; and
- any fees charged for witness intermediary services provided in court, reports in advance of the provision of such services and other work in preparation for or ancillary to court proceedings.

4.50 The LAA limits what it will pay in respect of experts to 45 pence per mile for travelling costs and £40 per hour travelling time. Substantive work by experts will be limited to the hourly rates/fixed fees for that expertise set out in the Civil Legal Aid (Remuneration) Regulations 2013 (see para 4.137 onwards below for more detail).

4.51 Family practitioners should note the Standard Civil Contract 2024 Specification Category Specific Rules: Family para 7.64, which states that:

> Court fees are an allowable disbursement under Family Help (Lower) only where such fees are incurred for the purpose of obtaining a consent order. In all cases, court fees may only be incurred where they are a reasonable and proportionate step which satisfies the reasonable private paying individual test (regulation 7 of the Merits Regulations).

4.52 This is slightly ambiguous, but it means that consent order fees are the only ones permitted and it must be reasonable to incur them.

4.53 This contrasts with licensed work, where court fees are an allowable disbursement, and with Legal Help, where court fees are never allowable.

Enhancements of costs

4.54 The enhancement of costs has two stages (threshold and factors) and is found in the Contract[38] and expanded upon under section 12 of the Costs Assessment Guidance. See chapter 15 at paras 15.67–15.71.

Help at Court

Scope

4.55 Help at Court is help and advocacy for a client in relation to a particular hearing, without formally acting as legal representative in the proceedings. Note that the work must be in scope.

> 'Help at court' means the provision of any of the following civil legal services at a particular hearing–
> (a) instructing an advocate;
> (b) preparing to provide advocacy; or
> (c) advocacy.[39]

---

38 Standard Civil Contract 2024 Specification paras 6.12–6.17.
39 Civil Legal Aid (Procedure) Regulations 2012 reg 5.

However, note that counsel may not be instructed under Help at Court.

4.56 The starting point as always is that the work must be allowed under LASPO (see chapter 2 for more information).

4.57 Ongoing formal representation can only be provided under a Legal Representation certificate.

4.58 Help at Court is useful for cases where a Legal Representation certificate would not be available. For example, it could be used to conclude a case where a client's means changes such that they would not be eligible for a legal aid certificate and it is reasonable to continue to provide Legal Help for a short time.

4.59 However, it is always preferable to provide representation under a Legal Representation certificate wherever possible as this provides costs protection for the client (para 4.83 below) and is better paid (at hourly rates in civil non-family categories).

4.60 See chapter 11 on housing for more on when Help at Court can be used.

Financial eligibility

4.61 As Legal Help, see above.

Merits test

The sufficient benefit test

4.62 See Legal Help, above.

4.63 The nature of the proceedings and the circumstances of the hearing must be such that representation will be of real benefit to the client.[40] This means the issue(s) must be more complex than the client could have explained to the court themself.

4.64 You must apply the test before every hearing and note the file with your justification. 'Sufficient benefit test met' is not an adequate justification.

Forms

4.65 The form is the CW1 Legal Help, Help at Court and Family Help (Lower) form (see Legal Help, above).

---

40 See Civil Legal Aid (Merits Criteria) Regulations 2013 reg 33: www.legislation.gov.uk/uksi/2013/104/contents/made.

4.66 If the client has already signed a Legal Help form to cover advice and assistance, they do not need to sign another form in relation to Help at Court.[41]

Funding

4.67 Advisers without rights of audience may provide informal advocacy and claim payment under Help at Court, as long as advocacy is justified, and the court agrees to hear them. Counsel may not be instructed.

4.68 There are no additional fixed fees to cover Help at Court. However, the additional work involved may make it more likely that the case will reach the escape threshold (three times the fixed fee).

4.69 Where advocacy is justified, you may claim travel and waiting to/from and at court, subject to costs assessment criteria,[42] as well as preparation and attendance, where appropriate. See chapter 15 for more information on payment schemes.

Help with Family Mediation

4.70 This level of controlled work was introduced from 1 April 2013 to pay for legal advice to clients who are participating, or have participated, in family mediation – see chapter 6 at para 6.68 for more information.

Ending a case

Overview

4.71 The Standard Civil Contract Specification 2024 para 3.64 sets out the circumstances in which you can close your file and claim your costs.

4.72 Most are obvious: the client decides not to proceed, or decides to take the matter forward themself; a representation certificate is granted, or you cannot act further due to a conflict of interest or other professional conduct issue; or the matter simply reaches a logical conclusion.

---

41 Standard Civil Contract 2024 Specification para 1.44.
42 *Costs Assessment Guidance: for use with the 2018 Standard Civil Contract*, v10, December 2023, paras 2.42–2.46 or *Costs Assessment Guidance for use with the Standard Contract 2024*: www.gov.uk/guidance/funding-and-costs-assessment-for-civil-and-crime-matters.

4.73 One is less obvious, which is where the client fails to give instructions for three months (unless the matter is on hold, eg, because you are waiting for a third party to act or you have agreed it with the client, in which case you should make a clear note on file). You have to watch out for this, because on a costs/contract compliance audit (see chapter 23) the LAA may say that the case terminated at that point and disallow all profit costs and disbursements after it. This is important in escape fee cases.

4.74 You cannot stop work or close a matter simply because the value of your costs is equal to, or more than, the fixed fee.[43] Equally, you should not delay making an application for a certificate that would otherwise be appropriate so that your costs cross the escape fee threshold.[44]

4.75 You should close and claim for your case as soon as you properly can, as apart from anything else, the date of the claim is when time starts to run to open a new matter start if the client subsequently needs further advice.

4.76 You have to submit a claim for controlled work standard fee matters within six months of the ending of the matter.[45]

4.77 Note that claims for escape fee cases have to be submitted within three months of the standard fee claim on that case.[46]

4.78 If you fail to submit claims within time limits 'persistently', you may receive a contract notice, which could lead to contract termination.[47]

Ending a case – monitoring

4.79 The LAA monitors organisations remotely, using the data they supply as a matter of course when applying for funding or claiming at the end of the case.

4.80 The Standard Civil Contract 2024 includes key performance indicators (KPIs). We will deal with all the KPIs in this section for completeness, although some relate to controlled work and some to licensed work. Some KPIs apply to all categories of law and a few are category-specific. Standard Civil Contract 2024 Specification paras 2.52–2.72 contains the detailed rules.

---

43 Standard Civil Contract 2024 Specification para 3.5.
44 Standard Civil Contract 2024 Specification para 3.6.
45 Standard Civil Contract 2024 Specification para 4.40.
46 Standard Civil Contract 2024 Specification para 4.20.
47 Standard Civil Contract 2024 Standard Terms clause 14.5.

4.81 Failure to meet KPIs can result in further audit or monitoring and could be taken into account when bidding for a new contract.[48] Therefore, it is important for caseworkers to be aware that their performance under the contract can affect the organisation as a whole.

Key performance indicators

4.82 KPIs are monitored on a rolling three-month basis, rather than on each individual case. They are set out in the Standard Civil Contract 2024 Specification from para 2.52 onwards. A summary of the KPIs is as follows:

KPI 1 – Controlled work (non-fixed fee) – assessment reduction – 10 per cent maximum

When your 'escape cases' are assessed (these are the cases that used to be called exceptional cases, where the costs on a time and item basis are 3 × the fixed fee), the costs claimed must not be reduced by more than 10 per cent. This includes disbursements but not VAT. This KPI will be calculated across a minimum of three months and a minimum of 10 cases.

KPI 2 – Licensed work – assessment reduction – 15 per cent maximum

This sets a similar target in relation to licensed work cases that are claimed on a time and item basis. This KPI will be calculated across a minimum of three months and a minimum of five cases.

KPI 3 – Fixed fee margin – 20 per cent maximum

The LAA is concerned that some organisations will select clients with straightforward cases that do not require much work, in order to retain a high surplus under each fixed fee case. This KPI can only be met if the total cost of cases under fixed fees when calculated in minutes and items is at least 80 per cent of the appropriate fixed fees.

This KPI applies to controlled work cases, and Family Private and Public Law Representation Scheme cases that are paid by way of fixed fees.

KPI 4 – Rejection rates for licensed work – five per cent maximum in the schedule period

Rejections occur when applications or claims are refused because of technical errors in form completion, or lack of enclosures, etc. This applies to applications for legal aid (known as applications for

---

48 Standard Civil Contract 2024 Standard Terms clauses 11.5 and 11.6.

determinations that an individual qualifies for legal aid in the post-LASPO scheme) and claims for payment. There are separate KPIs for applications for funding (KPI 4A) and for claims (KPI 4B).

KPI 5 – Refusal rates for licensed work – 15 per cent max in the schedule period

This applies to applications for legal aid which are refused because the LAA considers that the practitioner has failed to show that they meet the applicable means or merits test.

KPI 6 – Legal Representation outcomes – 30 per cent minimum

This KPI applies to all licensed work in the Clinical Negligence and Claims Against Public Authorities categories only.

KPI 7 – Quality – post-investigative success – substantive benefit
- claims against public authorities – 50 per cent; and
- clinical negligence – 60 per cent.

This applies to licensed work which proceeds beyond investigation in these two categories.

Legal aid representation certificates

Scope

4.83 Legal aid representation certificates are also known as 'full legal aid certificates'. They authorise the conduct of litigation and the provision of advocacy and representation, and generally – though not always[49] – include steps preliminary and incidental to proceedings, and steps to settle or avoid proceedings.

4.84 Clients in receipt of a legal aid certificate have a high degree of protection against costs being awarded against them.[50] Failure to advise clients of their ability to seek public funding where available could be a matter of professional misconduct[51] (though there is no obligation on any individual solicitor to take on a case under legal aid as opposed to privately or some other retainer, as long as the client is aware they could have obtained legal aid somewhere else).

---

49 For example, a certificate is generally not available in housing possession cases until proceedings have been issued: see chapter 11.
50 LASPO s26; and Civil Legal Aid (Costs) Regulations 2013.
51 Solicitors Regulation Authority (SRA) Principle 7 'act: in the best interests of each client': www.sra.org.uk/solicitors/standards-regulations/principles.

Investigative representation

4.85 This is a type of civil legal aid funding certificate (not available in family, mental health or immigration cases) limited to the investigation of a claim where the prospects of success are unclear without substantial investigative work; but it appears that once the investigative work is completed, the case would meet the merits test for a representation certificate[52] (see below). It is preferable to conduct investigation under this form of funding where possible rather than under Legal Help as it is paid by hourly rates and there is less uncertainty about payment than a Legal Help escape fee claim.

4.86 The Lord Chancellor's guidance on civil legal aid[53] suggests that substantial investigative work would be at least six hours of fee earner work or disbursements (including counsel's fees) of £400 or more (ex VAT). Therefore, an application needs to be very clear about the extent of work required. It may be possible to obtain a very brief opinion pro bono from counsel to confirm that merits are not clear, and counsel will need to consider the papers in full before advising on merits. It will not be necessary for counsel to give any advice on the actual details of the case itself at this stage.

Before you apply for a certificate

4.87 You need to ensure that the standard criteria are satisfied (see also para 4.95 below):

- The case must concern a matter of England and Wales (or Welsh) law, in an area permitted by LASPO (see chapter 2).
- The client must be an individual, and a party or proposed party to the proceedings or potential proceedings.
- You must be permitted by your contract to carry out the case.
- The client must not have acted unreasonably in this or any other application, or in these or any other proceedings (eg by concealing information or acting dishonestly to obtain funding – this criterion does not refer to a client's general character or notoriety).
- There must be no alternative funding available to the client, for example, through an insurance policy or trade union membership,

---

52 Civil Legal Aid (Merits Criteria) Regulations 2013 reg 40.
53 *Lord Chancellor's Guidance under Section 4 of the Legal Aid, Sentencing and Punishment of Offenders Act 2012*, May 2023, para 6.11.

or through another person or organisation the client could approach to fund the case.
- There must be no alternatives to litigation, or the client must have exhausted reasonable alternatives, such as complaints and ombudsman schemes and alternative dispute resolution mechanisms.
- The application should not be premature – that is, funding under Legal Help or Help at Court would not be more appropriate at this stage.
- It must be necessary for the client to be represented in the proceedings, and funding will be refused if it is not necessary, for example, if the case is straightforward and parties would ordinarily not be represented, or if the client does not need to be separately represented.
- Funding will be refused for cases allocated to the small claims track in the county court.[54]
- Representation will be refused if the case is suitable for a Conditional Fee Agreement (CFA) and the client is likely to be able to enter into a CFA, damages-based agreement or other litigation funding agreement.[55] This test is likely to be applied strictly.[56] See para 4.99 below.

Clients abroad

4.88 Although the case must be a matter of England and Wales (or Welsh) law, the client does not have to be resident in England or Wales to receive funding. Where clients abroad are entitled to access the courts in England and Wales, they remain eligible for legal aid subject to the usual scope, means and merits provisions. For example, legal aid is likely to be refused if any order obtained in England and Wales is likely to be ineffective, for example, if there is no reciprocal judicial protocol.

Clients abroad – procedures

4.89 Where the client is outside the UK, special procedures must be followed:

---

54 Civil Legal Aid (Merits Criteria) Regulations 2013 reg 39.
55 See Civil Legal Aid (Merits Criteria) Regulations 2013 reg 2 for definition of CFA.
56 See *Lord Chancellor's Guidance under Section 4 of the Legal Aid, Sentencing and Punishment of Offenders Act 2012*, May 2023, paras 7.16–7.21.

- the application must be made in English or French; and
- include a written statement of the individual's financial resources; and
- be verified by a statement that the individual believes that the facts stated in the application are true.[57]

Clients from abroad – public funds

4.90 Under Home Office guidelines,[58] legal aid is not classed as a 'public fund' for the purposes of those with 'no recourse to public funds'. Legal aid is available regardless of immigration status.

Children

4.91 Where the client is a child, you should note that (unlike controlled work) children cannot apply for funding direct. Where children are parties to litigation in the courts, they should be represented by litigation friends, and it is the litigation friend who should make the application for funding on behalf of the child. However, the application should be in the name of the child. Where the court orders that the child can be a party to the proceedings without a litigation friend, you should make the application on the child's behalf as the child's solicitor.[59]

4.92 The child's own means, not those of the litigation friend, are the means to be assessed, and you should therefore put the child's means into CCMS.[60] In cases where others might have an interest (eg in special educational needs (SEN) and public law cases), the LAA can require them to make a financial contribution.[61] Therefore, where you are submitting an application on behalf of a child, you should make clear whether you are seeking to justify non-aggregation of means and, if so, explain why it would be inequitable to aggregate, for example, because there is a conflict between the child and adult.

---

57 Civil Legal Aid (Procedure) Regulations 2012 reg 31(3).
58 See *Guidance: Public Funds*, last updated October 2023: www.gov.uk/government/publications/public-funds--2/public-funds.
59 Civil Legal Aid (Procedure) Regulations 2012 reg 30(2)(b).
60 Civil Legal Aid (Financial Resources and Payment for Services) Regulations 2013 reg 13.
61 Civil Legal Aid (Financial Resources and Payment for Services) Regulations 2013 reg 44(6).

Financial eligibility

4.93 See chapter 2. See also para 4.151 'Funding from the client's point of view', below. Where the client declares a bank account on the application, they will be required to provide three months' worth of up-to-date statements. Where the client is in employment, they will need to provide three months of up-to-date wage slips.

Merits test

4.94 Funding will not be granted unless the case passes the merits test. There is a number of different merits tests depending on the type of case – for those that apply in family, immigration and housing cases, see chapters 6, 7, 9 and 11; for all others, see below. The various merits tests are set out in the Civil Legal Aid (Merits Criteria) Regulations 2013, amended by the Civil Legal Aid (Merits Criteria) (Amendment) (No 2) Regulations 2015 and the Civil Legal Aid (Merits Criteria) (Amendment) Regulations 2016, and in each case you must satisfy both the standard criteria and the particular criteria applicable to the case.

The standard criteria

4.95 Before you apply for a certificate, you need to ensure that the standard criteria are satisfied:
(a) the individual does not have access to other potential sources of funding (other than a conditional fee agreement) from which it would be reasonable to fund the case;
(b) the case is unsuitable for a conditional fee agreement;[62]
(c) except in proceedings which concern a relevant application falling within paragraph 31A(2)(a) of Part 1 of Schedule 1 to the Act, there is no person other than the individual, including a person who might benefit from the proceedings, who can reasonably be expected to bring the proceedings;
(d) the individual has exhausted all reasonable alternatives to bringing proceedings including any complaints system, ombudsman scheme or other form of alternative dispute resolution;
(e) there is a need for representation in all the circumstances of the case including–
  (i) the nature and complexity of the issues;
  (ii) the existence of other proceedings; and

---
62 See *Lord Chancellor's Guidance under Section 4 of the Legal Aid, Sentencing and Punishment of Offenders Act 2012*, August 2021, para 7.16 for the approach the LAA will take to suitability for a CFA. See also para 4.99 below.

(iii) the interests of other parties to the proceedings; and
(f) the proceedings are not likely to be allocated to the small claims track.[63]

4.96 The first criterion requires you to consider whether the client has alternative methods of funding the case at their disposal, and you will need to explore with the client and consider whether the client has, for example, trade union membership or legal expenses insurance. Many household insurance policies include legal expenses insurance, and therefore if the client has a policy you will need to consider the certificates to satisfy yourself that the particular case is not covered (you will need to address this on the application form).

4.97 The LAA will ask people unconnected with the case (and possibly even unrelated to the client) to make declarations as to their means. This has forced clients to tell people they might not wish to know about their situation. The difficulty is that Civil Legal Aid (Financial Resources and Payment for Services) Regulations 2013 reg 16(5) allows the LAA to take the resources of persons other than the person applying for legal aid into account if it considers that they may be 'substantially maintaining' the client. However, this power is discretionary, and if there are valid reasons why it should not be applied in a particular case, the LAA should be asked to take these into account.

4.98 The LAA will also investigate this as part of its consideration of the standard criteria – in particular that there is no other person who can reasonably be expected to bring the proceedings. For example, the LAA will want evidence about the means of adults living in a property if it appears they would benefit from defending possession proceedings and could contribute to legal costs. If they are unable to contribute due to their own circumstances, the reason should be provided as 'extra information' in the means section of the CCMS application. The exemption to this criteria in Civil Legal Aid (Merits Criteria) Regulations 2013 reg 39(c), given at LASPO Sch 1 Part 1 para 31A(2)(a) is:

(a) an application made by the separated child or another person under the immigration rules for the grant of entry clearance, leave to enter or leave to remain in the United Kingdom (whether under or outside of the immigration rules);

4.99 The Director of Legal Aid Casework has to consider whether the case is 'unsuitable' for a CFA.[64] You therefore need to make sure you tick the 'yes' box on the CCMS form to confirm the case is **not** suitable

---

63 Civil Legal Aid (Merits Criteria) Regulations 2013 reg 39.
64 Civil Legal Aid (Merits Criteria) Regulations 2013 reg 39.

for a CFA, bearing in mind the guidance below. The Lord Chancellor's guidance on civil legal aid[65] says:

> 7.17 The test of unsuitability for a CFA is an objective one, rather than a question of whether an individual provider is willing to act under a CFA (although the test cannot be met if there is evidence of a CFA in fact having been offered or put in place for the applicant). In principle, a non-family case may be considered suitable for a conditional fee agreement if:
> - Prospects of success are considered at least at 60%;
> - The opponent is considered able to meet any costs and/or damages (or other sum of money) that might be awarded;
> - After-the-event insurance can be obtained by the applicant.
>
> 7.18 An applicant without after-the-event insurance seeking services otherwise considered suitable for a CFA will be expected to provide evidence of attempts to secure such insurance. Even where evidence is provided of refusals of insurance, the Director him/herself may make enquiries of insurers to see if they would support a CFA in the individual circumstances. Moreover, it will not always be sufficient for the applicant to allege that s/he cannot afford the after-the-event premium. If the proposed claim is for damages, then the applicant would need to demonstrate that it has not been possible to defer payment of the premium from any damages recovered.
>
> ...
>
> 7.20 If the proposed proceedings do not include a claim for damages or other money, however, particular considerations apply. An applicant for legal aid is unlikely to be able to pay an after-the-event premium or success fee from his/her own resources, and the case should not generally be considered as suitable for a CFA unless both:
> - the prospects of success are at least 80% (otherwise it would be unreasonable to expect the legal representative to act at risk in relation to costs without the prospect of a success fee or for the applicant to risk an adverse costs order); and
> - the case will not involve significant expenditure on disbursements (in particular experts' fees).
>
> Of course, if there is no likelihood of either damages or costs being awarded (for instance in seeking an injunction against an impecunious opponent) then there is no basis on which the case could be pursued under a CFA.
>
> 7.21 The fact that the applicant may wish to obtain legal aid rather than a CFA because of the potential deduction from damages in respect of a success premium or damages agreement and/or after-the-event insurance premium, will not of itself prevent a case being

---

65 *Lord Chancellor's Guidance under Section 4 of the Legal Aid, Sentencing and Punishment of Offenders Act 2012*, May 2023.

suitable for a CFA. The test is not whether the applicant or provider would prefer legal aid to a CFA, but is, in essence, whether the case could realistically be brought under a CFA in the absence of legal aid. It will be a question of fact on the individual circumstances of the case whether the need to meet an insurance payment from the likely damages would render the proceedings futile.

4.100 The removal of legal aid for most money claims means that para 7.20 above is cited extensively to deal with the CFA point. However, to prepare for cases where damages claims remain in scope you may wish to carry out a pre-emptive 'shopping around' exercise, attempting to obtain after the event (ATE) insurance in a couple of typical scenarios, so that you could use those as examples of why a CFA is not available. If you are a not for profit (NfP) agency that does not offer CFAs, you could try asking a friendly firm whether it would accept some typical case scenarios on a CFA basis and again use their response as evidence that such cases are not commercially attractive. If you are a private firm that does offer CFAs, you could set out your criteria for accepting CFAs and why the particular case does not meet them.

4.101 Two key criteria that must be addressed are the need for representation and the likely track allocation. The effect of these is that legal aid will not be available for the most simple and straightforward cases, including those likely to be small claims.

The various merits tests

4.102 Civil Legal Aid (Merits Criteria) Regulations 2013 reg 5 sets out the prospects of success – the likelihood of achieving a successful substantive outcome – and categorises them thus:
- **very good** – 80 per cent or above;
- **good** – 60 to 80 per cent;
- **moderate** – 50 to 60 per cent;
- **marginal** – 45 to 50 per cent;
- **poor** – less than 45 per cent;
- **borderline** – it is not possible, because of disputed law, fact or expert evidence, to decide that the chance of obtaining a successful outcome is 50 per cent or more but it cannot be categorised as 'unclear', 'poor' or 'marginal'; or
- **unclear** – the case cannot be assigned to any of the other categories because there are identifiable investigations to be carried out after which the prospects can be estimated.

4.103 Following assessment of the prospects of success, the following will apply:
- Where prospects of success are **moderate or better**, the prospects of success criterion will be met and so legal aid will be granted (subject to any other criteria that may apply in the individual case).
- Where prospects of success are **borderline** or **marginal**, the prospects of success criterion will only be met if the case is of significant wider public interest or of overwhelming importance to the individual.[66] See paras 4.104 and 4.107 below.
- Where prospects of success are **unclear**, it will generally be more appropriate to grant investigative representation than full representation, so that investigation can be carried out and the prospects clarified.
- Where prospects of success are **poor**, representation will be refused.

In addition, the value of the outcome must justify the costs. For damages claims, see below.

4.104 Besides the prospects of success test, there are other tests:
- The **proportionality test**[67] is met if:
 ... the Director is satisfied that the likely benefits of the proceedings to the individual and others justify the likely costs, having regard to the prospects of success and all the other circumstances of the case.
- The **significant wider public interest test**[68] is met if:
 ... the Director is satisfied that the case is an appropriate case to realise–
 (a) real benefits to the public at large, other than those which normally flow from cases of the type in question; and
 (b) benefits for an identifiable class of individuals, other than the individual to whom civil legal services may be provided or members of that individual's family.
- The **reasonable private paying individual test**[69] is met if:
 ... the Director is satisfied that the potential benefit to be gained from the provision of civil legal services justifies the likely costs, such that a reasonable private paying individual would be prepared to start or continue the proceedings having regard to the prospects of success and all the other circumstances of the case.

---

66 Civil Legal Aid (Merits Criteria) Regulations 2013 reg 43, as amended by Civil Legal Aid (Merits Criteria) (Amendment) (No 2) Regulations 2015 reg 2(4).
67 Civil Legal Aid (Merits Criteria) Regulations 2013 reg 8.
68 Civil Legal Aid (Merits Criteria) Regulations 2013 reg 6.
69 Civil Legal Aid (Merits Criteria) Regulations 2013 reg 7.

4.105 The **cost–benefit criteria** are:[70]
- If the case is primarily a claim for damages or other sum of money and not of significant wider public interest:
  - if prospects are very good, likely damages must exceed likely costs;
  - if prospects are good, likely damages must exceed likely costs by a ratio of 2:1; and
  - if prospects are moderate, the ratio must be 4:1.
- If the case is not primarily a claim for damages or other sum of money and not of significant wider public interest:
  - the reasonable private paying client test must be met.
- If the case is of significant wider public interest:
  - the proportionality test must be met.

4.106 The **multi-party action criteria** are:[71]
- the client's claim is the lead claim; and
- the case is of significant wider public interest.

4.107 A case is of **overwhelming importance to the individual** if it is not primarily a claim for damages or other sum of money and relates to the individual's life, liberty or physical safety (or that of a member of their family) or an immediate risk that the individual may become homeless.[72] For this to apply, that must be at issue in the proceedings and be more than merely academic. A claim for damages for false imprisonment post-dating release will not satisfy this test since liberty is no longer at stake, but a claim for habeas corpus will. If you are relying on the risk of homelessness to justify funding it must be immediate – so relate to occupation of property, not financial difficulties that may lead to later loss of occupation. Homelessness means lack of physical occupation of property, rather than the wider statutory definition of homelessness in Housing Act 1996 Part 7.[73]

4.108 The Regulations go on to set out a merits test that applies to general certificated cases, with variations for specific types of cases.

---

70 Civil Legal Aid (Merits Criteria) Regulations 2013 reg 42, as amended by 2015 Regulations reg 2(3) and 2016 Regulations reg 2(3).
71 Civil Legal Aid (Merits Criteria) Regulations 2013 reg 44.
72 Civil Legal Aid (Merits Criteria) Regulations 2013 reg 2.
73 *Lord Chancellor's Guidance under Section 4 of the Legal Aid, Sentencing and Punishment of Offenders Act 2012*, May 2023, paras 4.2.10–4.2.12.

The general merits test for full representation

4.109 The **general merits test** is set out in Civil Legal Aid (Merits Criteria) Regulations 2013 reg 41 and applies in all cases except those set out below. The test is that:
- the prospects of success criteria are satisfied;
- the cost–benefit criteria are satisfied; and
- if the claim is a multi-party action and is primarily a money claim but likely damages do not exceed £5,000, the multi-party action criteria are satisfied.

4.110 What this means in practice is that the case must fall into one of the following types:
1) A claim for damages or other sum of money with **no significant wider public interest** and which is **not of overwhelming importance to the individual**:
   a) prospects of success must be **very good** and likely damages exceed likely costs; or
   b) prospects of success must be **good** and likely damages exceed likely costs by 2:1; or
   c) prospects of success must be **moderate** and likely damages exceed likely costs by 4:1.
2) A claim other than for damages or other sum of money, or a defence to a claim, with **no significant wider public interest** and which is **not of overwhelming importance to the individual**:
   a) prospects of success must be **moderate or better**; and
   b) the **reasonable private paying client test** must be met.
3) A claim or defence to a claim which **has significant wider public interest**:
   a) prospects of success must be **marginal or better**; and
   b) the **proportionality test** must be met.
4) A case which **is of overwhelming importance to the individual**:
   a) the prospects of success must be **marginal or better**; and
   b) the *reasonable private paying client test* must be met.
5) A **multi-party action case**: the multi-party action criteria are satisfied.

Public law claims

4.111 For public law claims (defined in Civil Legal Aid (Merits Criteria) Regulations 2013 reg 2 as judicial review, habeas corpus and homelessness appeals), there are additions to the standard criteria:[74]

---

74 Civil Legal Aid (Merits Criteria) Regulations 2013 reg 53 and Civil Legal Aid (Merits Criteria) (Amendment) Regulations 2013.

Conducting a civil/family case 115

- the act, omission or matter complained of appears to be susceptible to challenge; and
- there are no alternative proceedings before a court or tribunal which are available to challenge the act, omission or other matter, except where the Director considers that such proceedings would not provide an effective remedy.[75]

4.112 The **merits test** for full representation in public law claims is:[76]
- the standard criteria are met (including the additional ones above);
- unless impracticable to do so, a letter before claim has been sent and the defendant given a reasonable time to respond;
- the proportionality test is met; and
- prospects of success are:
  - very good, good or moderate; or
  - borderline or marginal; and
    - the case is of significant wider public interest;
    - the case is of overwhelming importance to the individual; or
    - the substance of the case relates to a breach of convention rights.[77]

See para 7.35 onwards of the Lord Chancellor's guidance on civil legal aid[78] and chapter 13 in this Handbook for detailed guidance on public law claims.

Claims against public authorities

4.113 For claims against public authorities (LASPO Sch 1 Part 1 paras 21 and 22), the test is:[79]
- the proportionality test is met; and
- prospects of success are:
  - moderate or better; or

---

75 Civil Legal Aid (Merits Criteria) Regulations 2013 reg 53(b), as amended by Civil Legal Aid (Merits Criteria) (Amendment) Regulations 2013 reg 2.
76 Civil Legal Aid (Merits Criteria) Regulations 2013 reg 56, amended by Civil Legal Aid (Merits Criteria) (Amendment) (No 2) Regulations 2015 reg 2(5) and Civil Legal Aid (Merits Criteria) (Amendment) Regulations 2016 reg 2(5).
77 See *Lord Chancellor's Guidance under Section 4 of the Legal Aid, Sentencing and Punishment of Offenders Act 2012*, May 2023, chapter 5, 'Convention rights'.
78 *Lord Chancellor's Guidance under Section 4 of the Legal Aid, Sentencing and Punishment of Offenders Act 2012*, May 2023.
79 Civil Legal Aid (Merits Criteria) Regulations 2013, as amended by the 2015 and 2016 Regulations.

- borderline or marginal; and
    - the case is of significant wider public interest;
    - the case is of overwhelming importance to the individual; or
    - the substance of the case relates to a breach of ECHR rights.[80]

Other cases

4.114 For immigration, housing, mental health and family merits tests, see the appropriate chapters of this Handbook.

Changes to prospects of success or cost–benefit

4.115 As the case progresses, inevitably further information and evidence will come to light. If you consider that the merits test is no longer met, the case should be referred to the LAA for decision.

4.116 There is useful guidance on the difference of approach under the LASPO scheme which can be found in the Lord Chancellor's guidance on civil legal aid:

> 8.32 Regulation 42 [Civil Legal Aid (Procedure) Regulations 2012] addresses the ground and procedures for withdrawal of determinations. The grounds for withdrawal are set out at 42(1). These are expanded in comparison with those under the funding code. They include at 42(1)(k), the provisions in relation to the domestic abuse 'gateway' to civil legal services in family proceedings no longer being satisfied. This allows for determinations to be withdrawn in such circumstances where the forms of evidence supplied are no longer valid or successfully challenged and no longer stand. It includes, for example, evidence of a protective injunction for domestic abuse, obtained without notice to the respondent and subsequently set aside by the Court.
>
> 8.33 Regulation 42(3) provides for an equivalent of the 'show cause' procedure under the funding code procedures through notification of an intention to withdraw a determination. The scheme is different in that, if the determination is withdrawn as a result of this procedure, the withdrawal takes place with effect from the initial notification of intention (42(3)). That represents a difference from the position under the funding code in that:
> a) The client will not have cost protection, under the Civil Legal Aid (Costs) Regulations 2013, in the period from when the Director first notified an intention to withdraw the determination;

---

80 See *Lord Chancellor's Guidance under Section 4 of the Legal Aid, Sentencing and Punishment of Offenders Act 2012*, May 2023, chapter 5 'Convention rights'.

b) The provider can carry out work at risk in relation to whether the withdrawal does occur, whereas no work could be carried out within the show cause period under the funding code without express permission irrespective of the ultimate outcome of the show cause.

CCMS and forms

4.117 Applications for certificates for Legal Representation and for Investigative Representation are made to the LAA. Except in certain circumstances where urgent work is required (see below), solicitors do not have the power to grant or amend certificates directly. Special procedures also apply in urgent cases (see below).

4.118 The LAA made its electronic CCMS mandatory for all civil and family applications for certificates from April 2016, a date which was put back several times. There have been considerable difficulties with the system, including criticisms of its functionality. See chapter 5 for more information about how CCMS works. It has been said for some time that the applications stage of CCMS will be replaced by a system called 'Apply'. Apply is currently in use for applications in domestic abuse and Children Act cases.

4.119 CCMS has been created in such a way that the questions asked are to an extent dependent on answers to other questions and so the electronic screens do not mirror the paper forms which they replaced.

4.120 If you are unable to access CCMS due to a technical issue and you need an **urgent** decision (needed within 48 hours) on an **application or amendment**, you can submit a paper application. The LAA guidance is that it should be contacted by telephone for authorisation before contingency protocols can be used. The LAA will give you a contingency reference number, which should be quoted in subsequent correspondence.[81]

4.121 This process is not available where you have delegated functions allowing you to grant the application or amendment yourself.[82] For further details, see chapter 5.

4.122 When applying through CCMS, evidence of the client's means covering the last three months will also be required. See chapter 2 for details of financial eligibility. You will need to complete a statement

---

81 See: https://ccmstraining.justice.gov.uk/__data/assets/pdf_file/0015/8025/CCMS-Contingency-Process_v1_0.pdf.
82 See: www.gov.uk/guidance/bringing-civil-legal-aid-processing-online#ccms-contingency-arrangements.

of case, and this should be completed in as much detail as possible, as this is the part of the application that demonstrates that the criteria for granting a certificate are met. Do not forget that your client's statement is not the same as a statement of case. You have to explain to someone at the LAA, who has not met your client, why what the client says amounts to a cause of action and why it should be funded.

4.123 If you are applying for exceptional case funding (see chapter 3 and merits tests above), you can apply through CCMS. There is a CCMS quick guide to making exceptional case funding (ECF) applications, which will help you to follow the correct procedure. See chapter 3 for more information on ECF.

4.124 Low levels of rejects and refusals are KPIs under the Standard Civil Contract 2024 – see chapter 22 and para 4.79 onwards above.

Refusals and appeals

4.125 A refusal of a certificate on the basis of merit can be challenged, within 14 days of the decision – first by way of an application for a review by the Director, then by an appeal to an independent adjudicator.[83]

4.126 If successful on review, then the certificate will be granted from the date of the successful appeal. There is no provision for backdating to the original application.[84]

4.127 A refusal on financial grounds cannot be formally appealed, though a Director's review is available, and a fresh application can be made if circumstances change.

Funding

Overview

4.128 Civil legal aid representation certificates are funded on an hourly rate basis. Most family certificates are paid by way of standard fees. See chapter 15 for more information.

4.129 In almost every case, a funding certificate is only granted subject to two limitations:

---

83 Civil Legal Aid (Procedure) Regulations 2012 reg 44.
84 Civil Legal Aid (Procedure) Regulations 2012 reg 44(4).

1) a particular step in the proceedings, such as 'all steps up to the filing of a defence and thereafter obtaining counsel's opinion', or 'all steps up to a case management conference'; and
2) a costs limitation – costs limitations include profit costs (and any enhancement or uplift), counsels' fees and disbursements, but not VAT.

4.130 Standard costs limits vary by category:
- claims against public authorities – £6,000;
- community care – £3,500;
- immigration and asylum – £4,500;
- mental health – £5,000;
- Special Children Act cases – £25,000; and
- all other categories, and judicial review cases in the above categories – £2,250.

The above limits are the standard defaults, but it is open to you to apply for a larger initial limit where justified.

4.131 It is extremely important not to do work outside the scope of either limitation, as you will not be paid for it. It is particularly easy to lose track of counsels' fees and disbursements, and it really helps to keep all documents relating to financial issues together in the file. You are required to allocate fees to counsel in CCMS so that they can request payments on account, which can help to keep track of profit costs and counsel's fees as against the limitation. However, you need to keep separate track of disbursements to make sure you are within the costs limitation.

4.132 Limitations can be amended on application to the LAA.

Amendments to scope and costs

4.133 Requests for amendments to either scope or costs limitations are made to the LAA via CCMS. In making a request, the adviser will be obliged to demonstrate that the case continues to satisfy both the standard criteria and the case-based criteria of the merits test, and state what new scope or costs limitation is required. Therefore, there must be merit not only in the case as a whole but in each step of the proceedings.

4.134 Timing the application for an amendment has to be done with care, as the date an amendment takes effect is the date of the decision. If you leave your application until the last minute, you risk exceeding the current limitation and not being paid if the amendment is refused. On the other hand, you must justify why the work needs to be done at the particular time, as the LAA will refuse any amendment considered to be premature. It will also refuse an amendment that might become redundant due to some other event taking place.

Use of counsel and amendments for a KC

4.135 A representation certificate allows you to instruct one counsel; but if the case warrants second counsel or a KC, you must apply to the LAA for authority. In general, authority will only be granted in cases of exceptional complexity or importance, and you must be able to show that the interests of the client cannot properly be represented without the authority being granted. There is no automatic presumption that a KC will be granted for an appeal to the Court of Appeal, nor that where another party has a KC or more than one counsel it will be justified for a legally aided party to have the same level of representation. See the LAA's prior authority guidance at para 1.2 of *Guidance on authorities and legal aid for cases in courts outside England and Wales* for more information.[85]

4.136 Failure to obtain authority will mean that no payment can be made for the second counsel or KC. See also chapter 15.

Disbursements and prior authority

4.137 In many cases, disbursements can be large, and there is a risk to the organisation that they will not be allowed, or not be allowed in full, on assessment of the bill.

4.138 Therefore, the prior authority scheme allows you to apply to the LAA for authority to incur a disbursement in advance, if it is above £100 and is not an expert fee covered by the standard rates/hours introduced from 3 October 2011 and reduced from 2 December 2013.[86] The application is made via CCMS accompanied by a quote for the disbursement and reasons why it is necessary. The advantage of having authority is that no question as to the validity of the disbursement can be raised on assessment of the bill, unless and to

---

85 November 2022. Available at: https://assets.publishing.service.gov.uk/media/636b7d888fa8f5358665f4cd/Guidance_on_authorities_and_legal_aid_for_cases_in_courts_outside_England_and_Wales_November_2022.pdf.

86 Community Legal Service (Funding) (Amendment No 2) Order 2011 (for Access to Justice Act 1999 cases) and Civil Legal Aid (Remuneration) (Amendment) Regulations 2013 Sch 2 (for LASPO cases). Expert fees were reduced by 20 per cent on 2 December 2013 and so the rates in Civil Legal Aid (Remuneration) Regulations 2013 Sch 5 are no longer valid for cases started after that date.

Conducting a civil/family case 121

4.139 the extent that it exceeds the amount or scope of the authority. Prior authority therefore gives a measure of costs protection for expensive disbursements.

4.139 You may apply for prior authority if:
(a) that item of costs is either unusual in its nature or is unusually large;
(b) you propose to instruct a King's Counsel or more than one Counsel (see Paragraph 6.59(d));[87]
(c) prior authority is otherwise required under the Specification; or
(d) you seek to pay an expert higher rates than are set out in the Remuneration Regulations.[88]

If you do not apply for prior authority and (b), (c) or (d) above applies, you will not be paid in full or at all for the fees incurred.

Experts' fees

4.140 Experts' fees have been codified since October 2011. The Civil Legal Aid (Remuneration) Regulations 2013 set out applicable rates for experts in different areas of expertise. The fees were reduced by 20 per cent by the Civil Legal Aid (Remuneration) (Amendment) Regulations 2013. In some cases, there are fixed fees for reports, in others hourly rates. The hourly rates are a maximum, not a fixed rate.[89] The LAA has issued some useful guidance on experts' fees.[90]

4.141 There are 'London' and 'non-London' rates; which applies is determined by the location of the expert. Where an expert has offices both in and outside London, it is the location of the solicitor that determines the rate.[91]

---

87 For ease of reference, specification 6.59 (d) reads: 'you must not Claim for the fees of King's Counsel or more than one Counsel unless you have obtained prior authority to instruct King's Counsel or more than one Counsel under Paragraph 5.10(b). For the avoidance of doubt, prior authority to instruct a King's Counsel is required only where King's Counsel will act as such but not where King's Counsel chooses to act and be paid only at junior Counsel rates; . . .'
88 Standard Civil Contract 2024 Specification para 5.10.
89 The full list of rates can be found in Civil Legal Aid (Remuneration) Regulations 2013 Sch 5 for cases started before 2 December 2013 and in Civil Legal Aid (Remuneration) (Amendment) Regulations 2013 Sch 2 for cases started on or after that date.
90 See: www.gov.uk/guidance/expert-witnesses-in-legal-aid-cases and https://assets.publishing.service.gov.uk/media/66680933e8d5f2d4bdfcbb5a/Guidance_on_the_Remuneration_of_Expert_Witnessesv9_June_2024.pdf.
91 Costs Assessment Guidance para 3.46.

4.142 The rates cannot be exceeded unless the LAA has granted prior authority in advance. Prior authority will only be granted in exceptional circumstances, defined as being where:[92]
- the expert's evidence is key to the client's case and either:
  - the complexity of the material is such that an expert with a high level of seniority is required; or
  - the material is of such a specialised and unusual nature that only very few experts are available to provide the necessary evidence.

4.143 Applications for prior authority in certificate cases should be made via CCMS. Prior authority cannot be granted in Legal Help cases, and so where you instruct an expert at a higher rate in a Legal Help case you should justify in the file why you have done so. It would be unusual – and risky – to do this in a Legal Help case.

4.144 Where a particular type of expert is not specified in the regulations and therefore there are no codified rates, the LAA will assess rates on a case-by-case basis, but will 'have regard to' the codified rates.

4.145 Where either enhanced or non-codified rates are sought, the LAA will expect to see at least three[93] written quotes setting out the hourly rate, number of hours and total fee.

4.146 Where joint experts are instructed and all instructing parties are legally aided, the codified rates apply to the total instruction, not each party's share. Any application for prior authority need only be made by the lead solicitor in the instruction.

4.147 Where joint experts are instructed by both legally aided and non-legally aided parties, the LAA will take a pro rata approach. Where fixed fees are specified, the LAA will pay a share of the fee. Where an hourly rate is specified, the LAA will determine its share on the basis of hours rather than rates. It will pay – in a two-party case – half the time at the codified rate.[94]

4.148 For example, a surveyor is instructed jointly on behalf of a tenant and a landlord. If they take six hours to prepare their report, the LAA will pay for three hours, up to the maximum of £115 per hour (in London) – so £345. It will not pay six hours at £115 (£690) where the landlord also agrees to pay six hours at £115 – the approach is that the codified rate is the maximum the expert can charge to the fund

---

92 Standard Civil Contract 2024 Specification para 6.60.
93 Standard Civil Contract 2024 Specification para 4.27.
94 Costs Assessment Guidance para 3.43.

Conducting a civil/family case 123

and in a joint instruction the LAA will pay half the time taken to prepare the report. The other party can agree to pay the expert more, but that is a matter between them and the expert.

4.149 As a result of this, the LAA requires disbursement vouchers with a breakdown of time spent and hourly rates charged to accompany claims, even those assessed by the court. If the court has assessed an hourly rate higher than the codified rates without prior authority, the LAA will reject it and it will have to go back to the court for reassessment.[95] Other restrictions on experts' fees include:

- capping travel time to £40 per hour and costs to 45p per mile;
- a ban on claiming for administration costs;
- a ban on claiming a cancellation fee unless given less than 72 hours' notice of the cancellation; and
- requiring experts to time-record and itemise time spent on their invoices.

4.150 The codified rates also apply to attendance at court. Experts cannot charge half or full days for court attendance – they must charge the hourly rate.

Funding from the client's point of view

Contributions

4.151 Clients on passporting benefits (see chapter 2 at para 2.40) or with very limited means do not have to make contributions to the cost of their case during its lifetime; but they may need to make payment at the end of their case if money or property is recovered or preserved, under the statutory charge (see para 4.158 onwards below for more information). It is therefore easy for such clients to be lulled into feeling that their legal aid is going to be free, when it is not, and so it is even more important to ensure they understand the effect of the statutory charge and are given a costs estimate which is revised at every relevant point throughout the case.

4.152 If the client's capital is between the lower and upper thresholds, the client is required to pay a contribution. The amount of the contribution is the lower of: (a) the amount by which capital exceeds the lower threshold; and (b) the total estimated costs of the case.

4.153 If the client's disposable income is between the lower and upper threshold, a contribution will be payable. The amount of the

---

95 See: www.gov.uk/government/publications/civ-claim1-civil-claim-form-not-fixed-fee.

contribution depends on the amount by which income is above the lower threshold but is a fixed sum plus a percentage of the excess each month for the life of the certificate.

4.154 The Ministry of Justice has two online calculators for civil legal aid eligibility:
1) for members of the public: https://civil-eligibility-calculator.justice.gov.uk/ – or more directly here: www.gov.uk/check-legal-aid; and
2) for legal aid providers: https://check-your-client-qualifies-for-legal-aid.service.gov.uk.

4.155 If the client fails to pay a contribution, you will receive notification from the LAA, and although you do not have to stop work, you are at risk that legal aid will be withdrawn from the date of the notice[96] if the client does not make payment.

4.156 Should the amount paid in contributions exceed the final costs as assessed, the client will be entitled to a refund of the difference.

Changes in circumstances

4.157 Clients must be financially eligible on both capital and income. They must inform the LAA of any change in their means. A reassessment will then be carried out.

Statutory charge

4.158 The charge is governed by LASPO s25 and by the Civil Legal Aid (Statutory Charge) Regulations 2013. The statutory charge under certificates operates at all levels of service, and across all categories, except family mediation. It operates on both property recovered and property preserved.[97]

4.159 If a matter is funded by Legal Help **only**, the charge does not arise in any category.[98]

4.160 However, if a case is funded initially under Legal Help, Help with Mediation or Family Help (Lower) and goes on to a certificate, if the charge arises, it also applies to those costs.[99]

4.161 If money or property is at issue in the proceedings, then the successful client is at risk of the charge. A claimant client whose claim succeeds recovers property; a defendant client who resists a

---

96 See Civil Legal Aid (Procedure) Regulations 2012 regs 42 and 43.
97 LASPO s25.
98 Civil Legal Aid (Statutory Charge) Regulations 2013 reg 4(1).
99 Civil Legal Aid (Statutory Charge) Regulations 2013 reg 4(2).

4.162 claim preserves property.[100] Even if title to the property is not in issue, but possession of it is, the charge still arises.[101]

4.162 Where the proceedings result in recovery or preservation for someone other than the client, the charge arises.[102]

4.163 The charge gives the LAA first call on any money or property recovered in the proceedings. It is used to repay the costs of funding the case. You should note that even though damages in disrepair cases are out of scope under LASPO, the LAA takes the view that if the client has had the benefit of legal aid to enforce repairs, the statutory charge applies to the whole of the proceedings (see chapter 11 and para 4.179 below for more information). So, if a claimant in a housing disrepair case wins compensation of £5,000, and costs under the certificate and Legal Help were £1,500, then (assuming no costs were awarded from the other side) the charge would operate and the client would receive only £3,500 (recovery). On the other hand, if the client was defending a claim for a £5,000 share in property they owned and won the case, if the costs were £1,500, the client would be liable to pay £1,500 (preservation).

4.164 All monies due to a client in legal proceedings must be paid to their solicitor if the client is legally aided in any way.[103]

4.165 All property is caught by the charge, unless exempt by regulation. Exempt property is currently limited to:

- periodical payments of maintenance;
- sums paid under:
  - Matrimonial Causes Act 1973 s25B or 25C;
  - Inheritance (Provision for Family and Dependants) Act 1975 s5;
  - Family Law Act 1996 Part 4; and
  - Civil Partnership Act 2004 Sch 5 para 25(2) or 26;
- interim payments in Inheritance (Provision for Family and Dependants) Act 1975 proceedings;
- the first 50 per cent of a redundancy award;
- the client's clothes, household furniture or tools of the trade (except in exceptional circumstances); and
- state benefits and pensions, and any other property subject to a statutory prohibition on assignment.[104]

---

100 *Hanlon v Law Society* [1980] 2 All ER 199, HL.
101 *Parkes v Legal Aid Board* [1994] 2 FLR 850, FD.
102 LASPO s25(1)(a).
103 Civil Legal Aid (Statutory Charge) Regulations 2013 reg 13.
104 Civil Legal Aid (Statutory Charge) Regulations 2013.

4.166 Damages recovered from the state for breach of the claimant's human rights are not exempt and are caught by the operation of the charge in the same way as all other damages.[105]

4.167 The amount of the charge is calculated to compensate the LAA for funding the case and is therefore the amount of costs as assessed (less any contribution paid by the client), less costs recovered from the other side. Therefore, the amount is the net amount paid to the supplier by the LAA.

4.168 If the charge arises, the client will have a financial interest in the organisation's bill of costs. Clients should be advised of the potential effect of the charge at the outset of the case, be given regular costs updates, and at the end of the case be given a copy of the bill and advised of their right to make representations on the bill, including at any assessment hearing. The only elements of the bill that do not form part of the charge are the costs of assessment and costs of complying with Equality Act 2010 obligations to clients with disabilities,[106] as well as any settlement fees in family cases.[107]

Recovery of money

4.169 Civil Legal Aid (Statutory Charge) Regulations 2013 reg 13 provides that all monies owing to a funded client should be paid to their solicitor, not to the client direct. The only exceptions are periodic payments of maintenance and money paid into court to be invested for the client's benefit in the limited circumstances set out in reg 11. Regulation 15(1)(a) obliges the solicitor to report any recovery or preservation to the LAA straight away.

4.170 Once money is received, the solicitor may make a judgment as to whether it is exempt property. If it is, it may be paid to the client. If not, it must be paid to the LAA. In cases of doubt, the best course is to pay to the LAA, which can refund the client. If the solicitor fails to protect the LAA's charge and pays the money to the client without deducting it, the solicitor is liable.[108]

4.171 Regulation 15(3) entitles the solicitor to apply to the Director for permission to pay to the client money that is not required to satisfy the charge – for example, if £10,000 is recovered and costs will not exceed £5,000, an application can be made to return the extra £5,000 to the client.

---

105 *R (Faulkner) v Director of Legal Aid Casework* [2016] EWHC 717 (Admin).
106 Civil Legal Aid (Statutory Charge) Regulations 2013 reg 6.
107 Civil Legal Aid (Statutory Charge) Regulations 2013 reg 22.
108 Standard Civil Contract 2018 Standard Terms clause 14.15.

Conducting a civil/family case

4.172 Unless an application to defer the charge is being made (see below), the solicitor should complete form Admin 1 and send it to the client with the final bill for approval. The Awards section on CCMS within 'Record Outcome' needs to be completed and submitted. The statutory charge is paid to the LAA by BACS: Nat West Bank; Account name: LAA Receipts; Sort code: 60-70-80; Account number: 10014578. The reference is the funding certificate number. The balance can be returned to the client.

Recovery of property, and preservation cases

4.173 In such cases, money is unlikely to be paid to the solicitor. Instead, the solicitor will report recovery or preservation to the LAA. The LAA will pay the costs of solicitor and counsel and pursue the client for the costs.

Enforcement of the charge – the LAA's powers

4.174 The LAA has no power to waive the charge altogether, except in very limited circumstances (basically, where it was recognised as a wider public interest case from the start and the LAA funded this client but not others to act as a test case).[109]

4.175 In certain circumstances, enforcement of the charge can be postponed.[110] The conditions are:
- the property is the client's (or the client's dependant's) family home; or in family cases, money to be used to purchase a home for the client or dependants; and
- the LAA is satisfied that the home will provide sufficient security for the charge; and
- it would be unreasonable for the client to repay the charge.

4.176 If the charge is postponed, simple interest at eight per cent per annum will accrue from the date of registration. Interest is due on the lower of the value of the charge or the value of the home (Civil Legal Aid (Statutory Charge) Regulations 2013 reg 25). The charge must be registered at the Land Registry or equivalent steps taken.

4.177 Otherwise, the charge is payable immediately unless the LAA agrees to accept payment by instalment, and the LAA can enforce the charge, if necessary, by enforcement proceedings in the courts.

---

109 Civil Legal Aid (Statutory Charge) Regulations 2013 reg 9.
110 Civil Legal Aid (Statutory Charge) Regulations 2013 reg 22.

4.178 The solicitor should report to the LAA using the appropriate ADMIN form if the case is paper-based, or through CCMS as appropriate. There is a guide to reporting the statutory charge – on the LAA learning website search for 'statutory charge' under 'civil'.[111]

Related proceedings

4.179 The LAA takes the view that the statutory charge applies to the whole of proceedings, whether or not it funds the whole case. LASPO s25 says that the charge arises on 'any property recovered or preserved by the individual in proceedings, or in any compromise or settlement of a dispute, in connection with which the services were provided'.

4.180 There are two particular areas where practitioners have encountered difficulty: (a) housing disrepair; and (b) Human Rights Act (HRA) 1998 claims made by children and parents within care and wardship proceedings.

4.181 Disrepair claims (the position is different for counterclaims: see chapter 11) are only in scope to the extent that an injunction or claim for specific performance is sought to enforce repairs to a defect that carries a significant risk of harm. Any related damages claim – even if made within the same proceedings – is out of scope, and work done in relation to the damages must not be claimed for on the certificate. However, the LAA will recover the costs of the funded part of the claim – the remedy of the defect – as part of the statutory charge where damages are recovered in the non-funded part. The LAA's position is that even though that part of the proceedings was unfunded, the damages were recovered within the proceedings or in settlement of a dispute in connection with which services were provided.

4.182 As a result, some practitioners bring the entire claim under a CFA where practicable to do so.

4.183 There has been a number of cases relating to the welfare and protection of children, including care and wardship proceedings, where a local authority has fallen short in its obligations to the child or parents or both.

4.184 Damages are sometimes sought due to failings by local authorities in respect of children in their care, or in other family HRA 1998 cases. Following *Northamptonshire CC and another v Lord Chancellor (via the Legal Aid Agency)*,[112] the LAA issued a position statement[113]

---

111 See: https://legalaidlearning.justice.gov.uk.
112 [2018] EWHC 1628 (Fam).
113 At: www.gov.uk/guidance/funding-and-costs-assessment-for-civil-and-crime-matters (scroll down to 'other guidance').

to provide guidance on the circumstances in which the LAA will and will not apply a statutory charge to HRA 1998 damages. Judicial guidance set out in the statement explains the steps practitioners need to take if the statutory charge is not to be applied to the legally aided care case costs. This includes:

- seeking a separate legal certificate for HRA 1998 damages claims;
- making any applications for substantive relief under the HRA 1998 as a Part 8 claim following Civil Procedure Rules; and
- obtaining early confirmation from the LAA on whether the care proceedings statutory charge will apply to any HRA 1998 award.

Ending a case

4.185 Legal aid certificates come to an end in one of three ways: being discharged, revoked or when a final bill is submitted at the end of the case.

Discharge

4.186 When the LAA decides that a certificate should not continue because changing circumstances indicate that funding is no longer justified on the merits, or because the client is no longer financially eligible, the certificate will be discharged. The effect of this is that the client is no longer in receipt of legal aid. If discharge is at the instigation of the LAA, there is a right to appeal to an independent adjudicator. Once the certificate is discharged, the case is at an end and the file can be billed. At the end of a case, the adviser should usually apply for the certificate to be discharged.

Revocation

4.187 The effect of revocation[114] is not simply to end the funding of a case – revocation retrospectively removes funding from the client, so that they never had a valid legal aid certificate at all. The LAA will only revoke a certificate when information comes to light to suggest that it should never have been issued, for example, because a client concealed information about their resources and were never in fact eligible. The effect of revocation is that the client becomes liable for all costs incurred under the certificate.

---

114 Civil Legal Aid (Procedure) Regulations 2012 reg 42(2).

Submission of final bill

4.188 See chapter 15. A final bill can only be submitted after first discharging the certificate where there is an order for costs to be assessed.

Urgent cases

Scope

4.189 The LAA defines a case as urgent if it is necessary to carry out work before a substantive application can be made and determined. The LAA aims to process most substantive applications within four weeks. Therefore an emergency certificate is unlikely to be granted unless the work has to be carried out before a substantive certificate can be granted and cannot wait without serious adverse consequences to the client, for example, risk to the life, liberty or physical safety of the client or the client's family or the roof over their heads; or the delay will cause a significant risk of miscarriage of justice, or unreasonable hardship to the client, or irretrievable problems in handling the case; and in either case, there are no other appropriate options available to deal with the risk.

4.190 In 2019, powers were introduced to backdate the determination date of legal aid funding in an emergency situation where the client was eligible for legal aid and a practitioner needed to take action in their client's best interest but did not have delegated functions,[115] but note that this is a discretionary power. See chapter 5 for more details on delegated functions in emergency situations.

4.191 You should also consider whether it would be more appropriate to grant or amend a certificate under delegated functions (see para 4.202 below) before you submit an application to the LAA for decision.

Financial eligibility

4.192 See chapter 2. See also 'Funding from the client's point of view' at para 4.151 onwards above.

4.193 Emergency Representation may be granted without a full means assessment. There may be advantages for the client in getting legal

---

115 Civil Legal Aid (Procedure) Regulations 2012 reg 35(3).

Conducting a civil/family case

aid on an emergency basis, and getting their case progressed urgently, but there are also risks of a legal aid certificate being revoked.

Revocation

4.194 The client may turn out to be financially ineligible, may not co-operate with the means assessment, or may not accept an offer, should a contribution be required. In all of those circumstances, the emergency certificate will be revoked (ie cancelled and the client treated as though they were never in receipt of legal aid).

4.195 The client will be responsible for the full costs of their representation. In addition, the client will not have the protection from opponents' costs provided by a representation certificate. You must therefore advise the client of this and give a costs estimate. If the certificate is revoked, you should submit a bill in the usual way; the LAA will pursue the client for the costs.

Merits test

4.196 The appropriate merits test (see para 4.94 onwards above) must be satisfied, as well as the urgency criteria.

4.197 However, as the situation will be urgent, it may often be that only limited information is available. If so, Emergency Representation may be granted where it appears likely on the information available that the merits test will be satisfied.

Forms

4.198 Emergency applications for civil legal aid certificates are made via CCMS in the usual way. Emergency amendments to limitations on existing certificates may also be made via CCMS. See chapter 5 for more information about this.

4.199 The LAA must receive the substantive application within five working days of the emergency grant. If you fail to submit the application, the emergency certificate only covers work done within the first five working days, and you will not be paid for work beyond that period

Funding

4.200 Emergency certificates will usually be limited to £2,250 (profit costs, counsels' fees and disbursements, but not VAT), though you can

4.201 grant a higher limit, or amend to a higher limit, as long as you do not go above £10,000 and as long as the costs only relate to urgent work. Emergency certificates only last for eight weeks, so you must ensure that you are covered by a substantive certificate from that date, or else you will not be paid. This time limit cannot be extended.

Delegated functions

Scope

Overview

4.202 The delegated functions used to be listed in the Contract Specification but have been moved to a separate document called the Table of Delegated Authorities, which lists all the functions delegated by the Lord Chancellor to others.[116]

4.203 The LAA monitors the use of delegated functions and may suspend or terminate them if they have been seriously misused.[117]

4.204 Certificates can be granted for full Legal Representation in urgent cases. You may not use delegated functions to grant a certificate where there is an outstanding certificate or application at the LAA, or where a previous application has been refused and there is no clear and relevant change of circumstances to suggest that a reapplication would be granted.

4.205 You may not use delegated functions to grant exceptional case funding under LASPO s10 (see chapter 2 at para 2.25 and chapter 3 for more information), nor for judicial review cases (with limited exceptions, mainly for emergency homelessness cases, or unless you have specific authorisation). You must comply with any restrictions on your exercise of delegated functions set out in your schedule authorisation.[118]

---

116 See: https://assets.publishing.service.gov.uk/media/613f63d1e90e070434bbc00f/Table_of_Delegated_Authorities_Procedure_Regulations_September_2021_Update.pdf.
117 *Funding Code: decision-making guidance* section 12.8. Post-LASPO guidance has not been issued.
118 Standard Civil Contract 2024 Specification paras 5.2 and 5.3.

Steps for granting an emergency certificate

4.206 The LAA has issued guidance on emergency certificates which can be downloaded here: https://legalaidlearning.justice.gov.uk – select 'Civil' and search for 'emergency application'.

4.207 In CCMS you need to:
1. Select a matter type code.
2. Identify the wording code for the allowable proceedings. If there is no appropriate wording code, the relevant LAA processing office must be contacted.
3. Apply an appropriate scope limitation wording.
4. Apply a costs limitation.
   Costs limitations include profit costs, disbursements and counsels' fees, but *not* VAT.
   In emergency applications this will generally be £2250 and must not exceed £10,000.
5. Submit an application for a substantive certificate within five working days.

Amendments under delegated functions

4.208 Under Civil Legal Aid (Procedure) Regulations 2012 reg 39(3)(b), you can amend an emergency certificate as long as the LAA has not yet granted a substantive certificate and the amendment is required because of the urgency of the situation. In the event of a delegated function amendment to scope or costs, you can apply through the single step process so that the substantive certificate reflects the amendment you made using your delegated functions. There is an LAA quick guide to this. Go to: https://legalaidlearning.justice.gov.uk – select 'Civil' and search for 'Single stage emergency application'. See also chapter 5 at paras 5.35–5.45 for more information.

Refusals under delegated functions

4.209 A client has no right of appeal against your refusal to grant an emergency certificate.[119]

Financial eligibility

4.210 As 'Urgent cases', above.

---

119 Civil Legal Aid (Procedure) Regulations 2012 reg 53.

Merits test

4.211   As 'Urgent cases', above.

Funding

4.212   As 'Urgent cases', above.

Very expensive cases/special case work

4.213   Civil high cost cases are called 'special case work' under LASPO and are governed under Civil Legal Aid (Procedure) Regulations 2012 reg 54.

4.214   There are useful webinars for Family high cost cases on the LAA's Learning website: https://legalaidlearning.justice.gov.uk.

Scope

4.215   High cost civil cases are dealt with by two teams at the LAA. The Very High Cost Case (VHCC) Family Team (South Tyneside) deals with single counsel/advocate cases in private and public law family matters. The Exceptional and Complex Case Team (ECCT) family section (London) deals with KC/two-counsel cases in private and public law family matters; all high cost child abduction and Court of Protection cases; and all civil non-family high cost cases.

4.216   In civil cases, the LAA will agree individual case contracts for cases.

4.217   High cost cases fall into five types:
- individual VHCCs – where costs are expected to exceed £25,000, such as Children Act 1989, clinical negligence and judicial review cases;
- cases which might exceed £75,000 if they proceeded to contested trial, final hearing or the conclusion of any appeal stage before the Court of Appeal or Supreme Court;
- multi-party actions (MPAs) – these range from 10-claimant actions to 1,000-claimant actions;
- exceptional funding cases: when funding is approved outside LASPO provisions; and

Conducting a civil/family case 135

- 'community action' cases in relation to individuals who belong to an identifiable geographic community the members of which have a common interest in the proceedings.

4.218 The LAA can treat more than one set of proceedings or certificates as a single case when deciding whether the cost thresholds are reached, for example, in public law Children Act 1989 proceedings involving numerous parties.

4.219 Cases can be referred to the South Tyneside Family Team or the ECCT at any stage if it appears that they may meet the criteria.

Family high cost cases – Care Case Fee Scheme

4.220 In family, most high cost cases are subject to the 'Care Case Fee Scheme' (CCFS), which is a form of graduated/fixed fee, dependent on the number of hearing days and other events (as outlined in guidance). The benefit of the CCFS is that it avoids multiple revisions to detailed case plans, which is popular with practitioners and is often (but not always) considered preferable to an individually agreed case plan. From 1 October 2015 all single advocate care cases have been paid under CCFS unless you can show you would be paid at least 30 per cent more by claiming hourly rates with a case plan.

4.221 Prior to 3 June 2019, CCFS cases had an immediate limit of £25,000. From that date, the LAA increased the initial limit to £32,000, which applies as soon as the contract documentation is accepted by the LAA. This allows you to claim a payment on account (POA) up to the limitation. If costs will exceed £32,000, you need to apply for an extension. See chapters 7 and 15 for more detail.

Family KC and two-counsel cases

4.222 From 12 July 2019, the LAA took a similar approach to Family KC and two-counsel cases. Once you are granted prior authority for a KC/two-counsel, you should be asked to upload a signed High Costs Contract and Counsel Acceptance Form (where external counsel are used). If you accept, the case will be costed using CCFS. At the same time, you should submit a cost amendment for £60,000 where the authority covers a fact-finding hearing or a composite hearing. The LAA asks that if counsel is used, they are assigned to the case and allocated appropriate funds.

4.223 The LAA has issued guidance on high cost family cases: www.gov.uk/guidance/civil-high-cost-cases-family. See also chapters 7 and 15 for more detail.

Financial eligibility

4.224 See chapter 2 and para 4.151 onwards above. The LAA has a limited power to waive eligibility rules in relation to MPAs.[120]

Merits test

4.225 Only three types of case are automatically entitled to funding:
1) Special Children Act proceedings;
2) proceedings in which the client's life or liberty are at risk; and
3) judicial review proceedings in which:
   – the court has given permission for the case to continue, and
   – the case:
     – has a significant wider interest;
     – is of overwhelming interest to the client; or
     – raises significant human rights issues.

4.226 Cases concerning MPAs, appeals to the Supreme Court, breaches of ECHR rights (within the meaning of the HRA 1998) or a community action, may be subject to special controls.[121]

CCMS and forms

4.227 There is a quick guide to how to register a case as high cost using CCMS. Go to: https://legalaidlearning.justice.gov.uk/ – select 'Civil' and search for 'High Cost Case registration/query'.

4.228 If you need to submit a fully costed case plan, you need to submit:
- a statement of what the case is about;
- a statement of objectives – what is in issue and what is likely to be secured;
- a case analysis – this must include:
  – issues of law – favourable and unfavourable, setting out how any obstacles will be overcome;
  – issues of fact – favourable and unfavourable, assessing the evidence supporting each;
  – expert evidence required – and why;
  – costs in issue – for example, amount of claim for damages – special rules for clinical negligence, see below;

---

120 Civil Legal Aid (Procedure) Regulations 2012 reg 53.
121 Civil Legal Aid (Procedure) Regulations 2012 reg 58.

- key events and resources required – likely costs of solicitors, counsel, experts and disbursements;
- risk analysis – and how to deal with risks identified; and
- statement of prospects of success within the terms of the Funding Code;
• an assessment – addressing each relevant element of the merits criteria and stating how each is satisfied;
• a case theory – a short statement (five sentences or less) explaining why the client will win the case; and
• a broadly costed overall case plan, including:
    - when counsel and experts will be instructed;
    - when the case management conference will be held;
    - when the trial will take place;
    - forecast of cumulative costs – at key events and appropriate intervals and at 31 March each year;
    - fully costed plan for the next stage of the case, showing an overall price for the stage – also setting out costs of all elements of work to be performed and costs to be incurred;
    - breakdown of costs to date;
    - details of any costs-sharing agreements;
    - details of the person managing the case, and of the team (if any) who will be doing the work;
    - names of person managing the case and the team members;
    - what they will be doing;
    - evidence of their suitability; and
    - evidence of the firm's suitability to handle the work to its conclusion.

4.229 There is more information about what to submit (including sample case plans) on the LAA's website at: www.gov.uk/government/publications/high-cost-cases-non-family-civil.

Funding

4.230 The LAA has produced guidance, which can be downloaded from: www.gov.uk/civil-high-cost-cases-family for family cases, and www.gov.uk/government/publications/high-cost-cases-non-family-civil for non-family civil cases.

4.231 Funding is agreed as set out in the case plan. There is very little flexibility to move costs from one heading to another once they are agreed. It can also be difficult to get amendments to the case plan accepted.

4.232 For a case where inter partes costs are expected to be paid if successful, funding is provided on a risk-sharing basis. If it settles, recovery is at full inter partes rates; but if unsuccessful, the LAA will pay at specified hourly rates with no mark-up (normally £90 per hour for senior counsel, £70 for solicitors and £50 for junior counsel).

4.233 There are specific rates of payment for other contracted cases, which vary depending on the type of case, prospects of success and any exceptional circumstances.

4.234 Claims can be made, at the hourly rates applying, for costs to date at the start of the contract, and at the end of each stage. If a stage lasts longer than three months, a claim for costs can be made, but not more than twice in any 12-month period. These are applications for POA and made direct to the High Costs Cases Team.

4.235 At the end of the case, claims can be made in the same way as under an ordinary certificate (see chapter 15), though at the hourly rate agreed in the contract. If costs are recovered from the other side, the LAA is entitled to the recoupment of POAs. High cost case bills are always assessed by the LAA, not the courts.

CHAPTER 5

Client and Cost Management System

Edited by Simon Mullings and Vicky Ling

5.1	Introduction
5.4	**The logic of CCMS**
5.7	'Apply' for legal aid
	When civil Apply can be used • More information about Apply
5.15	**How to use CCMS in your practice**
5.21	**Who does what within CCMS?**
5.21	Overview
5.32	CCMS super users
5.34	**What application should you make?**
5.36	Emergency delegated function applications
5.46	Emergency non-delegated functions applications and backdating
5.51	Family legal aid cost limits
5.52	Urgent amendments
5.56	What if the client cannot be present to sign the CCMS application?
	Coronavirus (COVID-19): working with clients • Promissory declarations • Declaration against instructions
5.76	Exceptional case funding applications

continued

5.77	**Billing through CCMS**
5.90	**Contingency plans if CCMS is not available**
5.94	**Technical difficulties**
5.95	Clearing your browser cache
5.96	Copying-and-pasting: special characters

> **Key resources**
> - As we went to press, the LAA announced an Introduction to CCMS webinar. Search for it at: https://legalaidlearning.justice.gov.uk/civil
> - All the LAA resources explaining how to use CCMS can be found at: https://legalaidlearning.justice.gov.uk/civil
> - CCMS provider navigation contains information on how to find your way around the system: https://legalaidlearning.justice.gov.uk/ccms-provider-best-practice

> **Key points to note**
> - Have at least one CCMS 'super-user' within your practice who can train and support others. Having an in-house expert may resolve any difficulties more quickly than contacting the LAA.
> - Ensure you provide an introduction to CCMS for everyone joining your practice, even if they are an experienced practitioner. The interface between your case management system and what they are used to may be different.
> - Have CCMS as an agenda item at team meetings to ensure knowledge and experience are shared.

Introduction

5.1 This chapter is intended to provide useful oversight into how to best use the Client and Cost Management System (CCMS), which became mandatory in April 2016 (February 2016 for Special Children Act cases).

5.2 The Legal Aid Agency (LAA) has consolidated its training and support into one web-based catalogue on its training and support page.[1] The LAA is continually improving the resources available. All the materials can be accessed by selecting the Civil category and then using the search field. The website contains resources and training guides. These range from introducing you to the system; getting started and making an application; to uploading multiple bill submissions from your practice or case management system (PMS/CMS).

---

1 At: https://legalaidlearning.justice.gov.uk.

The training methods vary, including quick guides, interactive trainer-led sessions and live web chat during office hours. Some of the most useful guides are referenced in this chapter. However, the best approach is completing the training and using the website as an initial point of reference. LAA courses are run through the Eventbrite web booking platform.

5.3 Keeping up to date with changes made in CCMS will always be a sound investment. Changes to process are added to 'Quick Guides' accessed through the training and support page noted above. There is a dedicated section for CCMS service status, posted on the online portal page.[2] It is prudent to keep an eye on the planned maintenance updates when the portal is offline, as these maintenance sessions can be within what a legal aid lawyer would consider their working day.

The logic of CCMS

5.4 It is perhaps the logic of CCMS that has caused so much controversy in its development and application. CCMS was built to facilitate the digital delivery of the application and billing process of civil and family certificated legal aid work, but not to replicate the paper-based system. Despite applying the same regulations, the logic of the build of CCMS is very different, providing a digital platform to communicate the whole application and process.

5.5 Every process designed in CCMS follows the same regulations as the paper-based system, but due to the confines of the build of the digital platform, it has changed the way suppliers process their applications from start to finish. Perhaps the most frustrating element of CCMS when first using it is the linear structure it follows. Using a paper or eform provided the flexibility for suppliers to complete some of the form with their client present, enter further details off-site and part-prepare forms sufficiently in advance of an event that was likely to occur. With the fast pace of most casework and the vulnerability of many applicants for legal aid, paper helped you if you needed to issue emergency, time-sensitive applications without your client present. Front-loaded advice and action, printing off applications in advance of an event, was particularly useful for high-volume emergency work such as housing and immigration.

5.6 It appears there was little insight into workflows of how suppliers applied for funding, and why, during the development process of

2 At: https://bit.ly/2ZZNYje.

CCMS. As a result, applications are intended to be completed with a client present from start to finish (although promissory declarations can be used in some circumstances – see below) and despite the fantastic potential of a digital portal, unfortunately in practice CCMS restricts the application process. Changes to the style and navigation options of CCMS have improved the application experience with the ability to restart partially completed assessment for means in certain circumstances and to revisit answers completed before submission. The golden rule is always to be clear of the key proceedings, means and merits information before starting an application; further guidance is included below.

'Apply' for legal aid

5.7 'Apply' has been in use on a limited basis since 2019 for the submission of civil legal aid applications in domestic abuse cases. Apply replaces CCMS for the application process. Once legal aid is granted, the interface with the LAA is through CCMS.

5.8 Apply is intended to resolve two problems within CCMS: its complex processes and evidence requirements. Apply aims to simplify the application process by using existing information where possible and asking the right person the right question at the right time. The LAA has reported that passported applications take 15 minutes on average to complete compared with 60 minutes through CCMS, and rates of requests for further information by caseworkers have been significantly reduced.

5.9 Perhaps the most radical aspect of Apply involves the client by submission of digital evidence of means for non-passported applications.[3] In order to use Apply, the applicant must use online banking for all their current accounts. The application process, commenced by a provider, sends a link to the client where they can access and supply proof of means using open banking.

5.10 There were some issues concerning inconsistencies between addresses held on civil Apply and CCMS in late 2023, which led to the service being suspended until April 2024.

5.11 The LAA extended Apply to applications for criminal legal aid in 2024 and, by June, 98 per cent of crime applications were being made through the system.

---

3 Applications where a client is not in receipt of passporting benefits and therefore a full assessment of income is required. See chapter 2 at para 2.40 for a list of passporting benefits.

5.12   The LAA's most recent business plan at the time of writing states that that it intends to expand Apply to include civil public law cases.[4]

When civil Apply can be used

5.13   At the time of writing, civil Apply can be used for at least one domestic abuse proceeding and any combination of the following Children Act 1989 s8 proceedings:
- child arrangements order (contact);
- child arrangements order (residence);
- prohibited steps order; and
- specific issue order.

You cannot use the civil Apply service:
- for an emergency application unless delegated functions are used;
- if there is a partner who needs to be means tested; and
- if the client is self-employed.

More information about Apply

5.14   The LAA has provided a guide to Apply and a recorded video demo of the Apply process. These are available on the LAA's learning and development website https://legalaidlearning.justice.gov.uk.

How to use CCMS in your practice

5.15   In the light of the restrictions that CCMS places on the digital application and billing process, it is essential to spend some time getting the operations and set-up of users right. The matrix for roles and responsibilities below is useful to establish the appropriate rights to allocate to each user.

5.16   Whether you are setting up CCMS for the first time, adding new users or perhaps reviewing how it has been working, it is important to ensure that you are as efficient as possible at entering data and getting the results you want. Lack of training of new or current users can add delays, increase rejections and ultimately put your costs at risk. Users need to feel confident in what they need to do and the best way to achieve it. Using the wrong code for proceedings, or choosing a more

---

4 *LAA Business Plan 2023–24*, Milestone 5: www.gov.uk/government/publications/legal-aid-agency-business-plan-2023-24/legal-aid-agency-business-plan-2023-to-2024.

5.17 limited scope, can have drastic consequences for an application. Once a certain path has been chosen – for example, dual or single stage emergency application – it cannot easily be changed. If you choose the incorrect scope from a drop-down menu, it is highly likely to result in work being unpaid, if it is not noticed and remedied immediately.

5.17 The same was always true with a paper-based application; however, practitioners were much less likely to select incorrect proceedings, as solicitors were well-versed in the codes and wordings for proceedings and limitations. Within CCMS, some of the wordings appear slightly different, which can be confusing.

5.18 For example, in Housing Act statutory appeal cases, you should not use the wording 'HO11A' for first-instance Housing Act 1996 s204 appeals, even though that wording refers to appeals ('HO011' should be used instead). The reference to 'appeal' in the HO11A wording refers to a second appeal, and you should not use appeal versions of wordings generally, as proceedings are not intended to cover an appeal. 'Enforcement' (HSO11E) should be selected to enforce an original county court order.

5.19 Investing in CCMS training as part of every new starter's induction is therefore essential, regardless of whether they are new to the system or have joined you from another practice.

5.20 Work-arounds in CCMS are often solutions identified to resolve existing workflow challenges in the system. Sharing knowledge and the benefit of experience is also essential across your organisation. Often users do not sit in the same room, and information exchange within organisations can be sporadic. Adding CCMS updates as agenda items to regular departmental, practice area and supervision meetings is a way to ensure that no one within your organisation is having to work systems out for themselves, or equally has useful knowledge that is not being shared.

Who does what within CCMS?

Overview

5.21 It is often helpful for certain preparation work to be completed offline in advance of the application. A straightforward check of the means assessment and merits of the case can save time wasted in an abandoned application. Checking through papers and means evidence without a client present is often the best investment in time at the start of the process.

5.22 The Ministry of Justice has two online calculators for civil legal aid eligibility:
1) for members of the public: https://civil-eligibility-calculator.justice.gov.uk – or more directly here: www.gov.uk/check-legal-aid; and
2) for legal aid providers: https://check-your-client-qualifies-for-legal-aid.service.gov.uk.

5.23 It is advisable to use the calculator or the keycard[5] to check a client's means before setting up an application on CCMS as it can help to prevent going through the process for ineligible clients. At the same time as pausing to consider means and merits, consideration of the type of application to submit can prevent a rejection and the need to start again.

5.24 For legal aid applications, there are two main ways most firms operate; additionally, the LAA modelled CCMS assuming a third way:
1) A paralegal/trainee solicitor completes the majority of the admin process through CCMS in the same way they may have taken basic information essential to an application for funding on a paper form: they create the client, the new application and then fill in all the information up to and including means assessment, but not merits. The solicitor with conduct (who could be in a different location) then logs on to CCMS to add the merits information, including the statement of case. In this scenario, the solicitor has the opportunity to prepare a statement of case with reference to case papers that the client has provided, while means information is being entered, which can streamline the process.
2) It is also possible for a paralegal/trainee solicitor to undertake all of the work necessary in completing an application, all the way up to, but excluding, the submission of the application. The improved navigation within CCMS means you can move back and forward within sections of the application. It has always been good practice for a separate statement of case to be drafted, which can either be uploaded or pasted into CCMS, setting out the facts of the applicant's case, the law and the merits of the application to satisfy the criteria for funding. This could be completed by the solicitor in advance of the application, where possible, preventing the need for the solicitor to be involved at all in data input/form filling. Only an authorised litigator can submit an application in CCMS, and therefore it is necessary for such a person to approve the application, but their involvement in CCMS can be limited to the

---

5 At: www.gov.uk/guidance/civil-legal-aid-means-testing.

Client and Cost Management System 147

submission only. Often where urgent court work is required, this is the route chosen by practitioners, freeing up the solicitor to concentrate on drafting.
3) The method of submission the LAA assumed when designing CCMS is for a supervising solicitor to approve every application submitted. A solicitor/trainee solicitor/paralegal within a practice completes the application and the supervising solicitor logs in to approve and submit it. The LAA definition of 'supervisor' within CCMS is not one that corresponds with the way in which supervisors may work in practice, and is not the same as supervision as required by the Specialist Quality Mark/Lexcel and the contract. As can be seen from the table below, anyone who requires access to all areas of CCMS for completing an application requires a **Case Management** role, but the case manager cannot submit applications or bills in CCMS. A user needs the **Case Management Supervisor** role in order to submit an application.

5.25 Which method an organisation uses may depend on a number of factors, but the number and range of personnel is probably most determinative.

5.26 You will need to give 'supervisor' rights to every authorised litigator as well as case management rights. They will then be able to create and submit applications. It would perhaps be easier if the LAA had called the supervisor role the 'authorised litigator' role to avoid confusion.

5.27 The **Bill Preparation** and **Bill Supervisor** roles in the matrix below work in the same way for billing as for legal aid applications, but perhaps more logically. A biller or costs lawyer, external or internal, is allocated the bill preparation role, and so can draft but not submit the bill on CCMS. A bill supervisor in-house needs to approve their bills. If your biller is in-house and needs both to prepare and submit bills, they would need both roles allocated to them. Note, however, the guidance on bill preparation and submission below.

5.28 Finally, the roles of Office Manager, Cross Office Access and Firm Administrator need to be considered. As with 'supervisor', these are specific roles within the CCMS process and need not correspond with equivalent positions in your organisation.

5.29 The **Office Manager** role simply provides an overview of all cases, notifications and actions within an organisation, but does not allow the user to create or submit applications or bills. This is quite a useful function and could be used to ensure all outstanding notifications across the whole practice have been closed or replied to within the appropriate time limits. It is useful to allocate this role to supervising solicitors, heads of departments and billing managers.

5.30 The **Firm Administrator** role should be allocated to your CCMS administrator, the person who controls the set up and allocation of roles to all users within your practice. The remittance advice/BACS statements for the practice are only sent to the Firm Administrator, though they also need to be allocated the Office Manager role in order to receive them.

5.31 The final role is the **Cross Office Access** role: this is commonly used as an 'add on' privilege for all users to enable anyone entering data into CCMS to first check not just cases opened by them, but also any opened by their colleagues across the organisation. It can be built into your CCMS protocol to complete a wide search for the client across your organisation before entering the client as a new client within CCMS, to prevent duplicate entries if, for example, an existing client of another department returns with a new case. Organisations will often check for existing client entries in their own case management system before submission in routine cases. However, in urgent cases this may not be possible, and having Cross Office Access is another tool that can help prevent duplication and also help avoid conflicts of interest.

CCMS super users

5.32 There is still a huge variance in the time it takes different organisations to complete a CCMS application, with some taking significantly longer where only one person is involved in the process from start to finish. Admin support may not always be available; but planning your application around the availability of support can both reduce fee earner time taken and increase capacity to take on new cases. It can also improve the experience of the client, who will not need to be present while data entry is carried out.

5.33 Creating CCMS 'super users' within every team across the firm, or perhaps one 'super user' for a small organisation can also improve efficiency of creating and submitting applications. Frequent use of CCMS for repeated actions and familiarity of the navigation tools will improve the streamlining of the process. As with any routine, the more you use it the faster you become. CCMS super users could also have responsibility for updating the practice on new releases, trialling new upgrades, and feeding back to the LAA and representative bodies on enhancements needed.

Client and Cost Management System   149

Role	Case Management	Case Management Supervisor*	Bill Preparation*	Bill Supervisor*	Office Manager
Search for and view cases	•	•	•	•	•
View case details	•		•		
View case attachments	•	•	•	•	•
Search for client	•				
Register client/ amend client details	•				
Create new applications	•				
View proceedings	•		•		
Add/amend proceedings	•				
View, record and amend outcomes (incl undertaking)	•				
View actions and notifications	•	•	•	•	•
Add/amend case costs	•				
Request prior authority	•				
Submit new applications		•			
Submit amendments to applications/ outcomes		•			
Create bills/POAs[6]			•		
Submit bills/POAs				•	
Attach documents/ evidence	•		•		
Submit attached documents	•	•	•	•	•
Submit notifications	•	•	•	•	•
Bulk upload – claim upload pricing only			•		

6   Payment on account.

| Bulk upload – claim upload | | | | • | |
| Accessing remittance advice notifications | | | | | • |

* *The Cross Office Access role can be applied to users with these roles to allow the user to access all cases for the firm, as opposed to just those for which they are a named contact.*

CCMS *Provider: Roles and Responsibilities Guidance* https://legalaidlearning.justice.gov.uk/civil/user-roles-and-responsibilities

What application should you make?

5.34 Navigating the application process has historically been one of the most troubling issues for users. The information that follows is the up-to-date position at the time of writing. Where in doubt, always make reference to the CCMS guides on the LAA training and support website. Go to 'Civil' and use the search to find 'making a legal aid application' for general information or search using the terms in the table below.

5.35 Applications can be made in the following way depending on whether delegated functions can be exercised for all the work involved (see chapter 4 and subject-specific chapters for more on delegated functions):

Applications

1	Delegated functions	Dual stage emergency application
2	Delegated functions	Single stage emergency application
3	Delegated functions	Special Children Act application
4	Non-delegated functions	Emergency application
5	Non-delegated functions	Substantive application
6	Non-delegated functions	Exceptional case funding application

Emergency delegated function applications

5.36 A particular difficulty for many practitioners is the submission of emergency applications. In the table above, this includes numbers 1 and 2 where there is an emergency (urgent work to progress the case is required within four weeks, eg a hearing date or directions to comply with) and you have delegated functions permitted in your schedule authorisation for this type of case.

5.37 The purpose of CCMS in these cases is to communicate to the LAA the use of delegated functions rather than to seek funding. As you have the power to self-grant funding, you are reporting to the LAA that you have done so – you are not making an application for Emergency Representation.

5.38 There is a choice of two methods: the dual stage application or the single stage application. Practitioners have used the dual stage application because in urgent circumstances a client may not have all the documentation to support the application, either for the merits but more often the means stage. As the descriptions suggest, they allow the report of the exercise of delegated functions to be completed in a single stage or in two stages.

5.39 The training resources available on the CCMS website explain that the dual stage process is useful where you need more time to obtain evidence required in the single stage application but do not list what this evidence is. The resources also explain that one of the benefits of the dual stage process is that the limitations can be amended before the substantive application is submitted. Wherever possible, you should consider the type of application you are making alongside the nature of the emergency work to be done to minimise the need to amend the emergency application. This can be illustrated by considering examples of different sorts of emergency cases.

5.40 For example, in family proceedings you may make an initial application for a non-molestation order which you will rely on for a later application for linked proceedings. Where the second application is to be heard within five working days of the decision to use delegated functions for the non-molestation order, you can wait for the outcome of the hearing where the non-molestation order is granted and then submit one application with both proceedings. The same principle applies to a judicial review application where there will be interim relief and directions sought within five working days.

5.41 However, the main difference is that in family cases, the additional proceedings cannot be added unless you have the evidence required for the domestic violence gateway – which the non-molestation order will provide. However, for the judicial review case the initial limitation to proceedings chosen can reflect all work reasonably expected to be completed within the emergency period so as to avoid the need for emergency amendments in quick succession.

5.42 To take another example, in a housing case you might use a limitation up to a specified hearing date. If you consider the hearing has a likelihood of being adjourned to a date within the four-week emergency period, then add to the wording of the limitation 'any adjournment thereof'. This would then include any work completed for repeated adjournments of the hearing in the emergency period.

Clarification of the use of this wider scope should be made in your statement of case.

5.43 If, however, it is predicted that at the hearing an order will require filing of a defence and counterclaim, a limitation of all steps up to and including the filing of the defence and counterclaim could be used, as long as the work is predicted to be completed within the emergency four-week period justifying the exercise of delegated functions.

5.44 If you are satisfied that you can exercise delegated functions for the emergency application, your assessment of means and merits is sound, you are authorised to do so under your Contract Schedule and the case meets reg 46 of the Civil Legal Aid (Merits Criteria) Regulations 2013, then you need the easiest method of submitting the application which communicates your decision through CCMS.

5.45 Where there are no anticipated emergency amendments following the application, it is likely that the single stage application is the most appropriate. See the table below, which sets out an example of the options available where delegated functions are available:

Situation	Single stage	Dual stage
Client has the necessary evidence of means but limited case papers	Submit a single stage application and advise the LAA in the statement of case that you have been able to decide the merits based on the papers available, how and why. If requested, supply additional papers if they become available.	
Client in receipt of passported benefit and eligible based on capital assessment but does not have three months of bank statements	Submit a single stage application, upload the evidence you have available, fill in any gaps when requested at a later date when the application is processed by caseworkers. If your client is unlikely to be able to provide bank statements, let the LAA know in the statement of case or by a case enquiry to help the LAA caseworker process with the evidence available without asking questions you already know the answers to.	Submit a dual stage application, await bank statements, which may not be available before the date when the LAA request you submit the substantive amendment in any event.

Client has all the means and merits evidence needed, but the urgent work required within the initial four-week period of the emergency certificated includes potential changes to scope	Submit a single stage application with the scope limitation predicted for the whole of the emergency period rather than limited to a single stage or application. Explain the situation in your statement of case and why all of the emergency work is required beyond the first hearing.	Submit a dual stage application where you are less certain of what the outcome of urgent action will be and submit an amendment to the dual stage before submitting your substantive application amendment.
Client has all the means and merits evidence needed but there are amendments to proceedings and scope likely at the first hearing taking place within five days of the grant of emergency funding	Wait to make the application within the five working-day period once the hearing has taken place of the further application or when the order has been made. However, be aware of the risk you take as a provider that your client will come back to the office to sign the CCMS declaration.	Make a dual stage application and an application for an amendment in quick succession.

Emergency non-delegated functions applications and backdating

5.46 After the Legal Aid, Sentencing and Punishment of Offenders Act 2012 (LASPO) came into force, the LAA restricted delegated functions in many categories of work. The result is an increase in the number of non-delegated function applications being made. The time taken for the LAA to process these often-urgent applications can result in delays, and therefore close attention should be given to the options available. These are discussed below.

5.47 Changes to the process for applying for emergency non-delegated functions applications came into force on 20 February 2019. Previously it had been possible to make what was known as an 'out of hours application for funding', which commenced outside of CCMS. This process enabled urgent applications to be made and funding granted up to 8pm, often in immigration, community care and public law cases where funding was required to obtain interim relief in the Administrative Court.

5.48 Following the successful challenge in R *(Duncan Lewis Solicitors) v Lord Chancellor*,[7] the LAA introduced discretionary powers to backdate the grant of legal aid funding.[8] Urgent applications can now commence in CCMS, even if a decision is not communicated on funding, before immediate work is carried out.

5.49 However, it is important to note that the backdating power is a discretionary one and as such close scrutiny should always be applied to the regulation that enables the power to be exercised under Civil Legal Aid (Procedure) Regulations 2012 reg 35(3).

5.50 For non-delegated functions work:

1) **Submitting an emergency dual stage application on CCMS then contacting customer services if the application requires assessment within 48 hours of the application** (the LAA states it takes two hours for the system to upload the information and therefore asks you to wait two hours to call). The process is similar to submitting a delegated functions emergency dual stage application; however, when asked you select the drop-down for 'no' to the delegated functions box. Once the emergency application is processed, you will have five working days to submit the substantive application. It will be necessary to chase up the application by telephone at regular intervals and obtain clear information on timescales from the LAA.

2) **Making an application where work needs to commence before a determination is likely to be issued – backdating request.** As with all CCMS guidance in this chapter, the onus is on the earliest possible notification to the LAA of the work predicted. Where, for example, an urgent non-delegated functions application is made, and work will commence for injunctive relief immediately, the full nature of work should be predicted and a request for backdating of the determination included in the initial CCMS application. If in doubt when the application would be considered and whether therefore a backdate is requested, err on the side of caution and include the backdate request. Target turn arounds for

---

7 [2015] EWHC 2498 (Admin).
8 The Parliamentary and Health Service Ombudsman registered a finding of maladministration against the LAA in November 2021, for failing to backdate legal aid applications submitted by a law centre on behalf of three street homeless EU nationals facing deportation. See 'Barred from justice: vulnerable people locked out of legal aid to challenge unlawful deportation orders': www.ombudsman.org.uk/news-and-blog/news/barred-justice-vulnerable-people-locked-out-legal-aid-challenge-unlawful.

Client and Cost Management System 155

applications vary; where urgent work is predicted, a backdated request is sensible.

The application type selected will be 'emergency'. The application proceeds as normal until the merits section is reached. When completing the emergency details, you must select from the drop-down menu the reason for the emergency: ie injunctive relief sought/hearing date and then in the text-box enter the date you wish to backdate the application to and the justification.

If all the information cannot be included in the 'further information' box, reference can be made to an uploaded statement of case, which may detail the chronology of actions taken to date. The Director of Casework at the LAA has discretion to backdate the determination date where the application was made as soon as reasonably practical, it was in the interests of justice for the services to be carried out prior to the date of the determination and the services could not have been carried out as controlled work. Sufficient detail and justification need to be included.

3) **Requesting a backdate for an existing application for funding or amendment to a certificate.** Circumstances may change rapidly where work is required to be carried out which could not have been predicted when the application for funding was submitted on CCMS. In accordance with Civil Legal Aid (Procedure) (Amendment) Regulations 2019 reg 2(4), the application for funding must be made as soon as reasonably practical. A case enquiry should be submitted with the same detail as above of the details requested and justification for the backdating.

4) **Monitoring the success of backdated applications.** As with all changes to CCMS practice, practitioners may find it useful to introduce an in-house template making reference to the regulations when justifying the backdate. Due to the risk of commencing work and/or proceedings without a legal aid determination, you may want to include an approval process into any backdated application submission. Justifying the basis for backdated applications set against your own protocols is a great method of quality control. Keeping a central record of when backdating is required and responses from the LAA can help improve process for future applications.

Situation	Emergency application	Backdate request
Client needs representation for urgent work within 48 hours but work does not need to commence immediately	Submit a dual stage emergency non-delegated functions application and contact customer services two hours after the CCMS submission to ask for the application to be expedited.	
Client needs representation the same day your application is being made with immediate work required which cannot be completed under controlled work, ie representation at a hearing the same or next day and or applying for interim relief in the Administrative Court	Submit a dual stage emergency non-delegated functions application and contact customer services two hours after the CCMS submission to ask for the application to be expedited.	Include a fully detailed request for the backdating of the date of the determination. Set out the chronology of action to urgent work to be completed.
An application (initial funding application or amendment request) has been submitted where a backdated request was not made but immediate urgent work is now needed, eg an eviction date has been set, interim relief or an urgent application to maintain the status quo required		Submit a case enquiry including a fully detailed request for the backdating of the date of the determination. Set out the chronology of action to urgent work to be completed.

Family legal aid cost limits

5.51 In a move to streamline family work, applications from 19 April 2019 are granted an initial cost limit of £25,000 for some proceedings (see chapter 6 at para 6.108 for a list). All Special Children Act applications within CCMS will have a default cost limit already applied. However, for all other qualifying family proceedings, you should request the £25,000 limit in the Proceedings and Costs section of the

Client and Cost Management System 157

application. In the Requested Cost Limitation box simply overtype the default limitation provided. When you reach the Merits Assessment section you will be asked to justify the additional cost limit – you will need to use the following wording: 'We are applying for the new default cost limit.' The cost limits do not apply for certificates granted before 19 April 2019; however, the LAA may grant a single amendment to the cost limit up to £25,000 where justified.

Urgent amendments

5.52 As explained above, some emergency amendments can be predicted and, to avoid urgent amendments, a wider limitation included in the initial application, whether exercising delegated functions or not. Practitioners have reported that the LAA has discouraged applications for amendments to scope pending a substantive certificate being granted on the basis it can be applied for later and the cost limit will apply retrospectively. Any delay in applying for extensions to cost or scope limits places practitioners at risk. Should the LAA decide a substantive certificate is granted, but only limited to the emergency work, and then discharge the certificate (eg if new evidence of means comes to light suggesting the client is not eligible), the cost limit would never be amended. Regardless of the ability now to request backdating for determination dates, it is still best practice to ensure amendments are processed in the order they arise, even if this means a delay to a substantive certificate being granted. If the choice is whether to apply for the substantive certificate or increase costs, the cost increase should be pursued first. However, predicting the right cost limit with the initial application, rather than accepting a default limit, can dramatically reduce the need for cost amendments. Note below the changes for family cost limits in CCMS and changes to process needed.

5.53 Where delegated functions have been exercised and emergency work that was not predicted arises after submission of an emergency application and the substantive certificate has not yet been processed, you should contact the LAA Customer Service Team by telephone on 0300 200 2020 to determine what process to follow. It may be that the application is to be granted imminently and you can wait. Or it may be that the LAA will reject your substantive amendment, to enable you to submit an emergency amendment which will be considered before the substantive amendment.

5.54 If you submit a single stage application, the LAA can convert this to a dual stage application, which should result in your substantive amendment information being saved for future use. You can then submit the new emergency amendment to scope, and once this is considered, submit the substantive amendment within the deadline provided in subsequent notifications. This process can be difficult to understand; however, it follows the linear process of CCMS in that multiple amendments are not possible at the same time. They are dealt with in strict order, and so if a new amendment arises which is more urgent than an outstanding one, the outstanding one must be cancelled before the new one can be processed.

5.55 Similarly, you may grant multiple amendments pursuant to your contract schedule using delegated functions, but you can only communicate one at a time to the LAA via CCMS. It is therefore very important to anticipate all work needed in the emergency period from the date of the grant of any delegated functions where possible.

What if the client cannot be present to sign the CCMS application?

5.56 It is a requirement in CCMS that the client be present at the time the application is submitted. With both emergency delegated function applications and non-delegated function applications, there is a limited number of circumstances where a signature is not required before the application is submitted on the basis the client is not present. These are as follows.

Coronavirus (COVID-19): working with clients

5.57 The LAA has issued guidance on working with clients and making applications during the pandemic.[9] At the time of writing, the digital signature guidance is still applicable, described as 'retained until further notice in line with isolation requirements'. The LAA *Schedule of processes restarting after COVID-19 contingency* guidance[10] details the dates each measure will revert or has reverted to a pre-Covid-19 operational process.

5.58 The Contingency Guidance provides that digital signatures are acceptable as an alternative to handwritten 'wet' signatures and will meet contract requirements, where it is not possible to obtain a 'wet' signature due to Covid-19.

---

9 Available at: www.gov.uk/guidance/coronavirus-covid-19-legal-aid-agency-contingency-response.
10 Available at: www.gov.uk/guidance/schedule-of-processes-restarting-after-covid-19-contingency.

5.59 The LAA will accept all digital methods of signature that meet the requirements set out as Simple Contracts in the Law Society's practice note *Execution of a document using an electronic signature*.[11]

5.60 Section 4.1 of The Law Society's practice note provides:

> In the absence of any (usually statutory) requirement, there is no need under English law for contracts to be in any particular form.
>
> In fact, contracts can be entered into orally, provided there is offer and acceptance, consideration, certainty of terms, and an intention to be legally bound.
>
> Therefore, a simple contract may be concluded using an electronic signature.

5.61 The LAA makes it clear that text messages are not considered an acceptable method of digital signature and are not covered by the above practice note.

5.62 In practice, legal aid firms have relied on an exchange of emails as evidence of a digital signature. Where it is not possible to obtain a digital signature, a fully detailed file note should be kept explaining attempts made to obtain a signature and signed by a supervisor. Express evidence will need to be provided to establish that:

1) the client formed the appropriate intention to sign and submit the application form; or
2) you have been directly appointed by a court or tribunal to act for the client.[12]

5.63 You can still submit a claim where no signature was obtained where:

1) it is clear that reasonable attempts have been made to secure the client's signature and you have provided evidence of the client's intention to sign the form; or
2) you have been appointed to act for a client by a court or tribunal.[13]

5.64 The key to successfully claiming for legal aid work during the period of contingency guidance is to have robust processes for recording whether a digital signature has been obtained and where not, keeping a record of all communications and correspondence with the associated supervisor consideration and sign off.

---

11 Reviewed May 2020, at: www.lawsociety.org.uk/topics/business-management/execution-of-a-document-using-and-electronic-signature.
12 At: www.gov.uk/guidance/coronavirus-covid-19-working-with-clients.
13 At: www.gov.uk/guidance/coronavirus-covid-19-working-with-clients.

Promissory declarations

5.65 Promissory declarations are to be used only when you are granting an emergency certificate under delegated functions. There is no guidance specific to promissory declarations in the CCMS training materials, save for a quick guide of the same name; however, the guidance given for the use of Declaration Against Instructions will be useful as it provides a procedure you can follow for both methods of submitting applications. The most important part of both processes is the due diligence used to record the means and merits information that enables you to decide whether the applicant is eligible for legal aid. To this end, completing a thorough means assessment and being satisfied on disclosure of evidence of means is crucial. It would be sensible to have an office protocol for a supervisor to check and authorise the use of both declarations as they will be used infrequently. Particularly with promissory declarations where work commences before the CCMS declaration is signed, there is a heightened risk to your costs until the LAA issues a substantive application.

5.66 The promissory declaration can only be used when the client is reasonably unable to attend the office to sign the emergency application declaration in person. Examples given by the LAA include where the client is imprisoned or hospitalised; or there is an LAA system outage formally communicated to you by the LAA which prevents the client from being able to sign the client declaration on the CCMS emergency application. Therefore, the client is in the office but the relevant declaration page of their application cannot be printed off. Where the client cannot attend the office due to isolation requirements associated with the pandemic, the *Coronavirus (COVID 19): working with clients* guidance should be applied.[14] There will be other circumstances in addition to prison and hospitalisation that could prevent access to CCMS in emergency circumstances – for example, acting for a client with disabilities who cannot reasonably be expected to travel to the office. It may not be safe for an applicant to travel to the office, or an applicant may be homeless and destitute and only able to attend the office of a referrer within their locality, particularly in immigration and homeless cases.

5.67 Ultimately it is for you to decide (and, if necessary, justify on audit) whether the condition of 'unreasonable to travel to the office' is met. A clear attendance note referencing the reasons for your

---

14 At: www.gov.uk/guidance/coronavirus-covid-19-working-with-clients.

Client and Cost Management System 161

decision to use a promissory declaration and detailing the steps taken is essential.

5.68 The LAA provides a checklist for means to complete with your client to ensure you can fully complete the means application within CCMS later. Search 'means checklist' on the LAA training and support site. The checklist includes the mandatory fields in CCMS so that you can answer all means questions. Despite a client not attending the office in person, you still need to have seen adequate evidence to enable you reasonably to assess that your client is likely to be eligible for legal aid. Screenshots or using cameras on mobile phones can be a useful resource for clients to send images of either their online bank statements or letters received from the Department for Work and Pensions (DWP) when they cannot attend the office. Email copies may also be used.

5.69 In these cases, your client must still sign the CCMS declaration page from the application, which must be printed and a hard copy kept on file. The promissory declaration simply means they do not need to sign it at the point of submitting the application on CCMS; it can be completed later.

5.70 See chapter 4 for situations where a client cannot reasonably travel to the office at all and you need to use delegated functions. In an emergency case, there may be no time to travel to your client or you may not be able to secure a prison visit. Collating information to complete applications over the phone is never ideal, but where a referral agency, probation office or local advice centre is able to facilitate access to your client, they can be crucial in the process of obtaining a signed promissory declaration.

5.71 When submitting your application on CCMS and making the declaration at the end of the merits section, you will need to confirm you do not have a signed form and complete the free text-box to set out the circumstances. If the situation is complex, you may want to make reference to the further information contained within your statement of case. Finally, when you complete the application, you need to tick the box to confirm you have obtained the necessary signed declarations as the promissory declaration satisfies that criterion.

Declaration against instructions

5.72 The process for promissory declarations is only available for applications where you can use delegated functions to grant emergency funding. The declaration against instructions can be used where the client cannot attend the office for the same reasons detailed above and it is necessary to make the application for legal aid during the period when the client or their partner, for good reason, cannot attend your office in person, but you cannot use delegated functions. Examples given by the LAA include the imminent expiry of a limitation period or substantial detriment to the client; this could include urgent judicial review applications, for example, where access to the client and CCMS was not possible and delegated functions were not available due to the nature of the work.

5.73 LAA guidance is that the process is designed for use in a non-emergency situation where you attend your client and complete the full paper forms, uploading the information onto CCMS at a later date. Once you have completed the application on CCMS and uploaded the information you have relied upon, the application summary needs to be sent to the client to consider within 14 days of submission and any inaccuracies communicated. If there are any inaccuracies a further signed declaration will need to be obtained.

5.74 Whereas, with the promissory declaration you should tick 'yes' to certify you have the necessary declarations signed before submission on CCMS, you will not have a signature where you are using the declaration against instructions process. Therefore, in the means and merits assessments declaration box, you should specify that you will be printing the CCMS Application Summary screen and having the client sign this as their declaration. If you answer 'no' to having the signed declaration, you will then need to answer questions on how you satisfy the criteria for using the declaration of instructions process.

5.75 The LAA scrutinises use of this process, as it is only expected in a small minority of cases. You should keep a full attendance note detailing why and how you have followed the process, including attending your client for instructions and confirming the information provided as this will be crucial in justifying your actions on audit.

Exceptional case funding applications

5.76 CCMS is primarily used for applications for funding that are within the scope of LASPO. There is a quick guide on the LAA training website which sets out the exceptional funding application process.[15]

---

15 At: https://legalaidlearning.justice.gov.uk/pluginfile.php/1231/mod_resource/content/1/ECFApplication_v5.2.pdf.

Note that if part of your application for funding falls within scope of LASPO and part would be an exceptional funding application, both applications must be submitted separately; the LAA refers to such applications as 'blended' applications and there is no process within CCMS to submit one application with separate parts.

Billing through CCMS

5.77 A significant benefit of CCMS is the potential for improved cost control. All relevant data for a certificate including limitations, scope and allocation of costs to counsel are retained in the system. However, there are some additional digital processes that did not exist with a paper bill submission, and which if not dealt with promptly can slow down bill payment. This chapter deals with CCMS and billing issues; for a discussion of the rules that apply to claims for costs, see chapter 15.

5.78 The LAA did not develop CCMS billing functionality to rival existing billing software. You can report through CCMS, but the process is more time-consuming than the market-leading software widely available for legal aid billing. Line-by-line cost entry in CCMS is a laborious process which is not intuitive, so that save for the simplest of bills, mistakes may be made with incomplete submissions. If at all possible, you should avoid billing through CCMS and instead use billing software (either your case management software or dedicated digital billing tools) which produces an XML report to upload to CCMS.

5.79 Bills above £2,500 that were formerly always assessed by the court can be assessed by the LAA and uploaded through CCMS. You can choose the format of bill to upload/submit: Bill of Costs if the bill has already been created but not assessed, Claim 1/1A, accepted as a summary level claim or CCMS line-by-line hourly rate bill.

5.80 Whichever billing method you choose, the workflow to create the bill in CCMS requires you to select 'yes' when asked whether the bill has been assessed by the court. This is simply to ensure the bill is processed by the correct team. The date of the assessment can be entered as the date of submission of your bill to the LAA. If you select 'no' it is likely to take longer for the relevant team to receive it.

5.81 The upload functionality includes a price check before submission to ensure CCMS has matched the fields within your submission to pay what you expect.

5.82 While you will not be able to upload the billing bundle at the same time you submit the claim, it is sensible to prepare your billing bundle when the bill is uploaded. This ensures it is ready to upload when the request for required evidence is received and will prevent delay before the claim can be processed. This will enable you to work to the tight deadline for submission and receive payment sooner.

5.83 When uploading supporting papers, the LAA may list a number of items. Despite the guidance available on the LAA website, it is not necessary to separate out and individually update the documents requested. A paginated bundle with all the documents clearly listed in one upload is satisfactory and can save additional administrative time being added to the process.

5.84 Where you have linked certificates on CCMS, you will need to submit a nil bill for each of the linked certificates at the same time as submitting the bill on the main certificate. If you omit to submit the nil bills, this will delay your main bill being processed and paid.

5.85 When processing claims for travel, the LAA regularly seeks clarification of the reason for the travel if it is not clear on the claim. The same applies with regard to queries for any timed items on a claim that have an activity 'other'. It is sensible to provide any supporting documentation and an MS Word document setting out the reasons for travel, detailing the work listed as 'other' and providing a case narrative. This will prevent delay to payment of the claim. Anticipating any reasons for further queries, and front loading the information provided, can save valuable weeks in the billing process.

5.86 Before the LAA can process your bill, it needs first to have processed the outcome codes submission for the case. It is essential, therefore, that the outcome codes are completed as soon as the legal work on the case is concluded rather than waiting for the file to be billed. The LAA processing timetables only apply for billing to cases where the outcome code step has been completed.

5.87 Delays in counsel submitting bills and inaccurate counsel fee limits in CCMS can result in claims being rejected. Fees allocated by you through CCMS under the Family Advocacy Scheme (FAS) must reconcile with the final amount claimed by counsel before a bill is submitted. A check can be made of the Case Statement of Account Screen. If the final claim has been made by counsel and there is a positive balance in the Counsel Cost Ceiling Remaining line, an application should be made to amend the counsel cost limitation, so that the balance of costs remaining to counsel is £0.00 to ensure that there are no further claims from counsel.

5.88 For non-family claims where counsel is instructed, there is a tight time-limit for counsel to make and submit their claim on CCMS. Once your bill has been submitted, CCMS will create an automatic notification to counsel that their bill must be created and submitted in CCMS within 14 days. Where a claim is not submitted within 14 days, your claim will be rejected. The 14-day time-limit applies to all counsel claims. Where there are multiple counsel acting, it is vital that every claim is submitted. It can be tricky to negotiate submissions across chambers after your claim is made. Ensuring counsel's fees and submission dates are coordinated before you submit your claim will speed up claim processing and ultimately payment of all parties.

5.89 Initially, CCMS would enable you to upload a bill that was outside the scope of your client's funding. The bill would then be rejected at a later date when processed. The same was the case for uploading claims against emergency certificates where means had not yet been assessed. Improvements to CCMS now prevent any bill upload giving an error message if the claim does not match the scope of the funding or is before a substantive certificate is processed. This should prevent unnecessary rejections.

Contingency plans if CCMS is not available

5.90 Should CCMS be unavailable, the LAA guidance[16] is that practitioners should contact the online support team by telephone for authorisation to be given before contingency protocols can be used. Should the LAA accept the criteria for contingency is met, it will give you a contingency reference number, which should be quoted in subsequent contact.

5.91 If the contingency is with regard to an application or amendment and you have access to the case via CCMS, you will be sent a document request via CCMS. You will be expected to return the cover sheet with the relevant paper application by email to: contactcivil@justice.gov.uk marked as 'contingency' in the subject line. You will be expected to keep the original signed form.

5.92 When deciding whether to apply the contingency process, the LAA will consider the urgency of the application and whether delegated functions can be exercised.

---

16 At: www.gov.uk/guidance/bringing-civil-legal-aid-processing-online.

5.93 The LAA contingency guidance sets out the circumstances in which the contingency process will be invoked; however, it is advisable to take a screen shot of each and every attempt to submit your application on CCMS and to contact the LAA at the earliest opportunity. The LAA is alerted to CCMS outages by providers. It is imperative therefore that technical issues are reported and do not delay the grant of legal aid.

Technical difficulties

5.94 There are two well-known issues that can frustrate attempts to copy-and-paste into CCMS applications and access the CCMS platform: browser cache and special characters.

Clearing your browser cache

5.95 Clearing your browser cache can resolve a number of issues. Your browser cache is a temporary storage area on your computer that remembers your recent web-browsing history and can take you to frequented pages. Old passwords and temporary internet files can be saved automatically in your browser cache. This has been identified by the LAA technical team as potentially negatively impacting system performance. Pressing Ctrl/shift/delete while in your browser should bring up a window with options for deletion. See the LAA training site for the guide with more details.

Copying-and-pasting: special characters

5.96 When drafting any text to copy-and-paste into some CCMS upload screens, you should avoid the use of any 'special characters'. Most but not all the screens now accept special characters, but some rogue screens remain. To be certain you can copy and paste into any screen in CCMS, only a comma and full stop should be used. On some screens adding any others such as colons, speech marks, etc will slow down the process and can be prevent the pasting process altogether. The technical guide on the CCMS training and support website sets out how you can identify any hidden special characters to remove them. You can also copy-and-paste text into the note pad programme, which removes them before transferring onto CCMS.

CHAPTER 6

Conducting a family private law case

Edited by Vicky Ling

6.1	**Introduction**
6.5	**Scope of the scheme**
6.6	In scope with no need for evidence of abuse
	Inherent jurisdiction of the High Court • Unlawful removal of children • Domestic abuse • Respondents in domestic abuse cases • Other areas within scope without evidence of abuse
6.16	In scope with evidence of abuse
	Other private law matters arising out of a family relationship (LASPO Sch 1 Part 1 para 12) • Protection of children and family matters (LASPO Sch 1 Part 1 para 13)
6.21	Evidence of domestic abuse
6.29	Evidence that a child is at risk of abuse
6.30	Controlled work and licensed work
6.32	**Private family law – controlled work**
6.32	Introduction
6.33	Legal Help – level 1
	Overview • Scope • Hague Convention cases • Financial eligibility • Merits test • Forms • Funding
6.51	Family Help (Lower) – level 2
	Scope • Forms • Funding
6.68	**Help with Family Mediation**
6.68	Introduction
6.69	Scope

continued

6.71	Financial eligibility
6.72	Merits test
6.73	Forms
6.74	Funding
6.77	**Certificates – private family law**
6.77	Scope
6.81	Mediation
	Overview • Domestic violence and abuse
6.85	Final hearings
6.86	Financial eligibility
	Waiver in domestic abuse cases
6.90	Merits test – standard criteria
	Overview • Stage 1 – Prospects of success • Stage 2 – Cost-benefit/ successful outcome
6.95	Appealing refusals
6.96	Private law children cases – merits test
	CCMS and forms
6.104	Financial matters – merits test
	CCMS and forms • Funding
6.107	Grant and scope of a certificate
	Overview • Domestic abuse cases • Applying for a certificate – urgent cases

Key resources

Scope

- Legal Aid, Sentencing and Punishment of Offenders Act 2012 – Schedule 1 Part 1
- Lord Chancellor's Guidance under section 4 of the Legal Aid, Sentencing and Punishment of Offenders Act 2012, May 2023
- Legal Aid Sentencing and Punishment of Offenders Act (LASPO) 2012 Evidence Requirements for Private Family Law Matters, v11, March 2023

Fees and costs

- Civil Legal Aid (Costs) Regulations 2013 (costs against or in favour of a legally aided party).
- Civil Legal Aid (Remuneration) Regulations 2013 – Schedule 1 (fees)
- Costs Assessment Guidance: for use with the 2018 Standard Civil Contracts, v10, LAA, December 2023

Regulations

- Civil Legal Aid (Merits Criteria) Regulations 2013
- Civil Legal Aid (Procedure) Regulations 2012
- Civil Legal Aid (Financial Resources and Payment for Services) Regulations 2013
- Civil Legal Aid (Statutory Charge) Regulations 2013

Contract

- Standard Civil Contract 2024 Specification sections 1–6 (general) and Family Specification section 7

Key points to note

- From 1 March 2023, legal aid became available for parents or those with parental responsibility in relation to placement and adoption orders.[1] The merits test is 'it is appropriate for legal aid

---

1 Civil Legal Aid (Merits Criteria) Regulations 2013 reg 2 (interpretation) 'parental placement and adoption case'.

> to be granted when taking into account the circumstances of the case'.
> – It is non-means tested at representation level, whether the order is sought as part of care proceedings under the Children Act 1989 or whether an order is sought without any related care proceedings.[2] However, it remains means tested at Legal Help level.
> - From 1 May 2023, legal aid became available for special guardianship orders both for those with parental responsibility and prospective guardians,[3] subject to the public law merits test.[4]
>   – It is non-means tested for Legal Representation but is means tested at Legal Help level.[5]
> - In March 2023 the Public Law Project successfully challenged a decision that a child could only be a member of one household, which meant a domestic abuse survivor was ineligible for legal aid because there was no child disregard. The Legal Aid Agency had to reconsider its decision. More information is given at: https://publiclawproject.org.uk/latest/domestic-abuse-survivor-unlawfully-denied-legal-aid-in-case-against-ex-court-rules.

Introduction

6.1 This chapter deals with conducting family private law cases, that is where the issues are between private individuals rather than involving the state (in the shape of social services). There are separate chapters on the general rules that apply to all civil cases, as well as family public law, housing, immigration and mental health, as they have their own funding schemes and rules.

6.2 In chapter 2, we saw that there are three key stages in providing publicly funded services: to ensure that (a) the matter is within scope; (b) the client is financially eligible; and (c) the case meets the merits test. In addition, you need to ensure that applications are completed correctly and funding is obtained. The *Lord Chancellor's Guidance*

---

2 Civil Legal Aid (Financial Resources and Payment for Services) Regulations 2013 reg 12.
3 Legal Aid, Sentencing and Punishment of Offenders Act 2012 (LASPO) Sch 1 Part 1 para 1A.
4 Civil Legal Aid (Merits Criteria) Regulations 2013 reg 66.
5 Civil Legal Aid (Financial Resources and Payment for Services) Regulations 2013 reg 12.

Conducting a family private law case 171

6.3 under section 4 of the Legal Aid, Sentencing and Punishment of Offenders Act 2012[6] has a helpful section in relation to how LASPO applies. This chapter explains how these steps are taken successfully in respect of family private law. Where appropriate, you will be referred back to chapter 4, as that chapter sets out the general rules.

6.4 See appendix C for a summary of the Legal Aid Agency's (LAA's) Costs Assessment Guidance,[7] in respect of the most common queries raised by caseworkers.

Scope of the scheme

6.5 Scope is determined by LASPO – Schedule 1 Part 1 lists the services which may generally be provided in the family category.

In scope with no need for evidence of abuse

6.6 The following types of case are within scope without the need to produce evidence of domestic abuse or evidence that a child is at risk of abuse.

Inherent jurisdiction of the High Court

6.7 Inherent jurisdiction of the High Court in relation to children and vulnerable adults (LASPO Sch 1 Part 1 para 9) applications for wardship are covered by legal aid.

Unlawful removal of children

6.8 You can prevent removal from the jurisdiction but can only secure return of a child if unlawfully removed within the jurisdiction (LASPO Sch 1 Part 1 para 10). Unlawfully means removed by someone who does not have authority to do so, either because they do not have parental responsibility or because of a court order. The following are in scope:
- prohibited steps orders;
- specific issue orders; and

---

6 May 2023, available at: www.gov.uk/guidance/funding-and-costs-assessment-for-civil-and-crime-matters.
7 *Costs Assessment Guidance: for use with the 2018 Standard Civil Contracts*, v10, LAA, December 2023, available at: www.gov.uk/guidance/funding-and-costs-assessment-for-civil-and-crime-matters.

- orders for disclosure of a child's whereabouts under Family Law Act 1986 s33, under s34 for a child's return, and a requirement under s37 to surrender a passport of, issued to, or containing the particulars of a child.

Domestic abuse

6.9 Advice and representation in relation to home rights, occupation orders and non-molestation orders under Family Law Act 1996 Part 4, injunctions following assault, battery or false imprisonment, and inherent jurisdiction of the High Court to protect an adult (LASPO Sch 1 Part 1 para 11) are all in scope.

6.10 It is really important to note that this paragraph is not qualified – it is not necessary for the client to show or provide evidence of any previous abuse to be eligible for 'civil legal services'. Civil legal services include all forms of legal aid, so advice under Legal Help can be provided in relation to the issues concerning domestic violence/ abuse itself, and a warning letter drafted prior to, or instead of, applying to court for an injunction.

Respondents in domestic abuse cases

6.11 Legal aid may still be available to respondents in some cases, but it depends on the facts of the case. See below for an extract from the Lord Chancellor's guidance:

> **Respondents**
>
> 10.33 The prospects of success criteria ([Civil Legal Aid (Merits Criteria) Regulations 2013 reg] 67(2)) and the proportionality test ([Civil Legal Aid (Merits Criteria) Regulations 2013 reg] 67(3)) are unlikely to be satisfied by a respondent to non-molestation proceedings or a forced marriage protection order only, unless there are very serious allegations which are plausibly denied wholly or substantially. An exception is where there is any question of inability to defend, for example because of mental incapacity or age, in which case a grant is likely to be justified. When considering the proportionality test, the impact on the client of the order sought will be taken into account, including any impact on contact or other related family proceedings.
>
> 10.34 In cases where the allegations are less serious or are admitted to a significant extent the main issue may well be whether the respondent should give an undertaking to the court and what form that undertaking should take. Legal help will usually be more appropriate in such cases ([Civil Legal Aid (Merits Criteria) Regulations 2013 reg] 20).[8]

---

8 *Lord Chancellor's Guidance under section 4 of the Legal Aid, Sentencing and Punishment of Offenders Act 2012, May 2023*, available at: www.gov.uk/ guidance/funding-and-costs-assessment-for-civil-and-crime-matters.

Other areas within scope without evidence of abuse

6.12 Other areas within scope without evidence of abuse are:
- special guardianship orders as defined in section 14A of the Children Act 1989 (LASPO Sch 1 Part 1 para 1A);
- mediation (LASPO Sch 1 Part 1 para 14);
- representation of children who are themselves parties to family proceedings (LASPO Sch 1 Part 1 para 15);
- female genital mutilation (FGM) protection orders (LASPO Sch 1 Part 1 para 15A);
- forced marriage protection orders (LASPO Sch 1 Part 1 para 16);
- EU and international agreements concerning children (LASPO Sch 1 Part 1 para 17); and
- EU and international agreements concerning maintenance (LASPO Sch 1 Part 1 para 18).

6.13 From 1 March 2023, legal aid became available for parents or those with parental responsibility in relation to placement and adoption orders.[9] It does not include appeals from final orders made under the Adoption and Children Act 2002.

6.14 The merits test is 'it is appropriate for legal aid to be granted when taking into account the circumstances of the case'. It is non-means tested at representation level, whether the order is sought as part of care proceedings under the Children Act 1989 or whether an order is sought without any related care proceedings.[10] However, it remains means tested at Legal Help level.

6.15 From 1 May 2023, legal aid became available for special guardianship orders both for those with parental responsibility and prospective guardians,[11] subject to the public law merits test.[12] It is non-means tested for Legal Representation but is means tested at Legal Help level.[13]

In scope with evidence of abuse

6.16 Other than the above, private family law cases are only in scope where the applicant for legal aid can show that they are a victim of

---

9 Civil Legal Aid (Merits Criteria) Regulations 2013 reg 2 (interpretation) 'parental placement and adoption case'.
10 Civil Legal Aid (Financial Resources and Payment for Services) Regulations 2013 reg 12.
11 LASPO Sch 1 Part 1 para 1A.
12 Civil Legal Aid (Merits Criteria) Regulations 2013 reg 66.
13 Civil Legal Aid (Financial Resources and Payment for Services) Regulations 2013 reg 12.

domestic abuse, or that the services are required to protect a child from an adult other than the applicant for legal aid. In either case, evidence will be required – see para 6.21 below.

Other private law matters arising out of a family relationship (LASPO Sch 1 Part 1 para 12)

6.17 Legal aid (both advice and representation) for matters arising out of a family relationship is only available to people who can show in very specific ways (set out in Civil Legal Aid (Procedure) Regulations 2012 Sch 1) that they are the victims of domestic abuse. Examples include:
- financial matters and arrangements for children (eg maintenance or other financial arrangement orders, ancillary relief, transfer of tenancy);
- divorce, dissolution or nullity;
- child arrangement orders;
- declaration of parentage;
- parental responsibility orders;
- prohibited steps orders;
- specific issue orders; and
- orders under Family Law Act 1986 ss33 and 34 for disclosure of the child's whereabouts or return unless in relation to the unlawful removal of a child (in which case they are in scope under LASPO Sch 1 Part 1 para 10).

6.18 LASPO has the following wide definition of 'domestic violence' and 'abuse':

> 'domestic violence' means any incident, or pattern of incidents, of controlling, coercive or threatening behaviour, violence or abuse (whether psychological, physical, sexual, financial or emotional) between individuals who are associated with each other;[14]

Protection of children and family matters (LASPO Sch 1 Part 1 para 13)

6.19 Legal aid advice and representation is available in specified private family law matters:
- removal of a father's parental responsibility under Children Act 1989 s4(2A);
- termination of appointment of a guardian under Children Act 1989 s6(7);

---

14 LASPO Sch 1 Part 1 para 12(9).

- child arrangement orders, prohibited steps orders and specific issue orders;
- special guardianship orders under Children Act 1989 Part 2;
- orders under Family Law Act 1986 s33 for disclosure of the child's whereabouts; and
- orders under Family Law Act 1986 s34 for the return of a child.

6.20 Legal aid is only available to people who can show in very specific ways (set out in Schedule 2 to the Civil Legal Aid (Procedure) Regulations 2012) that the child is at risk of abuse from an adult who is not the applicant for legal aid. 'Abuse' means physical or mental abuse, including sexual abuse, and abuse in the form of violence, neglect, maltreatment and exploitation.[15]

Evidence of domestic abuse

6.21 Acceptable evidence of abuse is listed in Schedule 1 to the Civil Legal Aid (Procedure) Regulations 2012.

6.22 The LAA provides detailed guidance on the operation of the evidence requirements for private family law matters.[16] This specifies in detail what is required for each piece of evidence. It also confirms that full and satisfactory evidence must be provided **before** work starts, otherwise legal aid will be refused or Legal Help will be nil assessed (para 2.5 of the guidance). Where you are applying for a certificate, you should submit certified copies of the evidence and retain the originals (or a PDF of them) on file (para 1.11 of the guidance).

6.23 Where work on a case covers work automatically in scope (eg an application for a domestic violence injunction) and work only in scope on production of evidence (eg a prohibited steps order), you can only work on the first element until the evidence is obtained (whether through the initial in scope work or separately) (para 1.8 of the guidance).

6.24 The guidance includes the wording of the relevant regulation as well as a checklist setting out exactly what the LAA looks for in each document. As the LAA will reject any document that does not appear to match the wording of the regulation exactly, using this guide can save time and prevent delay.

---

15 LASPO Sch 1 Part 1 para 13(3).
16 *Legal Aid Sentencing and Punishment of Offenders Act (LASPO) 2012 Evidence Requirements for Private Family Law Matters*, v11, March 2023: www.gov.uk/guidance/funding-and-costs-assessment-for-civil-and-crime-matters.

6.25 Any of the following forms of evidence are acceptable. However, note that Legal Help is not available to assist the client to obtain the evidence or to pay the costs, for example GP's report fees, of obtaining it. The LAA has issued some standard letters which clients can ask the relevant agency to complete. It is advisable that they are used wherever possible, as the regulations are tightly drafted and unless the wording precisely covers all elements of the regulation, the LAA cannot accept it. However, it must be said that the LAA sometimes rejects evidence that appears to meet the requirements set out in the regulations and guidance. Letters and reports from health professionals are particularly vulnerable to this. Asking them to use the standard letters[17] provided by the LAA without amending them in any way will protect you from having the evidence rejected and ensure you get paid for the work you have done. However, medical professionals have their own professional reasons for amending the letters, so this continues to be a source of friction between legal aid practitioners and the LAA. Evidence that does not rely on opinion or explanation, such as protective injunctions, is the safest form of evidence of domestic abuse when it comes to protecting your fees.

6.26 You cannot grant Legal Help, nor will the client be eligible for a representation certificate for the private family law services listed at LASPO Sch 1 Part 1 para 12, without one of the following.[18] Note that A is the applicant for legal aid and B is the (alleged) perpetrator – see also children at risk below:

1. Evidence that B has been arrested for a relevant domestic violence offence.
2. A relevant police caution for a domestic violence offence.
3. Evidence of relevant criminal proceedings for a domestic violence offence which have not concluded.
4. A relevant conviction for a domestic violence offence.
5. Evidence of a court order binding over B in connection with a domestic violence offence.
6. A domestic violence protection notice issued under section 24 of the Crime and Security Act 2010 against B.
7. A relevant protective injunction.
8. An undertaking given in England and Wales under section 46 or 63E of the Family Law Act 1996 (or given in Scotland or Northern Ireland in place of a protective injunction) by B provided that a

---

17 See: www.gov.uk/government/collections/sample-letters-to-get-evidence-of-domestic-violence.
18 *The Legal Aid, Sentencing and Punishment of Offenders Act (LASPO) 2012 – Evidence Requirements for Private Family Law Matters*, LAA, v11, March 2023; Civil Legal Aid (Procedure) Regulations 2012 Sch 1.

cross-undertaking relating to domestic violence was not given by A.
9. A copy of a finding of fact, made in proceedings in the United Kingdom, that there has been domestic violence by B.
10. An expert report produced as evidence in proceedings in the United Kingdom for the benefit of a court or tribunal confirming that a person with whom B is or was in a family relationship, was assessed as being, or at risk of being, a victim of domestic violence by B.
11. A letter or report from an appropriate health professional[19] confirming that that professional, or another appropriate health professional–
    (a) has examined A in person, by telephone or video conferencing; and
    (b) in the reasonable professional judgement of the author or the examining appropriate health professional, or the appropriate examining health professional, A has, or has had, injuries or a condition consistent with being a victim of domestic violence.
12. A letter or report from–
    (a) the appropriate health professional who made the referral described below;
    (b) an appropriate health professional who has access to the medical records of A; or
    (c) the person to whom the referral described below was made;
    confirming that there was a referral by an appropriate health professional of A to a person who provides specialist support or assistance for victims of, or those at risk of, domestic violence.
13. A letter from any person who is a member of a multi-agency risk assessment conference (or other suitable local safeguarding forum) confirming that A, or a person with whom A is in a family relationship, is or has been at risk of harm from domestic violence by B.
14. A letter from an independent domestic violence advisor/advocate confirming that they are providing, or have provided, support to A.
15. A letter from an independent sexual violence advisor/advocate confirming that they are providing or have provided, support to A relating to sexual violence by B.
16. A letter from an officer employed by a local authority or housing association (or their equivalent in Scotland or Northern Ireland) for the purpose of supporting tenants containing–
    (a) a statement to the effect that, in their reasonable professional judgment, a person with whom B is or has been in a family relationship is, or is at risk of being, a victim of domestic violence by B;

---

19 Civil Legal Aid (Procedure) Regulations 2012 Sch 1 para 22 allows that a wide range of registered health practitioners can provide the evidence, including nurses, midwives, dentists and related professionals, paramedics, psychologists, radiographers, and social workers.

(b) a description of the specific matters relied upon to support that judgment; and
(c) a description of the support they provided to the victim of domestic violence or the person at risk of domestic violence by B.
17. (1) A letter from an organisation providing domestic violence support services.
(2) The letter must confirm that it–
(a) is situated in the United Kingdom;
(b) has been operating for an uninterrupted period of six months or more; and
(c) provided A with support in relation to A's needs as a victim, or person at risk, of domestic violence.
(3) The letter must contain–
(a) a statement to the effect that, in the reasonable professional judgment of the author of the letter, A is, or is at risk of being, a victim of domestic violence;
(b) a description of the specific matters relied upon to support that judgement;
(c) a description of the support provided to A; and
(d) a statement of the reasons why A needed that support.
18. A letter or report from an organisation providing domestic violence support services in the United Kingdom confirming–
(a) that a person with whom B is or was in a family relationship was refused admission to a refuge;
(b) the date on which they were refused admission to the refuge; and
(c) they sought admission to the refuge because of allegations of domestic violence by B.
19. A letter from a public authority confirming that a person with whom B is or was in a family relationship, was assessed as being, or at risk of being, a victim of domestic violence by B (or a copy of that assessment).
20. A letter from the Secretary of State for the Home Department confirming that A has been granted leave to remain in the United Kingdom as a victim of domestic violence.
21. Evidence which the Director is satisfied demonstrates that A has been, or is at risk of being, the victim of domestic violence by B in the form of abuse which relates to financial matters.

6.27 The guidance on evidence issued by the LAA[20] does not specify in detail what it will and will not accept in relation to evidence of financial abuse as the amendment is widely drafted, so other types of evidence should be accepted.

20 At: https://assets.publishing.service.gov.uk/media/63fc9fd6d3bf7f25f5948f22/Evidence_Requirements_for_Private_Family_Law_Matters_guidance_version_11__March_2023_.pdf.

Conducting a family private law case 179

6.28 The LAA suggests the following as non-exhaustive examples, although some seem unlikely to be available to an applicant for legal aid:
- copies of both the victim's and the perpetrator's bank statements and/or cancelled cheques;
- relevant letters from banks;
- credit card accounts;
- loan documents and statements;
- business financial statements;
- employee benefit records including insurance, stock options and bonuses;
- letter from a domestic violence support organisation;
- money order receipts;
- documentation with regard to any public assistance received;
- emails;
- text messages;
- diary kept by the victim;
- letters from employers or from an education or training institute;
- benefits or welfare history;
- application for universal credit split payment;
- evidence from foodbank; and
- exemption from child maintenance service fees.

Evidence that a child is at risk of abuse

6.29 In relation to the legal services listed in LASPO Sch 1 Part 1 para 13, acceptable evidence is listed in Civil Legal Aid (Procedure) Regulations 2012 Sch 2. Any of the following are acceptable:
1. Evidence that B has been arrested for a child abuse offence.
2. A relevant police caution for a child abuse offence.
3. Evidence of relevant criminal proceedings for a child abuse offence which have not concluded.
4. A relevant conviction for a child abuse offence.
5. A relevant protective injunction.
6. A copy of a finding of fact made in proceedings in the United Kingdom of abuse of a child by B.
7. A letter from a social services department in England and Wales (or its equivalent in Scotland or Northern Ireland) confirming that the child was assessed as being, or at risk of being, a victim of child abuse by B (or a copy of that assessment).
8. A letter from a social services department in England and Wales (or its equivalent in Scotland or Northern Ireland) confirming that

a child protection plan was put in place to protect the child from abuse or a risk of abuse by B (or a copy of that plan).
9. An application for an injunction described in paragraph 5 of this Schedule made with an application for a prohibited steps order against B under section 8 of the Children Act 1989 which has not, at the date of the application for civil legal services, been decided by the court.

For a full list of the work that can be done in the family category, see appendix B.

Controlled work and licensed work

6.30 Controlled work is granted by the solicitor/caseworker according to rules under the Standard Contract 2024. It is called 'controlled' because the LAA controls the number of matter starts that are allowed each year. The types of controlled work that are relevant to family practitioners are Legal Help and Family Help (Lower). Help at Court is not available in family work.

6.31 You need a representation certificate, sometimes known as a legal aid certificate, to represent a client in legal proceedings. This is called licensed work, as the organisation has a general licence to do such work, and numbers of matter starts are not limited. Certificates may be granted by the LAA or, in urgent circumstances, granted as a delegated function by the organisation.

Private family law – controlled work

Introduction

6.32 Under LASPO, much private family law was removed from scope unless the client can demonstrate that they are the victim of domestic abuse or that a child is at risk of abuse. Check carefully that the case you intend to take on remains in scope before granting controlled work (see the section on 'Scope' at para 6.5 above). This is particularly important, as if you grant controlled work in an out of scope case, you may be paid for it on your initial claim, as it will be submitted electronically and the LAA may not be able to identify your error through claim codes without seeing the file; but the LAA will seek to recover fees if an error comes to light on audit. You do not want the LAA to recover the fees it has paid and issue your organisation with a contract notice.

Legal Help – level 1

Overview

6.33 Legal Help allows you to provide legal advice and assistance in relation to a specific matter, but does not cover issuing proceedings, advocacy or instruction of an advocate (although you can obtain counsel's opinion, where justifiable). If you need to advise your client on issues arising from mediation and arbitration, see Help with Family Mediation (para 6.68 onwards).

6.34 Representation is not available in uncontested proceedings for divorce or judicial separation, except in very limited circumstances. Straightforward divorce work, where representation at court is not required, should be done under Legal Help, where it remains in scope for people who are the victims of domestic abuse (see 'Scope' at para 6.5 above for more information).

6.35 Legal Help is also known as level 1 in the family standard fees scheme.

Scope

6.36 See chapter 4 for information on the following:
- whether other funding may be available, and legal aid should therefore not be granted;
- what to do if your client has received previous advice from another organisation;
- what to do if your client has received previous advice from your organisation;
- clients from abroad or clients who are abroad; and
- clients who are children.

Legal Help is designed to cover cases that complete after little work beyond the first meeting with the client and covers the consequential letters to the client and any letters to a third party. If you do more work in relation to children or finance issues, you may be able to go on to grant Family Help (Lower) funding (see below).

Domestic abuse and child abduction cases

6.37 These cases are included in the controlled work standard fee scheme as far as level 1. Level 2 is not designed to cover these cases and you will often find that you need to issue proceedings under a certificate very quickly.

6.38 For evidence of domestic abuse that acts as a passport to private family law services, see 'Scope' above.

Hague Convention cases

6.39 The Hague Convention on the Civil Aspects of International Child Abduction 1980 is a multilateral treaty developed by the Hague Conference on Private International Law (HCCH) that facilitates the return of a child internationally abducted by a parent from one member country to another. Non-means tested legal aid is available to applicants in such cases; but legal aid for respondents is means tested.[21]

Wills and change of name cases

6.40 These cases are not in scope under LASPO.

Divorce petitioner cases

6.41 There is a 'stand-alone' fee that applies to divorce, nullity, judicial separation and proceedings to dissolve civil partnerships (assuming the work is brought into scope due to evidence of domestic abuse). This covers cases where the client requires advice to initiate proceedings, those are issued, and there are no children or finance issues that would justify the grant of Family Help (Lower). We will look at this in more detail later on.

Financial eligibility

6.42 See chapter 2 for more information on the following:
- passporting benefits;
- assessment of capital;
- assessment of income; and
- reassessment of means.

6.43 See chapter 4 for more information on the following:
- evidence of means;
- when you can start work without evidence of means; and
- reassessing the client's eligibility if their means change significantly.

Merits test

6.44 The Legal Help merits test is known as the 'sufficient benefit test', and in full states: 'there is likely to be sufficient benefit to the individual, having regard to all the circumstances of the case, including

---

21 Civil Legal Aid (Financial Resources and Payment for Services) Regulations 2013 reg 5(1)(h).

Conducting a family private law case 183

the circumstances of the individual, to justify the cost of provision of legal help.'[22] The question is whether a reasonable private paying individual would pay for the work.[23] In most family cases remaining within scope, the test will be met.

Forms

6.45 The form is the CW1 Legal Help, Help at Court and Family Help (Lower) form.[24] The assessment of means and client's details sections must be fully completed, and signed by the client, normally in the presence of someone from your organisation (although there are exceptions to this), before you start doing any legal work.[25] Under the Standard Civil Contract 2024, up to 50 per cent of controlled work matter starts may be provided to clients you do not meet in your office.[26] You may claim for the work done before the form is signed (eg by telephone, video or email) as long as the client signs and returns the form to you and provides acceptable evidence of means.[27]

How many Legal Help forms?

6.46 You can have more than one Legal Help matter open at the same time, but this is very unusual in family work. It may be permissible if your client has entirely separate family disputes.[28] The LAA gives the example of disputes in respect of different family relationships, where any potential proceedings would be separate. This would apply, for example, where your client was the mother of children with different fathers, each of whom was applying separately for residence.

Funding

6.47 Legal Help – level 1 is paid as two different standard fees.[29] The higher fee is only applicable when your client is the petitioner in a divorce and there are no significant children or finance issues and no other form of civil legal service is provided to your client. The higher

---

22 Civil Legal Aid (Merits Criteria) Regulations 2013 reg 32(b).
23 Civil Legal Aid (Merits Criteria) Regulations 2013 reg 7.
24 Available at: www.gov.uk/government/publications/cw1-financial-eligibility-for-legal-aid-clients.
25 Standard Civil Contract 2024 Specification para 3.9.
26 Standard Civil Contract 2024 Specification para 3.17.
27 Standard Civil Contract 2024 Specification para 3.18 onwards.
28 Standard Civil Contract 2024 Specification para 7.167.
29 Current fees and hourly rates are found in Civil Legal Aid (Remuneration) Regulations 2013 Sch 1.

fee can be claimed three months after proceedings are issued or when the proceedings are concluded (whichever is sooner).

6.48 In all other cases, the lower level 1 fee is payable (whether or not combined with a level 2 fee).

6.49 Divorce, child abduction and domestic abuse cases that exceed three times the fixed fee when calculated at hourly rates can be claimed in full (see chapter 15 for more information about claiming escape fee cases).

6.50 Other level 1 cases cannot be claimed as escape fee cases.

Family Help (Lower) – level 2

Scope

6.51 This covers the provision of ongoing assistance with some kinds of 'Family Dispute'.[30]

Private family law – conditions for level 2

6.52 Up to and including 8 May 2011, para 10.55 of the then Family Contract Specification required two meetings with the client in order to justify a level 2 fee. The then Legal Services Commission (LSC) removed the requirement for a second meeting from 9 May 2011, and instead practitioners had to show that 'substantive negotiations' had taken place and that you have been conducting the negotiations. This remains the position under the 2024 Standard Contract. However, practitioners report that it can be difficult to persuade some contract managers that 'substantive negotiations' have taken place, even when considerable work has been done on the file, for example, if the other party is acting in person and responds through their ex-partner rather than to the solicitors direct. However, contract managers should accept this: see the LAA's Costs Assessment Guidance Appendix 1 para 4.10 for more information.[31]

> **Criteria for Family Help (Lower) – meaning of 'significant family dispute' – Family Contract Specification 2024**[32]
>
> 7.58 You may only make a determination that a Client qualifies for Family Help (Lower) where all relevant criteria in the Merits Regulations, Financial Regulations and Procedure Regulations are

---

30 Standard Civil Contract 2024 Specification para 7.58.
31 *Costs Assessment Guidance: for use with the 2024 Standard Civil Contracts*, LAA, available at: www.gov.uk/guidance/funding-and-costs-assessment-for-civil-and-crime-matters.
32 Standard Civil Contract 2024 Specification para 7.58.

satisfied including the criteria in Paragraph 35 of the Merits Regulations. In addition, the fee for Family Help (Lower) may only be claimed for those Family Disputes:
(a) which involve more than simply taking instructions from and advising the Client, and providing any follow up written or telephone advice; and
(b) where you are involved in substantive negotiations with a third party (either by conducting the negotiations yourself or by advice and assistance in support of mediation); and
(c) where the dispute, if unresolved, would be likely to lead to family proceedings; and
(d) which do not primarily concern processing a divorce, nullity, judicial separation or dissolution of a civil partnership; and
(e) which do not primarily concern advice relating to child support.

Family Help (Lower) – children

6.53 This covers all work up to the issue of proceedings. It is not necessary to obtain a consent order to formalise any agreement in respect of children, although if you are claiming a settlement fee (see para 6.58 below) it is advisable to record the agreement in writing, so that the LAA can see that it was a 'genuine settlement to conclude that aspect of the case'.[33]

Family Help (Lower) – finance

6.54 This covers all work including the issue of proceedings and all work required to obtain a consent order.[34]

Family Help (Lower) – children and finance

6.55 Where a case involves children and finance issues meeting the criteria set out above, both the children and finance fees may be claimed. You claim two Family Help (Lower) fees, one for children and one for finance, where the merits criteria are met[35] (see merits test at para 6.90 below).

Forms

6.56 When claiming the level 2 fee you do not need another CW1 Legal Help, Help at Court and Family Help (Lower) form. Simply tick the 'yes' box at the bottom of page 15 of the form to confirm that the criteria for level 2 are met.

---

33 Standard Civil Contract 2024 Specification para 7.65(c).
34 Standard Civil Contract 2024 Specification para 7.65(d).
35 Standard Civil Contract 2024 Specification para 7.59.

Funding

6.57 Family Help (Lower) (level 2) is paid under standard fees, although cases that reach the escape threshold (three times the fixed fee at levels 1 and 2 combined) can be paid in full at hourly rates. For more information about claiming escape fee cases, see chapter 15.

Settlement fees

6.58 Settlement fees can be claimed for cases that conclude at this level, without the issue of proceedings (save to obtain a consent order – Standard Civil Contract Specification 2024 para 7.65). In order to be considered as 'settled', that aspect of the case (ie children or finance) must be fully resolved at that level and the client actively involved in a decision to accept a settlement. The agreement on financial issues must be recorded in writing or in a consent order. It is advisable to record the agreement in respect of children in writing as well.

6.59 If the client ceases to give instructions, dies, or the parties are reconciled, the settlement fee cannot be claimed.[36]

6.60 You must wait for 21 days after the case has been concluded before claiming the settlement fee. In relation to financial issues, if the settlement breaks down, and you become aware of the fact within six months, the settlement fee becomes repayable. In relation to children issues, the period is three months.[37]

> **Case study**
>
> Mrs Brown had been married for 11 years and has two children, James and Jennifer. She came to see us about her divorce. It transpired that her husband had been very controlling, preventing Mrs Brown from contacting her family and only permitting her access to small amounts of money, which had to be fully accounted for. This had resulted in Mrs Brown suffering from anxiety and depression, about which she had consulted her GP within the last two years. She was able to obtain a GP's letter to show that she was eligible on the basis of 'domestic abuse' under LASPO.
>
> Mr Brown refused to attend mediation; and also instructed solicitors on a private paying basis. Eventually we were able to finalise the divorce and obtain agreement to settlements in respect of the arrangements for the children and the finances.
>
> Our office is in Salisbury. What can we claim?

---

36 Standard Civil Contract 2024 Specification para 7.65(c).
37 Standard Civil Contract 2024 Specification para 7.65(b).

Conducting a family private law case 187

You can claim:	
Legal Help level 1	£86.00
Family Help (Lower) (children)	£199.00
Family Help (Lower) (finance)	£208.00
Settlement fee (children)	£119.00
Settlement fee (finance)	£125.00
	Total £737.00

6.61 For more information about when you can or should close a case, see chapter 4.

Funding from the client's point of view – the statutory charge

6.62 For information about the statutory charge,[38] see chapter 4. The statutory charge does not apply to cases completing at Legal Help (level 1), but if the case goes beyond level 1, the level 1 costs are included in the costs caught by the charge.

6.63 The home is exempt from the charge in cases completing under Legal Help, Help at Court or Family Help (Lower). The charge does not apply to maintenance payments. However, even where a lump sum is paid, the statutory charge does not apply to standard fee cases. This is a powerful incentive to clients to settle at level 2, as in most cases their legal aid will be free.

6.64 However, in escape fee cases, the charge applies, but only to costs above the escape threshold (ie those costs over three times the standard fee).

6.65 Where the charge arises only under Legal Help, Help at Court or Family Help (Lower), it is in favour of your organisation. You may apply to the LAA to waive it, if its operation would cause grave hardship or distress to the client, or where it would be unreasonably difficult to enforce.[39]

6.66 You should collect the appropriate sum from the client and claim the net costs from the LAA.

6.67 However, note that at level 3 (certificated work), the charge applies in favour of the LAA and includes the fees at levels 1 and 2.[40]

---

38 Civil Legal Aid (Statutory Charge) Regulations 2013.
39 Civil Legal Aid (Statutory Charge) Regulations 2013 reg 8.
40 Civil Legal Aid (Statutory Charge) Regulations 2013 reg 4(2).

Help with Family Mediation

Introduction

6.68 LASPO introduced a level of service to allow solicitors to provide legal advice to clients during and immediately following mediation. It is designed to assist the mediation process and give legal effect to any agreement reached. This covers the provision of any of the following legal services in relation to a family dispute:

(a) civil legal services provided in relation to family mediation; or
(b) civil legal services provided in relation to the issuing of proceedings to obtain a consent order following the settlement of the dispute following family mediation.[41]

Scope

6.69 Help with Family Mediation is controlled work.[42] Therefore, you need to use a matter start under your schedule to start a case.

6.70 Help with Family Mediation covers legal advice to a client who is undergoing or who has participated in family mediation within the last three months and can include the issuing of proceedings to obtain a consent order following the settlement of the dispute within family mediation.[43]

Financial eligibility

6.71 See 'Legal help' at para 6.45 onwards above.

Merits test

6.72 The merits test is the sufficient benefit test – see above. You will need evidence on the file that the client is, or has been within the last three months, participating in family mediation.[44]

---

41 Civil Legal Aid (Procedure) Regulations 2012 reg 8.
42 Civil Legal Aid (Procedure) Regulations 2012 reg 21(2).
43 Civil Legal Aid (Procedure) Regulations 2012 reg 8.
44 Standard Civil Contract 2024 Specification para 7.67.

Forms

6.73 The form is the CW5.[45] It has to be signed by the mediator as well as the client.

Funding

6.74 You may not claim for Help with Family Mediation if you have provided Family Help or Legal Representation in relation to the same family dispute within the previous six months. If a certificate is granted to a client in respect of the same family dispute within six months of your claim, your fee will be recouped.[46]

6.75 You may only claim one Help with Family Mediation fee per case, regardless of the number of clients you represented who took part in the mediation or the number of different issues covered by the mediation.[47]

6.76 There is a fixed fee of £150; but you can also claim a further £200 if you draft a consent order giving effect to a mediated agreement and which is approved by the court. There is no 'escape' from these flat fees.[48] As the fees are so low, and the work relatively high risk, particularly where you are asked to advise on finances, which may involve pension issues, very few practitioners are prepared to take on this work. Mediators report that it can be almost impossible to find firms to undertake CW5 work, and as a result, clients cannot obtain consent orders reflecting an agreement reached through mediation.

Certificates – private family law

Scope

6.77 A representation certificate authorises the conduct of litigation and the provision of advocacy and representation, and includes steps preliminary and incidental to proceedings, and steps to settle or avoid proceedings.

---

45 Available at: www.gov.uk/government/publications/cw5-financial-eligibility-form-for-clients-wanting-family-mediation.
46 Standard Civil Contract 2024 Specification para 7.70.
47 Standard Civil Contract 2024 Specification para 7.68.
48 Standard Civil Contract 2024 Specification para 7.3.

6.78 The then LSC introduced a standard fee funding scheme known as the Private Family Law Representation Scheme (PFLRS) from 9 May 2011. Under the PFLRS, there are two levels of funding:
- Family Help (Higher) – level 3: to cover all work up to the preparation for final hearing.
- Legal Representation – level 4: to cover all work from preparation for a final hearing up to and including all work to conclude a case after the final hearing, for example, application to the court of first instance for permission to appeal, and advice on the merits of an appeal against a final order.

6.79 The LSC introduced a standard fee scheme for advocacy, the Family Advocacy Scheme (FAS) from 9 May 2011. For more information on the fee schemes for litigators, see chapter 15. For more on the FAS, see chapter 19.

6.80 Before you apply for a certificate, see chapter 4:
- general criteria;
- clients who are abroad;
- clients from abroad; and
- clients who are children.

Mediation

Overview

6.81 Mediation is within the scope of legal aid. It is means and merits tested. The merits test is that 'the Director is satisfied that the mediator has assessed that, in all the circumstances of the case, the case is suitable for mediation'.[49] Prior to 2014, there was an obligation only on applicants for legal aid to prove their case was unsuitable for mediation before starting court proceedings; but Children and Families Act 2014 s10 made it compulsory for all separating couples to attend a Mediation Information and Assessment Meeting (MIAM) before starting proceedings in relation to money or children issues. Practitioners report that enforcement of this requirement varies considerably between different courts.

Domestic violence and abuse

6.82 The LAA does not consider the fact that domestic abuse or violence has taken place should automatically rule out consideration of medi-

---

49 Civil Legal Aid (Merits Criteria) Regulations 2013 reg 37.

ation. It will accept that it is not reasonable to consider mediation if an allegation of domestic abuse has resulted in a police investigation or the issuing of civil proceedings for the protection of the applicant within the last 12 months. In other circumstances, you will need to justify why it is not appropriate to involve the police – for example, where this might jeopardise the long-term financial or other interests of the family; or if you have reason to believe that the police will not be able to assist; or if they have been contacted but have failed to respond or to provide adequate assistance in the past.

6.83 It is unlikely that funding will be granted for committal proceedings if criminal proceedings have been instigated by the police. Breach of a non-molestation order became a criminal offence in 2007, and the LAA would ordinarily expect the client to report a breach to the police before seeking an amendment to the certificate for committal.

6.84 The LAA normally expects a warning letter to be sent to the respondent. However, this is not an absolute rule, for example, if you can show that a warning letter might endanger the client.[50]

Final hearings

6.85 Proceedings up to a final hearing are covered by a form of legal aid called Family Help (Higher). Final hearings are covered by a form of legal aid called 'Legal Representation'. In practice, you need to apply for an amendment to the certificate.

Financial eligibility

6.86 See chapter 2.

Waiver in domestic abuse cases

6.87 The LAA has discretion to waive the upper disposable income and capital limits for victims of domestic abuse seeking protection from the court.[51] It does not apply at Legal Help level. It is important to note that any contribution from income or capital that is applicable under the regulations cannot be waived. If granting a certificate as a

---

50 See *Lord Chancellor's Guidance under Section 4 of the Legal Aid, Sentencing and Punishment of Offenders Act 2012*, May 2023: www.gov.uk/guidance/funding-and-costs-assessment-for-civil-and-crime-matters para 10.30.
51 Civil Legal Aid (Financial Resources and Payment for Services) Regulations 2013 reg 12.

delegated function, you can assume the LAA will exercise its discretion in favour of granting a waiver; but when you submit the substantive application, you should make clear that the case is a domestic abuse case, and that you are seeking the waiver.

6.88 You should advise your client that although the upper limit may be waived, the liability to pay contributions is not. The usual rules on contributions will apply, so the client's funding will be revoked in the event of non-payment. Clients with income much above the upper limit who successfully obtain a waiver can find themselves paying quite substantial contributions, so you should clearly advise the client to expect that, for example, civil legal aid: means testing.[52]

6.89 This is particularly important in emergency cases, since if you grant an emergency certificate and the client is then offered a substantive certificate with contributions and declines the offer, they will be liable for the full costs you incur on the emergency certificate.

Merits test – standard criteria

Overview

6.90 Before you apply for a certificate, you need to ensure that the standard criteria are satisfied.[53] Those that apply in private family law cases are:
- the individual does not have access to other potential sources of funding from which it would be reasonable to fund the case;
- there is no other person besides the individual, including a person who might benefit from the proceedings, who can reasonably be expected to bring the proceedings;
- the individual has exhausted all reasonable alternatives to bringing proceedings, including any complaints system, ombudsman scheme or other form of alternative dispute resolution; and
- there is a need for representation in all the circumstances of the case including:
  – the nature and complexity of the issues;
  – the existence of other proceedings; and
  – the interests of other parties to the proceedings.

6.91 The first criterion requires you to consider whether the client has alternative methods of funding the case at their disposal, and you will need to explore with the client and consider whether, for example,

---

52 See: www.gov.uk/guidance/civil-legal-aid-means-testing.
53 Civil Legal Aid (Merits Criteria) Regulations 2013 reg 39.

the local authority would pay for adoption proceedings. You will need to address any potential sources which are not in fact available, in the application.

Stage 1 – Prospects of success

6.92 All cases must be put into one of the following categories according to its prospects of success:[54]
- **very good** – 80 per cent or above;
- **good** – 60 to 80 per cent;
- **moderate** – 50 to 60 per cent;
- **marginal** – 45 to 50 per cent;
- **poor** – less than 45 per cent;
- **borderline** – it is not possible, because of disputed law, fact or expert evidence, to assign the case to another category but it cannot be categorised as 'unclear'; or
- **unclear** – the case cannot be assigned to any of the other categories because there are identifiable investigations to be carried out after which the prospects can be estimated.

6.93 In the case *IS v Director of Legal Aid Casework and Lord Chancellor*[55] in the High Court, Collins J said that the standard to be applied in assessing the prospects of success is the prospects as they would be with the assistance of competent legal representation, not the prospects on the basis of material available but untested at the time of the application. This is to ensure that cases where competent representation would turn the case in the applicant's favour are not excluded from funding. Although the Court of Appeal overturned his declaration that the Civil Legal Aid (Merits Criteria) Regulations 2013 were unlawful, it did not specifically deal with this point.[56] In our view, and notwithstanding that the wider judgment was overturned, that must be the right approach.

Stage 2 – Cost-benefit/successful outcome

6.94 This varies according to the type of case, see below.

---

54 Civil Legal Aid (Merits Criteria) Regulations 2013 reg 5(1).
55 [2015] EWHC 1965 (Admin) at para 96, per Collins J.
56 *IS v Director of Legal Aid Casework and Lord Chancellor* [2016] EWCA Civ 464.

Appealing refusals

6.95 A refusal of a certificate on the basis of merit can be appealed, within 14 days of the decision, to the Independent Adjudicator. A refusal on financial grounds cannot be appealed, though a fresh application can be made if circumstances change.

Private law children cases – merits test

6.96 Private law children cases are proceedings concerning child arrangements, parental responsibility, financial provision for children, and other matters under the Children Act 1989 which are not Special Children Act or other public law proceedings.

6.97 You need to show that you are likely to obtain a 'successful outcome' – a significant improvement in the arrangements for children.

6.98 The merits test is as follows:

- prospects of success are very good, good, moderate, marginal or borderline;[57] and
- the reasonable private paying individual test is met:

    ... the potential benefit to be gained from the provision of civil legal services justifies the likely costs, such that a reasonable private paying individual would be prepared to start or continue the proceedings having regard to the prospects of success and all the other circumstances of the case.[58]

CCMS and forms

6.99 The LAA introduced mandatory use of its online Client and Cost Management System (CCMS) for all new applications from April 2016 (see chapter 5). CCMS has replaced the paper forms, which are retained for emergency use only, when authorised as such by the LAA (ie when CCMS is not available for a prolonged period of time).

6.100 See chapter 5 at para 5.90 for more information about:

- what to do if CCMS is not available; and
- claiming time spent using CCMS (see appendix C).

---

57 Civil Legal Aid (Merits Criteria) Regulations 2013 reg 68.
58 Civil Legal Aid (Merits Criteria) Regulations 2013 reg 7.

Conducting a family private law case 195

6.101 The client should attend an appointment with a mediator (MIAM) unless any of the exceptions set out in Family Procedure Rules Practice Direction 3A apply.

6.102 Representation will be refused if no reasonable attempts to settle without recourse to litigation (whether by negotiation or otherwise) have been attempted.

6.103 For CCMS cases, the client's signature cannot be obtained until the application is completed and must be done at that time unless CCMS is not available, for example, there is no internet access, in which case the client can sign a promissory declaration: see chapter 5 at para 5.65 for more information.

Financial matters – merits test

6.104 You need to show that you are likely to obtain a 'successful outcome' – a significant improvement in financial or other arrangements. The merits test is as follows:[59]

- Prospects of success are:
    - very good, good or moderate; or
    - borderline, marginal or unclear, and:
        - the case is of significant wider public interest;
        - the case is one with overwhelming importance to the individual; or
        - the substance of the case relates to a breach of Convention rights.
- Representation will be refused unless the likely benefits justify the likely cost, such that the reasonable private paying individual would be prepared to take or defend the proceedings in all the circumstances.

CCMS and forms

6.105 Again, before applying for funding, the client should attend mediation (unless the exceptions apply) and have attempted to settle, by negotiation or otherwise. Applications should be made via CCMS. If you need to apply using a paper form because CCMS is not available and this has been authorised by the LAA, use form CIVAPP3 with the appropriate MEANS form.

---

59 Civil Legal Aid (Merits Criteria) Regulations 2013 reg 69.

Funding

6.106 The PFLRS and the FAS have applied since 9 May 2011. For more information on the fee schemes, see chapter 15.

Grant and scope of a certificate

Overview

6.107 In almost every case, a certificate is only granted subject to two limitations. First, it is very rare for a certificate to be granted to cover the entirety of proceedings. Usually, it is limited to a particular step in the proceedings. Second, costs will be limited, usually to £2,250 plus VAT in the first instance.

6.108 From 19 April 2019, following a pilot which showed it did not increase final claims, the LAA changed its approach and applied an initial limit of £25,000 to a specific range of cases. However, if the subject matter of the case also includes an issue that falls outside the list below, the LAA will treat the case as though each aspect has a different limitation, so you will need to keep a careful eye on cost allocation.

Cases covered by the £25,000 limit

Public law	
Care proceedings	Discharge Care
Supervision proceedings	Vary/Discharge Supervision
Emergency Protection Order / Extend Emergency Protection Order	Contact Child in Care / Refuse Contact Child in Care
Secure Accommodation	Education Supervision Order
Section 37 Order* (standalone)	Child Assessment Order
Placement Order (standalone)	Vary/Discharge Placement Order (standalone)
Children	
Parental Responsibility (including vary/discharge)	Prohibited Steps (including vary/discharge)
Specific Issue (including vary/discharge)	Declaration of Parentage
Child Arrangements Order Contact (including vary/discharge)	Child Arrangements Order Residence (including vary/discharge)
Special Guardianship (including vary/discharge)	Adoption (standalone)

Remove Children from Jurisdiction	Enforcement of any Section 8 Order *
Disclosure of Child's Whereabouts under section 33*	Recovery of a Child under section 34*
Domestic abuse	
Non-Molestation (including vary/discharge)	Occupation (including vary/discharge)
Forced Marriage Protection Order	Female Genital Protection Order

*Children Act 1989.

6.109 Costs limitations include profit costs (and any enhancement or uplift), counsel's fees and disbursements, but not VAT. It is extremely important not to do work outside the scope of any limitation, as you will not be paid for it. You should note that payments to counsel under the FAS count towards the financial limitation on certificates.[60] It is particularly easy to lose track of counsel's fees and disbursements, and it really helps to keep all documents relating to financial issues together if using a paper file. CCMS helps in this area if you apportion part of your costs limit to counsel once instructed. If you have delegated functions, you have the power to amend the financial limitation on an emergency (but not substantive) certificate up to £10,000, but only to allow you to do work that is urgent.[61] If you exercise this power, you should inform the LAA via CCMS, or on form APP8 if CCMS is not available (and you have been authorised to do so by the LAA), that you have done so.

Domestic abuse cases

6.110 Representation is available to apply for an injunction under Family Law Act 1996 Part 4. This is covered by LASPO Sch 1 Part 1 para 11; therefore there is no need to produce evidence of previous domestic abuse as this only applies to services under para 12.

6.111 The merits test is as follows:[62]
- Prospects of success are:
  - very good, good, moderate, borderline or marginal.
- Representation will be refused unless the case meets the proportionality test: 'that the likely benefits of the proceedings to the individual and others justify the likely costs, having regard to the prospects of success and all the other circumstances of the case'.

60 Standard Civil Contract 2024 Specification para 7.29.
61 Civil Legal Aid (Procedure) Regulations 2012 reg 39(3)(b).
62 Civil Legal Aid (Merits Criteria) Regulations 2013 reg 67.

6.112 The LAA has made detailed guidance available on its website: see the *Lord Chancellor's Guidance under section 4 of Legal Aid, Sentencing and Punishment of Offenders Act 2012*.[63]

Applying for a certificate – urgent cases

6.113 You may exercise a delegated function to grant an emergency certificate. See chapter 4 for more information about delegated functions.

6.114 If a substantive certificate is refused (on means or merits) or made conditional on a contribution which the client refuses, the client is liable for all costs incurred under the emergency certificate. The client must therefore be advised of this at or before the time of the grant, and given a costs estimate. In these circumstances, the solicitor should bill the certificate in the usual way; the LAA will pursue the client for the costs.

- **Merits**: Emergency Representation may be granted as a matter of urgency where it appears to be in the interests of justice to do so.[64]
- **Means**: Emergency Representation may be provided where there has not yet been a detailed assessment of the client's resources, provided that they have provided sufficient financial information to demonstrate that it is likely that they will be found to be eligible.[65] In cases of doubt, for example, because of complex means, you can submit an urgent application via CCMS. See above for the LAA's power to waive the capital and income limits in domestic abuse cases.
- **Limitations**: You must apply both a scope and a costs limitation (see the standard limitations at 'Civil legal aid application forms: supporting guidance'[66]). Scope should be limited to the steps that need to be taken urgently. The initial scope limitation can be amended, provided the certificate remains limited to steps that need to be taken urgently. Costs will usually be limited to £1,350 plus VAT in the first instance, though this can be exceeded or amended where justifiable.
- **Application for substantive certificate**: The LAA must receive the substantive application within five working days of the emergency grant. In the event of a delegated function amendment to

---

63 At: www.gov.uk/funding-and-costs-assessment-for-civil-and-crime-matters. Scroll down to Other Guidance.
64 Civil Legal Aid (Procedure) Regulations 2012 reg 52(1)(b).
65 Civil Legal Aid (Procedure) Regulations 2012 reg 52(2).
66 At: www.gov.uk/government/publications/civil-legal-aid-application-forms-supporting-guidance.

scope or costs, you can apply through the single step process so that the substantive certificate reflects the amendment you made using your delegated functions. There is an LAA quick guide to this.[67] See also chapter 5 at para 5.36 onwards for more information.

6.115 It is important to ensure that an emergency certificate is replaced by a substantive certificate within 56 days, as emergency certificates expire at that point and any further work would not be funded. The time limit cannot be extended.

6.116 See chapter 4 for information about:
- amendments to certificates;
- refusals and appeals;
- use of counsel and amendments for a KC;
- changes to prospects of success or cost–benefit;
- disbursements and prior authority;
- contributions;
- high cost cases;
- ending a case;
- discharge of certificate; and
- evocation of certificate.

6.117 See chapter 15 for information about getting paid in family cases.

---

67 At: https://legalaidlearning.justice.gov.uk/single-stage-emergency-application.

CHAPTER 7

Conducting a family public law case

Edited by Vicky Ling

7.1	Introduction
7.4	**What is public family law?**
7.9	Scope
7.13	Controlled work and licensed work
7.15	**Public family law – controlled work**
7.15	Legal Help – level 1
	Scope • Merits test • Financial eligibility • Forms • Funding
7.25	Family Help (Lower) – level 2
	Scope • Merits test • Financial eligibility • Forms • Funding • Exceptional cases • Closing controlled work matters
7.34	**Certificates – public law cases**
7.34	Scope
7.35	Certificates
7.38	Financial eligibility
7.40	Merits test
7.42	CCMS and forms
7.46	Funding
	Advocacy under standard fees • Applying for a certificate – urgent cases
7.57	Very High Cost Cases
7.58	Care Case Fee Scheme
	KC and two-counsel cases
7.61	Exceptions to the CCFS

Key resources

Scope
- Legal Aid, Sentencing and Punishment of Offenders Act 2012 – Schedule 1 Part 1
- Lord Chancellor's Guidance under section 4 of the Legal Aid, Sentencing and Punishment of Offenders Act 2012, May 2023

Fees
- Civil Legal Aid (Remuneration) Regulations 2013 Sch 1
- Costs Assessment Guidance: for use with the 2018 Standard Civil Contracts, v10, LAA, December 2023

Regulations
- Civil Legal Aid (Merits Criteria) Regulations 2013
- Civil Legal Aid (Procedure) Regulations 2012
- Civil Legal Aid (Financial Resources and Payment for Services) Regulations 2013

Contract
- Standard Civil Contract 2024 Specification sections 1–6 (general) and Family Specification section 7.

Key points to note
- Once you become aware that costs are likely to exceed £25,000, you must contact the Legal Aid Agency (LAA) by general case enquiry informing it of this.
  - There is a quick guide on how to submit a case query: https://legalaidlearning.justice.gov.uk/ccms-provider-managing-live-cases-submit-a-case-query.
- High cost care cases under the Care Case Fee Scheme (CCFS) have an immediate limit of £32,500.
- For urgent high cost care cases, call the LAA's Customer Service Team: 0300 200 2020 and ask to speak to the High Cost Case Family Team (only for single counsel cases).
- There are some LAA recorded webinars on how best to work with the LAA on high cost cases: https://legalaidlearning.justice.gov.uk/ccms-provider-managing-live-cases-submit-a-case-query.

Introduction

7.1 This chapter deals with conducting family public law cases. There are separate chapters on the general rules that apply to all civil cases, as well as family private law, immigration, housing and mental health, as they each have their own funding schemes and rules.

7.2 In chapter 2, we saw that there are three key stages in providing publicly funded services: to ensure that (a) the matter is within scope; (b) the client is financially eligible; and (c) the case meets the merits test. In addition, you need to ensure that forms are completed correctly and funding is obtained. This chapter explains how these steps are taken successfully in respect of family public law.

7.3 See appendix C for a summary of the Legal Aid Agency's (LAA's) Costs Assessment Guidance,[1] in respect of the most common queries raised by caseworkers.

What is public family law?

7.4 Public family law includes Special Children Act proceedings and 'public law children cases'. These are defined in Civil Legal Aid (Merits Criteria) Regulations 2013 reg 2. The term 'Special Children Act' covers applications for funding from a child, parent or other person with parental responsibility in cases under Children Act 1989 ss31, 43, 44 and 45, and applications from a child under s25 (use of accommodation for restricting liberty), but not appeals from final orders made in cases under those sections.

7.5 'Public law children cases' are all other matters described in Legal Aid, Sentencing and Punishment of Offenders Act 2012 (LASPO) Sch 1 Part 1 paras 1 and 9, including care, protection and supervision matters that are not Special Children Act, and High Court inherent jurisdiction cases. It also includes parties other than the child or person with parental responsibility who are (or want to apply to be) joined to Special Children Act cases.

7.6 From 1 March 2023, legal aid became available for parents or those with parental responsibility in relation to placement and adop-

---

1 *Costs Assessment Guidance: for use with the 2018 Standard Civil Contracts*, v10, LAA, December 2023, available at: www.gov.uk/guidance/funding-and-costs-assessment-for-civil-and-crime-matters.

tion orders.[2] It does not include appeals from final orders made under the Adoption and Children Act 2002.

7.7 The merits test is 'it is appropriate for legal aid to be granted when taking into account the circumstances of the case'. It is non-means tested at representation level, whether the order is sought as part of care proceedings under the Children Act 1989 or whether an order is sought without any related care proceedings.[3] However, it remains means-tested at Legal Help level.

7.8 Note that special guardianship orders (SGOs) are private law family (under Children Act 1989 Part 2). From 1 May 2023, legal aid became available for SGOs both for those with parental responsibility and for prospective guardians,[4] subject to the public law merits test.[5] It is non-means tested for Legal Representation, but is means tested at Legal Help level.[6]

Scope

7.9 LASPO Sch 1 Part 1 para 1 brings within scope:
(a) orders under section 25 of the Children Act 1989 ('the 1989 Act') (secure accommodation);
(b) orders under Part 4 of the 1989 Act (care and supervision);
(c) orders under Part 5 of the 1989 Act (protection of children);
(d) approval by a court under paragraph 19 of Schedule 2 to the 1989 Act (arrangements to assist children to live abroad);
(e) parenting orders under section 8 of the Crime and Disorder Act 1998 ('the 1998 Act') or section 366 or 369 of the Sentencing Code;
(f) child safety orders under section 11 of the 1998 Act;
(g) orders for contact under section 26 of the Adoption and Children Act 2002 ('the 2002 Act');
(h) applications for leave of the court to remove a child from a person's custody under section 36 of the 2002 Act;
(i) placement orders, recovery orders or adoption orders under Chapter 3 of Part 1 of the 2002 Act (see sections 21, 41 and 46 of that Act);
(j) orders under section 84 of the 2002 Act (parental responsibility prior to adoption abroad).

2 Civil Legal Aid (Merits Criteria) Regulations 2013 reg 2 (interpretation) 'parental placement and adoption case'.
3 Civil Legal Aid (Financial Resources and Payment for Services) Regulations 2013 reg 12.
4 LASPO Sch 1 Part 1 para 1A.
5 Civil Legal Aid (Merits Criteria) Regulations 2013 reg 66.
6 Civil Legal Aid (Financial Resources and Payment for Services) Regulations 2013 reg 12.

Conducting a family public law case 205

- (k) orders under section 119 of the Social Services and Wellbeing (Wales) Act 2014 ('the 2014 Act') (secure accommodation);
- (l) approval by a court under section 124 of the 2014 Act (arrangements to assist children to live abroad).

7.10 LASPO Sch 1 Part 1 para 9 brings within scope:

(1) Civil legal services provided in relation to the inherent jurisdiction of the High Court in relation to children.[7]

See appendix B for a list of work that falls within the Family category under the legal aid standard contract.

7.11 Where appropriate, you will be referred back to chapter 4, as that chapter sets out the general rules.

7.12 See chapter 4 for information on the following:

- what to do if your client has received previous advice from another organisation;
- what to do if your client has received previous advice from your organisation;
- clients from abroad or clients who are abroad; and
- clients who are children.

For exceptional case funding for cases that are out of scope under LASPO, see chapter 3.

Controlled work and licensed work

7.13 Controlled work is granted by solicitors according to rules under the Standard Contract 2024. It is called 'controlled' because the LAA controls the number of matter starts that are allowed each year. The types of controlled work that are relevant to family practitioners are Legal Help and Family Help (Lower). Help at Court is not available in family work.

7.14 You need a representation certificate, sometimes known as a legal aid certificate, to represent a client in legal proceedings. This is called licensed work, as the organisation has a general licence to do such work, and numbers of matter starts are not limited. Certificates may be granted by the LAA, or, in urgent circumstances, granted as a delegated function by the organisation.

---

7 Vulnerable adults are also within scope but not in the family category.

Public family law – controlled work

Legal Help – level 1

Scope

7.15 This covers initial (ie pre-proceedings) advice and assistance in relation to any kind of public law family case, including the consequential letters to the client and any letters to a third party.

7.16 However, it is not designed to cover attending child protection conferences as a matter of course. The LAA believes that legal advice is only required in 'exceptional circumstances'.[8] If you attend a child protection conference, you will need to ensure that this is fully justified on your attendance note.

Merits test

7.17 The 'sufficient benefit test' applies to Legal Help: 'there is likely to be sufficient benefit to the individual, having regard to all the circumstances of the case, including the circumstances of the individual, to justify the cost of provision of legal help'.[9] The question is whether a reasonable private paying client would pay for the work.[10] It is hard to think of circumstances where it would not be met in such cases.

Financial eligibility

7.18 Legal Help is means tested, even in relation to care cases. See Family Help Lower, below, where the local authority has given notice of its intention to issue proceedings, as this is not means tested and has its own form.

7.19 See chapter 2 for more information on the following:
- passporting benefits;
- assessment of capital;
- assessment of income; and
- reassessment of means.

7.20 See chapter 4 for more information on the following:
- evidence of means;
- when you can start work without evidence of means; and

---

8 *Costs Assessment Guidance*, v10, December 2023, Appendix 1 'Family Fee Scheme Guidance (excluding advocacy)' para 3.2.
9 Civil Legal Aid (Merits Criteria) Regulations 2013 reg 32(b).
10 Civil Legal Aid (Merits Criteria) Regulations 2013 reg 7.

- reassessing the client's eligibility if their means change significantly.

Forms

7.21 The form is the CW1 Legal Help, Help at Court and Family Help (Lower) form (unless the local authority has given written notice of its intention to issue proceedings in which case CW1PL must be used, see below).

7.22 The assessment of means and client's details sections must be fully completed, and signed by the client, normally in the presence of someone from your organisation (although there are exceptions to this), before you start doing any legal work.[11] Under the Standard Civil Contract 2024, up to 50 per cent of controlled work matter starts may be provided to clients you do not meet in your office.[12] You may claim for the work done before the form is signed (eg by telephone, video or email) as long as the client signs and returns the form to you and provides acceptable evidence of means.[13]

How many Legal Help forms?

7.23 You can have more than one Legal Help matter open at the same time, but only if they relate to entirely separate family disputes where any proceedings would be issued and heard separately.[14] The LAA gives the example where there is a public law Legal Help matter in relation to concerns raised by the local authority and also a private law matter in relation to a divorce.[15]

Funding

7.24 Legal Help – level 1 is paid as a standard fee.[16] Cases that exceed three times the fixed fee when calculated at hourly rates can be claimed in full (see chapter 15 for more information about claiming escape cases).

---

11 Standard Civil Contract 2024 Specification para 3.9 (available at: www.gov.uk/government/publications/standard-civil-contract-2024).
12 Standard Civil Contract 2024 Specification para 3.17.
13 Standard Civil Contract 2024 Specification para 3.18 onwards.
14 Standard Civil Contract 2024 Specification para 3.30.
15 *Costs Assessment Guidance*, v10, December 2023, Appendix 1 'Family Fee Scheme Guidance (excluding advocacy)' para 2.5.
16 Current fees and hourly rates are found in Civil Legal Aid (Remuneration) Regulations 2013 Sch 1.

Family Help (Lower) – level 2

Scope

7.25 This level of funding covers advice and other work for parents or those with parental responsibility. It is intended that the focus of work at this level is on negotiation with the local authority to resolve disputes under the President's Public Law Outline. Therefore, it covers cases where the local authority has issued a notice of its intention to issue proceedings but no proceedings have yet been issued.

7.26 The letter before proceedings may suggest that a meeting is held between the client and the local authority to discuss the concerns raised in the letter and level 2 will cover attending this meeting (sometimes called a 'family meeting') with the client.

Extract from the Standard Civil Contract Specification 2024

7.27 The Standard Civil Contract 2024 Specification para 7.35 states:

> **Payment for Family Help (Lower)**
>
> 7.35 A determination that a Client qualifies for Family Help (Lower) may only be made where all criteria at Regulation 35 of the Merits Regulations are satisfied. In addition, in Public Law Work remuneration for Family Help (Lower) may only be claimed where the following conditions are satisfied:
> (a) the Local Authority has given written notice of potential s31 Care Proceedings in accordance with statutory guidance on court orders and pre-proceedings for local authorities, issued by the Department for Education or Welsh Assembly under the Local Authority and Social Services Act 1970 and regulations, but no proceedings have yet been issued (application for an Emergency Protection Order does not count as issue of proceedings for this purpose);
> (b) your Client is a Parent (as defined above) and 'Parent' for this purpose shall include either a mother or father of an unborn child in respect of whom proceedings are contemplated;
> (c) your Client requires advice and assistance with a view to avoiding the proceedings, or narrowing and resolving any issues with the local authority.

Merits test

7.28 Family Help (Lower) is not merits tested in public family law, as long as the requirements of Specification para 7.35 (reproduced above) are met.

Financial eligibility

7.29 Family Help (Lower) is not means tested in public family law.

Conducting a family public law case 209

Forms

7.30 There is a separate form for level 2 in public family law – the CW1PL.[17] It is designed to be used in relation to advice after the local authority has issued its notice of intention to issue proceedings (advice prior to this is covered under the CW1 Legal Help form). Key points are:
- it is not means tested;
- it has a box that allows you to record that the criteria for advice at level 2 were met; and
- the local authority's notice of intention to issue proceedings must be attached to it.

You tick the box at the top of page 2 of the Family Help (Lower) Public Law form, and attach a copy of the notice to show that the criteria are met.

Funding

7.31 Family Help (Lower) level 2 is paid as a standard fee. Whether you can claim it depends on the local authority issuing written notice of its intention to issue proceedings. This can be in an email, as long as the wording is unambiguous.

Exceptional cases

7.32 A case escapes the fixed fee in public law matters where the costs of all levels of advice provided at controlled work, calculated at hourly rates,[18] exceed three times the relevant fees. Therefore, where level 1 and level 2 advice has been provided, costs calculated at an hourly rate must exceed three times the level 1 and level 2 fees combined. If advice has only been provided at either level 1 or level 2, the exceptional limit will be three times the fees for that level of service.

Closing controlled work matters

7.33 For information about when you can or should close a case, see chapter 4.

---

17 Available at: www.gov.uk/government/publications/cw1-pl-family-help-lower-public-law#:~:text=Controlled%20work%20form%3A%20for%20when,child%20under%20section%2031%20proceedings.
18 Set out in Civil Legal Aid (Remuneration) Regulations 2013 Sch 1.

Certificates – public law cases

Scope

7.34 A representation certificate in family public law can only be granted when the local authority issues proceedings, and is therefore usually granted initially as an emergency certificate using delegated functions. It authorises the conduct of litigation and the provision of advocacy and representation.

Certificates

7.35 An application for funding in Special Children Act cases is granted automatically, without reference to means or merits. An application to extend the scope of the certificate to cover related proceedings (eg to make an application for a residence or contact order within the care proceedings, or to include representation in any other related proceedings which are being heard together) must be made, as the usual form of the certificate only covers proceedings under Children Act 1989 ss31, 43, 44 and 45, and applications from a child under s27.

7.36 Apart from 'related proceedings', certificates in this area are kept completely separate from all other work. Therefore, a separate application must always be made – an ordinary certificate cannot be amended to cover Special Children Act proceedings, and a Special Children Act certificate cannot be amended to cover anything else.

7.37 The application includes a question on whether separate representation is appropriate. Once funding has been granted, you have an ongoing duty to report any new information or changes of circumstance which might affect the terms of the certificate.[19]

Financial eligibility

7.38 Certificates in Special Children Act proceedings are not means tested. Certificates in other public law children cases are means tested, including interim care orders under Children Act 1989 s38.[20]

7.39 See chapter 2 for information about the means test.

---

19 Civil Legal Aid (Procedure) Regulations 2012 reg 40(1)(a).
20 Civil Legal Aid (Financial Resources and Payment for Services) Regulations 2013 reg 5.

Merits test

7.40 Certificates in Special Children Act proceedings are not merits tested.

7.41 Certificates in other public law children cases are subject to a limited merits test:[21]
- representation will be refused if:
  - alternative funding is available (eg in adoption, where the child is placed by the local authority that consents to the adoption, it would be reasonable to expect it to bear the costs of the application);
  - not necessary (eg because of the involvement of other parties or a professional guardian); or
  - it is unreasonable to provide representation, having regard to the importance of the case to the applicant; and
- if the applicant is making or supporting an appeal or application, the prospects of success of that appeal or application are:
  - marginal or better; or borderline.

CCMS and forms

7.42 As mentioned in chapter 4, the LAA introduced mandatory use of its online Client and Cost Management System (CCMS) for all new applications from April 2016. CCMS has replaced the paper forms as explained below but they may be used when CCMS is not available and the LAA authorises the alternative process.

7.43 See chapter 5 at para 5.90 for more information about:
- what to do if CCMS is not available; and
- claiming time spent on CCMS that exceeds time taken using a paper form (see also appendix C).

If you need to use a paper form, you use CIVAPP5[22] for Special Children Act proceedings and CIVAPP3[23] in other cases.

7.44 Apart from 'related proceedings', Special Children Act certificates are kept completely separate from all other work. Therefore, a separate application must always be made – an ordinary certificate cannot

---

21 Civil Legal Aid (Merits Criteria) Regulations 2013 reg 66.
22 Available at: https://assets.publishing.service.gov.uk/government/uploads/system/uploads/attachment_data/file/294555/legal-aid-civ-app-5.pdf.
23 Available at: www.gov.uk/government/publications/civ-app3-application-for-legal-aid-in-family-proceedings.

7.45 be amended to cover Special Children Act proceedings, and a Special Children Act certificate cannot be amended to cover anything else. See chapter 5 for more on CCMS.

Funding

7.46 Representation in respect of a child, parent or joined party in care and supervision proceedings (Children Act 1989 s31) and related proceedings[24] is covered by a standard fee scheme. The fees are based on the location of the solicitor's office and the nature and number of parties represented.

7.47 Fees refer to the LAA region where the fee earner was based during the case:[25]
- Wales;
- London, Brighton, Reading and Bristol – all claim the 'London and South' fee;
- Birmingham, Nottingham and Cambridge – all claim the 'Midlands' fee;
- Newcastle, Leeds, Liverpool and Manchester – all claim the 'North' fee.

The rates were reduced by 10 per cent for cases started on or after 22 April 2014. The fees shown in Civil Legal Aid (Remuneration) Regulations 2013 Sch 1 are the amended rates.

7.48 The standard fee scheme does not apply to other 'Special Children Act proceedings', ie under Children Act 1989 ss25–41 (when a child is brought before the court and wishes to be separately represented), s43 (a child assessment order), s44 (an emergency protection order) and s45 (extension or discharge of an emergency protection order).

7.49 It does not apply to other public law family proceedings, including appeals in Special Children Act cases, and proceedings under Parts 4 and 5 of the Children Act 1989, as well as adoption and High Court inherent jurisdiction cases.[26]

7.50 In Children Act 1989 s31 cases, funding under the Graduated Fee Scheme for Legal Representation certificates covers all stages up to the conclusion of the proceedings in the first instance (including representation on any interim appeal and/or advice on the merits of an appeal against a final order). Where Legal Representation is granted

---

24 Standard Civil Contract 2024 Specification para 7.46.
25 Standard Civil Contract 2024 Specification para 7.7 onwards.
26 Standard Civil Contract 2024 Specification paras 7.36 and 7.3.

to defend or bring an appeal against a final order, it is paid by way of hourly rates.[27]

7.51 Other public law family certificated cases are funded under hourly rates; but see below concerning Very High Cost Cases and the CCFS.

Advocacy under standard fees

7.52 The standard fees do not include advocacy. Where advocacy is provided, whether by counsel or a solicitor advocate, the claim is made under the Family Advocacy Scheme (FAS) (see chapter 19 for more information).

7.53 The LAA includes the following activities under the definition of advocacy for the purposes of the FAS preparation for advocacy:
- appearances as advocate before the court;
- travel to and from court and waiting time; and
- attendances by the advocate at court, including attendance at advocates meetings.

7.54 If you are a solicitor carrying out advocacy, it is helpful to keep a separate file for this aspect of the case as it helps you keep track of the advocacy fees to be charged on top of the applicable standard fee for other work. It also helps you identify whether you need to apply for an increase in the financial limitation as this includes all profit costs as well as disbursements, advocacy fees and VAT.

Applying for a certificate – urgent cases

7.55 Unless otherwise notified, under Standard Civil Contract Specification 2024 para 7.38 you have a delegated function to grant Legal Representation in Special Children Act cases. If authorised to use the alternative application process to CCMS, you use the CIVAPP5 form and complete the delegated functions section on page 6 of that form, stating the date on which the delegated function was exercised and confirming that the criterion as to separate representation is met.

7.56 See chapter 4 for more information about delegated functions, and also about:
- amendments to certificates;
- refusals and appeals;
- use of counsel and amendments for a KC;
- changes to prospects of success or cost–benefit;
- disbursements and prior authority;

27 Standard Civil Contract 2024 Specification para 7.49.

- contributions;
- high cost cases;
- ending a case;
- discharge of certificate; and
- revocation of certificate.

Very High Cost Cases

7.57 A Very High Cost Case (VHCC) is a case where total costs and disbursements are expected to be over £25,000 (not including VAT). Most of these cases are dealt with under a single case contract under the CCFS. From 3 June 2019, high cost care cases under the CCFS have an immediate limit of £32,500. Once you become aware that the costs are likely to exceed £25,000, you must contact the LAA by general case enquiry informing the LAA of this. The LAA will set up a case plan task on CCMS to which the provider must upload a signed contract and counsel acceptance form/s (if an external advocate is being used) and separately apply to amend the cost limitation to £32,500. A CCFS form (case plan) will not be required until the end of the case unless the costs will exceed the increased limit.

Care Case Fee Scheme

7.58 The LAA introduced the CCFS from 1 October 2015 (it was previously known as the 'Events Model'). It covers all single counsel care cases. Payment is made by reference to expected 'events' during the lifetime of the case. Examples of 'events' include the number of hearings, prehearing reviews and counsel conferences. Costs are calculated by totalling up these 'events'.

7.59 Some private law and other child cases, which follow a similar fact-finding route and have main hearings over 10 days, may qualify for the CCFS scheme (on request and when agreed by the LAA).

KC and two-counsel cases

7.60 From 12 July 2019, once you are granted prior authority for a KC/two-counsel, you should be asked to upload a signed High Costs Contract and Counsel Acceptance Forms (where external counsel are used). If you accept, the case will be costed using CCFS. At the same time, you should submit a cost amendment for £60,000 where the authority covers a fact-finding hearing or a composite hearing. The

Exceptions to the CCFS

7.61 If you can show you would be paid at least 30 per cent more by claiming hourly rates with a fully costed case plan rather than using the CCFS model, it can be an exception to the CCFS scheme. This needs to be fully justified with reasons.

7.62 The LAA has issued guidance on high cost Family cases: www.gov.uk/guidance/civil-high-cost-cases-family. See chapter 15 for more information about the CCFS and VHCCs.

CHAPTER 8
Family mediation

Edited by Vicky Ling

8.1	Introduction
	Scope of the scheme
8.9	**Contract**
8.11	**Financial eligibility**
8.15	The voucher scheme
8.18	**Merits test**
8.19	**Forms**
8.21	**Funding**

Key resources

Scope
- Legal Aid, Sentencing and Punishment of Offenders Act 2012 – Schedule 1 Part 1
- Lord Chancellor's Guidance under section 4 of the Legal Aid, Sentencing and Punishment of Offenders Act 2012, May 2023

Fees
- Civil Legal Aid (Remuneration) Regulations 2013 Sch 1

Regulations
- Civil Legal Aid (Merits Criteria) Regulations 2013
- Civil Legal Aid (Financial Resources and Payment for Services) Regulations 2013

Contract
- Standard Civil Contract 2024 Family Mediation Specification section 18.

Guidance
- Family Mediation Guidance Manual, v6, Legal Aid Agency, September 2024

Key points to note
- Do not forget the mediation voucher scheme. Originally set up during the pandemic to relieve pressures on the Family Court, it is not means tested.[1] A financial contribution will be provided of up to £500 towards the costs of mediation for the following issues:
  – a dispute/application regarding a child; and
  – a dispute/application regarding family financial matters where you are also involved in a dispute/application relating to a child.
- If the applicant is eligible for legal aid, legal aid will cover the cost of the Mediation Information and Assessment Meeting, see below.

---

1 See: www.gov.uk/guidance/family-mediation-voucher-scheme#can-i-get-a-voucher-if-i-am-eligible-for-legal-aid.

Introduction

8.1 This chapter deals with mediation – but mainly from the point of view of a lawyer, rather than a mediator or client. There is increased emphasis on resolving disputes through mediation rather than litigation, regardless of the way that cases are funded.

8.2 Used well, and complemented by legal advice, mediation helps clients find a solution to their problems in a more positive way. From April 2013, when the Legal Aid, Sentencing and Punishment of Offenders Act 2012 (LASPO) took effect, mediation and Help with Family Mediation (see chapter 6 at para 6.68) are the only legal aid services available to clients seeking to resolve private family disputes, unless the client is the victim of domestic abuse, or likely to be so, or there is evidence of child protection concerns (see chapter 6).

8.3 Family Mediation falls under the 2024 Standard Civil Contract and there is a specific Family Mediation Specification.[2]

Scope of the scheme

8.4 There are two types of mediation that can be funded by the Legal Aid Agency (LAA):

1) **family mediation**, where the LAA funds the mediator directly; and
2) **non-family mediation**, which can be funded as a disbursement under both Legal Help and representation certificates.[3]

8.5 LASPO Sch 1 Part 1 para 14 provides that mediation is only available for a 'family dispute', which is a matter arising out of a family relationship as defined in the Act. LAA guidance in its *Family Mediation Guidance Manual*[4] states that if there are no significant legal family issues in dispute and the role of the mediation is simply to improve communication and the relationship between the parties, then it does not fall within the scope of public funding:

---

2 See: www.gov.uk/government/publications/standard-civil-contract-2024 Section 18.
3 *Costs Assessment Guidance: for use with the 2024 Standard Civil Contracts*, LAA, para 3.6, available at: www.gov.uk/guidance/funding-and-costs-assessment-for-civil-and-crime-matters.
4 *Family Mediation Guidance Manual*, v5, LAA, September 2018, para 3.5 (available at: www.gov.uk/guidance/legal-aid-family-mediation).

As part of considering whether mediation is suitable for the dispute, the parties and all the circumstances, the mediator must consider whether the costs of mediation are themselves justified.[5]

8.6 Disputes that the LAA considers to be minor will not pass the merits test. The LAA gives the following list of examples where issues would be capable of giving rise to court proceedings and so family mediation would be appropriate:

- contact arrangements;
- residence and parental responsibility;
- child maintenance;
- property; and
- finance – savings, debts and pensions.[6]

8.7 The scheme includes the following:

- Mediation Information and Assessment Meetings (MIAMs) (which may be attended by one or both parties); and
- mediation:
  - all issues mediation;
  - child mediation; and
  - property and financial mediation.

8.8 The Children and Families Act 2014 was implemented on 22 April 2014. The Act makes it compulsory for people seeking to make applications in certain family proceedings to attend a MIAM before making an application unless they are exempt. The legal requirement is for the applicant to attend, and respondents are expected to do so.

Contract

8.9 Mediation is subject to the 2024 Standard Civil Contract and has its own specification.[7]

8.10 There is a detailed guidance document: *Family Mediation Guidance Manual*.[8]

---

5 *Family Mediation Guidance Manual* para 3.4.
6 *Family Mediation Guidance Manual* para 3.3.
7 See: www.gov.uk/government/publications/standard-civil-contract-2024 section 18.
8 *Family Mediation Guidance Manual*, v6, LAA, September 2024, available at: www.gov.uk/guidance/legal-aid-family-mediation.

Financial eligibility

8.11 In non-family mediation, the means test is carried out as usual for the type of funding – Legal Help or a representation certificate (see chapter 2).

8.12 In family mediation, the mediator carries out the eligibility test. If one of the parties qualifies for legal aid, then the cost of the MIAM will be met by the LAA.

8.13 Family mediation is means tested, but from 3 November 2014, non-financially eligible parties were exempted from the financial means test in respect of the first mediation session where the other party is financially eligible for legal aid.[9] The LAA will pay half a single session fee for the non-eligible party.

8.14 The idea is that the free 'taster' session will encourage the non-financially eligible party to fund their own mediation from then on.

The voucher scheme

8.15 In 2021, in response to Covid-19, to support recovery in the Family Court and to encourage more people to consider mediation as a means of resolving their disputes, where appropriate, the government set up a voucher scheme. This was described as a time-limited scheme when it was introduced, but it remains in operation at the time of writing. For more information see: www.gov.uk/guidance/family-mediation-voucher-scheme.

8.16 A financial contribution will be provided of up to £500 towards the costs of mediation for the following issues:

- a dispute/application regarding a child; and
- a dispute/application regarding family financial matters where you are also involved in a dispute/application relating to a child.

Vouchers are not available for finance issues alone.

8.17 Vouchers are claimed by the mediator. Only one £500 voucher is available per family/case.

Merits test

8.18 Mediation beyond the MIAM will only be provided where the mediator is satisfied that mediation is suitable in all the circumstances

---

9 Civil Legal Aid (Financial Resources and Payment for Services) Regulations 2013 reg 5(1)(gb).

of the case.[10] See the LAA's *Family Mediation Guidance Manual* (September 2024) for more information on how the LAA expects mediators to apply the test.

Forms

8.19 Family mediation is controlled work. The application form is the CW5.[11]

8.20 There are no forms for non-family mediation as this is claimed as a disbursement.

Funding

8.21 Where the parties are willing and the issues are suitable, the mediation should be able to deal with all the issues arising, including explanation of the law (but not advice), and disclosure.

8.22 From the client's point of view, family mediation is advantageous, as it is exempt from the statutory charge.

8.23 Robert Clerke, solicitor and mediator, has explained the stages of mediation in a typical family case:[12]

- setting the agenda/identification of the issues;
- disclosure;
- identification and exploration of options;
- impasse, and strategies to break through it;
- reality testing; and
- recording the outcome – hopefully a memorandum of understanding (MOU) and, where appropriate, an open financial statement (OFS).

8.24 A lawyer is needed to advise on the law and draw up the consent order and statement of information for the court: see 'Help with family mediation', chapter 6 at para 6.68.

---

10 Civil Legal Aid (Merits Criteria) Regulations 2013 reg 37.
11 Available at: www.gov.uk/government/publications/cw5-financial-eligibility-form-for-clients-wanting-family-mediation.
12 *Carter Survival Handbook*, Quay Books, 2008, chapter 5.

CHAPTER 9

Conducting immigration and asylum cases

Edited by Hilton von Herbert

9.1	Introduction
9.3	What immigration work is in scope of legal aid?
9.3	Overview
9.5	Separated children: immigration and citizenship matters
9.6	Immigration-related detention and bail
9.10	Victims of domestic violence: applications for indefinite leave to remain and residence cards
9.16	Asylum
9.20	Victims of human trafficking, modern slavery, servitude or forced labour: applications for leave to enter or remain
9.25	National Referral Mechanism advice
9.31	Group 2 Refugee decisions (the Differentiation Policy)
9.35	Terrorism Prevention and Investigation Measures
9.36	Claims for damages arising from immigration-related detention and bail
9.37	Special Immigration Appeals Commission
9.38	Exceptional case funding
9.42	Controlled Legal Representation and associated Legal Help
9.45	Immigration appeals and bail hearings before the First-tier Tribunal and Upper Tribunal
9.49	Judicial review

continued

9.57	**Definition of an immigration or an asylum matter**
9.59	**Who can carry out the work?**
9.59	Individual caseworkers
9.67	Organisations with exclusive immigration removal centre contracts
9.69	Clients detained otherwise than in an immigration removal centre
9.70	Scope
9.71	**Structure of immigration work**
9.76	Fee types
9.82	Matter starts and separate matters
9.88	Granting Legal Help
9.92	Granting Controlled Legal Representation
9.97	Refusing and withdrawing CLR
9.100	Change of supplier
9.102	**Conducting the case**
9.102	Overview
9.105	Attendance at interviews
9.108	Travel to detained clients
9.109	Bail
9.112	Attendance at hearings
9.116	Additional payments for online procedure advocacy services
9.117	Post-appeal work
9.120	Appeals to the Upper Tribunal
9.123	Higher Courts litigation
9.125	**Managing costs**
9.131	**Licensed work**

Key resources

Statutes

- Immigration Act 1971
- Nationality, Immigration and Asylum Act 2002
- UK Borders Act 2007
- Legal Aid, Sentencing and Punishment of Offenders Act 2012 – Schedule 1 Part 1
- Modern Slavery Act 2015
- Nationality and Borders Act 2022
- Illegal Migration Act 2023

Statutory instruments

- Civil Legal Aid (Procedure) Regulations 2012
- Civil Legal Aid (Immigration Interviews) (Exceptions) Regulations 2012
- Civil Legal Aid (Statutory Charge) Regulations 2013
- Civil Legal Aid (Remuneration) Regulations 2013
- Civil Legal Aid (Costs) Regulations 2013
- Civil Legal Aid (Financial Resources and Payment for Services) Regulations 2013
- Civil Legal Aid (Merits Criteria) Regulations 2013
- Civil Legal Aid (Merits Criteria) (Amendment) (No 3) Regulations 2013
- Civil Legal Aid (Procedure, Remuneration and Statutory Charge) (Amendment) Regulations 2018
- Civil Legal Aid (Procedure) (Amendment) Regulations 2020

EU Directives

- Council Directive 2001/55/EC of 20 July 2001
- Council Directive 2004/83/EC of 29 April 2004
- Council Directive 2005/85/EC of 1 December 2005

Costs and fees

- Costs Assessment Guidance: for use with the 2018 Standard Civil Contracts
- Escape Case Electronic Handbook

- Civil Legal Aid (Financial Resources and Payment for Services) Regulations 2013
- Civil Legal Aid (Costs) Regulations 2013
- Civil Legal Aid (Remuneration) Regulations 2013

Contracts

- 2024 Standard Civil Contract Standard
- 2024 Standard Civil Contract Specification
- 2024 Standard Civil Contract – Specification (General Provisions)
- 2024 Standard Civil Contract Category Definitions
- 2024 Standard Civil Contract Specification, Category Specific Rules: Immigration & Asylum

Lord Chancellor's Guidance

- Lord Chancellor's Exceptional Funding Guidance (non-inquests)
- Lord Chancellor's Guidance under section 4 of the Legal Aid, Sentencing and Punishment of Offenders Act 2012, May 2023
- Lord Chancellor's Guidance on Determining Financial Eligibility for Controlled Work & Family Mediation, April 2021

Miscellaneous

- Home Office Modern Slavery Statutory Guidance for England and Wales
- Legal Aid Agency's Quick Guide Key Card: https://legalaidlearning.justice.gov.uk/immigration-and-asylum-key-cards

Key points to note

- **Detained Duty Advice Scheme Surgeries** (DDAS) – You can now legitimately claim for DDAS work that has been carried out remotely.
- **Destitution Domestic Violence Concession** (DDVC) has been renamed – Migrant Victims of Domestic Abuse Concession (MVDAC) and brought within scope.
- **National Referral Mechanism (NRM) 'add-on' services** – You may provide and claim 'add-on' or 'bolt-on' services in relation to potential referrals into the NRM where (a) you are advising a client under a matter start in circumstances where add-on services may be provided under the Legal Aid Sentencing and

Punishment of Offenders Act 2012, and (b) you recognise indicators of the client being a potential victim of modern slavery. This will be claimed as a bolt-on fee of £150 to an existing legal help claim (Standard Civil Contract Specification Immigration and Asylum para 8.56). But note: the matter to which the add-on fee is applied can have been opened at any time. However, the NRM advice that gives rise to the add-on fee can only have been given on or after 1 April 2023. Also note that identifying trafficking indicators alone or ongoing advice through the NRM process are not in scope.
- **Non-means tested advice after Priority Removal Notice** (PRN) – from 1 April 2023 you are able to claim up to seven hours of non-means tested advice for a client after they receive a PRN from the Home Office. If you decide that the client has a substantive matter, you should conclude the PRN matter and open a new matter to conduct the follow-on work, which is defined as any substantive matter in scope (or out of scope where exceptional case funding is granted) identified as a result of the initial PRN advice given.
- **Controlled Legal Representation** (CLR) – from 1 April 2023 the escape fee threshold has been reduced from three times the standard fee to two times the standard fee for any CLR matter with a grant date on or after 1 April 2023. Also from that date, all newly opened CLR cases subject to the Standard Fee Scheme will use either 2(d) or 2(e) fee rates: 2(d) where there is no substantive hearing or 2(e) where there has been a substantive hearing.

Introduction

9.1 This chapter deals with work funded under the immigration and asylum category of law. You should read it in conjunction with chapters 2, 3 and 4 of this Handbook. Chapter 2 deals with general rules about taking on civil cases and applies to work in immigration and asylum as it does to all other work; chapter 3 deals with exceptional cases; and chapter 4 deals with the rules that apply to the conduct of all civil cases. The immigration and asylum-specific rules in this chapter usually build on, rather than replace, the general rules; where they do replace the general rules in chapters 2 and 4, we will say so.

9.2 See appendix C for a summary of the Legal Aid Agency's (LAA's) Costs Assessment Guidance,[1] in respect of the most common queries raised by caseworkers.

What immigration work is in scope of legal aid?

Overview

9.3 The Standard Civil Contract 2024 Category Definitions[2] paras 39–41 define asylum and immigration work as work covered by Legal Aid, Sentencing and Punishment of Offenders Act 2012 (LASPO) Sch 1 Part 1:

> 39. Legal Help on matters and all proceedings in relation to:
> (a) Immigration-related detention powers referred to in paragraph 25(1) of Part 1 of Schedule 1 to the Act;
> (b) Conditions of immigration bail under provisions referred to in paragraph 26(1) or 27(1) of Part 1 of Schedule 1 to the Act;
> (c) Conditions imposed on an individual under the provisions referred to in paragraph 27A(1) of Part 1 of Schedule 1 to the Act;
> (d) An application for indefinite leave by a victim of domestic violence (as described in paragraph 28 of Part 1 of Schedule 1 to the Act);
> (e) A residence card application by a victim of domestic violence (as described in paragraph 29 of Part 1 of Schedule 1 to the Act);
> (f) Rights to enter and to remain in the United Kingdom under the provisions referred to in paragraph 30(1) of Part 1 of Schedule 1 to the Act;
> (g) An application by a victim of human trafficking for leave to enter or remain in the United Kingdom (as described in subparagraph 32(1) of Part 1 of Schedule 1 to the Act);
> (h) A Terrorism Prevention and Investigation Measure notice (as described in paragraph 19 or paragraph 45 of Part 1 of Schedule 1 to the Act: August 2024
> (i) An application by a victim of slavery, servitude or forced or compulsory labour for leave to enter or remain in the United Kingdom (as described in subparagraph 32A(1) of Part 1 of Schedule 1 to the Act);

---

1 *Costs Assessment Guidance: for use with the 2018 Standard Civil Contracts*, v10 December 2023, available at: www.gov.uk/guidance/funding-and-costs-assessment-for-civil-and-crime-matters.
2 See appendix B. Available at: www.gov.uk/government/publications/standard-civil-contract-2018.

Conducting immigration and asylum cases 229

(j) A claim for damages arising from any of the powers listed in (a)–(c) of this paragraph 39 (as described in paragraphs 3, 21, 22, of 39) of Part 1 of Schedule 1 to the Act);
(k) All new services introduced by the Nationality and Borders Act 2022; and
(l) All new services introduced by the Illegal Migration Act 2023.

Also any LASPO s10 exceptional funding granted where the primary problem or issue is an immigration or asylum matter.

9.4 The descriptions within the Category Definitions should be read in conjunction with the exclusions set out in LASPO Sch 1 Part 2. The paragraphs in Part 2 exclude from the services (detailed below) those that are provided, among others, in relation to:

- personal injury or death;
- claims in tort in respect of negligence;
- claims in tort in respect of assault, battery or false imprisonment;
- claims in tort in respect of trespass to goods or to land;
- damage to property;
- defamation or malicious falsehood;
- claims in tort in respect of breach of statutory duty;
- claims for damages in respect of a breach of rights under the European Convention on Human Rights (ECHR) by a public authority (if relying on Human Rights Act (HRA) 1998 s7); and
- compensation under the Criminal Injuries Compensation Scheme.

Separated children: immigration and citizenship matters

9.5 Separated migrant children became eligible for legal aid to help with citizenship and non-asylum immigration applications and appeals from 25 October 2019. The Legal Aid, Sentencing and Punishment of Offenders Act 2012 (Legal Aid for Separated Children) (Miscellaneous Amendments) Order 2019 brings non-asylum immigration and citizenship matters into scope of legal aid for under 18-year-olds who are not in the care of a parent, guardian or legal authority. The relevant amendment is inserted in LASPO Sch 1 Part 1 para 31A.

Immigration-related detention and bail

9.6 Legal aid will be available on matters and all proceedings in relation to immigration-related detention and bail.[3] These provisions refer to

3 LASPO Sch 1 Part 1 paras 25(1), 26(1) and 27(1).

detention or control of persons: under the authority of an immigration officer; liable to deportation;[4] awaiting a decision of the secretary of state;[5] having served a period of imprisonment;[6] and granted or refused immigration bail.[7]

9.7 You can provide advice and assistance to an individual solely in relation to detention under immigration powers, such as applications for bail (and conditions on bail). You will not be able to claim for any non-detention work as part of the case unless this is itself in scope of immigration or asylum legal aid.

9.8 You can provide advice and assistance on bail conditions to a person who is liable to or has been released from detention, or to a person who has had conditions imposed on bail such as restriction to reside at a fixed address, reporting and employment.

9.9 In most cases, only the detention issue is in scope, not the substantive immigration case. For example, a person subject to deportation following imprisonment is entitled to legal aid in respect of their detention or bail conditions, but not in respect of deportation advice and proceedings themselves. You will need to be careful on your file to justify that work done is genuinely in relation to the in scope aspects, such as where it is necessary to consider the immigration history or offences leading to the deportation in order to assess bail or conditions.

Victims of domestic violence: applications for indefinite leave to remain and residence cards

9.10 Legal aid will be available on matters and all proceedings in relation to applications by migrant victims of domestic violence for indefinite leave to remain (ILR) and for a residence card under the Immigration (European Economic Area) Regulations 2016.[8] These provisions both rely on the following definition of domestic violence:

> 'domestic violence' means any incident, or pattern of incidents, of controlling, coercive or threatening behaviour, violence or abuse (whether psychological, physical, sexual, financial or emotional) between individuals who are associated with each other (within the meaning of section 62 of the Family Law Act 1996) . . .[9]

---

4 Immigration Act 1971 Sch 3.
5 Nationality, Immigration and Asylum Act 2002 s62.
6 UK Borders Act 2007 s36.
7 Immigration Act 1971 Sch 3 para 2(5).
8 LASPO Sch 1 Part 1 paras 28 and 29, respectively.
9 LASPO Sch 1 Part 1 paras 28(5) and 29(4).

Conducting immigration and asylum cases 231

9.11 You can provide advice and assistance to a victim of domestic violence in an application for ILR if the person has been granted leave to remain as a spouse or partner of a British citizen or person present and settled in the UK (probationary leave) and the relationship has broken down permanently due to domestic violence. This will include a person who has been granted leave to enter or remain outside the Immigration Rules as a partner or spouse of a British citizen or person present and settled in the UK (eg victims with leave to enter outside the Immigration Rules or with discretionary leave to remain). This is so long as the advice and assistance is solely in relation to an application for ILR under the domestic violence provisions.

9.12 The time you spent advising and assisting a victim with an application under the three-month Destitution Domestic Violence Concession (DDVC) can also be claimed as part of the substantive ILR application.

9.13 You can provide advice and assistance in relation to an application for a residence card to a person who has ceased to be a family member on the termination of a marriage/partnership (ie only if divorced), who was a victim of domestic violence or was a family member of the victim and the violence took place during the time that the marriage was subsisting.

9.14 Other than the above, the fact that the applicant is a victim of domestic violence does not generally entitle them to legal aid for immigration advice (eg those not on probationary leave, family members not divorced from their European Economic Area (EEA) spouse or those in durable relationships who were never married to EEA nationals in the first place).

9.15 Attendance at interviews conducted on behalf of the secretary of state with a view to reaching a decision on applications for ILR and for a residence card under the Immigration (European Economic Area) Regulations 2016, for victims of domestic violence, are not within scope.[10]

Asylum

9.16 Legal aid will be available on matters and all proceedings in relation to rights to enter and to remain in the UK arising from:[11]

1) the UN Convention relating to the Status of Refugees 1951 and the Protocol to that Convention 1967;

10 LASPO Sch 1 Part 1 paras 28(3) and 29(3).
11 LASPO Sch 1 Part 1 para 30(1).

2) ECHR Articles 2 and 3 (ie right to life and prohibition of torture and inhuman or degrading treatment or punishment, respectively);
3) the Temporary Protection Directive;[12]
4) the Qualification Directive.[13]

9.17 The above will include:
1) Controlled Work done on an asylum issue related to Special Immigration Appeals Commission (SIAC) proceedings;[14]
2) an application for ILR under the Refugee Settlement Protection policy.

9.18 Legal aid for advice and assistance on family reunion for refugees is not generally in scope. However, the Court of Appeal has said that where a claimant's family reunion case was particularly complex such that failure to provide exceptional funding would amount to a breach of ECHR Article 8 (right to respect for one's private and family life, home and correspondence), exceptional case funding (ECF) would be appropriate.[15] See chapter 3 for applying for ECF.

9.19 Attendance at interviews conducted on behalf of the secretary of state with a view to reaching a decision on a claim in relation to the rights mentioned in para 9.16 above is not within scope, except where regulations provide otherwise.[16]

---

12 Council Directive 2001/55/EC of 20 July 2001 on minimum standards for giving temporary protection in the event of a mass influx of displaced persons and on measures promoting a balance of efforts between member states in receiving such persons and bearing the consequences thereof.
13 Council Directive 2004/83/EC of 29 April 2004 on minimum standards for the qualification and status of third country nationals or stateless persons as refugees or as persons who otherwise need international protection and the content of the protection granted.
14 Standard Civil Contract 2024 Specification para 8.7(b).
15 *R (Gudanaviciene and others) v Director of Legal Aid Casework and Lord Chancellor* [2014] EWCA Civ 1622.
16 LASPO Sch 1 Part 1 para 30(3). The Civil Legal Aid (Immigration Interviews) (Exceptions) Regulations 2012 provide for attendance at asylum screening interviews and asylum interviews where the person is a child, or at an asylum interview where the person is either being detained at a specified immigration removal centre (IRC) or lacks mental capacity. See paras 9.105–9.107 (attendance at interviews) below.

Victims of human trafficking, modern slavery, servitude or forced labour: applications for leave to enter or remain

9.20 Legal aid will be available on matters and all proceedings in relation to applications for leave to enter or remain in the UK by: (a) victims of human trafficking and (b) victims of slavery, servitude or forced or compulsory labour.[17] These categories reflect different provisions within LASPO. However, the Home Office Modern Slavery Statutory Guidance uses the term 'modern slavery' to refer to human trafficking, as well as slavery, servitude and forced or compulsory labour.[18]

9.21 You can provide advice and assistance in relation to applications for leave to enter or remain by a victim of modern slavery (ie victim of trafficking and/or victim of slavery, servitude, or forced or compulsory labour). However, in order for you to assist, there must either be a conclusive determination that the person is a victim of modern slavery, or there must have been a determination that there are 'reasonable grounds' to believe that the person is a potential victim of modern slavery and there has not been a negative conclusive grounds determination.[19] These conditions reflect the two decisions that need to be made by the Single Competent Authority (SCA) once someone has been identified as a potential victim and referred to the National Referral Mechanism (NRM).[20] The NRM is the framework by which the UK implements relevant obligations under the 2005 Council of Europe Convention on Action against Trafficking in Human Beings.

9.22 Once a potential victim of modern slavery has been identified by the specified statutory authorities or non-governmental organisations and referred to the NRM, the SCA will make a 'reasonable grounds decision'. If there is a positive 'reasonable grounds decision' the SCA should go on to make a 'conclusive grounds decision'. After a positive 'reasonable grounds decision' you can provide advice and assistance on applications for leave to enter or remain.

---

17 LASPO Sch1 Part 1 paras 32(1) and 32A(1), respectively.
18 *Modern Slavery: Statutory Guidance for England and Wales (under s49 of the Modern Slavery Act 2015) and Non-Statutory Guidance for Scotland and Northern Ireland*, v2.3, Home Office, November 2021, paras 15.106, 15.110 and 15.113 (available at: www.gov.uk/government/publications/modern-slavery-how-to-identify-and-support-victims).
19 LASPO Sch 1 Part 1 paras 32(1)(a) and (b) and 32A(1)(a) and (b).
20 LASPO Sch 1 Part 1 paras 32(6)–(8) and 32A(6), (7) and (10). See also *Victims of modern slavery – Competent Authority guidance*, v7.0, Home Office, April 2019, p14.

9.23 There is no time restriction on the availability of funding to assist a person who has been determined a victim of modern slavery by the competent authority under controlled work. However, in licensed work, there is a time restriction of 12 months from the date of the 'conclusive grounds' determination that the person is a victim of trafficking or before the end of any leave outside the rules granted to the victim.[21]

9.24 Where a client has been determined a victim of modern slavery and is also making an asylum claim, you will need to treat the asylum work, and any 'associated' or 'additional' application for leave to remain on human rights grounds, as one asylum matter start under the Immigration specification.

National Referral Mechanism advice

9.25 From 1 April 2023 procedural advice work regarding the NRM is in scope. This includes advice regarding how a client can be referred into the NRM, how the NRM operates and how entry into the NRM can impact their asylum claim.[22]

9.26 This work is claimed as an add-on/bolt-on fee[23] to an existing matter and is only claimable for advice provided before the client entered the NRM.

9.27 Note that merely identifying indicators of trafficking and ongoing advice through the NRM process are not in scope.[24]

Priority Removal Notices

9.28 PRN work is now in scope from 1 April 2023 where a client receives a PRN from the Home Office. You may claim up to seven hours of non-means tested work.[25] This limit cannot be extended. If the limit is reached, consider carrying out any further work under alternative public funding.[26] A copy of the PRN must be retained on file.

9.29 Advice in relation to a PRN matter is a separate matter to any associated immigration or asylum matter. A CW1 form must be completed but you need not complete the means testing sections.[27] The work is claimed at hourly rates for the matter.[28]

---

21 Civil Legal Aid (Procedure) (Amendment) Regulations 2020 reg 31(8).
22 Standard Civil Contract 2024 Specification Immigration and Asylum para 8.56
23 Standard Civil Contract 2024 Specification Immigration and Asylum para 8.57
24 Standard Civil Contract 2024 Specification Immigration and Asylum para 8.58.
25 Standard Civil Contract 2024 Specification Immigration and Asylum para 8.61.
26 Standard Civil Contract 2024 Specification Immigration and Asylum para 8.62.
27 Standard Civil Contract 2024 Specification Immigration and Asylum para 8.60.
28 Standard Civil Contract 2024 Specification Immigration and Asylum para 8.63.

9.30 This work is in scope only to the point where it is determined that the client has a substantive matter. After that, the PRN advice matter should be closed and a new matter opened to deal with the follow-on substantive matter work.

Group 2 Refugee decisions (the Differentiation Policy)

9.31 The Nationality and Borders Act (NABA) 2022 introduced two groups of refugees (Group 1 and Group 2). Following asylum claims made on or after 28 June 2022, Group 1 are those who came to the UK directly without going through a safe third country (see NABA 2022 s12(2) and (3)). Group 2 are those who came here via a third country. If asylum/refugee status is granted, Group 1 would be granted five years' leave to remain while Group 2 claimants would be granted 30 months' (known as temporary refugee permission).

9.32 Advice work to rebut the Group 2 decision is in scope from 1 July 2022. This will be opened as a separate matter start[29] from the asylum matter, paid at hourly rates. You are allowed to run the two matters concurrently.

9.33 Note that on 17 July 2023 the Home Office suspended the Differentiation Policy. Asylum applicants will no longer be grouped into two different categories. All claimants will be given the rights enjoyed by Group 1 applicants. This change was applied retrospectively and the Home Office notified those with Group 2 decisions by letter advising them of their Group 1 status.

9.34 You must close the file and bill it, once the client receives notification of their Group 1 status.

Terrorism Prevention and Investigation Measures

9.35 Legal aid will be available on matters and all proceedings in relation to a Terrorism Prevention and Investigation Measure (TPIM) notice (see para 9.76(k) below) relating to the client that is being advised.[30]

---

29 Standard Civil Contract 2024 Specification Immigration and Asylum para 8.27.
30 LASPO Sch 1 Part 1 para 45(1). For authority of the secretary of state to impose TPIM notices, see Terrorism Prevention and Investigation Measures Act 2011 s2.

Claims for damages arising from immigration-related detention and bail

9.36 Legal aid will be available on matters and all proceedings in relation to a claim for damages arising from the powers related to immigration detention and bail, as referred to in paras 9.6–9.9 above.[31] In particular, this relates to civil legal services provided in relation to:
1) abuse of an individual that took place at a time when the individual was a child or vulnerable adult;[32]
2) abuse by a public authority of its position or powers;[33]
3) in respect of an act or omission by a public authority that involves a significant breach of ECHR rights by the authority;[34] and
4) a sexual offence, but only where the services are provided to the victim of the offence, or the victim of the offence has died and the services are provided to the victim's personal representative.[35]

Special Immigration Appeals Commission

9.37 Legal aid will be available for all proceedings before the SIAC. This will normally involve controlled work under Legal Help for any initial advice and licensed work for any preparation and representation on an SIAC appeal.[36]

Exceptional case funding

9.38 An ECF application to fund work that is not in scope may be made to the LAA under LASPO s10, but only where you can demonstrate that the following test is met:

> (3) ...
>   (a) that it is necessary to make the services available to the individual ... because failure to do so would be a breach of:
>   (i) the individual's Convention rights (within the meaning of the Human Rights Act 1998), or
>   (ii) any rights of the individual to the provision of legal services that are enforceable EU rights, or

---

31 LASPO Sch 1 Part 1 paras 25(1), 26(1) and 27(1).
32 LASPO Sch 1 Part 1 para 3(1).
33 LASPO Sch 1 Part 1 para 21(1).
34 LASPO Sch 1 Part 1 para 22(1).
35 LASPO Sch 1 Part 1 para 39(1).
36 LASPO Sch 1 Part 1 para 24(1); and Part 3 para 21.

9.39 In his original ECF guidance, the Lord Chancellor did not consider that immigration cases would come within the ambit of exceptional funding. However, in *R (Gudanaviciene) v Director of Legal Aid Casework*,[37] the Court of Appeal held that certain paragraphs of this guidance were incompatible with ECHR Article 6(1); and with Article 47 of the Charter of Fundamental Rights of the European Union; as well as, in immigration cases, incompatible with ECHR Article 8.

9.40 The court in *Gudanaviciene* also held that whether funding should be granted will depend on the facts of the case, including the importance and complexity of the issues and the person's ability to act on their own without legal assistance and any language difficulties. Since there is no appeal against an ECF determination, beyond a review by the Director, any challenge on a refusal of funding would be by way of judicial review.

9.41 Following *Gudanaviciene*, the Lord Chancellor issued new guidance which was amended to take account of the Court of Appeal judgment. In particular, the current guidance refers to the Court of Appeal's finding that 'Article 8 may give rise to a right to legal assistance in relation to immigration matters which engage the substantive right to respect for private and family life conferred by Article 8'.[38] In any event, before making any application for ECF you should carefully consider the judgment as well as the revised guidance (see chapter 3 for more on exceptional cases).

Controlled Legal Representation and associated Legal Help

9.42 From 1 April 2023 all CLR matters (appeals to the First-tier Tribunal) will be claimed under one of two new Standard Fee Scheme rates. These replaced the interim online appeals hourly rate.

9.43 The new Standard Fee claims are:

2(d) – where there was no substantive appeal hearing; and
2(e) – where there is a Substantive appeal hearing.

---

37 [2014] EWCA Civ 1622.
38 *Lord Chancellor's Exceptional Funding Guidance (Non-Inquests)* paras 27–29, available at: www.gov.uk/government/publications/legal-aid-exceptional-case-funding-form-and-guidance.

Note that the CLR rates for appeals that were 2(a), 2(b) and 2(c) and the interim hourly rates for online appeals will no longer be applicable for any CLR matter opened on or after 1 April 2023.

9.44 Also note that from 1 April 2023, a Legal Help matter/stage and the CLR matter/stage in a client's case will form two separate matter starts, where either is granted on or after 1 April 2023. The Legal Help matter can be claimed as soon as that stage of the work is completed. You do not have to wait until the CLR matter is completed before you submit your claim for the Legal Help matter.

Immigration appeals and bail hearings before the First-tier Tribunal and Upper Tribunal

9.45 Apart from Legal Help, if an area of immigration or asylum law is in scope, this will also include CLR and Legal Representation for appeal work.[39]

9.46 Advocacy in the First-tier Tribunal (FTT) and Upper Tribunal (UT) is in scope for five specific types of proceedings.[40] First, advocacy in appeals of decisions by the secretary of state to refuse a protection or human rights claim (or revoke protection status), is in scope.[41] Second, advocacy is also covered in proceedings before the FTT and UT related to Immigration Act 1971 Sch 2, ie administrative provisions as to control on entry.[42] Third, advocacy is also available in appeal proceedings in relation to applications for ILR and for a residence card under the Immigration (European Economic Area) Regulations 2006 by victims of domestic violence.[43] Fourth, advocacy is in scope in appeal proceedings in relation to applications for leave or enter by victims of modern slavery.[44]

9.47 Fifth, advocacy is available in the FTT and UT in appeals where a person is being deprived of British citizenship under British Nationality Act 1981 s40A and rights of residence under Immigration (European Economic Area) Regulations 2006 reg 26.[45] However, this is only to the extent that the appeal concerns a contravention of the Equality Act 2010. Although the Immigration (European Economic

---

39 Standard Civil Contract 2024 Specification Immigration and Asylum para 8.4.
40 LASPO Sch 1 Part 3 paras 11–13 and 15.
41 LASPO Sch 1 Part 3 para 11(b); and Nationality, Immigration and Asylum Act 2002 s82(1).
42 LASPO Sch 1 Part 3 para 11(a).
43 LASPO Sch 1 Part 3 para 13; and Part 1 paras 28–29.
44 LASPO Sch 1 Part 3 para 13; and Part 1 paras 32(1)–32A(1).
45 LASPO Sch 1 Part 3 para 12.

Area) Regulations 2016 replaced the 2006 Regulations from 1 February 2017 in respect of appeal rights, LASPO has not been updated to reflect this.[46]

9.48 If it arises from in scope work, any advocacy work in the High Court, Court of Appeal and Supreme Court is in scope as licensed work.[47]

Judicial review

9.49 Judicial review is in scope, but there are three types of restrictions.[48] First, and these restrictions apply to all categories, the judicial review must have the potential to produce a benefit for the individual, a member of the individual's family or the environment.[49]

9.50 Second, the judicial review may not relate to an immigration issue where:
   (a) the same issue, or substantially the same issue, was the subject of a previous judicial review or an appeal to a court or tribunal,
   (b) on the determination of the previous judicial review or appeal (or, if there was more than one, the latest one), the court, tribunal or other person hearing the case found against the applicant or appellant on that issue, and
   (c) the services in relation to the new judicial review are provided before the end of the period of 1 year beginning with the day of that determination.[50]

9.51 Third, the judicial review may not relate to removal directions in respect of an individual where the directions were given not more than one year after the latest of the following:
   (a) the making of the decision (or, if there was more than one, the latest decision) to remove the individual from the United Kingdom by way of removal directions;
   (b) the refusal of leave to appeal against that decision;
   (c) the determination or withdrawal of an appeal against that decision.[51]

9.52 Despite these restrictions, judicial review is still permitted in fresh asylum claims and other certified cases (effectively where there would be no appeal to the immigration tribunal against the decision).

---

46 LASPO Sch 1 Part 3 para 12(b).
47 LASPO Sch 1 Part 3 paras 1–3.
48 LASPO Sch 1 Part 1 para 19(1).
49 LASPO Sch 1 Part 1 para 19(3).
50 LASPO Sch 1 Part 1 para 19(5).
51 LASPO Sch 1 Part 1 para 19(6).

The latter two exclusions mentioned above do not apply when services are provided to an individual in relation to:
> (a) judicial review of a negative decision in relation to an asylum application (within the meaning of the EU Procedures Directive[52]) where there is no right of appeal to the First-tier Tribunal against the decision;
> (b) judicial review of certification under section 94 or 96[53] of the Nationality, Immigration and Asylum Act 2002 (certificate preventing or restricting appeal of immigration decision).[54]

9.53 Further, the latter two exclusions mentioned above do not apply when services are provided in relation to judicial review of removal directions in respect of an individual where prescribed conditions relating to either or both of the following are met:
> (a) the period between the individual being given notice of the removal directions and the proposed time for his or her removal;
> (b) the reasons for proposing that period.[55]

9.54 It is important to be clear about what funding is being sought in judicial review cases, and to ensure that the work is in scope and is not excluded under the above provisions. You will need to ensure that this is clearly spelt out in all funding applications to the LAA.

9.55 It is expected that all internal reviews and appeals are exhausted before any refusal of funding is challenged in court proceedings.[56]

9.56 Section 56 of the Illegal Migration Act 2023 makes various amendments to legal aid, including to LASPO Sch 1 to provide legal aid for judicial reviews regarding removals following the refusal of a human rights claim where Article 2 or 3 ECHR is in issue. The Act also makes provision for legal aid services with regard to PRNs and suspensive claims.

Definition of an immigration or an asylum matter

9.57 The Standard Civil Contract 2024 Specification Category-Specific Rules: Immigration and Asylum[57] paras 8.7 and 8.8 (as amended)

---

52 Council Directive 2005/85/EC of 1 December 2005 on minimum standards on procedures in member states for granting and withdrawing refugee status.
53 Respectively, unfounded human rights or asylum claims or certification on the basis of an earlier right of appeal.
54 LASPO Sch 1 Part 1 para 19(7).
55 LASPO Sch 1 Part 1 para 19(8).
56 *Rrapaj and others v Director of Legal Aid Casework* [2013] EWHC 1837 (Admin).
57 Available at: www.gov.uk/government/publications/standard-civil-contract-2018.

Conducting immigration and asylum cases 241

divide work in the immigration category into asylum and immigration matter types. It is important that you correctly report new matter starts and claims as asylum or immigration, both as part of your contractual obligation and also because the funding limits are different.

9.58 The Contract Specification says:

Contract Work covered by this Specification
8.7 For the purposes of Controlled Work, a Matter should proceed and be reported under this Specification as an 'Asylum Matter' where:
  (a) it relates to civil legal services in respect of the rights set out in paragraph 30 of Part 1 of Schedule 1 of the Act ('Immigration: rights to enter and remain');
  (b) it relates to an asylum issue and is proceeding under paragraph 24 of Part 1 of Schedule 1 to the Act ('Special Immigration Appeals Commission').
8.8 For the purposes of Controlled Work, a Matter should proceed and be reported as an 'Immigration Matter' where it relates to civil legal services in respect of the rights mentioned in:
  (a) paragraph 25 of Part 1 of Schedule 1 to the Act ('Immigration: detention');
  (b) paragraph 26 of Part 1 of Schedule 1 to the Act ('Immigration: conditions of immigration bail: persons liable to examination or removal');
  (c) paragraph 27 of Part 1 of Schedule 1 to the Act ('Immigration: conditions of immigration bail (deportation));
  (d) paragraph 27A of Part 1 of Schedule 1 to the Act ('Immigration: conditions imposed under other provisions')
  (e) paragraph 28 of Part 1 of Schedule 1 to the Act ('Immigration: victims of domestic violence and indefinite leave to remain');
  (f) paragraph 29 of Part 1 of Schedule 1 to the Act ('Immigration: victims of domestic violence and residence cards');
  (g) paragraph 32 of Part 1 of Schedule 1 to the Act (Victims of trafficking in human beings') insofar as civil legal services relate to an application by the individual for leave to enter, or to remain in, the United Kingdom;
  (h) paragraph 24 of Part 1 of Schedule 1 to the Act ('Special Immigration Appeals Commission') where it relates to an immigration issue;
  (i) paragraph 45 of Part 1 of Schedule 1 to the Act ('Terrorism prevention and investigation measures etc');
  (j) paragraph 32A of Part 1 of Schedule 1 to the Act ('Victims of slavery, servitude or forced or compulsory labour') in so far as civil legal services relate to an application by the individual for leave to enter, or to remain in, the United Kingdom.

Who can carry out the work?

Individual caseworkers

9.59 Immigration work is unique in legal aid, in being completely subject to an accreditation scheme (ie the Immigration and Asylum Accreditation Scheme (IAAS)).[58] Other areas of legal aid also use accreditation, for example, to qualify as a supervisor, and even restrict work by accreditation type, for example, criminal police station work, but only immigration funding is subject to a category-wide restriction. Note that IAAS accreditation is a separate matter from that provided by the Office of the Immigration Services Commissioner (OISC).

9.60 Unless you are IAAS accredited, you will not be paid for doing any legal aid work in the immigration category at all.[59] There are several levels of accreditation:

- Trainee Caseworker (formerly level 1 probationer);
- Casework Assistant (formerly level 1 accredited caseworker);
- Senior Caseworker (level 2 accredited);
- Advanced Caseworker (level 3 accredited); and
- Accredited Supervisor.

9.61 The contract reserves certain types of work to caseworkers of a particular level or above, as set out at para 9.62 below.[60] You should note that the Contract Specification restricts representation of any child to a senior caseworker,[61] who must hold a valid (ie within two years) enhanced Disclosure and Barring Service (DBS) certificate.[62]

9.62 Under the Contract Specification, both Legal Help and CLR cases must be conducted by a senior caseworker. However, individual tasks at both levels can be delegated to assistant and trainee caseworkers (except in cases involving children, detention and mental capacity issues):[63]

---

58 This scheme is now referred to by the Law Society as 'Immigration and Asylum Accreditation' (IAA). However, Standard Civil Contract 2018 Specification para 8.13(a) still refers to it as the 'IAAS'.
59 Standard Civil Contract 2018 Specification paras 8.13 and 8.20.
60 Standard Civil Contract 2024 Specification para 8.18.
61 Standard Civil Contract 2024 Specification paras 8.13 and 8.18.
62 Standard Civil Contract 2024 Specification para 8.13(c).
63 Standard Civil Contract 2024 Specification para 8.18.

Type of contract work	Level of accreditation
Conduct of Legal Help Matters and Legal Representation	Senior Caseworker Trainee Casework Assistants (who have passed the relevant examination required by the IAAS at that level) and Casework Assistants can conduct tasks delegated by the Senior Caseworker, except Reserved Matters
Reserved Matter 1 – Use of Delegated Functions to make a determination that an individual qualifies for CLR; and conduct of CLR cases	Senior Caseworker and above
Reserved Matter 2 – All Contract Work for clients who lack capacity within the meaning of section 2 of the Mental Capacity Act 2005	Senior Caseworker and above
Reserved Matter 3 – All Contract Work carried out for a Child or an unaccompanied asylum-seeking child (UASC)	Senior Caseworker and above
Reserved Matter 4 – All Contract Work for clients detained in IRCs	Senior Caseworker and above
Conduct of any other Contract Work not covered above	Senior Caseworker and above

9.63 What work can be done by caseworkers of each level is defined by the contract and the accreditation work restrictions.

9.64 In this context, 'conduct' means 'having responsibility for and control of the progression of the case'.[64] So a casework assistant can carry out tasks on an appeal conducted by a senior caseworker, whereas all work on the file of an unaccompanied child must be carried out by a senior caseworker or above. In addition to this broad rule, you must comply with the work restrictions, as set out in the text-box at para 9.62 above.

9.65 Work carried out by advanced caseworkers attracts an uplift of five per cent on the payment rates on all controlled work paid at hourly rates and personally undertaken by an advanced caseworker.[65]

---

64 Standard Civil Contract 2024 Specification para 8.19.
65 Standard Civil Contract 2024 Specification para 8.103.

9.66 The Contract Specification requires each of your offices to maintain a ratio of at least one full-time equivalent senior caseworker for every two trainee caseworkers or casework assistants.[66]

Organisations with exclusive immigration removal centre contracts

9.67 You may only provide advice and representation to clients in an IRC if you have been granted schedule authorisation to do so,[67] with the following four exceptions:[68]

(a) the Client is a close family member of an existing Client and knowledge of the family's circumstances is material to the new Client's case (a close family member for the purpose of this rule is a member of the family who is the Client's spouse, partner, child, sibling, parent, grandparent or grandchild); or
(b) in the case of a Client detained in an IRC only, the Client is an existing Client on whom you have attended in the UK and carried out at least five hours work . . . prior to the Client's detention . . .;
(c) there are no providers with Schedule authorisation in the IRC Procurement Area where the Client is detained; or
(d) your Client has an appeal listed at a designated Fast Track location.

9.68 Providers with authorisation have either a contract to carry out work by way of: (a) the Detained Duty Advice Scheme in an IRC; and/or (b) the Detained Fast Track Scheme/Detained Asylum Casework Scheme.[69] The schedule authorisation does not apply to licensed work (ie work that is in scope and that is carried out under a funding certificate in higher court proceedings).

Clients detained otherwise than in an immigration removal centre

9.69 You can provide advice and representation to clients detained in prisons and other places of detention that are not IRCs without special authorisation.[70] Where you do so, your advice must include advice on bail. Where you act for a client in detention, or who becomes detained during the case, you must continue acting until:

---

66 Standard Civil Contract 2024 Specification para 8.15.
67 Standard Civil Contract 2024 Specification para 8.5.
68 Standard Civil Contract 2024 Specification para 8.6.
69 Standard Civil Contract 2024 Specification para 8.5.
70 Standard Civil Contract 2024 Specification para 8.52.

- the client formally ceases to give instructions;
- the client is released from detention;
- the client is dispersed from the area;
- the client is removed from the country; or
- you can no longer act because of a conflict of interest or other good professional conduct reason.[71]

Scope

9.70 See chapter 4 for information on the following:
- whether other funding may be available, and public funding should not be granted;
- what to do if your client has received previous advice from another organisation;
- what to do if your client has received previous advice from your organisation;
- clients from abroad or clients who are abroad; and
- clients who are children.

Structure of immigration work

9.71 In general, immigration work can be divided into four stages:
1) advice and assistance on entry clearance and leave to remain applications;
2) advice and representation on appeals to the FTT;
3) advice and representation on appeals to the UT; and
4) litigation in the UT and higher courts.

9.72 Stage 1 is funded by Legal Help. Stage 2 is funded by CLR (though different rules apply and it helps to think of them as different types of work). Stages 3 and 4 are funded by a legal aid representation certificate (certificated work).

9.73 The Contract Specification does not create any additional rules for certificated work in the higher courts, and this is therefore not dealt with to any great extent in this chapter. See chapter 4 for the general rules that apply.

9.74 The various funding types are consecutive as the case progresses. For example, where a client's entry clearance/leave to remain application is refused, you should consider whether there is merit for an

---

71 Standard Civil Contract 2024 Specification para 8.53.

appeal under CLR, and, if so, grant it. CLR should be applied for as soon as practicable after the right to appeal has arisen. Once CLR is granted or refused, the Legal Help comes to an end and no further Legal Help work may be done on that matter.[72] Post-appeal work will form part of the CLR.[73]

9.75 Where you take an appeal to the Court of Appeal, the issue of a certificate to conduct the appeal brings the controlled work matter to an end. If the Court of Appeal then remits the case back to the Immigration and Asylum Chamber (IAC), a new matter start will be required to do the remitted appeal, which will be paid at hourly rates.[74] If during either stage 1 or stage 2, it is necessary to do work under a certificate while the relevant stage remains pending, then either the Legal Help or the CLR, as applicable, may be kept open to deal with that work.

Fee types

9.76 Immigration work is paid as standard fees or at hourly rates. Different rules apply to standard fee work and hourly rates work. Therefore, it is important to determine at the start of the case which category the work falls into.[75]

9.77 The Contract Specification lists all hourly rates work:
(a) Asylum Matters opened under this Contract which relate to an Asylum application (including 'NAM' or 'Legacy'), made to the UKBA prior to 1 October 2007;
(b) a fresh claim/further application for Asylum opened under this Contract where the original Asylum application was lodged, whether concluded or not, prior to 1 October 2007;
(c) advice in relation to the merits of lodging an application for permission to appeal to the Upper Tribunal (where advice has not been received under Stage 2 of the Standard Fee);
(d) Bail applications;
(e) advice and applying for a determination that a Client qualifies for civil legal services provided as Licensed Work, including complying with any pre-action protocol;
(f) initial advice in relation to an Asylum application prior to claiming Asylum at the Asylum Screening Unit where you then cease to be instructed. This will also apply where the Client returns after attendance at the Asylum Screening Unit but where it is confirmed that the Client will be dispersed and will not continue to instruct you;

---

72 Standard Civil Contract 2024Specification para 8.74.
73 Standard Civil Contract 2024Specification paras 8.79(e) and 8.80.
74 Standard Civil Contract 2024 Specification para 8.139.
75 Standard Civil Contract 2024 Specification paras 8.71.

(g) Escape Fee Cases under the Standard Fee;
(h) advice in relation to a Client who is an UASC;
(i) cases remitted, reviewed or referred from the Court of Appeal or the Upper Tribunal to the First Tier Tribunal;
(j) where you hold a Schedule authorisation any Matters opened under the Detained Duty Advice Scheme or for a Detained Fast Track or a DAC Scheme Client;
(k) advice in relation to Terrorism Prevention and Investigation Measures Orders;
(l) applying for a determination that an individual qualifies for civil legal services provided as Licensed Work in relation to Terrorism Prevention and Investigation Measures Orders;
(m) applying for a determination that an individual qualifies for civil legal services provided as Licensed Work in relation to the Special Immigration Appeals Commission.
(n) Immigration advice in relation to a client who is a Separated Child; and
(o) CLR (excluding Online Procedure Advocacy Services) where:
  (i) CLR was granted on or before 6 October 2020 and you have not elected to claim a Stage 2(c) Standard Fee; or
  (ii) CLR was granted between 7 October 2020 and 31 March 2023; the matter has progressed using:
    (i) the Pre Online Procedure where you have chosen to claim Online Procedure Hourly Rates rather than the Stage 2(c) Standard Fee; or
    (ii) the Post Online Procedure Hourly Rates.
(p) where you provide 30 minutes advice to a client at a prison without reference to the client's financial eligibility pursuant to Paragraph 8.186;
(q) advice on an application to rebut Group 2 Refugee Status pursuant to Paragraph 8.26;
(r) advice in relation to Age Assessment Appeals;
(s) up to 7 hours advice to a client in receipt of a PRN;
(t) any follow-on work that is conducted for a client after receiving advice in relation to Paragraph 8.101(s); and
(u) Illegal Migration Act Matters.[76]

9.78 Contract work payable at hourly rates, with the exception of para 8.101(d), will be subject to cost limits as described at paras 8.106–8.109 and 8.112–8.115. The relevant hourly rates are set out in the Civil Legal Aid (Remuneration) Regulations 2013.

9.79 All other work not included in para 8.101 of the Contract Specification is payable as standard fees.

---

76 Standard Civil Contract 2024 Specification para 8.101.

9.80 Where the substantive matter is standard fee, nonetheless any bail, UT work, remittals, applications for funding certificates and pre-action work under the same matter will always be paid at hourly rates. In this situation, the hourly rates work is an additional payment. By contrast, where the substantive matter is hourly rates, bail, applications for funding certificates and pre-action work all fall under the costs limit of the substantive matter. The costs limit for UT and remittals work is explained later in this chapter.

9.81 You should be especially careful when dealing with the case of a UASC. If the child turns 18 before CLR is granted, the CLR work on this matter will be standard fee. The Legal Help work on the matter will still all be hourly rates.[77] If the child turns 18 after CLR is granted, then both the Legal Help and CLR work on this matter will remain at hourly rates.

Matter starts and separate matters

9.82 A 'matter' is all work done on a single case for a client. A matter can pass through Legal Help and CLR but can now be treated as two separate matters.[78]

9.83 The following paragraphs in the Specification explain when only one matter should be opened and when more than one matter should be opened:

> 8.25 An Asylum application and any Asylum appeal other than Standard Fee Stage 2(a), 2(b) or 2(c) Claims will constitute separate Matters. The appropriate UKVI unique Client number for both Matters will be that of the original Asylum application.
>
> 8.26 An Asylum application and any Asylum appeal attracting a Standard Fee Stage 2(a), 2(b) or 2(c) Claim will constitute one Matter. The appropriate UKVI unique Client number will be that of the original application given by the UKVI.
>
> 8.26A All advice in relation to a Client's Illegal Migration Act Matter will constitute one Matter. The Appropriate UKVI unique Client number will be that of the original application given by the UKVI. Any application to appeal at the Upper Tribunal or representation at the Upper Tribunal, if permission is granted, will constitute Licensed Work.

---

77 *Escape Case Electronic Handbook*, v2.3, LAA, August 2023, para 13.8 p88 (available at: www.gov.uk/government/publications/submit-an-escape-fee-case-claim).
78 Standard Civil Contract Specification 2024 para 8.25.

Conducting immigration and asylum cases 249

8.27 Advice in relation to an application (including advice on merits) to rebut a provisional decision to recognise an individual as a Group 2 Refugee by UKVI made prior to a final decision on the asylum application will constitute one Matter.

8.28 A Matter Start under Paragraph 8.27 is a separate Matter Start to the original Asylum application and a separate Claim may be submitted for this work.

8.29 An Age Assessment Appeal will constitute one Matter.

8.30 A Matter Start under Paragraph 8.29 is a separate Matter Start to any associated Immigration or Asylum Matter.

8.31 Advice in relation to obligations under a Priority Removal Notice is a separate Matter Start to any associated Immigration or Asylum Matter.

8.32 An Immigration application and any Immigration appeal other than Standard Fee Stage 2(a), 2(b) or 2(c) Claims will constitute separate Matters. The appropriate UKVI unique Client number for both Matters will be that of the original application given by the UKVI. January 2024

8.33 An Immigration application and any Immigration appeal attracting a Standard Fee Stage 2(a), 2(b) or 2(c) Claim will constitute one Matter. The appropriate UKVI unique Client number will be that of the original application given by the UKVI. 8.34 Any associated or additional application to an application within scope of Part 1 of Schedule 1 to the Act on human rights grounds will also form part of the same Asylum Matter. 8.35 Where a Client has made or wishes to make a fresh application for Asylum then this new application would constitute a new Matter Start.

8.36 Any associated advice in relation to the National Referral Mechanism will not constitute a separate Matter from the original Matter and you may not open a separate Matter Start.

8.37 Where you have an ongoing Matter, work undertaken in relation to a determination that the Client qualifies for civil legal services provided as Licensed Work including complying with any pre-action protocol may be undertaken as part of the same Matter.

- Where a client applies to enter or remain in the UK under more than one category, or applies to switch status while the first application remains outstanding, this will be one matter.[79] However, where the first application is at appeal stage and a different additional application is made, the second application will be a new matter.[80]

---

79 Standard Civil Contract 2024 Specification para 8.40.
80 Standard Civil Contract 2024 Specification para 8.41.

- Where you transfer cases between your own offices, either because of dispersal or other reason, you must continue the case under the same matter start and not open a new one.[81]
- If you are acting for several clients in relation to the same case, this should generally be one Legal Help matter. For example, where you have an asylum claim with a principal applicant and a family member who is dependent, then this should usually be one matter. However, if there needs to be separate applications or appeals for each family member, then separate matters may be opened. To determine that separate applications or appeals are needed, you must consider that each family member has a separate and distinct legal interest for which there is sufficient benefit to justify a separate matter. For example, where the family members are claiming asylum each in their own right, there should normally be separate matters.

9.84 A second matter start for the same client would not be justified on the same case unless:
- at least six months have elapsed since the first matter was closed; or
- there has been a material development or change in the client's instructions and at least three months have elapsed.[82]

9.85 If the client fails to give instructions and you close the file, and then the client returns, that is not a change in instructions. A decision, response, etc from a third party to an application, representations, correspondence, etc made in the first matter is not a material development.[83]

9.86 Where further work is justified but you cannot start a new matter under the rule, new disbursements can be claimed, as can profit costs if the case is an hourly rate case. You may claim new disbursements and profit costs if the case is an hourly rate case, or an escape fee case if the new work plus the old work would make it an escape fee claim. However, note that the previous relevant upper costs and disbursements limits will apply and you will need to apply for extensions where necessary.

9.87 See chapter 2 for more information on how to report further work on a revived case and where a new matter would be justified.

---

81 Standard Civil Contract 2024 Specification para 8.38.
82 Standard Civil Contract 2024 Specification para 3.35.
83 Standard Civil Contract 2024 Specification para 3.36.

Granting Legal Help

9.88 The means test for Legal Help as set out in chapter 2 must be applied. The only difference in the immigration category is that support granted under section 4 or 95 of the Immigration and Asylum Act 1999 (referred to as National Asylum Support Service (NASS) support) is treated as passporting support (see chapter 2 at para 2.40).[84]

9.89 In all controlled work cases, the means of minors should not be aggregated with those of their foster carer or social worker.[85] Proof of means will be required. Many asylum-seekers and migrants without leave who are not in receipt of section 4 or 95 support may be accommodated and maintained by friends and relatives. Where that is the case, you will need to get proof, usually in the form of a letter signed by the person accommodating the client and setting out the nature and extent of support being given (and quantifying it if it includes money). It is very important that the letter is signed and dated and makes it clear that the support has covered the whole of the month prior to the date the form was signed and how much support (financial and accommodation address) is being provided. It would also help to have the signatory's contact telephone number and/or email address on the letter. Letters that do not specify a time period since the support began have not been allowed as acceptable evidence of means at audit. Alternatively, you may use the LAA's optional form for third parties providing support.[86]

9.90 Note that neither section 98 support (Immigration and Asylum Act 1999) nor Schedule 10 support (Immigration Act 2016) are passporting support for legal aid purposes. You might consider applying for ECF if necessary.

9.91 The merits test is the sufficient benefit test – see chapter 2 for further information on the means test, and chapter 4 for further information on the merits test.

---

84 Civil Legal Aid (Financial Resources and Payment for Services) Regulations 2013 reg 6(1).
85 *Lord Chancellor's guidance on determining financial eligibility for Controlled Work and Family Mediation*, September 2023, para 9 (available at: www.gov.uk/guidance/civil-legal-aid-means-testing). Note that the text states that it would 'usually be inequitable' to do so (para 9.1(2)).
86 See: www.gov.uk/government/publications/cw1-financial-eligibility-for-legal-aid-clients.

Granting Controlled Legal Representation

9.92 CLR is subject to the means test. The test is the same as for Legal Help, except that the capital limit for CLR is £3,000 for all non-asylum appeal work, rather than the £8,000 that applies to all other levels of civil funding.

9.93 CLR has its own merits test, which should be applied and kept in mind throughout, once CLR has been granted. This test, in addition to the standard criteria (see chapter 4), requires that:
1) if the case is not of significant wider public interest, the **reasonable private paying individual test** is met; or
2) if the case is of significant wider public interest, the **proportionality test** is met; and
3) in either of these two scenarios, the prospects of success for the case are:
    a) **very good, good or moderate**; or
    b) **borderline, marginal** or **unclear**, and:
        i) the case is of **significant wider public interest**;
        ii) the case is one with overwhelming importance to the individual; or
        iii) the substance of the case relates to a breach of Convention rights.[87]

9.94 The bold terms in the above-mentioned CLR merits test are defined elsewhere in the relevant statutory instrument as follows (emphasis added):

- The **reasonable private paying individual test** is met if the Director is satisfied that the potential benefit to be gained from the provision of civil legal services justifies the likely costs, such that a reasonable private paying individual would be prepared to start or continue the proceedings having regard to the prospects of success and all the other circumstances of the case.[88]
- The **proportionality test** is met if the Director is satisfied that the likely benefits of the proceedings to the individual and others justify the likely costs, having regard to the prospects of success and all the other circumstances of the case.[89]

---

87 Civil Legal Aid (Merits Criteria) Regulations 2013 reg 60(2)–(3).
88 Civil Legal Aid (Merits Criteria) Regulations 2013 reg 7.
89 Civil Legal Aid (Merits Criteria) Regulations 2013 reg 8.

Conducting immigration and asylum cases 253

- **'Borderline'** means that the case is not 'unclear' but that it is not possible, by reason of disputed law, fact or expert evidence, to:
  - decide that the chance of obtaining a successful outcome is 50 per cent or more; or
  - classify the prospects as marginal or poor.[90]
- **'Unclear'** means where there are identifiable investigations which could be carried out, after which it should be possible to give a reliable estimate of the prospects of success.[91]
- **'Marginal'** means a 45 per cent or more chance, but less than a 50 per cent chance, of obtaining a successful outcome.[92]
- A case is of **significant wider public interest** if the Director is satisfied that the case is an appropriate case to realise:
  - real benefits to the public at large, other than those which normally flow from cases of the type in question; and
  - benefits for an identifiable class of individuals, other than the individual to whom civil legal services may be provided or members of that individual's family.[93]
- A case with **'overwhelming importance to the individual'** means a case that is not primarily a claim for damages or other sum of money and which relates to one or more of the following:
  - the life, liberty or physical safety of the individual or a member of that individual's family; or
  - the immediate risk that the individual may become homeless.[94]

9.95 The merits test applies to both FTT and UT appeals.

9.96 Where you are satisfied that the merits are either very good, good or moderate,[95] you should sign the CLR form – it is your signature (the client having already signed the form) that gives effect to the grant – since you are making the determination on behalf of the Director of Legal Aid Casework.[96]

---

90 Civil Legal Aid (Merits Criteria) Regulations 2013 reg 5.
91 Civil Legal Aid (Merits Criteria) Regulations 2013 reg 5.
92 Civil Legal Aid (Merits Criteria) Regulations 2013 reg 5.
93 Civil Legal Aid (Merits Criteria) Regulations 2013 reg 6.
94 Civil Legal Aid (Merits Criteria) Regulations 2013 reg 2.
95 See Civil Legal Aid (Merits Criteria) Regulations 2013 reg 5(1)(a), (b) and (c) for the respective definitions of these terms.
96 Civil Legal Aid (Merits Criteria) Regulations 2013 reg 3.

Refusing and withdrawing CLR

9.97 Where you believe the merits test is not, or is no longer, satisfied, you should refuse or withdraw CLR as appropriate and complete form CW4[97] setting out the date and reasons for your decision.[98]

9.98 A copy of the form must be provided to the client within five days of your decision, and you must also advise the client of their right to appeal against your decision.[99]

9.99 The client can either appeal direct to the LAA or instruct you to do so on their behalf.[100] This work is normally carried out under Legal Help.

Change of supplier

9.100 A person's remedy against a refusal of CLR would be to appeal to the LAA against a provider's decision to refuse or withdraw CLR. If an appeal to the Independent Funding Adjudicator (IFA) is being considered, the applicant will have 14 days by which to submit the appeal to the Director of Legal Aid Casework.

9.101 Where you are asked to take on a transfer following refusal of CLR, generally you should advise the client to appeal to the IFA. However, there may be occasions where your specific experience and knowledge compel you to take a different view on the merits and grant CLR funding on this basis. You will need to follow the usual rules for transfers of funding (see chapter 4). If you reassess and decide to grant funding, without your client having to appeal to an IFA, you will need to record details of your revised determination in the relevant case details and merits criteria section of the CW2(Imm)[101] form.

Conducting the case

Overview

9.102 Once you have determined that the case is in scope and Legal Help or CLR, as appropriate, has been granted (and assuming there is sufficient merit on an ongoing basis), you can conduct the case.

---

97 Available at: www.gov.uk/government/collections/controlled-work-application-forms.
98 Standard Civil Contract 2024 Specification para 8.48.
99 Standard Civil Contract 2024 Specification para 8.48.
100 Standard Civil Contract 2024 Specification para 8.48.
101 Available at: www.gov.uk/government/collections/controlled-work-application-forms.

9.103 You are generally permitted to take instructions, take witness statements, make applications and representations, conduct appeals, and so on.

9.104 There are rules that govern certain aspects of the conduct of cases, which we will look at in this section.

Attendance at interviews

9.105 As mentioned in paras 9.15 and 9.19 above, attendance at interviews is excluded under LASPO unless allowed by regulations. The relevant regulations provide for attendance at: (a) asylum screening interviews and asylum interviews where the person is a child;[102] or (b) at an asylum interview where the person is either being detained at a specified IRC[103] or lacks mental capacity.[104] In respect of attendance at an interview of a child, 'child' does not include a child whose age is being disputed at the time of the interview unless the Home Office has said that it is nevertheless going to treat the person as a child for the purpose of the interview.[105]

9.106 Payment for attendance at an interview is not determined by the age of the child at the time of signing controlled work, but by whether the child is a still a child at the date of the actual interview.

9.107 Where you attend in a standard fee case, you can claim the interview additional fee. In an hourly rate case, the contract states that attendance at a substantive interview is outside the relevant costs and disbursement limits.[106]

Travel to detained clients

9.108 You can now claim for travelling time and waiting time to attend a detained duty advice surgery under a schedule authorisation,[107] and you can claim for travel and waiting costs to visit a client in

---

102 Civil Legal Aid (Immigration Interviews) (Exceptions) Regulations 2012 regs 2 and 3.
103 Following the amendment of the relevant regulations by the Civil Legal Aid (Immigration Interviews) (Exceptions) (Amendment) Regulations 2017, these are, currently, Colnbrook House IRC, Harmondsworth IRC and Yarl's Wood Immigration IRC.
104 Civil Legal Aid (Immigration Interviews) (Exceptions) Regulations 2012 reg 4.
105 Civil Legal Aid (Immigration Interviews) (Exceptions) Regulations 2012 regs 2(b) and 3.
106 Standard Civil Contract 2024 Specification para 8.109.
107 Standard Civil Contract 2024 Specification para 8.52.

detention.[108] However, travel time is capped to a maximum of three hours for both legs of the journey. Travel and waiting time and associated disbursements are excluded from any applicable costs limit, and in a standard fee case payable on top of the relevant fee.

Bail

9.109 When attending a client in detention you must always advise the client in relation to bail and record the outcome of this advice in the file. You must ensure that the client receives advice on the appropriateness of making an application at any particular time (including when appeal rights have been exhausted).[109]

9.110 Bail applications to the tribunal are covered by CLR funding[110] (Home Office bail and bail restrictions are covered under Legal Help). If you do not already have CLR open for an appeal, you should grant CLR to cover bail.[111] If you are already conducting an appeal, you should extend the scope of CLR to cover the bail application. The merits test for bail is the same for CLR generally, except that it will be specifically related to the prospects of a successful bail application.

9.111 Bail work is always paid at hourly rates.[112] See below for costs limits in bail matters.

Attendance at hearings

9.112 Appeals work is out of scope of Legal Help but is covered by CLR. You may instruct an advocate (within or outside your organisation) to attend any hearing if CLR has been granted.

9.113 The advocate's time should be included on your claim as if it were your profit costs, and it will be paid at the relevant hourly rate or as part of the standard fee – in a standard fee case, their time will count towards the escape threshold. Where an advocate is instructed, you cannot make a claim for time spent accompanying them to the hearing.[113]

---

108 Standard Civil Contract 2024 Specification para 8.179.
109 Standard Civil Contract 2024 Specification para 8.42.
110 Standard Civil Contract 2024 Specification para 8.45.
111 Standard Civil Contract 2024 Specification para 8.45.
112 Standard Civil Contract 2024 Specification para 8.101(d).
113 Standard Civil Contract 2024 Specification paras 8.138, 8.73 and 8.101.

9.114 You can apply to the LAA for an uplift to increase the rates payable to advocates (including advocates employed by you) if the case raises an exceptionally complex or novel point of law (eg country guidance cases) or if there is a significant wider public interest (as defined by the regulations). Any enhanced rates that may be granted apply to advocacy, attendance and preparation only.[114]

9.115 Time spent instructing advocates and in conference is properly claimable if reasonable in the circumstances of the case.

Additional payments for online procedure advocacy services

9.116 Where applicable,[115] the standard fees for advocacy services as set out in the Civil Legal Aid (Remuneration) Regulations 2013 are payable at the end of the CLR as set out in Standard Civil Contract 2024 Specification para 8.86 for each relevant attendance. When claiming for advocacy work the following rules apply:

1) Advocacy fees are payable whether the relevant advocacy services are carried out by you or counsel and whether remotely or in person.
2) Only one advocacy fee for a substantive hearing in the FTT may be claimed per matter. If the hearing goes into a second day, either part heard or re-listed, an additional day's substantive hearing fee may be claimed for the second and each subsequent day.[116]
3) Advocacy fees are inclusive of time for travel and waiting.

Post-appeal work

9.117 The scope of Legal Help ends at the point of the Home Office decision and consideration of CLR merits.[117] Therefore, by definition, Legal Help cannot be used for post-appeal follow-up work, such as chasing of status papers and advice on status.

9.118 The CLR will cover advice on the outcome of the appeal, including on the rights conferred by a grant of status, together with any post-appeal advice and assistance that does not justify a new matter start (see above for rules on matter start boundaries).[118]

---

114 Standard Civil Contract 2024 Specification paras 8.104 and 8.135–8.137.
115 Standard Civil Contract 2024 Specification para 8.87(a)–(c).
116 Standard Civil Contract 2024 Specification para 8.104.
117 Standard Civil Contract 2024 Specification paras 8.79 and 8.80.
118 Standard Civil Contract 2024 Specification paras 8.79 and 8.80.

9.119 Stage 2 CLR will end when a determination is made that a client does or does not qualify for licensed work in relation to the submission of application for permission to appeal to the UT or where the matter otherwise ends earlier.[119]

Appeals to the Upper Tribunal

9.120 Work on an application for permission to appeal to the UT, and, if granted, the appeal itself and any subsequent remittal back, is licensed work and you must apply on the Client and Cost Management System (CCMS) for a certificate before any work can be done.[120] The work carried out on the initial application to the FTT for permission to appeal to the UT on the application is payable at the hourly rates set out in the regulations for FTT work. However, work carried out on a direct application to the UT for permission to appeal and all subsequent work in that forum is payable at the hourly rates specified for licensed work in the Higher Courts.[121]

9.121 If you apply for permission to appeal and permission is refused, you may not claim any costs related to the application or appeal, but may claim any disbursements incurred, including interpreters' fees.[122]

9.122 Where the application for permission is lodged by the Home Office, or where the case is subject to the Detained Fast Track Scheme or the Detained Asylum Casework Scheme (see para 9.68 above), work done is not at risk, and is contract work not licensed work.[123]

Higher Courts litigation

9.123 Onward litigation will usually take the form of an appeal to the Court of Appeal against a decision of the UT. In this case, a full representation certificate is required. See chapter 4 for information on applying for a legal aid certificate. The issue of the certificate will end the controlled work matter. Therefore, remittal back to the tribunal would be a new matter.

9.124 The main difference in the immigration category to the usual rules on certificate applications is that you do not have the delegated function to grant emergency certificates in judicial review claims

---

119 Standard Civil Contract 2024 Specification para 8.74.
120 Standard Civil Contract 2024 Specification para 8.142.
121 Standard Civil Contract 2024 Specification para 8.145.
122 Standard Civil Contract 2024 Specification paras 8.142 and 8.144.
123 Standard Civil Contract 2024 Specification para 8.143.

Conducting immigration and asylum cases 259

unless you have specifically been granted that power by the LAA – the reverse of that position is seen in other categories, where suppliers have the power by default. You therefore need to submit an application for emergency funding to the LAA. All applications must be made via the CCMS, including, from 1 February 2018, out of hours emergency applications (see chapter 5 at para 5.46 for more information about emergency non-delegated function applications and backdating).

Managing costs

9.125 The amount of any costs limit depends on the stage of the case and the type of funding.

9.126 In standard fee cases, save for disbursements, only the standard fee is payable unless the matter becomes an escape fee case. There is a limit on disbursements. Hourly rate cases are limited by both profits costs and disbursements. Review and reconsideration cases before the UT are not subject to costs limits for either costs or disbursements, since they are subject to assessment on a case-by-case basis by the LAA.

9.127 These are the applicable costs limits:
- Standard fee stage 1 (Legal Help):
  – £400 disbursements;[124]
  – no profit costs limits.
- Standard fee stage 2 (CLR):
  – £600 disbursements;[125]
  – no profit costs limits.
- Hourly rates Legal Help:
  – £800 profit costs (asylum); £500 profit costs (non-asylum);[126]
  – £400 disbursements.[127]
- Hourly rates CLR:
  – £1,600 combined costs and disbursements in asylum;
  – £1,200 combined costs and disbursements in non-asylum.[128]

---

124 Standard Civil Contract 2024 Specification para 8.110.
125 Standard Civil Contract 2024 Specification para 8.106.
126 Standard Civil Contract 2024 Specification para 8.106.
127 Standard Civil Contract 2024 Specification para 8.110.
128 Standard Civil Contract 2024 Specification para 8.112.

- Bail work:
  - £500 for all bail work, inclusive of disbursements (where CLR has not already been granted for an appeal; where it has, bail work forms part of the main £1,600/£1,200 limit; if CLR has already been granted for bail, when it is granted for a substantive appeal, the costs already spent on bail count towards the £1,600/£1,200).[129]
- Illegal Migration Act 2023 matters (Legal Help):
  - £1,500 combined costs and disbursements.[130]

9.128 Any of the above limits can be extended on application to the LAA. In addition, there are limits for specific case stages:

1) Where a client instructs you prior to making an application at the Asylum Screening Unit (ASU) and following attendance at the ASU you cease to be instructed – £100 including disbursements.
2) Where advice is given on the merits of an appeal to the UT under Legal Help (usually because the case has transferred to you at this stage, otherwise such advice would be part of CLR stage 2b) – £100 including disbursements.
3) Where you provide initial advice in relation to an asylum application which the client decides not to make or ceases to provide instructions before making – £100 including disbursements.

9.129 The Legal Help Cost Limit set out in 1) above cannot be extended. In contrast, the cost limits set out in 2) and 3) above may be extended by submitting the relevant contract report form to the LAA. However, costs are only payable within the cost limits that applied at the point they were incurred. Cost limits cannot be extended retrospectively.[131]

9.130 For details of making claims for costs, see chapter 15.

Licensed work

9.131 For the details of how licensed work operates, see chapter 3. However, note that from 1 September 2018 all UT work should be covered by a licensed work certificate. CLR funding is no longer applicable for UT work. This is facilitated by the Civil Legal Aid (Procedure, Remuneration and Statutory Charge) (Amendment) Regulations 2018 (see reg 5).

---

129 Standard Civil Contract 2024 Specification paras 8.107 and 8.112.
130 Standard Civil Contract 2024 Specification para 8.110A.
131 Standard Civil Contract 2024 Specification para 8.114.

9.132 The merits tests for licensed work in the immigration and asylum category are the same as those for CLR, ie the standard criteria combined with the test set out in paras 9.92 and 9.93 above.[132]

9.133 In a judicial review in relation to a transfer decision within the meaning of the Dublin III Regulation (ie Regulation (EU) No 604/2013 of the European Parliament and of the Council of 26 June 2013 establishing the criteria and mechanisms for determining the Member State responsible for examining an application for international protection lodged in one of the Member States by a third-country national or a stateless person),[133] the general merits criteria do not apply. Instead the merits test is whether the Director of Legal Aid Casework is satisfied that the case has a tangible prospect of success.[134]

---

132 Civil Legal Aid (Merits Criteria) Regulations 2013 reg 60(2)–(3). The LAA has produced a guidance document: *Immigration and Asylum Upper Tribunal Appeals: Background Information on the transfer of Immigration and Asylum Upper Tribunal work from Controlled Legal Representation to Licensed Work*, v1, November 2018, available at: https://assets.publishing.service.gov.uk/government/uploads/system/uploads/attachment_data/file/759115/Immigration_and_Asylum_Upper_Tribunal_Background_Information.pdf.
133 Civil Legal Aid (Merits Criteria) (Amendment) (No 3) Regulations 2013 reg 2.
134 Civil Legal Aid (Merits Criteria) Regulations 2013 reg 56A.

CHAPTER 10

Conducting a mental health case

Edited by Jonathan Wilson[1]

10.1	**Introduction**
10.4	**What is mental health work?**
10.7	**Overview**
10.11	Mental health supervisors
10.14	Advocacy
10.16	Use of counsel
10.18	**Levels of funding**
10.18	Overview
10.19	Standard fees for controlled work
10.24	Granting Legal Help
	Introduction • Means • Merits
10.31	Granting CLR
	Introduction • Means • Merits
10.34	**Operating under standard fees**
10.34	Non-Mental Health Tribunal cases
10.36	Mental Health Tribunal cases

1 Jonathan would like to thank Richard Charlton (Richard Charlton Solicitors) for writing and updating this chapter in previous editions of the Handbook, and also Karen Wolton (Wolton & Co), Jade Cassidy (Campbell Law), and Najmus Madarbux, Jake Kraft and Graham McDonald (Legal Aid Agency) for commenting on drafts of this updated chapter.

continued

10.43	**Escape fee cases**
10.49	**Separate matters**
10.55	**Disbursements**
10.58	**Licensed work**
10.61	**Contact with the LAA**

> **Key resources**
>
> **Statutes**
>
> - Mental Health Act 1983
> - Mental Capacity Act 2005
>
> **Contracts**
>
> - Standard Civil Contract 2024 Specification – sections 1–6[2]
> - Standard Civil Contract 2024 Specification – section 9 (Mental Health)

> **Key points to note**
> - Increased lot value per procurement area (see para 10.9).
> - Changes to supervisor standards (see para 10.11).
> - Replacement of 'designated accredited representative' provisions (see para 10.15).
> - Level 1 fee payable when Tribunal Procedure (First-tier Tribunal) (Health, Education and Social Care Chamber) Rules 2008 rule 11(7)(a) client refuses to engage (see para 10.38).
> - New rule about disbursements and alternative arrangements (see para 10.57).

Introduction

10.1 This chapter deals with the funding of mental health cases, and should be read alongside chapters 2, 3 and 4. In this chapter we set out the rules specific to mental health work which are in addition to and build on the general rules applicable to all civil work, and are mostly set out in section 9 of the Contract Specification. See also appendix C for a summary of costs issues applicable to all civil work.

10.2 Specific mental health peer review guidance to work in this field has been published by the Legal Aid Agency (LAA), now in its sixth edition.[3] Particular attention should be paid to pages 2 and 3 regarding

---

2 Available at: www.gov.uk/government/publications/standard-civil-contract-2024.
3 Peer Review Quality Guide for Mental Health: *Improving Your Quality in Mental Health: A guide to common issues identified through Peer Review*, LAA, March 2021, available at: www.gov.uk/guidance/legal-aid-agency-audits.

'major concerns'. The Independent Peer Review Process Document describes the peer review process itself, including in relation to mental health.[4] In addition, invaluable guidance as to attendance and appropriate work is to be found in the Law Society's practice note *Representation before mental health tribunals*.[5]

10.3 Some of the flexible working arrangements introduced during the coronavirus pandemic have been retained. These are set out on the LAA's website,[6] and are mentioned in this chapter where relevant.

What is mental health work?

10.4 The mental health category of law is defined as:[7]

> 42. Legal Help and all proceedings in relation to:
> (a) cases under the Mental Health Act 1983, the Mental Capacity Act 2005, and paragraph 5(2) of the Schedule to the Repatriation of Prisoners Act 1984 (as described in paragraph 5 of Part 1 of Schedule 1 to the Act);[8]
> (b) the inherent jurisdiction of the High Court in relation to vulnerable adults (as described in paragraph 9 of Part 1 of Schedule 1 to the Act);
> (c) the inherent jurisdiction of the High Court in relation to children (as described in paragraph 9 of Part 1 of Schedule 1 to the Act) where the case relates to a decision on medical treatment.
>
> 43. For the avoidance of doubt, except as permitted by paragraph 13 above[9] the Mental Health Category does not include any civil legal services made available under paragraphs 21 or 22 of Part 1 of Schedule 1 to the Act,[10] including, but not limited to, matters arising from an individual's detention under the Mental Health Act 1983 or the Mental Capacity Act 2005. Nor does it [include] services under the Mental Health Act 1983 that are required to be made available under sections 13, 15 and 16 of the Act (criminal legal aid).

---

4 *Independent Peer Review Process Document*, v5, LAA, November 2021, available at: www.gov.uk/guidance/legal-aid-agency-audits.
5 23 February 2024. At: www.lawsociety.org.uk/topics/private-client/representation-before-mental-health-tribunals.
6 At: www.gov.uk/guidance/schedule-of-processes-restarting-after-covid-19-contingency.
7 LAA, Category Definitions 2024, August 2024, para 42.
8 Legal Aid, Sentencing and Punishment of Offenders Act 2012 (LASPO).
9 Under the heading 'Damages under the Human Rights Act 1998'.
10 Under the headings 'Abuse of position or powers by public authority' and 'Breach of Convention rights by public authority', respectively.

10.5 Court of Protection work is permitted by virtue of the inclusion of the Mental Capacity Act (MCA) 2005, but advocacy in the Court of Protection is only permitted where the proceedings concern:[11]

- right to life;
- liberty or physical safety;
- medical treatment;
- capacity to marry, enter a civil partnership or enter sexual relations; or
- right to family life.

10.6 For any other Court of Protection matter, advice will be in scope but not representation (advocacy). Where representation can be justified, an application for exceptional funding can be made (see chapter 3), and the Category Definitions confirm that will be treated as mental health work.

Overview

10.7 Under the Standard Civil Contract 2024, mental health contracts were let by geographical procurement area.

10.8 To do any mental health work at all, you must have a schedule authorisation for at least one procurement area and meet the appropriate supervisor requirements.

10.9 In the procurement process for the 2024 Contract, lot boundaries were increased: lot 1 allowed 300 matter starts and required one FTE panel member per area; lot 2 allowed 500 matter starts for two panel members per area; and lot 3 allowed 700 for three panel members per area.

10.10 You can take on cases as you see fit, subject to means and merits tests where applicable. However, in each schedule period, you must use at least 70 per cent of your matter starts for a procurement area for clients who were physically located in the procurement area at the time the matter start is opened.[12]

---

11 LASPO Sch 1 Part 3 para 4; Civil Legal Aid (Merits Criteria) Regulations 2013 reg 52(3).
12 Standard Civil Contract 2024 Specification para 9.13.

44. To the extent that any relevant grant of exceptional funding is made (in accordance with section 10 of the Act), this category also includes advocacy for matters arising under the Mental Capacity Act 2005 (as described in paragraph 5 of Part 1 of Schedule 1 to the Act) that are not listed in paragraph 4 of Part 3 of Schedule 1 to the Act.

Mental health supervisors

10.11 Under the Standard Civil Contract 2024 Specification, there are two legal competence standards for supervisors. These are:
1) the **MHT Legal Competence Standard** for supervisors who predominately supervise mental health contract work in relation to the Mental Health Act 1983;[13] and
2) the **Mental Health and Mental Capacity Legal Competence Standard** for supervisors who supervise a mixture of contract work under the Mental Health Act 1983 and MCA 2005.[14]

10.12 The Legal Competence Standard for these two different supervisor standards is summarised in the table below:

Mental health	Mental health and mental capacity
Member of Law Society Mental Health Accreditation Scheme	Member of Law Society Mental Health Accreditation Scheme
Representation at five MHTs	Five case files involving under the MCA 2005 (including at least two Court of Protection applications) **or** mental welfare (capacity) accreditation

10.13 The Standard Civil Contract 2024 includes a clause that states that the LAA may implement further requirements for performing contract work under the MCA 2005. These would only be introduced with the express agreement of the Consultative Bodies and providers will be given 12 months' notice of any changes before they come into effect.[15]

Advocacy

10.14 All advocates before the Mental Health Tribunal (MHT), except self-employed counsel, must be members of the Law Society's Mental Health Accreditation Scheme.[16]

10.15 The 2018 Contract's concept of 'designated accredited representatives' has been removed in the 2024 Contract. Instead, the 2024 Specification states:[17]

---

13 Standard Civil Contract 2024 Specification paras 9.18–9.22.
14 Standard Civil Contract 2024 Specification paras 9.24–9.30.
15 Standard Civil Contract 2024 Specification para 9.7.
16 Standard Civil Contract 2024 Specification para 9.8.
17 Standard Civil Contract 2024 Specification para 91.2

Where you instruct Agents and/or self-employed Counsel to conduct advocacy before the MHT you must: (a) comply with rules on working with third parties in Clause 3 and Paragraphs 2.5 to 2.7; (b) ensure that any third party you appoint has the appropriate skills, experience and knowledge to advocate on behalf of Clients before the MHT; and (c) you ensure that as far as possible any third parties you appoint have familiarised themselves with the Client's case before they provide any advocacy.

Use of counsel

10.16 You are entitled to instruct counsel to represent clients before the tribunal. Where you instruct counsel, you will still only be entitled to the level 3 fee (see para 10.40 below), and it is a matter for you to negotiate how much of that fee to pay to counsel. Counsel's fees do not count as a disbursement.[18] The same principle applies to instructing agents.

10.17 However, in unusually complex cases, you can apply to the LAA to pay counsel as a disbursement at an hourly rate above the standard hourly rates in the contract. The LAA will grant prior authority, specifying the hourly rate and the maximum costs limit, if the case poses unusually complex evidential problems or novel or difficult points of law. This cannot be retrospective. The LAA considers it highly unlikely that such issues will arise at MHT level.[19]

Levels of funding

Overview

10.18 The following forms of civil legal aid services apply to mental health work:[20]

- Legal Help – advice and assistance, but excluding representation before the tribunal;
- Help at Court – funding for representation for victims under the Domestic Violence, Crime and Victims Act 2004;
- Controlled Legal Representation (CLR) – representation before the tribunal; and

---

18 Standard Civil Contract 2024 Specification paras 9.60–9.62.
19 Standard Civil Contract 2024 Specification para 9.61.
20 Standard Civil Contract 2024 Specification para 9.3.

- Legal Representation (certificate) – appeals to the Upper Tribunal and representation in the higher courts, including the Court of Protection.

Standard fees for controlled work

10.19 Mental health work is covered by standard fixed fees for almost all controlled (ie non-certificate) work – the sole exception being Help at Court for victims, which is always paid at hourly rates.[21]

10.20 There are four main fees:[22]
- the non-MHT fee, for all work that does not involve the tribunal;[23]
- MHT fee level 1 – initial advice;[24]
- MHT fee level 2 – negotiation and preparation once an application to the MHT has been made;[25] and
- MHT fee level 3 – representation before the MHT, and follow-up work.[26]

You cannot claim both the non-MHT fee and any level of MHT fee in the same matter for a client.

10.21 A fee may be claimed for each stage through which the matter passes. Disbursements incurred are in addition to the fixed fees (but see para 10.16 above in relation to counsel's fees).

10.22 Subject to certain conditions being met, an adjourned hearing fee can be claimed for face-to-face or remote hearings that are adjourned, postponed or otherwise cancelled on the day of the hearing.[27] The reasons behind the adjournment, postponement or cancellation of a remote hearing should be documented on file along with a justification, and any relevant evidence, that the circumstances warrant the adjourned hearing fee to be claimed.[28]

10.23 In theory there is an additional fee for travel to any hospital that the LAA has designated on its website as a remote hospital[29] (at the time of writing, none had been designated).

---

21 Standard Civil Contract 2024 Specification para 9.66.
22 Standard Civil Contract 2024 Specification para 9.66.
23 Standard Civil Contract 2024 Specification para 9.71 onwards.
24 Standard Civil Contract 2024 Specification para 9.77 onwards.
25 Standard Civil Contract 2024 Specification para 9.79 onwards.
26 Standard Civil Contract 2024 Specification para 9.84 onwards.
27 Standard Civil Contract 2024 Specification paras 9.85 and 95A.
28 Standard Civil Contract 2024 Specification para 9.85B.
29 Standard Civil Contract 2024 Specification para 9.88.

> **Case study**
>
> *I have granted CLR to my client. I made an application to the tribunal. I prepared the case and attended a hospital managers' review with my client, but he then decided he didn't want to proceed to a full hearing yet. What can I claim?*
>
> Level 1 (initial advice) and level 2 (negotiation and preparation). You only claim level 3 if there is an MHT hearing.

Granting Legal Help

Introduction

10.24 The general rules set out in chapters 2 and 4 apply to the granting of Legal Help in the Mental Health category.

10.25 Where relevant, a person acting or proposing to act as litigation friend (or someone else when there is a good reason for that not being possible) may make an application for controlled work.[30] Exceptionally, where the client's condition is such that they will not sign the application form, you may annotate the form to that effect and a supervisor may sign it.[31] The reasons should be noted on the form.

10.26 In any case, a claim can be made without a client signature if 'it is clear reasonable attempts have been made to secure the client's signature and you have provided evidence of the client's intention to sign the form' or 'you have been appointed to act for a client by a court or tribunal'. The LAA will accept digital signatures. Detailed guidance was published during the Covid-19 pandemic and remains in force.[32]

10.27 The Specification allows you to provide advice remotely prior to obtaining a signature,[33] and/or to receive the signed application form by post or other means.[34] The limit to this is 50 per cent of total matters in any schedule period, though cases where it was required under the Equality Act 2010 are not counted in that calculation.[35] It is obviously much better practice to see clients in person when possible.

---

30 Civil Legal Aid (Procedure) Regulations 2012 reg 22(4).
31 Standard Civil Contract 2024 Specification para 9.59.
32 *Coronavirus (COVID-19): working with clients*, LAA, April 2022: www.gov.uk/guidance/coronavirus-covid-19-working-with-clients.
33 Standard Civil Contract 2024 Specification para 3.18 onwards.
34 Standard Civil Contract 2024 para 3.15.
35 Standard Civil Contract 2024 para 3.17.

Means

10.28 The usual means test for Legal Help will apply – see chapter 2 for details. Note that the guidance on evidence of means, states:

> It will often be impracticable to obtain evidence of income from patients with mental health problems who are in hospital (for example, those detained under the Mental Health Act). Providers should however attempt to obtain oral or written confirmation of the position (eg type of benefit received) from the ward manager or social worker where practicable.[36]

10.29 However, where the client is a patient whose case is the subject of proceedings or potential proceedings before the MHT, no means test is required[37] – the client is automatically eligible. Where the case starts as an MHT matter but subsequently covers advice on non-MHT issues, it will be all one matter and therefore no means test needs to be carried out.[38]

Merits

10.30 The usual merits test for Legal Help – the 'sufficient benefit test' – will apply. See chapter 4 for details of the sufficient benefit test.

Granting CLR

Introduction

10.31 CLR is granted by your signature on a form already signed by the client (subject to the same provisions set out above for Legal Help where the client is unable or refuses to sign). Since a grant of CLR is a requirement in any case that goes to the MHT, and therefore very much standard practice in most cases, it can become easy to overlook the necessity actually to sign the form. In our experience, some firms have suffered on costs audit as a result. You may wish to consider incorporating a reminder into your file checklist.

---

36 *Lord Chancellor's Guidance on determining financial eligibility for Controlled Work and Family Mediation*, September 2023, para 12.2(11), available at: www.gov.uk/guidance/civil-legal-aid-means-testing.
37 Civil Legal Aid (Financial Resources and Payment for Services) Regulations 2013 reg 5(1)(f); Standard Civil Contract 2024 Specification para 9.32(a).
38 Standard Civil Contract 2018 Specification para 9.33.

Means

10.32 CLR for representation before the MHT is available without the need for a means test.[39]

Merits

10.33 The merits test applicable to CLR in the Mental Health category is set at a very low threshold, given that the client's liberty is at stake. The test is that the Director of Legal Aid Casework (in practice, you) must be satisfied that it is reasonable in the particular circumstances of the case for CLR to be granted.[40] The contract makes clear that it would be unusual for it to be unreasonable to grant CLR.[41] CLR is available to the patient, and if the nearest relative is the applicant to the tribunal, to the nearest relative.[42]

Operating under standard fees

Non-Mental Health Tribunal cases

10.34 All cases that do not concern an application or potential application to the MHT are deemed to be non-MHT cases and attract the non-MHT fee.[43] Only Legal Help is available.

10.35 Initial advice in an MCA 2005 case can be claimed as a non-MHT matter,[44] including making an application for a certificate for representation before the Court of Protection.

Mental Health Tribunal cases

10.36 MHT cases divide into three fee levels.

10.37 **Level 1** is funded by Legal Help and covers initial advice to the client, including a visit to the client and follow-up work up to and including making an application to the MHT. The Contract Specification specifies that the fee:

---

39 Civil Legal Aid (Financial Resources and Payment for Services) Regulations 2013 reg 5(1)(f); Standard Civil Contract 2024 Specification para 9.32(a).
40 Civil Legal Aid (Merits Criteria) Regulations 2013 reg 51.
41 Standard Civil Contract 2024 Specification para 9.54.
42 Standard Civil Contract 2024 Specification para 9.52.
43 Standard Civil Contract 2024 Specification para 9.71.
44 Standard Civil Contract 2024 Specification para 9.47.

... covers the work done in making an initial visit to the Client, including all advice and assistance provided to the client at your first attendance, and follow-up work such as:
(a) preparing and sending initial letters of instruction;
(b) making the application to the MHT if none has been made; and/or
(c) applying to withdraw an existing MHT application if this is agreed as part of the initial advice (eg at the first attendance or as part of the immediate follow-up work).[45]

10.38 The level 1 fee can be claimed after appointment as a representative by the tribunal under Tribunal Procedure (First-tier Tribunal) (Health, Education and Social Care Chamber) Rules 2008 rule 11(7)(a)[46] even if you are unable to make contact with the client or the client refuses to engage with you, as long as you make sufficient and reasonable attempts to obtain instructions. The Specification sets out what justification and paperwork must be kept on file.[47]

10.39 Once it becomes clear that the case is to be considered by the MHT, you should grant CLR[48] and continue work at **level 2**. You can only claim level 2 when substantial legal work (defined as an additional 30 minutes of preparation or advice or separate communication with other parties on legal issues) has been done since the level 1 threshold.[49] This stage covers all work up to, but not including, the substantive hearing, including preparation of the case generally and for the hearing, negotiation with third parties, attendance at managers' reviews and other meetings where appropriate, as well as taking instructions from the client and instructing experts.[50]

10.40 **Level 3** covers representation at the tribunal hearing. Level 3 also includes work done in applying to the tribunal for a review of its decision under Tribunals, Courts and Enforcement Act 2007 s9, or applying for permission to appeal under s11.[51]

10.41 Where the tribunal sets aside its decision, you are still in level 3 but may claim an additional adjourned hearing fee.[52] However, where an appeal or review goes to the Upper Tribunal, you will need to

---

45 Standard Civil Contract 2024 Specification para 9.77.
46 Mental Health Tribunal for Wales Rules 2008 r13(5)(a)(i) in Wales.
47 Standard Civil Contract 2024 Specification para 9.105 onwards.
48 Standard Civil Contract 2024 Specification para 9.55.
49 Standard Civil Contract 2024 Specification paras 9.80 and 9.81.
50 Standard Civil Contract 2024 Specification para 9.82.
51 Standard Civil Contract 2024 Specification para 9.101.
52 Standard Civil Contract 2024 Specification para 9.101.

Conducting a mental health case 275

apply for a certificate for representation at that stage.[53] If the challenge results in further MHT proceedings, you can choose whether to open a new matter start or continue with the existing one.

10.42 Where a client transfers their case to you, you are entitled to claim the full mental health fee for each of the levels of work you undertake, including initial advice and negotiation/preparation.[54]

Escape fee cases

10.43 Where the amount of any claim as calculated on the basis of hourly rates exceeds three times the relevant mental health fee(s) payable, it becomes an escape fee case and is paid at hourly rates.

10.44 The LAA provides the following example of how this is calculated:

> In an MHT case with work at levels 1, 2 and 3 and two adjourned hearings, in order to become an Escape Fee Case the costs would need to be greater than or equal to:
>
> (3 × (Level 1 Fee + Level 2 Fee + Level 3 Fee)) + (2 × Adjourned Hearing Fee).[55]

10.45 For work covered by the non-MHT fee or the MHT fee level 1, the relevant hourly rate is that for Legal Help.

10.46 For work covered by MHT fee level 2 and MHT fee level 3, the relevant hourly rate is that for CLR.

10.47 An EC1 claim form must be submitted, which may be done electronically.[56] Bill preparation time of 30 minutes is considered reasonable in the majority of cases, but this time does not count towards the costs when calculating whether the case has 'escaped'.[57]

10.48 Escape fee claims are not paid automatically: they are paid in full or in part, or not at all, following an assessment by the LAA. There is an appeal process which can be used when payment is not made in full.[58]

---

53 Standard Civil Contract 2024 Specification para 9.3.
54 Standard Civil Contract 2024 Specification para 9.99.
55 Standard Civil Contract 2024 Specification para 9.96.
56 *Guidance for electronic submission of Escape Case Claims*, May 2021, at: https://assets.publishing.service.gov.uk/media/60afad6cd3bf7f43560e3227/Guidance_for_electronic_submission_of_Escape_Case_Claims.pdf.
57 *Escape Cases Electronic Handbook*, v2.3, Aug 2023, para 7.4.
58 *Escape Cases Electronic Handbook*, chapter 9.

Separate matters

10.49 Each time a client becomes eligible to make an application to the tribunal, the client enters a 'period of eligibility'. This is defined in the preliminaries to the Mental Health Contract Specification as:

> ... the period during which the Client is eligible to apply to the MHT under the applicable provisions in Part V of the Mental Health Act 1983 relating to their particular circumstances.[59]

10.50 Generally, all work done for a client within a period of eligibility, on both MHT and non-MHT matters, is 'rolled up' into one matter start.[60]

10.51 However, you may start a new matter, even if you have an existing ongoing matter, when:[61]

- there is more than one (non-concurrent) set of MHT proceedings within the same period of eligibility (ie separate MHT proceedings fees can be claimed for each); or
- the client withdraws from the MHT, and within the same period of eligibility applies again in the same period of eligibility. This applies if the withdrawal and re-application were carried out in good faith and made with the client's consent and/or in the client's best interests and you have noted down the reasons for withdrawal and re-application on your file. If reinstatement would have been an alternative, then you must justify why this course was not taken.[62]

10.52 Generally, you must open a new matter start for any work on a new legal issue when a client is in a new eligibility period. However, this does not include any issue that originally arose within a previous period of eligibility (such as ongoing tribunal proceedings or a hospital managers renewal hearing).[63] Note that a hospital managers renewal hearing belongs to the 'old' period of eligibility and should be billed as part of that period, which requires a new matter start if there is no pre-existing file for that period.

---

59 Standard Civil Contract 2024 Specification para 9.1.
60 Standard Civil Contract 2024 Specification para 9.39.
61 Standard Civil Contract 2024 Specification para 9.41.
62 Standard Civil Contract 2024 Specification para 9.42.
63 Standard Civil Contract 2024 Specification para 9.43.

10.53 However, note that communicating the decision of the MHT, advising the client about it and about aftercare is part of the same matter as the MHT.[64]

10.54 Where an MCA 2005 matter is open, and then the client is sectioned or otherwise requires MHT advice, a separate MHT matter may be opened.[65]

Disbursements

10.55 Disbursements may be incurred in the usual way in the mental health category.

10.56 You can make a claim for payment on account of disbursements (not including counsel's fees) during the life of a case, but only where the matter has been open for at least three months and if there has been a previous application for payment on account, at least three months have elapsed since that application was made.[66]

10.57 Under the 2024 Contract, where you hold a schedule authorisation based on an 'alternative arrangement' rather than permanent presence, all costs and disbursements (including travel and mileage) must be calculated from the relevant alternative arrangement and not any other location (eg permanent presence or fee earner's home address) unless it would reduce costs.[67]

Licensed work

10.58 See chapter 4 for the general principles applicable to licensed work. See also paras 10.4–10.6 above in relation to work under the MCA 2005.

10.59 The merits test for certificates to be granted for mental capacity work is:[68]

- the standard criteria apply (see chapter 4); and
- the Court of Protection has ordered, or is likely to order, an oral hearing; and
- it is necessary for the individual to be provided with full representation in the proceedings.

---

64 Standard Civil Contract 2024 Specification para 9.44.
65 Standard Civil Contract 2024 Specification para 9.48.
66 Standard Civil Contract 2024 Specification para 9.68.
67 Standard Civil Contract 2024 Specification para 9.5A.
68 Civil Legal Aid (Merits Criteria) Regulations 2013 reg 52(1) and (2).

10.60 Non-means tested representation is available for the protected person and their responsible person's representative in an application under MCA 2005 s21A.

Contact with the LAA

10.61 All work in the mental health category, with the exception of high cost cases, is handled by the Liverpool Office of the LAA. All claims and applications, including certificate applications, together with any queries, should be directed to:

Mental Health Unit/Immigration and Asylum
Controlled Work and Escaped Fee Claims
Legal Aid Agency
Level 6, The Capital
Union Street
Liverpool L3 9AF

Phone: 0300 200 2020
Email: mhu-ec@justice.gov.uk

CHAPTER 11

Conducting a housing case

Edited by Simon Mullings

11.1	Introduction
11.5	**What housing work is in the scope of legal aid?**
11.5	Overview
11.6	Possession cases
	Overview • Counterclaims • Mortgage possession proceedings
11.21	Homelessness and allocations
	Housing Act 1996 and Housing (Wales) Act 2014 • Accommodation by way of community care services • Accommodation for asylum-seekers
11.35	Unlawful eviction
11.41	Housing conditions and disrepair
	Overview • Freestanding disrepair and housing conditions claims • Disrepair counterclaims
11.60	Harassment
11.62	Anti-social behaviour
11.71	Other housing work
11.72	**Housing Loss Prevention Advice Service (HLPAS)**
11.72	Overview
11.83	Post-Covid-19 provisions
11.87	Operation of the Scheme
	Stage One – In Court Duty Scheme overview • Agents • Forms
11.93	Stage Two – Early Legal Advice
	Making a claim for payment

Key resources

Statutes and statutory instruments

- Legal Aid, Sentencing and Punishment of Offenders Act 2012 – Schedule 1 Part 1
- Civil Legal Aid (Procedure) Regulations 2012
- Civil Legal Aid (Statutory Charge) Regulations 2013
- Civil Legal Aid (Merits Criteria) Regulations 2013
- Civil Legal Aid (Financial Resources and Payment for Services) Regulations 2013
- Civil Legal Aid (Remuneration) Regulations 2013 and Civil Legal Aid (Remuneration) (Amendment) Regulations 2013

Contracts

- 2024 Standard Civil Contract Standard
- 2024 Standard Civil Contract Specification
- 2024 Standard Civil Contract Specification (General Provisions)
- 2018 Standard Civil Contract Table of Amendments – from January 2024
- 2024 Standard Civil Contract Category Definitions
- 2018 Standard Civil Contract Specification Category Specific Rules – see relevant area of law

Lord Chancellor's Guidance

- Lord Chancellor's Guidance under section 4 of the Legal Aid, Sentencing and Punishment of Offenders Act 2012, May 2023
- Lord Chancellor's Guidance on Determining Financial Eligibility for Controlled Work & Family Mediation
- Lord Chancellor's Guidance on Determining Financial Eligibility for Certificated Work
- Costs Assessment Guidance: www.gov.uk/guidance/funding-and-costs-assessment-for-civil-and-crime-matters
- Guidance on the Remuneration of Expert Witnesses: https://assets.publishing.service.gov.uk/media/66680933e8d5f2d4bdfcbb5a/Guidance_on_the_Remuneration_of_Expert_Witnessesv9_June_2024.pdf
- Housing Loss Prevention Advice Service (HLPAS) Provider Guidance: www.gov.uk/government/publications/housing-loss-prevention-advice-service-hlpas

Other
- Frequently Asked Questions: Civil Legal Aid Reforms, v1.4, Legal Aid Agency, May 2013, FAQ 98 – this document is no longer on the LAA website, but is available at: https://assets.publishing.service.gov.uk/government/uploads/system/uploads/attachment_data/file/375631/legal-aid-reform-faq.pdf
- Apply for legal aid for breach of Part 1 injunctions under the Anti-Social Behaviour Crime and Policing Act 2014: Guidance for providers: www.gov.uk/guidance/apply-for-legal-aid-for-anti-social-behaviour-injunction-breaches

Key points to note
- Housing law cases often have other issues such as welfare benefits, debt, community care, immigration and other areas of law at their heart. Unfortunately, many of these areas of law are out of scope. Be clear about what you can and cannot do for you client under legal aid rules and within your organisation. If possible, try to have good referral and signposting arrangements for the things you cannot do.
- The Client and Cost Management System (CCMS) can be tricky for housing cases and much of the language used within CCMS shows a lack of understanding of how housing law cases work. Make sure you know the right scope limitations to use and that you know how to do single and dual stage applications, and how to manage counterclaim cases in CCMS.
- In disrepair/housing conditions cases there is a particular need to be aware of what work you can do in what circumstances and also the effect of the statutory charge. It is essential that you cover these issues in your advice to your client and that you have a clear record of having done so.
- In housing cases delegated functions can be a critical part of the service to clients. Make sure you understand when you can and cannot use them.
- The Housing Loss Prevention Advice Service (HLPAS) is a new service and the Early Legal Advice part of it is likely to be changed over time as the scheme 'beds in'. Make sure you keep abreast of changes.

Introduction

11.1 This chapter deals with work done in the Housing category. You should read it in conjunction with chapters 2 and 4. Chapter 2 deals with general rules about taking on civil cases and applies to work in housing as it does to all other work; chapter 4 deals with the rules that apply to the conduct of all civil cases. The housing-specific rules in this chapter usually build on, rather than replace, the general rules; where they do replace the general rules in chapters 2 and 4 we will say so. Out of scope housing cases may be funded as exceptional cases – see chapter 3 for more on exceptional funding.

11.2 At the time of writing, some Covid-19 contingency arrangements remain in place and some have become permanent. None of these apply **solely** to housing category work, but the provisions in respect of legal aid most relevant to housing advisers are 'Coronavirus (COVID-19): working with clients', available at: www.gov.uk/guidance/coronavirus-covid-19-working-with-clients.

11.3 Included in this chapter is advice about counterclaims in housing proceedings. You should keep in mind that when you apply for a representation certificate, a counterclaim is treated as separate proceedings and so you need to add the counterclaim as a proceeding in your application. For example, housing possession proceedings with a disrepair counterclaim should have two sets of proceedings, namely:

- Recover possession – tenant – Housing; and
- Bring a counterclaim – Housing,

and each should have appropriate scope and costs limitations. Also keep in mind that where there is any damages claim you will need to advise your client of the operation of the Legal Aid Agency's (LAA's) statutory charge (see chapter 4).

11.4 In respect of claiming for legally aided housing law cases, see appendix C for a summary of the LAA's Costs Assessment Guidance,[1] dealing with some of the most common queries raised by solicitors and caseworkers.

---

1 Costs Assessment Guidance: www.gov.uk/guidance/funding-and-costs-assessment-for-civil-and-crime-matters.

What housing work is in the scope of legal aid?

Overview

11.5 The Category Definitions in the Standard Civil Contract 2024[2] define housing work as:
- **possession** of the home, other than mortgage possession and orders for sale;[3]
- **homelessness**:
  - provision of accommodation and assistance under Housing Act 1996 Parts 6 and 7 (although not mentioned in the Category Definitions, includes Part 2 of Housing (Wales) Act 2014) for an individual who is homeless or threatened with homelessness;
  - provision of accommodation by way of community care services to an individual who is homeless or threatened with homelessness; and
  - accommodation and support for asylum-seekers, etc;
- **eviction**, including unlawful eviction, and planning eviction and closure orders not arising from criminal conduct;
- **housing conditions and disrepair**, to the extent it is in scope;
- injunctions under the **Protection from Harassment Act 1997** arising from housing matters;
- applications to vary or discharge an injunction under Housing Act 1996 s153A – this provision has been repealed and effectively replaced by the **Anti-social Behaviour, Crime and Policing Act 2014**; while the definition has once again not been updated in the Category Definitions, document guidance makes clear that the new provisions are in scope for legal aid;
- proceedings in relation to accommodation provided under section 4 or 95 of the Immigration and Asylum Act 1999 and section 17 of the Nationality, Immigration and Asylum Act 2002; and
- **exceptional funding grants** on any other matter concerning the possession, status, terms of occupation, repair, improvement, eviction from, quiet enjoyment of, or payment of rent or other charges for premises (including vehicles and sites they occupy)

---

2 At paras 37 and 38. See appendix B; and/or for the current version: www.gov.uk/government/publications/standard-civil-contract-2024 or https://assets.publishing.service.gov.uk/media/6569c0739462260013c567df/Draft_Category_Definitions_2024__Dec_2023__.pdf.

3 Mortgage possession and orders for sale are in the debt category. The telephone gateway has been withdrawn – see para 11.19 onwards below.

that are occupied as a residence, including the rights of leaseholders, allocation, transfers and the provision of sites for occupation.

Possession cases

Overview

11.6 Defences to claims for possession of the home are in scope and in the Housing and Debt category. Legal Help is available for initial advice, and you can apply for a certificate for investigative help and/or representation in court should that become necessary. See also the section below on HLPAS.

11.7 Possession of 'the home' includes houses, caravans, houseboats and other vehicles that are the individual's only or main residence, together with the land on which they are located.[4]

11.8 Legal aid is not available to defend possession proceedings brought against squatters – that is, where there are no grounds for arguing that the individual is occupying otherwise than as a trespasser, **and** no grounds for arguing that their occupation began otherwise than as a trespasser. The conjunction word 'and' is important here as it means that legal aid is available to person who had licence or consent to enter the premises but later became a trespasser.[5]

11.9 Defences based on whether it is reasonable for a possession order to be made and/or defences on public law/human rights/Equality Act 2010 grounds are included. Help at Court and Investigative Help are also available in appropriate cases.

11.10 LASPO Sch 1 Part 1 para 33 says that civil legal services in relation to court orders for possession are in scope. This does not mean that you have to wait until proceedings are issued before any legal aid becomes available, though there must be a real prospect of proceedings being commenced. The LAA has said that 'formal written notification that proceedings will be issued (such as a section 8 or section 21 notice)' will be enough. There is no reason to think that where a tenant has received a letter[6] with a credible threat to bring proceedings they should not receive Legal Help just because the landlord has

---

4 Legal Aid, Sentencing and Punishment of Offenders Act 2012 (LASPO) Sch 1 Part 1 para 33(9) and (11).
5 LASPO Sch 1 Part 1 para 33(10).
6 *Frequently Asked Questions: Civil Legal Aid Reforms*, v1.4, LAA, May 2013, FAQ 98 – this document is no longer on the LAA website, but is available at: https://assets.publishing.service.gov.uk/government/uploads/system/uploads/attachment_data/file/375631/legal-aid-reform-faq.pdf.

erroneously not served a notice. A representation certificate will not be granted, however, until proceedings have actually been issued. Prior to that, you may grant Legal Help.

11.11 Therefore, general advice on the theoretical possibility of possession proceedings, or advice on the implications of a client's rent arrears at an early stage, will be out of scope. However, once the landlord has issued any kind of notification of intent to take proceedings, legal aid in the form of Legal Help will be available. Once proceedings have actually been issued, you can apply for a certificate,[7] using delegated functions if necessary, as long as the client has a defence (or a realistic prospect of arguing that it would not be reasonable to make a possession order). If not, you can still attend court to offer mitigation using Help at Court. The timescales of housing possession cases means that Investigative Help is rarely required, but it should be borne in mind that it is available in appropriate cases.

11.12 The **merits test** for the grant of a certificate in possession proceedings is:[8]

- the standard criteria are met (see chapter 4 at para 4.94);
- the individual has a defence (including that it would be unreasonable for the court to make an order for possession in the circumstances); and
- prospects of success are:
  - borderline, or marginal or better; and
  - the proportionality test is met (see chapter 4 at para 4.104).

11.13 Many possession cases involving rent arrears will have, as the underlying cause or a contributor to it, problems with housing benefit or the housing element of universal credit. LASPO Sch 1 Part 1 para 33(3)

---

7 In relation to accelerated possession proceedings under Civil Procedure Rules 1998 (CPR) 55.11 onwards it appears there has been varying practice. The writer (and others we surveyed on this point) had been of the view that in those cases you must provide advice under Legal Help, including work to file a defence form, and could not move to a representations certificate until a hearing is listed. We think this arose from indication given by LAA officers in cases some considerable time ago. However, we are grateful to Jeinsen Lam of South West London Law Centre for pointing out that nothing in the Specifications or Guidance says you cannot do that work under a certificate, and practitioners also report this is their practice.

8 Civil Legal Aid (Merits Criteria) Regulations 2013 reg 61, amended by Civil Legal Aid (Merits Criteria) (Amendment) Regulations 2014 to provide that the prospects of success test to be applied is that in reg 43 of the 2013 Regulations. Regulation 43 was amended by Civil Legal Aid (Merits Criteria) (Amendment) Regulations 2016 reg 2(4) to allow for grants in the borderline and marginal, but not poor, categories.

applies the Part 2 scope exclusions, including the welfare benefits exclusion. The effect of this is that work done in relation to the possession proceedings is in scope, but work done in relation to welfare benefits is out of scope. You can investigate the housing benefit or universal credit position to prepare a defence to the possession matter – which may include preparing witness statements, or even summonsing housing benefits or Department for Work and Pensions (DWP) officers – and can seek an adjournment for the client to resolve the benefits matter themselves. However, any work in assisting the client with that resolution will not be claimable.[9] Often work of that kind will be necessary and will be done to assist your client to resolve matters and so good, properly apportioned attendance notes will help with costs assessment. See also the section on HLPAS below where we show that benefits work can be done under the Early Legal Advice Scheme.

11.14 Judicial review of housing benefit and other local authority financial assistance is in scope, though would fall into the welfare benefits and public law categories – see chapters 3 and 13. Exceptional case funding (ECF) for welfare benefits cases is possible. Practitioners who apply for this will do well to consult the guidance from the Public Law Project.[10] See also chapter 3.

11.15 Where there is a claim for possession based wholly or in part on allegations of anti-social behaviour, including mandatory grounds, then legal representation to defend the possession proceedings is made in the usual way, selecting the appropriate scope in the CCMS. However, applications for injunctions under the Anti-social Behaviour, Crime and Policing Act 2014 and committal proceedings based on a breach of such injunctions are dealt with separately in this chapter at para 11.62 onwards below.

11.16 Where a client does not have a full or partial defence to the proceedings (including the defence that it would be unreasonable for the court to make an order for possession in the circumstances and/ or on public law/human rights/Equality Act 2010 grounds), it is unlikely that a certificate would be justified, though Help at Court may be granted where informal advocacy is justified by way of mitigation at court hearings. The guidance[11] states that 'typically this will

---

9 *Frequently Asked Questions: Civil Legal Aid Reforms*, LAA, FAQ 107.
10 See: https://publiclawproject.org.uk/exceptional-case-funding.
11 *Lord Chancellor's Guidance under Section 4 of the Legal Aid, Sentencing and Punishment of Offenders Act 2012*, May 2023, para 6.9(b), available at: www.gov.uk/guidance/funding-and-costs-assessment-for-civil-and-crime-matters. See chapter 4 at para 4.55 for more on Help at Court.

be in possession proceedings where the client has no defence to possession but seeks to influence the discretion of the court in relation to postponing possession or suspending eviction'. Practitioners should consider (a) whether there is a defence and (b) whether that defence has sufficient merits under the rules, rather than be inhibited from applying because a suspended order is a possible outcome. Difficulties sometimes arise when LAA caseworkers misunderstand the nature of a defence in possession proceedings, particularly in Housing Act 1988 s21 cases, and so it is important to set out the nature of the defence carefully in the application and to appeal bad decisions where necessary.

11.17 Where legal aid is required to apply to suspend a warrant of eviction, then in all appropriate cases an application for Legal Representation should be made, not least because the certificate affords the client costs protection. Formal representation can be made on behalf of the client, adjournments with directions can be obtained for exchange of statements along with relevant medical reports, and for the hearing to be allocated sufficient time for proper judicial consideration.

Counterclaims

11.18 Where legal aid has been granted in possession proceedings, it can also be granted to cover work done on a counterclaim (see para 11.3 above), even if the subject of the counterclaim would otherwise be out of scope as a freestanding claim, including discrimination, declaration of tenancy and Equality Act 2010 claims. The LASPO Sch 1 Part 2 exclusions of assault, battery and false imprisonment claims; trespass to goods and trespass to land; damage to property; and breach of statutory duty do not apply to counterclaims in possession proceedings, so all may be pleaded and claimed for.[12] However, from the authors' experience, the LAA considers claims for personal injury (which are excluded by LASPO Sch 1 Part 2 para 2) are not in scope (because personal injury is not re-included for counterclaims by LASPO Sch 1 Part 1 para 33(6)) and that is the case even when personal injury would be the subject of a counterclaim which is re-included, such as a claim for breach of statutory duty. In that case, ECF is the only route to litigate a personal injury counterclaim with legal aid funding. There is more on housing conditions and disrepair counterclaims at para 11.55 onwards below.

12 LASPO Sch 1 Part 1 para 33(7).

Mortgage possession proceedings

11.19 Mortgage possession claims are also in scope but are in the Debt category. Each housing contract is actually a housing and debt contract and includes a notional four debt matter starts per year, as well as a licence to do debt certificated work. Up to May 2020, Debt was a mandatory gateway category, meaning that a client needing Legal Help or Help at Court had to go through the gateway unless they were exempt. From 15 May 2020, clients in need of mortgage possession proceedings advice, assistance, and investigative help and representation can, subject to eligibility, access face-to-face services directly.[13]

11.20 In the context of mortgage possession proceedings it is also worth noting that there have also been amendments to assessments of capital for homeowners by way of the Civil Legal Aid (Financial Resources and Payment for Services) (Amendment) Regulations 2020.[14] Those regulations amended Civil Legal Aid (Financial Resources and Payment for Services) Regulations 2013[15] reg 37, removing the £100,000 cap on the deductions from capital to be applied in relation to a mortgage. So the position from 28 January 2021 has been that the entire amount of the debt secured by the mortgage or charge is deducted for the purposes of assessing capital.

Homelessness and allocations

Housing Act 1996 and Housing (Wales) Act 2014

11.21 Both Legal Help and, in appropriate cases, Legal Representation, are available to individuals who are homeless or threatened with homelessness[16] and seeking assistance under Housing Act 1996 Part 6 or 7.

11.22 In Wales, the law on allocations is the same (Housing Act 1996 Part 6), but the law on homelessness is different and contained in Housing (Wales) Act 2014 Part 2. There is a separate Welsh Code of Guidance for both Housing Act 1996 Part 6 and Housing (Wales) Act 2014 Part 2. Although homelessness cases in Wales are in scope for

---

13 Civil Legal Aid (Procedure) Regulations 2012, amended by the Civil Legal Aid (Procedure) (Amendment) Regulations 2020.
14 At: www.legislation.gov.uk/uksi/2020/1584/contents/made.
15 At: www.legislation.gov.uk/uksi/2013/480/regulation/37/2013-04-01.
16 As defined in Housing Act 1996 s175, as amended by Homelessness Reduction Act 2017 s1(2) and Housing (Wales) Act 2014 s55(4).

legal aid, the LAA's regulations, guidance and CCMS system do not refer to the Housing (Wales) Act 2014. For example, CCMS does not have scope limitations referring to the Welsh Act. Practitioners are forced therefore to 'read across' provisions when dealing with homelessness cases in Wales, for example, a Housing (Wales) Act 2014 s88 appeal is treated as a Housing Act 1996 s204 appeal.

11.23 LASPO Sch 1 Part 1 para 34(1) says that 'Civil legal services ... in relation to the provision of accommodation and assistance for the individual' are within scope. This is relatively broad and will cover advice on entitlement and suitability of accommodation for homeless people (although legal aid is not available in relation to allocations and suitability of accommodation to people who do not fall within the definition of 'homeless' as set out above), as well as assistance with making an application and any statutory review and appeal that may follow. All such work should be carried out under one matter start except when (a) as a result of a Housing Act 1996 s204 appeal (Housing (Wales) Act 2014 s88) the matter is, by order or agreement, remitted back to the council for a further decision; (b) the review is a suitability review pursuant to Housing Act 1996 s202(1)(f) (Housing (Wales) Act 2014 s85(3)); or (c) judicial review is contemplated in relation to the council's failure to protect possessions under Housing Act 1996 ss211 and 212 (Housing (Wales) Act 2014 ss93 and 94). In those cases a further matter start may be used.[17]

11.24 Legal Help will cover initial advice, the application and any review. The decisions that may be reviewed and therefore which may be the subject of Legal Help are set out in Housing Act 1996 s202 (as amended) and are the subject of guidance at chapter 19 of the Homelessness Code of Guidance.[18] In Wales, the equivalent provisions are at Housing (Wales) Act 2014 s85 and chapter 20 of the Welsh Code of Guidance.[19]

---

17 Standard Civil Contract 2024 Specification, para 10.13: https://assets.publishing.service.gov.uk/media/64c24f02331a650014934cb7/2018_Standard_Civil_Contract_Category_Specification_Housing_and_Debt_Section_10_HLPAS_August_2023.pdf.
18 *Homelessness code of guidance for local authorities*, Department for Levelling Up, Housing and Communities, February 2018, updated June 2024: www.gov.uk/guidance/homelessness-code-of-guidance-for-local-authorities/chapter-19-review-of-decisions-and-appeals-to-the-county-court.
19 *Code of Guidance for Local Authorities on the Allocation of Accommodation and Homelessness*, Welsh Government, March 2016: https://gov.wales/sites/default/files/publications/2019-03/allocation-of-accommodation-and-homelessness-guidance-for-local-authorities.pdf.

11.25 A certificate for Legal Representation will cover an appeal to the county court, or a judicial review. The merits test for homelessness cases is the same as for public law more generally.[20] The test is:
- the standard criteria are met (see chapter 4 at para 4.94);
- all administrative appeals and alternatives to court have been exhausted;
- a letter before claim has been sent (only relevant to judicial review);
- the proportionality test is met (see chapter 4 at para 4.104); and
- prospects of success are:
  – moderate or better; or
  – borderline or marginal, and the case of significant wider public interest, of overwhelming importance to the individual or the substance of the case relates to a breach of European Convention on Human Rights (ECHR) rights.[21]

The borderline or marginal criteria will often be satisfied in cases involving homelessness.

11.26 Inexplicably the default scope limitation for a homelessness appeal in CCMS is for counsel's opinion only and so in order to comply with the 21-day appeal deadline practitioners should add a limitation under delegated functions, which covers lodging the appeal.

11.27 There is a lack of clarity as to whether an appeal and/or application under Housing Act 1996 s204A (Housing (Wales) Act 2014 s89) should be progressed under a separate certificate or under the same certificate as the section 204 appeal. In this situation practitioners are advised to telephone the LAA for advice and keep a good note of the advice given. At the time of writing the advice given by the LAA on this was that a section 204A appeal (and any section 204A(4)(a) application for an injunction) should be done under the same certificate as the section 204 appeal, but there is no official rule or guidance to this effect.

11.28 You can use delegated functions to grant emergency legal aid in homelessness cases, and in judicial review cases involving homelessness.[22]

---

20 Civil Legal Aid (Merits Criteria) Regulations 2013 reg 2 – see definition of 'public law'.
21 Civil Legal Aid (Merits Criteria) Regulations 2013 reg 56, as amended, most recently by the Civil Legal Aid (Merits Criteria) (Amendment) Regulations 2016.
22 Standard Civil Contract 2024 Specification para 5.2.

Accommodation by way of community care services

11.29 Legal aid (both Legal Help and Legal Representation) is available in the Housing category to provide advice and representation to individuals seeking accommodation under certain community care provisions (as set out at LASPO Sch 1 Part 1 para 6). The main provisions that housing practitioners use include:

- Children Act 1989 s17 for families with children;
- Children Act 1989 s20 for homeless children;
- Children Act 1989 ss22A, 22B, 22C, 23, 23B, 23C, 24, 24A and 24B (the 'leaving care' provisions) for young people previously accommodated by children's services;
- Mental Health Act 1983 s117 (after-care services for individuals previously detained under Mental Health Act 1983 s3); and
- Care Act 2014 Part 1 for individuals who have care and support needs.

Organisations that hold housing and community care contracts will be aware that the community care fixed fee for Legal Help is higher.

11.30 Legal Help will cover initial advice and assistance, including consideration of any assessments carried out by local authorities and drafting pre-action letters under the Judicial Review Pre-Action Protocol. A certificate for Legal Representation will cover a judicial review. The **merits test** for community care cases is the same as for public law more generally.[23] The test is:

- the standard criteria are met (see chapter 4 at para 4.94);
- all administrative appeals and alternatives to court have been exhausted;
- a letter before claim has been sent (only relevant to judicial review);
- the proportionality test is met (see chapter 4 at para 4.104); and
- prospects of success are:
  - moderate or better; or
  - borderline or marginal, and the case of significant wider public interest, of overwhelming importance to the individual or the substance of the case relates to a breach of ECHR rights.[24]

---

23 Civil Legal Aid (Merits Criteria) Regulations 2013 reg 2 – see definition of 'public law'.
24 Civil Legal Aid (Merits Criteria) Regulations 2013 reg 56, as amended, most recently by the Civil Legal Aid (Merits Criteria) (Amendment) Regulations 2016.

11.31 Practitioners do not have delegated functions to grant emergency funding in these cases, save for Children Act 1989 s20 and the provision of urgent services pending completion of an assessment under Care Act 2014 s9(3). If the individual needs emergency funding for other cases (including temporary accommodation under Children Act 1989 s17) the practitioner must make an emergency application for a certificate on the CCMS. It is advisable to telephone the LAA, after making the application online, to ask it to make a decision on the application. It is also advisable to be persistent and continue to chase the determination of the application. Full details of the CCMS procedure are outlined in chapter 5; and community care in chapter 12.

Accommodation for asylum-seekers

11.32 Legal Help is available to individuals who apply for accommodation from the Home Office under Immigration and Asylum Act 1999 s4 (for destitute failed asylum-seekers) and s95 (for those with ongoing asylum claims or failed asylum-seekers with children under 18). This can include advice on making an application, challenging the suitability of the offered accommodation (including location and type), and drafting letters before claim under the Judicial Review Pre-Action Protocol for delays in processing applications or failure to provide appropriate accommodation. Assistance can also be provided to draft a notice of appeal and appeal submissions to the First-tier Tribunal (Asylum Support). However, legal aid is not available for representation at the tribunal itself.

11.33 Legal Help is not available under the Housing category to individuals who apply for subsistence-only support under Immigration and Asylum Act 1999 s98. However, where the Home Office makes an unlawful decision advice and assistance may be provided under the Public Law category.

11.34 Practitioners do not have delegated functions to grant emergency funding for judicial review in asylum support accommodation cases. See chapter 5 at para 5.46 for emergency non-delegated functions applications and backdating.

Unlawful eviction

11.35 Legal aid is available for unlawful eviction claims, which includes claims for damages only.[25] In most cases, the eviction will have happened and so an emergency grant of legal aid using delegated

25 LASPO Sch 1 Part 1 para 33.

Conducting a housing case 293

functions will be appropriate (unless the client is simply seeking damages, not reinstatement). However, a 'reasonably alleged' threat of unlawful eviction will be in scope,[26] including by way of withdrawal of services such as utilities,[27] and in such a case Legal Help to advise and issue a warning letter may be more appropriate.

11.36 That being said, Legal Representation may be granted under delegated functions in appropriate cases in order to apply to the court for an injunction prohibiting the landlord from carrying out an unlawful eviction where there is a credible threat to do so. Justification should be set out clearly in the application.

11.37 The **merits test** for Legal Representation is:[28]
- the standard criteria are met (see chapter 4 at para 4.94);
- the proportionality test is met (see chapter 4 at para 4.104);
- prospects of success are:
  – moderate or better; or
  – borderline or marginal, and the case is of significant wider public interest or of overwhelming importance to the individual; and
- the landlord or other person responsible for the matter complained of has been notified of the complaint (except where this is impracticable) and, where notice has been given, has had a reasonable opportunity to resolve the matter.

11.38 Where a claim is primarily for damages rather than reinstatement, it is still in scope, but you will need to explain on the legal aid application why a Conditional Fee Agreement (CFA) is not appropriate. The Lord Chancellor's guidance suggests a CFA will be considered suitable – and so legal aid refused – if:[29]
- prospects of success are at least 60 per cent;
- the opponent is considered able to meet any costs and damages awarded; and
- after the event (ATE) insurance can be obtained.

---

26 *Frequently Asked Questions: Civil Legal Aid Reforms*, FAQ 84.
27 *Frequently Asked Questions: Civil Legal Aid Reforms*, FAQ 105.
28 Civil Legal Aid (Merits Criteria) Regulations 2013 reg 63. Note that the prospects of success criterion is contained in reg 43, which was amended by Civil Legal Aid (Merits Criteria) (Amendment) Regulations 2016 reg 2(4) to allow for grants in the borderline and marginal, but not poor, categories.
29 *Lord Chancellor's Guidance under Section 4 of the Legal Aid, Sentencing and Punishment of Offenders Act 2012*, May 2023, para 7.17.

11.39 Note that where you are relying on the non-availability of ATE insurance, you will be expected to provide evidence of having tried and failed to obtain it (see chapter 4 at para 4.100 for more information).

11.40 Remember that in any claim for damages you must advise your client as to the operation of the LAA's statutory charge.

Housing conditions and disrepair

Overview

11.41 For legal aid purposes, disrepair and housing conditions cases can be considered separately as (a) freestanding claims and (b) counterclaims, respectively. Each has their own distinct rules.

11.42 Freestanding claims and counterclaims brought pursuant to the Homes (Fitness for Human Habitation) Act 2018 will be in scope for legal aid in the same way and to the same extent as disrepair claims. In this chapter, then, we refer to 'disrepair and housing conditions' to mean traditional disrepair claims **and** claims brought under the amendments to Landlord and Tenant Act 1985 ss8–10 by the 2018 Act.

Freestanding disrepair and housing conditions claims

11.43 Disrepair and housing conditions claims are in scope, but only in limited circumstances. LASPO Sch 1 Part 1 para 35 says:

(1) Civil legal services provided to an individual in relation to the removal or reduction of a serious risk of harm to the health or safety of the individual or a relevant member of the individual's family where–

(a) the risk arises from a deficiency in the individual's home,
(b) the individual's home is rented or leased from another person, and
(c) the services are provided with a view to securing that the other person makes arrangements to remove or reduce the risk.

Exclusions

(2) Sub-paragraph (1) is subject to–

(a) the exclusions in Part 2 of this Schedule, with the exception of paragraphs 6 and 8 of that Part, and
(b) the exclusion in Part 3 of this Schedule.

Definitions

(3) For the purposes of this paragraph–

(a) a child is a relevant member of an individual's family if the individual is the child's parent or has parental responsibility for the child;
(b) an adult ('A') is a relevant member of an individual's family if–

(i) they are relatives (whether of the full blood or half blood or by marriage or civil partnership) or cohabitants, and
(ii) the individual's home is also A's home.
(4) In this paragraph–
'adult' means a person aged 18 or over;
'building' includes part of a building;
'child' means a person under the age of 18;
'cohabitant' has the same meaning as in Part 4 of the Family Law Act 1996 (see section 62(1) of that Act);
'deficiency' means any deficiency, whether arising as a result of the construction of a building, an absence of maintenance or repair, or otherwise;
'harm' includes temporary harm;
'health' includes mental health;
'home', in relation to an individual, means the house, caravan, houseboat or other vehicle or structure that is the individual's only or main residence, together with any garden or ground usually occupied with it.

11.44 The **merits test** for a disrepair claim is:
- the standard criteria are met (see chapter 4 at para 4.94);
- the proportionality test is met (see chapter 4 at para 4.104);
- prospects of success are:
  – moderate or better; or
  – borderline or marginal, and the case is of significant wider public interest or of overwhelming importance to the individual; and
- the landlord or other person responsible for the matter complained of has been notified of the complaint (except where this is impracticable) and, where notice has been given, has had a reasonable opportunity to resolve the matter.

11.45 Therefore, legal aid is only available to remove or reduce a serious risk of harm to the client or a member of their family. This means that it is available to force repairs to be done and/or work to make the premises fit for habitation, but not to claim damages.

11.46 In order to be eligible for legal aid, there must at least be a credible allegation that there is such a risk.[30] Once that threshold is crossed, Legal Help will be available to investigate further, including by obtaining expert reports. If after investigation it transpires that there was no serious risk of harm, then legal aid should be withdrawn, though the costs of the investigation will be claimable.

---

30 *Lord Chancellor's Guidance under Section 4 of the Legal Aid, Sentencing and Punishment of Offenders Act 2012,* May 2023, para 12.6; Standard Civil Contract 2024 Specification para 10.10.

11.47 The costs of expert reports should be limited to the maximum set out in the Remuneration Regulations and guidance[31] and if they are, you do not need to apply for prior authority. However, if you need to go above those levels, you can apply for prior authority to do so if working under a certificate. There is no way of applying for prior authority in Legal Help cases, and so you should make a note on the file explaining why you believe the exceptional circumstances criteria are met.[32] The criteria are that the complexity of the material is such that an expert with a high level of seniority is required, or the material is so specialised and unusual that only very few experts are available.[33] These criteria are unlikely to be met in most disrepair and housing conditions cases.

11.48 Any expert instructed should generally be a joint expert in accordance with the Pre-Action Protocol for Housing Conditions Claims (England) or Pre-Action Protocol for Housing Disrepair Cases (Wales),[34] though additional medical evidence may be necessary to show that there is a serious risk of harm in the particular client's circumstances. The LAA recognises that the risk may vary from individual to individual – the risk, for example, arising from damp is higher for a tenant with a respiratory illness than a tenant without one.[35] There is, however, no specific evidential requirement to establish a serious risk of harm.[36] If the LAA does not agree that there is a serious risk, and so considers funding is not justified, there is a right to request a review by the Director, but no right of appeal to an independent funding adjudicator.[37] Any further challenge would have to be by way of judicial review.

---

31 The current rates can be found in Civil Legal Aid (Remuneration) (Amendment) Regulations 2013 Sch 2, and the guidance is at: https://assets.publishing.service.gov.uk/media/66680933e8d5f2d4bdfcbb5a/Guidance_on_the_Remuneration_of_Expert_Witnessesv9_June_2024.pdf. This guidance is still headed 'Family Cases' but actually applies to all civil cases.
32 *Frequently Asked Questions: Civil Legal Aid Reforms*, FAQ 86.
33 Civil Legal Aid (Remuneration) Regulations 2013 Sch 5 para 2.
34 *Lord Chancellor's Guidance under Section 4 of the Legal Aid, Sentencing and Punishment of Offenders Act 2012*, May 2023, para 12.7. The guidance predates the changes in the protocols and therefore simply refers to the 'Housing Disrepair Pre-Action Protocol'.
35 *Lord Chancellor's Guidance under Section 4 of the Legal Aid, Sentencing and Punishment of Offenders Act 2012*, May 2023, para 12.9.
36 *Frequently Asked Questions: Civil Legal Aid Reforms*, FAQ 79.
37 *Frequently Asked Questions: Civil Legal Aid Reforms*, FAQ 80.

11.49 The Lord Chancellor's guidance says that all relevant factors will be taken into account in determining whether there is a serious risk of harm, including the following (non-exhaustive) list of examples:[38]

- whether harm has already resulted;
- whether, as a result of the deficiency, an existing health condition has been exacerbated;
- whether the individual or any family members are in a high risk group, such as the elderly or very young children;
- whether the individual or any family member is vulnerable due to a disability, either because of risk to them, or damage to medical equipment;
- whether there are relevant environmental conditions – such as broken heating in winter;
- whether there are multiple deficiencies that could, taken cumulatively, be of greater seriousness;
- whether a single deficiency poses multiple risks;
- whether a deficiency affects shared rooms or areas;
- whether an instructed expert reports that future deterioration is likely; and
- whether the local authority has identified hazards.

11.50 Freestanding damages claims (ie claims for monetary compensation) are out of scope under LASPO. Where you claim both for enforcement of repairs and other works, and for damages, perhaps under a CFA, you should separate the work done on the file and ensure that you do not claim any work done in respect of the damages aspect on your legal aid bill.

11.51 However, it should also be noted that the LAA takes the view that the statutory charge applies to the whole proceedings, not just the funded part.[39] So if you recover damages as part of a case for which you have legal aid, even if the damages part was out of scope and you have made no claim for work done in respect of it, your client will be required to pay the costs of the in scope part of the case out of any damages recovered. See also chapter 4 at para 4.158, and chapter 4 of Luba, O'Donnell and Peaker, *Housing Conditions: Tenants' Rights*.[40]

11.52 It may therefore be in the client's best interests to bring a claim where the damages element is more than purely nominal under a CFA. In any event, the LAA will probably take the view that a claim

---

38 *Lord Chancellor's Guidance under Section 4 of the Legal Aid, Sentencing and Punishment of Offenders Act 2012*, May 2023, para 12.10.
39 *Frequently Asked Questions: Civil Legal Aid Reforms*, FAQ 81.
40 LAG, sixth edition, 2019.

involving a substantial damages element is likely to be suitable for a CFA, and so refuse a certificate on that basis. See chapter 4 at paras 4.99–4.100 for more on suitability for a CFA.

11.53 Where a client is eligible for legal aid, the work to gather evidence to consider whether a case is suitable for a CFA or not can usefully be done under Legal Help. It can then be decided what is the best way to progress the claim further. However, always bear in mind the absolute duty to advise clients of the availability of legal aid and also the costs protection afford by legal aid.

11.54 Statutory nuisance proceedings under Environmental Protection Act 1990 s82 are in scope.[41] However, the combined effect of LASPO Sch 1 Part 1 para 35(2)(b) and Part 3 is to exclude the provision of advocacy services in the magistrates' court. Likewise, LASPO Sch 1 Pt 1 para 35 makes clear that Legal Help can be provided to a leaseholder in respect of disrepair/housing conditions, but legal aid is not available for representation because representation in the property tribunal where leasehold cases are dealt with is out of scope.

Disrepair counterclaims

11.55 Disrepair and housing conditions counterclaims in possession proceedings are in scope (see para 11.3 above), and unlike with freestanding claims, counterclaims for damages are included.[42] The LASPO Sch 1 Part 2 exclusions of assault, battery and false imprisonment claims; trespass to goods and trespass to land; damage to property; and breach of statutory duty do not apply to counterclaims in possession proceedings, so all may be pleaded and claimed for.[43] As set out above at para 11.18, personal injury counterclaims are excluded and so ECF would be needed if that were to be pursued.

11.56 However, if a tenant withholds rent in order to provoke possession proceedings, and then counterclaims for disrepair and/or housing conditions, legal aid is likely to be refused.[44] This is because legal aid will only be granted if the Director is satisfied it would be reasonable to do so in light of the applicant's conduct.[45] We have

---

41 *Frequently Asked Questions: Civil Legal Aid Reforms*, FAQ 104.
42 LASPO Sch 1 Part 1 para 33(6)(a).
43 LASPO Sch 1 Part 1 para 33(6).
44 *Lord Chancellor's Guidance under Section 4 of the Legal Aid, Sentencing and Punishment of Offenders Act 2012*, May 2023, para 7.4(c).
45 Civil Legal Aid (Merits Criteria) Regulations 2013 reg 11(6).

11.57 The Part 2[47] exclusions of assault, battery and false imprisonment claims, trespass to goods and trespass to land, damage to property, and breach of statutory duty do not apply to claims for unlawful eviction, so all may be pleaded and claimed for.[48] Personal injury counterclaims are not re-included for counterclaims and so are not in scope – see para 11.18 above.

11.58 Many practitioners have found bringing a counterclaim a useful way to bring funded disrepair and housing conditions cases where there has previously been a possession order but before execution of the warrant. If the counterclaim is successful to the extent of extinguishing the arrears, an application can be made to discharge the possession order. *If a counterclaim exceeds any rent or other set-off, then the statutory charge would apply to the excess amount in the normal way. Because of this, clients must be informed for the potential operation of the statutory charge at the outset of the case.*

11.59 Clients will also need to be advised that if possession proceedings are withdrawn or otherwise disposed of without a possession order and works of repair are completed, then legal aid may at that point be withdrawn because all that would be left in proceedings would be a claim for damages, which is not in the scope of legal aid by itself.

Harassment

11.60 Legal aid is available to victims of harassment to bring an application for an order under Protection from Harassment Act 1997 s3 or 3A, and to defend against such an application. It will only be in the Housing category where the injunction arises out of a housing issue, such as harassment by a landlord or arising out of a neighbour dispute. The merits test for Legal Representation is:[49]

- the standard criteria are met (see chapter 4 at para 4.94);
- the proportionality test is met (see chapter 4 at para 4.104);

---

46 See Jan Luba KC and Sara Stephens, 'Sorting myths from facts over housing cases', November 2014, *Legal Action* 10: www.lag.org.uk/article/202414/sorting-myths-from-facts-over-housing-cases.
47 LASPO Sch 1 Part 2.
48 LASPO Sch 1 Part 1 para 33(7).
49 Civil Legal Aid (Merits Criteria) Regulations 2013 reg 63. Note that the prospects of success criterion is contained in reg 43, which was amended by Civil Legal Aid (Merits Criteria) (Amendment) Regulations 2016 reg 2(4) to allow for grants in the borderline and marginal, but not poor, categories.

- prospects of success are:
  - moderate or better; or
  - borderline or marginal, and the case is of significant wider public interest or of overwhelming importance to the individual; and
- the landlord or other person responsible for the matter complained of has been notified of the complaint (except where this is impracticable) and, where notice has been given, has had a reasonable opportunity to resolve the matter.

11.61 Legal Help will be available to advise prior to proceedings and to issue a warning letter.

Anti-social behaviour

11.62 Injunctions under the Anti-social Behaviour, Crime and Policing Act (ASBCPA) 2014 are in scope, but even where they arise out of a housing issue they are in the 'Miscellaneous' category. Advice funded by Legal Help, and representation in the county court or youth court by certificate will be available in the usual way. Even though applications for injunctions against under-18s are dealt with in the youth court, they are still deemed to be civil cases for the purposes of legal aid. Where you have general authorisation to do so, you can grant an emergency certificate using delegated functions. If not, you can apply to the LAA in the usual way for a certificate. However, you can only grant Legal Help if you have sufficient 'Miscellaneous' matter starts on your contract schedule.

11.63 If the only proceedings are possession proceedings brought on grounds of anti-social behaviour, then just as with any other possession proceedings a certificate with the proceeding wording *Recover Possession – tenant – Housing* is all that is required.

11.64 If only ASBCPA 2014 injunction proceedings are in play, then you will simply need a certificate with the ASBO proceedings wording, which is '*ASBO – Housing*'. The acronym ASBO is still used by the LAA even though it is out of date.

11.65 If an injunction application is being made in the same proceedings as possession is sought, then you will need to apply for a certificate with both *Recover Possession – tenant – Housing* proceeding wording and *ASBO* wording, much like the procedure for applying for *Counterclaim* proceedings alongside *Recover Possession* proceedings as described at para 11.3 above.

11.66   If there are separately issued proceedings for an ASBCPA 2014 injunction, on the one hand, and possession proceedings, on the other, then you will need to apply for a separate certificate for each set of proceedings, each with an appropriate proceedings wording.

11.67   Breach of an injunction order, although dealt with in the county court (for adults), is deemed by the LAA to fall within the Crime category and the provisions of the Crime Contract. Civil practitioners whose firm does not have a crime contract can apply for an individual case contract (ICC) to represent an existing individual client. Where there are conjoined injunction and possession proceedings and within those proceedings an application for committal for breach of an ASBCPA 2014 injunction is made, the practitioner should apply for a criminal representation order from the LAA to be covered for the work carried out on the breach proceedings.

11.68   Funding of breach proceedings is paid by way of a fixed fee under the crime provisions (see chapter 16 for more details). Counsel is assigned automatically and so will be paid at hourly rates. There is no means test for breach proceedings.

11.69   Application for funding of breach proceedings is by way of the LAA Apply online portal or by email in the case of an ICC – see *Apply for legal aid for breach of Part 1 injunctions under the Anti-Social Behaviour, Crime and Policing Act 2014: Guidance for providers.*[50]

11.70   Civil legal aid only covers ASBCPA 2014 Part 1, so because closure orders arising out of alleged criminal conduct do not come under Part 1 they are excluded. You would need to refer your client to a criminal practitioner to deal with closure order proceedings. However, to be clear, you can grant legal aid under the possession proceedings wordings to defend possession proceedings which rely on Housing Act 1988 Sch 2 ground 7A and Housing Act 1985 s84A.

Other housing work

11.71   All other housing cases are outside the scope of legal aid. However, applications for exceptional funding can be made – see chapter 3.

---

50 LAA, August 2024, available at: www.gov.uk/guidance/apply-for-legal-aid-for-anti-social-behaviour-injunction-breaches.

Housing Loss Prevention Advice Service (HLPAS)

Overview

11.72 The HLPAS Scheme (previously Housing possession Court Duty Scheme and other informal names) is now in two parts:

11.73 Stage Two – In Court duty Scheme – this is similar to the traditional court duty scheme.

11.74 Stage One – Early Legal Advice – this is an entirely new service by which providers with a HLPAS contract can provide non-means tested legal advice to people facing the loss of their home through possession proceedings.

11.75 We will tackle these out of order, discussing Stage Two first and then Stage One. This is because the Stage Two In Court Duty Scheme will be relatively familiar to readers, so we think it will be helpful to outline that before going on to set out how the new Stage One Early Legal Advice Scheme works.

11.76 The key documents for understanding HLPAS are:

1) 2024 Standard Civil Contract Specification – Category Specific Rules: Housing and Debt;[51] and
2) Housing Loss Prevention Advice Service Guidance for Service Providers[52] ('the Guidance').

11.77 The main landing page for HLPAS is: www.gov.uk/government/publications/housing-loss-prevention-advice-service-hlpas.

11.78 While those who have or who wish to have a HLPAS contract will get most out of this section, we would encourage all housing providers to be familiar with the HLPAS Scheme in its entirety because you will want to refer prospective clients or enquiries to the scheme.

11.79 With that in mind, the easiest way to find a HLPAS provider is at the government website, at: https://find-legal-advice.justice.gov.uk. You will see that you can enter a postcode and then tick the box marked 'Housing Loss Prevention Advice Service'. A list of HLPAS providers will then appear ranked in order of proximity to the postcode you entered.

---

51 At: https://assets.publishing.service.gov.uk/media/64ff37f657e8840013e12872/5_2024_Housing_and_Debt_Category_Specific_Rules.pdf.
52 At: https://assets.publishing.service.gov.uk/media/64baa4962059dc00125d27d2/Housing_Loss_Prevention_Advice_Service_-_Provider_Guidance_-_August_2023_.pdf.

Conducting a housing case 303

11.80 If you want to know what organisation(s) cover which courts then you will need to go to: www.gov.uk/government/publications/housing-loss-prevention-advice-service-hlpas and click on 'Current HLPAS Provider List'.

11.81 The HLPAS Scheme commenced in August 2023 and the second contract runs from 1 September 2024. In order to hold a HLPAS contract the provider must also hold a face-to-face Housing and Debt contract.

11.82 The contract schedule sets out the allocated volume of HLPAS acts of assistance for each court and provides for a 10 per cent buffer if you go over your allocation. If you require more than is allowed under the 10 per cent buffer you must seek permission from your contract manager.

Post-Covid-19 provisions

11.83 Many readers will be aware that between September 2020 and October 2021, residential possession proceedings in the county court were subject to the provisions of the Master of the Rolls' *Overall Arrangements for Possession Proceedings*.[53]

11.84 From 1 November 2021, the Overall Arrangements were brought to an end and possession proceedings are again subject to local decisions as to how to list possession claims, subject to the Civil Procedure Rules (CPR) and practice directions (PDs). Duty advisers will need to be in close contact with the court(s) where they operate in order to understand the local arrangements.

11.85 The current HLPAS guidance[54] simply states, in relation to historical Covid-19 measures:

> Review hearings were introduced under Covid-19 pandemic Judicial arrangements. In most courts Review hearings are no longer being used. They have been included in this guidance for completeness and to ensure arrangements are clear where a court may still be using such hearings.

11.86 Headline changes that were brought about from 20 September 2020 and which remain in place are:

- Duty advice on a review date can be provided remotely.
- There is now no requirement to complete a proxy means test (prior to 20 September 2020 providers had to complete a

---

53 September 2020.
54 At: https://assets.publishing.service.gov.uk/media/64baa4962059dc00125d27d2/Housing_Loss_Prevention_Advice_Service_-_Provider_Guidance_-_August_2023_.pdf.

means test for each client although the scheme was not means tested).

From 1 November 2021:

- It became possible for a client to sign a Legal Help form to receive further advice and assistance after advice under the Duty Scheme as well as claiming the duty fee.
- It became possible to make a claim for two fees per session if you see no clients and only one client in a session. See para 11.98 below.

Operation of the Scheme

Stage One – In Court Duty Scheme overview

11.87 The In Court Duty Scheme provides for free legal advice and representation for anyone who is facing possession proceedings in the county court (where a HLPAS contract is in place) regardless of their finances, which means that the service is not means tested. The assistance has to be given on the day of the hearing for a claim for payment to be made.

11.88 The fee is contained in the Civil Legal Aid (Remuneration) Regulations 2013 Sch 1 table 6 – and is at the time of writing £75.60 plus VAT in London and £71.55 plus VAT outside of London.

11.89 You can advise and represent the same client at more than one hearing and receive payment for each – ie at subsequent adjourned hearings. You will, however, not get paid for advising the client before a hearing date or in between any subsequent hearings. For that work see the section on Early Legal Advice, below.

11.90 If the client has a substantive defence, then this should where possible be funded under a certificate of legal aid, because of costs protection for your client and higher rates of pay for your organisation. Any substantive work should be progressed by way of emergency legal aid under delegated functions if directions need to be complied with urgently.

Agents

11.91 The HLPAS schedule sets out whether you can use agents in the delivery of the service. Check table 4 in your schedule. If the use of agents is permitted, those agents must fulfil the essential experience requirement of either having a professional legal qualification or

Conducting a housing case 305

undertaking 12 hours of case work per week. The LAA, recognising some of the challenges of the new arrangements, has proved to be permissive about new agency arrangements, where applied for, and that should be done through your contract manager.

Forms

11.92 For every client you represent at court you must fill out an HPCDS monitoring form and send an advice letter confirming the outcome of the hearing. Until recently both documents had to be retained on file, but in 2024 the LAA accepted that once the HLPAS reporting sheet had been submitted there was no need to keep the monitoring form. You must keep the advice letter and should keep your notes from the hearing. Your LAA contract manager may ask for copies of these documents during your annual contract management review. In addition, HLPAS cases must be part of your organisation's supervision and file review procedures

Stage Two – Early Legal Advice

11.93 Stage 2 of the HLPAS Scheme allows for the provision of early legal advice (Legal Help), in person or remotely, to individuals at risk of possession proceedings and loss of their home. Full details are set out at para 2.1 of the Guidance, but the early legal advice can be provided in relation to housing, debt and welfare rights issues. Critically, the client must be able to demonstrate that they have written evidence of a risk of possession proceedings, but the early legal advice need not be explicitly in relation to those potential proceedings or the loss of home issues (though normal scope requirements apply).

11.94 The provision of early legal advice under the HLPAS Scheme is not means tested and can be provided from the moment an individual is informed that possession of their home is being sought and continue up to the first substantive possession hearing. This means that early legal advice under Stage One of the HLPAS Scheme will almost certainly end when Stage Two Representation at Court is triggered.

Making a claim for payment

11.95 In order to make a claim for payment from the LAA for work commenced before 31 August 2024, you must complete the HLPAS

11.96 reporting spreadsheet.[55] The spreadsheet is currently the method to claim for In Court Duty Scheme cases and Early Legal Advice cases.

11.96 For cases commenced on or after 1 September 2024 early legal advice claims for payment must be made via the LAA's Contracted Work and Administration (CWA) system, but the In Court Duty advice claims for payment must continue to be made using the HLPAS Contract Report form, v2.0. See the Guidance at section 5 (para 80).

11.97 To report and claim payment for each client, all fields must be completed. Only one claim can be made where more than one client is being advised in relation to a single hearing (eg where there are joint tenants and/or multiple defendants). However, where no client was seen at a session or only one client was seen at a session, two claims for payment can be made. If a duty day at court includes a morning session and an afternoon session, then up to four 'nil' claims can be made. See the Guidance at para 2.7 for examples of how this works in practice in respect of substantive and review hearings.

11.98 In respect of claiming, the following rules apply:[56]

- You can claim both the HLPAS In Court Duty Scheme fee and the Legal Help matter start fee when a client assisted through the In Court Duty Scheme goes on to be assisted under Legal Help.
- Where you attend court for a possession listing and no clients are seen, ie a nil session, or only one client is seen, you can claim as though you have seen two clients – ie two HPCDS fees will be claimed and paid. Where you attend court for a morning and an afternoon session, that counts as two sessions. Therefore, if you see no clients at all in the morning or in the afternoon, you can claim a total of four fees. If you see one client in the morning and one client in the afternoon you still claim as though you had seen four clients. The LAA sees this is a way to try to incentivise HLPAS work and make it sustainable. Readers can be the judge as to whether it is successful in that regard.

11.99 The Guidance[57] says the following about disbursements in relation to the In Court Duty Scheme:

---

55 Available at the time of writing at: https://assets.publishing.service.gov.uk/media/64baa4c3ef537100147af0ce/HLPAS_Contract_Report_Form_v1.0.xls but probably subject to change.
56 See: www.gov.uk/government/news/civil-news-changes-to-the-hpcds-contract.
57 At: https://assets.publishing.service.gov.uk/media/64baa4962059dc00125d27d2/Housing_Loss_Prevention_Advice_Service_-_Provider_Guidance_-_August_2023_.pdf paras 73 and 74.

73. There are no additional payments for travel or waiting for the In Court Duty Scheme. No additional payments will be made beyond the individual HLPAS Stage two: in court duty scheme fee other than for disbursements incurred in representing a client at a remote hearing.

74. Disbursements will cover the cost for an individual case to be heard remotely e.g., the cost of setting up a call to dial into a hearing using e.g., BT Meet Me. It would not cover a general administrative cost e.g., purchasing a Zoom license or phone contract.

11.100 HLPAS work is to be reported electronically by completing the HLPAS Contract Report form and submitting it via e-mail to HousingLossPreventionAdviceService@justice.gov.uk or uploading it to Secure File Exchange. Details on how to register and use Secure File Exchange can be found at Secure File Exchange – GOV.UK (www.gov.uk).

11.101 The Guidance states that the report (which triggers the claim) should be submitted electronically to the LAA by the 10th of each following month.

11.102 Although this is not an absolute deadline, the Guidance suggests that the report must be submitted in a timely manner, and delayed reports will mean delayed payments.

CHAPTER 12
Conducting a community care case

By Silvia Nicolaou Garcia

12.1	Introduction
12.3	What is community care law?
12.6	What community care law is within the scope of legal aid?
12.9	Who can do community care law?
12.10	Levels of funding for community care work
12.13	How to conduct a community care case
12.13	Overview
12.16	Mental Health Act 1983 s117
12.18	Children Act 1989
	Main provisions of the Act • Means in Children Act 1989 cases • Children Act 1989 s17 • Children Act 1989 s20 • Age assessment cases • Children Act 1989 leaving care • Children Act 1989 s24
12.34	Care Act 2014
12.37	Community care for people from abroad
12.40	The use of litigation friends
12.42	Community care damages claims

Key resources

Statutes

- Children Act 1989
- Care Act 2014
- Mental Health Act 1983
- Social Services and Well-being (Wales) Act 2014
- Legal Aid, Sentencing and Punishment of Offenders Act 2012 – Schedule 1 Part 1

Legal aid regulations

- Civil Legal Aid (Procedure) Regulations 2012
- Civil Legal Aid (Merits Criteria) Regulations 2013
- Civil Legal Aid (Merits Criteria) (Amendment) (No 3) Regulations 2013
- Civil Legal Aid (Procedure) (Amendment) Regulations 2020

Costs and fees

- Costs Assessment Guidance: for use with the 2024 Standard Civil Contract: www.gov.uk/guidance/funding-and-costs-assessment-for-civil-and-crime-matters
- Escape Case Electronic Handbook
- Civil Legal Aid (Financial Resources and Payment for Services) Regulations 2013
- Civil Legal Aid (Costs) Regulations 2013
- Civil Legal Aid (Remuneration) Regulations 2013

Contracts

- Standard Civil Contract 2024 Specification Category Specific Rules – Community Care
- Standard Civil Contract 2024 Specification – General Rules

Lord Chancellor's Guidance

- Lord Chancellor's Guidance under section 4 of the Legal Aid, Sentencing and Punishment of Offenders Act 2012

Miscellaneous

- Standard Civil Contract 2024 Tender process: www.gov.uk/government/publications/civil-2024-contract-procurement-process

- Check if your client qualifies for legal aid: https://check-your-client-qualifies-for-legal-aid.service.gov.uk

Key points to note
- Practitioners continue to experience difficulties obtaining investigative representation.
- Practitioners sometimes forget it is possible to delegate functions for Care Act 2014 s19(3) cases. It is not possible to delegate functions to Children Act s17 cases.

Introduction

12.1 This chapter deals with work done in the Community Care category. You should read it in conjunction with chapters 2 and 4. Chapter 2 deals with general rules about taking on civil cases and applies to work in community care as it does to all other work; chapter 4 deals with the rules that apply to the conduct of all civil cases. The community care rules in this chapter usually build on, rather than replace, the general rules: where they do replace the general rules in chapters 2 and 4, we will say so.

12.2 See appendix C for a summary of the Legal Aid Agency's (LAA's) Costs Assessment Guidance,[1] in respect of the most common queries raised by caseworkers.

What is community care law?

12.3 Community care law covers access to health and social services from the National Health Service (NHS) or local authorities. Community care cases affect adults and children alike. They often relate to an individual's care and wellbeing, but can also relate to decisions about policy and strategy, such as increased charging or reductions in service provision.[2]

12.4 Most community care cases cover legal advice and challenges relating to:

1 *Costs Assessment Guidance: for use with the 2024 Standard Civil Contract*, available at www.gov.uk/guidance/funding-and-costs-assessment-for-civil-and-crime-matters.
2 Funding regimes for Court of Protection cases are outside the scope of this chapter.

- the provision of services by local authority social departments, both to children and young people (generally under the Children Act 1989[3]) and to adults, now largely under the framework of the Care Act 2014;
- the provision of services by local authority social services departments and clinical commissioning groups (CCGs) in relation to aftercare services under Mental Health Act (MHA) 1983 s117.

12.5 Cases are often sensitive and urgent, and it is important for practitioners to know the community care funding regime and to satisfy themselves that the work is within scope before undertaking community care legal aid work.[4]

What community care law is within the scope of legal aid?

12.6 Under Legal Aid, Sentencing and Punishment of Offenders Act 2012 (LASPO) Sch 1 Part 1 para 6, 'community care services' are defined as:
- MHA 1983 s117 (after-care);
- Children Act 1989 s17 (provision of services for children in need);
- Children Act 1989 s20 (provision of accommodation for children);
- Children Act 1989 ss22A, 22B, 22C (accommodation and maintenance for children in care and looked after children);
- Children Act 1989 ss23B and 23C (local authority functions in respect of relevant children);
- Children Act 1989 ss24, 24A and 24B (provision of services for persons qualifying for advice and assistance);
- Care Act 2014 Part 1 (local authority's functions of meeting adults' needs for care and support);
- Social Services and Well-being (Wales) Act 2014 s15;
- Social Services and Well-being (Wales) Act 2014 Part 4;
- Social Services and Well-being (Wales) Act 2014 s76;
- Social Services and Well-being (Wales) Act 2014 ss79, 80 and 81; and
- Social Services and Well-being (Wales) Act 2014 ss105–116.

---

3 Excluding matters within the family public law category – see chapter 7 and appendix B.
4 Standard Civil Contract 2024 Category Specific Rules section 11 – Community Care Specification, available at: www.gov.uk/government/publications/standard-civil-contract-2024.

Conducting a community care case 313

12.7 Examples of community care cases within scope which practitioners often encounter could include:
- a family not getting the help that they need to care for a severely disabled child;
- a 16-year-old who has fled an abusive home and has nowhere to sleep that night;
- a 21-year-old challenging a local authority's refusal to grant retrospective Children Act 1989 s20 status;
- a family with no recourse to public funds (NRPF) who have finally exhausted the resources of the friends on whose floors they have been sleeping;
- an unaccompanied asylum-seeking minor child whose age is disbelieved by the Home Office and/or the local authority is being wrongly treated as an adult and who is homeless and in need of support and accommodation;
- a 17-year-old in a young offender institution who has been approved for early release but has nowhere safe to go;
- a care-leaver who is not being given the support they need to pursue their education;
- an adult previously detained under MHA 1983 s3 who has not been provided with adequate aftercare services on discharge; and
- an adult receiving Care Act 2014 support challenging an increase in charges.

12.8 This chapter will deal with some of the most common types of community care work in scope in more detail.

Who can do community care law?

12.9 Under para 2.32 of the 2024 Standard Civil Contract Specification General Rules, community care contracts were commissioned by procurement area and require part-time presence. To do community care work at all, you must have a schedule authorisation for at least one procurement area.

Levels of funding for community care work

12.10 Legal Help will cover initial advice and assistance including: taking instructions, consideration of any assessments carried out by local authorities and drafting pre-action protocol letters under the Judicial

Review Pre-Action Protocol. A certificate for Legal Representation (also known as full representation to distinguish it from a certificate for investigative representation, see chapter 4 at para 4.83) will cover an application for judicial review. The **merits test** for a full representation certificate in community care cases is the same as for public law cases more generally.[5] The test is:

- for the standard criteria to be met (see chapter 4 at para 4.94);
- for a letter before claim to have been sent to the proposed defendant (except where impracticable) and for the defendant to have been given a reasonable time to respond;
- for the proportionality test to be met (see chapter 4 at para 4.104); and
- for the prospects of success to be: very good, good or moderate; or, borderline and for the case to be of significant wider public interest or of overwhelming importance to the individual or the substance of the case relates to a breach of European Convention on Human Rights (ECHR) rights.

12.11 The merits test for an investigative representation certificate in community care cases is the same as for public law cases generally.[6] The test is:

- for the standard criteria in Civil Legal Aid (Merits Criteria) Regulations 2013 reg 40 to be met (see chapter 4 at para 4.94): unclear prospects of success and substantial investigative work required before those prospects can be determined; once the investigative work is completed, the case will satisfy the criteria for full representation and will meet the cost–benefit criteria; if it is a claim for damages that does not meet £5,000, the case must be of significant wider public interest; and
- for the claimant to have notified the proposed defendant of the potential challenge and given reasonable time for the defendant to respond (unless impracticable).

12.12 Some practitioners report that it is very difficult to obtain investigative representation for community care challenges. When applying for investigative representation, practitioners need to show that they are in a position to consider whether the prospects of success in relation to a claim for judicial review are unclear (and substantial work

---

5 Civil Legal Aid (Merits Criteria) Regulations 2013 reg 56.
6 Civil Legal Aid (Merits Criteria) Regulations 2013 reg 57, as amended by the Civil Legal Aid (Merits Criteria) (Amendment) (No 2) Regulations 2015 and the Civil Legal Aid (Merits Criteria) (Amendment) Regulations 2016.

needs to be done to ascertain the merits of a case), rather than at the early stage of taking initial instructions from their client, as this initial work would fall under the ambit of the Legal Help scheme rather than a funding certificate.

How to conduct a community care case

Overview

12.13 There are distinct statutory frameworks governing community care for children and for adults. Both, however, follow the same basic pattern: in certain defined circumstances, a local authority will have (a) a duty to assess a person's needs; and (b) a duty or a power to formulate and implement a plan to meet certain of those needs by providing services.

12.14 Challenges can be brought regarding:
- a failure or a delay to assess needs;
- an inadequate assessment of needs;
- an unlawful plan to meet needs; or
- a failure to implement a care plan.

12.15 Work will normally be started on a Legal Help file and full representation will be applied for later on, after either sending a pre-action protocol letter, giving the defendant enough time to reply and/or after putting the defendant on notice. If the merits of the case are unclear, and substantial work needs to be done to ascertain the merits of the case, then investigative representation should be applied for (see chapter 4 for further details of investigative and full representation). Where possible, delegated functions should be used.

Mental Health Act 1983 s117

12.16 Persons who cease to be detained under certain provisions of the MHA 1983 (ss3, 37, 45A and 48) are entitled to aftercare services from the relevant CCG and local authority, until both organisations are satisfied that the person is no longer in need of such services. Aftercare services comprise any service within reason necessary to meet a need arising from a person's continued mental disorder, including medication, counselling and accommodation, plus care and social support. The Care Act 2014 amended MHA 1983 s117 to make it clearer which authority bears responsibility for the provision of aftercare services.

12.17 Challenges to failures to provide support under MHA 1983 s117 are in scope and in the Community Care category. Legal Help will cover initial advice and assistance, including travel to the hospital, taking instructions, considering any assessments and drafting Judicial Review Pre-Action Protocol letters. Legal aid (full representation or investigative representation) could then be applied for by making an application on the Client and Cost Management System (CCMS). Delegated functions cannot be used in section 117 cases.[7]

Children Act 1989

Main provisions of the Act

12.18 Legal aid (both Legal Help and Legal Representation) is available in the Community Law category to provide advice and representation to individuals seeking accommodation and support under certain community care provisions (as set out in LASPO Sch 1 Part 1 para 6). The main provisions of the Children Act 1989 that are in scope are:

- section 17: provision of services for children in need and their families;
- section 20: provision of accommodation for homeless children;
- sections 22A, 22B, 22C;
- sections 23B, 23C; and
- sections 24, 24A and 24B: the leaving care provisions.

Means in Children Act 1989 cases

12.19 For Legal Help cases, when assessing the means of a child, the resources of a parent, guardian or other person who is responsible for maintaining the child, or who usually contributes substantially to the child's maintenance, must be taken into account, as well as any assets of the child. There is a discretion not to aggregate assets in this way if it appears inequitable to do so, having regard to all the circumstances, including the age and resources of the child and any conflict of interest between the child and the adult(s). For example, it might be inequitable to aggregate the resources of a 17-year-old child who is

---

7 See *Work out who qualifies for civil legal aid: Legal aid providers: test scope, merits and means; access legislation and regulations; use the civil legal aid calculator and manual*, LAA, www.gov.uk/guidance/work-out-who-qualifies-for-civil-legal-aid.

12.20 estranged from his parents and living separately from them and who is fully financially independent from his parents.[8]

For Legal Representation cases, financial determination will normally be carried out using the child's resources. However, where the application is made in respect of family proceedings, the resources of a parent, guardian or any other person who is responsible for maintaining the child, or who usually contributes substantially to the child's maintenance, are required to be treated as the child's resources (ie they are aggregated), unless having regard to all the circumstances, including the age and resources of the child and any conflict of interest, it appears inequitable to do so. A legal aid application on behalf of a child must be made by: (a) the person who is or proposes to be the child's litigation friend, professional children's guardian or parental order reporter; or (b) the proposed practitioner in proceedings which the child may conduct without a children's guardian or litigation friend in accordance with Family Procedure Rules 2010 16.6 or Civil Procedure Rules 1998 (CPR) 21.2.[9]

12.21 Practitioners report having mixed experiences when working on community care cases on behalf of children. For initial work done on Legal Help, the parents' means will be aggregated, unless there are exceptional reasons as to why this should not be the case, for example, a conflict of interest. For Legal Representation cases, the means for the children should not be aggregated to the parents' means. It is important to note that the LAA will seek to aggregate parental means. Practitioners appealing decisions from the LAA should bear in mind that for the parents' means not to be aggregated, it is important to show that the cause of action will benefit the child and that it is appropriate only for the child to bring the claim, not for the parent. For large-scale policy challenge cases, the LAA will seek to aggregate the parents' means.

Children Act 1989 s17

12.22 The provision of services to children 'in need' lies at the heart of local authority duties towards children and families. The duty to provide services to children 'in need' and their families arises following an assessment, which must be concluded in accordance with the

---

8 See *Lord Chancellor's guide to determining financial eligibility for controlled work and family mediation*, September 2023, para 9.1, available at: www.gov.uk/guidance/funding-and-costs-assessment-for-civil-and-crime-matters.
9 Civil Legal Aid (Procedure) Regulations 2012 reg 30(2).

relevant statutory guidance.[10] It is only following assessment that a local authority can decide whether it is necessary to provide a child or family member with services. Common challenges under Children Act 1989 s17 include: failure to conduct an assessment; failure to accommodate and support pending an assessment; withdrawal of section 17 support; and accommodation out of area.

12.23 Practitioners acting for children and families in need of section 17 support should ensure that they gather enough evidence in relation to the means of their clients. If the clients and their families have been supported by family members, friends or community groups, it will be necessary to get a statement of support from each of these individuals. This will be required for both Legal Help and Legal Representation work. In September 2018, a change was made to allow the use of delegated functions in Children Act 1989 s17 homeless judicial reviews. The LAA has clarified its position in relation to the scope of delegated functions to grant Emergency Representation for urgent homelessness judicial reviews. The position reverts back to the position before September 2018. Delegated functions cannot be used in Children Act 1989 s17 judicial reviews.[11]

Children Act 1989 s20

12.24 Children Act 1989 s20(1) places local authorities under a 'specific' statutory duty to provide accommodation for any child in need within their area who requires accommodation as a result of:

1) there being no person who has parental responsibility for the child;
2) the child being lost or having been abandoned; or
3) the person who has been caring for the child being prevented (whether or not permanently, and for whatever reason) from providing the child with suitable care accommodation or care.

---

10 *Working together to safeguard children 2023: statutory guidance*, Department for Education, December 2023.
11 See V Ling, 'Keeping up with delegated functions', at: www.lag.org.uk/article/206294/keeping-up-with-delegated-functions; and 'Authorisations given pursuant to section 6, for the purposes of section 5(2) and section 5(4), of the Legal Aid, Sentencing and Punishment of Offenders Act 2012 (LASPO), in relation to functions of the Lord Chancellor and the Director under the Civil Legal Aid (Procedure) Regulations 2012 (SI 2012/3098)', at: https://assets.publishing.service.gov.uk/government/uploads/system/uploads/attachment_data/file/1017081/Table_of_Delegated_Authorities_Procedure_Regulations_September_2021_Update.pdf.

12.25 The law concerning the duties and powers contained in Children Act 1989 s20 is clear following the landmark House of Lords case of *R (G) v Southwark LBC*.[12] It is therefore surprising that 15 years after these cases, local authorities still misunderstand the nature of the Children Act 1989 s20 duty. It is often necessary to send a Judicial Review Pre-Action Protocol letter or even issue proceedings, to secure appropriate accommodation for child clients who are street homeless, about to become street-homeless, 'sofa-surfing' or in unsuitable accommodation (eg asylum support accommodation for adults or bed and breakfast accommodation). There are a number of specific issues arising from particular categories of children requiring accommodation, such as:

- children in custody;
- children at risk of gang violence;
- unaccompanied asylum-seeking children (UASCs);
- trafficked children;
- child victims of sexual abuse; and
- children at risk of going missing.

Because of this, practitioners will be involved in section 20 challenges that often relate to not just the requirement of a roof over the child's head, but also to the suitability of the section 20 accommodation.

12.26 Children Act 1989 s20 cases are often very urgent, and practitioners have delegated functions to grant emergency funding in these cases[13] (see chapter 4).

Age assessment cases

12.27 Community care practitioners will also often act for children from abroad whose age has not been correctly determined, either by the Home Office or by a local authority.

12.28 Challenges to local authority age assessments, to failures to conduct age assessments, and to failures to support and accommodate pending challenges to age assessments are within scope, given that a failure to conduct a lawful age assessment on a UASC will result in no services being provided to the child under the Children Act 1989.[14]

12 [2009] UKHL 26.
13 'Civil news: delegated functions for emergency homelessness JRs', LAA, 11 January 2019, at: www.gov.uk/government/news/civil-news-delegated-functions-for-emergency-homelessness-jrs.
14 Services under Children Act 1989 Part 3 are only available to children under 18 and their families; therefore the assessment of a young person's age is a central issue for UASCs claiming to be children.

Children Act 1989 leaving care

12.29 Care leavers are a particularly vulnerable group, more prone to homelessness and unemployment than other young adults. If a child is accommodated by a local authority for 13 weeks between the ages of 14 and 18 with at least one day being on or after the child's 16th birthday, they become entitled to a wide range of long-term support set out in Children Act 1989 ss23A–23CA.

12.30 Common challenges for practitioners acting for this client group include:
- challenges to the failure of support and accommodation;
- challenges to pathway plans, including failure to support and assist to the extent that the young person's education, training or welfare requires;
- failure to appoint a personal adviser; and
- retrospective Children Act 1989 s20 cases, for young adults who should have been looked after under section 20 by a local authority and were not.

12.31 Delegated functions cannot be used for leaving care cases.[15]

Children Act 1989 s24

12.32 Many children and young people who spend time in care will not accumulate the requisite period of 13 weeks spent as a 'looked after' child in order to qualify for the full leaving care package. However, they may qualify for a more limited form of 'advice and assistance' under Children Act 1989 s24 from the responsible local authority, sometimes referred to as 'aftercare'. This work is in scope.

12.33 Delegated functions cannot be used for Children Act 1989 s24 cases.[16]

Care Act 2014

12.34 Adult social care in England is now largely governed by the Care Act 2014. The preamble to the Act describes it as:

> ... an Act to make provision to reform the law relating to care and support for adults and the law relating to support for carers; to make

---

15 'Civil news: delegated functions for emergency homelessness JRs', LAA, 11 January 2019.
16 'Civil news: delegated functions for emergency homelessness JRs', LAA, 11 January 2019.

12.35 Care Act 2014 Part 1 is within the scope of legal aid[17] and sets out the general responsibilities of local authorities for care and support, and safeguarding, in relation to adults, carers and children becoming adults. Some sections came into force on 1 October 2014, but most of Part 1 came into force on 1 April 2015. Common challenges community care practitioners will work on are:

- failure to assess an adult's needs for care and support;
- failure to assess a carer's needs for support;
- refusal to assess;
- failure to accommodate and support pending assessment; and
- failure to safeguard adults at risk of abuse or harm.

12.36 Delegated functions can be used for Care Act 2014 s19(3) cases.[18]

Community care for people from abroad

12.37 In the last few years, a number of reported community care cases have involved the interaction of immigration, community care and human rights law.[19] Nationality and immigration status might restrict the community care support clients get from local authorities.[20] In these types of cases, practitioners must ensure that their clients do not fall foul of Nationality, Immigration and Asylum Act 2002 Sch 3. In such cases, practitioners whose clients are excluded by Schedule 3 will have to show that support is necessary to avoid a breach of their client's human rights. In some cases, practitioners will ask local authorities to use their powers under Localism Act 2011 s1 to provide accommodation and support to their clients who are not entitled to accommodation under the Care Act 2014 and who would otherwise

---

17 LASPO Sch 1 Part 1 para 6(n).
18 'Civil news: delegated functions for emergency homelessness JRs', LAA, 11 January 2019.
19 *R (SL) v Westminster City Council* [2013] UKSC 27; *R (GS) v Camden LBC* [2016] EWHC 1762 (Admin); *R (SG) v Haringey LBC* [2017] EWCA Civ 322; *R (AR) v Hammersmith and Fulham LBC* [2018] EWHC 3453 (Admin); *R (TMX) v LB Croydon LBC and Secretary of State for the Home Department* [2024] EWHC 129 (Admin).
20 Nationality, Immigration and Asylum Act 2002 Sch 3 para 1.

have their ECHR rights breached. These cases will normally be opened as community care cases and not public law cases.

12.38 Challenges to asylum support provided by the Home Office to asylum-seeking clients (also known as asylum support challenges) should be conducted under a public law contract. See para 13.23 below.

12.39 When seeking evidence of means from clients from abroad for community care cases, it is important to obtain letters or statements of support from individuals supporting the client before commencing work on the case, even where only non-cash support is being provided to the client, such as food, clothes or travel money. Practitioners report that the LAA is refusing to pay for work unless there is enough evidence of means, including letters or statements of support.

The use of litigation friends

12.40 Many community care clients will require a litigation friend. Litigation friends make decisions about a court case for either:
- an adult who lacks the mental capacity to manage their own court case either with or without a solicitor; or
- a child.

12.41 As such, practitioners need to be aware of the rules that apply to taking instructions from litigation friends, in particular as to who should be signing the legal aid forms and whose resources should be taken into account when assessing financial eligibility. See chapters 2 and 4 for more information.

Community care damages claims

12.42 Claims for damages against social services do not fall within the community care contract and may come within the claims against public authorities (CAPA) category or, if it is a claim under the Human Rights Act 1998, within the public law category.

CHAPTER 13
Conducting a public law case

By Silvia Nicolaou Garcia

13.1	Introduction
13.2	Public law and judicial review
13.7	Overlaps between categories
13.9	What public law work is within the scope of legal aid?
13.10	Judicial review
	Overview • Judicial reviews that benefit the individual and/or the individual's family or the environment • R (Liberty) v Director of Legal Aid Casework • Immigration judicial reviews
13.20	Writs of habeas corpus • Human Rights Act 1998 claims
13.23	Examples of public law cases
13.25	**Who can do public law?**
13.26	**Levels of funding for public law work**
13.32	**Common reasons for refusal of funding in legal aid cases**
13.39	**How to conduct a public law case**
13.39	Steps in a judicial review case
13.44	Payment for judicial review work
13.47	Administrative Court and Judicial Review Guidance
13.50	Habeas corpus

> **Key resources**
> - Costs Assessment Guidance: for use with the 2024 Standard Civil Contracts (v1)
> - Standard Civil Contract 2024 Category Definitions
> - Civil Legal Aid (Merits Criteria) Regulations 2013 – regs 2, 18, 39, 40, 53 and 54
> - Legal Aid, Sentencing and Punishment of Offenders Act 2012 – Schedule 1 Part 1 para 19
> - Lord Chancellor's Guidance under section 4 of the Legal Aid, Sentencing and Punishment of Offenders Act 2012
> - Civil Legal Aid (Procedure) Regulations 2012 – reg 38
> - Civil Legal Aid (Remuneration) Regulations 2013 – reg 5A
> - Civil Legal Aid (Remuneration) (Amendment) Regulations 2015
> - Administrative Court and Judicial Review Guide 2024
> - Lord Chancellor's Guidance on Determining Financial Eligibility for Controlled Work and Family Mediation, September 2023

> **Key point to note**
> - Practitioners continue to experience difficulties obtaining investigative representation.

Introduction

13.1 This chapter deals with work done in the public law category. You should read it in conjunction with chapters 2 and 4. Chapter 2 deals with general rules about taking on civil cases; chapter 4 deals with the rules that apply to the conduct of all civil cases. The public law rules in this chapter usually build on, rather than replace, the general rules: where they do replace the general rules in chapters 2 and 4 we will say so. See appendix C for a summary of the Legal Aid Agency's (LAA's) Costs Assessment Guidance[1] in respect of the most common queries raised by caseworkers.

---

1 *Costs Assessment Guidance: for use with the 2024 Standard Civil Contracts*, v1, LAA, September 2024, available at: https://assets.publishing.service.gov.uk/media/66f13cfa76558d051527abb9/Costs_Assessment_Guidance_2024_SCC_-_Version_1a-_23_September_2024.pdf.

Public law and judicial review

13.2 Public bodies (eg government departments and local authorities), and certain private organisations exercising a public function, have to obey the law. The type of law governing the conduct of public bodies is known as 'public law'.

13.3 Judicial review is a tool that enables individuals or groups to go to court to hold public bodies to account and determine whether decision-makers have acted:

- lawfully;
- rationally;
- fairly;
- in good faith;
- only using the powers that they have for their proper purposes; and
- compatibly with the human rights of those affected by their actions.

Every decision-maker must respect these public law principles.

13.4 When a public body acts unlawfully, there is a number of ways in which individuals affected can challenge the decision. These include:

- using a public bodies' complaints procedures or the ombudsman;
- exercising the right of appeal to a tribunal;
- asking a public body to review its decision; and
- issuing judicial review proceedings.

13.5 Decision-makers have to respect laws that protect fundamental rights and interests such as the Human Rights Act (HRA) 1998, the Data Protection Act 1998, the Equality Act 2010 and retained EU law. These laws help to ensure that individual's rights are protected, that personal information is not misused and that individuals are not discriminated against because of a protected characteristic.[2]

13.6 Of all civil representation applications granted, around 3,000 a year relate to judicial review. Over half of judicial reviews are for public law.[3]

Overlaps between categories

13.7 The legal aid categories are drafted to ensure that the majority of cases fall within one category or another. However, some cases arise

---

2 See: www.equalityhumanrights.com/equality/equality-act-2010/protected-characteristics.
3 Available at: www.gov.uk/crime-justice-and-law/legal-aid-for-providers (scroll down).

as a result of a number of different underlying issues, so many cases fall within more than one category.[4] For example, sometimes community care work might fall under both the Community Care and the Public Law contract categories. When choosing what category of law to use when opening a file, practitioners should choose the overall substance or predominant issue of the case when taken as a whole.

13.8 Practitioners should be clear when they open Legal Help and legal aid files what categories of law they are using, as this will have a bearing on many things, including the number of matter starts used and the applicable Legal Help standard fee.

What public law work is within the scope of legal aid?

13.9 According to Civil Legal Aid (Merits Criteria) Regulations 2013 reg 2:

> 'public law claim' means any matter which is described in any of the following paragraphs of Part 1 of Schedule 1 to the Act [Legal Aid, Sentencing and Punishment of Offenders Act 2012 (LASPO)] (civil legal services)–
>
> (a) paragraph 19 (judicial review) . . .;
> (b) paragraph 20 (habeas corpus); or
> (c) paragraph 34 (homelessness);[5]

Judicial review

Overview

13.10 Public law work within the scope of legal aid includes 'judicial review of an enactment, decision, act of omission' of public bodies, as described in LASPO Sch 1 Part 1 para 19. This is subject to the general exclusions under Parts 2 and 3 of Schedule 1 to LASPO.[6]

13.11 According to para 19(10), 'judicial review' means:

> (a) the procedure on an application for judicial review (see section 31 of the Senior Courts Act 1981), but not including the procedure

---

4 Standard Civil Contract 2024 Category Definitions, issued by the Legal Aid Agency (LAA), available at: https://assets.publishing.service.gov.uk/media/66e40af3718edd8177131704/Category_Definitions_2024__September_2024_.pdf.
5 Civil Legal Aid (Merits Criteria) Regulations 2013.
6 With the exception of the paragraphs referred to in LASPO Sch 1 Part 1 para 19(2)(a).

after the application is treated under rules of court as if it were not such an application, and
(b) any procedure in which a court, tribunal or other person mentioned in Part 3 of this Schedule is required by an enactment to make a decision applying the principles that are applied by the court on an application for judicial review;

Judicial reviews that benefit the individual and/or the individual's family or the environment

13.12 According to LASPO Sch 1 Part 1 para 19(3) and (4), services provided to an individual in relation to a judicial review that does not have the potential to produce a benefit for the individual, a member of the individual's family or the environment are excluded from Schedule 1 para 19. This does not exclude services provided in relation to a judicial review where the judicial review ceases to have the potential to produce such a benefit after the civil legal services have been provided in relation to the judicial review.[7]

R (Liberty) v Director of Legal Aid Casework[8]

13.13 LASPO Sch 1 Part 1 para 19(3), (4) and (10)(a) and (b) has been the subject of recent litigation. In 2018, Liberty brought a judicial review against the Director of Legal Aid Casework for blocking access to justice for residents seeking to take local authorities to court.[9] Public spaces protection orders (PSPOs) allow councils to ban activities they deem to have a 'detrimental effect' on the lives of others. Many PSPOs have been used to ban rough sleeping. Anti-social Behaviour, Crime and Policing Act (ASBCPA) 2014 s66 created a specific statutory appeal route for those who wish to challenge a local authority's decision to introduce a PSPO, for which there is no permission stage. The grounds for such a challenge can be:

1) that the local authority did not have power to make the order or variation, or to include particular prohibitions or requirements imposed by the order; or
2) that a requirement under the statute was not complied with in relation to the order.

7 LASPO Sch 1 para 19(3) and (4).
8 [2019] EWHC 1532 (Admin).
9 S Marsh and P Greenfield, 'Legal Aid Agency taken to court for refusing to help rough sleepers', *Guardian*, 23 October 2018: www.theguardian.com/society/2018/oct/23/legal-aid-agency-taken-to-court-for-refusing-to-help-rough-sleepers.

13.14 The ASBCPA 2014 prohibits interested persons from challenging a PSPO by any route other than the section 66 procedure. Judicial review jurisdiction is still an option for those who do not have interested person status. Anyone seeking to challenge a PSPO faces a significant risk of an adverse costs order if they lose.

13.15 The LAA had taken the position that statutory appeals under ASBCPA 2014 s66 were not within scope for legal aid purposes for two reasons:

- An ASBCPA 2014 s66 challenge is not a 'judicial review' within the meaning given to that term in LASPO Sch 1 Part 1 para 19(10).
- The proceedings do not have the potential to produce a 'benefit' for Liberty's client within the meaning given to that term in LASPO Sch 1 Part 1 para 19(3).

13.16 On 17 June 2019, Murray J dismissed[10] Liberty's attempt to secure legal aid on behalf of its client, Ms Ward, so that she could pursue a challenge to a PSPO made by the Borough of Poole. He held that:

1) the potential to produce a benefit for an individual or a member of their family was a mixed question of fact and law (para 43 of the judgment).
2) that the ordinary meaning of the word 'benefit' was a broad one and that it was not necessary for the Director or the court to consider the quality of the benefit, but that the benefit must be of substance, and must be real, direct and material for the individual or a member of her family (paras 44–45).
3) the elimination of the hypothetical risk that Ms Ward might find herself homeless was not sufficient to constitute a benefit in the sense required by para 19(3) of Schedule 1 (para 47).
4) her experience of working in homelessness services and desire to avoid the criminalisation of the homeless was also an insufficient benefit as it was not sufficiently direct, personal and material to Ms Ward or a member of her family to constitute the sort of benefit that would distinguish the section 66 challenge from what is, in essence, a representative action (para 53).

13.17 In view of his conclusion, the judge decided it was not necessary for him to decide whether the section 66 challenge fell within the definition of 'judicial review' at para 19(1) for legal aid purposes. Liberty sought permission to appeal this decision in the Court of Appeal.

10 *R (Liberty) v Director of Legal Aid Casework* [2019] EWHC 1532 (Admin).

Permission was refused by the Rt Hon Lord Justice Leggatt on 8 October 2019.

13.18 In another recent judicial review (*R (FF) v Director of Legal Aid Casework*[11]) the claimant succeeded and the judge found that the proposed judicial review proceedings were not excluded by para 19(3).

Immigration judicial reviews

13.19 Judicial reviews in respect of an issue relating to immigration where the conditions in LASPO Sch 1 Part 1 para 19(5)(a)–(c) are met are also excluded from Schedule 1 Part 1 para 19. Similar exclusions apply in judicial review of removal directions,[12] unless they are services provided to an individual in relation to: a judicial review of a negative decision in relation to an asylum application where there is no right of appeal to the First-tier Tribunal against the decision; judicial review of certification under Nationality, Immigration and Asylum Act 2002 s94 or 96; and judicial review of removal directions where the conditions in LASPO Sch 1 Part 1 para 19(8) are met. Practitioners working on immigration judicial reviews should read this chapter in conjunction with chapter 9.

Writs of habeas corpus

13.20 'Civil legal cases provided in relation to a writ of habeas corpus ad subjiciendum'[13] are also covered by the public law category, subject to the exclusions in LASPO Sch 1 Parts 2 and 3.

Human Rights Act 1998 claims

13.21 Claims for damages under the HRA 1998 fall exclusively within the claims against Public Authorities category of law or the Public Law category, depending on the facts of the claim.[14] This includes:

- damages claims made within proceedings not described in LASPO Sch 1 Part 1, except para 21 ('Abuse or position of powers by public authority') or 22 ('Breach of Convention [European Convention on Human Rights (ECHR)] rights by public authority'); and
- all freestanding claims for damages under HRA 1998 s7(1)(a).

---

11 [2020] EWHC 95 (Admin).
12 See LASPO Sch 1 Part 1 para 19(7).
13 LASPO Sch 1 Part 1 para 20(1).
14 Standard Civil Contract 2024 Category Definitions.

13.22 Legal Help and all proceedings in relation to:
- abuse of a child or a vulnerable adult (as described in LASPO Sch 1 Part 1 para 3);
- abuse of position of power by a public authority (as described in LASPO Sch 1 Part 1 para 21);
- significant breach of ECHR rights by a public authority (as described in LASPO Sch 1 Part 1 para 22); and
- sexual offences,

will fall within the Claims Against Public Authorities category where the conditions set out in para 21 of the LAA Category Definitions in the Standard Civil Contract 2024 apply.[15]

Examples of public law cases

13.23 Examples of public law cases within scope that practitioners often encounter can include:
- a judicial review of a council's decision to cut a special educational needs (SEN) budget without conducting a local consultation and without making sufficient enquiries;
- challenges to central government policies;
- an ECHR Article 8 (right to respect for private and family life, home and correspondence) claim against a local authority for failing to secure a long-term placement for a looked after child;
- an unlawful detention judicial review;
- a challenge to the Home Office's failure to give adequate reasons to unaccompanied asylum-seeking children (UASC) not accepted into the UK from France;
- challenges to secure access to the adequacy of financial support victims of trafficking receive;
- a breach of ECHR Article 4 (prohibition of slavery and forced labour) for failing to protect a victim of trafficking;
- challenges to secure access to subsistence support for destitute asylum-seekers;
- judicial review claims against the Crown Prosecution Service (CPS) and the Independent Police Complaints Commission (IPCC);
- challenges to planning decisions and environmental challenges; and
- claims to secure access to medical treatment.

15 Standard Civil Contract 2024 Category Definitions paras 20 and 21.

13.24 This chapter deals with some of the most common types of public law work in scope in more detail.

Who can do public law?

13.25 Under the Standard Civil Contract 2024, public law contracts are let by procurement area and require permanent residence. To do public work at all, practitioners must have a schedule authorisation for at least one procurement area. The 2024 Standard Specification Rules for Public Law must be met.[16]

Levels of funding for public law work

13.26 Legal Help will cover initial advice and assistance, including: taking instructions from the client; reviewing documentation on the case; and drafting pre-action protocol letters under the Judicial Review Pre-Action Protocol. The issue and conduct of legal proceedings are not permitted under Legal Help.[17]

13.27 A certificate for Legal Representation (full representation) will cover an application for judicial review. The **merits test** for full representation in public law cases can be found in Civil Legal Aid (Merits Criteria) Regulations 2013 reg 53; see chapter 4 on conducting a civil/family case:
- for the standard criteria to be met (see chapter 4 at para 4.94);
- for a letter before claim to have been sent to the proposed defendant (except where impracticable) and for the defendant to have been given a reasonable time to respond;
- for the proportionality test to be met (see chapter 4 at para 4.104);
- for the prospects of success to be: very good, good or moderate, **or** borderline; and
- for the case to be of significant wider public interest (SWPI) or of overwhelming importance to the individual or the substance of the case relates to a breach of ECHR rights.

13.28 The merits test for an investigative representation certificate in public law can be found in Civil Legal Aid (Merits Criteria) Regulations 2013 reg 54. The test is:

---

16 Standard Civil Contract 2024 Specification Category Specific Rules: Public Law.
17 Costs Assessment Guidance para 6.1.

- For the standard criteria in reg 40 to be met: unclear prospects of success and substantial investigative work required before those prospects can be determined; once the investigative work is completed the case will satisfy the criteria for full representation and will meet the cost–benefit criteria; if it is a claim for damages that does not meet £5,000, the case must be of significant wider public interest.
- For the claimant to have notified the proposed defendant of the potential challenge and given a reasonable time for the defendant to respond (unless impracticable).

13.29 Some practitioners report that it is now more difficult to obtain investigative representation for public law challenges. When applying for investigative representation, practitioners need to show that they are in a position to consider whether the prospects of success in relation to a claim for judicial review are unclear (and substantial work needs to be done to ascertain the merits of a case), rather than at the early stage of taking initial instructions from their client, as this initial work would fall under the ambit of the Legal Help scheme rather than a funding certificate.

13.30 Since 2013, practitioners have not had delegated functions[18] to grant emergency applications for judicial reviews, though some homelessness housing and community care matters are exempt from this. Delegated functions can only be used in judicial reviews under the following:
- Housing Act 1996 Part 7;
- National Assistance Act 1948 s21;
- Children Act 1989 s20;
- National Health Service and Community Care Act 1990 s47(5);
- Care Act 2014 s19(3); and
- Social Services and Well-being (Wales) Act 2014 s36.[19]

13.31 Delegated functions can no longer be used in Children Act 1989 s17 cases (homelessness challenges).[20]

---

18 The power providers have to grant representation certificates in some circumstances – see chapter 4.
19 *Tables of Delegated Authority*, LAA and Ministry of Justice, https://assets.publishing.service.gov.uk/government/uploads/system/uploads/attachment_data/file/1017081/Table_of_Delegated_Authorities_Procedure_Regulations_September_2021_Update.pdf.
20 V Ling, 'Keeping up with the new rules on delegated functions', June 2019 *Legal Action* 16.

Common reasons for refusal of funding in legal aid cases

13.32 Civil Legal Aid (Merits Criteria) Regulations 2013 reg 39 states that an individual may qualify for Legal Representation only if the Director of Legal Aid Casework is satisfied that:
- the individual does not have access to other potential sources of funding from which it would be reasonable to fund the case;
- the case is unsuitable for a Conditional Fee Agreement (CFA);
- there is no person other than the individual who can reasonably be expected to bring the proceedings; and
- the individual has exhausted all reasonable alternatives to bringing proceedings, including any complaints system, ombudsman scheme or other form of alternative dispute resolution.

13.33 Practitioners report that the LAA commonly refuses funding in public law cases where there are alternative sources of funding available.

13.34 The Lord Chancellor's Guidance[21] provides examples of potential sources of funding, such as other interested parties, trade unions or insurers. With the cuts to public funding, crowdfunding has arisen as an alternative source of funding in the last few years. Crowdfunding connects litigants with sponsors who are prepared to contribute funds to cases. Some practitioners report that legal aid funding has been refused if no attempts to crowdfund have been made. Practitioners should continue to challenge these refusals of funding. According to CrowdJustice (a crowdfunding platform designed specifically for funding legal action), crowdfunding should not be seen as an alternative to legal aid.[22]

13.35 Practitioners also report refusals of funding in public law cases on the basis that that cases should be on CFAs with after the event (ATE) insurance obtained on a deferred basis. Practitioners are encouraged to appeal these decisions by relying on the general lack of ATE funding for judicial reviews. This is because the prospects of success are often difficult to predict and because any relief granted is

---

21 *Lord Chancellor's Guidance under section 4 of Legal Aid, Sentencing and Punishment of Offenders Act 2012*, May 2023, available at: https://assets.publishing.service.gov.uk/media/6447d753529eda00123b0420/Lord_Chancellor_s_Guidance_Under_s4_of_LASPO_May2023.pdf.

22 'We're no replacement for legal aid, says crowdfunder pioneer', *Law Gazette*, 22 November 2018: www.lawgazette.co.uk/law/were-no-replacement-for-legal-aid-says-crowdfunding-pioneer/5068408.article.

within the discretion of the court. ATE insurance premiums are also very expensive. See chapter 4 at para 4.100 onwards for more information.

13.36 Other refusals of funding in public law judicial review cases sometimes refer to the possibility that another body (eg the Equality and Human Rights Commission (EHRC)) brings the judicial review in question. In human rights cases, the EHRC does not need to be a 'victim' of the affected violation. The Commission might bring judicial review cases rather than a victim where the actual or potential victims do not have access to lawyers, or the government announces a change in the law which the EHRC believes will lead to violations of human rights.

13.37 It will be very difficult in practice for solicitors to obtain evidence of all of the above when applying for emergency public funding or appealing decisions close to limitation deadlines, so practitioners are encouraged to gather generic evidence in support of applications and/or appeals and to liaise with colleague practitioners in relation to this.

13.38 Other common reasons for refusing funding in public law cases include premature applications and/or failure to exhaust all reasonable alternatives to bringing proceedings. In urgent cases or cases issued shortly before limitation deadlines, this will not be appropriate.

How to conduct a public law case

Steps in a judicial review case

13.39 There are various stages to a judicial review case. The first step involves writing a pre-action protocol letter to the proposed defendant, setting out the proposed claim and remedy sought. This is normally done under the Legal Help scheme, although in some very exceptional cases it will be done under the Investigative Representation scheme.

13.40 A response is normally sought within 14 days. However, in very urgent cases an abridged timescale will be sought. In planning cases, there is a 6-week time limit to issue a claim, so a shorter and abridged timescale is also normally sought.

13.41 If the defendant does not concede at this stage, a claim can be lodged in the High Court or the tribunal with the relevant fee. A public funding application for full representation will have to be made using the Client and Cost Management System (CCMS)[23] in

---

23 See chapter 5.

order to cover work related to getting the claim issued in court. This will include counsel's fees and the court fee. Full representation is needed in order to issue judicial proceedings.[24] Generally, proceedings cannot be issued on investigative representation, although there are some exceptions to this rule, which are set out at Civil Legal Aid (Merits Criteria) Regulations 2013 reg 18(3):

- to obtain disclosure of information relevant to the prospects of success of the proceedings;
- to protect the position of the individual or legal persona applying for investigative representation in relation to an urgent hearing; or
- to protect the position of the individual or legal person applying for investigative representation in relation to the time limit for the issue of the proceedings.

13.42 The court or tribunal where proceedings are issued must be provided with a copy of the legal aid certificate.[25] Once proceedings are issued, the defendant files its summary grounds of defence to explain why they are unarguable and permission should not be granted. The papers are then sent to a judge for a decision to be made on the papers. The test for permission is that a case is an arguable one. If permission is refused on the papers, it can be 'renewed' in open court. An application will need to be made to the LAA to request that the legal aid certificate covers the renewal hearing.

13.43 If permission is granted, the claim proceeds to a full substantive hearing. A further amendment to the certificate will need to be made at this stage to cover work done between permission and the final hearing and to cover the payment of the permission fee. Sometimes, particularly in urgent cases, a judge may order that both the permission stage and the substantive stage be heard at the same time ('a rolled-up hearing').

Payment for judicial review work

13.44 Payment for work in a judicial review case is dependent on what occurs in the case.

13.45 Civil Legal Aid (Remuneration) Regulations 2013 reg 5A sets out the circumstances in which legal aid providers are paid for their work having issued a claim for judicial review. When reg 5A first came into

---

24 Civil Legal Aid (Merits Criteria) Regulations 2013 reg 18(2).
25 Civil Legal Aid (Procedure) Regulations 2012 reg 38.

force, it provided for a blanket ban on payment when a claim for judicial review had been refused permission to proceed to full judicial review, unless permission was later granted. The regulation was partially amended after the case of *R (Ben Hoare Bell Solicitors and others) v Lord Chancellor*[26] in 2015, in which the Divisional Court held that the blanket prohibition was unlawful as it included instances where the failure to obtain permission was based on events that occurred 'beyond the control' of the providers and only came to light after the initial merits assessment.

13.46 Following this case, the LAA re-introduced regulations.[27] Duncan Lewis brought a judicial review case challenging the Lord Chancellor's interpretation of the regulations, which settled in December 2018.[28] As part of the basis of the settlement, the Lord Chancellor undertook to produce a clarification of the effect of reg 5A.[29] See also chapter 15 at paras 15.72–15.81.

Administrative Court and Judicial Review Guidance

13.47 The latest *Administrative Court Judicial Review Guide* was published in October 2024.[30] Paragraph 4.5 of this guidance deals with the type of Legal Representation available in civil cases.

13.48 The guidance also explains (at para 25.10) the issue of cost orders when the claimant has the benefit of legal aid. Costs orders can be made against persons who have the benefit of legal aid. Where the court makes such an order, it will order that the person with the benefit of legal aid must pay the costs of the requesting party and the court may set the amount to be paid, but the court will note that the person with the benefit of legal aid is subject to costs protection in accordance with LASPO s26.

13.49 As a result of the costs protection, the person with the benefit of legal aid is not automatically liable for the costs. However, practition-

---

26 [2015] EWHC 523 (Admin).
27 Civil Legal Aid (Remuneration) (Amendment) Regulations 2015.
28 *R (Duncan Lewis Solicitors) v Lord Chancellor* CO/1551/2018.
29 *Clarification on Payment for Civil Legal Services under Regulation 5A of the Civil Legal Aid (Remuneration) Regulations 2013*, LAA and Ministry of Justice, available at: www.gov.uk/government/publications/judicial-review-discretion-pro-forma.
30 *The Administrative Court Judicial Review Guide 2024*, available at: www.judiciary.uk/courts-and-tribunals/high-court/administrative-court/administrative-court-judicial-review-guide-2024.

ers acting for individuals from abroad should be aware of the Home Office's *Suitability: unpaid litigation costs* guidance.[31] The latest version of this guidance was published in February 2024, and states that the Home Office has the power to refuse some applications for entry clearance, leave to enter or leave to remain on the basis of litigation debt, but that if an individual is publicly funded, no further action will be taken.

Habeas corpus

13.50 Although rarely used nowadays, a writ of habeas corpus is still to be considered a fundamental instrument for safeguarding individual freedom against arbitrary and lawless state action. Writs of habeas corpus are sometimes used in the context of age assessment judicial reviews where the age-disputed child is being detained under immigration powers. This was discussed in the Supreme Court case of *R (AA (Afghanistan)) v Secretary of State for the Home Department*.[32] Practitioners should be wary of applying for writs of habeas corpus when there are other remedies available or to avoid the jurisdiction of the Upper Tribunal.[33]

13.51 If practitioners who are acting for individuals who are being detained send a CW1 Legal Help form by post or fax to the client, or if they travel out of the office to visit the client, they need to provide the circumstances justifying this in accordance with the relevant rule in the Contract Specification.[34] Only once the declaration has been fully understood and signed by the client can the practitioner open a file and begin work. Detailed guidance as to what evidence of means is required is set out in the LAA Controlled Work Guidance,[35] which should be followed by all practitioners. Further details can be found

---

31 *Suitability: unpaid litigation costs*, v7.0, Home Office, February 2024, available at: www.gov.uk/government/publications/litigation-debt/suitability-unpaid-litigation-costs-accessible.
32 [2013] UKSC 49 paras 52–53.
33 See, for example, *R (Ajani and others) v Secretary of State for the Home Department* [2018] EWHC 913 (Admin) where the case was referred to the Solicitors Regulation Authority (SRA) for full investigation.
34 Legal Help Form, p15; Standard Civil Contract 2024 Specification para 3.15.
35 *Lord Chancellor's guidance on determining financial eligibility for Controlled Work and Family Mediation*, September 2023, available at: https://assets.publishing.service.gov.uk/media/64f1d047fdc5d100102849bf/Lord_Chancellor_s_guide_to_determining_financial_eligibility_for_controlled_work_and_family_mediation__September_2023_.pdf.

in chapter 2. It may be impracticable for clients in detention to supply evidence of means. In such cases, eligibility can be assessed without evidence. However, the attendance note must give the reason why evidence could not be obtained, and providers must be prepared to justify this on audit if necessary.[36]

---

36 *Lord Chancellor's guidance on determining financial eligibility for Controlled Work and Family Mediation*, para 12.2(10) and (11).

CHAPTER 14

Conducting a criminal case

By Itpal Dhillon

14.1	Introduction
14.5	**General rules**
14.5	Unique file numbers
14.9	Disbursements
14.18	**Work in the investigations class**
14.18	Overview
14.19	Police station cases
	Scope of work • Sources of work • Permitted work • Who may carry out work? • Starting a case • Conducting work • Warrants of further detention • Applications in relation to police bail
14.49	Advice and Assistance for Pre-Charge Engagement
	Overview • Scope of work • Qualifying criteria • Application process
14.60	Advice and assistance (freestanding)
	Overview • Means test • Merits test • The application process • Conducting work
14.75	Separate matters
14.77	**Work in the proceedings class**
14.79	Court duty solicitor work
14.85	Representation orders – magistrates' court
	Scope • Financial eligibility • Merits test • Funding in the absence of an order • Disbursements and prior authority • Counsel

continued

14.120   Separate matters
14.123   Co-defendants and conflict of interest
14.126   Transfer cases
14.129   Matter ends
14.130   Representation in the Crown Court
         The merits test
14.134   Means testing
         Overview • Applications • Assessing case costs • Effects of Crown Court means testing • Disbursements • Prescribed proceedings in the Crown Court • Appeals to the Crown Court • Recovery of defence costs orders

14.178   Appeals and reviews
14.178   Scope
14.179   Case stated
14.182   Advice and assistance in the appeals class
14.188   Representation orders in the Court of Appeal

14.191   Prison law work
14.203   Scope of prison law work

14.206   Associated civil work

14.210   Very High Cost Cases

Key resources

Statutes

- Legal Aid, Sentencing and Punishment of Offenders Act 2012

Contract

- Draft Standard Crime Contract 2025
- Draft Standard Crime Contract Specification 2025
- Standard Crime Contract 2022
- Standard Crime Specification 2022

Regulations

- Criminal Legal Aid (Remuneration) Regulations 2013
- Criminal Legal Aid (General) Regulations 2013
- Criminal Legal Aid (Financial Resources) Regulations 2013
- Civil and Criminal Legal Aid (Amendment) Regulations 2015
- Criminal Legal Aid (Determinations by a Court and Choice of Representative) Regulations 2013
- Criminal Legal Aid (Recovery of Defence Costs Orders) Regulations 2013
- Criminal Legal Aid (Contribution Orders) Regulations 2013

Fees and costs

- Criminal Bills Assessment Manual
- Criminal Legal Aid (Remuneration) Regulations 2013
- Criminal Legal Aid (General) Regulations 2013
- Criminal Legal Aid (Financial Resources) Regulations 2013
- Civil and Criminal Legal Aid (Amendment) Regulations 2015

Other

- Attorney General's Guidelines on Disclosure Annex B
- Criminal Legal Aid Keycard No 48

Key points to note

- The Standard Crime Contract is due to be replaced by the 2025 contract on 1 October 2025. At the time of writing, only a draft contract has been published and therefore it is important to

> ensure that any references made to the 2022 Contract are checked against the 2025 Contract for accuracy.
> - Advice and Assistance for Pre-Charge Engagement has now been extended to cover preparatory work to determine whether Pre-Charge Engagement would be beneficial following the first PACE interview.
> - Several upper costs limits have been increased and the Regulations should be checked as to each amount where relevant.
> - Where Advice and Assistance (other than Police Station Advice and Assistance) or Advocacy Assistance is provided to a child, the child must sign the application form themselves. The child will not be subject to any Financial Eligibility Test.

Introduction

14.1 The Standard Crime Contract 2022,[1] extended to 30 September 2025 by the Legal Aid Agency (LAA) in May 2024, governs criminal work where representation is granted after 1 October 2022. The contract comprises the Standard Terms and the Specification.

14.2 Criminal work is divided into classes by the contract:[2]

- **investigations** – work done pre-charge;
- **proceedings** – post-charge court work appeals and reviews;
- **post-conviction work** on appeals and reviews of convictions or sentences that do not fall into any other class;
- **prison law** – work in relation to parole, treatment or discipline in the prison system; and
- **associated civil work** – judicial review, habeas corpus and some Proceeds of Crime Act 2002 work.

In addition, 'Very High Cost Cases' (VHCCs) can be regarded as an extra class of work.

14.3 A case may move through several classes. For example, a client arrested and charged with burglary will start in the investigations class, then move into the proceedings class; if convicted, the client may have further cases in the appeals and prison law classes. Each of those classes of work has separate rules and funding mechanisms,

---

1 Available at: www.gov.uk/government/publications/standard-crime-contract-2022.
2 Standard Crime Contracts 2022 and 2025 Specification para 1.3.

Conducting a criminal case 343

14.4 At the time of writing, the 2022 Standard Crime Contract will come to an end on 30 September 2025. The LAA started the procurement process for the 2025 Standard Crime Contract in September 2024 for services to commence on 1 October 2025. We have included references from the version published by the LAA at the time of writing. Contracts are marked 'draft' until they come into effect. However, it is very unusual for the LAA to make more than minor changes once a contract has been published unless there is significant change in government policy. Practitioners should refer to the final 2025 Contract for accuracy. Unless otherwise stated, any reference to paragraphs in the 2022 Contract are the same paragraphs as the Draft 2025 Contract. There is a number of minor changes to the 2022 Contract, which are highlighted where relevant. Any further updates or changes can be checked via the LAA's website.[3]

General rules

Unique file numbers[4]

14.5 The contract requires you to assign a unique file number (UFN) to every case. The case will retain the UFN throughout its life as it moves through the classes of work. Where you act for more than one client on the same case, each client will have their own UFN. Where you submit a consolidated claim (see chapter 16), it will be under one 'lead' UFN. Where you act for one client on more than one case, each case will have its own UFN.

14.6 All UFNs must be in the format set out in the contract – DDMMYY/NNN, where DDMMYY is the date the client first instructed you on that matter. and NNN is a sequential number unique to that day which will return to 001 at the beginning of each day. No two clients or cases should have the same number.

14.7 So, for example, the first client to instruct you on 1 February 2019 would have the UFN 01022019/001, the second would then be 01022019/002, and so on.

14.8 The purpose of the UFN is to allow the LAA to track and, where necessary, check all work done for a particular client. You are therefore

---

3 See: www.gov.uk/government/publications/crime-contract-2025-tender.
4 Standard Crime Contract 2022 Specification paras 4.40 and 4.41 and Standard Crime Contract 2025 Specification paras 4.34 and 4.35.

required to record the UFN on file, use it for all applications and claims to the LAA and, since the LAA will use it when communicating with you, ensure that you can search your database against it.

Disbursements

14.9 Disbursements – that is, expenses incurred in the course of a client's case – are generally permitted where it is in the best interests of the client to incur the disbursement for the purpose of giving advice, and the amount of the disbursement is reasonable.[5]

14.10 This amounts to a three-stage test:
1) Is it in the best interests of the client?
2) Is it for the purposes of giving advice or representation?
3) Is the amount reasonable?

14.11 The client's best interests will be served by incurring expenditure that is necessary for you to conduct the case, or that will assist (or may assist) in achieving the best outcome. For example, travel expenses may be in the client's best interests, even though the client does not benefit directly, because it is necessary for you to incur them to get to court. An expert report may or may not assist the client's case – that would depend on what the expert says – but where it has the potential to do so, it would likely be in the client's best interests to obtain it. This test should not be applied with the benefit of hindsight; the question is, what was reasonable based on what was known at the time?

14.12 'For the purpose of advice or representation' describes the nature and purpose of the expense. To use the preceding example, travel expenses to court are justifiable as being for the purpose of providing representation. A medical report to comment on a client's medical situation would be for that purpose, since it is evidence that could be put before the court, but paying for the client to see a medical expert to obtain treatment would not, since it is not necessary for the purpose of giving advice for the client to be treated, only for you to know what their condition is.

14.13 Finally, the amount of the disbursement must be reasonable. The rates for expert witnesses, save in defined exceptional circumstances prescribed by Criminal Legal Aid (Remuneration) Regulations 2013 Sch 5, as amended, are to be found in that Schedule. Although it is not

---

5 Standard Crime Contract 2022 Specification para 5.38 and Standard Crime Contract 2025 Specification para 5.36.

mandatory to obtain prior authority to incur disbursements,[6] doing so is advisable where substantial sums are to be incurred as prior authority generally ensures that, unless the scope of the disbursement is not as authorised, it will be paid and not questioned on audit.[7]

14.14 Where disbursements are incurred, you should retain a receipt or invoice on file.[8]

14.15 Where you incur mileage, the contract rate is 45 pence per mile.[9] However, this rate will only be paid where use of a motor vehicle was necessary (eg because no public transport was available), or where a considerable saving of time is made (eg where the fee earner would have been required to stay overnight or leave and return at unreasonable hours if public transport was used) or the use of a private motor vehicle was otherwise reasonable. Where there is no justification for the use of a private motor vehicle, the cost of public transportation, or notional public transport mileage rate (25p), may be applied.[10]

14.16 The LAA has power to fix the maximum payments that may be paid to third parties such as experts.[11] Limits have been set to experts' fees in Schedule 5 to the Criminal Legal Aid (Remuneration) Regulations 2013. These fees may be exceeded only in exceptional circumstances.[12] You must require third parties to keep a record of their time spent on a case if the fees will exceed £250.[13]

14.17 Witness expenses to attend court cannot generally be funded under the contract, unless the court has directed that they may not be recovered from central funds (the usual source of witness expenses, including fees of professional witnesses) and they are not recoverable from any other source.[14]

---

6 Standard Crime Contract 2022 Specification para 5.32 and Standard Crime Contract 2025 Specification para 5.30.
7 Standard Crime Contract 2022 Specification para 5.29 and Standard Crime Contract 2025 Specification para 5.27.
8 Standard Crime Contract 2022 Specification para 5.40 and Standard Crime Contract 2025 Specification para 5.37.
9 Standard Crime Contract 2022 Specification para 5.48 and Standard Crime Contract 2025 Specification para 5.43.
10 LAA, *Criminal Bills Assessment Manual*, v19, April 2024, para 3.9(20).
11 Standard Crime Contract 2022 Standard Terms para 3.6 and Specification para 5.37 and Standard Crime Contract 2025 Standard Terms 3.11 and Specification para 5.35.
12 Criminal Legal Aid (Remuneration) Regulations 2013 reg 16(2) and (3), as amended.
13 Standard Crime Contract 2022 Standard Terms para 3.7 and Standard Crime Contract 2025 Specification para 3.12.
14 Standard Crime Contract 2022 Specification para 5.47 and Standard Crime Contract 2025 Specification para 5.42.

Work in the investigations class

Overview

14.18 Investigations work is work done pre-charge or in the police station, and covers:[15]
- police station telephone advice;
- police station attendance;
- advice and assistance for pre-charge engagement;
- advice and assistance outside the police station; and
- advocacy assistance:
  - on a warrant of further detention;
  - on an application to a magistrates' court to vary police bail conditions or oppose the extension of pre charge bail; and
  - at an armed forces custody hearing.

Police station cases

Scope of work

14.19 Police station work will consist of telephone advice, attendance in person at the police station, or both. It is generally available to anyone attending a police station, whether under arrest or as a volunteer, during the course of a criminal investigation.[16] The exceptions to this rule are:
- where the matter falls within the scope of the Criminal Defence Direct Scheme (eg arrests for non-imprisonable offences);[17] and
- advice and assistance to a witness (which is covered in certain circumstances by the Advice and Assistance Scheme).[18]

Police station work is not means tested.[19]

14.20 Police station work can also be carried out post charge, for example, to deal with identification procedures, arrest on warrant or for breach of bail, or for caution or re-charge following discontinuance or dismissal. However, only post-charge work carried out at the police

---

15 Standard Crime Contracts 2022 and 2025 Specification para 1.3.
16 Standard Crime Contracts 2022 and 2025 Specification para 9.1.
17 Standard Crime Contract 2022 Specification para 9.9 and Standard Crime Contract 2025 Specification para 9.2.
18 Standard Crime Contract 2022 Specification paras 9.3 and 9.4 and Standard Crime Contract 2025 Specification paras 9.46 and 9.47.
19 Criminal Legal Aid (General) Regulations 2013 Part 2; and Criminal Legal Aid (Financial Resources) Regulations 2013 Part 2.

station can be claimed under the criminal investigations class of work,[20] rather than as part of the claim in the criminal proceedings.

14.21 For these purposes, a 'police station' is a place where a constable is present, and a 'constable' is an official with a power of arrest conferred by virtue of their office.[21] For example, an officer of HM Revenue and Customs (HMRC) is a constable, but a Department for Work and Pensions (DWP) benefit fraud investigator is not; therefore, a client arrested by HMRC is entitled to police station representation, but a client being interviewed by the DWP is not. However, such a client may be entitled to advice and assistance if the relevant criteria are met. See below for more on advice and assistance.

> **Case study**
>
> *One of our clients has been invited to attend the DWP to be interviewed about an allegation that he has been working and claiming benefits. What should I do?*
>
> This will be an interview under the Police and Criminal Evidence Act 1984 (PACE) and so a criminal lawyer should attend. Since an officer of the DWP does not have a power of arrest, your client would not be entitled to police station legal aid. However, subject to means, your client would be entitled to advice and assistance. You should get the client to sign forms CRM1 and CRM2 and provide proof of means, and then you will be funded to attend the interview with the client. You will have a costs limit of £314.81, but this can be extended on application to the LAA if necessary.

Sources of work

14.22 All requests by persons seeking advice under the police station scheme must, to qualify for public funding, be placed through the Defence Solicitor Call Centre (DSCC).

14.23 The DSCC records the basic details of the alleged offence before passing the case on to the own solicitor requested, the duty solicitor or Criminal Defence Direct. Criminal Defence Direct provides telephone advice to clients detained for less serious matters such as drink-driving offences, non-imprisonable offences, breaches of bail and warrants.

---

20 Standard Crime Contract 2022 Specification para 9.105 and Standard Crime Contract 2025 Specification para 9.102.
21 Standard Crime Contracts 2022 and 2024 Standard Terms para 1.1 (Definitions).

14.24 Where an attendance is likely to be necessary, Criminal Defence Direct will not deal with the matter and the case will be passed to the own solicitor (if requested) or the duty solicitor.

14.25 However, you may also be contacted direct by a third party, for example, the relative of a client, and requested to take on the case. You may also be contacted by a client direct, for example, a client who is aware that the police are looking for them and wants to surrender. In such a situation you can take on the case and provide telephone advice and attendance as appropriate, but must, within very short time limits, report to the call centre that you have taken the case.[22]

> **Case study**
>
> *My client's wife phoned to say that he has been arrested for theft and wants me to go to the police station. Can I go?*
>
> Yes. You can attend the police station when instructed to do so by a third party. However, you must notify the DSCC that you have taken the case. You must notify it before you contact the client and obtain a reference number. You must notify the DSCC in advance for third party instructions, and within 48 hours where you are at a police station and instructed direct, or where a client instructs you direct to attend a surrender or bail date. The 48-hour time limit, which includes weekends and bank holidays, is strictly enforced.

Permitted work

14.26 Whatever the source of the case, you should consider whether or not to attend the police station. Attendance at the police station is mandatory where:

- the client has been arrested and is to be interviewed;
- there is to be an identification procedure (except a video parade, attendance at which is discretionary[23]); or
- the client complains of serious maltreatment by the police.[24]

14.27 You cannot claim for payment for attendance at the police station where:

22 Standard Crime Contract 2022 Specification para 9.20 and Standard Crime Contract 2025 Specification 9.14.
23 Standard Crime Contract 2022 Specification para 9.40 and Standard Crime Contract 2025 Specification para 9.36.
24 Standard Crime Contract 2022 Specification para 9.38 and Standard Crime Contract 2025 Specification para 9.34.

- the client has been arrested solely for non-imprisonable offences;
- the client has been arrested on a warrant for failure to appear unless you have clear documentary evidence that would result in the client's release, for example, a bail form showing that the client is not in fact in breach of a condition;
- the client has been arrested for offences under Road Traffic Act 1988 s4, 5, 6, 7 or 7A (driving while unfit, drunk in charge of a vehicle, driving with excess alcohol or failure to provide a specimen); or
- the client has been detained in relation to breach of police or court bail conditions.[25]

14.28 However, attendance in a prohibited case will be permitted (or mandatory, as the case may be) if one of the exceptions apply and the sufficient benefit test (see below) is satisfied:[26]
- there is to be an interview or identification procedure;
- the client requires an appropriate adult;
- the client is unable to communicate over the telephone;
- the client complains of serious maltreatment by the police;
- the client is being investigated for an additional offence not covered by the above list;
- you are already at the same police station (but in this case you may only claim the telephone advice fixed fee);
- the advice relates to an indictable offence; or
- the request is identified as a 'Special Request'[27] by the DSCC. A special request will be identified by the DSCC as such; for instance, because Criminal Defence Direct considers an attendance to be required.

14.29 In all other cases, attendance at the police station is at your discretion, and you should consider whether the 'sufficient benefit' test is met. This is the merits test for police station work and states that work may only be done where 'there is sufficient benefit to the client, having regard to the circumstances of the matter, including the personal circumstances of the client, to justify work or further work being carried out'.[28]

25 Standard Crime Contract 2022 Specification para 9.9 and Standard Crime Contract 2025 Specification para 9.3.
26 Standard Crime Contract 2022 Specification para 9.10 and Standard Crime Contract 2025 Specification para 9.4.
27 Standard Crime Contracts 2022 and 2025 Specification para 1.2.
28 Standard Crime Contracts 2022 and 2025 Specification paras 3.10 and 10.2; see also Specification paras 1.2 and 3.10–3.16.

14.30 The test would be automatically satisfied where the client has a right to advice under PACE, or where the client is a volunteer, or under equivalent military legislation – but only in relation to initial advice; you must apply the test to determine the extent of advice, and particularly whether attendance (as opposed to telephone advice) is necessary.[29]

14.31 Where you intend to attend the police station and it is not one of the mandatory attendances outlined above, you should be satisfied that the attendance is necessary for the purpose of giving advice that could not be given over the telephone and is expected to progress the case materially. Specifically, the contract says that it might be reasonable to remain at the police station post charge to provide advice or make representations on bail, but unless the client is particularly vulnerable it would not be reasonable to stay for photographs, fingerprints and DNA samples.[30]

Who may carry out work?

14.32 Although almost all work comes through the DSCC, there is a distinction between 'own client' and 'duty' work – own client being cases where you or your firm were specifically requested, and duty work where the client requested the duty solicitor and the case was allocated to you.

14.33 In order to carry out police station work, you must be accredited and registered by the LAA. Only an accredited person or solicitor with Police Station Qualification (PSQ) may undertake duty work.[31] An accredited representative is a person who has passed the PSQ, which is administered by the LAA and consists of a two-part portfolio of cases, an oral examination known as the critical incidents test and a written examination (which need not be taken by a representative who has a legal qualification).

14.34 To become a probationary representative, you must pass the written examination (if required) and part one of the portfolio; you then have one year to pass the remaining elements to become fully accredited. The accreditation process is no longer bypassed by qualification as a solicitor; everyone must be accredited (by obtaining the

---

29 Standard Crime Contract 2022 Specification para 9.14 and Standard Crime Contract 2025 Specification para 9.8.
30 Standard Crime Contract 2022 Specification para 9.16 and Standard Crime Contract 2025 Specification para 9.10.
31 Standard Crime Contract 2022 Specification para 9.28 and Standard Crime Contract 2025 Specification para 9.25.

Police Station Representative Accreditation Scheme (PSRAS) or PSQ) to do duty solicitor police station work. The training and quality assurance of probationary and accredited representatives must be documented.[32]

14.35 To do own client work, a person must either be a solicitor or be accredited or a probationary representative. Probationary representatives cannot do duty cases and cannot do cases where the offence under investigation is indictable only; fully accredited representatives can do all cases.[33] See chapter 22 for the obligations of those who manage and supervise representatives.

Starting a case

14.36 Police station work is not means tested,[34] and the client is not required to complete any application form.

14.37 A case will be initiated when you are contacted, either by the DSCC or by the client or a third party, and requested to provide advice.

14.38 When you take on a case where the client has been arrested and is at the police station, you must make first contact with the client within 45 minutes of being notified of the case.[35] This is a target set out in the contract which should be met in at least 80 per cent of cases, and to enable monitoring of the target[36] your file should contain a note of the time the case was accepted and the time of first contact, together with a note of why contact was not possible inside the 45 minutes, if applicable.[37]

14.39 Where a client has previously received police station advice on the same matter within the past six months from another firm, you cannot provide further advice on the same matter unless:

- there is a gap in time and a material change in circumstances between the first and second occasions;

---

32 Standard Crime Contract 2022 Specification para 9.33 and Standard Crime Contract 2025 Specification para 9.26.
33 Standard Crime Contract 2022 Specification paras 9.26–9.37 and Standard Crime Contract 2025 Specification paras 9.23–9.25.
34 Standard Crime Contract 2022 Specification para 9.15 and Standard Crime Contract 2025 Specification para 9.9.
35 Standard Crime Contract 2022 Specification para 9.23 and Standard Crime Contract 2025 Specification para 9.16.
36 Standard Crime Contract 2022 Specification para 9.24 and Standard Crime Contract 2025 Specification para 9.19.
37 Standard Crime Contract 2022 Specification para 9.25 and Standard Crime Contract 2025 Specification para 9.21.

- the client has reasonable cause to transfer; or
- the first supplier confirms they will not make a claim.[38]

14.40 You should make reasonable enquiries of the client to find out whether there has been previous advice, and if there has been and the exceptions are not met you cannot make a claim. Reasonable cause for transfer will not be made out where the client finds sound advice unpalatable and wants a second opinion.[39] Where you take on a transfer case, you should note the reason on the file.

Conducting work

14.41 Once you have accepted a case, you can continue to do such work as is necessary and complies with the requirements above. Where the client is bailed to return to the police station, attendance at the bail to return is funded on the same basis as the initial attendance and will be included in the same fixed fee – you should ensure that the sufficient benefit test is satisfied and that you are permitted to attend.

14.42 There is no costs limitation for police station work.

14.43 Police station work will come to an end at the point the client is charged or cautioned, the police decide to take no further action or the case is otherwise ended. Uncertainty over cases where a suspect remains under investigation or is released on pre-charge bail means most firms bill after one month. If the case revives, you may not make another claim on the same matter until you reach the threshold fee for a full claim to be made. A bill should be submitted at that point[40] – see chapter 16 for details of costs and the billing procedure.

Warrants of further detention

14.44 Where a client is detained and the police seek an extension to the detention under PACE s43 or 44, or under Terrorism Act 2000 Sch 8 para 29 or 36, you can provide advocacy assistance to represent the client at the hearing of the application.[41]

---

38 Standard Crime Contract 2022 Specification para 9.67 and Standard Crime Contract 2025 Specification para 9.64.
39 Standard Crime Contract 2022 Specification para 9.70 and Standard Crime Contract 2025 Specification para. 9.67.
40 Standard Crime Contract 2022 Specification para 9.104 and Standard Crime Contract 2025 Specification para 101.
41 Standard Crime Contract 2022 Specification para 9.166 and Standard Crime Contract 2025 Specification para 9.161.

Conducting a criminal case 353

14.45 Advocacy assistance is not means tested[42] and the client is not required to sign an application form, but you should record on the file that you have granted funding.[43] The scope of advocacy assistance includes any reasonable preparation and follow-up work.[44] However, counsel may only be instructed in applications before the High Court or a senior judge.[45] There is an extendable upper limit of £1,574.06.[46]

14.46 Similar provisions apply to armed forces custody hearings.[47]

Applications in relation to police bail

14.47 In certain circumstances, where the police have the power to impose bail conditions (or 'street bail' conditions) or wish to extend bail time limits, a client can make an application to a magistrates' court to vary the conditions or oppose the extension.[48]

14.48 You can grant advocacy assistance to represent such a client.[49] It is not means tested,[50] and no application form is required, though a note of the grant should be made on the file.[51] The scope of advocacy assistance includes any reasonable preparation and giving of any advice on appeal.[52] Counsel may be instructed but, if so, you are responsible for paying them out of your fee.[53] There is an extendable upper limit of £1,574.06.[54]

---

42 Criminal Legal Aid (Financial Resources) Regulations 2013 Part 2; Standard Crime Contract 2022 Specification para 9.168 and Standard Crime Contract 2025 Specification para 9.163.
43 Standard Crime Contract 2022 Specification paras 9.169–9.171 and Standard Crime Contract 2025 Specification paras 9.164–9.166.
44 Standard Crime Contract 2022 Specification para 9.172 and Standard Crime Contract 2025 Specification para 9.167.
45 Standard Crime Contract 2022 Specification para 9.173 and Standard Crime Contract 2025 Specification para 9.168.
46 Criminal Legal Aid (Remuneration) Regulations 2013 Sch 4 para 3(2) and (3), as amended.
47 Standard Crime Contract 2022 Specification paras 9.179–9.191 and Standard Crime Contract 2025 Specification para 9.161.
48 PACE ss30CB and 47(1E).
49 Standard Crime Contract 2022 Specification para 9.203 and Standard Crime Contract 2025 Specification para 9.161.
50 Criminal Legal Aid (Financial Resources) Regulations 2013 Part 2.
51 Standard Crime Contract 2022 Specification paras 9.183–9.184 and Standard Crime Contract 2025 Specification paras 9.164–9.166.
52 Standard Crime Contract 2022 Specification para 9.185 and Standard Crime Contract 2025 Specification para 9.167.
53 Standard Crime Contract 2022 Specification para 9.186 and Standard Crime Contract 2025 Specification para 9.167.
54 Criminal Legal Aid (Remuneration) Regulations 2013 Sch 4 para 3(4), as amended.

Advice and Assistance for Pre-Charge Engagement

Overview

14.49 Following the *Attorney General's Guidelines on Disclosure*[55] in 2020, the contract has been amended to include Advice and Assistance for Pre-Charge Engagement. You may only provide advice and assistance under this unit of work after the first (PACE) interview.[56] This is essentially preparatory work to determine whether pre-charge engagement would be beneficial or a voluntary agreement between the parties to an investigation to undertake pre-charge engagement.

Scope of work

14.50 You may only provide advice and assistance for pre-charge engagement where there is an agreement (either formally or informally) between the client and the prosecutors and or investigators to undertake pre-charge engagement or no agreement has been made and preparatory work has been undertaken to determine whether pre-charge engagement will be beneficial to the client.[57]

14.51 There is no definitive guide on what work is covered by pre-charge engagement; however, the Attorney General's guidelines provide a non-exhaustive list:[58]

   a. Giving the suspect the opportunity to comment on any proposed further lines of inquiry.
   b. Ascertaining whether the suspect can identify any other lines of inquiry.
   c. Asking whether the suspect is aware of, or can provide access to, digital material that has a bearing on the allegation.
   d. Discussing ways to overcome barriers to obtaining potential evidence, such as revealing encryption keys.
   e. Agreeing any key word searches of digital material that the suspect would like carried out.
   f. Obtaining a suspect's consent to access medical records.
   g. The suspect identifying and providing contact details of any potential witnesses.

---

55 Available at: www.gov.uk/government/publications/attorney-generals-guidelines-on-disclosure-2020.
56 Standard Crime Contract 2022 Specification para 9.114 and Standard Crime Contract 2025 Specification para 9.109.
57 Standard Crime Contract 2022 Specification para 9.113 and Standard Crime Contract 2025 Specification para 9.109.
58 *Attorney General's Guidelines on Disclosure*, Annex B.

h. Clarifying whether any expert or forensic evidence is agreed and, if not, whether the suspect's representatives intend to instruct their own expert, including timescales for this.

14.52 This unit of work does not cover further PACE interviews.[59]

14.53 There is an extendable upper limit of £314.81.[60] See chapter 16 for more on getting paid for criminal work.

Qualifying criteria

14.54 The sufficient benefit test (explained further below) must always be satisfied before providing this work, and can only be satisfied where there has been a formal agreement between the respective parties to undertake pre-charge engagement or preparatory work to determine whether it would be beneficial to the client to undertake pre-charge engagement. You must maintain a record on the client's file to demonstrate your reasons for undertaking such work.[61]

14.55 This unit of work is not means tested.[62]

Application process

14.56 You are delegated the function to self-grant legal aid in matters in this unit of work. A determination that an individual qualifies for advice and assistance may be made without a formal application. This determination must, however, be made by a qualified solicitor who is a designated fee earner or a supervisor (excluding a prison law supervisor).[63]

14.57 You must also record the following information on the file prior to the work being carried out or, if provided at short notice, as soon as practicable thereafter:

1) the client's name and address;
2) the UFN; and
3) details of the relevant unit of work and confirmation that there has been (either formally or informally) agreement between the

---

59 Standard Crime Contract 2022 Specification para 9.132 and Standard Crime Contract 2025 Specification para 9.128.
60 Criminal Legal Aid (Remuneration) Regulations 2013 Sch 4 para 3A, as amended.
61 Standard Crime Contract 2022 Specification paras 9.115–9.116 and Standard Crime Contract 2025 Specification paras 9.111–9.112.
62 Standard Crime Contract 2022 Specification para 9.117 and Standard Crime Contract 2025 Specification para 9.113.
63 Standard Crime Contract 2022 Specification para 9.119 and Standard Crime Contract 2025 Specification para 9.115.

14.58 Where a client has received previous advice and assistance on the same matter within the last six months, there are restrictions on when you can accept a further application that would involve a change of solicitor.[65] You cannot accept such an application unless:

- there is a gap in time and a material change in circumstances;
- the client has reasonable cause to transfer from the first supplier;
- the first supplier confirms they are making no claim; or
- previous advice and assistance was police station advice only.

14.59 You should make reasonable enquiries of the client to find out whether there has been previous advice and assistance. If so, and if you can justify the change of solicitor, there should be a clear note to that effect on the file.

Advice and assistance (freestanding)

Overview

14.60 Advice and assistance can also be given to a client who meets the means and merits tests, to advise and assist in respect of a criminal investigation – that is, before the client is charged, requisitioned or summoned for an offence. It will include representing the client at interviews with non-police agencies, such as the DWP in a benefit fraud matter, as well as general advice, case preparation and related work.

Means test

14.61 In order to qualify for advice and assistance, the client must pass the means test.[66] There are two elements to the test – income and capital – and the client must pass both parts. You are responsible for assessing the client's means and deciding whether the test is met.

14.62 Where the client is directly or indirectly in receipt of any of the following 'passporting' benefits, they automatically qualify for advice and assistance without the need for an assessment of income or capital:

---

64 Standard Crime Contract 2022 Specification para 9.120 and Standard Crime Contract 2025 Specification para 9.116.
65 Standard Crime Contract 2022 Specification para 9.121 and Standard Crime Contract 2025 Specification para 9.117.
66 Criminal Legal Aid (Financial Resources) Regulations 2013 reg 8.

- income support;
- income-based jobseeker's allowance (JSA);
- income-based employment and support allowance (ESA);
- guarantee pension credit; or
- universal credit paid under Welfare Reform Act 2012 Part 1.[67]

A person is indirectly in receipt of a benefit if they are included in another person's claim, for example, if a partner receives it on the basis of a couple.

14.63 'Capital' means all the client's assets and resources, excluding household furniture and effects, clothes, and the tools of the client's trade. Where the client owns property, the value to be taken into account is the equity after disregarding any mortgage, though only up to the value of £100,000. The first £100,000 of any equity is also disregarded, and the remainder is the capital value.[68] Where the client has a partner, the partner's capital should also be taken into account.

> **Case study**
>
> My client has a flat worth £120,000, with a mortgage of £90,000. He has £650 in savings and his wife has £300 in her account. Is he eligible on capital?
>
> The flat is worth £120,000. Disregard up to £100,000 of the mortgage – so the equity is £30,000. Disregard up to £100,000 of equity – so the capital is nil. Aggregate his and his wife's savings, so the total capital is £950, so the client is eligible on capital.

14.64 'Income' means all income from any source that the client may reasonably expect to receive within the seven days up to and including the day of their application[69] – with the following exceptions:
- any tax and National Insurance paid;
- any contributions paid under Social Security Contributions and Benefits Act 1992 Part 1;
- disability living allowance (DLA);
- attendance allowance;
- constant attendance allowance;
- any payment out of the social fund;

67 Criminal Legal Aid (Financial Resources) Regulations 2013 reg 2.
68 Criminal Legal Aid (Financial Resources) Regulations 2013 reg 13.
69 Criminal Legal Aid (Financial Resources) Regulations 2013 reg 6.

- so much of any back to work bonus received under Jobseekers Act 1995 s26 as is, by virtue of that section, to be treated as payable by way of a JSA;
- any direct payments made under regulations made under Care Act 2014 ss31–33 (direct payments); Children and Families Act 2014 s49(3) (personal budgets and direct payments); Carers and Direct Payments Act (Northern Ireland) 2002 s8(1) (direct payments); or Social Services and Well-being (Wales) Act 2014 ss50–53;
- any reasonable living expenses provided for as an exception to a restraint order under Proceeds of Crime Act 2002 s41;
- any personal independence payment (PIP) paid under Welfare Reform Act 2012 Part 4;[70]
- any payments made under Universal Credit (Transitional Provisions) Regulations 2014 reg 17 (2016 NI Regs reg 17);
- any payment on account of universal credit;
- any PIPs.
- any Windrush connected payment;
- a payment made under the Social Security (Additional Payments) Act 2022; and
- a payment made to an individual under section 13 or 15 of the Energy Prices Act 2022.

Where the client has a partner, the partner's income should also be taken into account.[71] Where the client has a partner or other dependant member of the household, you should deduct the standard allowance for each member.[72]

14.65 The thresholds for capital and income, and the standard dependants' allowances can be found on Keycard No 48 on the LAA website.[73] The levels are very occasionally uprated, and you should check the website for the most up-to-date figures.

14.66 Evidence of the client's means will be required and should be retained on file.[74] This is a key issue on audit. There is a power to assess means without evidence where it is not practicable to obtain it before the form is signed, but it should be obtained at a later stage, and if it is not, any claim should be limited to the equivalent of two

---

70 Criminal Legal Aid (Financial Resources) Regulations 2013 reg 11.
71 Criminal Legal Aid (Financial Resources) Regulations 2013 reg 9.
72 Criminal Legal Aid (Financial Resources) Regulations 2013 reg 12.
73 See: www.gov.uk/guidance/criminal-legal-aid-means-testing.
74 Standard Crime Contract 2022 Specification para 9.140 and Standard Crime Contract 2025 Specification para 9.136.

hours.[75] You cannot make a claim if you do not seek to obtain the relevant evidence. Only in defined exceptional circumstances may you dispense with evidence altogether, if the client's circumstances make it impracticable to obtain it at any point.[76]

Merits test

14.67 Assuming the client qualifies on means, you should go on to consider whether there is merit. The merits test is the 'sufficient benefit' test – is there 'sufficient benefit to the client, having regard to the circumstances of the matter, including the personal circumstances of the client, to justify work or further work being carried out'.[77]

14.68 The sufficient benefit test must be applied throughout the case to determine the extent of the advice required,[78] and the provision of advice must cease if it becomes apparent that the test is no longer satisfied.[79]

The application process

14.69 The client must complete and sign the application forms – CRM1[80] and CRM2[81] – and you should retain the original copies of them on file (this may be in electronic format).[82] Advice and assistance is granted by you, with no application to the LAA required, and so the presence of the signed forms on file is sufficient to effect the grant.

14.70 The usual rule is that the client comes to you to sign the forms. However, there will be situations where that is not possible, and therefore the contract allows for exceptions where certain criteria are met:

- A **postal application** can be accepted where it is reasonable to do so (eg where there is good reason why the client cannot attend your offices). However, you cannot accept a postal application where a client is temporarily resident outside the EU and the

---

75 Standard Crime Contracts 2022 and 2025 Specification paras 3.5–3.8.
76 Standard Crime Contracts 2022 and 2025 Specification paras 3.6–3.7.
77 Standard Crime Contracts 2022 and 2025 Specification para 3.10.
78 Standard Crime Contracts 2022 and 2025 Specification paras 3.11 and 3.15.
79 Standard Crime Contracts 2022 and 2025 Specification para 3.12.
80 Available at: www.gov.uk/government/publications/crm1-collect-client-details-in-legal-aid-cases.
81 Available at: www.gov.uk/government/publications/crm2-apply-for-advice-and-assistance-awaiting-police-interview.
82 Standard Crime Contracts 2022 and 2025 Standard Terms para 8.10.

matter can be delayed until they return, or another person in England and Wales could apply for advice and assistance on the same matter.[83]
- Where the client cannot attend immediately but can telephone you, **telephone advice** can be given before the form is signed[84] and you can claim for that advice. In order to qualify, there has to be good reason why the client cannot attend the office, but the client must later sign the form and be eligible. This power can be combined with one of the others; for example, you could give telephone advice to a client in prison and then post the form to them.
- Where **the client lacks capacity**, you can accept an application on behalf of a child or protected party (a person lacking mental capacity under the Mental Capacity Act 2005)[85] from another person, such as a parent, guardian, deputy or attorney, litigation friend, or any other person where there is good reason why one of the above-named persons cannot make the application. The form will be signed by the authorised person but completed in the name of the client, and it will be the client's means that should be assessed and evidenced.
- You can also accept an application from **a child direct**[86] where the client is entitled to defend proceedings themself (which is true of almost all criminal work), or where you are satisfied that there is good reason why none of the authorised persons in the previous paragraph can make the application, and the child is old enough to give instructions and understand the nature of the advice, or where the child is seeking police station advice only.

Where a client cannot attend the office for one of the good reasons outlined above, you may claim for outward travel expenses;[87] and where the client is in custody, detention or hospital, travel time[88] for

---

83 Standard Crime Contract 2022 Specification para 4.31 and Standard Crime Contract 2025 Specification para 4.25.
84 Standard Crime Contract 2022 Specification para 9.146 and Standard Crime Contract 2025 Specification para 9.142.
85 Standard Crime Contract 2022 Specification para 4.25 and Standard Crime Contract 2025 Specification para 4.20.
86 Standard Crime Contract 2022 Specification paras 4.28–4.30 and Standard Crime Contract 2025 Specification paras 4.23–4.24.
87 Standard Crime Contract 2022 Specification para 9.147 and Standard Crime Contract 2025 Specification para 9.143.
88 Standard Crime Contract 2022 Specification para 9.148 and Standard Crime Contract 2025 Specification para 9.144.

travelling to see the client before the form is signed in order to get the form signed.

14.71 Where a client has received previous advice and assistance on the same matter within the last six months, there are restrictions on when you can accept a further application that would involve a change of solicitor.[89] You cannot accept such an application unless:

- there is a gap in time and a material change in circumstances;
- the client has reasonable cause to transfer from the first supplier;
- the first supplier confirms they are making no claim; or
- previous advice and assistance was police station advice only.

You should make reasonable enquiries of the client to find out whether there has been previous advice and assistance. If so, and if you can justify the change of solicitor, there should be a clear note to that effect on the file.

Conducting work

14.72 Once you have confirmed that the client is eligible and the form has been signed, you can proceed to work on the client's case.

14.73 Advice and assistance covers all necessary work (other than work in the police station or advice and assistance for pre-charge engagement) up to the point at which the client is charged with, summoned or requisitioned for an offence. It will cover you for attendance and advice to the client, case preparation, taking witness statements with a view to preserving memory, or avoiding charge, and so on. It will also cover attendance at interviews with non-police agencies.

14.74 Costs are limited to £314.81, though an application may be made to the LAA to extend that limit.[90] The limit includes both time and disbursements. Where advice and assistance runs alongside police station work, you may not make a separate claim for the advice and assistance; all work under this unit of work is covered by the police station fixed fee. However, the costs limit will continue to apply and you will need to be within the limit or have a granted extension for advice and assistance costs to count towards exceptionality. See chapter 16 for more on getting paid for criminal work.

---

89 Standard Crime Contract 2022 Specification para 9.150 and Standard Crime Contract 2025 Specification para 9.146
90 Criminal Legal Aid (Remuneration) Regulations 2013 Sch 4 para 3(1), as amended; and Standard Crime Contract 2022 Specification para 9.164 and Standard Crime Contract 2025 Specification para 9.160.

Separate matters

14.75 All work for a client that constitutes one matter will require one application and will lead to one claim. Where, however, work is a genuinely separate matter, a separate application and a separate claim will be required.

14.76 All work in respect of a single investigation constitutes one matter and therefore one claim for costs, even if the investigation is subsequently extended to cover other offences. However, work may be treated as a separate matter if it amounts to a generally separate problem requiring separate advice,[91] unless the client requires advice on one occasion only.[92]

> **Case study**
>
> *I had a client who was arrested for theft and taken to the police station, where it was found he was also wanted for a separate incident of criminal damage, and he was further arrested for that. Is that one matter or two?*
>
> It depends on the outcome of the case. If he were charged with both offences and bailed to the same court date, that would be one matter and one claim. This is because the two allegations required advice on one occasion only. However, if he were charged with theft and bailed to return on the criminal damage, that would constitute two matters, if you could reasonably attend on the bail to return, since they would require separate advice on more than one occasion.

Work in the proceedings class

14.77 The proceedings class runs from the point of charge/summons/requisition and includes all magistrates' court work and most Crown Court proceedings. The main funding types in the proceedings class are:
- advice and assistance/advocacy assistance as court duty solicitor, or in a virtual court;[93] and
- representation orders.

---

[91] Standard Crime Contract 2022 Specification para 4.43 and Standard Crime Contract 2025 Specification para 4.37.

[92] Standard Crime Contract 2022 Specification para 4.46 and Standard Crime Contract 2025 Specification para 4.40.

[93] Standard Crime Contract 2022 Specification paras 10.21–10.35. This has been removed from the Standard Crime Contract 2025 Specification on the basis that Virtual Court schemes are no longer in existence

14.78 You must be able to work with the Crown Court Digital Case System[94] and Common Platform digital case management system.[95] This enables you digitally to receive and serve papers and applications.[96]

Court duty solicitor work

14.79 A duty solicitor is a solicitor who has previously been a member of a scheme under a previous contract or is a current member of the Law Society's Criminal Litigation Accreditation Scheme and undertaken the police station qualification.[97]

14.80 Duty solicitors whose firms have successfully bid in a procurement area will be allocated sessions as a duty solicitor whose role is to advise and assist otherwise unrepresented defendants.

14.81 Technically speaking, two different funding types are available to a court duty solicitor – Advice and Assistance and Advocacy Assistance, to advise the client outside court and represent the client in court respectively. In practice, however, there is no distinction, and a single consolidated claim is made for all work done for all clients on a duty day.

14.82 Court duty advice is available to clients whose cases qualify for assistance without regard to their means, and no application form is needed. However, a file note of the details of the client and the case will be needed.[98]

14.83 However, clients can only be represented where their case comes within the scope of the scheme:

- The duty solicitor must in all circumstances:[99]
    - advise any client who requests it who is in custody;
    - make a bail application where a client in custody requires a bail application and such an application has not previously been made by a duty solicitor;

---

94 See: https://crowncourtdcs.caselines.co.uk.
95 See: www.gov.uk/guidance/hmcts-services-common-platform.
96 Standard Crime Contract 2022 Standard Terms para 7.24 and Standard Crime Contract 2025 Standard terms para 7.19 require the use of CJS online once operational. You must be able to use CJS online, which is the online system for accessing and serving material between parties within the criminal justice system including courts, police, prosecution and defence. This system includes the Crown Court Digital Case System and Common Platform.
97 Standard Crime Contracts 2022 and 2025 Standard Terms para 1.1.
98 Standard Crime Contract 2022 Specification para 10.6 and Standard Crime Contract 2025 Specification para 10.5.
99 Standard Crime Contract 2022 Specification para 10.7 and Standard Crime Contract 2025 Specification paras 10.7–10.8. Note the distinctions between advice and representation throughout these provisions.

- advise a client before the court in connection with 'prescribed proceedings' (civil orders deemed to be criminal for legal aid purposes); the full list of prescribed proceedings appears at para 14.86 below;[100] and
- cross-examine, save in exceptional circumstances, under Youth Justice and Criminal Evidence Act 1999 s38 if appointed to do so by the court.[101]
- The duty solicitor must also:[102]
  - advise and represent any client who is in custody on a plea of guilty and wishes the case to be concluded that day;
  - advise and represent any client before the court for failure to pay a fine or other sum or to obey an order of the court, and such failure may lead to the client being at risk of imprisonment;
  - advise and represent a client not in custody in connection with an imprisonable offence where, in the opinion of the duty solicitor, such a client requires advocacy assistance;
  - help a client in making an application for a representation order, whether the nominated solicitor is the duty solicitor or another solicitor;
  - advise and represent a client seeking to vary police-imposed bail conditions pre-charge; and
  - advise and represent a client subject to an application by the police to extend police bail under section 47ZF or 47ZG of PACE.
- The duty solicitor must not:
  - represent at a not guilty trial or in relation to a non-imprisonable offence unless within the provisions above;[103] or
  - advise or represent a client who has had the services of a duty solicitor at a previous hearing in the proceedings (except where they are before the court this time as a result of failure to pay a fine or other sum or comply with an order imposed previously).[104]

---

100 Criminal Legal Aid (General) Regulations 2013 reg 9.
101 Standard Crime Contracts 2022 and 2025 Specification para 10.15.
102 Standard Crime Contract 2022 Specification para 10.8 and Standard Crime Contract 2025 Specification paras 10.7–10.8.
103 Standard Crime Contract 2022 Specification para 10.9 and Standard Crime Contract 2025 Specification para 10.6.
104 Standard Crime Contract 2022 Specification para 10.10 and Standard Crime Contract 2025 Specification para 10.9.

14.84 As duty solicitor, with the client's permission you are entitled to take on the case and apply for a representation order. However, you must not apply for a representation order where the case concludes on the day of the duty or make any claim for a sending hearing fixed fee if the matter is sent to the Crown Court.[105]

Representation orders – magistrates' court

Scope

14.85 A representation order is the main method of funding proceedings in the magistrates' court.

14.86 It covers representation of clients charged, summoned, or requisitioned for criminal offences, and also covers proceedings deemed to be criminal for the purpose of legal aid funding, as set out in Criminal Legal Aid (General) Regulations 2013 reg 9:[106]

- (a) civil proceedings in a magistrates' court arising from a failure to pay a sum due or to obey an order of that court where such failure carries the risk of imprisonment;
- (b) proceedings under sections 14B, 14D, 14G, 14H, 21B and 21D of the Football Spectators Act 1989 in relation to banning orders and references to a court;
- (c) proceedings under section 5A of the Protection from Harassment Act 1997 in relation to restraining orders on acquittal;
- (d), (e) [Revoked.]
- (f) proceedings in relation to parenting orders made under section 8(1)(b) of the Crime and Disorder Act 1998 where an order under section 330 of the Sentencing Code or a sexual harm prevention order under section 103A of the Sexual Offences Act 2003 or Chapter 2 of Part 11 of the Sentencing Code is made;
- (fa) proceedings under sections 342H and 342I of the Sentencing Code in relation to serious violence reduction orders;
- (g) proceedings under section 366 of the Sentencing Code in relation to parenting orders made on the conviction of a child;
- (h) proceedings under section 9(5) of the Crime and Disorder Act 1998 or section 374 of the Sentencing Code to discharge or vary a parenting order made as set out in sub-paragraph (f) or (g);
- (i) proceedings under section 336(10) of the Sentencing Code in relation to an appeal against a parenting order made as set out in sub-paragraph (f) or (g);

---

105 Standard Crime Contracts 2022 and 25 Specification para 10.14.
106 As amended by the Criminal Legal Aid (General) (Amendment) Regulations 2013, the Civil and Criminal Legal Aid (Amendment) Regulations 2015 and the Sentencing Act 2020.

(j) proceedings under section 368 of the Sentencing Code in relation to parenting orders for failure to comply with orders under section 90 of that Code;

(ja) proceedings, in a youth court, (or on appeal from such a court) in relation to a breach or potential breach of a provision in an injunction under Part 1 of the Anti-social Behaviour, Crime and Policing Act 2014 where the person subject to the injunction is under 14.

(k) proceedings under sections 80, 82, 83 and 84 of the Anti-social Behaviour, Crime and Policing Act 2014 in relation to closure orders made under section 80(5)(a) of that Act where a person has engaged in or is likely to engage in behaviour that constitutes a criminal offence on the premises;

(ka) proceedings under paragraph 3 of Schedule 2 to the Female Genital Mutilation Act 2003 in relation to female genital mutilation protection orders made other than on conviction and related appeals;

(kb) proceedings under paragraph 6 of Schedule 2 to the Female Genital Mutilation Act 2003 in relation to female genital mutilation protection orders made under paragraph 3 of that Schedule;

(l) proceedings under sections 20, 22, 26 and 28 of the Anti-social Behaviour Act 2003 in relation to parenting orders–
  (i) in cases of exclusion from school; or
  (ii) in respect of criminal conduct and anti-social behaviour;

(m) proceedings under sections 97, 100 and 101 of the Sexual Offences Act 2003 in relation to notification orders and interim notification orders;

(n) proceedings under sections 103A, 103E, 103F and 103H of the Sexual Offences Act 2003 or sections 345, 350 and 353 of the Sentencing Code in relation to sexual harm prevention orders;

(o) [Revoked.]

(p) proceedings under sections 122A, 122D, 122E and 122G of the Sexual Offences Act 2003 in relation to sexual risk orders;

(q) [Revoked.]

(r) proceedings under section 13 of the Tribunals, Courts and Enforcement Act 2007 on appeal against a decision of the Upper Tribunal in proceedings in respect of–
  (i) a decision of the Financial Conduct Authority;
  (ia) a decision of the Prudential Regulation Authority;
  (ii) a decision of the Bank of England; or
  (iii) a decision of a person in relation to the assessment of any compensation or consideration under the Banking (Special Provisions) Act 2008 or the Banking Act 2009;

(s) proceedings before the Crown Court or the Court of Appeal in relation to serious crime prevention orders under sections 19, 20, 21 and 24 of the Serious Crime Act 2007;

(t) proceedings under sections 100, 101, 103, 104 and 106 of the Criminal Justice and Immigration Act 2008 in relation to violent offender orders and interim violent offender orders;
(u) proceedings under sections 26, 27 and 29 of the Crime and Security Act 2010 in relation to–
 (i) domestic violence protection notices; or
 (ii) domestic violence protection orders;
(ua) proceedings under sections 14(1)(b) and (c), 15 and 20 to 22 of the Modern Slavery Act 2015 in relation to slavery and trafficking prevention orders;
(ub) proceedings under sections 23 and 27 to 29 of the Modern Slavery Act 2015 in relation to slavery and trafficking risk orders,
(uc) [Revoked.]
(ud) proceedings under sections 1, 4, 5 and 7 of the Stalking Protection Act 2019 in relation to stalking protection orders and interim stalking protection orders;
(ug) proceedings under sections 21, 28 or 29 of the Public Order Act 2023 in relation to a serious disruption prevention order; and
(v) any other proceedings that involve the determination of a criminal charge for the purposes of Article 6(1) of the European Convention on Human Rights.

14.87 Subparagraph (v) includes contempt other than in the face of the court, at all levels of court in all proceedings, including criminal, family and civil, and on appeal. (In the High Court see *King's Lynn and West Norfolk BC v Bunning*;[107] in the county court see *Brown v Haringey LBC*;[108] and in the Court of Appeal and generally see *Devon CC v Kirk*.[109]) Respondents to committal proceedings in courts other than the magistrates' court are entitled to non-means tested legal aid (*CH v CT (committal: appeal)*,[110] approved by *Re O (committal: legal representation)*[111]). Applications for legal aid in the High Court should be made to the LAA; applications in relation to the Court of Appeal are made to that court.

> **Case study**
>
> My client is in arrears on council tax. She has been summoned to appear at the magistrates' court. I cannot represent her. Can I advise her to see the court duty solicitor?

---

107 [2013] EWHC 3390 (QB).
108 [2015] EWCA Civ 483.
109 [2016] EWCA Civ 1221.
110 [2018] EWHC 1310 (Fam).
111 [2019] EWCA Civ 1721.

> She is in principle eligible to see the duty solicitor, since she is before the court for failure to pay a sum due. Whether she can use the duty solicitor depends on whether she is at risk of imprisonment, which is the merits test. That will depend on the facts of her case and is more likely if she is in wilful default or has shown culpable neglect.

14.88 An order also covers advice on appeal, and any related bail proceedings in the Crown Court or High Court.[112]

Financial eligibility

14.89 Representation orders are means tested. Therefore, a full application for a representation order (including means information) must be completed in all cases.

14.90 Applications for representation orders are made to the LAA, which will apply the means test to decide whether the client is eligible. However, you will need an understanding of the test in order to advise clients whether they are likely to be eligible. You can use the LAA's 'Financial eligibility calculator for criminal legal aid' on its webpage 'Criminal legal aid: means testing' at: www.gov.uk/guidance/criminal-legal-aid-means-testing.

14.91 The details of the test, together with the eligibility limits applying from time to time, can be found in the Criminal Legal Aid (Financial Resources) Regulations 2013, as amended. The eligibility limits are very occasionally amended, and the discussion that follows is based on the limits applying since June 2016. There is guidance in the *Criminal Legal Aid Manual* and on the LAA website at: www.gov.uk/guidance/criminal-legal-aid-means-testing.

14.92 Eligibility for a representation order is based solely on income – capital is not taken into account except where there is a conviction at the Crown Court. There are three stages to the test:
1) Is the client under the age of 18, or directly or indirectly in receipt of a passporting benefit? (See para 14.62 above.)
2) If not, is the client's gross income below the initial test threshold?
3) If not, is the client's disposable income below the full means test threshold?

If the answer to all three questions is no, the client is automatically not eligible.

---

112 Standard Crime Contract 2022 Specification para 10.36 and Standard Crime Contract 2025 Specification para 10.20.

14.93 The means of the client's partner should always be taken into account, unless the partner has a contrary interest in the proceedings (eg is a victim or prosecution witness), together with the resources of any other person which have been or are likely to be made available to the client.[113]

14.94 The passporting benefits are:[114]

- income support;
- income-based JSA;
- guarantee state pension credit;
- income-related ESA; and
- universal credit.

If the client is directly or indirectly in receipt of any of these, they will automatically be eligible for legal aid. 'Indirectly in receipt' means that the client is included as a dependant on another person's claim.

14.95 If the client is not passported, you will need to proceed to the two-stage means test. If gross income is below the initial threshold, currently £12,457, then they are eligible. If gross income is over £22,325, they are not eligible.[115] If gross income is between those two figures, then a full means test to determine disposable income will be required. Following that test, if disposable income is less than £3,398 the client will be eligible. All figures are annual.

14.96 'Gross income' is all income from all sources, excluding certain benefits:[116]

- attendance allowance;
- severe disablement allowance;
- carer's allowance;
- DLA;
- constant attendance allowance;
- housing benefit;
- council tax benefit;
- payments out of the social fund;
- direct payments under the Care Act 2014; Children and Families Act 2014; Carers and Direct Payments Act (Northern Ireland) 2002; and Social Services and Well-being (Wales) Act 2014;
- exceptionally severe disablement allowance;

---

113 Criminal Legal Aid (Financial Resources) Regulations 2013 reg 19.
114 Criminal Legal Aid (Financial Resources) Regulations 2013 reg 2.
115 Criminal Legal Aid (Financial Resources) Regulations 2013 reg 18.
116 Criminal Legal Aid (Financial Resources) Regulations 2013 reg 20.

- service pensions paid under the Naval, Military and Air Forces Etc (Disablement and Death) Service Pensions Order 2006;
- independent living funds payments;
- financial support paid for the foster care of a child;
- reasonable living expenses provided for as an exception to a restraint order under Proceeds of Crime Act 2002 s41;
- universal credit payments on account;
- PIPs;
- any Windrush connected payment; and
- a payment made to an individual under section 13 or 15 of the Energy Prices Act 2022.

14.97 Where the client has a partner or children in the same household, the gross income threshold increases according to the following weighting:[117]

Person	Weighting
Partner	0.64
Child 0–1 year	0.15
Child 2–4 years	0.30
Child 5–7 years	0.34
Child 8–10 years	0.38
Child 11–12 years	0.41
Child 13–15 years	0.44
Child 16–17 years	0.59

14.98 To calculate the weighting, add the relevant factors to 1 and divide household income by the result.

> **Case study**
>
> *My client earns £25,000 per year. He lives with his partner and their children, aged 6 and 3. Is he eligible for a representation order?*
>
> The client has a partner and two children, so the weighting is 1 + 0.64 + 0.30 + 0.34 = 2.28. Weighted income = £25,000 divided by 2.28 = £10,964.91. The gross income threshold is £12,457 and the weighted income is below that, so your client is eligible.

---

117 Criminal Legal Aid (Financial Resources) Regulations 2013 Sch 1.

14.99 Where the client is not eligible on gross income, but the (weighted) household income is below the upper threshold, you will need to consider whether the client is eligible on disposable income.[118]

14.100 'Disposable income' is gross income **minus**:
- tax and National Insurance paid;
- council tax paid;
- rent, mortgage, etc;
- childcare costs;
- maintenance payments; and
- living expenses allowance.

14.101 The 'living expenses allowance' is a notional cost of living allowance, currently £5,676 per year. Where the client has a partner and/or children, the allowance is increased using the scale in the table above – so, in the case study, the allowance would be £5,676 x 2.28 = £12,941.28.

14.102 Proof of means will always be required to accompany the application, except where the client is in custody, in which case a statement of truth (now incorporated within form CRM15[119]) should be signed instead, or unless the client's sole income is state benefits, in which case the courts can use its direct computer link with the DWP to check against the client's National Insurance number that the means information is correct.

14.103 Where the client is not financially eligible but can demonstrate that to pay privately would cause the client real hardship, an application can be made for hardship funding. This application is made to the LAA, and whether to grant is at the LAA's discretion. See: www.gov.uk/guidance/criminal-legal-aid-means-testing#exceptional-circumstances-hardship-and-eligibility-reviews.

Merits test

14.104 The merits test for the grant of representation orders is the 'interests of justice' test. The test is set out in Legal Aid, Sentencing and Punishment of Offenders Act 2012 (LASPO) s17(2), which says:

> In deciding what the interests of justice consist of [in relation to any individual], the following factors must be taken into account–
>   (a) whether, if any matter arising in the proceedings is decided against the individual, the individual would be likely to lose his

---

118 Criminal Legal Aid (Financial Resources) Regulations 2013 reg 18.
119 Available at: www.gov.uk/government/publications/criminal-legal-aid-application-forms.

or her liberty or livelihood or to suffer serious damage to his or her reputation,
(b) whether the determination of any matter arising in the proceedings may involve consideration of a substantial question of law,
(c) whether the individual may be unable to understand the proceedings or to state his or her own case,
(d) whether the proceedings may involve the tracing, interviewing or expert cross-examination of witnesses on behalf of the individual, and
(e) whether it is in the interests of another person that the individual be represented.

Note that this list is not exhaustive, merely examples of what can be taken into account. Guidance on the merits test as applied by the courts contains helpful information about factors that are considered.[120] Where reliance is placed on the existence of previous convictions, the LAA requires evidence of these from either the Initial Details of Prosecution Case (IDPC) or older files. Significant regard is paid to sentencing guidelines.

14.105 Applications for representation orders should be made to the LAA, electronically. The LAA's contract with eforms ended in September 2024 and therefore the LAA developed a new digital replacement in-house service to replace CRM forms. 'Applying for criminal legal aid' service can be accessed via the LAA portal. There is more information about electronic submission of crime forms on the LAA website: www.gov.uk/government/news/digital-developments-in-applying-for-criminal-legal-aid. If your client is present when you submit the electronic forms, they can sign the applicant's declaration for online submissions available from the LAA. In all other cases, it is important that the completed application is kept on file for audit purposes. Where your client is not in custody, full evidence of means will be required. Where the client is in custody, the online declaration can be signed instead – this is a statement of truth that the information regarding means is accurate.

14.106 An application should be submitted as soon as possible after charge. Orders are deemed to be granted on the date a properly

---

120 *Interests of Justice: Guidance on the Consideration of Defence Representation Order Applications*, May 2018, available at: www.gov.uk/government/uploads/system/uploads/attachment_data/file/314453/LAA-guidance-consideration-defence-representation-order-applications.pdf.

completed application was received, which will be immediately if submitted electronically.[121]

14.107 Where an application is granted, funding for the magistrates' court element of the case is in place and preparation can begin.

14.108 Where the application is refused on means, there is no right of appeal, although applicants can ask for a recalculation if they believe that an error has been made, and a fresh application can be submitted at any time, for example, if there is a change of circumstances). Where the application is refused on the merits, there is a right of appeal to the magistrates' court, which will either confirm the original decision or grant an order.[122]

Funding in the absence of an order

Pre-order costs

14.109 The general rule is that no work can be done, and no costs claimed, until such time as a representation order has been granted.

14.110 However, an order can be backdated so that a claim can be made for pre-order work where:[123]

- urgent work was required (defined as being a hearing within 10 working days of taking initial instructions);
- there was no undue delay in making the application (that is, it was submitted no more than five working days after taking initial instructions); and
- an order is subsequently granted.

If all these conditions are granted, you are able to claim for work done from the time of initial instructions onwards – or, if later, from the point of charge onwards. In order to enable the LAA to decide whether pre-order work may be claimed and/or allowed, you must note on file the date of initial instruction; the date the application for a determination that an individual qualifies for representation was lodged with the court and the date of the court hearing.

Early Cover

14.111 Where an order is subsequently refused, you can nevertheless make a claim for work done in certain circumstances:

---

121 Criminal Legal Aid (General) Regulations 2013 reg 23.
122 Criminal Legal Aid (General) Regulations 2013 reg 29.
123 Standard Crime Contract 2022 Specification para 10.40 and Standard Crime Contract 2025 Specification para 10.28.

- Where the application is refused on means, an Early Cover[124] fixed fee of £78.71 may be claimed if:
  - the application was submitted by 9 am on the sixth working day following initial instructions;
  - you have taken all reasonable steps to assist the client to complete the forms and provide appropriate evidence;
  - no decision had been made on the application by the first hearing;
  - you represent the client at the first hearing, and that hearing moves the case forward and any adjournment is justified; and
  - the eventual decision is that the case passes the interests of justice test but the client fails the means test.
- Where the application has been refused on the merits, a Pre-Order Cover[125] claim, must be made at the hourly rates and subject to the limit set out in the Criminal Legal Aid (Remuneration) Regulations 2013 and may be made if:
  - a qualified solicitor documents on file why it was believed the interests of justice test was passed; and
  - no claim for early cover is made.[126]
- You can claim a means test form completion[127] fixed fee of £26.23 where:
  - you complete an application for a determination that a client qualifies for representation;
  - you advise the client that although the interests of justice test is in all probability satisfied, the client would fail the means test and the file is marked accordingly;
  - such advice was given within 10 working days of charge or summons;
  - the client does not go on to instruct you privately; and
  - you do not make a claim for early cover or pre-order cover.

Disbursements and prior authority

14.112 Disbursements can be incurred in accordance with the general rules – see above. When you are considering large expenditure, you

---

124 Standard Crime Contract 2022 Specification para 10.122 and Standard Crime Contract 2025 Specification para 10.105.
125 Standard Crime Contract 2022 Specification para 10.115 and Standard Crime Contract 2025 Specification para 10.98.
126 Standard Crime Contract 2022 Specification para 10.116 and Standard Crime Contract 2025 Specification para 10.99.
127 Standard Crime Contract 2022 Specification para 10.124 and Standard Crime Contract 2025 Specification para 10.107.

can apply to the LAA for prior authority to incur the disbursement.[128] The effect of prior authority is that, provided the expenditure does not exceed the terms or amount of the authority, no question can normally be raised as to it on assessment – in other words, you are generally guaranteed to be paid.[129] If authority is refused by the LAA, or not granted in full, the application automatically goes before a costs assessor, but beyond that there is no appeal – though there is nothing to stop you making a further application at any time.[130]

14.113 If authority is refused, that does not prevent you from incurring the disbursement; it merely means that you do not have the security of knowing it will be paid on assessment.

14.114 Prior authority will be refused, and so will the disbursement if incurred, where it is a disbursement that should have come out of central funds, for example, a court ordered report in consideration of a Mental Health Act 1983 disposal.[131] Privilege does not attach to such reports, and it is normally preferable for you to obtain the report for which authority may then be given.

14.115 Where an application for prior authority has been made and refused, and the client nevertheless instructs you to incur the expense, you may accept payment from the client or a third party for that expense.[132] This is an exception to the rule that legal aid is complete remuneration for the case and no additional charge may be made to the client or a third party.[133]

Counsel

14.116 A representation order for work in the magistrates' court is usually limited to representation by solicitor only. This does not mean that you cannot instruct counsel at all; it just means that counsel is not assigned by the order and therefore the rules regarding unassigned

---

128 Standard Crime Contract 2022 Specification para 5.27 and Standard Crime Contract 2025 Specification para 5.25.
129 Standard Crime Contract 2022 Specification para 5.29 and Standard Crime Contract 2025 Specification para 5.27.
130 Standard Crime Contract 2022 Specification para 5.28 and Standard Crime Contract 2025 Specification para 5.26.
131 Standard Crime Contract 2022 Specification para 5.35(a) and Standard Crime Contract 2025 Specification para 5.33(a).
132 Standard Crime Contracts 2022 and 2025 Specification para 8.43.
133 Standard Crime Contracts 2022 and 2025 Specification para 8.41.

counsel apply.[134] This means that you are responsible for agreeing and paying counsel's fees.[135]

14.117 In more serious cases, you can apply to the court for counsel (or an independent solicitor advocate) to be assigned. Where counsel is assigned, they are entitled to be paid directly by the LAA at the rates prescribed in the contract, though you should submit their bill with your own[136] – see chapter 16.

14.118 Whether or not counsel is assigned, you must provide them with the UFN and a copy of the representation order when briefing them.[137]

14.119 For more details on the instruction of counsel, refer to chapter 20.

Separate matters

14.120 All work done in the proceedings class is described by the LAA as a case. Excluding the sending fixed fee (see below) only one bill can be submitted per case.[138] A case is all work done for all clients in respect of:
- one offence;
- more than one offence where the charges are laid at the same time;
- more than one offence where the charges are founded on the same facts; or
- more than one offence where the charges form a series of offences.[139]

14.121 'Founded on the same facts' covers situations where one charge is withdrawn and replaced by another, or where two charges are laid as alternatives.

14.122 'Series of offences' means offences of a similar nature. For example, where a client is charged with two separate offences which

---

134 Standard Crime Contract 2022 Specification paras 10.46–10.55 and Standard Crime Contract 2025 Specification paras 10.34–10.43.
135 Standard Crime Contract 2022 Specification para 10.46 and Standard Crime Contract 2025 Specification para 10.34.
136 Standard Crime Contract 2022 Specification para 10.44 and Standard Crime Contract 2025 Specification para 10.32.
137 Standard Crime Contract 2022 Specification para 10.43 and Standard Crime Contract 2025 Specification para 10.33.
138 Standard Crime Contract 2022 Specification para 10.59 and Standard Crime Contract 2025 Specification para 10.47.
139 Standard Crime Contract 2022 Specification para 10.69 and Standard Crime Contract 2025 Specification para 10.56.

could be tried together, that would constitute one case. Similarly, where two clients are charged with the same offence (assuming you act for both), that would also be one case. There is no hard and fast rule here; the contract does not offer definitive guidance, and it is a matter for your judgment (subject to LAA audit) whether you decide there is one case or two.[140]

Co-defendants and conflict of interest

14.123 Note that the Criminal Legal Aid (Determinations by a Court and Choice of Representative) Regulations 2013 say that where an individual who is granted a right to representation is one of two or more co-defendants whose cases are to be heard together, that individual must select the same litigator as a co-defendant unless there is, or is likely to be, a conflict of interest.[141] Therefore, if you are making an application for a representation order on behalf of a client whose co-defendant is separately represented, you should ensure that you demonstrate on the application form why there is a potential conflict requiring separate representation.

14.124 There is a practice note on the Law Society's website,[142] *Conflicts of interest in criminal cases*, which deals with many examples of possible conflict in criminal cases. Although the Solicitors Regulation Authority's (SRA's) 2007 Code of Conduct has been superseded,[143] the guidance to the old rule 3 may still be helpful. It stated:

> ... the regulations are not intended to put solicitors in a position where they are asked by the court to act contrary to their professional responsibilities. If asked by the court for your reasons why you cannot act for both defendants, you must not give information which would breach your duty of confidentiality to your client(s). This will normally mean that you can say no more than that it would be unprofessional for you to continue to act.

14.125 Therefore, you do not have to disclose reasons why a potential conflict of interest exists which prevents you from acting for more than one

---

140 Standard Crime Contract 2022 Specification para 10.72 and Standard Crime Contract 2025 Specification para 10.59; and see chapter 16.
141 Reg 13.
142 December 2019: www.lawsociety.org.uk/topics/criminal-justice/conflicts-of-interest-in-criminal-cases.
143 The SRA Solicitors' Code of Conduct 2007 (part of the SRA Handbook) was replaced on 6 October 2011 by the SRA Code of Conduct 2011; the SRA Handbook was replaced by the SRA Standards and Regulations on 25 November 2019.

defendant. However, where such a reason exists, you should make clear on the application that there is a (potential) conflict, to avoid you being appointed for both defendants or to avoid delay while the court makes further enquiries.

Transfer cases

14.126 Where the client wants to transfer from one solicitor to another, that can only happen if the court agrees to the transfer of the order.

14.127 Transfers are governed by regulation, not by the contract. The regulations say that the court may grant an application to transfer where:

- the solicitor appointed under the order considers themself under a professional duty to withdraw;
- there is breakdown in the relationship between solicitor and client such that effective representation can no longer be provided;
- through circumstances beyond their control, the authorised solicitor can no longer represent the client; or
- there is some other substantial compelling reason.[144]

14.128 Note that any explanation will be strenuously tested by the courts. Solicitors must exercise a proper and independent judgment when considering the applicant's grounds.[145]

Matter ends

14.129 A matter ends, and a bill must be submitted, when the case comes to an end in the proceedings class. This will happen when:

- the case has concluded (eg by acquittal, sentence or committal);
- it is known that no further work will be needed (eg where the client has transferred);
- it is unclear whether further work will be required but at least one month has elapsed since the last work was done;[146]
- the LAA notifies you that the case is a VHCC; or
- the representation order is withdrawn.[147]

---

144 Criminal Legal Aid (Determinations by a Court and Choice of Representative) Regulations 2013 reg 14.
145 *R (Sanjari) v Birmingham Crown Court* [2015] EWHC 2037 (Admin).
146 Standard Crime Contract 2022 Specification para 10.62 and Standard Crime Contract 2025 Specification para 10.50.
147 Standard Crime Contract 2022 Specification para 10.56 and Standard Crime Contract 2025 Specification para 10.44.

Representation in the Crown Court

14.130 Cases in the Crown Court are generally funded by representation orders.

The merits test

14.131 The merits test for a Crown Court representation order is the interests of justice test, just as in the magistrates' court – see above.[148]

14.132 Where a case goes from the magistrates' court to the Crown Court, except on appeal, the magistrates' court representation order will automatically continue into the Crown Court,[149] and no application to extend or amend the order is required (although additional supporting evidence as to means may have to be provided). If a case is sent to the Crown Court (but not on an appeal), the interests of justice test is deemed to be met.[150] Even if counsel were not assigned under the order in the magistrates' court, once the case goes to the Crown Court the order is deemed to include representation by one junior advocate (that is, any advocate other than a KC) automatically.[151]

14.133 For more information on the instruction of advocates in the Crown Court, see chapter 20.

Means testing

Overview

14.134 Representation orders in the Crown Court are means tested. However, the means test takes into account both a client's income and capital.

14.135 Depending on their means, clients may be:
- granted an order without any financial contribution;
- required to make payments towards the cost of their representation, either immediately or following the conclusion of their case if they are convicted; or
- refused legal aid.[152]

14.136 Certain clients are still passported. These are the same clients who would be passported in the magistrates' court, ie those under 18 or in

---

148 Criminal Legal Aid (General) Regulations 2013 reg 21.
149 Criminal Legal Aid (General) Regulations 2013 reg 24.
150 Criminal Legal Aid (General) Regulations 2013 reg 25.
151 Criminal Legal Aid (General) Regulations 2013 reg 18.
152 Criminal Legal Aid (Contribution Orders) Regulations 2013.

receipt of income support, income-based JSA, guarantee state pension credit, income-related ESA or universal credit.

14.137 For those who are not passported, the client's means must be considered. In the Crown Court, unlike in the magistrates' court, this involves assessment of the client's capital as well as income. The means test is the same as in the magistrates' court, save that if the household disposable income is £37,500 or more, the applicant is not eligible for legal aid. The means test can be considered in two stages – income and capital – as follows.

Income

14.138 When the case becomes a Crown Court case, the client who is eligible with a contribution will be required to make monthly contributions towards the cost of their representation for the first five months after the case is sent to the Crown Court. The client's annual disposable income will be divided by 12 and the client will be asked to pay 90 per cent of the monthly figure each month for the first five months. Alternatively, the client can pay all five payments up-front in one lump sum.

14.139 Late payment of any of the five monthly contributions will result in an additional month's payment, ie the client will have to pay the same amount again for a sixth month.

14.140 There is a cap on **income** contributions, which is determined by the type of offence. If a client's contributions reach the maximum level, the client will be notified and will not be required to make any further income contributions.[153]

14.141 If a client's case concludes within the first five months of being transferred to the Crown Court, the client will not be required to continue paying income contributions.

14.142 Assuming the case continues beyond five (or six) months from transfer to the Crown Court, the client will not be required to make any further contributions until the conclusion of their case.

14.143 If the client is acquitted, they will not be required to make any further payments at all, and the their income contributions will be refunded in full with interest (currently set at a rate of two per cent annual compound interest). (Note that any costs associated with late payment may be deducted, and very occasionally a client may be required to make a contribution towards their defence costs where, eg the client has misled the prosecution or the court or brought the

---

153 Criminal Legal Aid (Contribution Orders) Regulations 2013 reg 16.

prosecution on themselves by their own conduct. This would be a matter for the judge to decide.)

14.144 However, if the client is convicted, the client's position will depend on the costs of their case. If the client's income contributions have exceeded the actual costs of the case, the overpayment will be refunded with interest (again, subject to any deduction associated with late payment). However, if the income contributions are less than the actual costs incurred, the client's capital will then be considered.

Capital

14.145 A client will only be required to contribute from their capital[154] at the conclusion of their case if:

- the client is convicted;
- any payments already made from income do not cover the client's defence costs; and
- the client has more than £30,000 of assets (eg savings, equity in property, shares or Premium Bonds).[155]

Not only can this result in a further payment towards profit costs, but significantly, towards high cost disbursements.

14.146 A client with less than £30,000 worth of assets will not be required to make any further contribution, even if the client's income contributions have not covered their defence costs. (Note, however, that this threshold may be removed if evidence of the client's assets has not been provided.)

14.147 A client with more than £30,000 worth of assets whose income contributions have not accounted for the full costs will be required to make up the shortfall from their assets. The costs may be recovered in various ways. For example, the LAA may apply an interest-bearing or non-interest-bearing charge to a property or, as a last resort, apply for an order for sale.

14.148 If a client, liable for any contribution either from income or capital, is acquitted of some but not all charges, it is critical that the court is asked to make an apportionment order identifying the percentage of the costs for which the defendant is liable. There is a strict 21-day time limit for applications for such orders.[156]

---

154 Criminal Legal Aid (Contribution Orders) Regulations 2013 reg 27.
155 Criminal Legal Aid (Contribution Orders) Regulations 2013 reg 28.
156 Criminal Legal Aid (Contribution Orders) Regulations 2013 reg 26; *R (Khan) v Director of Legal Aid Casework* [2018] EWHC 3198 (Admin).

Applications

14.149 If the order was not granted at the magistrates' court stage, Crown Court means testing says that a complete application for a representation order using the online portal must be submitted to the LAA.

14.150 The same rules apply in the Crown Court as in the magistrates' court regarding applications from children and vulnerable adults.

14.151 A major difference between applications for funding in the magistrates' court and in the Crown Court is that clients who are in custody cannot self-declare as to their means when their case is in the Crown Court.

14.152 This does not mean that all evidence (payslips, bank statements, tax returns, share certificates, and so on) must be provided with the initial application, although the application must contain all of the required information. Provided the application has been submitted, a representation order will be issued. The client then has 14 days in which to provide the required documentary evidence. If the required documents are not provided in this time, sanctions may be imposed with respect to both income and capital:

- If evidence of income is not provided, the client's monthly contribution could increase to £900 or 100 per cent of the client's monthly disposable income, whichever is higher.
- If evidence of capital is not provided (or the information provided is subsequently found to be incorrect), the LAA may remove the £30,000 capital threshold and require a client who has less than this amount in capital to pay towards the costs of their defence.

14.153 Where the evidence required is over and above what would normally be required for a magistrates' court legal aid application, you may be able to claim an evidence provision fee for helping the client to provide this evidence. For standard applications a fee of £45 plus VAT can be claimed. For more complex applications, involving five or more pieces of evidence, or a self-employed client whose application is referred to the National Crime Team, a fee of £90 plus VAT can be claimed.

14.154 When the completed application has been assessed, the client will be issued with a contribution notice or order alongside the representation order, detailing how much they will be required to pay and the sanctions for late or non-payment.

14.155 A client can also apply for a review on the grounds of hardship if they feel that they have higher than usual outgoings or would suffer financial hardship as a result of the means assessment. A hardship application must be submitted. This can be submitted either at the same time as applying for legal aid or afterwards.

Assessing case costs

14.156 Case costs in the Crown Court will vary considerably, depending on the type of case, the volume of evidence, the need for expert witnesses, and so on. Therefore, at the outset of a case it may be difficult to foresee whether a client's contributions will match the actual case costs.

14.157 The cap imposed on income contributions is intended to prevent clients from paying substantially more than the likely case costs up front, although it should be noted that according to the LAA figures, the cap is well above the average cost to trial in all categories of cases.

14.158 The actual case costs will be calculated at the end of the case, and will include the total litigator and advocate fees and any payments to expert witnesses and other disbursements. At the end of the case, this amount will be compared with the amount the client has already paid in income contributions: if the client has already paid more than the actual costs, the difference will be refunded with interest; if the client has paid less, the client may be required to contribute further from capital as described above. The client will be notified of the position and any amount they owe once the full costs have been established at the end of the case.

Effects of Crown Court means testing

14.159 Because of the potentially high costs of Crown Court cases and the obligation to keep the client informed of the potential costs,[157] it is essential that the cost implications of any step in the proceedings are thoroughly considered. This will be particularly important in cases where, for example, expert evidence is required: the client should be advised of the cost implications prior to the instruction of any expert and cost considerations may have an impact on the conduct of the case.

14.160 Clients may also be more reluctant to instruct a solicitor at all, and therefore it will be important to advise clients at the outset as to the potential costs (given the type of case), the advantages of being represented and, if appropriate, the possibility of a hardship applica-

---

157 SRA Code of Conduct for Solicitors, RELs and RFLs para 8.7 (formerly Code of Conduct 2011, O1.13).

tion. Such an application takes account of the potential private client rates to see if the applicant has sufficient funds to meet them.

14.161 The supporting evidence requirements for a Crown Court legal aid application are more onerous than those in the magistrates' court. Therefore, where a case is sent to the Crown Court and evidence has not already been provided, it is essential that this evidence is obtained as quickly as possible, as failure to provide this evidence within 14 days may have serious financial consequences for the client (see above).

Disbursements

14.162 Disbursements may be incurred in exactly the same way as in the magistrates' court. The test as to whether they are justified is the same, and applications for prior authority may be made.[158] The process is exactly the same as for magistrates' court cases: applications are made directly to the LAA.

14.163 Where the disbursement exceeds £100, you have prior authority and have in fact incurred the disbursement, you can make an application for payment on account of that disbursement at any time. Provided that the amount and scope of the prior authority have not been exceeded, payment should be made.[159] See also chapter 16.

Prescribed proceedings in the Crown Court[160]

14.164 Some civil proceedings have been deemed to be criminal for the purposes of legal aid[161] (designated 'prescribed proceedings'), and where orders are imposed in the magistrates' court, the appeal lies to the Crown Court. Examples include stand-alone parenting orders, football banning orders and Sexual Offences Act 2003 orders. The full list is given at para 14.86 above.

14.165 Where a stand-alone order is made by the magistrates' court and the client wants to appeal it to the Crown Court, this will also be funded on an application by way of a representation order.

14.166 As for other representation orders in the Crown Court, funding for such cases is means tested and the client will need to submit an

---

158 Criminal Legal Aid (Remuneration) Regulations 2013 reg 13.
159 Criminal Legal Aid (Remuneration) Regulations 2013 reg 14.
160 Standard Crime Contract 2022 Specification paras 10.144–10.155 and Standard Crime Contract 2025 Specification paras 10.126–10.137.
161 Criminal Legal Aid (General) Regulations 2013 reg 9, as amended; see para 14.86 above for the full list.

application on the online portal in this situation even if a representation order had been granted for the magistrates' court proceedings.

14.167 Claims are made as part of the normal monthly return and not by graduated fees. There is an upper limit to the costs that can be claimed for such work. Unless extended, this is £1,574.06.[162]

Appeals to the Crown Court

14.168 Other appeals to the Crown Court from the magistrates' court, whether against conviction, sentence or other order, require a fresh application for funding. The means test is similar to that applied in the magistrates' court.

14.169 Clients who are passported or pass the means test will not be required to pay any contribution towards the cost of their appeal.

14.170 Clients who do not pass the means test will be required to pay a defined contribution in the following appeals:

- £500 if an appeal against conviction is dismissed or abandoned;
- £250 if an appeal against conviction is dismissed but sentence is reduced; and
- £250 if an appeal against sentence or order is dismissed or abandoned.

14.171 All applications for funding will also be subject to the interests of justice test.

Recovery of defence costs orders

14.172 Privately paying clients in the magistrates' court are entitled to apply to recover their legal costs under a recovery of defence costs order (RDCO) if they are acquitted.[163] However, the amount recoverable is limited to the amount that would be payable under specified legal aid rates.

14.173 In the Crown Court, privately paying clients who have been acquitted can only apply to recover costs if they have been refused legal aid. It is important to note that it is a requirement that the LAA has made a determination of financial ineligibility in relation to the proceedings. To ensure that your client is entitled to recover costs in the event of their acquittal, you must apply for, and be determined to be ineligible for, legal aid.[164]

---

162 Criminal Legal Aid (Remuneration) Regulations 2013 Sch 4 para 7, as amended.
163 Prosecution of Offences Act 1985 s16A(4)(a), as amended.
164 Prosecution of Offences Act 1985 s16A, as amended.

14.174 Any costs recoverable will be limited to the amount that would be payable under specified legal aid rates.

14.175 Those who choose to instruct you privately cannot recover their costs.

14.176 RDCOs may also be imposed to recover legal costs in the Court of Appeal and Supreme Court.[165]

14.177 It is therefore very important that clients are advised as to the cost implications should they be seeking to instruct you privately.

Appeals and reviews

Scope

14.178 Work in the appeals and reviews class covers representation in the High Court on an appeal by way of case stated, advice on an application to the Criminal Cases Review Commission (CCRC), and advice on appeals to the Court of Appeal.

Case stated

14.179 Where the client seeks an appeal to the High Court by way of case stated, the appeal is funded by a representation order. The original order in the magistrates' court (or, as the case may be, the Crown Court) covers advice on appeal,[166] including the application to the magistrates' court to state a case.[167]

14.180 Once the case is lodged at the High Court, an application for representation in the appeal should be made to the High Court.[168] It is an application for a criminal representation order. There is no means test, and the merits test is deemed to be met.[169] If the appeal is unsuccessful, a recovery of defence costs order can be considered by the court.[170]

---

165 Prosecution of Offences Act 1985 s16A(4)(b), as amended.
166 Standard Crime Contracts 2022 and 2025 Specification para 11.3.
167 Standard Crime Contract 2022 Specification paras 11.44–11.61 and Standard Crime Contract 2025 Specification paras 11.44–11.52.
168 Standard Crime Contracts 2022 and 2025 Specification paras 11.48–11.49; Criminal Legal Aid (Determinations by a Court and Choice of Representative) Regulations 2013 reg 7.
169 Criminal Legal Aid (General) Regulations 2013 reg 21.
170 See the Criminal Legal Aid (Recovery of Defence Costs Orders) Regulations 2013.

14.181 Where disbursements are needed, you can make an application to the LAA for prior authority under the 2022 Contract, although it should be noted that this paragraph is currently not in the 2025 Draft contract.[171] Counsel may be instructed under the order.[172]

Advice and assistance in the appeals class

14.182 Advice and assistance may be granted to assist a client with an application to the CCRC, or to appeal against conviction and/or sentence.

14.183 The representation order in the magistrates' court or Crown Court includes the provision of advice on appeal,[173] up to the point where an appeal is lodged, and therefore where you represented a client in the magistrates' court or Crown Court under legal aid, the advice on appeal should be given under the order. It would not be appropriate to grant advice and assistance for that.

14.184 Similarly, where a representation order is available from the Court of Appeal,[174] advice and assistance should not be used as an alternative to, or to supplement, the Court of Appeal's powers to grant a representation order where only counsel has been authorised.[175]

14.185 Therefore, the primary use of advice and assistance is in cases where the client was not represented or was represented and seeks a second opinion on the appeal. This would apply whether the client is entitled to go direct to the Court of Appeal or would make an application to the CCRC.

14.186 The general rules on advice and assistance (see the investigations class, above) will apply. The work is means tested[176] and subject to the sufficient benefit test.[177] Costs are limited to an extendable upper limit of £314.81 (£524.69 in the case of a CCRC application).[178]

14.187 When you are dealing with a CCRC case, the LAA recognises that substantial work may be required, particularly where you are not the

---

171 Currently only in the Standard Crime Contract 2022 Specification para 11.57.
172 Standard Crime Contract 2022 Specification para 11.54 and Standard Crime Contract 2025 Specification para 11.53.
173 Standard Crime Contracts 2022 and 2025 Specification para 11.3.
174 Under Criminal Legal Aid (Determinations by a Court and Choice of Representative) Regulations 2013 reg 8.
175 Standard Crime Contracts 2022 and 2025 Specification para 11.7.
176 Standard Crime Contracts 2022 and 2025 Specification para 11.9.
177 Standard Crime Contract 2022 Specification para 11.8.
178 Standard Crime Contract 2022 Specification para 11.42 and Standard Crime Contract 2025 Specification para 11.43; and Criminal Legal Aid (Remuneration) Regulations 2013 Sch 4 para 8.

solicitor who acted at the trial. This may include obtaining the prosecution and defence files, considering transcripts,[179] commissioning further expert evidence and conducting further investigations. However, you should screen the case at as early a stage as possible, and where there is no reasonable prospect that it will meet the CCRC's criteria, refuse to carry out further work.[180]

Representation orders in the Court of Appeal

14.188 The Court of Appeal has the power to grant a representation order, but not until notice of appeal or application for leave to appeal has been submitted.[181]

14.189 The court can grant a representation order to an advocate alone,[182] and indeed this is usual practice. Applications for litigators will usually only be granted to undertake some specific step in the proceedings, such as to interview a witness, rather than for the appeal as a whole.

14.190 For Court of Appeal representation orders, the interests of justice test is deemed to be met.[183] There is no means test, but RDCOs may be made.

Prison law work

14.191 Work in the prison law class is divided into two funding types:
1) advice and assistance; and
2) advocacy assistance.

14.192 Assistance under these two categories may be provided to prisoners (including those on remand and those released on licence or parole, where appropriate) in the following types of cases:

---

179 Standard Crime Contract 2022 Specification para 11.23 and Standard Crime Contract 2025 Specification para 11.19.
180 Standard Crime Contract 2022 Specification para 11.22 and Standard Crime Contract 2025 Specification para 11.24.
181 The earlier Criminal Defence Service (General) (No 2) Regulations 2001 reg 10(5) was so interpreted in *Revenue and Customs Prosecution Office v Stokoe Partnership* [2007] EWHC 1588 (Admin): now the Criminal Legal Aid (Determinations by a Court and Choice of Representative) Regulations 2013 reg 8.
182 Criminal Legal Aid (Determinations by a Court and Choice of Representative) Regulations 2013 reg 8.
183 Criminal Legal Aid (General) Regulations 2013 reg 21.

- sentence cases;
- review of category A classification;
- application of Prison Rules 1999 rr46 and 46A in relation to close supervision centres and separation centres;
- disciplinary cases;
- Parole Board cases, including reconsideration cases;[184]
- review of an individual's classification as a restricted status prisoner or inmate; and
- review of the classification of a Young Offender Institution (YOI) inmate's classification as a category A inmate whose escape would be highly dangerous to the public, police or national security, and for whom the aim is to make escape impossible.

14.193 The general rules on advice and assistance apply (see above in the investigations class), including the means test[185] and the test that there is a sufficient benefit to the client, having regard to the circumstances of the matter, including the personal circumstances of the client, to justify work or further work being carried out. There should be a realistic prospect of a positive outcome that would be of real benefit to the client.[186]

14.194 There are complex rules on the number of matters that may be opened.[187] An application for Parole Board reconsideration is treated as part of the original Parole Board case, but a separate claim should be made if a reconsideration hearing is listed or directed.[188]

14.195 There are restrictive rules on when and how much travel and waiting time can be claimed,[189] and a requirement to obtain prior authority to incur a disbursement in excess of £500.[190] You can use

---

184 Standard Crime Contract 2022 Specification paras 12.68–12.80, 12.81–12.89, 12.90–12.100 and 12.101–12.112 and Standard Crime Contract 2025 Specification paras 12.87–12.103.
185 Standard Crime Contract 2022 Specification paras 12.13–12.14 and Standard Crime Contract 2025 Specification paras 12.8–12.9.
186 Standard Crime Contract 2022 Specification paras 12.5–12.12 and Standard Crime Contract 2025 Specification paras 12.2–12.7, 12.76, 12.82 and 12.90.
187 Standard Crime Contract 2022 Specification paras 12.23–12.31 and Standard Crime Contract 2025 Specification paras 12.18–12.19.
188 Standard Crime Contract 2022 Specification paras 12.114–12.115 and Standard Crime Contract 2025 Specification paras 12.95–12.96.
189 Standard Crime Contract 2022 Specification paras 12.32–12.37 and Standard Crime Contract 2025 Specification paras 12.26–12.31.
190 Standard Crime Contract 2022 Specification para 12.38 and Standard Crime Contract 2025 Specification para 12.32.

agents[191] (subject to the general rules in the contract about using agents). If counsel is used to give advice and assistance, there are specific rules on how their fees are to be claimed.[192]

14.196 Advice and assistance is limited to a fixed fee of £200.75 unless effective and waiting time costs (calculated at specified hourly rates) exceed £602.25, in which case the costs will be assessed.[193]

14.197 Advocacy assistance for disciplinary cases and Parole Board cases is paid under a standard fee scheme. This is similar to the fee scheme for magistrates' court cases, in that you may claim a lower standard fee, a higher standard fee or a non-standard fee depending on whether your profit and waiting time costs (but not travel) fall below, between or above two standard fee limits. Details of the limits are given in Criminal Legal Aid (Remuneration) Regulations 2013 Sch 4 para 11, as amended.

14.198 Both advice and assistance and advocacy assistance are granted by you, rather than by application to the LAA.

14.199 The client must complete the relevant forms (CRM1 and CRM2 or CRM3) and must pass the means test. Means are limited by both capital and disposable income, and the eligibility levels can be found on Keycard No 48 on the LAA website.[194] 'Disposable income' means all income received by the client and their partner, less tax, National Insurance and the dependants' allowances set out on the keycard.

14.200 In all cases within scope, the sufficient benefit test must be satisfied, and in addition advocacy assistance may not be provided in disciplinary cases where:

- it appears unreasonable to grant in the particular circumstances of the case; or
- (where required) permission to be legally represented has not been granted by a governor or other prison authority, where appropriate.[195]

14.201 In all cases, you should record on the file how the merits test has been and continues to be met.[196]

191 Standard Crime Contract 2022 para 12.40 and Standard Crime Contract 2025 para 12.59.
192 Standard Crime Contract 2022 Specification paras 12.41–12.44 and Standard Crime Contract 2025 Specification paras 12.34–12.47.
193 Criminal Legal Aid (Remuneration) Regulations 2013 Sch 4 para 11, as amended.
194 See: www.gov.uk/guidance/criminal-legal-aid-means-testing.
195 Standard Crime Contract 2022 Specification para 12.94 and Standard Crime Contract 2025 Specification para 12.79.
196 Standard Crime Contracts 2022 and 2025 Specification para 12.7.

14.202 Counsel may be instructed under advocacy assistance, but you may not claim for accompanying them to a hearing.[197] If you instruct counsel, you are responsible for agreeing a fee with them and paying them directly. There are restrictions on what can be recovered.[198]

Scope of prison law work

14.203 Advice and assistance may be provided regarding reviews of an individual's classification as a restricted status prisoner or inmate, and of reviews of a YOI inmate's classification as a category A inmate whose escape would be highly dangerous to the public, police or national security and for whom the aim is to make escape impossible. Advice and representation may be provided in sentence cases where the case is about the calculation of the total time to be served before a prisoner is eligible for automatic release or for consideration of release by the Parole Board;[199] in cases involving the review of category A classification; and the application of Prison Rules 1999 rr46 and 46A in relation to close supervision centres and separation centres.[200]

14.204 Advice and representation is available in all Parole Board cases including reconsideration cases.[201]

14.205 Advice and representation is only available in disciplinary cases that involve the determination of a criminal charge for the purposes of the right to a fair trial provisions of European Convention on Human Rights (ECHR) Article 6(1), or where the governor has exercised the discretion to allow advice and assistance.[202]

---

197 Standard Crime Contract 2022 Specification para 12.47 and Standard Crime Contract 2025 Specification para 12.40.
198 Standard Crime Contract 2022 Specification paras 12.43 and 12.46 and Standard Crime Contract 2025 Specification paras 12.34–12.47.
199 Criminal Legal Aid (General) Regulations 2013 reg 12, as amended by the Criminal Legal Aid (General) (Amendment) Regulations 2013; Standard Crime Contract 2022 Specification paras 12.68–12.80 and Standard Crime Contract 2025 Specification paras 12.70–12.74.
200 Criminal Legal Aid (Amendment) Regulations 2017; Standard Crime Contract 2022 Specification paras 12.81 and 12.68–12.80 and Standard Crime Contract 2025 Specification paras 12.70–12.74.
201 Standard Crime Contract 2022 Specification paras 12.101–12.112 and Standard Crime Contract 2025 Specification paras 12.87–12.103.
202 Criminal Legal Aid (General) Regulations 2013 reg 12, as amended by the Criminal Legal Aid (General) (Amendment) Regulations 2013; Standard Crime Contract 2022 Specification para 12.90 and Standard Crime Contract 2025 Specification para 12.78.

Associated civil work

14.206 Associated civil work is civil work arising out of criminal proceedings – for example, judicial review or habeas corpus, the obtaining of anti-social behaviour injunctions in the youth court, or certain civil work under the Proceeds of Crime Act 2002. Although you are permitted to do this work if you have a Standard Crime Contract, even if you do not have a Civil Contract, it is fundamentally civil work and the usual civil rules apply.[203] See chapters 2, 4 and 15 for more details of civil funding.

14.207 Criminal offences under the Proceeds of Crime Act 2002 are dealt with in the same way as all other criminal offences. Confiscation as part of criminal proceedings forms part of the criminal case, so where confiscation is sought against a defendant you can deal with that under the representation order.

14.208 Where confiscation is sought as part of criminal proceedings, but which affects a third party (eg someone who jointly owns property with a defendant), that party can apply for civil legal aid to be represented in the confiscation, notwithstanding that it is part of criminal proceedings in the Crown Court.

14.209 The availability of legal aid is defined by LASPO Sch 1 Part 1 para 40. See appendix A.

Very High Cost Cases

14.210 Criminal proceedings which, if the case were to proceed to trial, would likely last more than 25 days may qualify as VHCC.

14.211 VHCCs may be subject to individual case contracts.[204] If you potentially have such a case, you are obliged to report it to the LAA National Courts Team within five working days of the earliest date at which the court sets a trial estimate or you identify that the case will be or is likely to be a VHCC.[205]

14.212 If you are required to do so, you can only continue with the case if you enter into a contract with the LAA in relation to the individual case.

14.213 Further information on the arrangements for VHCCs can be found in the Standard Contract Terms and the 2013 VHCC guidance document, all published on the legal aid website at: www.gov.uk/guidance/high-cost-cases-crime.

---

203 Standard Crime Contract 2022 Specification paras 13.3 and 13.19 and Standard Crime Contract 2025 Specification paras 13.3 and 13.13.
204 Standard Crime Contracts 2022 and 2025 Specification para 7.1.
205 Standard Crime Contracts 2022 and 2025 Specification para 7.3.

CHAPTER 15

Getting paid for civil and family work

By Paul Seddon

With Daniel M Grütters (immigration and asylum fees)

15.1	Introduction
15.9	Terms of assessment and guidance
15.15	Exceptional case funding
15.18	**Disbursements**
15.32	Apportionment of experts' fees
15.37	**Controlled work**
15.46	**Legal aid representation certificates**
15.46	Rejected claims and erroneous document requests
15.49	Payments on account
15.53	Prior authority and payment on account for disbursements
15.56	Assessment of the final bill
15.65	Civil contempt proceedings and Anti-social Behaviour, Crime and Policing Act 2014 breach proceedings
15.67	Enhanced rates
15.72	Conditional payment for judicial review
15.82	Allowances for CCMS tasks

continued

15.83   Assessment of costs by the LAA
        Claims to the LAA • Claims on CCMS • Use it or lose it – inactivity on CCMS • When counsel fees are also claimed on CCMS • Claims over £2,500 assessed by the LAA

15.98   Costs appeals
        Generally • Points of principle of general importance

15.107 Assessment of costs by the courts – legal aid only

15.119 Costs between the parties and the indemnity principle (inter partes costs)

15.123 Assessment of costs by the courts – inter partes
        The procedure • The LAA and inter partes costs • Apportioned inter partes costs and legal aid only costs

15.144 **Recoupment and limitation**

15.148 **Pro bono costs orders**

15.156 **Family**

15.156 Overview

15.158 Controlled work
        Family – controlled work escape fee cases

15.162 Licensed work
        Overview • Family – public law fee scheme • Family – private law fee scheme • Family – public and private law standard fee schemes: enhancement of hourly rates • Family – public and private law standard fee schemes: client transfers • Family – public and private law standard fee schemes: advocacy • Family – Very High Cost Cases

15.207 **Immigration and asylum**

15.207 Introduction

15.209 Standard Fee cases

15.213 Immigration and asylum fee stages

15.219 Immigration and asylum – additional payments

15.220 Immigration and asylum – counsel

15.222 Immigration and asylum – disbursements

15.226 Immigration and asylum – escape fee cases

15.229 Immigration and asylum – hourly rates cases

15.234 Upper Tribunal cases

Key resources

Statutes

- Legal Aid, Sentencing and Punishment of Offenders Act 2012 – Schedule 1 Part 1

Statutory instruments

- Civil Legal Aid (Remuneration) Regulations 2013
- Civil Legal Aid (Costs) Regulations 2013
- Civil Legal Aid (Statutory Charge) Regulations 2013
- Civil Legal Aid (Procedure) Regulations 2012
- Civil Procedure Rules Parts 44 and 47
- Family Procedure Rules Part 28
- Supreme Court Rules 2024 Part 8; and UKSC PD 13

Contracts

- 2024 Standard Civil Contract Standard
- 2024 Standard Civil Contract Specification
- 2024 Standard Civil Contract – Specification sections 1–6 (General Provisions)
- 2024 Standard Civil Contract – Specification section 7 (Family)
- 2024 Standard Civil Contract – Specification section 8 (Immigration and Asylum)
- 2024 Standard Civil Contract – Specification section 10 (Housing and Debt)
- 2024 Standard Civil Contract – Specification section 12 (Welfare Benefits)
- Individual Case Contract 2018 Specification (High Cost Case)

Guidance

- Costs Assessment Guidance: for use with the 2024 Standard Civil Contract
- Civil Finance Electronic Handbook
- Escape Case Electronic Handbook
- Guidance on the Remuneration of Expert Witnesses in Family Cases
- Ministry of Justice Guidance on Remuneration of Clinical Negligence Experts 2013

- Guidance on Remuneration Rates for Expert Services Determined as Risk Assessments 2013
- Care Case Fee Scheme (CCFS) Information Packs, available at: www.gov.uk/guidance/civil-high-cost-cases-family
- Client and Cost Management System (CCMS) Quick Guide 'Claiming 100% Payment on Account for the Very High Cost Care Case Fee Scheme', available at: https://legalaidlearning.justice.gov.uk

Useful websites/pages

- www.gov.uk/guidance/funding-and-costs-assessment-for-civil-and-crime-matters
- www.gov.uk/guidance/legal-aid-high-cost-cases
- www.gov.uk/government/publications/submit-an-escape-fee-case-claim
- www.gov.uk/guidance/legal-aid-eforms
- www.gov.uk/government/publications/cwa-codes-guidance
- www.gov.uk/guidance/submitting-your-claim-civil-and-family-cases
- www.legalaidlearning.justice.gov.uk
- www.gov.uk/guidance/transfer-of-claims-assessed-at-court-to-the-legal-aid-agency
- www.gov.uk/legal-aid-points-of-principle-of-general-importance-pop

Case-law

- *Crane v Canons Leisure Centre* [2007] EWCA Civ 1352
- *Harold v Smith* (1860) 5 H&N 381, Exch
- *R (Bahta) v Secretary of State for the Home Department* [2011] EWCA Civ 895
- *R (Burkett) v Hammersmith and Fulham LBC* [2004] EWCA Civ 1342
- *Haji-Ioannou v Frangos and others* [2006] EWCA Civ 1663
- *MG v Cambridgeshire CC (SEN)* [2017] UKUT 172 (AAC)
- *Legal Services Commission v Henthorn* [2011] EWCA Civ 1415
- *Raftopoulou v Revenue and Customs Commissioners* [2015] UKUT 630 (TCC)
- *JG v Lord Chancellor and others* [2014] EWCA Civ 656
- *Brown v Haringey LBC* [2015] EWCA Civ 483

- *Re Children Act 1989 (taxation of costs)* [1994] 2 FLR 934, Fam, also known as *London Borough of A v M and SF* [1994] Costs LR (Core) 374
- *R (Ben Hoare Bell Solicitors and others) v Lord Chancellor* [2015] EWHC 523 (Admin)

Key points to note
- Since the last edition of this Handbook, the Civil Legal Aid (Financial Resources and Payment for Services and Remuneration) (Amendment) Regulations 2023 and the Civil Legal Aid (Remuneration) (Amendment) Regulations 2023 have both added new hourly rates for providers and counsel for work described in para 31C of Part 1 of Schedule 1 to the Legal Aid, Sentencing and Punishment of Offenders Act 2012 (LASPO), which was brought into scope of legal aid by an amendment to LASPO made by the Illegal Migration Act 2023. This includes new hourly rates for routine letters out and telephone calls; preparation and attendance; attendance at court or conference with counsel; advocacy; and travelling and waiting time.

Introduction

15.1 This chapter deals with billing and payment for civil and family work. You should refer to chapters 2–14 for information on conducting cases.

15.2 This chapter does not deal with contract management (which is covered in Part C), but with the rules and processes for billing individual cases.

15.3 See chapters 18 and 19 for more information on payment for civil and family advocacy.

15.4 See chapter 10 for detailed information on conducting a mental health case and getting paid.

15.5 See appendix C for a summary of the Legal Aid Agency's (LAA's) Costs Assessment Guidance,[1] in respect of the most common queries raised by caseworkers.

---

1 *Costs Assessment Guidance: for use with the 2018 Standard Civil Contracts*, v10, LAA, December 2023 and *Costs Assessment Guidance: for use with the 2024 Standard Civil Contracts*, available at: www.gov.uk/guidance/funding-and-costs-assessment-for-civil-and-crime-matters.

15.6   Most payment rates are to be found in the Civil Legal Aid (Remuneration) Regulations 2013. Some of the rates have been amended and so the latest rates are in the following instead:

- Civil Legal Aid (Remuneration) (Amendment) Regulations 2013 – reduced fees for experts for all certificates applied for on or after 2 December 2013, removed separate hourly rates for controlled work in the Upper Tribunal (Immigration and Asylum Chamber) where permission granted to client (non-fast track), and changed/reduced advocacy fees for non-family counsel harmonising them with providers' schedule ('franchise') rates including percentage enhancements;
- Civil Legal Aid (Remuneration) (Amendment) Regulations 2014 – set rates for welfare benefits work under 2014 contracts, including introducing a higher standard (fixed) fee for controlled work;
- Civil Legal Aid (Remuneration) (Amendment) (No 2) Regulations 2014 – implemented remuneration changes arising from the introduction of the single Family Court;
- Civil Legal Aid (Remuneration) (Amendment) (No 4) Regulations 2014 – implemented to apply to bundle payments in the Family Advocacy Scheme (FAS) for hearings from 31 July 2014;
- Civil Legal Aid (Procedure, Remuneration and Statutory Charge) (Amendment) Regulations 2014 – set rates for community care and mental health work under 2014 contracts;
- Civil and Criminal Legal Aid (Remuneration) (Amendment) Regulations 2015 – amended the regulations to prescribe payment rates for orders under the Anti-social Behaviour, Crime and Policing Act (ASBCPA) 2014 from 24 March 2015;
- Civil Legal Aid (Remuneration) (Amendment) Regulations 2015 – implemented conditional payment for judicial review work done pre-permission for all certificates applied for on or after 27 March 2015;
- Civil and Criminal Legal Aid (Amendment) Regulations 2015 – amended regulations to exclude advocacy services in civil proceedings concerning female genital mutilation protection orders from FAS (non-advocacy family work is also excluded from the Higher Standard Fee Scheme under the contract) for all certificates applied for on or after 17 July 2015;
- Civil Legal Aid (Remuneration and Statutory Charge) (Amendment) Regulations 2016 – set rates for welfare benefits work under 2016 contracts;

Getting paid for civil and family work 399

- Civil Legal Aid (Procedure, Remuneration and Statutory Charge) (Amendment) Regulations 2018 – set rates for work under the 2018 contract;
- Civil Legal Aid (Remuneration) (Amendment) (No 2) (Coronavirus) Regulations 2020 – (a) provided a new definition of online procedure advocacy services and new immigration and asylum fees and rates where online procedure is used, (b) changed arrangements for payments on account to counsel, and (c) revoked the first 2020 Amendment Regulations;
- Civil Legal Aid (Immigration Interviews (Exceptions) and Remuneration) (Amendment) Regulations 2022 – (a) added the 2018 Standard Civil Contract to para 2A, which had previously been omitted, (b) made a number of minor and insubstantial corrections to the Remuneration Regulations, for example, correcting fees which are currently 'per hour' where they should be 'per item', (c) added four new fees for work done through HM Courts and Tribunals Service's (HMCTS's) new online procedure and added a new additional fixed fee for providers who provide advice on referral into the National Referral Mechanism
- Civil Legal Aid (Financial Resources and Payment for Services and Remuneration) (Amendment) Regulations 2023 – added new hourly rates for providers and counsel for work described in para 31C of Part 1 of Schedule 1 to LASPO, which was brought into scope of legal aid by an amendment to LASPO made by the Illegal Migration Act 2023; and
- Civil Legal Aid (Remuneration) (Amendment) Regulations 2023 – added more new hourly rates for providers and counsel for work described in para 31C of Part 1 of Schedule 1 to LASPO, which was brought into scope of legal aid by an amendment to LASPO made by the Illegal Migration Act 2023, previously omitted from the first set of 2023 amending regulations.

15.7 Payment rates not prescribed under the Civil Legal Aid (Remuneration) Regulations 2013 (as amended) are:
- family counsel fees falling outside the family fixed fee schemes;
- events fees under the Care Case Fee Scheme – these are provided within the Very High Cost Case (VHCC) Contract Guide (Information Pack) and also now under the Specification to the individual case contract (ICC); and
- 'risk rates' paid on Special and High Cost Cases where a costs order against the other side is anticipated. Risk rates (given in the

VHCC Information Packs – Non-Family) are agreed under the ICC that the practitioner must sign for such cases.

15.8 Solicitors situated in a London borough receive prescribed rates approximately 5 to 10 per cent higher for non-routine preparation work (and advocacy in family work), as well as on routine communications in controlled work.

Terms of assessment and guidance

15.9 Once a case has concluded, the final bill should be submitted to the court or LAA for assessment, as appropriate (see below).

15.10 Assessment of costs is governed by the Contracts, the Civil Legal Aid (Remuneration) Regulations 2013 (as amended) and the Civil Procedure Rules (CPR). Sections 4 and 6 of the Specifications to the contracts are of particular relevance, and provide for the payment and assessment of controlled work and licensed work, respectively. For Civil Legal Advice (CLA)[2] contracts see section 6 of Annex 1, and Annex 3: Payments and Disbursements of their respective Specifications. The transitional provisions of the Specifications (section 1) provide that subject to category-specific rules and the transitional provisions of secondary legislation, they apply to all work done under their particular contract (including procedures for assessment of remuneration). This does not apply to any matter started or certificate applied for before 1 October 2007. This means, for example, that once you start working under a new contract, any disbursements you incur from that date are subject to the list of excluded disbursements under the corresponding specification to that contract.

15.11 Both the court and the LAA are to refer to the LAA Costs Assessment Guidance (defined under the contract as a 'Costs Assessment Manual') when assessing civil legal aid costs to be paid by the LAA.[3] The guidance provides for how both controlled and licensed work is assessed, including what may be or is unclaimable.

15.12 The court does not have jurisdiction to allow costs falling outside the terms of the contract. Therefore, if the contract and/or documents of contractual authority (such as the Costs Assessment Guidance) excludes an item of costs whether because it is out of

---

2 That is, work undertaken under contract for the LAA's telephone service: www.gov.uk/civil-legal-advice.
3 See: Standard Civil Contract 2024 Standard Terms clause 1.1 – see Costs Assessment Manuals.

15.13 Civil legal aid costs to be paid by the LAA (rather than another party) must be assessed on the standard basis.[4] The Guidance provides that many of the basic principles governing assessments are contained in the CPR, and also cites CPR 44.3(2) (proportionality) and CPR 44.4 (factors to be taken into account in deciding the amount costs, in particular the 'Seven/Eight Pillars of Wisdom').

15.14 The LAA also produces and releases internal guidance on how it will assess controlled work and licensed work. These are the *Escape Case Electronic Handbook*[5] (for controlled work) and the *Civil Finance Electronic Handbook*[6] (for licensed work). While these provide a lot of information and can be very helpful, they are created specifically for LAA caseworkers and are not comprehensive guidance – they are not subject to consultation by the consultative bodies and do not have contractual authority. They refer to authorities and provide the LAA Finance Team's interpretation of them.

Exceptional case funding

15.15 Like any other work not within scope under LASPO, you can charge privately for making an application for exceptional case funding (ECF). However, you cannot do this once ECF is granted, and you must refund any payment made for costs that become retrospectively covered under ECF.[7]

15.16 There is no special payment scheme for ECF cases; they are paid under the same schemes as non-ECF cases.[8]

15.17 When Legal Help is granted to investigate the possibility of a further ECF application being made to cover substantive services sought, the onus is on you to show that each disbursement is necessary for the work covered, based on the information available to you at the time, rather than for use in potential proceedings for which

---

4 Standard Civil Contract 2024 Specification para 6.9.
5 At: www.gov.uk/government/publications/submit-an-escape-fee-case-claim.
6 Available at: www.gov.uk/guidance/funding-and-costs-assessment-for-civil-and-crime-matters.
7 Standard Civil Contract 2024 Specification para 1.38.
8 Standard Civil Contract 2024 Specification paras 4.51, 6.84, 7.1, 8.12, 10.17 and 12.23.

ECF might be granted. Substantial disbursements will be considered unreasonable unless it has been established that the substantive application likely meets the ECF criteria. An application for investigative representation under ECF should be considered if a disbursement would be £400 or more.[9]

Disbursements

15.18 On 3 October 2011, codified (set) rates and fees for experts and other third-party suppliers were introduced under secondary legislation and are found in the Civil Legal Aid (Remuneration) Regulations 2013, as amended. They are commonly referred to as 'expert fees' by the LAA, although not all of them are experts: for example, interpreters and process servers. Where a rate is codified, only the LAA has discretion to increase this upon an application for prior authority (or justification of 'exceptional circumstances' on a claim under the 2021 CLA Education and Discrimination Contracts[10]), and the court can only direct a recommendation and give reasons.[11]

15.19 The LAA's guidance on the recommended number of hours that experts should incur on a case is also strictly applied (see 'Prior authority and payment on account for disbursements', at para 15.53 onwards below).

15.20 The codified rates for experts and others outside of London boroughs are generally higher than if they are inside London boroughs. A non-London rate is set by the location of the 'expert' rather than your own office.

15.21 Adequate details should be given on an 'expert's' invoice to show the breakdown of work, including the postcode where the expert was travelling from and to when claiming travel time and expenses. Omission can result in the claim being rejected.

15.22 Since the 2018 Contract, you must use interpreters with specified qualifications (listed in the contract) and a note must be placed on the client's case file confirming that the interpreter or the agency through which the interpreter is supplied holds such a qualification and which qualification it is. A 'non-qualified interpreter' can be used in exceptional circumstances (a non-exhaustive list is provided),

---

9 Costs Assessment Guidance para 3.55.
10 CLA (Discrimination) Contract 2021/CLA (Education) Contract 2021 Specification para 6.17.
11 Standard Civil Contract 2024 Specification para 6.60 and *A Local Authority v DS* [2012] EWHC 1442 (Fam).

but you must record on file what these circumstances are and why there was no alternative. The LAA can also require you only to use interpreters under its nominated translation framework upon giving you three months' notice.[12]

15.23 Specified costs and expenses of the expert, including administrative support and subsistence, and cancellation fees where notice is given over 72 hours before the hearing/appointment, will not be paid. Mileage is capped at 45p per mile and travel time is capped at £40 per hour or the codified rate if less.[13] The LAA imposes a discretionary cap on travel and waiting time at two-thirds of the codified rate if that rate is under £40 (note: it cannot reject, only assess, a claim that seeks a full codified rate of £40 or under). The LAA imposed this on waiting time for interpreters at court, but impracticality forced it to concede to pay the full rate; however, it may impose a two-thirds rate for interpreters' court waiting time incurred before 1 April 2019.[14] The LAA's only response to objections raised by the Association of Costs Lawyers about imposing this transitional provision date is that assessments reducing rates can be appealed.

15.24 Since the 2018 Contract, when you incur a non-codified disbursement you must obtain at least three quotes (unless the LAA agrees this is inappropriate) and select the one that you believe to be the best value for money in the circumstances, including but not limited to the need for speed and competence/expertise of the provider. If you cannot do this, then you must advise the LAA and provide it with further information it reasonably requires.[15]

15.25 Witness intermediaries were added to excluded disbursements listed in the 2018 Contract and remain excluded.[16] The LAA has confirmed that it will not fund assessment reports for the need for witness intermediaries. See chapter 4 at para 4.49 for the full list of excluded disbursements.

15.26 When other legal aid practitioners are instructed as legal experts, even when directed by the court, to advise or give evidence on a case, such as immigration advice on the status of children in care proceedings, practitioners' legal aid rates will still apply.[17]

---

12 Standard Civil Contract 2024 Specification paras 2.47–2.51.
13 Civil Legal Aid (Remuneration) Regulations 2013 Sch 5 para 4.
14 *Civil Finance Electronic Handbook* section 10.18 p92; and *Escape Case Electronic Handbook* section 5.16 p32.
15 Standard Civil Contract 2024 Specification para 4.27.
16 Standard Civil Contract 2024 Specification para 4.28.
17 Costs Assessment Guidance para 2.49.

15.27 No payment of fees for client's records requested under a subject access request will be paid, unless the organisation in receipt of the request considers it to be 'manifestly unreasonable or excessive', pursuant to the UK General Data Protection Regulation (UK GDPR) and the Data Protection Act (DPA) 2018. The LAA initially misconstrued the GDPR and the DPA 2018 to mean any request, including police disclosure or medical records even when required by an expert, but it then changed its internal guidance better to align with them,[18] although providers should still ensure that they properly understand and utilise the provisions of the legislation, in particular DPA 2018 Sch 2 Part 1 para 5(2) and (3).

15.28 With regard to covering travel expenses to court for clients who are destitute, rather than simply eligible for legal aid, the LAA now acknowledges that under Family Procedure Rules 2010 (FPR) 27.3 the parties governed by the FPR must attend any hearing or directions appointment of which they have been notified.[19]

15.29 The LAA's *Guidance on the Remuneration of Expert Witnesses in Family Cases* includes the codified rates for all civil and criminal cases, the number of hours that an expert can incur before a prior authority should be made in family cases, specific expert remuneration arrangements and payment on account (POA) of experts. The guidance provides a lot of helpful information for all civil cases and gives an indication of what the LAA may consider reasonable hours of instruction in non-family cases. There is also specific guidance on remuneration of clinical negligence experts and risk assessments.[20]

15.30 For CLA work (including Discrimination and Education), payment of each disbursement is limited to £250 excluding VAT unless approved at the LAA's discretion prior to incurring it, and copies of receipts must be kept at the front of the case file. Some disbursements cannot be claimed. Under the 2018 CLA Contract, travel time incurred under disbursements is limited to two hours at the prescribed/codified rate.[21]

---

18 *Civil Finance Electronic Handbook* section 10.29 p101; and *Escape Case Electronic Handbook* section 5.27 p39.
19 Costs Assessment Guidance para 3.31.
20 *Ministry of Justice Guidance on Remuneration of Clinical Negligence Experts*, LAA, 2013; and *Guidance on Remuneration Rates for Expert Services Determined as Risk Assessments*, Ministry of Justice and LAA, 2013; both are available at: www.gov.uk/guidance/expert-witnesses-in-legal-aid-cases.
21 CLA Contract 2018 Specification Annex 3: Payments and Disbursements paras 11–25; CLA Contract 2018/CLA (Discrimination) Contract 2021/CLA (Education) Contract 2021 Specification Annex 3: Payments and Disbursements paras 11–24.

15.31 On CLA work, counsel's fees are deemed unusual and claimed as a disbursement, but must meet a high threshold to justify instruction. While it is still for you to agree counsel's fees and pay them directly, there is no express exclusion from their prescribed rates and their work is subject to the limits as detailed at para 15.30 above.[22]

Apportionment of experts' fees

15.32 Following the Court of Appeal's decision of *JG v Lord Chancellor and others*,[23] the Access to Justice Act 1999 and LASPO do not prevent the court from having discretion in private law Children Act 1989 proceedings to depart from the order that it would otherwise have made ('normal order'),[24] in apportioning more or all of joint experts' costs to a legally aided party where other parties (who are not legally aided) cannot afford to pay all or part of their share, if there will be a breach of rights under the European Convention on Human Rights (ECHR). The judgment is also useful in other proceedings where similar situations may arise, for example, in the Court of Protection.

15.33 As with a determination for ECF, the test of exceptionality is that there is (or sometimes might be) a breach of ECHR rights; there is no separate requirement. Further, just because another party will benefit from a report that they have to pay less or nothing at all for, this does not justify a violation of a child's Convention rights by the state refusing to provide legal aid for it. Whether there is a breach will depend on the individual facts, and most likely not only the nature of the application but also the nature of the report will be a relevant circumstance.

15.34 In determining impecuniosity, the court does not have to undertake the highly technical analysis of establishing that a non-legally aided party would be financially eligible for legal aid. Although if said party is eligible then this can be indicative, but it is only one relevant factor.

15.35 When a court can reach final determination about whether to depart from a normal order can vary depending on the facts. If

---

22 CLA Contract 2018 Specification/CLA Contract 2018/CLA (Discrimination) Contract 2021/CLA (Education) Contract 2021 Specification Annex 3: Payments and Disbursements paras 25/26–27.
23 [2014] EWCA Civ 656.
24 The Court of Appeal found there is no normal rule of equal apportionment of single joint experts' costs in Children Act 1989 proceedings, that FPR 25.12(6) is merely a default position in the absence of the court directing otherwise, and emphasised the importance of tailoring the order to the facts of the case.

reaching that decision will cause harmful delay and the other parties can provide cogent evidence that they cannot pay their share, then the court can order the guardian to instruct the expert (the costs being met under the child's legal aid certificate) in the first instance, and then the other party be found liable to pay a share, on proper financial information, later by means of a conventional costs order.

15.36 It should also be noted that the judgment recommends that a prior authority should still be obtained.

Controlled work

15.37 Controlled work cases are billed individually, but they are paid by way of a monthly payment from the LAA. Each month, the organisation submits claims and receives a monthly payment (known as a 'standard monthly payment' (SMP)), with the aim that bills and payments balance each other out over the course of the financial year, or a 'variable monthly payment' (VMP) based on what it has billed that month. See chapter 23 for more information on this process (known as reconciliation) and on the management of civil contracts generally. Organisations can opt for the payment system that suits them best. The LAA's *Guidance for reporting Controlled Work and Controlled Work matters* is a substantive guide regarding the various fields and codes for completion via the Contracted Work and Administration (CWA) when submitting controlled work; it is found on the LAA's CWA Codes Guidance page.[25]

15.38 Standard fees are paid for controlled work. These are shown net of VAT and disbursements, which may be claimed in addition. You need to submit a claim for the standard fee within six months of the conclusion of a matter,[26] other than CLA matters which is within three months of conclusion or one month in the event of a determination being made.[27] Standard fees are claimed by submitting an online claim within 20 days of the end of each month.

15.39 Escape fee cases (known under pre-LASPO contracts as 'exceptional cases'), are defined under the 2024 Standard Civil Contract as those where costs exceed three times the fixed fee and may be claimed

---

25 V37, LAA, October 2024, available at: www.gov.uk/government/publications/cwa-codes-guidance.
26 Standard Civil Contract 2024 Specification para 4.40.
27 CLA Contract 2018/CLA (Discrimination) Contract 2021/CLA (Education) Contract 2021 Specification Annex 3: Payments and Disbursements para 6.

in full. Under the CLA contracts, they are defined as exceeding 900 minutes on the 2018 Contract and Discrimination Contracts, and 450 minutes on the Education Contracts; under the Discrimination and Education exclusive contracts claiming such cases at hourly rates is mandatory.[28]

15.40 You can instruct counsel on Legal Help (not Help at Court) and Family Help (Lower). However, on non-CLA contract cases their fee cannot be claimed as a disbursement in addition to a standard fee, and it cannot be used to escape the standard fee. However, if a case does escape, then their fee can be claimed as a disbursement. Prescribed counsel's hourly rates do not apply. As detailed in paras 15.30–15.31 above, on CLA contract cases counsel's fee counts as a disbursement and again cannot be used to escape the standard fee; there is also no express exclusion from prescribed hourly rates. On any case, you must record your justification for instruction, counsel must set out details of time spent, and you must pay counsel the full fee claimed regardless of any reduction on assessment.[29] See further details of instructing counsel under controlled work for family in the 'Family' section at para 15.160 onwards below.

15.41 In escape cases, you need to submit an EC Claim 1 form (there are separate EC Claim 1 forms for immigration, mental health and CLA work) with your file in order to be credited with the balance above the fixed fee. You must submit claims for escape fee cases within three months of reporting the end of the case and claiming the standard fee.[30] Electronic web-based EC Claim 1 forms were launched in 2017, and the LAA encourages you to use them. While there is no change to the assessment process, it is intended that the paper-based forms will eventually be withdrawn.

15.42 If costs are reduced on assessment, you can appeal (see costs appeals, para 15.98 onwards below and chapter 17).

15.43 Since the 2018 Contract, costs audits have been amended. Findings of 'mis-claiming' and 'over-claiming' have been introduced. 'Mis-claiming' means claiming in a manner that the LAA considers to be 'clearly contrary to the Contract and where no discretion arises as to payment. For instance, claiming using the wrong rates, or

28 CLA Contract 2018/CLA (Discrimination) Contract 2021/CLA (Education) Contract 2021 Specification para 6.3.
29 Standard Civil Contract 2024/Standard Civil Contract (Education and Discrimination) 2018 Specification paras 3.58–3.61; CLA Contract 2018/CLA (Discrimination) Contract 2021/CLA (Education) Contract 2021 Specification paras 5.42–5.44.
30 Standard Civil Contract 2024 Specification para 4.20.

15.44 incorrectly claiming VAT'. 'Over-claiming' means claiming more than the LAA determines to be reasonable on assessment, but where discretion arises as to the amount allowable.[31]

15.44 A sample of at least 20 files can be requested. For mis-claiming, the sample period has been increased from one year to two (after the claims have been submitted), or up to six years prior where an official investigation is underway or the LAA considers it reasonable to do so upon receiving a report. For over-claiming, the period is since the last contract compliance audit, or the 12 months before the date the sample is requested.[32]

15.45 Although the basic systems for claiming immigration/asylum and mental health controlled work fees are the same as other civil and family work, they have more complex fee schemes. Family cases also have their own schemes. More information is given below.

Legal aid representation certificates

Rejected claims and erroneous document requests

15.46 Rejected claims (which can include report outcomes) can count against key performance indicators (KPIs) (see chapter 22 for more information).

15.47 If you believe that your claim should not have been rejected or a non-automated CCMS document request is made where information is already provided or is not required as evidence of the claim, you can use the LAA's Claimfix service[33] to review the rejection/document request and reverse it if the LAA considers it is erroneous. You email laacivilclaimfix@justice.gov.uk. The turnaround is often very fast, usually within 24 hours.

15.48 In August 2019 the LAA revised the categories of rejects, moving many scenarios that would have resulted in a document request to a reject. The distinction between KPI and non-KPI rejects was removed from 1 October 2021. This is laid out in the LAA's internal guidance.[34]

---

31 Standard Civil Contract 2024 Specifications Definitions.
32 Standard Civil Contract 2024 Specification paras 4.47–4.50.
33 Send an email with details to: laacivilclaimfix@justice.gov.uk.
34 *Civil Finance Electronic Handbook* section 16.

Payments on account

15.49 The Standard Civil Contract[35] allows you to claim on account profit costs incurred not earlier than three months after the issue of a legal aid representation certificate. Thereafter, you can apply for further POAs, provided that you make no more than four applications in any 12-month period, which runs from the date that the first profit costs POA is authorised (rather than the anniversary of the certificate). On non-CCMS cases, use form CIVPOA1, which providers can submit as an eform via the LAA CWA online portal.[36] Counsel must still submit their claims for POAs on non-CCMS cases by paper only.

15.50 Cases where the certificate was applied for through CCMS have to be claimed through CCMS. To claim profit costs POAs on CCMS, you need to submit a copy of the time ledger, ie full details of the case's running costs incurred to date (unless the case is covered by a standard fee scheme and has not escaped the fee). CCMS sends a notification (document request) for you to upload a copy of the ledger shortly after you have submitted the bill. In family cases, FAS should be included in the claim; neither these nor different fixed fee aspects are claimed separately. The system then calculates 80 per cent of the costs and a caseworker (not CCMS) will check the POA's value against the supporting evidence. You will be paid the amount to bring the total POAs made to 80 per cent of your profit costs to date. 100 per cent profit costs POAs can be paid in CCFS (events) cases (see para 15.203 below).

15.51 It should be noted that claims for POAs (whether for profit costs or disbursements) are not assessed and do not form quasi gross sum bills, no matter how much supporting information may be requested for them. POAs simply form debit amounts under the certificate that will be deducted from the total amount payable under the interim/final bill, so if the amount allowed under that bill is not greater than or equal to the total amount paid on account there will be a debit balance owed to the LAA when the bill is paid. However, there have been disputes between the LAA (and its predecessors) and practitioners regarding old POAs and whether final bills were ever received or paid. See 'Recoupment and limitation' at para 15.144 onwards below.

15.52 See below for information about POAs under the family law fee schemes.

---

35 Standard Civil Contract 2024 Specification para 6.21; Standard Contract 2018 Specification para 7.25.
36 At: www.gov.uk/guidance/legal-aid-eforms.

Prior authority and payment on account for disbursements

15.53 You can apply to the LAA for authority to incur a disbursement in advance if it is above £100 and is not covered by the standard rates/hours for experts introduced from 3 October 2011.[37] The LAA has set out guidance for the number of hours it considers reasonable for different types of expert reports in family cases (also a likely indication for non-family cases), and will only consider a prior authority application if it is for more hours than in the guidance, or of a type not included.[38] The application must include a quote for the disbursement and set out the reasons why it is necessary. The application is made via CCMS or using form CIVAPP8A if it is a pre-CCMS case.

15.54 You may apply for prior authority if:[39]

1) an item of costs is either unusual in its nature or is unusually large – this means that it is outside the guidance referred to above;
2) you wish to instruct a KC or more than one counsel;
3) prior authority is required under the specification; or
4) you wish to instruct an expert at higher rates than are set out in the Remuneration Regulations.

If you do not apply for prior authority and 1), 3), or 4) above applies, you may not be paid in full or at all for the fees incurred.

15.55 POAs of disbursements can be claimed at any time, subject to disbursements being individually or cumulatively above £100. For non-CCMS cases, the form is the CIVPOA1, as for profit costs above. It can be submitted as a paper form, or as an eform using the legal aid online facility. The latter is recommended, not least because payment is made more quickly. See: www.gov.uk/legal-aid-eforms. In CCMS cases claims are made via CCMS. An invoice showing the hourly rate and number of hours claimed must accompany a claim for expert fees.

---

37 Community Legal Service (Funding) (Amendment No 2) Order 2011, now in the Civil Legal Aid (Remuneration) (Amendment) Regulations 2013.
38 See *Guidance: Expert witnesses in legal aid cases*, LAA, last updated September 2024: www.gov.uk/guidance/expert-witnesses-in-legal-aid-cases.
39 Standard Civil Contract 2018/Standard Civil Contract 2018 (Education and Discrimination Specification) para 5.10.

Assessment of the final bill

15.56 Once a case has concluded, the final bill should be submitted to the court or LAA for assessment, as appropriate (see below).

15.57 The contract currently still allows certain cases to be assessed by the court. These are principally claims where assessable costs exceed £2,500 excluding VAT ('the assessment limit') in cases where proceedings have been issued and conclude before a judge (rather than a magistrate). Assessable costs are any costs, whether profit costs, counsel's fees or disbursements, that are not subject to standard and graduated fees (ie fixed fees). Unlike FAS, for the purposes of assessment, payments to counsel under the Family Graduated Fees Scheme (FGFS) are considered a disbursement and form assessable costs. Where the only assessable costs are disbursements, this was (and presumably still is) deemed a 'special circumstance' disapplying the assessment limit and making an LAA assessment mandatory.

15.58 In late May 2020, the LAA announced that it had received HMCTS approval to remove the courts as an assessing body and bring all assessments in-house, as already permitted under the contracts. From 1 June 2020, the LAA gave providers the option to have claims that are eligible for court assessment be assessed by the LAA instead. The LAA only provided a short consultation on the operational implementation and withdrew the option for court assessments from 17 August 2020. However, as part of a settlement of a judicial review claim brought by The Law Society, the LAA reintroduced the option on 15 January 2021, pending the outcome of a fresh full public consultation on the removal of court assessments. Furthermore, as part of the settlement the LAA introduced an interim 'hybrid' system, whereby if a provider is unhappy with the outcome of an assessment by the LAA of an eligible claim submitted from 17 August 2020 onwards, they can seek a fresh assessment of their bill by the court. In November 2021, the Ministry of Justice (MoJ) announced that the arrangements set out above would continue until November 2022, to allow data to be collected, and a further consultation would take place to establish the medium- to long-term process. As at the time of writing the LAA has still made no move to change the situation.

15.59 All provisions relating to when a court assessment did and did not apply (including 'special circumstances' and the consideration of FGFS fees as a form of assessable costs), were removed from section 14 of the Costs Assessment Guidance shortly before the initial removal of court assessments in August 2020 and (at the time of writing) have not been reinstated. So, there are at the time of writing no express provisions identifying claims eligible for court assessment. The procedure for assessment of legal aid costs will remain for legal aid only costs being assessed in concurrence with inter partes costs (see below).

15.60 There are two expressly provided exceptions to the presumed assessment limit:

1) where there is an element of inter partes costs and a detailed assessment of those costs is carried out by the court, in which case the court will also assess the legal aid only costs regardless of the amount;[40] and
2) costs under a VHCC contract – these must be assessed by the LAA,[41] even when there are inter partes costs assessed by the court and the LAA has authorised that legal aid only costs be paid in addition to them.

15.61 It should be noted that both the LAA and the court require authority to assess the bill. The authority to assess is either a final order requiring costs to be assessed or other authority as detailed in the contract (which mirrors those under CPR 47.7),[42] or in the absence of this a discharged certificate.[43] Therefore, if the final order makes no mention of costs, a discharge should be sought before submitting the bill. If applying to the LAA for assessment, you can apply for discharge at the same time, but if the reasons for discharge are contentious the LAA will implement the show cause procedure and return the claim to the practitioner to be resubmitted when the certificate is discharged.[44]

15.62 Where the court is responsible for assessment, you must first submit a detailed bill of costs for assessment by the court; and when that is complete, make a claim for payment from the LAA within three months of the legal aid assessment certificate (HMCTS form EX80A, or EX80B where costs include those subject to/escape family fixed fee(s)) being received from the court.

---

40 Standard Civil Contract 2024 Specification para 6.36(a).
41 Individual Case Contract 2018 Specification High Cost Case para 5.12.
42 Standard Civil Contract 2024 Specification para 6.33(b)(i)–(iv); Costs Assessment Guidance paras 15.2–15.3 (Court Assessment).
43 Standard Civil Contract 2024 Specification para 6.33(b)(iv) (LAA Assessment); Costs Assessment Guidance para 15.4 (Court Assessment).
44 Costs Assessment Guidance para 15.6.

15.63 Where the LAA is responsible for assessment, you must submit a claim within three months of the right to claim accruing.[45]

15.64 Frequent submission of late claims may lead to contract sanctions.[46] If the client has a financial interest and you fail to submit your claim in time, the LAA may serve notice requiring you to do so within two months. If you then do not submit within two months and do not provide a satisfactory explanation why, the LAA can disallow your claim to the amount of the client's financial interest. You can appeal this disallowance under the costs appeals procedure (see below), regardless of whether the LAA has assessed the claim or the court has.[47]

Civil contempt proceedings and Anti-social Behaviour, Crime and Policing Act 2014 breach proceedings

15.65 Civil contempt committal proceedings are classed as criminal under LASPO s14(h) and thus the provisions of the Crime Contract apply. Following the decision of *Brown v Haringey LBC*,[48] civil providers can obtain criminal legal aid for contempt committal in civil proceedings, including breaches of the ASBCPA 2014, by way of a representation order. The Civil and Criminal Legal Aid (Remuneration) (Amendment) Regulations 2015 amended scope of the criminal regulations to encompass proceedings in the county court and introduced bespoke standard fees and corresponding rates under *Representation in the Magistrates Court* for ASBCPA 2014 breach proceedings[49] dealt with in the county court (for adults). All other civil contempt committal proceedings are paid under hourly rates falling within LASPO s14(h).[50] Counsel is paid under the Criminal Legal Aid (Remuneration) Regulations 2013 also,[51] and is always assigned automatically and so will be paid at hourly rates. Further breaches of the same order (whether ASBCPA 2014 or other) count as a series of offences and an amendment is made to the existing

---

45 Standard Civil Contract 2024 Specification para 6.33.
46 Standard Civil Contract 2024 Standard Terms clause 14.5.
47 Standard Civil Contract 2024 Specification para 6.35.
48 [2015] EWCA Civ 483.
49 Criminal Legal Aid (Remuneration) Regulations 2013 Sch 4 para 5A, as amended.
50 Criminal Legal Aid (Remuneration) Regulations 2013 Sch 4 para 7, as amended.
51 Criminal Legal Aid (Remuneration) Regulations 2013 Sch 4 para 12, as amended.

representation order; thus the date of the original representation order determines the applicable rate (eg rates and fees between 1 July 2015 and 31 March 2016 are 8.75 per cent lower). Providers holding a criminal contract claim ASBCPA 2014 via their crime monthly submission/CRM 7. Providers without a criminal contract use the bespoke CRMCLAIM11 (not to be confused with the CRM11) and can use pages 5 and 6 of the CIV CLAIM1 if the schedule of work provided is too small. All other civil contempt committal proceedings are claimed on CRMCLAIM11 regardless of whether the provider has a criminal contract. Counsel's fees are claimed using a CRM8, which should be submitted with the CRMCLAIM11.

15.66 Further information on both ASBCPA 2014 and other civil contempt can be found at: www.gov.uk/guidance/apply-for-legal-aid-for-civil-contempt-cases.

Enhanced rates

15.67 In certain circumstances, you can apply for payment of the prescribed hourly rate at a discretionary enhanced rate. The LAA/court will consider whether enhancement is justified and, if so, will increase the hourly rates for some or all of the work done on the case. It would be very unusual for enhanced rates to be allowed on routine items (short letters and telephone calls) and travel and waiting (this would usually only be applicable for exceptional speed).

15.68 The two-stage criteria for enhancement (threshold and factors) are provided in the contract[52] and expanded upon under section 12 of the Costs Assessment Guidance.

15.69 The threshold test for enhancement is one of exceptionality, within the normal meaning of unusual or out of the ordinary,[53] that:

1) the work was done with exceptional **competence, skill or expertise**;
2) the work was done with exceptional **speed**; or
3) the case involved exceptional **circumstances or complexity**,

compared with the generality of proceedings to which the relevant rates apply.[54] So, the comparison is not just cases within the same category of law, but all cases paid at that rate. However, the excep-

---

52 Standard Civil Contract 2024 Specification paras 6.13–6.15.
53 Costs Assessment Guidance para 12.8.
54 Standard Civil Contract 2024 Specification para 6.17; and Costs Assessment Guidance para 12.11.

tional criterion/criteria must have actually had an effect on the fee earner's work in the qualitative or quantitative sense.[55]

15.70 Where the threshold test is met, the LAA may allow a percentage increase to the relevant hourly rate not exceeding 50 per cent, or in cases in the Upper Tribunal, High Court, Court of Appeal and Supreme Court not exceeding 100 per cent.[56] The original allowance of 100 per cent and 200 per cent (Senior Courts and Supreme Court) was halved from 3 October 2011/1 February 2012, but this is interpreted as a cap to be applied after the enhancement sought is assessed, rather than a general 50 per cent reduction.[57] From the 2018 Contract onwards, the provision to apply a level of enhancement where the threshold test is met is no longer binding on the LAA and is permissive. The amount of the percentage increase will be determined by having regard to seven factors grouped into three areas:

1) the **degree of responsibility** accepted;
2) the **care**, **speed** and **economy** with which the case was prepared; and
3) the **novelty**, **weight** and **complexity** of the case.

In short: 1) is about you and the expertise/experience you brought to the case; 2) is about what you had to do and the way you did it; and 3) is about the issues affecting the case. These factors are explored in more detail in the Costs Assessment Guidance. It is not only the number of factors present, but also the strength of those individual factors that will determine the amount to be claimed on assessment.

15.71 It is rare to apply an enhancement across the board for all pieces of work, but rather enhancements should only be applied to what is affected, for example, 40 per cent on all work (including routine and travel/waiting) for urgency and complexity up to first hearing, and then 20 per cent for complexity for all non-funding non-routine work (excluding travel/waiting) afterwards. However, preparing appeals to reductions to multi-layered enhancements on CCMS claims can be disproportionately laborious. Every enhancement claim is fact-specific and detailed grounds must be given.

---

55 *Re Children Act 1989 (taxation of costs)* [1994] 2 FLR 934, FD, also known as *London Borough of A v M and SF* [1994] Costs LR (Core) 374.
56 Civil Legal Aid (Remuneration) Regulations 2013 reg 6(3).
57 Costs Assessment Guidance para 12.2.

Conditional payment for judicial review

15.72 For cases started on or after 22 April 2014, payment for work done between issue of proceedings and grant of permission in judicial review cases was made conditional on either:[58]

- the court granting permission; or
- notwithstanding that no permission was granted, the LAA agreeing to discretionary payment.

15.73 The LAA would only agree to payment of pre-permission work in cases where permission was not granted if the court had neither granted nor refused permission and it considered it was reasonable to pay in the circumstances of the case. Work on interim relief was duly confirmed as payable regardless, to reflect the MoJ's consultation response on conditional payment in judicial review. This, along with investigative work (including counsel's advice) and reasonable disbursements such as experts' fees (but not including counsel's fees), is clarified in the LAA's pro forma application for discretionary payments (see below) as being paid regardless.

15.74 However, on 3 March 2015 the High Court found the regulations to be irrational in the case of *R (Ben Hoare Bell Solicitors and others) v Lord Chancellor*.[59] The regulations were quashed on 24 March 2015, meaning that the above amendments to the Civil Legal Aid (Remuneration) Regulations 2013 were of no effect.

15.75 Rather than appeal the judgment, the Lord Chancellor accepted it but immediately laid new regulations that affected all certificates granted on or after 27 March 2015, which effectively reinstated the quashed regulations with some amendments aimed at alleviating the grounds on which the court found against them.

15.76 The Civil Legal Aid (Remuneration) (Amendment) Regulations 2015[60] provide that, for all certificates applied for on or after 27 March 2015, payment for judicial review work done pre-permission is conditional on one of the following:

- the court giving permission;
- the defendant withdrawing the decision to which the application for judicial review relates, resulting in the court refusing permission or making no decision on permission;

---

58 Civil Legal Aid (Remuneration) (Amendment) (No 3) Regulations 2014.
59 [2015] EWHC 523 (Admin).
60 Reg 2 inserts reg 5A into the Civil Legal Aid (Remuneration) Regulations 2013.

- the court ordering an oral permission hearing or an oral hearing of an appeal against a refusal of permission;
- the court ordering a rolled up hearing; or
- the court neither granting nor refusing permission but the Lord Chancellor considers it reasonable to pay remuneration in the circumstances of the case, taking into account, in particular:
  – the reason why no costs order or agreement was obtained;
  – the extent to which, and why, the outcome sought was achieved; and
  – the strength of the application for permission at the time it was filed, based on the law and on facts which the provider knew or ought to have known at the time.

15.77 In settlement of a judicial review brought by Duncan Lewis, the Lord Chancellor issued a clarification in February 2019 that cases could be paid where permission was refused on papers and oral renewal was sought but the matter then concluded before a decision was made by the court, and further also if the defendant withdraws the decision being challenged either before the court decides on permission on papers or after the matter has moved beyond refusal of permission on papers. This clarification can be found on the same LAA webpage as the 'Judicial review discretion pro-forma' (see below).

15.78 Existing certificates granted before, but to which new judicial review proceedings are added on or after 27 March 2015 are also subject to these rules, but other judicial review cases under certificates applied for before this must be paid by the LAA without reference to any conditional funding arrangement under the regulations.

15.79 If you want to claim costs that are only payable at the Lord Chancellor's discretion, an application must be made to the LAA for this to be considered, and any representations received from counsel should accompany this. Only once such an application is successful should a claim or court bill be prepared.

15.80 Where the certificate is issued under CCMS, a 'JR Discretionary Payment Req' should be submitted via a case enquiry on the CCMS case, and upon receipt of this a document request for any additional supporting paperwork will be made. If it is a pre-CCMS certificate, then an application can be made by using the 'Judicial review discretion pro-forma' letter which also includes guidance on making the application. The letter can be found here: www.gov.uk/government/publications/judicial-review-discretion-pro-forma.

15.81 The Lord Chancellor's discretion is not required for the following work and will be payable regardless:

- work on the earlier stages of a case to investigate the prospects of strength of a claim (including advice from counsel on the merits of the claim) and work under the Pre-Action Protocol for Judicial Review procedure;
- disbursements (but not counsel's fees); and
- work carried out on an application for interim relief.

Allowances for CCMS tasks

15.82 After a short consultation process with the Association of Costs Lawyers Legal Aid Group and other representative bodies, allowances were added in September 2018 for time to prepare the means assessment and other CCMS tasks, including allocation of costs to counsel (see appendix C for a summary).[61]

Assessment of costs by the LAA

Claims to the LAA

15.83 As detailed above, the LAA will now assess all claims, including those over £2,500 (excluding VAT), although at the time of writing you can still request a court assessment for eligible claims. The form used for claims assessed by the LAA that are eligible to be assessed by the court is detailed below.

15.84 Claims to the LAA are made via CCMS for certificates granted via CCMS and on form CIV CLAIM1 (or CIV CLAIM1A in certain family cases and CIV CLAIM2 where inter partes costs have also been recovered – see relevant sections below for more details) for pre-CCMS cases. Paper claims must be completed in full and are now submitted via email to CIS-SFE@Justice.gov.uk. The supporting papers required with a claim (submitted via a document request when a claim is submitted on CCMS) vary:

- Counsels' fee notes are only required with paper claims when FAS/FGFS fees are not being claimed, or on CCMS non-family claims if you and counsel have chosen that the balance fees (after POAs) will be paid directly to the provider and forwarded to counsel.
- Where solicitor's FAS fees claimed – an order providing full details of hearing (advocates attending, times, bolt-ons, etc) or Advocate's Attendance Form (EX506), attendance notes for advocates' meetings and orders for same if more than two per case.

61 Costs Assessment Guidance paras 2.61–2.63.

Getting paid for civil and family work 419

- Expert's invoices and disbursement vouchers (or if train then tickets/booking receipts) for any disbursement of £20 **including** VAT or more must be provided, this includes experts' expenses, for example, train and hotel. For court fees and mileage, the LAA will accept a copy of the accounts ledger instead, although a copy of the covering letter to the court referring to the court fee and amount is usually accepted.
- Where DNA and/or alcohol tests are claimed, copies of the court orders for these are required unless there is prior authority.
- The file of papers is only required on claims for:
  - mental health cases;
  - judicial review and immigration cases if the profit costs excluding VAT exceed £1,000;
  - other cases if the profit costs excluding VAT exceed £2,500; and
  - family cases where costs have escaped the fixed fee.

  If a CCMS claim, the document request should specify exactly what they require in terms of file papers. For paper claims with paper files, only attendance notes for entries over three hours is required (see guide for electronic submission of paper bills referred to above). The standard request for the file of papers on CCMS will ask for all correspondence and attendance notes. However, it has been found by many providers that submitting attendance notes for entries over three hours will suffice, although this is no guarantee that the request will not be more stringently enforced by the LAA in the future.
- For line-by-line CCMS bills for claims eligible for assessment by the court – attendance notes for entries over three hours (see CCMS quick guide referred to at para 15.97 below).

15.85 There are useful checklists found on each claim form page on the LAA website, to ensure the claim is correctly submitted.

15.86 If the client has a financial interest and wishes to make written objections to the LAA, then the certificate on the claim form will need to be altered (it assumes that the client does not wish to raise objections).

Claims on CCMS

15.87 Where the file of papers is required as detailed above, and the claim is submitted on CCMS, a document request will generally ask for just the preparation notes, file notes and 'third party documents' (documents from a third party to support an unusually high claim, eg an unusually high expert's report fee).

15.88   In August 2019, the LAA introduced a checklist for CCMS claims with a two-stage process, with the claim being rejected for amendment after one 'fail' on Stage 1 and then rejected for amendment or document request made for additional information at Stage 2. This was introduced in conjunction with the changes to categories of rejects, moving many scenarios that would have resulted in a document request to a reject as laid out in the LAA's internal guidance.[62]

15.89   There is a useful checklist found on the LAA website,[63] to ensure the claim is correctly submitted. There are also 'Quick guides' to submitting bills on the civil section of the LAA's training and support website:[64]

15.90   For CCMS cases, unlike paper claims, the outcomes are not included within the claim and are reported separately on CCMS. The outcomes must be reported before a final bill can be submitted on CCMS. Outcomes are not reported when submitting an interim bill for a transferred case, or a non-final stage of a VHCC case plan. The final bill will be 'parked' until the outcomes are processed, which may take some time if statutory charge issues have to be investigated. If a CCMS claim is still pending assessment, then omitted costs can be added by submitting an adjustment bill. An adjustment bill request must be submitted via a case query, and if the LAA grants this then a notification will be sent to submit one – there is a Quick guide on the Civil section of the LAA's training and support website. If omitted costs are identified after a CCMS claim is reduced on assessment and an appeal is being made for these, then the omitted costs can be included in the appeal bill (see 'Costs appeals' at para 15.98 onwards below) but must be identified as such in appeal submissions along with reasons for the omission.

15.91   Where the client has a financial interest, CCMS will not allow you to prepare the draft claim on its interface without answering that the client has been sent the bill on a specified date, even before the bill itself has been created. This is due to an oversight in the way CCMS was developed and is the only way around this problem. You must then remember to alter this in the bill once the bill has actually been sent to the client, together with any response that the client may have made.

15.92   Where you represent multiple parties on a family case, the certificates must be linked on CCMS and the claim will be submitted

---

62 *Civil Finance Electronic* Handbook section 16.
63 At: www.gov.uk/guidance/submitting-your-claim-civil-and-family-cases.
64 At: https://legalaidlearning.justice.gov.uk.

under the lead certificate (which holds the total costs limitation). Outcomes and nil bills must still be submitted on the linked certificates. Where multiple certificates cover a non-family case, these can be linked on CCMS, but this does not automatically result in a lead costs limitation and must be done manually with agreement of the LAA, for example, on VHCCs. The LAA has confirmed to the Association of Costs Lawyers that as long as there is a sufficient costs limitation under a single certificate, a single claim can be submitted under it rather than preparing multiple claims apportioning disbursements and time on each line entry.

Use it or lose it – inactivity on CCMS

15.93 Draft claims on the CCMS interface can be left untouched for up to 84 days, but if there is no activity on the claim after this it will be deleted from the system and all the data will be lost. If a CCMS claim is submitted and rejected by the assessment team, a copy will remain on the CCMS case billing page indefinitely until it is amended and/ or submitted.

When counsel fees are also claimed on CCMS

15.94 Family counsel (whether paid under FAS or hourly rate) must claim their fees on CCMS before solicitors can submit their claim. Significant outstanding balances under their costs allocation will result in queries from the LAA and possibly a rejection of your claim.

15.95 For non-family counsel, unless you have opted that their fees are included within your claim to be paid directly to you and then forwarded to them, once your claim is received counsel will be notified to submit their claim for fees on CCMS. You must ensure that they have adequate allocation under the costs limitation before your claim is submitted and authorised.

Claims over £2,500 assessed by the LAA

15.96 Claims eligible for assessment by the court (as detailed in para 15.56 above) can be submitted to the LAA for assessment instead. For CCMS matters, there are three options:
1) submit a line-by-line bill as you would for any other LAA assessed claim;
2) submit a 'court bill' which will be assessed by the LAA; or
3) submit a Claim 1 on CCMS.

15.97 If using option 2 or 3, this is submitted using the Court Assessed Bill claim on CCMS, as detailed in para 15.114 below, which will allow you to upload the 'court bill' or Claim 1 with the document request. It is advisable to highlight in the accompanying message on CCMS whether the claim is for LAA assessment or payment of a bill that has actually been assessed by the court.

15.97 See the *Court assessed claims guidance: Guidance on voluntary submission of court assessed claims to LAA for assessment*, 30 March 2020; and CCMS quick guide *CCMS Provider: Advanced Guide – Bills Formerly Submitted Under Court Assessed Process*, v1.0, 22 May 2020 – both of which can be found on the LAA website.[65]

Costs appeals

Generally

15.98 If costs escape or are not subject to a fixed fee in either controlled work or licensed work and are reduced on assessment, you can appeal. You may want to do this, even if the effort of preparing the appeal seems disproportionate to the reduction in fees, if a successful appeal would improve your KPIs (see chapter 22).

15.99 If the LAA assessed claim was eligible to be assessed by the court, then rather than appeal the LAA assessment you can seek a fresh assessment by the court instead, following the procedure detailed in the section 'Assessment of costs by the courts – legal aid only' at para 15.107 onwards below. You should notify the LAA in advance of seeking the fresh assessment, to allow it to note that the existing payment is to be treated as a POA in the interim and to expect a further claim. For more information, see the LAA's *Court Assessed Claims Guidance – Guidance on Submitting a Claim Where You Have Sought to Set Aside LAA's Original Assessment*, v1.1, 4 February 2021.[66]

15.100 Appeals must be made in writing within 28 days of receipt of the assessment; you can request an extension of up to 14 days if there is a good reason and it is made within 21 days. The appeal must be accompanied by any supporting papers returned with the assessment. An LAA internal reviewer will carry out a formal and detailed review of the original decision, and if they do not concede to the

---

65 At: www.gov.uk/guidance/transfer-of-claims-assessed-at-court-to-the-legal-aid-agency.

66 At: www.gov.uk/guidance/transfer-of-claims-assessed-at-court-to-the-legal-aid-agency.

Getting paid for civil and family work 423

appeal then it will be referred to an Independent Costs Assessor (ICA). The ICA is an experienced solicitor, CILEx Fellow, barrister or regulated costs lawyer in private practice, and not a member of the LAA's staff. The ICA may confirm, increase or decrease the amount assessed. See chapter 17 for more information on appeals to ICAs.

15.101 On pre-CCMS licensed work, an appeal can be made using the APP10 form returned with the assessment, although use of this form is not mandatory and an electronic appeal can be made using the LAA's appeals proforma (see below). On CCMS cases, an appeal bill must be completed, and representations are uploaded to the subsequent document request received. A CCMS appeal bill must consist of only the balance of work/amounts reduced on the original claim, for example, if one hour of preparation is removed from a line entry on assessment then it is that one hour that is entered, or the hearing unit reduction on FAS, or balance disbursement that was reduced. The balance reduced for an enhancement is claimed through the disbursement screen, either as a single-line entry if the same amount is reduced for the same reasons, or multiple lines if different amounts and/or for different reasons. 'Quick guides' are found on the Civil section of the LAA's training and support website.

15.102 There are optional appeal proformas that can be used for certificated and controlled work. This negates the requirement to return all papers on non-CCMS cases. It can be used as an appeal submissions document on CCMS Appeals (an appeal must still be prepared and submitted on CCMS). For non-CCMS claims it can be emailed to: ContactCivil@Justice.gov.uk; and for controlled work emailed to: mhu-ec@justice.gov.uk. The proforma for certificated cases can be found on the LAA's Claim1A form webpage and for controlled work cases the EC Claim 1 form webpage.

15.103 The LAA can make written representations (in addition to those contained in the original assessment) and must send these to you no less than 21 days before the appeal is sent to the ICA. You can provide a written response to these within 14 days of receiving them.

15.104 Any appeal to an ICA is considered on paper, although either party can make a written request (setting out full reasons) to the ICA for an oral hearing. Such requests are rarely granted.

15.105 See the Standard Civil Contract 2024 Specification paras 6.71–6.81 for more information on costs appeals.

Points of principle of general importance

15.106 Under the 2013 and previous Civil Contracts[67] there was a further right of appeal. Where applicable, you could apply for a point of principle of general importance (POP) to be certified. The provision still applies to cases opened under contracts where there was the right to apply for a POP. See the relevant contract for more information. The text of POPs and the procedure for applying for one are set out in the POP Manual – this manual was withdrawn by the LAA on 2 September 2021, but a link to it can currently still be found on the applicable webpage and the POPs therein may still be persuasive.[68] Without a further right of appeal to the LAA, the only route to challenge a costs decision would be by way of judicial review.

Assessment of costs by the courts – legal aid only

15.107 Civil and family legal aid costs are assessed by the courts under CPR Part 47 (detailed assessment, called taxation pre-CPR), as summarised in the *Senior Court Costs Office guide* sections 4 and 24. CPR Part 47 applies to proceedings under other civil court and tribunal procedure rules by those rules delegating to the CPR for detailed assessment.

15.108 The bill must be drawn up in the prescribed form.[69] Although the CPR do not expressly exclude legal aid only court bills in multi-track proceedings subject to a costs budget (CPR Practice Direction (PD) 47 Schedule of Costs Precedents: Precedent H) from having to be prepared as a phased bill, and in electronic form for any work done on or after 6 April 2018, it is highly unlikely that the courts will require this when no inter partes costs are being assessed, because the budget (prepared for inter partes recovery only) would not be a useful comparator to refer to. A costs lawyer or draftsman's fee is included in the bill and can be claimed as profit costs falling under solicitor's work.[70]

15.109 Bills are subject to provisional assessment (assessment on papers) under CPR 47.18, which is separate to inter partes provisional assessment under CPR 47.15. The procedure is:

---

67 There was no right to apply for POPs under the 2014 or 2015 Contracts.
68 See: www.gov.uk/legal-aid-points-of-principle-of-general-importance-pop.
69 CPR Part 47 PD paras 5.7–5.22; and Part 44 PD paras 2.1–2.11.
70 *Crane v Canons Leisure Centre* [2007] EWCA Civ 1352.

1) Within three months of the right to detailed assessment arising, the bill of costs is lodged for provisional assessment with a request for detailed assessment – HMCTS form N258A (or D258A for family law proceedings), together with:
   - the document giving right to detailed assessment (eg order for detailed assessment or discharged certificate[71]);
   - copies of counsel's and expert's fee notes;
   - written evidence of any disbursement exceeding £500 (if your bill includes the optional certificate as to disbursements of £500 or less);
   - legal aid certificate;
   - a statement of the client's address and contact details should they have a financial interest and wish to be heard on the assessment; and
   - the court fee.

   An oral detailed assessment will only be listed if the request form asks for a client with financial interest to be heard. The file of relevant papers (as specified under the CPR[72]) must not be lodged unless the court requests them,[73] and contrary to the inclusion on the D258A checklist, this applies to the Senior Court Costs Office (SCCO), which also assesses cases of the Central Family Court (previously the Principal Registry of the Family Division (PRFD)).

2) The original assessed bill is returned with an N253 'Notice of Amount Allowed on Provisional Assessment'.

3) You must notify counsel of any reduction to their fees within seven days.[74]

4) If you object to reductions, then you can request a hearing within 14 days of receiving notice of provisional assessment. It is common for written objections to be sent. However, while some courts will list a hearing to hear further submissions if the provider is dissatisfied with the response to written submissions, some may not. Any costs of an appeal will only be payable to the extent that the court hearing it orders.[75]

5) If you object to the outcome of a hearing and wish to proceed further, you must follow the same route as other costs under CPR Part 47, and appeal under CPR Part 52 or 47.21–47.24 if heard by

---

71 Costs Assessment Guidance paras 15.2–15.4.
72 CPR Part 47 PD para 13.12.
73 CPR Part 47 PD para 17.2(2).
74 Standard Civil Contract 2024 Specification para 6.43.
75 Standard Civil Contract 2024 Specification para 6.40.

an authorised court officer (referred to in the SCCO as costs officer); see para 15.133 below for further information.

6) If you consent to the assessment, or after outcome of a hearing and/or appeal, you must return the bill of costs with a completed legal aid assessment certificate HMCTS form EX80A (or EX80B where costs are subject to or escape family fixed fees). You must retain a copy of the assessed bill. There is no separate court fee for approving the certificate (it was combined with the assessment fee in July 2013).

7) The legal aid assessment certificate is approved (sealed) by the court and returned – the bill of costs is meant to be retained on the court file.

15.110 The costs of detailed assessment (except preparation of the bill of costs) fall outside of the costs limitation and statutory charge.[76] Profit costs which the LAA will recognise as costs of detailed assessment are detailed in their internal guidance *Civil Finance Electronic Handbook*:

- completing N258A/D258A (request for detailed assessment);
- letter out to court;
- diarising;
- completing EX80A/B/legal aid assessment certificate;
- drawing up the bill of costs following assessment;
- considering points of dispute and preparation of replies;
- attendance on the detailed assessment; and
- time spent checking any provisional assessment.

15.111 The contract requires that costs of detailed assessment of legal aid only costs must be assessed within the detailed assessment itself.[77] This means that these costs have to be included within the bill of costs (apart from the court assessment fee). However, this does create a conflict with the CPR, which provides that they should not be[78] because CPR Part 47 is principally for the assessment of inter partes costs, where the liability for costs of detailed assessment must be determined upon the outcome of those proceedings and is summarily assessed. However, for legal aid only assessments the bill is the only available mechanism to recover these costs which you have a right to be paid under the contract.

---

76 Standard Civil Contract 2024 Specification para 6.42.
77 Standard Civil Contract 2024 Specification para 6.38.
78 CPR Part 47 PD para 5.19.

15.112 The bill and request, etc must be lodged at the 'appropriate office' as specified under the CPR.[79] While the PD provides that for London County Court proceedings this is the SCCO, this does not apply where there are only legal aid costs, and these are assessed in the county court (unless the SCCO agrees to carry out the assessment instead). In family proceedings the 'appropriate office' is the Designated Family Court for the Designated Family Judge area.[80] However, where there are only legal aid costs, proceedings in the Central Family Court, East London, North London and West London Family Courts are all now assessed by costs officers in the SCCO.

15.113 While there is a sliding scale of court assessment fees for inter partes costs, there is a separate single court fee for detailed assessment of legal aid non-family and family costs, respectively.[81] Fees for detailed assessment for family proceedings were not increased in 2016, 2021 and 2024. In fact, the assessment fee for legal aid costs in family proceedings was more than halved in 2020 after an MoJ review of court fees.

15.114 Once the assessment process is completed, you must then submit your claim for payment of the bill of costs to the LAA. If this is a CCMS case, a summary level bill is submitted. You can enter a breakdown of disbursements, which allows you to enter the hourly rates incurred by the expert if applicable, but this is optional. Solicitor's FAS must be broken down by using the FAS Unit Entry screen, the same as a claim assessed by the LAA. The 'Court Assessment Result Date' is the date that the legal aid assessment certificate is sealed. Once the claim is submitted, a document request will be sent asking for:

1) the sealed legal aid assessment certificate;
2) a copy of the assessed bill of costs;
3) counsels' fee notes, but only for a non-family case where you and counsel have opted for the balance fees (after POAs) be paid directly to the provider and forwarded to counsel;
4) where solicitor's FAS fees claimed – an order providing full details of hearing (advocates attending, times, bolt-ons, etc) or Advocate's Attendance form (EX506), attendance notes for advocates' meetings and orders for same if more than two per case.
5) expert's invoices and disbursement vouchers (or if train then tickets/booking receipts) of £20 **including** VAT or more, this

---

79 CPR Part 47 PD paras 4.1–4.3.
80 Family Procedure Rules Part 28 PD 28A para 2.8.
81 Civil Proceedings Fees Order 2008 Sch 1 para 5.1, as amended; and Family Proceedings Fees Order 2008 Sch 1 para 9.1, as amended.

includes experts' expenses, for example, train and hotel. For court fees and mileage, the LAA will accept a copy of the accounts ledger instead, although a copy of the covering letter to the court referring to the court fee and amount is usually accepted;

6) where DNA and/or alcohol tests are claimed, copies of the court orders for these are required unless there is prior authority; and

7) disbursement list, numbered and cross-referenced against the vouchers, court orders, ledgers (only if the disbursements have not been broken down in the CCMS claim).

A quick guide 'Court Assessed Bill' is found on the Civil section of the LAA's training and support website.[82]

15.115 If a pre-CCMS case, then a form CIV CLAIM 1, CIV CLAIM 1A (or CIV CLAIM2 when inter partes costs recovery has also been made) is sent to the LAA together with the documentation detailed above, except for the disbursement list but including counsels' fee notes unless counsel has been paid under FAS/FGF. This is now done via email (see para 15.84 above).

15.116 Family counsel (whether paid under FAS or hourly rate) must claim their fees on CCMS before you submit your claim. Significant outstanding balances under their costs allocation will result in queries from the LAA and possibly a rejection of your claim.

15.117 For non-family counsel, unless you have opted that their fees are included within your claim to be paid directly to you and then forwarded to them, once your claim is authorised counsel will be notified to submit their claim for fees on CCMS. You must ensure that they have adequate allocation under the costs limitation before your claim is submitted and authorised.

15.118 If the assessed costs (excluding costs of detailed assessment) exceed the costs limit, then you can either limit these when preparing the legal aid assessment certificate, or the LAA states within its internal *Civil Finance Electronic Handbook* that it will reduce the claim accordingly rather than rejecting the claim and requiring the bill and legal aid assessment certificate to be redrawn. However, if profit costs of detailed assessment have not already been properly split from the rest of the profit costs and claimed as such within your claim, it is unlikely that the LAA will spend time ringfencing these from the costs limitation for you.

---

82 At: https://legalaidlearning.justice.gov.uk.

Costs between the parties and the indemnity principle (inter partes costs)

15.119 The contract requires that you seek costs against another party (inter partes costs) just as you would with any non-legally aided case and to protect the interests of public funds on any inter partes costs assessment.[83] An inter partes costs order is an order that one party indemnify another party's loss/liability for legal costs, so if there is no lability there is nothing to indemnify, ie there is nothing to pay.[84] This is called the 'indemnity principle', and it limits what can be claimed/recovered inter partes to the terms of the client's retainer. A legal aid provider can recover costs on behalf of their client at market rates rather than legal aid rates, because the indemnity principle is disapplied from costs funded under civil legal aid (including family) to the extent of the rates and costs limit but not the scope.[85] This was first done for licensed work in 1994 when civil legal aid rates were first prescribed (at that time these were roughly 10 per cent less than market rates), and for controlled work in 2000. Today, the disparity between legal aid rates and market rates means that recovering inter partes costs where possible has never been more vital to the survival of many legal aid practices, and there is no reason not to pursue and obtain applicable costs awards for your client even when the paying party is a publicly funded body.[86]

15.120 Debts against the client can be ordered to be set off against their inter partes costs; such debts are often damages or adverse costs within the same proceedings, but they do not always have to be. An order for set-off against a legally aided party's costs is commonly known as a Lockley order. Costs protection under legal aid does not prevent a set-off up to the amount of the client's inter partes costs, and the costs order belongs to the client rather than the solicitor or the LAA, even though the client is legally aided.[87] Unfortunately, this means that if there is a set-off against inter partes costs, you can either elect to keep the balance recovered or pay this into the fund and claim the costs of the entire action from the LAA at legal aid rates.

---

83 Standard Civil Contract 2024 Specification para 6.57.
84 *Harold v Smith* (1860) 5 H&N 381, Exch.
85 Civil Legal Aid (Costs) Regulations 2013 reg 21(3); and Standard Civil Contract 2024 Specification para 1.40.
86 *R (Bahta) v Secretary of State for the Home Department* [2011] EWCA Civ 895.
87 *R (Burkett) v Hammersmith and Fulham LBC* [2004] EWCA Civ 1342.

15.121 If the order or agreement only allows for a single sum for both damages and costs and does not specify the proportion of that sum which relates to costs, you cannot keep any of this money for your costs but rather should claim them from the LAA at the applicable legal aid rates/fees.[88]

15.122 Where CPR 44.9 applies, a party is liable to pay costs even when an order is not specifically made by the court, for example, when a claim is struck out, when a Part 36 offer is accepted or when the claim is discontinued. Equally, you should try to ensure that there is an order as to costs in every interim order in the case (eg 'Costs in the case'), because (where CPR 44.10 applies) without this no inter partes costs can be claimed in relation to that order (eg costs of the hearing at which the order was made) regardless of the order for costs made at the end of the case; that is unless (in civil cases) it is an order granting permission to appeal or for judicial review or any other order sought without notice which is silent as to costs, in which case these are deemed orders for costs.

Assessment of costs by the courts – inter partes

The procedure

15.123 Civil and family inter partes costs are assessed by the courts under CPR Part 47 (detailed assessment, called taxation pre-CPR), as summarised in the *Senior Court Costs Office guide*. Part 47 applies to proceedings under other civil court and tribunal procedure rules by those rules delegating to the CPR for detailed assessment. There is a separate procedure for detailed assessment in the Supreme Court, including a different form of bill, a requirement to file the bill at court with an upfront court fee at the outset of proceedings with much stricter requirement to do so in time and differing deadlines.[89]

15.124 Inter partes costs funded under legal aid are precluded from summary assessment under the CPR,[90] and while this provision does not directly apply to tribunal proceedings, there is case-law that says it should be followed for licensed work.[91] However, summary assessments of inter partes costs funded under legal aid are sometimes carried out (usually on interim hearings), and the LAA's *Civil*

---

88 Standard Civil Contract 2024 Specification para 1.42.
89 Supreme Court Rules 2024 Part 8; and UKSC PD 13.
90 CPR Part 44 PD para 9.8.
91 *MG v Cambridgeshire CC (SEN)* [2017] UKUT 172 (AAC).

Finance Electronic Handbook details how such a recovery should be dealt with, particularly where legal aid family fixed fees apply.

15.125 The detailed assessment procedure is analogous to the civil fast-track procedure, but with default case management steps as to disclosure and evidence removed:

1) Notice of commencement of detailed assessment proceedings (claim form);
2) Bill of Costs in the prescribed form[92] (Particulars of Claim);
3) Points of Dispute (PoDs) in the prescribed form[93] (Defence);
4) Optional Replies in the prescribed form[94] (Reply);
5) assessment either by provisional assessment with oral review, or oral detailed assessment (Trial); and
6) Final Costs Certificate (Money judgment which can be used for enforcement).

15.126 For cases where proceedings are not issued, and costs are payable pursuant to an agreement and the quantum of those costs is the only issue in dispute, an order for costs must be obtained first. This is done under costs-only proceedings.[95] Applicable cases are usually under controlled work and are rare under post-LASPO civil legal aid, so problems have arisen when the parties cannot agree on quantum, or the paying party reneges on the agreement, and the LAA refuses to grant Legal Representation for costs-only proceedings on the basis that they are not within eligible scope.

15.127 Proceedings are commenced by serving the notice (HMCTS form N252) and a copy of the bill together with other specified enclosures.[96] Unless a payment of interim costs is sought, or some other application is made, the court is rarely involved until the point that assessment is requested. In the majority of cases a settlement is reached before this point. Commencement is required within three months of the right to costs arising (ie order for costs or deemed order for costs), although this can be extended or shortened either by agreement or by the court. The exception to the three-month period is where the right arises in the interim of the principal case, and the general rule is that the principal case must conclude first before detailed assessment proceedings can be commenced. Proceedings are *not* automatically stayed pending an appeal. If the receiving party

---

92 CPR Part 47 PD paras 5.1–5.1A and 5.7–5.22; and Part 44 PD paras 2.1–2.11.
93 CPR Part 47 PD para 8.2; and Schedule of Costs Precedents: Precedent G.
94 CPR Part 47 PD Schedule of Costs Precedents: Precedent G.
95 CPR 46.14.
96 CPR Part 47 PD para 5.2.

fails to commence after three months, the paying party can apply for an unless order disallowing all or part of the costs that would otherwise be allowed if the receiving party fails to commence within a specified time, or if the paying party does not make such an application the court may disallow interest on costs that can accrue from the date of the costs order, although often only the interest for the period of delay is disallowed. The court can also disallow all or part of the costs claimed on the basis of misconduct, but commencing late when this is not deliberate or wilful does not in and of itself meet this criterion.[97] The assessment must be requested within three months of the expiry of the period for commencing proceedings (ie six months after the right to detailed assessment arises) and there are identical sanctions for failure to comply. These are the only applicable sanctions for delay in commencing proceedings and requesting assessment under CPR Part 47.

15.128 The paying party has 21 days to serve PoDs (although this can be extended or shortened by agreement or the court) together with an open offer. The open offer can be nil, and usually any figure given is only for the maximum amount conceded to in the PoDs. There are no sanctions for failure to serve an open offer. If the paying party misses the deadline to serve PoDs, a default costs certificate (default money judgment) for the full amount sought in the notice can be applied for from the court, with fixed costs of £80 plus the court fee,[98] and if it is issued before the PoDs are served then it is enforceable. If the PoDs are served out of time the paying party may not be heard further in the proceedings, unless the court gives permission which it generally will.

15.129 Replies can be served within 21 days of receipt of the PoDs, but these are optional.

15.130 The receiving party recovers costs of detailed assessment unless the court orders otherwise. The amount sought within the bill does not include these costs (except those exclusive to legal aid only costs as detailed above), which will include costs of negotiations and optional replies. These are usually summarily assessed at the end of the assessment (even when they are a legally aided party's). This distinction between the claim (for costs) and costs of the claim is often overlooked by receiving parties. Part 36 offers may be made within detailed assessment proceedings.[99] However, paying parties

---

97 *Haji-Ioannou v Frangos and others* [2006] EWCA Civ 1663.
98 CPR Part 47 PD para 10.7.
99 CPR 47.20.

will often make non-Part 36 without prejudice save as to costs offers instead, which of course do not carry a predetermined liability for costs of the (detailed assessment) proceedings to be paid. The CPR provide that any offer made within detailed assessed proceedings will include costs of preparing the bill, VAT and interest, unless the offer expressly states otherwise,[100] but the provision omits any reference to inclusion of costs of detailed assessment (apart from preparation of the bill) within the offer. It should be noted that negotiations made on a 'without prejudice' basis (whether oral or on papers) which miss off 'save as to costs', cannot be disclosed to the court after the assessment is concluded. If adverse costs of detailed assessment are made against your client, these may be set off against their costs of the principal case under a Lockley order (see above).

15.131 If interim costs are agreed or the proceedings are settled and you are concerned that the paying party will not actually pay, you can apply for an interim or final costs certificate under CPR 47.10 so that the agreement can be enforced.

15.132 A detailed or provisional assessment is requested on HMCTS form N258. Claims for costs up to £75,000 (including VAT) are subject to provisional assessment, unless the court orders otherwise. The procedure is under CPR 47.15 and is separate to the procedure for provisional assessment of legal aid only costs under CPR 47.18, although both sets of costs will be assessed by the court and the court fee for inter partes assessment covers the legal aid only assessment (at an oral assessment they will be assessed at the end of the hearing[101]). Costs of provisional assessment are capped at £1,500 excluding VAT and court fees. The request for provisional assessment must be lodged with documents specified under CPR Part 47 PD para 14.3, which will include your statement of costs (N260) for detailed assessment proceedings, the paying party's open offer, and any Part 36/without prejudice save as to costs offers in a sealed envelope for the court to open when determining the liability of costs of detailed assessment. Under provisional assessment, the rules do not require you to file your file of relevant papers in support of the bill (as specified under the CPR[102]), but the SCCO may request it if it is not already lodged with the request for provisional assessment; post-Covid-19 there may be a return to requiring this on every case. Other courts may do the same. The provisionally assessed bill will be sent to

---

100 CPR Part 47 PD para 19.
101 Standard Civil Contract 2024 Specification para 6.46.
102 CPR Part 47 PD para 13.12.

both parties and they have 14 days to agree the calculation of the assessed figures or make written submissions on any dispute about this. Any dispute as to liability for costs of the provisional assessment process will also be dealt with by written submissions and determined without a hearing. Each party also has 21 days from receipt of notice of provisional assessment to request an oral review of the assessment. The request must specify which items within the bill are to be reviewed and the court can (and does) refuse to review anything that is not specified within the request. Because the oral review is technically not an appeal, it is heard by the same judge or authorised court officer who provisionally assessed the bill. For the requesting party to obtain costs of the oral review and not incur adverse costs of the same, they must vary the total provisionally assessed sum by at least 20 per cent in their favour unless the court orders otherwise. Of course, you will not be successful on review if your costs have been reduced by less than 20 per cent on the provisional assessment. Consequently, you must carefully consider whether it is worth pursuing an oral review, because after incurring further own costs and adverse costs, you may end up worse off even if your claim is increased.

15.133 If the assessment is made by an authorised court officer (referred to in the SCCO as a costs officer), their decision is appealed under CPR 47.21–47.24 to a costs judge or a district judge of the High Court. Such appeals do not require permission but must be made no more than 21 days after the date of the decision being made, and the detailed assessment proceedings will be re-heard. An appeal from a judge must be made under CPR Part 52 and is limited to review of the decision under appeal rather than a re-hearing of the whole proceedings (CPR 52.21(1)).

The LAA and inter partes costs

15.134 For licensed work, there is deemed cover for detailed assessment proceedings for the client as the receiving party under the certificate even after it is discharged;[103] however, since the 2010 Contract there has been an express term providing for a conditional funding arrangement, meaning that the LAA will not pay you costs of detailed assessment that your client is not awarded when the inter partes costs of the principal case are recovered.[104] Therefore, should costs of detailed assessment not be recovered on a successful inter partes

103 Standard Civil Contract 2024 Specification para 6.38; and Costs Assessment Guidance para 15.14.
104 Standard Civil Contract 2024 Specification para 6.39.

Getting paid for civil and family work 435

recovery, these cannot be claimed from the LAA even at legal aid rates, although the court fee may be paid.

15.135 Where interest is recovered, you must pay the LAA the proportion of interest on the costs recovered as calculated at legal aid rates, and you may keep any excess.[105] For example, you recover £10,000 costs with interest thereon and at legal aid rates those costs would be worth £3,000, so the proportion of the interest accrued on that £3,000 must be paid to the LAA. When calculating the LAA's share of interest, discretionary enhancements should not be applied to the legal aid rates used to calculate what the costs would be worth.

15.136 Once payment is received from the paying party, if you are not claiming legal aid only costs in addition, then you have two months to report the recovery;[106] however, where multiple recoveries at different times are being made under a certificate, for example, where there are costs of the first instance and appellate proceedings, the LAA acknowledges that the recoveries can only be reported after the final recovery. For CCMS cases, you must report the recovery under your outcomes and any claim for legal aid only costs is made separately with a normal CCMS bill. On non-CCMS cases, a form CIV CLAIM2 is used to report the recovery and claim any legal aid only costs.

15.137 There is no deemed cover to enforce the costs certificate if the paying party fails to pay, and an amendment must be sought under the certificate to obtain a retainer to do this.[107] You do not have to carry out enforcement; instead you can claim your costs from the LAA, but this will be at legal aid rates. If you have already discharged the legal aid certificate, then you will not be able to obtain cover for enforcement and your only option will be to claim costs at legal aid rates from the LAA and rely upon the LAA to pursue enforcement. You will need to obtain a costs certificate to enable pursuit of enforcement: without this the LAA will not pay your claim. Where a court assessment is an option, you will need to lodge your inter partes bill for a legal aid only assessment with an accompanying schedule of the items in the bill calculated at legal aid rates (a legal aid schedule) in the prescribed form.[108] The legal aid assessment certificate must be completed and this is the only time that Box A of the EX80 form is completed to show the costs being paid by the LAA for which an

---

105 Standard Civil Contract 2024 Specification para 6.53.
106 Standard Civil Contract 2024 Specification para 6.48.
107 Standard Civil Contract 2024 Specification para 1.41.
108 CPR Part 47 PD paras 17.6–17.9.

inter partes costs order has been made. For CCMS cases you use the Awards Summary of the Outcomes section to report the award, any partial recovery, the paying party's details and amount due. For non-CCMS cases where there is no recovery the form CIV CLAIM2 is not used, but forms CIV CLAIM1 or CIV CLAIM1A instead, which also have relevant pages for awards unrecovered and debtor's details.

Apportioned inter partes costs and legal aid only costs

15.138 In cases where inter partes costs are possible, it is not uncommon for costs to be ordered or negotiated on the basis of payment of part of the costs of the case. If so, it is important that you are clear as to the terms of the order or agreement, because although you can claim the balance from the legal aid fund;[109] if it is a VHCC then you must specifically apply to the LAA case manager for authorisation to do so.[110] The Standard Civil Contract 2024 (and previous contracts) allows you to claim from the legal aid fund any costs not payable by another party (legal aid only costs), but only if certain conditions are met.[111]

15.139 The Specification defines 'legal aid only' costs – costs that can be claimed from the legal aid fund even where inter partes costs are recovered – as:
   a) contract work not covered by a client's costs order or agreement;
   b) costs of completing legal aid forms and communicating with the LAA;
   c) certain limited types of costs disallowed or not agreed.

15.140 Where a costs order or agreement specifies that another party should pay a proportion of the client's costs (but not a fixed sum), the same proportion of the total work that is not covered is legal aid only costs.

15.141 To take a practical example, say total costs on the case are £2,000 at legal aid rates and £4,000 at inter partes rates. If the other side agree to pay your costs in the sum of £2,000, that could be expressed in one of three ways:

1) £2,000 as the total agreed costs of the case (you agree it is only worth £2,000 rather than £4,000);
2) agreement to pay costs between x and y dates, totalling £2,000; or
3) agreement to pay 50 per cent of the costs, 100 per cent of this being £4,000 at market rates.

---

109 Standard Civil Contract 2024 Specification para 6.44.
110 Individual Case Contract 2018 (High Cost Case) Specification paras 5.3–5.11.
111 Standard Civil Contract 2024 Specification paras 6.50–6.51 (in para 6.51, para 6.48 is erroneously referred to rather than para 6.50).

None of the agreed costs include work done relating to legal aid funding, which is solicitor–client/funding work and therefore comes under both categories a) and b) of legal aid only costs (para 15.139 above).

15.142 In each case, you receive £2,000 from the other side. In the first case, that £2,000 represents the total costs of the case, so there are no legal aid costs (apart perhaps from £100 or so for completing the application for legal aid and so on). In the second case, costs outside the agreed dates are not subject to the costs order, so you can claim those costs from the LAA in addition to the £2,000 inter partes costs you have received. In the third case, the other side has agreed to pay 50 per cent of your costs, so the other 50 per cent are legal aid only costs, so you can claim the other 50 per cent from the LAA at legal aid rates plus the full amount for work completing the application for legal, etc from the LAA, in addition to the £2,000 from the other side.

15.143 Claiming legal aid only costs at a percentage is relatively uncommon and none of the LAA claim forms, both paper and electronic, are designed to cater for this. For a single claim on a non-CCMS case with only one set percentage being claimed, ie 50 per cent with no full costs for solicitor client/funding work, a CIV CLAIM 2 can be used, showing the costs at the full claim within the schedules and then an addendum set of figures showing at 50 per cent. If there are multiple percentages and/or it is a CCMS case, then agreement as to how to claim should be sought from the LAA before preparing it. This may be by using separate schedules or forms for each percentage rate. The LAA has accepted paper forms for CCMS cases where there is a percentage claim, because the CCMS pricing system for hourly rates cannot be set at a percentage of the price, let alone multiple percentage rates within a single claim. Splitting the amounts by time – for example, 50 per cent of the full time claimed for each piece of work – is inadvisable, because the full amount must be given in order to assess what is reasonable and proportionate and then the percentage rate applied afterwards.

Recoupment and limitation

15.144 The authority in relation to the limitation period in which the LAA can recover funds paid as POAs is *Legal Services Commission v Henthorn*.[112] The then Legal Services Commission (LSC) pursued

112 [2011] EWCA Civ 1415.

recoupment of POAs from a retired barrister, Aisha Henthorn. The cases dated back to between 1992 and 1998, with the LSC's claim issued in 2006. Henthorn argued that the six-year limitation period ran from the end of the case, and therefore the LSC was out of time in bringing the case against her. The High Court agreed and the LSC appealed. The Law Society and the Bar Council intervened in the Court of Appeal.

15.145 The Master of the Rolls held that time begins to run not at the end of the case, but only once the assessment process has been completed, and therefore once there has been a determination of how much the LSC owes solicitor/counsel, or how much they owe the LSC by way of recoupment of POAs. He further held that the LSC's claim was not an abuse of process, nor was it unreasonable in public law terms, and that on the facts of the individual payments, Ms Henthorn had no defence to the claims. The LSC was therefore entitled to recovery of POAs.

15.146 The effect of this case is that once a final bill is assessed, time starts to run for the purposes of the limitation period and the LAA cannot demand repayment of unrecouped POAs more than six years after the date of final assessment. However, if no final bill was ever submitted, limitation never starts to run and so the LAA can recover POAs at any time.

15.147 It is therefore critical that organisations hold good records regarding the discharge and final payments of claims and keep those for at least six years, until claims for the refund of POAs become statute barred under the Limitation Act 1980.

Pro bono costs orders

15.148 Pro bono is of course no replacement for legal aid, but many legal aid providers find themselves carrying out legal work, including representation, without legal aid to cover fees, and consequently fees for the work cannot be recovered from another party who is ordered to pay costs because of the indemnity principle. If this work and/or period without cover can be identified when the issue of costs liability arises in the applicable court (see below), then you can ask the court to make a pro bono costs order for this work, if costs are awarded to your client or include this within a settlement. In many civil litigation cases this can also avoid the other side being in a position of strength, because they know that they will not be excused from the expense of having to pay your client's costs if they lose.

15.149 Pro bono costs recovered must be paid to the Access to Justice Foundation ('the Foundation'), which is the prescribed charity.[113] The Foundation distributes the money to agencies and projects giving free legal help (where legal aid is unavailable) to those in charitable need, and can also help fund organisations that further access to justice more broadly. If such a front-line agency recovers costs under a pro bono costs order, it can apply to receive up to 50 per cent of this. The Foundation also provides grants to Legal Support Trusts.

15.150 Pro bono costs orders are made pursuant to Legal Services Act 2007 ss194, 194A and 194B. Pro bono costs orders can be made pursuant to s194(3) and CPR 46.7 in the Civil Division of the Court of Appeal, High Court, the Family Court or County Court (CPR 46.7 applies in the Family Court via FPR 28.1), and pursuant to s194B for relevant appeals in the Supreme Court. Since 28 June 2022, s194A of the 2007 Act came into force enabling pro bono costs orders to be made for costs incurred since that date in the First-tier Tribunal, the Upper Tribunal, an employment tribunal, the Employment Appeal Tribunal and the Competition Appeal Tribunal.

15.151 A pro bono costs order is in most ways like any other order for costs and is subject to the same restrictions and considerations when making one. If CPR Part 45 applies, the costs will be limited to the relevant fixed fees. The key differences are that: (a) the order must provide for payment of pro bono costs to be made to the Foundation; (b) the costs are not restricted by the terms of a retainer; and (c) the costs cannot be set off against adverse costs and payments cannot be returned from the Foundation in this event. It is prudent to ask for reserved costs on interim orders with a note on the court file that a pro bono costs award would otherwise have been made, so that this can be considered when making one determination on costs at the end of proceedings. Also, a pro bono costs order cannot be made against a party who was at all times in receipt of either pro bono or legal aid representation. The procedure for obtaining a pro bono costs order in the Civil Division of the Court of Appeal, High Court, the Family Court or County Court is provided under CPR 46.7 and the costs can be subject to either summary or detailed assessment. While CPR 46.7 does not require you to put the other party on special notice that you might be seeking a pro bono costs order, the accompanying PD para 4.1 does require that you file and serve a statement of costs equivalent to the same fees had the work been charged for. No

---

113 Legal Services Act 2007 s194(8) and s194C and The Legal Services Act 2007 (Prescribed Charity) Order 2008.

15.152 deadline is specified to do this, but the usual deadlines applying to statements of costs for summary assessment should be observed. There is provision under UKSC PD 13 for the making pro bono costs orders and assessment of such costs in the Supreme Court, but there appear to be no express procedural provisions for them in tribunals.

15.152 If costs are summarily assessed, the prescribed form for other summary assessments in the Civil Division of the Court of Appeal, High Court, the Family Court or County Court (N260) is not required (CPR Part 46 PD para 4.1 applies instead), but can be used, although the certificate as to the indemnity principle should be removed. The Foundation also provides templates for a draft order and skeleton argument for a pro bono costs order to be made, and a costs schedule that can be used, instead of an N260, that complies with PD para 4.1.

15.153 If the costs are subject to detailed assessment, the costs of detailed assessment which can be identified as solely attributable to the pro bono costs cannot be paid to you but can be recovered under a further pro bono costs order and paid to the Foundation.

15.154 CPR 46.7(3) requires you to send a copy of the pro bono costs order to the Foundation within seven days of receipt. There are no sanctions for failing to comply with this rule. The subsequent money judgment (eg default costs certificate) can be enforced as normal. The client can enforce in their own name, or alternatively the Foundation will enforce.

15.155 More information and helpful quick guides including guides for litigators and advocates can be found on the Access to Justice Foundation website: www.atjf.org.uk/pro-bono-costs-orders.

Family

Overview

15.156 There are two family payment schemes: public family law and private family law.

Public law

Fee level	Form of civil legal service	Provided as	Escape threshold
1	Legal Help	Controlled work	x3 Fixed fee
2	Family Help (Lower)	Controlled work	x3 Fixed fee
3	Legal Representation	Licensed work	x2 Fixed fee

Private law

Fee level	Form of civil legal service	Provided as	Escape threshold
1	Legal Help	Controlled work	x3 Fixed fee
2	Family Help (Lower)	Controlled work	x3 Fixed fee
3	Help with Family Mediation	Controlled work	N/A
4	Family Help (Higher)	Licensed work	x3 Fixed fee
5	Legal Representation	Licensed Work	x3 Fixed fee

15.157 The rates and fee amounts are provided under the Remuneration Regulations and the provisions for the schemes are in section 7 of the Contract Specification. All controlled work is subject to fixed fees and must 'escape' them before it can be claimed at hourly rates. Most licensed work is subject to fixed fees but there are exclusions. Fixed fees do not apply to public family law non-advocacy licensed work other than Children Act 1989 s31 proceedings (see below). A useful matrix of the non-advocacy fees is provided under the Specification section 7 para 7.3. Family advocacy is dealt with separately in chapter 19.

Controlled work

15.158 Claims for Legal Help and Family Help (Lower) in both private and public family schemes and Help with Family Mediation claims are paid and claimed as other civil categories, described above.

15.159 In public family law, controlled work is provided for work preceding the issue of applications for a care order or supervision order under Children Act 1989 s31. See chapter 7 for more information.

Family – controlled work escape fee cases

15.160 The escape threshold for Legal Help and Family Help (Lower) in both private and public family schemes is that profit costs calculated on an hourly rate basis must exceed three times the aggregate fixed fee (combined standard fees), but excluding the settlement fees under the children and finance aspects. The settlement fees cannot be claimed in addition to an escape case claim. The settlement fees under children and finance aspects do not form part of the aggregate fee. Help with Family Mediation cannot escape its standard fee.

15.161 You can instruct counsel on both Legal Help and Family Help (Lower), but their fee cannot be claimed as a disbursement in addition to a standard fee, and it cannot be used to escape the standard fee either. However, if a case does escape then counsel's fee can be claimed as a disbursement, but it is limited to the equivalent FAS fee. You must pay counsel within 28 days of receiving their fee note.[114]

Licensed work

Overview

15.162 The general rules and procedures for claiming licensed work costs are described above. Standard fee claims are submitted to the LAA as above. In cases where proceedings have not been issued, the LAA always assesses the costs.

15.163 Where proceedings have been issued, concluded before a judge and assessable costs exceed £2,500 (excluding VAT), you can opt to have the court assess them. The common special circumstance that means the LAA will assess costs over the assessment limit is where the only assessable costs exceeding £2,500 (excluding VAT) are disbursements, for example, a Children Act 1989 s31 care fixed fee plus substantial disbursements.

15.164 Proceedings that conclude before lay justices (magistrates) are assessed by the LAA regardless of the level of assessable costs. This does not include proceedings concluding before a district judge of the magistrates' court. Further, such judges are now defined as 'judges of district judge level' for the purposes of the Family Fixed Fee Scheme[115] and hearings before them attract a higher FAS fee than they did before the introduction of the single Family Court on 22 April 2014.

15.165 The requirement that claims for advocacy under the FAS be supported by an appropriately completed advocates attendance form (EX506) was removed in 2023. Instead, full details of the FAS claim (including bolt-ons) should be recorded in the recitals of the court order (see the introduction of chapter 19 for further details). Absent a recorded order or EX506 in support, the claim(s) will only be paid at the unit 1 rate for interim hearings and no fee will be paid for a final hearing. If older orders for remote hearings in the initial year of Covid-19 do not have the proper details, an attendance note may possibly be accepted.

---

114 Standard Civil Contract 2024 Specification paras 7.170–7.172.
115 Civil Legal Aid (Remuneration) (Amendment) (No 2) Regulations 2014 reg 2(1).

Getting paid for civil and family work

15.166 Private law proceedings heard with public law proceedings or where a private law order is sought within public law proceedings, for example, when an application for a child arrangements order is made within care proceedings, are called 'related proceedings'. Related proceedings are remunerated under the public law fees scheme as part of the public law case and no separate standard fee is claimable. The 2018 Contract now expressly clarifies that private law proceedings cannot be related proceedings simply because an order is being sought which may avoid public law proceedings when those public law proceedings do not exist.[116]

15.167 Cases are paid at hourly rates, and are not subject to a fixed fee, if:
1) you are instructed for less than 24 hours;
2) where the client has previously instructed a different provider in respect of the same work and the certificate has not been transferred; or
3) where you act for a client whose application to be joined in proceedings is refused.[117]

15.168 Work on an appeal against a final order is also paid at hourly rates instead of a fixed fee, apart from work up to the conclusion of the first instance proceedings, which is within any applicable standard fee and includes:
1) representation on any interim appeal;
2) any advice on the merits of an appeal against the final order; and
3) an application to the court of first instance for permission to appeal.[118]

15.169 Claims for cases on CCMS must be made via CCMS. With non-CCMS cases you must use form CIV CLAIM1A if the provider's fixed fees are claimed or a case escapes the fixed fee, or form CIV CLAIM1 if the only fixed fees claimed (if any) are for counsel.

15.170 Where there are multiple clients on a case and these are under CCMS, the certificates must be linked. There will be a lead certificate which will hold the costs limitation for all certificates (one full costs limit plus half of that costs limit again for each linked certificate). The claim must be made on the lead certificate, but outcomes must be reported and nil bills submitted on all other certificates.

---

116 Standard Civil Contract 2024 Specification paras 7.46–7.47.
117 Standard Civil Contract 2024 Specification para 7.19.
118 Standard Civil Contract 2024 Specification paras 7.48–7.49 and 7.98–7.99.

Family – public law fee scheme

15.171 Within public family law, there is only a non-advocacy standard fee for proceedings under Children Act 1989 s31 – the Legal Representation standard fee, also known as the Care Proceedings Graduated Fees Scheme (CPGFS). Non-advocacy work in all other public law proceedings is paid at hourly rates.

15.172 The escape threshold for Legal Representation standard fee is that profit costs calculated on an hourly rate basis must exceed twice the fixed fee. This calculation cannot include enhancements on the hourly rate, even the guaranteed minimum for panel members. Only once 'base costs' have escaped can you add the percentage enhancement. Do not forget that advocacy is claimed separately and in addition to the fixed fee, so advocacy costs do not count towards reaching the escape threshold.[119]

15.173 The Legal Representation standard fee is applied by reference to the level of judge before whom the proceedings conclude (or if you cease to provide the service before conclusion then the relevant level of judge hearing the case at that time),[120] the status of the client in the proceedings and the region where the solicitor's office is located.

Parties

15.174 The parties are as follows:
- **'Child'** applies where you represent the child who is the subject of the proceedings.
- **'Parent'** applies where you represent the parent of such a child or a person who has parental responsibility for such a child.
- **'Joined party'** applies to all other clients in Children Act 1989 s31 care proceedings (unless the client's application to be joined to the proceedings is refused, in which case must be claimed at hourly rates).

15.175 There is a higher fee where two parents or two+ children are represented. There is one fixed fee per case, not per client, unless the client is a joined party to the proceedings (for which there is only a single-party fixed fee available). Where there are separate section 31 care proceedings for another child and these are not consolidated, then a separate Legal Representation standard fee is claimable. However, if the proceedings are consolidated, then these are claimed

---

119 Standard Civil Contract 2024 Specification paras 7.50–7.52.
120 Standard Civil Contract 2 Specification para 7.9.

under one fee and if a CCMS case then the certificates will need to be linked.

15.176 Where you act for a client whose status changes during the proceedings, you must claim the higher fee available. For example, if you act for a grandparent who loses parental responsibility and continues as a joined party, the standard fee (and the relevant escape threshold) for a parent will apply.

Regions

Regional Fee	LAA Regional Office of Provider
North	North Western Region (Manchester)
	North Eastern Region (Newcastle)
	Yorkshire & Humberside Region (Leeds)
	Merseyside Region (Liverpool)
Midlands	West Midlands Region (Birmingham)
	East Midlands Region (Nottingham)
	Eastern Region (Cambridge)
South (including London)	South Eastern Region (Reading) / London Region (London)
	South Western Region (Bristol)
Wales	Wales Region (Cardiff)

15.177 Remember that the region is dictated by the location of the provider's address on the legal aid certificate. As with all costs, it is the retainer that is key, so this is a matter decided by where the client instructs the solicitor.

Family – private law fee scheme

15.178 The Higher Standard Fee Scheme, also known as the Private Family Law Representation Scheme (PFLRS), divides private family law into three aspects: (a) domestic abuse; (b) children; and (c) finance. The aspects will be funded under one certificate per client (except child abduction proceedings, which cannot cover any other proceedings[121]).

15.179 There are two levels under the Higher Standard Fee Scheme:
- level 4 – Family Help (Higher); and
- level 5 – Legal Representation.

---

121 Standard Civil Contract 2024 Specification para 7.75.

Pre-LASPO these were levels 3 and 4 (Help with Family Mediation was added as level 3) and are still commonly referred to as such and are still labelled as these on the CCMS Billing interface. Family Help (Higher) is provided in children and finance for all work excluding preparation for and representation at final hearing (any hearing listed to make a final determination). Legal Representation is provided for work up to and including final hearing and is issued from the outset on domestic abuse, although upon initial grant the scope may be limited to the first interim hearing.

15.180 The Higher Standard Fee is applied by reference to the level of judge that the first instance proceedings conclude before (or if you cease to provide the service before conclusion then the relevant level of judge hearing the case at that time),[122] and whether the solicitor's office is located within a London borough.

15.181 The escape threshold for the Higher Standard Fee Scheme is that profit costs calculated on an hourly rate basis must exceed three times the aggregate fixed fee (combined standard fees under a single aspect) but excluding the settlement fee under the finance aspect. Work cannot be combined to escape different aspects. For example, if three times the domestic abuse fee is £1,521 but the domestic abuse work is £500 below this, and three times the children fee is £1,176 and the children work is £501 above this, you cannot combine the two to escape both fees, but rather you must claim the domestic abuse fee and only claim the children work at hourly rates. As above, enhancements (including guaranteed minimum for panel members) cannot be included to escape the fee, only once 'base costs' have escaped can you add the percentage enhancement. Advocacy is also excluded when calculating the escape threshold.

15.182 There are various proceedings excluded from the Higher Standard Fee Scheme,[123] so they are always claimed at hourly rate. The exclusions are identical to those for FAS:

- child abduction proceedings;
- proceedings under the Inheritance (Provision for Family and Dependants) Act 1975;
- proceedings under the Trusts of Land and Appointment of Trustees Act 1996;
- proceedings in which you provide separate representation of a child in proceedings that are neither Specified Proceedings (as

---

122 Standard Civil Contract 2024 Specification para 7.9.
123 Standard Civil Contract 2024 Specification para 7.74.

defined in Children Act 1989 s41(6)) nor proceedings which are being heard together with Specified Proceedings;
- applications for forced marriage protection orders under the Forced Marriage (Civil Protection) Act 2007;
- defended proceedings for divorce, judicial separation, dissolution of a civil partnership or the legal separation of civil partners;
- nullity proceedings (including proceedings for annulment of a civil partnership);
- proceedings under the inherent jurisdiction of the High Court in relation to children;
- applications for parental orders under the Human Fertilisation and Embryology Act 2008; and
- applications in relation to female genital mutilation protection orders under the Female Genital Mutilation Act 2003.

15.183 Upon settling ongoing litigation with the National Centre for Domestic Violence (NCDV) in December 2018, the LAA has stated that it will not pay providers for the £178.50 plus VAT fee charged by NCDV to produce a bundle of documents, including witness statements and draft order. The LAA also reminded providers that they are prohibited from paying referral fees.

Family – public and private law standard fee schemes: enhancement of hourly rates

15.184 A discretionary enhancement can be claimed on family cases where hourly rates are claimable rather than a fixed fee, as detailed above in 'Enhanced rates'.

15.185 In family cases (whether paid under family or non-family remuneration rates), there is a guaranteed minimum enhancement of 15 per cent for all work done (including routine items, travel and waiting) by a member of the following panels:[124]
- Resolution Accredited Specialist Panel;
- the Law Society's Children Panel;* and
- the Law Society Family Law Panel Advanced.

* Under previous contracts, a certificate had to include proceedings relating to children in order for a Children Panel member to qualify for the 15 per cent minimum, but this requirement was removed from the 2018 Contract onwards.

15.186 Where a discretionary higher amount is sought, the 15 per cent minimum cannot be claimed in addition to that amount, but rather

124 Standard Civil Contract 2024 Specification para 7.23.

forms part of it.[125] So, care should be taken when wording the justification in order to avoid any implication of the former, for which the LAA finds the claim falls outside the contractual terms and consequently the court's discretion where the court has carried out the assessment.

Family – public and private law standard fee schemes: client transfers

15.187 If your fees on an hourly rates basis (excluding enhancement) are equal to or greater than the standard fee, you claim the standard fee.[126] If your fees on an hourly rates basis are less than the standard fee, you claim half the standard fee. The only exception to this is where you continue to act for one or more clients is a private family law matter, then every provider can claim the full standard fee(s) regardless. You cannot combine the amount of your actual costs with those of the other provider to escape the standard fee.

15.188 Where all clients transfer instructions to you from another provider:
- where your own actual costs are **less** than the full standard fee(s), you will claim **half** of the standard fee; and
- where your own actual costs are **equal to or greater** than the full standard fee(s), you will claim the **full** standard fee(s), or hourly rates if your own actual costs reach the escape threshold.

15.189 Where multiple clients instruct you in a private family law case and one or more transfers, and one or more remains:
- One client transfers to another solicitor, and one client remains:
  – first provider gets a full relevant fee unless escapes; and
  – subsequent provider(s) gets a full relevant fee unless escapes (but this may only be a level 5 fee if the case has already moved to level 5, **even** if there is cover for level 4 on the certificate).

15.190 Where multiple clients instruct in section 31 care proceedings and one or more transfers and one or more remains:
- first provider gets a full standard fee (which is 2+ fee if more than one client was represented at one or more hearings) unless escapes; and
- subsequent provider(s) gets relevant fee, which will be half the fee if actual costs are less than the fee, the full fee if actual costs are

---

125 Costs Assessment Guidance para 12.23.
126 Standard Civil Contract 2024 Specification paras 7.43 and 7.96.

equal to or greater than the full standard fee, or hourly rates if the actual costs reach the escape threshold.

Family – public and private law standard fee schemes: advocacy

15.191 The standard fees for both private and public law cases do not include advocacy. The LAA defines 'advocacy' to include not only appearances as advocate before the court, but also any associated travel and waiting time and attendance as advocate at advocates' meetings in public law matters, as well as preparation for advocacy. The exception to this is preparation by a provider when the hearing does not go ahead (so no FAS can be claimed), which can then be claimed under the standard fee. Time spent instructing counsel is part of the standard fee too.[127]

15.192 See chapter 19 for information on FAS.

Family – Very High Cost Cases

15.193 A VHCC is a case where total costs and disbursements are expected to be over £25,000 (not including VAT) and/or one defined as 'Special Case Work'[128] requiring an ICC. If you represent more than one party and the combined costs limitations are more than £25,000 the LAA will restrict payment to £25,000 unless the case has been registered as a VHCC. However, you need to be aware of the financial limitation (costs limit) when you apply for a case contract (whichever type), because the LAA will not increase it pending approval of the case as exceptional and/or agreement of the case plan/Care Case Fee Scheme (CCFS) form, and if the case is at hourly rates ('Fully costed case plan') then your costs up to the date of registration of the VHCC ('pre-contract costs') will be limited to the costs limit. There is a legislated list of circumstances when an application/amendment for civil legal services will be treated by the LAA as an application for special case work, including appeals to the Supreme Court.[129]

15.194 All single-advocate Children Act 1989 s31 care cases registered from 1 October 2015 are paid under the CCFS (previously known as the Events model). This is unless you can show you would be paid at least 30 per cent more by claiming hourly rates (including enhancements) with a fully costed case plan; this is referred to as an 'exceptional case' but should not be confused with a case under ECF (see

---

127 Standard Civil Contract 2024 Specification paras 7.45 and 7.78.
128 Civil Legal Aid (Procedure) Regulations 2012 Part 6 (regs 54–59).
129 Civil Legal Aid (Procedure) Regulations 2012 reg 54(3).

above). The CCFS model is used in section 31 care cases to avoid multiple revisions to detailed case plans. You can also request your non-section 31 VHCC be paid under CCFS if it follows the Public Law Outline or is being managed in a similar way. If the case concludes before a High Court-level judge, then all events will change to High Court events, and vice versa if a case concludes before a judge of a lower level. Costs incurred when a case temporarily escalates (ie for an appeal hearing) are paid at hourly rates rather than events. CCFS is a form of graduated/fixed fee, dependent on the number of hearing days and other events. The event fees are based on detailed analysis of the average costs and hours in these types of expensive/complex cases.

15.195 There is a separate CCFS for cases using two counsel/advocates or leading counsel, which is similar to the One Advocate Scheme. Two Counsel CCFS is not mandatory if a two-counsel case becomes high cost, and you can choose to be paid under a fully costed case plan instead, but it must be submitted within 20 working days otherwise the CCFS Two Counsel model will apply regardless. Upon grant of prior authority for KC or two counsel, the LAA assumes that the case will exceed £25,000 and will be subject a VHCC contract unless the provider confirms otherwise. One Advocate (aka Single Counsel) CCFS was calculated using FAS. The Two Counsel CCFS was calculated using the FGFS. The slight differences between how events are triggered on them are detailed below. See chapter 19 for more information about payment for advocacy in family VHCC cases.

15.196 VHCC Contracts are composed of the ICC, ICC Specification, and Contract Guides, which are labelled as Information Packs and detail the specific terms of the various schemes.

15.197 A fixed fee is paid to you for each event (eg hearing day or advocates' meeting) based on the predicted case timetable. As the case progresses, revised CCFS forms are submitted for agreement if the case timetable is increased and/or further disbursements are required. At the end of the case, the final costs are adjusted to reflect the final actual timetable. Event fees are paid to counsel only if the main hearing (including split hearings) is listed for more than 10 days, otherwise they are paid under FAS on Single Counsel or FGFS on Two Counsel.

15.198 There are slight differences between the Single Counsel and Two Counsel models, which can become confusing when alternating between them on different cases:

Event fee	Single Counsel case	Two Counsel case
Hearing day event fee for litigator solicitor	Event fee as shown in the fees matrix.	Only the event fee as shown in the fees matrix **if** the solicitor attends court with the advocate. Otherwise, £900 a day (section 8 of the Information Pack).
Substantive conferences with the client	Two event fees available, and then only to the attending advocate, but specific authorisation can be sought for more.	Two event fees available, and then only to the attending advocate, but a further two event fees are available on split hearings at welfare/disposal stage.
Advocates' meetings	Available for every advocates' meeting ordered in advance by the court, but they must be evidenced with an order or judicial email.	Two event fees available, even when the court orders more, unless, like conferences, there is split hearing and then a further two are available at welfare/disposal stage. Although not stated in the Information Pack, the LAA asserts that an event fee is only payable to the litigator if they attend with or in place of the advocate.
Judge's reading day	Only when the advocate is on standby and then called to court. Only then will this count towards a main hearing that exceeds 10 days, **unless** in between a group of days that the advocate is ordered to attend court, for example, not a Monday morning.	Only when the advocate is on standby and then called to court. Only then will this count towards a main hearing that exceeds 10 days.
Written submissions	Only if the judge sets aside a day, and only to the individual advocate preparing the submissions. Will not count towards the 10-day threshold.	Only if the judge sets aside a day, and only to the individual advocate preparing the submissions. The day set aside must be on a hearing exceeding 10 days.

15.199 Acceptance of retrospective recording of advocates' meetings in orders, as provided under remote hearings guidance issued during the Covid-19 lockdown, does not extend to events. So, while counsel will be paid a FAS fee on a single counsel case for such an advocates' meeting, the litigator will not be paid the significantly higher event fee. If counsel is on events then they too will be paid nothing.

15.200 The information packs and case plans for CCFS were revised on 3 June 2019. At the same time, in response to concerns raised by the

Family Law Bar Association (FLBA) regarding large amounts of outstanding fees due to counsel under section 31 VHCCs, an automatic limit of £32,500 for all CCFS cases (regardless of when they were registered) was introduced, and this was later extended to £60,000 for Two Counsel CCFS cases. Upon registration of the section 31 case (or other case deemed by LAA as suitable for CCFS), rather than an interim case plan being prepared, a generic VHCC contract and counsel's acceptance form are downloaded and populated with case details by the provider, signed and uploaded to the Case Plan notification thread on CCMS (see para 15.202 below). An application to increase the case plan to £32,500/£60,000 can then be immediately submitted and will be authorised accordingly. You do not have to submit a case plan under CCFS within the normal four weeks of registration, and you can wait up until three months after the case has concluded to submit your CCFS form. However, your automatic costs limit of £32,500/£60,000 will remain, restricting what you can claim on account and fees that counsel can submit if you exceed it. If you submit a CCFS form before the case has concluded, the 'FAST' procedure for an interim case plan will apply and you should not have to provide all of the supporting documentation at this point. However, a final case plan with supporting documentation will still need to be provided and agreed before a final claim can be made.

15.201 There are different fees available if you are instructing counsel or doing the advocacy yourself. If you are seeking to agree a Single Advocate section 31 case be paid outside CCFS, there are strict deadlines to submit a fully costed case plan and final claim for pre-contract costs.

15.202 If the case is on CCMS, then the case plan and contract will be agreed and uploaded on a case notification thread labelled 'Case Plan'. Previous providers can agree their case plan independently and this will be dealt with through a Case Plan thread activated under the case notifications on their CCMS account. Their final bill will also be submitted via the Billing thread on their CCMS account. However, CCFS was revised before functions on CCMS were considered and communication and coordination are needed between the providers. The final provider must apply on CCMS to increase the costs limit once the case plan is agreed (CCMS will not allow the LAA to increase the limit without this) and allocate costs for previous providers and their counsel once the costs limitation is increased. This can be a staggered process because the case plans for each provider will not be agreed at exactly the same time – no established procedure for this has been provided by the LAA.

15.203 POAs can be made for all costs and counsels' fees once a VHCC contract is signed and lodged with the LAA, and further POAs for profit costs and counsels' fees can be made every six months or if six events have occurred since the last POA was paid.[130] 100 per cent POAs will be paid on events but on CCMS cases providers must use the 'Non Expert Disbursement' POA type rather than profit costs[131] and counsel must email a CIV POA1 form to: counsel_events_POA@legalaid.gsi.gov.uk, otherwise only the usual 80 per cent of the claim will paid. Further, the LAA must flag it properly on CCMS.

15.204 The CCFS form includes a final claim page to be added and submitted as a final claim for non-CCMS cases. For CCMS cases, a separate electronic claim must be submitted for the final claim. A quick guide 'High Cost Billing' is found on the Civil section of the LAA's training and support website. If there is more than one provider, interim bills for the previous providers are submitted, then the outcomes are reported by the final provider afterwards and their claim is submitted as the final bill.

15.205 The benefit of the CCFS is that it avoids multiple revisions to detailed case plans, which is popular with practitioners and is often (but not always) considered preferable to an individually agreed case plan. Unlike certificates, you only produce and agree a single case plan (whether CCFS or fully costed) per case, not per client. This is revised as the case changes, in the usual way. The LAA recommends that you consider registration when your fees reach £12,000. It is also worth considering whether to register a case at an earlier stage; but you need to be confident that there are enough 'events' to show costs will exceed £25,000. If it is not clear it will be a VHCC case, the LAA will reject the application as premature.

15.206 All VHCCs are assessed by the LAA. You can find out more information at: www.gov.uk/guidance/legal-aid-high-cost-cases.

Immigration and asylum

Introduction

15.207 This section describes payment for Legal Help and Controlled Legal Representation (CLR) cases. For licensed work in the Immigration category, see the general principles above. Legal representation of a

---

130 CCFS Information Packs section 17 (Interim Payments).
131 CCMS Quick Guide 'Claiming 100% Payment on Account for the Very High Cost Care Case Fee Scheme'.

client in any application (including for permission) to the Upper Tribunal for judicial review or appeal, either to the Court of Appeal or Supreme Court, is paid for as licensed work and cannot be carried out under controlled work.[132]

15.208 Immigration and asylum controlled work is remunerated according to either standard fees or hourly rates, as set out in the relevant regulations. However, in 2020 HMCTS introduced an 'online procedure', which enabled parties to deal with appeals online. If a case is lodged through the online procedure, CLR matters are renumerated depending on when CLR was granted.[133] If granted on or before 6 October 2020, you may elect either one of two options (ie Standard Fee Stage 2(c) or Online Procedure Hourly Rates, Additional Payments for Advocacy Services[134] available in both options). If granted between 7 October 2020 and 31 March 2023, you may only claim Online Procedure Hourly Rates and Additional Payments for Advocacy Services.[135] If granted on or after 1 April 2023, it will depend on whether there has been a substantive hearing (ie Standard Fee Stage 2(d) if not, and Standard Fee Stage 2(e) if there has).

Standard Fee cases

15.209 Work at both the Legal Help and CLR stages can claim a standard fee.[136] The fee for Stage 2(a) is applicable where there has **not** been a substantive hearing, where the Online Procedure was not used, and CLR was granted on or before 31 March 2023. The fee for Stage 2(b) is applicable where there **has** been a substantive hearing. Claims can be made for either Stage 2(a) or 2(b), not for both,[137] and the fee for Stage 2(b) is only claimable where there was attendance at the hearing.[138]

15.210 There is also a standard fee for Stage 2(c), where the Online Procedure was used and CLR was granted on or before 6 October

---

132 Standard Civil Contract 2024 Specification para 8.70.
133 Standard Civil Contract 2024 Specification para 8.86.
134 These would be claimed in accordance with the fees in table 4(c) in Schedule 1 to the Civil Legal Aid (Remuneration) Regulations 2013.
135 These would be claimed in accordance with the fees in table 4(ca) in Schedule 1 to the Civil Legal Aid (Remuneration) Regulations 2013.
136 Standard Civil Contract 2024 Specification para 8.72.
137 Standard Civil Contract 2024 Specification para 8.84.
138 Standard Civil Contract 2024 Specification para 8.85.

2020.[139] Claims cannot be made for Stage 2(c) and for Stage 2(a) or Stage 2(b) in relation to the same matter.[140]

15.211 The scope of the Standard Fee Scheme is not defined in the contract, except by exclusion. The Specification simply lists hourly rates cases, all others – when in scope under LASPO as detailed in chapter 9 – being standard fee cases.[141] Therefore, the standard fee applies to all cases other than:

a) Asylum Matters opened under this Contract which relate to an Asylum application (including 'NAM' or 'Legacy'), made to the UK Border Agency (UKBA) prior to 1 October 2007;
b) a fresh claim/further application for Asylum opened under this Contract where the original Asylum application was lodged, whether concluded or not, prior to 1 October 2007;
c) advice in relation to the merits of lodging an application for permission to appeal to the Upper Tribunal (where advice has not been received under Stage 2 of the Standard Fee);
d) Bail applications;
e) advice and applying for a determination that a client qualifies for civil legal services provided as Licensed Work, including complying with any pre-action protocol;
f) initial advice in relation to an Asylum application prior to claiming Asylum at the Asylum Screening Unit where you then cease to be instructed. This will also apply where the client returns after attendance at the Asylum Screening Unit but where it is confirmed that the Client will be dispersed and will not continue to instruct you;
g) Escape Fee Cases under the Standard Fee;
h) advice in relation to a client who is an unaccompanied asylum-seeking child (UASC);
i) cases remitted, reviewed or referred from the Court of Appeal or the Upper Tribunal to the First Tier Tribunal;
j) where you hold a Schedule authorisation any Matters opened under the Detained Duty Advice Scheme or for a Detained Fast Track or a DAC Scheme Client;
k) advice in relation to Terrorism Prevention and Investigation Measures Orders;
l) applying for a determination that an individual qualifies for civil legal services provided as Licensed Work in relation to Terrorism Prevention and Investigation Measures Orders; and

---

139 Standard Civil Contract 2024 Specification para 8.72. See also Civil Legal Aid (Remuneration) (Amendment) (No 2) (Coronavirus) Regulations 2020 reg 4, dealing with the transitional provision.
140 Standard Civil Contract 2024 Specification para 8.86.
141 Standard Civil Contract 2024 Specification para 8.101.

m) applying for a determination that an individual qualifies for civil legal services provided as Licensed Work in relation to the Special Immigration Appeals Commission.
n) immigration advice in relation to a client who is a Separated Child; and
o) CLR (excluding Online Procedure Advocacy Services) where:
   i) CLR was granted on or before 6 October 2020 and you have not elected to claim a Stage 2(c) Standard Fee; or
   ii) CLR was granted between 7 October 2020 and 31 March 2023;
p) where you provide 30 minutes advice to a Client at a prison without reference to the Client's financial eligibility;
(q) advice on an application to rebut Group 2 Refugee status;
(r) advice in relation to Age Assessment Appeals;
(s) up to 7 hours advice to a Client in receipt of a PRN;
(t) any follow-on work that is conducted for a Client after receiving advice in relation to receipt of a PRN; and
(u) Illegal Migration Act Matters.

15.212 Exceptional fee cases are paid at hourly rates rather than through the Standard Fee Scheme. However, in the Immigration and Asylum category, providers must make an application for an exceptional fee payment, which can only be made by those with a schedule authorisation in this category,[142] unless the case satisfies the effective administration of justice test.[143]

Immigration and asylum fee stages

15.213 Fees are split into Stages 1, 2(a), 2(b), 2(c), 2(d) and 2(e). While different fees apply at each stage in asylum matters and in immigration (non-asylum) matters, the stages are the same for both. Currently, the standard fees for Stages 1, 2(a) and 2(b) in asylum matters are £413, £227 and £567, respectively.[144] The standard fee for Stage 2(c) is £627.[145] The standard fees for Stages 1, 2(a) and 2(b) in immigration (non-asylum) matters are £234, £227 and £454, respectively. The standard fee for Stage 2(c) is £527.

---

142 Standard Civil Contract 2024 Specification para 8.12.
143 Civil Legal Aid (Procedure) Regulations 2012 reg 31(5).
144 Civil Legal Aid (Remuneration) Regulations 2013 Sch 1 table 4(a).
145 Civil Legal Aid (Remuneration) Regulations 2013 Sch 1 table 4(a). Note that the column for Stage 2c (ie Online Procedure CLR) was removed by virtue of the Civil Legal Aid (Remuneration) (Amendment) (No 2) (Coronavirus) Regulations 2020, but in substance continues to apply by virtue of reg 4.

15.214 Stage 1 covers the Legal Help stage of the case, and ends when CLR is granted or refused, or when the matter ends, whichever is earlier.[146]

15.215 Stages 2(a) and 2(b) cover the CLR phase of the matter. CLR standard fees for matters that did not use the Online Procedure are split into two sub-stages. Depending on the point at which the matter ends, either the fee for Stage 2(a) or Stage 2(b) (but not both) will be payable. The Stage 2(a) fee will be payable where the case does not proceed to – or, at least, representation is not provided at – a substantive hearing.[147] Stage 2(b) is payable where the case does proceed to a substantive hearing.[148] As noted above, Stage 2(c) concerns matters pursued through the Online Procedure where CLR was granted prior to 7 October 2020.[149]

15.216 Stage 2 will end at the point that a determination is made whether the client qualifies for licensed work in relation to the submission of an application for permission to appeal to the Upper Tribunal or where the matter otherwise ends, whichever is earlier.[150] As detailed in point e) in para 16.210 above, advice on and applying for a determination that a client qualifies for licensed work is paid at hourly rates.

15.217 See the Standard Civil Contract 2024 Specification paras 8.73–8.81 for full definitions of each stage and examples of what work is included.

15.218 For all matters, a controlled work claim (including additional payments if incurred) must be made within six months of the end of both Stage 1 and Stage 2, as well as after all submissions have been made and a client has been interviewed, in cases when an asylum application has been lodged.[151]

Immigration and asylum – additional payments

15.219 Where applicable, Immigration and Asylum Outline Procedure Advocacy Services Standard Fees are payable at the end of Stage 2, in addition to the appropriate standard fee, for each relevant attendance:[152]

---

146 Standard Civil Contract 2024 Specification para 8.74.
147 Standard Civil Contract 2024 Specification para 8.79.
148 Standard Civil Contract 2024 Specification para 8.80.
149 Standard Civil Contract 2024 Specification para 8.72.
150 Standard Civil Contract 2024 Specification para 8.82.
151 Standard Civil Contract 2024 Specification para 8.139.
152 Civil Legal Aid (Remuneration) Regulations 2013 Sch 1 table 4(ca).

- at an in-person (£166) and telephone (£90) case management review hearing;
- advocacy services at a substantive First-tier Tribunal hearing (£302 for asylum, £237 for immigration); and
- advocacy services for an additional day for a substantive hearing, including when it has been either part heard or re-listed (£161 for both asylum and immigration).

Immigration and asylum – counsel

15.220 As listed above, specific CLR work – ie where granted on or before 6 October 2020 without a claim of a Stage 2(c) Standard Fee, or where CLR was granted between 7 October 2020 and 31 March 2023 – is payable at hourly rates,[153] set by the Civil Legal Aid (Remuneration) Regulations 2013,[154] which are payable at the end of CLR. Preparation, attendance and advocacy are charged at £51.62 per hour for the London rate and £47.30 per hour for the non-London rate. Travel and waiting time are charged at £27.27 and £26.51 per hour, respectively.

15.221 When claiming for advocacy work, it should be noted that advocacy fees are payable regardless of whether the relevant advocacy services are carried out by counsel and whether remotely or in person. However, only one advocacy fee for a substantive hearing in the First-tier Tribunal may be claimed per matter; if such a hearing goes into a second day, either part heard or re-listed, an additional day's substantive hearing fee may be claimed for the second and each subsequent day.[155]

Immigration and asylum – disbursements

15.222 All (reasonably incurred) disbursements are payable in addition to the standard fee, subject to the relevant disbursement limits. Disbursements at the Legal Help stage should not exceed £400 and at the CLR stage should not exceed £600.[156] However, disbursement limits cannot be amended retrospectively.[157]

---

153 Standard Civil Contract 2024 Specification para 8.101(o).
154 Schedule 1 table 7(d).
155 Standard Civil Contract 2024 Specification para 8.87.
156 Standard Civil Contract 2024 Specification para 8.88.
157 Standard Civil Contract 2024 Specification para 8.90.

Getting paid for civil and family work 459

15.223 If the case is payable at hourly rates, then, at the Legal Help stage the costs limit, inclusive of disbursements, is £100 where you provide initial advice and the client either ceases to instruct you or does not make an application. The rate is £500 for immigration matters and £800 for asylum matters (where it has progressed beyond initial advice).[158]

15.224 At the CLR stage, costs and disbursements together should not exceed £1,600 (asylum), £1,200 (immigration) or £500 (bail only).[159] These limits could also be extended by submitting the relevant extension request form to the LAA before incurring the costs.[160] However, the costs of waiting time where there is a significant delay on the day of a hearing, which is no fault of yours or your client, provided you apply for an extension to the cost limit as soon as practicable thereafter, can be the basis for retrospective amendment of the cost and disbursement limits.[161]

15.225 A claim can be made in respect of unpaid disbursements. This claim can be made if at least three months have elapsed since the start of the matter and, if you have become entitled to make a controlled work claim or have previously applied for payment under this provision, at least three months have elapsed since that entitlement arose or application was made.[162]

Immigration and asylum – escape fee cases

15.226 Cases may escape the Standard Fee Scheme and become payable solely by hourly rates. This will occur when a case, following the conclusion of Stage 2 or when the matter ends, whichever is earlier, the value of the controlled work, when calculated as if it were paid at the appropriate hourly rate, is three times the applicable standard fee for the matter – where the relevant Legal Help form was signed, or CLR was granted, on or before 31 March 2023 – or two times the applicable standard fee for the matter – where the relevant Legal Help form was signed, or CLR was granted, on or after 1 April 2023.[163]

---

158 Standard Civil Contract 2024 Specification para 8.106.
159 Standard Civil Contract 2024 Specification para 8.112.
160 See: www.gov.uk/government/publications/cw3-extension-of-upper-cost-limit-in-controlled-work-cases.
161 Standard Civil Contract 2024 Specification para 8.114.
162 Standard Civil Contract 2024 Specification para 8.141.
163 Standard Civil Contract 2024 Specification para 8.98.

15.227 The calculation for determining whether escape fee payments can be made is relatively complicated. You must:[164]
1) identify the total hours spent on the matter up to the end of Stage 2 or when the matter concludes (whichever is earlier), including any advocacy services but excluding services which are outside the standard fee and are always payable at hourly rates;
2) calculate the total costs for the hours spent on such services using the hourly rates set out in the Civil Legal Aid (Remuneration) Regulations 2013 to determine the 'gross total' (Total A);
3) from Total A, deduct all the claims for additional payments paid or payable, to determine the 'reduced total' (Total B);
4) identify the standard fees claimable for the matter (note: only one standard fee is payable at each stage); add these standard fees together and multiply that total by three to determine the 'escape threshold' (Total C); then
5) if Total B exceeds Total C the matter has escaped the Standard Fee Scheme and is therefore an escape fee case payable at hourly rates.

15.228 Claims for escape fee cases are subject to an individual cost assessment by the LAA.[165] The claim must be submitted on an EC-Claim 1 IMM form.[166]

Immigration and asylum – hourly rates cases

15.229 All cases excluded from the Standard Fee Scheme (see above) are payable by hourly rates.

15.230 In hourly rates cases (except those that become so by escaping from the Standard Fee Scheme), there are costs limitations which may be extended on application to the LAA.

15.231 For Legal Help, the limit (excluding VAT and disbursements) is £800 in asylum cases and £500 in (non-asylum) immigration cases.[167]

15.232 For CLR, the limit (excluding VAT, but including disbursements and counsel) is £1,600 for asylum cases, £1,200 for (non-asylum) immigration cases and £500 for stand-alone bail applications (where

---

164 Standard Civil Contract 2024 Specification para 8.99.
165 Standard Civil Contract 2024 Specification para 8.94.
166 See: www.gov.uk/government/publications/escape-fee-case-claim-forms. See Immigration section in *Escape Case Electronic Handbook* for guidance.
167 Standard Civil Contract 2024 Specification para 8.106.

a substantive appeal includes a bail application, bail is included in the £1,600/£1,200).[168]

15.233 Legal Help claims must be submitted within six months of submission of a fresh application for asylum (fresh claim cases only), or within six months of the Home Office decision (all other cases), and then within six months of the end of the case. CLR claims should be submitted within six months of the first tribunal decision, and then within six months of the end of the case.[169]

Upper Tribunal cases

15.234 Before any work in connection with applying for an appeal to the Upper Tribunal is carried out, a licensed work certificate must be in place. The costs of interpreters and experts are payable regardless of the outcome of the application.[170] However, the costs of solicitor and counsel are only payable if permission is granted.[171]

15.235 Payment rates will be at the rates set out in the regulations for work in the First-tier Tribunal. Work carried out on the initial application to the First-tier Tribunal for permission to appeal to the Upper Tribunal will be paid at the hourly rates (specified in the relevant regulations) for licensed work in the First-tier Tribunal. However, work carried out on a direct application to the Upper Tribunal for permission to appeal and all subsequent work in that forum will be paid at the hourly rates (specified in the relevant regulations for licensed work in the Higher Courts).[172]

15.236 However, where the Home Office applies for permission to appeal, or the case is dealt with under the Detained Fast Track Scheme, you may claim costs under the contract.[173]

---

168 Standard Civil Contract 2024 Specification para 8.112.
169 Standard Civil Contract 2024 Specification para 8.139.
170 Standard Civil Contract 2024 Specification para 8.144.
171 Standard Civil Contract 2024 Specification para 8.142.
172 Standard Civil Contract 2024 Specification para 8.145. See also Civil Legal Aid (Remuneration) Regulations 2013 Schs 1 and 2.
173 Standard Civil Contract 2024 Specification para 8.143.

CHAPTER 16

Getting paid for criminal work

By Itpal Dhillon

16.1	Introduction
16.10	Remuneration Regulations
16.12	**Investigations class work**
16.12	Introduction
16.13	Police station telephone advice only
16.16	Free-standing advice and assistance
16.20	Police station attendance
16.24	**Payment rates and escape fee cases**
16.24	Overview
16.33	Pre-charge engagement
16.37	Advocacy assistance
16.38	**Proceedings class work**
16.38	Virtual court claims
16.39	Court duty claims
16.42	Representation orders in the magistrates' court
16.46	**Standard fees**
16.57	Counsel
16.59	Separate matters
16.62	Enhanced rates

continued

16.66	Representation orders – matters sent to the Crown Court for trial
16.69	Other contract work
16.77	**The claiming process**
16.82	**Crown Court – litigator fees**
16.94	Payments on account
16.99	Coronavirus provisions on hardship
16.100	**Crown Court – advocates' fees**
16.104	**Very High Cost Cases**
16.106	**Topping up criminal legal aid fees**

Key resources

Contract
- Draft Standard Crime Contract 2025
- Draft Standard Crime Specification 2025
- Standard Crime Contract 2022
- Standard Crime Specification 2022

Regulations
- Criminal Legal Aid (Remuneration) Regulations 2013
- Criminal Legal Aid (General) Regulations 2013
- Criminal Legal Aid (Determinations by a Court and Choice of Representative) Regulations 2013

Fees and costs
- Criminal Bills Assessment Manual
- Criminal Legal Aid (Remuneration) Regulations 2013
- Criminal Legal Aid (General) Regulations 2013

Key points to note
- The LAA's contract with eForms ended on 31 August 2024 and applications should now be made via 'Applying for criminal Legal Aid' on the LAA Portal.
- A police station bill can now be submitted to the LAA when it is unclear whether further work will be required and a minimum of one month has elapsed since the last work in the matter was undertaken. This includes where the client has been released under investigation or on pre-charge bail and it is unclear whether further work will be required. For the avoidance of doubt, where a client has an outstanding bail back, this will form part of the same matter as the original attendance.
- Several upper costs limits have been increased and the Regulations should be checked as to each amount where relevant.

Introduction

16.1 This chapter deals with billing and payment for criminal work. See appendix D for a summary of the Legal Aid Agency's (LAA's) *Criminal Bills Assessment Manual*,[1] in respect of the most common queries raised by caseworkers.

16.2 The LAA has also identified a number of regular issues that cause difficulty on audit. These are italicised in the text below. They are often raised long after the event, so good record-keeping on file is critical.

16.3 *There must be adequate attendance notes to show how time has been used with some precision as to the work carried out. An explanation should be recorded. If this is longer than might normally be expected (eg with clients with a disability) an explanation should be recorded. A lack of adequate notes can cause difficulties on audit when claiming higher standard fees in criminal and prison law cases.*

16.4 *No more can be earned, either as profit costs or as a disbursement, by using a fee earner from a more distant office, or by an agent or unassigned counsel, than would have been paid had the firm itself undertaken the work from its most local office. This is known by the LAA as the 'maximum fee principle'.*

16.5 *Where travel time is claimed, this must be recorded and justified as the contract limits the amount of travel in a number of circumstances. The use of a private car as opposed to public transport should be explained. The distance cannot exceed that from the provider's office or home, whichever is closer. Explanations should be given for all travel costs so that even if the time cannot be recovered, the justification for the distance is on file.*

16.6 Most criminal work is paid for through the monthly contract payment, the biggest exception being work done in the Crown Court.[2]

16.7 Thus, although contract cases are billed individually, they are not directly paid. Instead, each firm or office, generally has a fixed monthly payment set by the LAA. Each month, the firm submits bills which are offset against the payment, with the aim that bills and payments balance each other out over the course of the financial year. See chapter 23 for more information on this process (known as

---

1 Available at: www.gov.uk/guidance/funding-and-costs-assessment-for-civil-and-crime-matters.
2 Standard Crime Contracts 2022 and 2025 Standard Terms para 14.8; Specification 2022 paras 5.20 and 5.25 and Specification 2025 paras 5.17 and 5.23 (all available at: www.gov.uk/government/publications/standard-crime-contract-2022).

reconciliation), and on the management of criminal contracts generally. Crown Court bills in cases funded by representation orders are individually paid.[3]

16.8 This chapter does not deal with contract management (which is covered in Part C), but with the rules and processes for billing individual cases. For information about conducting criminal cases, see chapter 14.

16.9 This is of necessity a brief overview of a complex subject. The detail is of significance and a full understanding will reduce the number of issues on audit.

Remuneration Regulations

16.10 Remuneration rates are set out in the Criminal Legal Aid (Remuneration) Regulations 2013. These have been amended as follows:

- Criminal Legal Aid (General) (Amendment) Regulations 2013 – changed the scope of prison law;
- Criminal Legal Aid (Remuneration) (Amendment) Regulations 2013 – codified Very High Cost Case (VHCC) rates and reduced expert fees for cases started on or after 2 December 2013;
- Criminal Legal Aid (Remuneration) (Amendment) Regulations 2014 – reduced most rates (the main exception being Advocates' Graduated Fee Scheme (AGFS) rates) by 8.75 per cent from 20 March 2014;
- Criminal Legal Aid (Remuneration) (Amendment) (No 2) Regulations 2014 – introduced additional interim payments and removed some cases from fixed fees;
- Civil and Criminal Legal Aid (Remuneration) (Amendment) Regulations 2015 – prescribed rates for civil injunctions under the Anti-social Behaviour, Crime and Policing Act 2014;
- Criminal Legal Aid (Remuneration) (Amendment) Regulations 2015 – prescribed for payments to be made to trial rather than to instructed advocates;
- Criminal Legal Aid (Remuneration etc) (Amendment) Regulations 2015 – imposed a (in the result time limited) further 8.75 per cent cut (again except in AGFS cases) from 1 July 2015 and made amendments to the fee structures applying from 11 January 2016;

---

3 Standard Crime Contract 2022 Specification para 5.25 and Standard Crime Contract 2025 Specification para 5.23.

- Civil and Criminal Legal Aid (Amendment) Regulations 2015 – further provisions on civil injunctions;
- Civil and Criminal Legal Aid (Amendment) (No 2) Regulations 2015 – amended definitions;
- Criminal Legal Aid (Remuneration etc) (Amendment) (No 2) Regulations 2015 – delayed the effect of the Criminal Legal Aid (Remuneration etc) (Amendment) Regulations 2015 above, postponing the second 8.75 per cent fee cut;
- Criminal Legal Aid (Remuneration) (Amendment) Regulations 2016 – effectively repealed the Criminal Legal Aid (Remuneration etc) (Amendment) Regulations 2015;
- Criminal Legal Aid (Standard Crime Contract) (Amendment) Regulations 2017 – extended advice and assistance and advocacy assistance to 'magistrates' court applications relating to police bail' as opposed to bail conditions from 1 April 2017;
- Criminal Legal Aid (Amendment) Regulations 2017 – re-introduced some prison law to scope and prescribe the payment rates;
- Criminal Legal Aid (Remuneration) (Amendment) Regulations 2018 – amended the fees payable under the AGFS; and Criminal Legal Aid (Remuneration) (Amendment) (No 2) Regulations 2018 – further amended the fees payable under the AGFS;
- Criminal Legal Aid (Coronavirus, Remuneration) (Amendment) Regulations 2020 – amended criteria for hardship payments in light of the Covid-19 pandemic;
- Criminal Legal Aid (Remuneration) (Amendment) Regulations 2020 – introduced additional payments for consideration of unused material under the Litigators' Graduated Fee Scheme (LGFS) and AGFS; introduced a sending fee for cases sent to the Crown Court and amended fees payable under the AGFS;
- Criminal Legal Aid (Remuneration) (Amendment) Regulations 2021 – amended the fees payable under LGFS and AGFS;
- Criminal Legal Aid (Remuneration) (Amendment) (No 2) Regulations 2021 – introduced additional payments for pre-charge engagement;
- Criminal Legal Aid (Remuneration) (Amendment) Regulations 2022 – amended various fees payable;
- Criminal Legal Aid (Remuneration) (Amendment) (Amendment) Regulations 2022 – increased various fees within the Regulations by 15 per cent;
- Criminal Legal Aid (Remuneration) (Amendment) (Amendment) (No 2) Regulations 2022 – amended the fees payable under the LGFS and AGFS;

Getting paid for criminal work

- Criminal Legal Aid (Remuneration) (Amendment) (No 2) Regulations 2022 – amended the fees payable under the LGFS and AGFS;
- Criminal Legal Aid (Remuneration) (Amendment) Regulations 2023 – introduced additional payment to a trial advocate in a case where a special measures direction provides for a video recording to be admitted under section 28 of the Youth Justice and Criminal Evidence Act 1999;
- Criminal Legal Aid (Remuneration) (Amendment) (No 3) Regulations 2023 – revoked the Criminal Legal Aid (Remuneration) (Amendment) (No 2) Regulations 2023 and provided additional payments under the AGFS; and
- Criminal Legal Aid (Remuneration) (Amendment) (No 4) Regulations 2023 – amended fee payable under AGFS and police station work.

16.11 Audits suggest that firms are often not claiming the correct fees. It is not always easy to work out which rates apply to which cases. You should start with the main 2013 Regulations, and then check later Regulations to see whether there have been amendments relevant to your particular case. Unfortunately, no single consolidated set of rates exists. For cases where the unique file number (UFN) (for advice and assistance and advocacy assistance) or the date of the representation order (for representation cases) is on or after 19 October 2020, the rates, where set out in this edition, are correct at the time of writing.

Investigations class work

Introduction

16.12 A bill should be submitted when:
1) the criminal investigation has been concluded, either by way of the client being charged or reported for summons, or the matter has been disposed of in any other way;
2) it is known that no further work will be undertaken for the client in the same matter;
3) it is unclear whether further work will be required and a minimum of one month has elapsed since the last work in the matter was undertaken. This includes where the client has been released under investigation or on pre-charge bail and it is unclear whether

further work will be required. For the avoidance of doubt, where a client has an outstanding bail back this will form part of the same matter as the original attendance; or

4) post-charge work has been undertaken that is within the scope of this unit of work, and is not the subject of a claim under the representations unit of work.

One bill should be submitted for all work done in the class (subject to the exceptions set out below).

Police station telephone advice only

16.13 Where a client is at the police station and you provide telephone advice but do not attend, you can claim the telephone advice fee.[4]

16.14 The fee is not claimable in a case in which Criminal Defence Direct were involved,[5] and is triggered by a telephone call during which you speak to the client. Only one fee is payable per investigation.[6]

16.15 The value of the fee is set out in the Criminal Legal Aid (Remuneration) Regulations 2013, and is currently £31.74 (£33.00 for London firms). *This fee is deemed to be included in the fixed attendance fee if an attendance is made in the matter, and should not be claimed separately.*

Free-standing advice and assistance

16.16 In cases where you provide advice and assistance to a client outside the police station but do not attend the police station with the client, you can claim for the costs of the advice and assistance at the hourly rates set out in the contract and in addition to a telephone fee. *Where the case also involves attendance at the police station, the costs of advice and assistance are included within the police station fixed attendance fee and must not be claimed separately.*[7]

---

4 Standard Crime Contract 2022 Specification para 9.111 and Standard Crime Contract 2025 Specification para 9.107.
5 Standard Crime Contract 2022 Specification para 9.110 and Standard Crime Contract 2025 Specification para 9.106.
6 Standard Crime Contract 2022 Specification para 9.112 and Standard Crime Contract 2025 Specification para 9.106.
7 Standard Crime Contract 2022 Specification para 9.160 and Standard Crime Contract 2025 Specification para 9.156 (2022 and 2025 Specifications available at: www.gov.uk/government/publications/standard-crime-contract-2022 and www.gov.uk/government/publications/standard-crime-contract-2025).

16.17 A single claim for all work done (except pre-charge engagement or advocacy assistance, which should be claimed separately) in the investigations class should be submitted when:
- the investigation has concluded, whether by charge, summons, requisition or other disposal;
- it is known no further investigations work will be undertaken for the client;
- it is unclear whether further work will be required and a minimum of one month has elapsed since the last work in the matter was undertaken. This provision will not apply where a client has an outstanding bail back in the matter, unless it is known that further work will not be undertaken on that occasion; or
- post-charge work at the police station has been undertaken that is within the scope of this unit of work.[8]

16.18 Where you have acted for more than one client in the same investigation, you should make a separate claim for each client, apportioning the work between them if necessary.[9]

16.19 The hourly rates applicable to this work are set out in the Criminal Legal Aid (Remuneration) Regulations 2013. You should apply the rates to all work done, subject to any costs limit. The costs limit for advice and assistance is £314.81 to cover both profit costs and disbursements; this limit can be extended on application to the LAA.[10]

Police station attendance

16.20 All work done at the police station is subject to a fixed fee regime. The fee is triggered whenever there is attendance upon the client at the police station. However, in the 2022 Contract it does not include attendance for an ineffective bail to return if you did not check whether it would be effective prior to attending.[11]

16.21 Where triggered, the fee will cover all work done in the investigations class. Therefore, where, for example, you carry out free-standing

---

8 Standard Crime Contract 2022 Specification para 9.161 and Standard Crime Contract 2025 Specification para 9.157.
9 Standard Crime Contract 2022 Specification para 9.162 and Standard Crime Contract 2025 Specification para 9.158.
10 Standard Crime Contract 2022 Specification para 9.164 and Standard Crime Contract 2025 Specification para 9.160.
11 Standard Crime Contract 2022 Specification para 9.2 and Standard Crime Contract 2025 Specification para 9.89.

16.22 advice and assistance outside the police station for eligible clients (such as between bails to return) or have given telephone advice, that work will also be covered by the fixed attendance fee, until you reach the threshold fee for an escape fee claim to be made.

16.22 There is a separate fee for each duty scheme area, and the fees are set out in the Criminal Legal Aid (Remuneration) Regulations 2013. Only one fee is payable per client per matter (even if you attend the police station on more than one occasion).[12] Where, however, work is a genuinely separate matter, then a separate claim may be made if you attend the client at the police station on a separate occasion in relation to one of the matters after another has concluded. *It will be a separate matter if the client has genuinely separate legal problems requiring separate advice*[13] *on more than one occasion.* This test is carefully applied on audit. *A file note should be made setting out any justification for claiming more than one fixed fee.*[14] If, for example, the client is charged with one offence and you reasonably attend on the bail to return to the police station on another, separate fees should be claimed in relation to each offence.[15]

16.23 A separate Defence Solicitor Call Centre (DSCC) reference number must be obtained for each matter.

> **Case study**
>
> *I had a client who was arrested for theft and taken to the police station, where it was found he was also wanted for a separate incident of criminal damage, and he was further arrested for that. Is that one matter or two?*
>
> It depends on the outcome of the case. If he were charged with both offences at the same time, that would be one matter and one claim. This is because the two allegations required advice on one occasion only. However, if he were charged with theft and you reasonably attended on the bail to return on the criminal damage, that would constitute two matters since they require separate advice on more than one occasion.

---

12 Standard Crime Contract 2022 Specification para 9.86 and Standard Crime Contract 2025 Specification para 9.83.
13 Standard Crime Contract 2022 Specification para 9.80 and Standard Crime Contract 2025 Specification para 9.77.
14 Standard Crime Contracts 2017 and 2022 Specification para 9.80 and Standard Crime Contract 2025 Specification para 9.77.
15 Standard Crime Contracts 2017 and 2022 Specification para 9.82 and Standard Crime Contract 2025 Specification para 9.79.

Payment rates and escape fee cases[16]

Overview

16.24 Although police station work is payable by fixed fee, you should record all the time spent on the case and report the value of that time at the appropriate hourly rates to the LAA. The applicable rates are set out in the Criminal Legal Aid (Remuneration) Regulations 2013. Where the value of the case at hourly rates exceeds the escape fee threshold for the appropriate area, the case is deemed to be exceptional, and you can apply to the LAA for an additional payment.

16.25 The categories of rates for attendance are:
- own or duty solicitor;
- duty solicitor unsocial hours;
- duty solicitor serious offence social hours; and
- duty solicitor serious offence unsocial hours.

Similar categories (except those for serious offences) apply for travel and waiting time.

16.26 For these purposes, social hours are between 9.00 am and 5.30 pm on a business day – that is, any day other than Saturday, Sunday, Christmas Day, Good Friday or any other bank holiday.[17]

16.27 Serious offences are:[18]
- treason;
- murder;
- manslaughter;
- causing death by dangerous driving;
- rape;
- assault by penetration;
- rape of a child under 13;
- assault of a child under 13 by penetration;
- robbery;
- assault with intent to rob;
- arson;
- perverting the course of justice;
- conspiracy to defraud;

---

16 Standard Crime Contract 2022 Specification paras 9.95–9.100 and Standard Crime Contract 2025 Specification paras 9.92–9.95.
17 Standard Crime Contracts 2022 and 2025 para 1.1 define Business Hours and Business Day. Unsocial hours are those outside those definitions.
18 Standard Crime Contract 2022 Specification para 9.99(a) and Standard Crime Contract 2025 Specification para 9.96 (a).

- kidnapping;
- wounding/grievous bodily harm (GBH) – sections 18 and 20 of the Offences Against the Person Act 1861;
- conspiracy, solicitation, incitement or attempt of any of the above;
- any offence if the client is also accused of possession of a firearm, shotgun or imitation firearm; and
- any offence if the client is detained under section 41 of the Terrorism Act 2000.

16.28 In order to claim duty rates, the case must be a duty case – that is, referred as a duty case by the call centre or conducted during a duty period, and the work done by an accredited fee earner.[19] To claim serious offences rates, the work must be done by a duty solicitor,[20] and you must not be a confirmed category 3 firm (costs audit) in relation to your crime contract.[21]

16.29 To calculate whether the case is exceptional, you calculate the value of all time spent at the appropriate hourly rate. This will include any free-standing advice and assistance outside the police station for an eligible client. You should also include any telephone advice fixed fee[22] or a Criminal Defence Direct acceptance fee[23] (where a former Criminal Defence Direct matter was referred to you for police station attendance). This will give you a total value for the case. If the total value is more than the relevant exceptional threshold set out in the Criminal Legal Aid (Remuneration) Regulations 2013, you can make an application to the LAA to treat it as an escape fee case.[24]

16.30 In order to do that, you should complete the form (CRM18) and submit it along with the relevant bundle. The LAA will assess the claim, and if following assessment it is confirmed that the case is worth more than the escape fee threshold, the case will be treated as an escape fee case.

---

19 Standard Crime Contract 2022 Specification para 9.98 and Standard Crime Contract 2025 Specification para 9.95.
20 Standard Crime Contract 2022 Specification para 9.99 and Standard Crime Contract 2025 Specification para 9.96.
21 Standard Crime Contract 2022 Specification para 9.100 and Standard Crime Contract 2025 Specification para 9.97.
22 Standard Crime Contract 2022 Specification para 9.84 and Standard Crime Contract 2025 Specification para 9.81.
23 Standard Crime Contract 2022 Specification para 9.94 and Standard Crime Contract 2025 Specification para 9.91.
24 Standard Crime Contract 2022 Specification para 9.95 and Standard Crime Contract 2025 Specification para 9.92.

16.31 However, you will still not be paid the full value of the case. Instead, you will only be paid the fixed fee, plus the amount by which the case exceeds the threshold.[25]

> **Case study**
>
> I represented a client at a central London police station on a case of murder over a weekend. It was a duty case, and I spent in total 14 unsocial hours in attendance at the police station, plus six hours' travel and waiting (all unsocial). I also incurred a telephone fee. What will I be paid?
>
> The Central London scheme has a fixed fee of £272.84 plus VAT. It was a duty case and a weekend, so London duty unsocial serious case rates apply: £83.95 per hour for attendances, £72.46 for travel and waiting, and telephone attendance fee of £33.00.
>
> Your time is worth (£83.95 × 14) + (£72.46 × 6) = £1,175.30 + £434.76 + £33.00 = £1,643.06. The fixed fee is £272.84, and the threshold is £924.35. Therefore, you are over the threshold and the case is exceptional.
>
> You will be paid (subject to assessment) the value of the fixed fee plus the amount by which the threshold is exceeded: £272.84 + (£1,643.06 − £924.35) = £991.55.
>
> You should send your exceptional claim to the LAA who will assess the bill.

16.32 Escape fee cases will not be paid direct. Instead, the value allowed on assessment will count towards your standard monthly payment.

Pre-charge engagement

16.33 Pre-charge engagement advice and assistance is one of the exceptions to the rule that all investigation work be billed together. A single claim must be submitted separately. This work is not subject to a fixed fee and hourly rates applicable to this work are set out in the Criminal Legal Aid (Remuneration) Regulations 2013. Travel and waiting times may not be claimed.[26] You should apply the rates to the claimable work done, subject to any costs limit. The costs limit of

---

25 Standard Crime Contract 2022 Specification paras 9.96–9.97 and Standard Crime Contract 2025 Specification paras 9.93–9.94.
26 Standard Crime Contract 2022 Specification para 9.136 and Standard Crime Contract 2025 Specification para 9.132.

£314.81 is to cover both profit costs and disbursements; this limit can be extended on application to the LAA.[27]

16.34 Where police station advice and assistance or free-standing advice has already been provided to the same client for the same matter, the same UFN must be assigned but the pre-charge engagement work must be claimed separately at the appropriate rates.[28]

16.35 A claim must only be submitted when:
- the investigation has concluded, whether by charge, summons, requisition or other disposal;
- it is known that no further investigations work will be undertaken for the client; or
- it is unclear whether further work will be required, especially for cases that remain under investigation, but at least one month has elapsed since the last work.[29]

16.36 Where you have acted for more than one client in the same investigation, you should make a separate claim for each client, apportioning the work between them if necessary.[30]

Advocacy assistance

16.37 Advocacy assistance – of whatever type – is also one of the exceptions to the rule that all investigations work be billed together. Any claim for advocacy assistance should be submitted separately. This work is not subject to fixed fees, and the hourly rates set out in the contract will apply subject to the extendable costs limit of £1,574.06. A single claim for advocacy assistance on a case should be made[31] at the end of the investigations stage, or when it is known that no further work will be undertaken for the client in the same matter or it is unclear whether further work will be required and a minimum of one month has elapsed since the last work in the matter was undertaken..[32] The

---

27 Standard Crime Contract 2022 Specification para 9.136 and Standard Crime Contract 2025 Specification para 9.133.
28 Standard Crime Contract 2022 Specification para 9.132 and Standard Crime Contract 2025 Specification para 9.128.
29 Standard Crime Contract 2022 Specification para 9.133 and Standard Crime Contract 2025 Specification para 9.129.
30 Standard Crime Contract 2022 Specification para 9.134 and Standard Crime Contract 2025 Specification para 130.
31 Standard Crime Contract 2022 Specification paras 9.174, 9.187 and 9.198 and Standard Crime Contract 2025 Specification para 9.169 onwards.
32 Standard Crime Contract 2022 Specification paras 9.175, 9.188 and 9.199 and Standard Crime Contract 2025 Specification para 9.170d.

2025 Contract allows a separate claim to be submitted for advocacy and assistance undertaken for each separate application to extend pre-charge bail under section 47ZF or 47ZG of the Police and Criminal Evidence Act 1984 (PACE). Where police station advice and assistance, or free-standing advice and assistance, has already been provided, the same UFN must be used, although the work must be claimed separately.[33]

Proceedings class work

Virtual court claims[34]

16.38 Rates of remuneration are specified in Criminal Legal Aid (Remuneration) Regulations 2013 Sch 4, as amended. These claims have been removed in the 2025 Crime Contract on the basis that the virtual court scheme will no longer exist.

Court duty claims[35]

16.39 You should claim any work done as court duty solicitor at the end of the duty session. You should make one claim per session, rather than one claim per client.[36] The applicable payment rates are set out in the Criminal Legal Aid (Remuneration) Regulations 2013.

16.40 *If a claim exceeds eight hours, a special note should be kept for use on audit to explain what had occurred on the day. Similarly, any travel should be justified in accordance with the standard crime contract.*

16.41 You cannot claim for travel time or expenses to get to court, except where you are acting on a non-business day (eg a Saturday or bank holiday sitting), or where you are called to court having not been on the rota or having attended on a rota and been released and then asked to return.

---

33 Standard Crime Contract 2022 Specification paras 9.189 and 9.200 and Standard Crime Contract 2025 Specification para 9.171.
34 Standard Crime Contract 2022 Specification paras 10.21–10.35.
35 Standard Crime Contract 2022 Specification paras 10.1–10.20 and Standard Crime Contract 2025 Specification para 10.19.
36 Standard Crime Contracts 2022 and 2025 Specification para 10.18.

Representation orders in the magistrates' court

16.42 See chapter 14 for details on conducting work under a representation order.

16.43 Magistrates' court work should be billed at the end of the magistrates' court stage of the case. All claims under a representation order must be submitted together (other than sending fees[37]). There is no provision for interim payments, so the bill will be submitted when one of the defined end-points occurs:

- the case has concluded;
- it is known that no further work will be required;
- it is unclear whether further work will be required and at least a month has elapsed since the last work was undertaken;[38] or
- a warrant of arrest was issued and at least six weeks, but not more than 19 weeks, have elapsed since.[39]

16.44 Another exception to this is where sentence is deferred; you may submit a bill when sentence is deferred and another when the client returns to be sentenced.[40] Bills must be submitted within three months of the end of the case.

16.45 Where you act for more than one client in a case, you should submit a single bill covering work done for all clients,[41] though you will need a separate representation order for each one.[42]

Standard fees

16.46 Most magistrates' court work is covered by the standard fee regime. There are three categories of fee – 1A, 1B and 2 – and in each category a lower and a higher standard fee.

16.47 There are two types of fee:

---

37 Standard Crime Contracts 2022 and 2025 Specification para 8.4.
38 Standard Crime Contract 2022 Specification para 10.62 and Standard Crime Contract 2025 Specification para 10.50.
39 Standard Crime Contract 2022 Specification para 10.67 and Standard Crime Contract 2025 Specification para 10.54.
40 Standard Crime Contract 2022 Specification para 10.66 and Standard Crime Contract 2025 Specification para 10.53.
41 Standard Crime Contract 2022 Specification paras 10.60 and 10.64 and Standard Crime Contract 2025 Specification paras 10.48 and 10.52.
42 Standard Crime Contract 2022 Specification para 10.37 and Standard Crime Contract 2025 Specification para 10.21.

1) If your office is in an area designated by the contract, or if it is not but the court named in the representation order is, you should claim the **designated area** standard fee.[43]
2) If not, you should claim the **undesignated area** standard fee.[44]

16.48 The designated areas[45] are the criminal justice areas of:
- Greater Manchester;
- London;
- West Midlands;
- Merseyside; and
- the local authority areas of:
  – Brighton and Hove;
  – Bristol;
  – Cardiff;
  – Derby and Erewash;
  – Kingston upon Hull;
  – Leeds and Bradford;
  – Leicester;
  – Nottingham;
  – Portsmouth;
  – Newcastle-upon-Tyne and Sunderland (including Gateshead, North Tyneside and South Tyneside);
  – Sheffield; and
  – Southampton.

16.49 The difference between designated and undesignated is that in a designated area, the fees are slightly higher but you cannot claim for any travel and waiting time,[46] whereas in an undesignated area you can claim travel and waiting[47] but the standard fees are lower. Even if you cannot claim travel and waiting, you are still required to record the waiting time (though need not record travel).[48]

---

43 Standard Crime Contract 2022 Specification para 10.77 and Standard Crime Contract 2025 Specification para 10.64.
44 Standard Crime Contract 2022 Specification para 10.77 and Standard Crime Contract 2025 Specification para 10.64.
45 Standard Crime Contracts 2022 and 2025 Specification para 1.2.
46 Standard Crime Contract 2022 Specification paras 10.80 and 10.85 and Standard Crime Contract 2025 Specification paras 10.67 and 10.72.
47 Standard Crime Contract 2022 Specification para 10.83 and Standard Crime Contract 2025 Specification para 10.70.
48 Standard Crime Contract 2022 Specification para 10.87 and Standard Crime Contract 2025 Specification para 10.73.

16.50 In either case, the structure of the fees is the same. Whatever the category of your case, you calculate your core costs (all profit costs except travel and waiting time).[49] If the core costs do not exceed the lower limit for the category of case, you claim the lower standard fee. If core costs are above the lower but do not exceed the higher limit, you claim the higher standard fee. If core costs are above the higher limit, you claim a non-standard fee – that is, you claim your costs in full as incurred.[50]

16.51 You should decide which category of fee to claim based on the nature and outcome of the case. There are complexities in the correct identification which significantly affect the appropriate fee:

- Category 1A[51] is:
  - either way guilty pleas (including thefts from a shop of goods valued at under £200);
  - indictable only cases heard in the youth court;
  - proceedings relating to either way offences which are discontinued or withdrawn or where the prosecution offer no evidence; and
  - proceedings relating to either way offences which result in a bind over.
- Category 1B[52] is:
  - summary only guilty pleas;
  - uncontested proceedings arising out of a breach of an order of a magistrates' court;
  - proceedings relating to summary offences which are discontinued or withdrawn or where the prosecution offers no evidence;
  - proceedings relating to summary offences which result in a bind over;
  - proceedings arising out of a deferment of sentence (including any subsequent sentence hearing) under Powers of Criminal Courts (Sentencing) Act 2000 s1;
  - proceedings prescribed under Criminal Legal Aid (General) Regulations 2013 reg 9 (see chapter 14 at para 14.86), except

---

49 Standard Crime Contract 2022 Specification para 10.79 and Standard Crime Contract 2025 Specification para 10.66.
50 Standard Crime Contract 2022 Specification para 10.88 and Standard Crime Contract 2025 Specification para 10.74.
51 Criminal Legal Aid (Remuneration) Regulations 2013 Sch 4 para 5.
52 Criminal Legal Aid (Remuneration) Regulations 2013 Sch 4 para 5.

where the case was listed and fully prepared for a contested hearing to decide whether an order should be made; and
- proceedings relating to either way offences which must be tried in a magistrates' court in accordance with Magistrates' Courts Act 1980 s22.
- Category 2[53] is:
  - contested trials;
  - proceedings which were listed and fully prepared for trial in a magistrates' court but are disposed of by a guilty plea on the day of trial before the opening of the prosecution case;
  - proceedings which were listed and fully prepared for trial in a magistrates' court but are discontinued or withdrawn, or where the prosecution offers no evidence or which result in a bind over on the day of trial before the opening of the prosecution case;
  - contested proceedings relating to a breach of an order of a magistrates' court (including proceedings relating to a breach of a Crown Court community rehabilitation order, community punishment order or suspended sentence);
  - proceedings where mixed pleas are entered; and
  - proceedings prescribed under Criminal Legal Aid (General) Regulations 2013 reg 9 where the case was listed and fully prepared for a contested hearing to decide whether an order should be made (see chapter 14 at para 14.86).

16.52 Where proceedings have not concluded but a warrant of arrest has been issued, the proceedings will be treated as category 1 proceedings.[54]

16.53 Bail applications (including to the Crown Court) and appeals against bail are included in the standard fee of the substantive case.[55]

16.54 Where more than one category is possible, you should select the one that will pay the highest fee.[56]

16.55 On a change of solicitor, the old firm should claim a category 1 fee, and the new firm should claim in the usual way. The exception

---

53 Criminal Legal Aid (Remuneration) Regulations 2013 Sch 4 para 5.
54 Standard Crime Contract 2022 Specification para 10.94 and Standard Crime Contract 2025 Specification para 10.79.
55 Standard Crime Contract 2022 Specification para 10.73 and Standard Crime Contract 2025 Specification para 10.60.
56 Standard Crime Contract 2022 Specification para 10.91 and Standard Crime Contract 2025 Specification para 10.76.

to this is where the conducting solicitor moves firms and takes the case – if this happens, only the new firm can claim, but should claim for both firms' work. The firms should seek to agree in advance how payments will be distributed between them.[57]

16.56 Where you have claimed a fee and then a further claim is required – for example, you claimed a category 1 fee when a client absconds and a warrant is issued, and then continued to represent the client following arrest on the warrant –you should calculate the total costs due for the whole of the case, deduct the amount previously claimed, and claim the balance.[58] The exact provision does not appear in the 2025 Contract as the LAA relies on para 10.54:

> 10.54 Where proceedings in a magistrates' court have not been concluded but a warrant of arrest has been issued, a Claim for costs in respect of work done under a Representation Order must be made not earlier than six weeks and not later than 19 weeks from the date of issue of the warrant. A supplemental Claim amendment may be made for any further work undertaken after the original Claim has been submitted if the Client is arrested or surrenders. The original Claim will then be recalculated.

Case study

My office is in Manchester. My client was charged with theft, indicated a not guilty plea and elected summary trial. He was convicted following trial, and sentencing was deferred for six months. What should I claim?

Manchester is in a designated area, so you should be claiming the designated area standard fee. Your client took the case to a trial, so the case is in category 2. You should calculate your core costs (all time excluding travel and waiting) to see whether a lower, higher or non-standard fee is claimable.

When your client comes back to be sentenced in six months' time, you can claim a further category 1B standard fee.

---

57 Standard Crime Contract 2022 Specification paras 10.92 and 10.93 and Standard Crime Contract 2025 Specification paras 10.77 and 10.78.
58 Standard Crime Contract 2022 Specification para 10.97.

Counsel

16.57 Unassigned counsel are treated as if they were employed by you, and you should include their times on your bill as if they were your profit costs.

16.58 Where counsel are assigned, their costs are separate from yours. Rates for assigned counsel are set out in the Criminal Legal Aid (Remuneration) Regulations 2013, and counsel should prepare a bill at those rates.[59] They will be paid direct by the LAA, but you should submit their bill alongside yours.[60]

Separate matters

16.59 One standard fee is payable per case. A case consists of all work for all clients in respect of:
- one offence; or
- more than one offence, where:
    - they are charged at the same time;
    - they are founded on the same facts; or
    - they form part of a series of offences.[61]

16.60 Offences 'charged at the same time' is a straightforward test. 'Founded on the same facts' is intended to cover situations where two charges are brought as alternatives, or where one charge is substituted for another – common examples include theft and handling stolen goods, or actual bodily harm (ABH) and common assault.

16.61 A 'series of offences' refers to offences which have similarities or form a pattern of offending, that could be tried together. Each potential series of offences has to be considered on its own facts and definitive guidance cannot be given. However, there is a discussion at section 6.6 of the LAA's *Criminal Bills Assessment Manual*.[62] The key principle is that the offences are sufficiently related to have been tried on the same indictment had they been indictable offences. For example, offences that are based on a system of conduct, are similar in nature, or where evidence of one is admissible at the trial of

---

59 Standard Crime Contract 2022 Specification para 10.44 and Standard Crime Contract 2025 Specification para 10.32.
60 Standard Crime Contract 2022 Specification para 10.45 and Standard Crime Contract 2025 Specification para 10.33.
61 Standard Crime Contract 2022 Specification para 10.69 and Standard Crime Contract 2025 Specification para 10.56.
62 V19, LAA, April 2024, available at: www.gov.uk/guidance/funding-and-costs-assessment-for-civil-and-crime-matters.

another, may all form part of a series. Even though some hearings may be held at different times, or in different courts, that would not prevent a series being established. However, cases linked only for sentence do not thereby become a series.

Enhanced rates

16.62 In certain circumstances, you can apply for payment at an enhanced rate. The LAA will consider whether enhancement is justified and, if so, will increase the hourly rates for some or all of the work done on the case. It would be very unusual for enhanced rates to be allowed on routine items such as travel and waiting (where payable) or letters and telephone calls.

16.63 The test for enhancement is that:
- the work was done with exceptional competence, skill or expertise;
- the work was done with exceptional dispatch; or
- the case involved exceptional circumstances or complexity compared with the generality of proceedings.[63]

16.64 Where the test is met, the LAA will allow a percentage increase to the relevant hourly rate not exceeding 100 per cent.[64] The amount of the percentage increase will be determined by having regard to:
- the degree of responsibility accepted;
- the care, speed and economy with which the case was prepared; and
- the novelty, weight and complexity of the case.[65]

16.65 Enhancement of the hourly rates takes the case out of the standard fee regime, so you should submit an individual bill to the LAA, accompanied by a note setting out why you believe the criteria for enhancement are met and justifying the percentage sought. It is important to remember that what seems obvious to you may not be so to an assessor. So, for example, you should not assume that because the court granted a certificate for counsel you will automatically obtain an uplift if you have decided to do the advocacy yourself. You will need to address the criteria explicitly and show how your advocacy was exceptional.

---

63 Standard Crime Contract 2022 Specification para 10.99 and Standard Crime Contract 2025 Specification para 10.82.
64 Standard Crime Contract 2022 Specification para 10.102 and Standard Crime Contract 2025 Specification para 10.85.
65 Standard Crime Contract 2022 Specification para 10.101 and Standard Crime Contract 2025 Specification para 10.84.

Representation orders – matters sent to the Crown Court for trial

16.66 A fixed sending hearing fee of £208.61 can be claimed for preparation and attendance under a representation order in relation to proceedings that are committed to or sent to the Crown Court for trial under Crime and Disorder Act 1998 s51.[66]

16.67 This fee applies to matters with a representation order dated on or after 19 October 2020.[67]

16.68 The rules on claiming are as follows:

- You may only submit a claim when your client's sending hearing has concluded, but it may be claimed before the conclusion of the case in the Crown Court.[68]
- Only one fee is payable if you are representing multiple defendants whose cases are sent to the Crown Court for trial at the same hearing.[69]
- Disbursements are payable in addition to the sending fee.[70]
- If you are representing the client as duty solicitor, you cannot claim a sending fee.[71]

Other contract work

16.69 Advice and assistance in the appeals and prison law classes, and advocacy assistance in the prison law class, is claimed under the contract in the same way as free-standing advice and assistance in the investigations class (see above, and see also sections 11 and 12 of the Contract Specification). There must be evidence to show that the sufficient benefit test has been met. The Criminal Legal Aid (Remuneration) Regulations 2013 provide details of the fixed fees and standard fees applicable to prison law cases.

---

66 Standard Crime Contract 2022 Specification paras 10.131–10.143 and Standard Crime Contract 2025 Specification paras 10.114–10.125.
67 Criminal Legal Aid (Remuneration) Regulations 2013 Sch 4 para 5(6), as amended.
68 Standard Crime Contract 2022 Specification para 10.137 and Standard Crime Contract 2025 Specification para 10.120.
69 Standard Crime Contract 2022 Specification para 10.140 and Standard Crime Contract 2025 Specification para 10.123.
70 Standard Crime Contract 2022 Specification para 10.136 and Standard Crime Contract 2025 Specification para 10.119.
71 Standard Crime Contracts 2022 and 2025 Specification para 10.14.

16.70 It is critical to correctly identify the client's eligibility for the work in question. Both income and capital positions must be checked, even for those in prison. The eligibility must be documented.

16.71 The scope of prison law has been significantly reduced and then expanded again so the scope rules applicable at the time and section 12 of the Specification should be checked. Where work is within scope, this must be documented, for instance, to show that disciplinary proceedings were held before an adjudicator.

16.72 Similarly, the rules on the number of cases that can be claimed, particularly in sentencing cases, can cause difficulty on audit.

16.73 Representation in judicial review or habeas corpus proceedings, proceedings in the youth court for anti-social behaviour injunctions (ASBIs), or civil proceedings under the Proceeds of Crime Act 2002, is claimed as all other civil legal aid: see chapter 14 of this Handbook and section 13 of the Specification to the Standard Crime Contract.

16.74 Representation in other civil proceedings associated with criminal proceedings (eg where papers from a civil case are relevant to a criminal case) is funded by representation order and requires prior authority. However, it is claimed under the same remuneration provisions as apply to civil legal representation. See the Standard Crime Contract 2022 Specification paras 10.164–10.175 and Standard Crime Contract 2025 Specification paras 10.145–10.156.

16.75 Representation on an appeal by way of case stated is funded by representation order (issued by the High Court) and claimed in the same way as in the proceedings class, except that there are no standard fees. See the Standard Crime Contract Specification section 11.

16.76 Special provision is made by the Standard Crime Contract[72] for representation in proceedings for breach of injunctions under Part 1 of the Anti-Social Behaviour, Crime and Policing Act 2014 in whatever court those proceedings take place. Remuneration levels are set out in the Criminal Legal Aid (Remuneration) Regulations 2013. The proceedings at which those injunctions are obtained (including in the youth court) are civil and require civil legal aid. Criminal legal aid, however, is available in proceedings for breach of these injunctions in all courts. See also chapter 14.

---

72 Standard Crime Contract 2022 Specification paras 10.181–10.191 and Standard Crime Contract 2025 Specification paras 10.160–10.169.

The claiming process

16.77 Contract work is claimed by submitting details of the bills to the LAA. With the exception of magistrates' court non-standard fees, you do not need to send in the file of papers, and bills will not be individually assessed.

16.78 Each month, you should submit form CRM6 to the LAA using the legal aid online portal: https://portal.legalservices.gov.uk. Each line on the CRM6 represents one bill. There is a series of codes you should use to differentiate between different types of cases, different offences and scheme areas (for police station fee purposes). The LAA then sets off each bill against your contract payments, with the overall aim being that payments match claims, within acceptable reconciliation boundaries, if you are being paid under standard monthly payments – see chapter 23. The codes can be found on the legal aid website at: www.gov.uk/government/publications/cwa-codes-guidance.

16.79 Non-standard fees in the magistrates' court are subject to individual assessment by the LAA. You should complete form CRM7 with details of the case and the amount claimed, plus justification for the costs, and submit it as an eform through LAA online: https://portal.legalservices.gov.uk.[73] The LAA will assess the bill and return details of the amount allowed, which will be credited to your contract account rather than paid to you direct.

16.80 If you disagree with the assessment, there is a right of appeal to an Independent Costs Assessor (ICA), who is a solicitor independent of the LAA. The ICA will consider the file, the LAA assessment and your representations and will reduce, confirm or increase the amount allowed by the LAA. There is a 28-day time limit to appeal, and appeals will generally be dealt with on the papers. Full details of the appeal process are set out in the contract.[74] See also chapter 17 for more information on costs appeals.

16.81 There is no right of appeal beyond the ICA under the 2022 and 2025 Crime Contracts. While ICAs must take Points of Principle (POPs) published by the LAA into account, no new POPs will be certified from April 2017.

---

73 Standard Crime Contract 2022 Specification para 10.74 and Standard Crime Contract 2025 Specification para 10.61.
74 Standard Crime Contract 2022 Specification paras 8.19–8.29 and Standard Crime Contract 2025 Specification paras 8.20–8.30.

Crown Court – litigator fees

16.82 Although all Crown Court work is included within the scope of the contract, the payment rates and rules are governed by the Criminal Legal Aid (Remuneration) Regulations 2013, as amended. See para 16.10 above.

16.83 The scheme makes a distinction between fixed fees and graduated fees. There are fixed fees for cases that involve either way offences when the magistrates' court accepted jurisdiction but the defendant elected trial on indictment; and for cases that do not involve trial on indictment, such as committal for sentence, breaches and appeals. Graduated fees apply to all other cases heard on indictment.

16.84 Graduated fees are determined by a number of factors:
- the classification of the offence – offences are classified into 11 classes (A–K);
- the category (outcome) – whether a guilty plea (plea entered before or at the first hearing at which the defendant enters a plea), a cracked trial (guilty plea or no evidence offered after the first hearing at which the defendant enters a plea) or trial (including Newton hearings);
- the length of the main hearing – the trial or hearing at which pleas were entered;
- the number of pages of prosecution evidence (including unused material) served – this can in defined circumstances include pages served electronically;[75] and
- the number of defendants represented by you.

To calculate the fee, you should first categorise your case by the offence. Where there is more than one charge on the indictment, select the one which would result in the higher fee.

16.85 For each outcome type, there is a basic fee which varies depending on the classification of the offence, and to which an uplift is added depending on the number of pages of evidence (including time spent considering unused material) and the length of the main hearing.

16.86 As a result, there are thousands of variables and the tables set out in Criminal Legal Aid (Remuneration) Regulations 2013 Sch 2 and amendments thereto are lengthy and complex. However, the LAA

---

75 Criminal Legal Aid (Remuneration) Regulations 2013 Schs 1 and 2 para 1(2)–(5), as amended.

has made available a spreadsheet into which the classification, trial length, page count and outcome can be entered, and which then calculates the appropriate fee – see: www.gov.uk/government/public ations/graduated-fee-calculators.

16.87 All work done on a case is covered by the graduated fee – the exceptions are: work done in connection with confiscation following conviction;[76] work classified as 'special preparation' (considering more than 10,000 pages of evidence or exhibits, or electronic evidence which does not qualify as pages of prosecution evidence (often referred to as PPE)), which is payable at hourly rates in addition to the fee;[77] and consideration of unused material.[78]

16.88 In relation to the consideration of unused material, for matters other than a guilty plea with a representation order dated on or after 17 September 2020, a fixed fee of £74.38 is payable for viewing material for up to three hours[79] (regardless of whether any material has actually been considered).

16.89 Material considered in excess of three hours is payable at an hourly rate (based on grade of fee earner) and may be claimed in addition to the fixed fee for the first three hours.

16.90 Claims for litigator fees are to be made through the LAA online billing system.

16.91 Claims are assessed item by item by the LAA, which will compare the information on your claim with that held by the Court Service.

16.92 There is a right to redetermination of an assessment provided for in Criminal Legal Aid (Remuneration) Regulations 2013 reg 28. The request must be made in writing within 21 days of receipt of the assessment. You cannot challenge the fee scheme itself, but can challenge the calculation in any individual case, such as by appealing the classification of the offence or the allowed page count. On redetermination, the fee may be confirmed, reduced or increased.

16.93 If you remain dissatisfied with the assessment, you can apply for written reasons within 21 days, and then within 21 days of receipt of the reasons request a hearing before a costs judge.

---

76 Criminal Legal Aid (Remuneration) Regulations 2013 Sch 2 para 26, as amended.
77 Criminal Legal Aid (Remuneration) (Amendment) Regulations 2017 Sch 2 para 20.
78 Criminal Legal Aid (Remuneration) Regulations 2013 Sch 2 para 20A, as amended.
79 Criminal Legal Aid (Remuneration) Regulations 2013 Sch 2 para 20A(2A), as amended.

Payments on account

16.94 Where you have been granted prior authority by the LAA and have incurred a disbursement of more than £100 you can apply for a payment on account of the disbursement at any time.[80]

16.95 A litigator may make a claim for an interim payment of profit costs at one or both of two stages in proceedings.[81]

16.96 The first stage is where a not guilty plea is entered following a pre-trial preparation hearing (PTPH) (unless it was on a defence election), or alternatively, where a retrial is ordered and representation has been transferred to a new litigator. The interim payment at PTPH stage of proceedings is set at 75 per cent of the cracked trial rate plus any uplifts. Where a retrial is ordered and representation transferred to a new litigator, the payment is set at 50 per cent. The determination of the cracked trial rate will depend on the number of pages of prosecution evidence served on the court and the classification of the offence into which the case falls.

16.97 The second stage is where a trial has commenced that is expected to last for 10 or more days. The trial is presumed to last one day, and the claim is for the fee payable at that stage.

16.98 There is no other provision for payment on account of profit costs unless you can show financial hardship. When applying under hardship provisions, you will have to provide evidence of hardship, usually in the form of a bank statement or letter from your bank.[82]

Coronavirus provisions on hardship

16.99 As a result of the coronavirus pandemic, the Criminal Legal Aid (Remuneration) Regulations 2013 have been amended to allow a hardship application to be made if it has been one month since being instructed.

Crown Court – advocates' fees

16.100 The scheme for advocates in mainstream criminal cases is similar to that applying to litigators. The applicable rules and fees are set out in Criminal Legal Aid (Remuneration) Regulations 2013 Sch 1, as amended. Further amending regulations are expected to be laid shortly.

---

80 Criminal Legal Aid (Remuneration) Regulations 2013 reg 14.
81 See Criminal Legal Aid (Remuneration) (Amendment) (No 2) Regulations 2014.
82 Criminal Legal Aid (Remuneration) Regulations 2013 reg 21, as amended.

16.101 Each case will have a trial advocate, who is responsible for claiming fees on behalf of all advocates instructed in the case. Payment will be made to the trial advocate.

16.102 The scheme provides for a basic fee based on the classification of the offence, to which is added an uplift for the length of the trial. There are higher fees for a trial and some cracked trials and a lower fee for guilty plea case. Additional fees can be claimed for other hearings and specified work.

16.103 In prescribed proceedings where criminal legal aid is granted in relation to civil proceedings in accordance with Criminal Legal Aid (General) Regulations 2013 reg 9, hourly rates apply subject to an extendable upper fee limit.

Very High Cost Cases

16.104 Cases accepted by the LAA as VHCCs (ie cases in which a representation order was granted on or after 3 October 2011 and, if the case were to proceed to trial, would likely last more than 40 days (60 for advocates)) may be subject to individual case contracts. The rates will depend on the category of case (seriousness) and the level of fee earner (dependent on experience). Standard rates for each category and level of fee earner are set out in the Specification to the VHCC Standard Contract.

16.105 For further information refer to the guidance on the legal aid website 'Crime high cost case arrangements and contract documents' at: www.gov.uk/government/publications/high-cost-case-arrangements-and-contract-documents.

Topping up criminal legal aid fees

16.106 Once legal aid has been granted, Legal Aid, Sentencing and Punishment of Offenders Act 2012 (LASPO) s28 provides:

> (2) A person who provides services under arrangements made for the purposes of this Part must not take any payment in respect of the services apart from–
> (a) payment made in accordance with the arrangements, and
> (b) payment authorised by the Lord Chancellor to be taken.[83]

---

83 Confirmed by Standard Crime Contract 2022 Standard Terms 7.18 and Specification para 8.41 and Standard Crime Contract 2025 Standard Terms 7.13 and Specification para 8.41.

16.107 The Standard Crime Contracts 2022 and 2025 allow[84] for payment by a client, provided that an application for prior authority to incur that expenditure has been refused and express authority has been obtained from the client, to:
   a) prepare, obtain or consider any report, opinion or further evidence, whether provided by an expert witness or otherwise; or
   b) obtain or prepare any transcripts or recordings of any criminal investigation or proceedings, including police questioning; or
   c) instruct counsel other than where an individual is entitled to counsel (as may be determined by the court) in accordance with Criminal Legal Aid (Determinations by a Court and Choice of Representative) Regulations 2013 regs 16 and 17.

16.108 This paragraph is wider than Criminal Legal Aid (Remuneration) Regulations 2013 reg 9, which restricts payments to a) and b), but appears to amount to an authority, in relation to magistrates' court work, within LASPO s28(2)(b).

---

84 Standard Crime Contracts 2022 and 2025 Specification para 8.43.

CHAPTER 17

Appeals to Independent Funding Adjudicators and Costs Assessors in civil cases

By Paul Keeley

17.1	**Introduction**
17.3	**When might you need to appeal?**
17.4	**Appeals to Independent Funding Adjudicators**
17.4	Introduction
17.6	Before you appeal to an IFA
	Can you make a new application?
17.7	Internal review
	Overview • Internal review: exceptional case funding decisions • Internal review: licensed work
17.18	Funding appeals: controlled work immigration cases
17.24	Funding appeals: licensed work
17.26	Powers of the IFA
17.29	Submission of further information
17.30	Oral hearings and panels
17.32	LAA decision upheld for different reasons
17.33	Backdating licensed work: post 20 February 2019

continued

17.35	Nil assessment appeals in controlled work cases
17.46	**Appeals to Independent Costs Assessors**
17.46	Introduction
17.47	Appeals to ICA: procedure
17.53	Some tips for appeals to ICAs
17.54	**Special casework decisions**
17.55	**Family mediation**
17.56	**Further challenges**

> **Key resources**
> - Civil Legal Aid (Procedure) Regulations 2012 – regs 44–48, 53, 59, 65, 69
> - Legal Aid Agency's Appeals Manual[1]

> **Key points to note**
> - Mastering appeals to Independent Funding Adjudicators (IFAs) and Independent Costs Assessors (ICAs) is essential for securing full and proper payment. We talk about the rights of appeal in more detail below, but the following scenarios are when you might typically appeal:
> - You might want to appeal when the Legal Aid Agency (LAA) refuses to grant a legal aid certificate in a licensed work matter, for example, to bring a judicial review, or an appeal to the Court of Appeal, on the grounds that there are insufficient prospects of success.
> - At the end of the case, or after an audit, when the LAA has assessed your costs, you might want to appeal against a decision to reduce payment for some or all of the work carried out. For example, where the LAA decides that you spent too much time on a particular task, or it might decide that you were wrong to grant legal aid in the first place.

Introduction

17.1 This chapter deals with appeals to IFAs following a determination by the LAA that an individual does not qualify for legal aid and appeals to ICAs following a reduction of remuneration by the LAA.

17.2 This chapter also deals with the right to internal review of LAA decisions.

---

1 At: https://assets.publishing.service.gov.uk/government/uploads/system/uploads/attachment_data/file/1114734/LAA_Appeals_Manual_October_2022.pdf.

When might you need to appeal?

17.3 We will talk about the rights of appeal in more detail below, but first we will set out the scenarios when you might typically appeal:
- You might want to appeal when the LAA refuses to grant a legal aid certificate in a licensed work matter, for example, to bring a judicial review, or an appeal to the Court of Appeal, on the grounds that there are insufficient prospects of success.
- At the end of the case, or after an audit, when the LAA has assessed your costs, you might want to appeal against a decision to reduce payment for some or all of the work carried out. For example, where the LAA decides that you spent too much time on a particular task, or it might decide that you were wrong to grant legal aid in the first place.

Appeals to Independent Funding Adjudicators

Introduction

17.4 IFAs primarily decide appeals against decisions of the LAA to refuse or withdraw funding on the grounds of merits or related matters such as the cost–benefit ratio.

17.5 IFAs also decide appeals against decisions of suppliers to refuse or withdraw legal aid on merits grounds in some Controlled Legal Representation (CLR) cases (eg asylum appeals).

Before you appeal to an IFA

Can you make a new application?

17.6 Before appealing, you should consider whether you can make a new application. If, for example, you could have provided more evidence to support your application for legal aid, or put your case in different terms, it may be quicker to make a new application. It is usually possible to submit new evidence or arguments as part of an appeal, but it can often take longer to get your case before an IFA than to get a new decision, so making a new application is often the best first step.

Internal review

Overview

17.7 Although you might focus on the appeal, the right of internal review process can be just as, if not more, important. That is because, in some cases, there is no right of appeal at all. In cases where there is a right of appeal, it is, in practice, usually the case that if the LAA maintains its decision, the case is automatically passed on to the IFA for a decision,[2] so your grounds for internal review, will effectively become your grounds of appeal. You should therefore prepare your application for internal review as your grounds of appeal.

17.8 In most cases, the deadline for an internal review is 14 days.

Internal review: exceptional case funding decisions

17.9 In matters falling outside the scope of the Legal Aid, Sentencing and Punishment of Offenders Act 2012 (LASPO), there is a right of internal review of decisions:[3]

1) to refuse to grant exceptional case funding (ECF) generally, either because the LAA decides that the case does not meet the exceptional case threshold, or that, for some other reason (such as being financially ineligible), the individual does not qualify for legal aid;
2) that the wider public interest test is not satisfied in relation to inquest matters, or that, for some other reason (such as being financially ineligible), the individual does not qualify for legal aid in such a case;
3) to amend or refuse to amend a limitation or condition attached to a grant of ECF; and
4) to withdraw ECF.

17.10 The deadline to apply for internal review on an ECF case is 14 days, and any such application must be made on form APP9E and include written representations in support of the application.[4]

---

2 This is despite LAA policy stating that practitioners should be notified of a decision upheld following an internal review – see LAA guidance *Appeals: civil merits* at: www.gov.uk/guidance/appeals-civil-merits.
3 Civil Legal Aid (Procedure) Regulations 2012 reg 69(1)(b).
4 Civil Legal Aid (Procedure) Regulations 2012 reg 69(2). Form APP9e can be found at: www.gov.uk/government/publications/legal-aid-exceptional-case-funding-form-and-guidance.

17.11 The application should be sent by email to ContactECC@justice.gov.uk.[5]

17.12 Unless the LAA has specified otherwise, where the decision under review was to withdraw ECF, and that decision is overturned following an internal review, the decision takes effect as though the original withdrawal decision had not been made – ie work carried out in the interim would be payable.[6]

17.13 There is no right of appeal to an IFA against a final decision to refuse ECF. The next step would be to apply for judicial review. Judicial review falls within the scope of LASPO, so it may be possible to obtain legal aid to bring such a challenge.

Internal review: licensed work

17.14 Except in cases of Emergency Representation refusals,[7] before reaching a decision to withdraw legal aid on the ground of means or merits, the LAA must first invite written representations within a specified time limit and consider those representations before reaching a final decision.[8]

17.15 If the LAA then goes on to refuse legal aid, there is a right to internal review against a decision:

1) that a case does not fall within the scope of LASPO;[9]
2) that an individual does not qualify for the civil legal aid services (eg on means or merits grounds);[10]
3) that an individual qualifies for civil legal aid services but not on the terms requested (ie subject to a limitation or condition);[11]
4) to amend or refuse to amend a limitation or condition;[12] or
5) to withdraw legal aid.[13]

17.16 The deadline for internal review is 14 days.[14]

---

5 *Exceptional Cases Funding – Provider Pack*, LAA, September 2022, p7, available at: https://assets.publishing.service.gov.uk/government/uploads/system/uploads/attachment_data/file/1114082/ECF_Provider_Pack_September_2022_Amendments.pdf.
6 Civil Legal Aid (Procedure) Regulations 2012 reg 69(4).
7 Civil Legal Aid (Procedure) Regulations 2012 reg 50(3).
8 Civil Legal Aid (Procedure) Regulations 2012 reg 42(3).
9 Civil Legal Aid (Procedure) Regulations 2012 reg 44(1)(a).
10 Civil Legal Aid (Procedure) Regulations 2012 reg 44(1)(b).
11 Civil Legal Aid (Procedure) Regulations 2012 reg 44(1)(c).
12 Civil Legal Aid (Procedure) Regulations 2012 reg 44(1)(d).
13 Civil Legal Aid (Procedure) Regulations 2012 reg 44(1)(e).
14 Civil Legal Aid (Procedure) Regulations 2012 reg 44.

Appeals to IFAs and Costs Assessors

17.17 Where the LAA goes on to withdraw legal aid, the withdrawal takes effect from the date that the written representations were requested, not at the date of the final decision to withdraw, so any work carried out in the interim would be at risk of non-payment.[15]

Funding appeals: controlled work immigration cases

17.18 In asylum and in scope immigration CLR cases, the power to make decisions to refuse or withdraw legal representation[16] lies with you, the practitioner.[17] In such cases, the client has a right of appeal against **your** decision to refuse legal aid. The same would apply to an ECF case where you decided to withdraw CLR after the LAA had decided to grant it.

17.19 Where you have decided to refuse or withdraw CLR (other than on grounds of financial eligibility) you must complete and retain a copy of form CW4. The form must clearly state the date and reason for your decision.

17.20 As soon as possible, and in any event within five days of the decision, you must provide the client with a copy of the CW4 form and tell them of their right to appeal your decision and details of how to do this (the form provides the details of how to appeal). You can, if instructed to do this, help your client appeal against your decision, making clear any grounds for urgency such as a hearing date.

17.21 There is no deadline for the client to bring such an appeal.

17.22 The powers of the IFA in such cases are the same as in licensed work (see below).

17.23 If you are instructed by a client who has had such a refusal made by another practitioner, you are not prevented from taking on the case in the absence of a successful appeal, because the decision to grant legal aid is yours to make. However, a successful appeal to an IFA would protect you against the LAA stating at the end of case that you were wrong to grant legal aid.

Funding appeals: licensed work

17.24 In licensed work, there is a right of appeal against **all** decisions to refuse or withdraw legal aid, **unless** the decision to refuse is made on the basis that:[18]

---

15 Civil Legal Aid (Procedure) Regulations 2012 reg 42(4).
16 Civil Legal Aid (Procedure) Regulations 2012 reg 28(1).
17 Immigration Specification 2018 paras 8.47–8.51.
18 Civil Legal Aid (Procedure) Regulations 2012 reg 45(1).

1) the case does not fall within the scope of LASPO; or
2) the individual does not qualify on the grounds of means.

17.25 In the case of a refusal of Emergency Representation, there is no right of appeal against a decision made on the basis of limited information and documents[19] – ie if the LAA takes the view that you have not provided a complete set of papers. There is also no right of appeal against a refusal made solely on the basis that the time limit to bring the case in question has expired.[20]

Powers of the IFA

17.26 On the following matters, an IFA's decision replaces that of the LAA:
1) prospects of success;
2) costs–benefit criteria;
3) whether the case is of overwhelming importance to the individual; and
4) whether a determination that someone qualifies for legal aid should be withdrawn or revoked in light of their conduct.[21]

17.27 In relation to all other appealable decisions, an IFA can only consider whether the decision was unlawful or unreasonable and refer it back to the LAA for a new decision.[22] In such cases, the LAA must reconsider its decision, taking into account the IFA's decision and any new information provided following the review.[23]

17.28 Where the IFA upholds the LAA's decision, the IFA must give written reasons, and the LAA must notify the individual of that decision.[24]

Submission of further information

17.29 Guidance IFAs suggests that additional information submitted at the time of the appeal may be taken into account,[25] although as stated

---

19 Civil Legal Aid (Procedure) Regulations 2012 reg 53(1)(a).
20 Civil Legal Aid (Procedure) Regulations 2012 reg 53(1)(a).
21 Civil Legal Aid (Procedure) Regulations 2012 reg 46(1)(a), read with reg 47(1).
22 Civil Legal Aid (Procedure) Regulations 2012 reg 46(1)(b), read with reg 47(1).
23 Civil Legal Aid (Procedure) Regulations 2012 reg 48(1).
24 Civil Legal Aid (Procedure) Regulations 2012 reg 47(2).
25 *Appeals Manual 2013*, p25, available at: https://assets.publishing.service.gov.uk/government/uploads/system/uploads/attachment_data/file/1114734/LAA_Appeals_Manual_October_2022.pdf.

Oral hearings and panels

17.30 It is very rare for an oral hearing to be held. The presumption is that appeals to IFAs will be decided without a hearing unless it is in the interests of justice to have a hearing.[26]

17.31 The IFA or LAA may refer the appeal to a panel of two or more adjudicators where it considers that the appeal is of exceptional complexity or importance.[27]

LAA decision upheld for different reasons

17.32 Where, following an appeal to an IFA, the decision of the LAA is upheld but for reasons that are materially different from the reasons for the decision under appeal, you may appeal once again to an IFA, but this may not happen a further time.[28]

Backdating licensed work: post 20 February 2019

17.33 Unless the LAA specifies otherwise, in all cases where an IFA has overturned a decision to **withdraw** legal aid, work done in the interim is claimable.[29]

17.34 In relation to decisions to **refuse** legal aid made from 20 February 2019 onwards, it is possible to claim work carried out in the interim – between the refusal and the successful appeal – where:[30]

1) the application for legal aid was made as soon as reasonably practical;
2) it was in the interests of justice that work was carried out prior to the final decision;
3) the work could not have been carried out as controlled work; and
4) having regard to all the circumstances, including information that was available to the practitioner when the application for legal aid was made, it is appropriate for payment to be backdated.

---

26 Civil Legal Aid (Procedure) Regulations 2012 reg 45(2).
27 Civil Legal Aid (Procedure) Regulations 2012 reg 45(3).
28 Civil Legal Aid (Procedure) Regulations 2012 reg 48(4).
29 Civil Legal Aid (Procedure) Regulations 2012 reg 48(5).
30 Civil Legal Aid (Procedure) Regulations 2012 reg 35, as amended by the Civil Legal Aid (Procedure) (Amendment) Regulations 2019.

Nil assessment appeals in controlled work cases

17.35 What we have called 'nil assessment' appeals are challenges to decisions taken by the LAA at the end of a case or after an audit that you did not carry out a sufficient merits, or, more often means, assessment. The result being that all the work carried out was not claimable and payment is reduced to nil. Because this happens at the end of a case, it can mean losing payment for considerable work and disbursements. There are some helpful tips to deal with such decisions. For those reasons, we give such appeals specific consideration.

17.36 First, have you been granted ECF? If so, it is the LAA, not you, that made the grant of legal aid. The error, if there is one, is the LAA's, and you are entitled to claim for legal aid granted by the LAA, subject to any changes not made known to the LAA.

17.37 Second, if you are to appeal, it is possible to submit evidence of means that was not available at the time the LAA made the decision to nil assess. An example of this could be if the LAA nil assess the claim on account of one payslip being missing in a series of payslips, there are good reasons this was missing at the time, and you can obtain the missing payslip to submit at the time of the appeal. Even if there was no good reason that the payslip was missing, if you can obtain it at the time of the appeal, you should ask that it be considered. Practice shows that the LAA and IFAs are generally willing to consider evidence obtained after the grant of legal aid, so long as evidence covers the computation period.

17.38 If you were responsible for the grant of legal aid (in non-ECF controlled work cases), the LAA or IFA may only depart from your assessment that the merits test is satisfied where your decision was 'manifestly unreasonable', or where the assessment was:

> ... plainly unreasonable, such that no reasonably competent solicitor, in light of their then knowledge, could have concluded that the relevant merits test was met rather than because an assessor has simply made a different, although equally valid, decision about merits.[31]

Although this quote from the Costs Assessment Guidance refers to 'merits', to assess merits under the Civil Legal Aid (Merits Criteria) Regulations 2013 also includes an assessment as to whether a client has access to other sources of funding – ie an assessment of their

---

31 *Costs Assessment Guidance: for use with the 2018 Standard Civil Contracts*, LAA, section 6, available at: www.gov.uk/guidance/funding-and-costs-assessment-for-civil-and-crime-matters.

17.39 None of this, of course, overrides your duty to carry out an assessment of means and merits according to the relevant regulations, but where there is any element of discretion, such as assessing an individual's claim to have no income, the decision lies with you, and so the LAA and IFA should only overturn your decision where it was manifestly unreasonable.

17.40 A sensible approach to the assessment of incomplete means can be seen in *R (Duncan Lewis Solicitors) v Lord Chancellor*.[32] Although this case was under the Access to Justice Act 1999, the principles apply equally here.

17.41 Duncan Lewis had assessed its client as being financially eligible for legal aid on the basis of a letter from social services stating that the client was supported financially under the Children Act 1989. The letter stated the amount of money received by the client and, on assessment, was accepted as adequate.[33] However, when the case moved on to another form of legal aid, and an updated letter was provided, it did not state the amount given by social services to the client, but it was clear that support under the Children Act 1989 continued.[34]

17.42 The LAA 'nil assessed' the claim, meaning Duncan Lewis could not claim for work done at the later stage of the case. An IFA upheld that decision, stating that because the letter did not state the amount received by the client, the assessment of means was inadequate.[35]

17.43 When the case went to judicial review, Cranston J held that the IFA had asked himself the wrong question.[36] While Duncan Lewis had a clear obligation to assess means, the combination of the two letters made it clear that the client was in receipt of support from social services, and in any event Duncan Lewis would have been aware how much is received by such a client supported by social services, which would not have been anywhere near the legal aid financial eligibility threshold.[37]

17.44 The Lord Chancellor accepted that the crux of the case was whether this evidence was satisfactory,[38] and Duncan Lewis had to

32 [2015] EWHC 2498 (Admin).
33 At paras 3–4.
34 At paras 4 and 7.
35 At para 11.
36 At para 28.
37 At paras 29–30.
38 At para 31.

'make a judgment whether they had satisfactory evidence', and in doing so they could consider the evidence before them which was to be 'read against the background of their extensive knowledge' of the people in their client's position.[39] The question was not whether the letter stated the specific amount received but whether, when read in light of Duncan Lewis's extensive knowledge of people in their client's position, the evidence was 'reasonably sufficient'.[40]

17.45 The *Duncan Lewis* case is particularly useful in appeals where the issue is whether you were right to accept a piece of evidence (or right to assess legal aid in the absence of some information or evidence) from the client as to their means.

Appeals to Independent Costs Assessors

Introduction

17.46 Appeals to ICAs are appeals against decisions of the LAA to reduce payment for work done. They can occur at the end of a case, or, even later, after an audit.

Appeals to ICA: procedure

17.47 Following an assessment of costs made by the LAA at the end of a case, if either you (the supplier) or counsel are dissatisfied with that assessment, there is a right of appeal to an ICA.[41]

17.48 The appeal must be made within 28 days of notification of the decision, and must be accompanied by the file. The LAA can extend the time limit for up to 14 days, where an application is made providing good reason for an extension, and the application itself is made within 21 days.[42]

17.49 If you appeal, the LAA has the right to make additional written representations to the ICA. The LAA must do this 21 days before the appeal is sent to the ICA, allowing you 14 days to provide a written response to it. However, be aware that the LAA often does not provide a copy of such reasons, so you should watch out for this as a ground for further challenge.

---

39 At para 33.
40 At paras 31, 33.
41 Standard Civil Contract 2024 Specification para 6.71.
42 Standard Civil Contract 2024 Specification para 6.72.

17.50 The ICA has the power to review the assessment, whether by confirming, increasing or decreasing the amount assessed. In a controlled work assessment, the ICA may apply their findings generally across files outside the sample before them.[43] The same or similar powers existed in the 2013 Contract.

17.51 In reaching a decision, the ICA will be bound by the Costs Assessment Guidance, the Standard Contract Terms and the category-specific rules, and must decide what work was reasonably done, the reasonable time to be spent in relation to that work and what reasonable remuneration should be.

17.52 There is a presumption that there will be no right to an oral hearing or to be represented before the ICA, but you may make an application for an oral hearing at the time your appeal, demonstrating exceptional circumstances.[44]

Some tips for appeals to ICAs

17.53 To succeed in appeals before an ICA or, even better, to avoid the need to do so in the first place, there are a few simple tips as follows:

- Always record work done at the time that you did it, even if briefly. If, for example, you read documents while you drafted, note down the documents, and ideally state how long they were, with a brief note on any complexities (eg if medical or technical), or matters that might have added time (eg if the document was handwritten or you needed to cross-refer to other items).
- Refer to the Costs Assessment Guidance to be clear on what work you can and cannot claim for. See appendix C for common queries in relation to the Costs Assessment Guidance.
- Compare the work you did against what the Costs Assessment Guidance states is reasonable to claim for. Take the example of drafting a two-page letter that took you one hour to draft. The LAA, with little information to go on, might reasonably suggest that one hour was too long and reduce the amount paid. However, had you made clear that you had read 16 pages of complex medical documents and the rate for reading the most simple prepared document is two minutes per page, and the rate for drafting the most straightforward document is 6–12 minutes, it is far easier to justify your work.

---

43 Standard Civil Contract 2018 Specification para 6.80.
44 Standard Contract 2018 para 6.75; see also the Appeals Manual at p16 (this is internal guidance for IFAs and is not on the LAA website).

Special casework decisions

17.54 In relation to decisions on special casework matters, special provisions apply which include that appeals are to a specially appointed panel, not to an IFA.[45]

Family mediation

17.55 In family mediation, there is a right to apply for internal review, and no right of appeal to an IFA.[46] No time limit is specified for such an application.

Further challenges

17.56 If you have come to the end of the road with either an internal review or a funding appeal, the next step is to bring a judicial review.

---

45 Civil Legal Aid (Procedure) Regulations 2012 regs 58–59.
46 Civil Legal Aid (Procedure) Regulations 2012 reg 65.

PART B

Legal aid advocacy

CHAPTER 18

Advocacy in civil cases

Edited by Simon Mullings

18.1	Introduction
18.5	General principles
18.8	**Help at Court**
18.8	Scope
18.12	Merits test
	The sufficient benefit test
18.16	Specific areas of work
	Housing cases
18.21	Who can provide advocacy?
18.22	Payment for advocacy services
18.23	**Controlled Legal Representation**
18.24	**Representation certificates**
18.29	**Payment for advocacy services**
18.29	Work done by a solicitor
18.30	Work done by counsel – cases started prior to 2 December 2013
18.32	Work done by counsel – cases started on or after 2 December 2013
18.38	Payment on account of counsel's fees
18.43	High Cost civil cases
18.47	Unpaid fees
18.50	Inter partes costs and legal aid only costs
	Legal aid only costs

Key resources

Statute and regulations
- Legal Aid Sentencing and Punishment of Offenders Act 2012 – Schedule 1 Part 1
- Civil Legal Aid (Procedure) Regulations 2012
- Civil Legal Aid (Merits Criteria) Regulations 2013
- Civil Legal Aid (Remuneration) Regulations 2013 and Civil Legal Aid (Remuneration) (Amendment) Regulations 2013

Contracts
- 2024 Standard Civil Contract Standard Terms
- 2024 Standard Civil Contract – Specification (General Provisions)
- 2018 Standard Civil Contract Table of Amendments – from January 2024
- 2024 Standard Civil Contract Category Definitions
- 2018 Standard Civil Contract Specification, Category Specific Rules – see relevant area of law

Lord Chancellor's Guidance
- Lord Chancellor's Guidance under section 4 of the Legal Aid, Sentencing and Punishment of Offenders Act 2012, May 2023
- Costs Assessment Guidance – www.gov.uk/guidance/funding-and-costs-assessment-for-civil-and-crime-matters

Other
- Standard Contractual Terms for the Supply of Legal Services by Barristers to Authorised Persons 2020, Bar Council, available at: www.barcouncilethics.co.uk/documents/contractual-terms

Key points to note
- For details of advocacy under the Housing Loss Prevention and Advice Service (HLPAS) see chapter 11.
- It is important to know under what type of funding advocacy can and cannot be provided, and rules are different for different areas of law. Make sure you know or know where to look for the rules for your area(s) of law.

- If you are a solicitor or caseworker, you will still need to know how the remuneration of barristers works under legal aid, even if you are not doing any advocacy work yourself. This is because overall you are responsible for barristers' fees. In this chapter we set out what you will need to do in the course of a case where a barrister is instructed.
- However, if you are doing advocacy work yourself under a legal aid certificate as a solicitor or caseworker, make sure you consider claiming enhancements to your hourly rates (see chapter 15).
- Keeping on top of scope limitations and costs limitations is essential to make sure any advocacy work, whether conducted by yourself or by a barrister, is covered by legal aid.

Introduction

18.1 This chapter deals with the conduct of and payment for advocacy in civil cases and the general rules applying to both civil and family cases.

18.2 In general, we use the term 'advocate' to refer to anyone who has a right of audience to appear in the relevant court or who the court is willing to hear where the scheme makes no distinction between solicitor and counsel. Where there is a difference according to whether advocacy is conducted by solicitor or by counsel, we will use the terms 'solicitor' and 'counsel' as appropriate.

18.3 This chapter only deals with the advocacy aspects of cases. For more information on the conduct of litigation, see Part A of this Handbook. For information on the particular rules applying in family and criminal cases, see chapters 19 and 20.

18.4 We deal separately with the In Court Duty Scheme under the Housing Loss Prevention Advice Service (HLPAS) in chapter 11 and only mention it here where relevant.

General principles

18.5 Advocacy can only be conducted under the following levels of service:
- Help at Court;
- Controlled Legal Representation (CLR) (immigration and mental health only);
- Legal Representation (certificated work);
- specific contracts, such as a HLPAS contract.

18.6 Advocacy can only be carried out by a person who has a general right of audience or who has been given permission to be heard by the court in the specific case.

18.7 Advocacy funded by legal aid can only be carried out in matters before a court, whether remotely or in person, and before certain limited tribunals. The full list is set out in Legal Aid, Sentencing and Punishment of Offenders Act 2012 (LASPO) Sch 1 Part 3.

Help at Court

Scope

18.8 Work must be allowed within scope of the scheme (see chapters 2 and 4 for more information).

18.9 Help at Court is help and advocacy for a client in relation to a particular hearing, without formally acting as legal representative in the proceedings or being on the record at the court.[1] Help at Court only covers informal advocacy, usually by way of mitigation at individual court hearings. Ongoing representation can only be provided under a Legal Representation certificate.

18.10 Help at Court is particularly useful for cases where a Legal Representation certificate would not be available, for example, where a client does not have a defence to a possession claim but does need an experienced adviser to set out repayment proposals to the court. Note, however, that if it would be unreasonable for the court to make an order for possession in the circumstances; that can be treated as a defence to the claim for possession and a certificate should, assuming means and merits tests are met, be available. See chapter 11 for more information.

18.11 Help at Court can also be used to represent a client on an application for enforcement of an order where the client is the applicant. It is not a stand-alone level of funding, but can only be granted as an add-on to a pre-existing Legal Help matter.

---

1 Civil Legal Aid (Procedure) Regulations 2012 reg 5; see also *Lord Chancellor's Guidance under Section 4 of the Legal Aid, Sentencing and Punishment of Offenders Act 2012*, May 2023, para 6.9, available at: www.gov.uk/guidance/funding-and-costs-assessment-for-civil-and-crime-matters.

Merits test

The sufficient benefit test

18.12 The merits test is that:
- it is reasonable to provide funding, taking into account the availability of alternative (ie non-legal aid) funding;
- there is likely to be sufficient benefit, having regard to all the circumstances of the case, including the circumstances of the client, to justify the costs; and
- the nature and circumstances of the client, the proceedings and the particular hearing are such that advocacy is appropriate and would be of real benefit.[2]

18.13 You must apply the test before every hearing and note the file with your justification. 'Sufficient benefit test met' is not an adequate justification.

18.14 There are no additional fixed fees to cover Help at Court. However, the additional work involved may make it more likely that the case will reach the Legal Help escape threshold (three times the fixed fee).

18.15 Where advocacy is justified, you may claim travel and waiting to/ from and at court, as well as preparation and attendance, where appropriate. See chapter 15 for more information on payment schemes.

Specific areas of work

Housing cases

18.16 The (now defunct) Funding Code Guidance, at section 19.3, provided specific guidance on the use of Help at Court in housing cases. You may still find it helpful to consult it if your organisation has a pre-LASPO copy of the Legal Services Commission (LSC) Manual (eg that dated December 2012, vol 3) – an online version is available in the archived version of the old LSC website.[3]

18.17 Before making an application for a full certificate, you should consider the availability of Help at Court. This may be more appropriate where the client has no defence but seeks to influence the discretion of the court in relation to postponing possession or

---

2 Civil Legal Aid (Merits Criteria) Regulations 2013 reg 33.
3 *Funding Code – Non-Family Guidance*, archived on 3 April 2013: http:// webarchive.nationalarchives.gov.uk/20130403152321/http://www.justice.gov. uk/legal-aid/funding/funding-code/non-family-guidance.

suspending eviction.⁴ In the latter case, Help at Court should not be used where a certificate would be more appropriate (unless one has been applied for and refused) as formal representation can be made on behalf of the client, directions obtained for exchange of statements and relevant medical reports, and the hearing allocated sufficient time for judicial consideration.

18.18 A full certificate should be applied for where the client has a substantive defence to the possession proceedings, or where there is a substantial issue of fact or law or where the client should be formally represented in the proceedings.

18.19 Neither should Help at Court be used where it is not justified, for example because it would achieve no more than would explaining to the client what steps they could take themselves or writing a letter on their behalf under Legal Help.

18.20 See chapter 11 for more information on housing cases.

Who can provide advocacy?

18.21 Solicitors can attend court under Help at Court in circumstances where they have rights of audience; since it will almost always be the county court, that will be most cases. Advisers without rights of audience may provide advocacy and claim payment under Help at Court, as long as advocacy is justified, and the court agrees to hear them. Counsel may not be instructed under Help at Court.⁵

Payment for advocacy services

18.22 Advocacy under Help at Court – and associated preparation, attendance, travel and waiting – is claimable as part of the main Legal Help matter. The costs are included within the fixed fee and may be taken into account in determining whether the case becomes an escape fee case – if it does, the costs will be payable at hourly rates.

---

4 *Lord Chancellor's Guidance under Section 4 of the Legal Aid, Sentencing and Punishment of Offenders Act 2012* para 6.9(b).
5 Standard Civil Contract 2024 Specification para 3.61, available at: www.gov.uk/government/publications/standard-civil-contract-2024.

Controlled Legal Representation

18.23   CLR is only available in the immigration and mental health categories, and advocacy under those levels of service is dealt with in chapters 9 and 10, and payment in chapter 15.

Representation certificates

18.24   Where a certificate is issued to a solicitor covering proceedings before a court, it will in principle be possible to provide and claim for advocacy services under the certificate at all hearings in the case, though like every other step in the proceedings attendance at hearings is subject to there being merit in taking that step. You should also make sure that the particular hearing is within the limitation of the certificate; final hearings, for example, are generally not included within the scope of a certificate when first issued, and an amendment is needed to include trial/final hearing in the limitation.

18.25   Advocacy under a certificate can be undertaken by a solicitor (subject to rights of audience in the higher courts) or by counsel. An advocate can be employed by your organisation or be in independent practice, either as a freelance solicitor or solicitor agent or as counsel in chambers. Under para 7.3 of the Standard Civil Contract 2024,[6] you must consult your client regarding the use and selection of counsel or in-house advocate, unless it is not practical or appropriate to do so.

18.26   There is general authority to instruct one junior advocate under a certificate;[7] the instruction of more than one junior, or of Kings' Counsel (KC) acting as such, requires an application for prior authority to be made.[8] Unless the authority is granted, no claim can be made by a second advocate appearing at any hearing or by a KC for acting as such (it is always open to a KC to accept instructions to appear as a junior and to be paid on that basis).[9] In a case where the statutory charge applies, you also require the informed consent of your client to the incurring of the extra costs of instructing a KC or

---

6   Available at: www.gov.uk/government/publications/standard-civil-contract-2024.
7   Standard Civil Contract 2024 Specification para 5.12.
8   Standard Civil Contract 2024 Specification para 5.10(b).
9   Standard Civil Contract 2024 Specification para 6.59(d).

second counsel,[10] and costs officers will be looking to see that on your file.[11]

18.27 Where you instruct counsel, the brief must include a copy of the certificate and a copy of any prior authority to instruct counsel.[12] Where the certificate has not yet been issued, you should provide counsel with a copy within 14 days of receipt.[13]

18.28 You can instruct a solicitor not employed by your organisation to provide advocacy services.[14]

Payment for advocacy services

Work done by a solicitor

18.29 Advocacy work, and associated preparation, attendance, travel and waiting, done by a solicitor is payable at the hourly rates set out in the Civil Legal Aid (Remuneration) Regulations 2013. This is true whether the solicitor is employed by your organisation or is acting as an independent solicitor advocate. Their times should be included on your bill along with all other profit costs and will be assessed in the usual way. See chapter 15 for details of the assessment process. The fact that a solicitor has undertaken the advocacy themselves rather than instruct counsel, especially in a complex case, will assist in justifying an enhancement to the hourly rates.

Work done by counsel – cases started prior to 2 December 2013

18.30 Barristers' fees are codified in all cases started on or after 3 October 2011. For cases started after that date, but before 2 December 2013, there are hourly rates applicable in all courts and for three categories of barrister – KCs and senior and junior counsel (respectively, 10 years' call or more and less than 10 years' call). The location of chambers, not the court, determines whether the London or non-London rate should be claimed (only junior counsel in the county court have

---

10 *Practice Note (Solicitors: taxation of costs)* [1982] 2 All ER 683.
11 *Costs Assessment Guidance: for use with the 2018 Standard Civil Contract*, para 13.8, available at: www.gov.uk/guidance/funding-and-costs-assessment-for-civil-and-crime-matters.
12 Standard Civil Contract 2024 Specification para 5.13(a) and (b).
13 Standard Civil Contract 2024 Specification para 5.14.
14 Standard Civil Contract 2024 Specification para 2.5.

separate London and non-London rates).[15] See Civil Legal Aid (Remuneration) Regulations 2013 Sch 2 for the rates. They apply to barristers in independent practice but not solicitor advocates or barristers employed by solicitor firms, both of whom claim at solicitor rates.

18.31 There is a discretion for junior counsel in the county court to be paid at higher rates than those set out in the Civil Legal Aid (Remuneration) Regulations 2013. The regulations merely say that the Legal Aid Agency (LAA) can do so if it is 'reasonable' to do so. The Costs Assessment Guidance applicable at the time[16] went on to say that the decision lies with the LAA, even if the court has assessed fees at the higher rate, and that factors to be taken into account include:

- the complexity of case – for example, the gravity of the case, points of law or contested evidence;
- novel areas of law – a case requiring unusually specialised knowledge or skill or that is likely to set a precedent or have a wider impact;
- where an opponent has instructed a QC;[17]
- a case requiring considerable amount of out of hours work;
- where a client has mental health problems, learning difficulties, social impairment or language difficulties that may impact on the approach taken;
- where the case involves an unusually large number of parties represented at a contested final hearing;
- where a hearing requires the cross-examination of more than one expert on technical issues, for example in clinical negligence cases; and
- a fully contested hearing lasting more than two days.

Work done by counsel – cases started on or after 2 December 2013

18.32 For cases started on or after 2 December 2013, payment rates for counsel were reduced, in most cases, to the rates applicable to

15 *Costs Assessment Guidance: for use with the 2013, 2014, 2015, 2018 and 2024 Standard Civil Contracts*, para 13.9. www.gov.uk/guidance/funding-and-costs-assessment-for-civil-and-crime-matters.
16 This was formerly in Costs Assessment Guidance para 13.12, but has been removed from the current edition, presumably as these provisions are not in force for certificates granted after December 2013.
17 Reference to QC applicable for the guidance at that time.

solicitors doing the same work where the case is in the High Court or below, or in the Upper Tribunal. The location of chambers, not the court, determines whether the London or non-London rate should be claimed.[18] Where chambers has more than one address, the solicitor's location will be taken into account in determining the applicable rates.

18.33 There are separate rates for counsel appearing in the Court of Appeal and Supreme Court, which depend on the level of counsel's seniority. Those rates also apply to KCs acting as such and appearing in any court (assuming authority for a KC has been granted). The rates are set out in Civil Legal Aid (Remuneration) (Amendment) Regulations 2013 Sch 1. There are no prescribed rates for work done in tribunals other than the Upper Tribunal (where in scope or as part of exceptional funding), but in determining the rate paid costs officers should have regard to the prescribed rates.[19]

18.34 Where junior counsel is paid at prescribed rates in the High Court or below, an application for an enhancement of the rates may be made on the bill.[20] The criteria for enhancement are that the work done by counsel (either a particular item of work or hearing, or on the case as a whole):

- was done with exceptional competence, skill or expertise;
- was done with exceptional speed; or
- involved exceptional circumstances or complexity.

18.35 In calculating the percentage enhancement, costs officers will have regard to the degree of responsibility accepted by counsel, the care, speed and efficiency with which counsel prepared the case, and its novelty, weight and complexity. Assessment of the care with which counsel prepared the case includes the skill with which the work was carried out and in particular the case shown to a vulnerable client, while the weight of the case means the volume of documentation, the number of issues arising or the importance of the case to the client.[21]

18.36 The percentage enhancement can never exceed 100 per cent in the Upper Tribunal or High Court and 50 per cent in the county court. In determining what is exceptional, regard is to be had to the

---

18 *Costs Assessment Guidance: for use with the 2018 and 2024 Standard Civil Contracts* para 13.9: www.gov.uk/guidance/funding-and-costs-assessment-for-civil-and-crime-matters.
19 Civil Legal Aid (Remuneration) Regulations 2013 reg 7(4).
20 Civil Legal Aid (Remuneration) Regulations 2013 reg 7(3).
21 Civil Legal Aid (Remuneration) Regulations 2013 reg 7(5).

generality of proceedings to which the prescribed rate to be enhanced applies.

18.37 In practice, similar considerations apply to the enhancement of counsels' fees as to apply to the enhancement of solicitors' fees. See chapter 15 for more information; and the criteria contained in the Costs Assessment Guidance.[22]

Payment on account of counsel's fees

18.38 Counsel can apply direct to the LAA via the Client and Cost Management System (CCMS) for a payment on account of their costs.[23] An application can be made on each anniversary of the issue of the certificate, with a window of two months before and four months after the relevant date. However, the fees need to have been allocated on CCMS (see chapters 5 and 15) and so provider organisations will find that chambers are keen for that to be done and have it confirmed to them.

18.39 An application can also be made at any point if:
- the proceedings have continued for more than 12 months;
- it appears unlikely that an order will be made for the costs of the case to be assessed within the next 12 months; and
- delay in the assessment will cause hardship to counsel.

18.40 An application can also be made if:
- the proceedings have concluded or counsel is otherwise entitled to payment; and
- six months have elapsed since then and counsel has not been paid.

18.41 On application, the LAA will pay up to 80 per cent of counsel's reasonable fees. If the final payment is less than the amount of any payments on account, the outstanding balance will be recouped from counsel.[24]

---

22 *Costs Assessment Guidance: for use with the 2018 and 2024 Standard Civil Contracts* section 12: www.gov.uk/guidance/funding-and-costs-assessment-for-civil-and-crime-matters.
23 Civil Legal Aid (Remuneration) Regulations 2013 reg 11.
24 Civil Legal Aid (Remuneration) Regulations 2013 reg 12.

> **Case study**
>
> I am instructed in a case where my solicitor's certificate was issued on 1 April 2020 and the case is still ongoing. When can I make a payment on account application?
>
> You can apply on the anniversary of the issue of the certificate, but there is a window either side to allow some flexibility – two months before and two months after the date. So you could have applied for a payment on account at any point between 1 February and 1 June 2021. If the case continues into 2022, you can apply again at any time between 1 February 2022 and 1 June 2022, and so on into 2023 if applicable.
>
> At any time, you should put your total costs to date into CCMS, and the LAA will pay 75 per cent of that (subject to reasonableness), less any payment you have already received. So, for example, if you were paid £1,000 on account in 2020 and by 1 February 2022 your costs have reached £5,000, you should put £5,000 on the form and will be paid £2,750 (75 per cent of £5,000 = £3,750, less £1,000 already received).

18.42 These provisions do not apply to family proceedings where the Family Advocacy Scheme (FAS) applies – see chapter 19 on FAS.

High Cost civil cases

18.43 Where the case is a High Cost case (see chapter 4), any advocacy work will also be part of the individual case contract.

18.44 Any contract will be with the solicitor, but where an external advocate is instructed, they will need to agree to the payment rates and case/stage plans.

18.45 The rates payable to counsel depend on the classification of the case. Where there is a possibility that, if successful, inter partes costs will be recovered, the case is deemed to be 'at risk' and the rates will be £50 per hour for junior counsel and £90 per hour for senior counsel. Where prospects of success are only borderline but the case is nonetheless being funded because of its overwhelming importance to the client, wider public interest or significant human rights issues, the rates will be £65 and £117, respectively. Where there is no prospect of inter partes costs, standard remuneration rates will apply.[25] The first £5,000 of counsel's fees will always be paid at standard rates rather than High Cost case contract rates.

18.46 See chapter 15 for claiming costs in High Cost civil cases.

Unpaid fees

18.47 Counsel can only claim fees through solicitors. In certificated cases, solicitors must include counsel's fees in the bill, and must submit the bill to the court or LAA for assessment within the three-month time limit. See chapter 15 for details of the process.

18.48 Where the solicitor fails to submit the bill, counsel will not be paid, as there is no provision for counsel to bill the LAA directly. Counsel can, to some extent, protect themselves by using the payment on account scheme to recover 75 per cent of the costs. Counsel can place solicitors on the List of Defaulting Solicitors, and can complain, through the Bar Council, to the Solicitors Regulation Authority (SRA). Note that the Bar Council's Standard Terms of Business[26] do not apply to legal aid work.

18.49 It is a term of the Standard Civil Contract that bills be submitted within the three-month time limit (which runs from the date of the right to claim accruing);[27] failure to do so is a breach of contract, and repeated failure may lead to sanctions up to and including termination. Counsel may wish to draw a solicitor's failure to submit a bill to the attention of the LAA. Conversely, solicitors are not paid in CCMS cases if counsel have not submitted their bill, so it is much appreciated if this is done quickly.

Inter partes costs and legal aid only costs

18.50 In cases where inter partes costs are possible, it is not uncommon for costs to be ordered or negotiated on the basis of payment of part of the costs of the case. If so, it is important that you are clear as to the terms of the order or agreement, as in some cases but not others you may be able to claim the balance from the legal aid fund. The Standard Civil Contract allows you to claim from the legal aid fund

---

25 *VHCC – Solicitors Information Pack (Non-Family)*, v4, LAA, September 2017, section 12, available at: www.gov.uk/government/publications/high-cost-cases-non-family-civil.
26 *Standard Contractual Terms for the Supply of Legal Services by Barristers to Authorised Persons 2021*, Bar Council, available at: www.barcouncilethics.co.uk/documents/contractual-terms.
27 Standard Civil Contract 2024 Specification para 6.33.

Legal aid only costs

18.51 The Specification defines 'legal aid only' costs – costs that can be claimed from the legal aid fund even where inter partes costs are recovered – as:
- costs of completing legal aid forms and communicating with the LAA;
- certain limited types of costs disallowed or not agreed; and
- costs of work not covered by a costs order or agreement.

18.52 Where a costs order or agreement specifies that another party should pay a proportion of the client's costs (but not a fixed sum), the same proportion of the total work that is not covered is legal aid only costs.[28]

18.53 To take a practical example, say total costs on the case are £2,000 at legal aid rates and £4,000 at inter partes rates. If the other side agree to pay your costs in the sum of £2,000, that could be expressed in one of three ways:
- £2,000 as the total agreed costs of the case;
- agreement to pay costs between X and Y dates, totalling £2,000; or
- agreement to pay 50 per cent of the costs, being £2,000.

18.54 In each case, you receive £2,000 from the other side:
- In the first case, that £2,000 represents the total costs of the case, so there are no legal aid costs (apart perhaps from £100 or so for completing an application and other tasks on CCMS and so on).
- In the second case, costs outside the agreed dates are not subject to the costs order, so you can claim those costs in addition to the inter partes costs you have received.
- In the third case, the other side has agreed to pay 50 per cent of your costs, so the other 50 per cent is legal aid only costs, so you can claim £1,000 (50 per cent of £2,000 at legal aid rates) from the LAA in addition to the £2,000 from the other side.

See also chapter 15 at para 15.134 onwards.

---

28 Standard Civil Contract 2024 Specification paras 6.50 and 6.51.

CHAPTER 19
Advocacy in family cases

By Samantha Little

19.1	Introduction
19.6	**Merits test**
19.7	**Family cases started prior to 9 May 2011**
19.7	Overview
19.8	Scope of the FGFS
19.10	**Family cases started on or after 9 May 2011**
19.10	Introduction
19.11	Scope of the FAS
	Overview • Escape fee cases • Mixed categories
19.20	Hearing fees
19.22	Interim hearing units
19.28	Final hearings
19.33	Cancelled hearings
19.34	Bolt-ons
	Overview • Public law • Private law • Court bundles • Exceptional travel • Payments for counsel only • Opinion fees
19.57	Assessment
19.58	CCMS and forms
19.62	FAS in High Cost cases

> **Key resources**
> - Community Legal Service (Funding) (Counsel in Family Proceedings) Order 2001
> - Civil Legal Aid (Remuneration) Regulations 2013
> - Standard Civil Contract 2024
> - Standard Civil Contract 2024 Specification and Standard Civil Contract Category Specific Rules –Family – section 7
> - Costs Assessment Guidance (frequently updated so always refer to the latest version – www.gov.uk/guidance/funding-and-costs-assessment-for-civil-and-crime-matters

> **Key points to note**
> - Family Advocacy Scheme Advocates' attendance forms are no longer required. Orders must set out the time taken for the hearing and the bolt-ons to evidence the advocacy claim.
> - There have been difficulties with care cases when a deprivation of liberty order application is made within care proceedings concerning the payment for the advocacy on the deprivation of liberty – this is now resolved and updated guidance received. See para 19.19 onwards below.
> - The position regarding when the hearing is an interim and when it is a final is sometimes confusing. Always refer to the Specification and the Costs Assessment Guidance if you are in doubt.
> - Advocates commonly overlook claiming bolt-ons. These are valuable so be vigilant about claiming them when they apply as they will increase your advocacy fee.
> - Self-employed advocates can claim for a cancelled hearing (but employed advocates cannot).

Introduction

19.1 This chapter deals with the particular rules that apply to conduct of and payment for advocacy in family cases. See chapter 15 for the general rules applying to both civil and family cases.

19.2 Advocacy can only be conducted under Legal Representation certificates in family work as Help at Court and Controlled Legal Representation (CLR) are not available in the family category.

19.3 In general, we use the term 'advocate' to refer to anyone who has a right of audience to appear in the relevant court or whom the court is willing to hear, where the scheme does not make a distinction between solicitor and counsel. Where there is a difference according to whether advocacy is conducted by solicitor or by counsel, we will use the terms 'solicitor' and 'counsel' as appropriate.

19.4 This chapter only deals with the advocacy aspects of family cases. For more information on the conduct of litigation, see Part A of this Handbook. For information on the rules applying to advocacy in criminal cases, see chapter 20; and chapter 18 for other civil cases.

19.5 In March 2020, the global Covid-19 pandemic affected the way we work. In relation to advocacy, almost all hearings at the start of the pandemic were held remotely (prior to this, a remote video or telephone hearing was extremely rare). Despite concerns at the outset, the costs of setting these hearings up were borne by HM Courts and Tribunals Service (HMCTS). Following the pandemic some cases are still heard remotely, both for case management and for substantive hearings. Where the pandemic has affected Family Advocacy Scheme (FAS) claims we have noted the differences, which by way of summary are:

- During the pandemic, the Legal Aid Agency (LAA) accepted the court order as evidence of the times of hearing and the existence of bolt-ons and Advocates Attendance Forms (AAFs) were not needed.
- After the pandemic, initially it was not clear whether AAFs would be needed for attended hearings, but it has been confirmed that AAFs are not needed for any hearing now and advocates can rely on the court order to evidence times, bolt-ons and bundle size. Attendance notes can be requested for hearings and advocates meetings in escape cases, so it is important that you keep your notes and evidence the times on those notes.
- Guidance has been provided to the judiciary about the FAS and this includes the standard wording for court orders to reflect court

times (*The Family Advocacy Scheme – Information for Judiciary*, LAA, October 2022).[1]
- As will be seen, the key times are the start of pre-hearing discussion and the time the hearing ended, **including** time for settling the court order, ie the only time you need to state is the total time for the hearing, including the time taken for the order. Therefore, you no longer have to record working through lunch, although you may choose to continue to record this.
- Times for remote hearings run as for attended hearings, ie from the time listed in the notice of hearing/order.

Merits test

19.6 See chapter 4 for the merits tests relevant to Legal Representation and chapters 6 and 7 for their operation in family cases.

Family cases started prior to 9 May 2011

Overview

19.7 The Family Graduated Fees Scheme (FGFS) continues to apply to these cases. The provisions of the scheme are set out in the Community Legal Service (Funding) (Counsel in Family Proceedings) Order 2001, as amended. It is unlikely that there are many, if any, outstanding cases to which this scheme applies, but for details see the 2011/12 edition of this Handbook.

---

1 **FAS Funding Recitals:**
UPON this hearing having taken place in person / remotely by CVP / telephone / Teams / as a hybrid hearing by order of the Court [*delete as appropriate*];
AND UPON the court noting the following provisions for FAS:
Family Court before: [*Judge*]
Hearing date: Court type: [*e.g. Magistrates, County Court, High Court*]
Case type: Type of Hearing: [*e.g. Directions, Case Management, Finding of Fact, Final Hearing*]
Bundle: [*number of pages*]
Pre-hearing discussions began at:
Start time of the hearing: End time, including time to agree an order:
TOTAL LENGTH OF THE HEARING: [*hours and minutes, deduct any adjournment*]
Bolt-ons and uplifts:
Advocates meetings:

Scope of the FGFS

19.8 The FGFS applies only to counsel. Solicitor advocates claim under the appropriate standard fee or hourly rate scheme, depending on whether the case is public or private law, and whether the case started prior to 1 October 2007.

19.9 Payments under the FGFS are essentially fixed or standard fee payments, with a range of base fees for different pieces of work. These fees are set according to the nature of the proceedings, the work to be done, whether junior or leading counsel is employed, and venue. There is also a range of additional payments that may be added to the fee due, to reflect special features and complexity. The permutation of possible payments is quite complex.

Family cases started on or after 9 May 2011

Introduction

19.10 The FAS applies to cases where the certificate was granted following an application made on or after 9 May 2011. The provisions of the scheme are set out in the Civil Legal Aid (Remuneration) Regulations 2013 Sch 3[2] and in section 7 of the Standard Civil Contract 2024 Specification (specifically Part D).[3]

Scope of the FAS

Overview

19.11 The fees apply to most advocacy, and the majority of fees can be claimed equally by solicitors and counsel, although the fees for providing opinions or advising in conference can only be claimed by counsel. The scheme uses the term 'advocate' when any advocate can claim a payment and 'counsel' when only the latter (or a self-employed solicitor or CILEx equivalent) can claim:

---

2 These regulations have been amended a number of times subsequent to their release in 2013, so ensure you consult the latest and amended version of them.
3 Available at: www.gov.uk/government/publications/standard-civil-contract-2024.

'Counsel' means either a barrister in independent practice; or a solicitor or Fellow of the Institute of Legal Executives who does not work in a partnership and does not hold a contract with us.[4]

19.12 Solicitors claim payment from the LAA in the usual way, and if you instruct a solicitor advocate freelancer or one from another firm, they act as an agent and you are responsible for their fees. Counsel claim FAS fees directly from the LAA.[5]

19.13 The advocacy fee includes all preparation for a hearing (including the preparation of a position statement), travel to and waiting at court, time spent in discussions, and in advocacy itself. The advocacy fee can only be claimed by the legal representative providing advocacy at a hearing. If a solicitor's representative attends with an advocate, they cannot also claim the fee (but can claim the time under the fixed fee for the casework, if justifiable).

19.14 Some types of advocacy are paid under hourly rates because they do not fall under the FAS.[6] Proceedings excluded from the FAS are given in para 7.107 of the Standard Civil Contract 2024 Specification:

(a) Child abduction proceedings;
(b) proceedings under the Inheritance (Provision for Family and Dependants) Act 1975;
(c) proceedings under the Trusts of Land and Appointment of Trustees Act 1996;
(d) proceedings in which you provide separate representation of a Child in proceedings other than Specified Proceedings (as defined in section 41(6) of the Children Act 1989) and proceedings which are being heard together with Specified Proceedings;
(e) applications for Forced Marriage Protection Orders under the Forced Marriage (Civil Protection) Act 2007;
(f) defended proceedings for divorce, judicial separation, dissolution of a civil partnership or for the legal separation of civil partners;
(g) nullity proceedings (including proceedings for annulment of a civil partnership);
(h) proceedings under the inherent jurisdiction of the High Court in relation to the children;
(i) applications for Parental Orders under the Human Fertilisation and Embryology Act 2008;
(j) applications in relation to female genital mutilation protection orders under the Female Genital Mutilation Act 2003.

---

4 Standard Civil Contract 2024 Specification para 7.117.
5 Standard Civil Contract 2024 Specification para 7.119.
6 Standard Civil Contract 2024 Specification para 7.107.

19.15 The following are also excluded[7]:
- advocacy in relation to appeals against final orders (but note that appeals of interim orders are covered within FAS unless they are in the Court of Appeal or Supreme Court. Applications to the court of first instance for permission to appeal are in the scope of FAS[8]);
- advocacy provided under a high costs case contract;[9]
- advocacy by King's Counsel (KCs); and
- advocacy before the Court of Appeal or Supreme Court.

19.16 The scheme is split into five categories of case:
1) care and supervision proceedings, including applications made within such proceedings or related proceedings;
2) other public law cases (including adoption);
3) private law children proceedings;
4) finance cases; and
5) domestic abuse cases.

Escape fee cases

19.17 There are no escape fee cases or uplifts payable under FAS, irrespective of the total number of days the hearing lasts. This is because the payments are based on time periods.

Mixed categories

19.18 Where work covers more than one of the categories above within a single set of proceedings, the advocate can choose which fee to claim:[10]
- In family cases, the certificate will often either be issued to cover a number of proceedings or be subsequently amended to add or substitute proceedings during the life of the certificate.
- When the continuing proceedings fall within more than one category, an advocate must, for the purpose of payment under FAS, choose under which single category they wish to be paid for all the advocacy services performed when making a claim for payment. Usually, an advocate will claim at the category that pays the highest rate. For example, in a Children Act 1989 s8

---

7 Standard Civil Contract 2024 Specification paras 7.108 and 7.109.
8 Standard Civil Contract 2024 Specification paras 7.109 and 7.110.
9 But note that in public law cases the LAA will often contract based on the 'events model' rather than at hourly rates and has, in some cases, contracted based on FAS.
10 Costs Assessment Guidance appendix 2 para 12.2.

application that subsequently involves allegations of abuse to a degree that the local authority issues care proceedings, at the point at which a new certificate is issued, an advocate can claim all future work (including issues as to contact) at the higher care proceedings rate.[11]
- Where an advocacy service includes work from two categories but it falls within a single set of proceedings, only one fee will be paid – for example, if a single hearing covers both private law children and financial issues, then only one hearing fee will be payable and the advocate can choose which hearing fee to claim.[12]

19.19 There is a particular problem we have recently resolved which relates to cases for care orders during which there are applications for deprivation of liberty (DoL) orders. It is now very common for DoL orders to be applied for during the lifetime of a care case. DoL orders come within means and merits assessed legal aid, whereas care proceedings are non-means/non-merits tested legal aid. Therefore, complications have arisen where the two sets of proceedings are not consolidated and/or where there is a stand-alone DoL hearing. It is possible to amend the care certificate to cover the DoL application, but we had encountered difficulties when applying for an amendment for a parent where the LAA had indicated that if a parent has previously agreed to a DoL order, they will not be granted an amendment to the care certificate as the matter is not contested. We have also encountered difficulties where the proceedings are not consolidated and even when the care certificate has been amended, that did not appear to cover a stand-alone DoL hearing, which means that the FAS fee is not covered. Recent discussions have happily resolved this issue and the LAA now appear to accept that a DoL application made within care proceedings is treated as 'related proceedings' and this will mean that:

(i) you only need to get one amendment to the care certificate even if there are a number of DoL applications in the case;
(ii) you are covered even if the DoL application has a separate case number to the care case and/or if there is a DoL only hearing and/or even when in the separate national DoL court;
(iii) parents will no longer have difficulty amending their certificate on the basis of a merits issue.

---

11 Costs Assessment Guidance appendix 2 para 12.2.
12 Costs Assessment Guidance appendix 2 para 12.3.

You will still need a means and merits tested legal aid certificate if the DoL application is free standing and there are no care proceedings or if the DoL application runs on after the Care Case has finished. Children don't have a means test if they are under 18 but there will a merits test, albeit we would expect it to be a light merits test.

Hearing fees

19.20 Fees vary according to whether a hearing is interim or final, as stated in the Standard Civil Contract 2024 Specification:

> **Interim and Final Hearings**
>
> 7.127 A Final Hearing is any hearing which the court has listed for the purpose of making a final determination, either of the whole case or of all issues relating to an Aspect of the case (Domestic Abuse, Children or Finance). Subject to paragraph 7.130, there can only be one Final Hearing per Aspect and a hearing listed only to determine particular facts or issues is not a Final Hearing. A hearing listed with a view to the issues being dealt with under a consent order, or which is otherwise not expected to be effective or contested, is not a Final Hearing. Any hearing which is not a Final Hearing is an Interim Hearing.
>
> 7.128 The following hearings are also deemed to be Final Hearings for the purposes of the FAS only:
>
> (a) In Public Law proceedings, if a case is concluded at an Issues Resolution Hearing and therefore does not proceed further, the Issues Resolution Hearing will be treated as a Final Hearing.

However, note that a recent enquiry to the LAA about what happens when you have multiple children and the case for one child finishes at the Issues Resolution Hearing (IRH) by agreement whilst the other children continue to a final hearing, has confirmed that the IRH for the one child would not be treated as a final hearing for that one child and would be remunerated as an interim hearing and the hearing at which final orders are made for the other children would be remunerated as the final hearing.

> (b) Subject to Paragraph 7.129, in Private Law Children proceedings, a hearing listed for the purpose of findings of fact pursuant to the 'Practice Direction: Residence and Contact Orders: Domestic Violence and Harm' issued by the President of the Family Division on 14 January 2009.[13]

---

13 Note that this practice direction was updated by Practice Direction 12J in December 2017, but the LAA specification still refers to the 2009 Practice Direction.

7.129 If a Final Hearing is listed for a split hearing in a Public Law matter with certain issues being heard and/or determined in advance of other issues, this must be claimed as a Final Hearing, rather than as an Interim Hearing plus a Final Hearing.

Note our comments above about the position when the case finishes for one child at an agreed IRH and not the others.

7.130 It is possible for more than one Final Hearing fee to be claimed under a single certificate. In particular this can occur where a Final Hearing has taken place but subsequent enforcement proceedings are listed at first instance. Provided the enforcement issues are listed to be finally determined at the further hearing, an additional Final Hearing fee may be justified.

19.21 Interim hearings are paid by a series of interim hearing units; final hearings are paid by a fixed daily rate. Bolt-on payments may apply to interim and final hearing payments (see below).

Interim hearing units

19.22 The fee payable depends on the length of the hearing. There are two interim hearing units:

- hearing unit 1: one hour or less; and
- hearing unit 2: more than one hour but less than 2.5 hours.

19.23 If a hearing exceeds 2.5 hours, multiples of unit 2 fees will be paid (rounded up – eg two unit 2 fees will be paid for a hearing that lasts four hours). You cannot claim multiples of hearing unit 1, or claim both unit 1 and unit 2 for the same hearing.

19.24 The applicable hearing time is the time at which the hearing is listed to start (unless the court specifically directs the advocate to attend earlier) until the time the hearing concludes:[14]

7.131 The fee payable under the FAS for an Interim Hearing depends on its length. For this purpose the length of hearing is measured from the time that the hearing is listed at court to start (or such earlier time as the court specifically directs the advocate to attend) to the time that the hearing concludes, disregarding any period in which the court is adjourned overnight or for a lunch break. Time spent when a hearing or resumed hearing is delayed because the court is dealing with other business may however be taken into account. In the case of an Interim Hearing taking place by telephone or video link, time only runs from the time the call is made. If for an emergency hearing the court has not listed a time for the hearing or a time for the advocate to attend

---

14 Standard Civil Contract 2024 Specification para 7.131.

Advocacy in family cases 533

and the papers were only issued by the court on the day of the proposed hearing (so that the advocate must wait at court to be heard in the matter), the length of hearing may be measured from the time that the papers were issued.

19.25 Note that if you have worked through lunch, this can be included as FAS time and needs to be included in the times set out on the order. The times set out on the order will also include any time allowed to settle the order.

19.26 The Costs Assessment Guidance gives additional guidance in relation to interim hearings:

> 14.6 ... Where for an emergency hearing the court has not listed a time for the hearing and the papers are only issued by the court on the day of the proposed hearing so that the advocate must wait at court to be heard the length of the hearing will be measured from the time that the papers were issued.
>
> 14.7 Where a court directs a party to adjourn for further discussions at court then that time will be included in the calculation of the interim hearing fee.
>
> 14.8 A hearing may take place by any method directed by the court eg by either video or telephone conference without attendance at court. If the court directs an alternative method of hearing then the advocate will receive the appropriate fee as if the hearing had taken place at court. However, in these cases the hearing time will start from the time that the telephone call/video conference is first attempted rather than the time that the hearing was listed.[15] Bolt-ons may be claimed for telephone/video hearings if appropriate although due to the nature of these hearings bolt-ons are less likely to be applicable. It is unlikely, for example, that the criteria for the expert bolt-on would be met. As there will be no Advocates Attendance Form, detailed notes of the hearing will need to be recorded and the claim justified on the CLAIM 1A or CLAIM 5A.[16]

19.27 Note that this guidance now appears somewhat out of date bearing in mind the provisions for remote hearings and their payment; the time for remote hearings starts from the time directed by the court for pre-hearing discussions – it is therefore essential that this is stated clearly on each order/notice of hearing listing a hearing.

> 14.9 Where a case is resolved at an Issues Resolution Hearing held under the Public Law Outline (PLO) and no further hearings take place then this hearing will be paid as a final hearing.

15 This was the provision in place before the global Covid-19 pandemic. Since March 2020, most hearings have taken place remotely and the time allowed to start the hearing has been the time listed in the notice of hearing or order – as with in-person hearings.
16 Costs Assessment Guidance appendix 2.

14.10 In Private Law Children cases where a 'finding of fact hearing' is held in accordance with the Practice Direction 12J of the Family Procedure Rules 2010: Residence and Contact Orders: Domestic Violence and Harm, it will be paid as a final hearing.

Final hearings

19.28 Final hearings are paid under daily rates. A full daily fee is payable, regardless of the length of the hearing on that day.[17] A reading day will not be a hearing day unless the court has also required actual attendance at court for case management issues. The court can designate a hearing day for the writing of submissions, but this must be clearly endorsed on the order.

19.29 Finding of fact hearings in private and public law proceedings will be paid for as final hearings. Issues resolution hearings in public law cases will be paid for as final hearings (if the case concludes at that hearing).[18]

19.30 There is some additional guidance in relation to final hearings in the Costs Assessment Guidance:

14.11 In care proceedings, the main hearing will be the hearing at which the court determines whether or not a section 31 order is made. If a final hearing is listed for a split hearing with certain issues being heard and/or determined in advance of other issues (for example, findings of fact and/or threshold criteria), this must be claimed as a final hearing rather than an interim hearing plus a final hearing. In ancillary relief proceedings, it is likely to be the hearing at which the court determines the form of relief entitlement and in family injunctions, the on notice hearing which will determine the form and continuation of the without notice injunction order made. The definition includes all preparation or incidental work relating to the hearing including preparation, travel to court and waiting at court as well as the advocacy within the hearing itself.[19]

19.31 See also Civil legal aid, Costs Assessment Guidance appendix 2:

15.9 A directions hearing that concludes the case does not make the hearing a 'final hearing'.

15.10 On the making of an order the court may decide to review the position after an interval of some months. That subsequent review is not a continuation of the final hearing but an interim hearing. The court may make further directions, continue or vary the order. None

---

17 Standard Civil Contract 2024 Specification para 7.133.
18 Standard Civil Contract 2024 Specification para 7.128.
19 Costs Assessment Guidance appendix 2 para 14.11.

of these circumstances turn that later hearing into either the continuation of the final hearing or a new final hearing.

15.11 It is possible in certain circumstances for more than one final hearing fee to be paid in a case. In particular this can occur where a final hearing has taken place but subsequent enforcement proceedings are issued which are required to be finally determined or where an earlier fact finding hearing has taken place.

19.32 Note that if acting in a private law children or finance case, you will not be able to claim for a final hearing if the certificate scope is limited and does not permit attendance at a final hearing.

Cancelled hearings

19.33 Counsel and self-employed advocates may claim a fee for cancelled hearings. They must have done at least 30 minutes' preparation in order to claim a hearing unit 1 fee (for interim hearings) or half a final hearing fee (for final hearings).[20] An employed advocate may not claim a cancellation fee through FAS but may include wasted time in preparation for the hearing as part of the preparation costs of the case and such costs may count towards the case becoming exceptional.[21]

Bolt-ons

Overview

19.34 Additional bolt-on fees are available for more complex cases in public and private law children cases. Claims must be verified by the judge, magistrate or legal adviser who approves the order. Bolt-ons must therefore be recorded on the order and the attendance note. Bolt-on fees cannot be claimed for cancelled hearings. Bolt-ons are not available in finance cases and domestic abuse cases, apart from court bundles in finance cases and exceptional travel in both finance and domestic abuse cases, where applicable.[22]

Public law

19.35 In public law cases, bolt-ons are claimable where:

---

20 Standard Civil Contract 2024 Specification para 7.134; and Costs Assessment Guidance appendix 2 para 14.15.
21 Costs Assessment Guidance appendix 2 para 14.16.
22 Standard Civil Contract 2024 Specification paras 7.142–7.155.

- you are acting for a parent or others against whom allegations of serious harm to a child are made by the local authority;
- the client has difficulty giving instructions/understanding advice; and
- expert(s) has/have to be cross-examined.[23]

19.36 Bolt-on payments are cumulative, ie you get 25 per cent uplift for each that applies (thus the total that your fee can be increased in public law is 75 per cent).

Client – allegations of significant harm

19.37 Paragraph 7.145 of the 2024 Specification states:

> This Bolt-on Fee is claimable only where your Client is facing allegations that he or she has caused significant harm to a Child. It applies only so long as those allegations remain a live issue in the proceedings. For this purpose only the following conditions constitute significant harm:
> (a) death;
> (b) significant head and/or fracture injuries;
> (c) burns or scalds;
> (d) fabricated illness;
> (e) extensive bruising involving more than one part of the body;
> (f) multiple injuries of different kinds;
> (g) other significant ill-treatment (such as suffocation or starvation) likely to endanger life;
> (h) sexual abuse.

Client – lack of understanding etc

19.38 Paragraph 7.147 of the 2024 Specification states:

> This Bolt-on applies to hearings in Public Law proceedings where:
> (a) your Client has difficulty in giving instructions or understanding advice,
> (b) this is attributable to a mental disorder (as defined in section 1(2) of the Mental Health Act 1983) or to a significant impairment of intelligence or social functioning, and
> (c) the Client's condition is verified by a medical report from either a psychologist or psychiatrist.

Cross-examination of expert

19.39 This bolt-on applies to all advocates when cross-examination is undertaken by any party. It can also be claimed if the expert was stood down within 72 hours of the hearing and preparation has been

23 Standard Civil Contract 2024 Specification paras 7.156–7.158.

Advocacy in family cases 537

carried out, or if the expert attended the hearing but did not give evidence.[24]

Advocates' meetings

19.40 In public law cases, a separate fee is available for advocates attending an advocates' meeting, where such a meeting is directed by the court in accordance with the Public Law Outline. Where in section 31 care proceedings (Children Act 1989 s31) advocates are able to discuss all relevant matters without the need for a formal advocates' meeting directed by the court, half the standard fee is payable (without any bolt-ons).[25]

19.41 There is additional guidance in the Costs Assessment Guidance in relation to advocates' meetings:

> 14.18 Although it would usually be expected that two advocates' meetings would take place in accordance with the PLO, provided that the advocates' meeting is held as directed by the court and in accordance with the PLO there is no limit to the number of these fees that may be claimed. No fees for advocates' meetings will be payable in Private Law Children cases.
>
> 14.19 The definition of advocates' meeting includes meetings held by video conference, webcam or telephone where this is appropriate in the circumstances.
>
> 14.20 It is not envisaged under the PLO that an advocates meeting would take place on the same day as a hearing. However, if an advocates meeting does take place on the same day as an interim hearing then it may be claimed only if the meeting takes place outside of any time period that is taken into account in calculating the fee for the interim hearing.[26]

Private law

19.42 In private law children cases, bolt-ons are claimable where:

- you are acting for a parent or others against whom allegations of significant harm to a child are made;[27] and

---

24 Standard Civil Contract 2024 Specification para 7.156
25 Standard Civil Contract 2024 Specification paras 7.135 and 7.136.
26 Costs Assessment Guidance appendix 2.
27 Standard Civil Contract 2024 Specification para 7.144.

- expert(s) has/have to be substantially challenged in court (but note the uplift is 20 per cent, not 25 per cent as in public law cases).[28]

19.43 In private law finance cases, an early resolution fee can be claimed for cases which settle at the first appointment or Financial Dispute Resolution (FDR) hearing, as long as the advocate materially assisted in the settlement, it is recorded in a consent order and it lasts for six months (as far as you are aware).[29] The 2024 Specification states:

> **Early Resolution Fee**
>
> 7.152 This Bolt-on Fee is claimable only in Private Law Finance cases which settle at the first appointment or Financial Dispute Resolution ('FDR') hearing. It may only be claimed by an advocate who is entitled to the Hearing fee for that hearing but only if the following conditions are satisfied:
> (a) the Finance Aspect of the case has been fully concluded at the first appointment or FDR hearing;
> (b) the advocate attending that hearing materially assisted in the settlement;
> (c) the Finance Aspect of the case does not proceed further to a new Form of Civil Legal Services within six months of the settlement, either with you or, so far as you are aware, another Provider;
> (d) there has been a genuine settlement to conclude that Aspect of the case, rather than, for example, a reconciliation between the parties or one party dying or disengaging from the case;
> (e) the settlement is recorded in a form of a Consent Order approved by the Court, either at the hearing itself or subsequently.

Court bundles

19.44 Additional fees may be claimed for cases involving larger bundles, known as advocates' bundle payments or ABPs:[30]

ABP 1 – over 350 pages (interim and final);
ABP 2 – over 700 pages (interim and final); and
ABP 3 – over 1,400 pages (final hearings only).

19.45 Family Procedure Rules (FPR) Practice Direction (PD) 27A sets out the content and format of the court bundle in family proceedings and introduced a maximum 350-page limit on the size of the court bundle

---

28 Standard Civil Contract 2024 Specification paras 7.156–7.158; and Costs assessment Guidance para 14.32.
29 Standard Civil Contract 2024 Specification para 7.152.
30 Standard Civil Contract 2024 Specification para 7.148.

in family cases. From that date, the LAA amended the regulations[31] so that bundle payments were claimed by reference to the advocate's bundle rather than the court bundle. The Specification continues to refer to 'court bundle payments' and 'CBPs', but claims should be based on the advocate's bundle.

19.46 The amended regulations set out that the advocate's bundle may only include:

- those documents relevant to the case that have been served by the parties to the proceedings to which the hearing relates;
- notes of contact visits if included in the court bundle; and
- a paginated index agreed by the parties to those proceedings.

19.47 The Costs Assessment Guidance states that advocates must also include a written explanation of how the documents included in the bundle are relevant and necessary to the case, and that advocates should keep a copy of the index for the relevant hearing to show the number of pages in the advocate's bundle. There was some anxiety when these changes came in about the required explanations and keeping indices. However, in our experience the explanation and/or production of the index has not been requested by the LAA and the significant step now in the absence of the AAF is the judge's approval of the order, which must have the confirmation of the page numbers for the bundle.

19.48 There are restrictions on the circumstances and number of times within a set of proceedings that a court bundle payment may be claimed for interim hearings, set out in the 2024 Specification:

> 7.149 . . . In Public Law proceedings, court bundle payments may be claimed for no more than two Interim Hearings and each of these must be either a Case Management Conference, an Issues Resolution Hearing or otherwise a hearing which is listed for the hearing of contested evidence. A court bundle payment may never be claimed more than once per hearing.
>
> 7.150 In Private Law proceedings court bundle payments may only be claimed at one Interim Hearing per case. For this purpose the Children and Finance Aspects of a case will be treated separately.
>
> 7.151 Court bundle payments may not be claimed in Domestic Abuse proceedings, either for Interim or Final Hearings.

---

31 The Civil Legal Aid (Remuneration) (Amendment) (No 4) Regulations 2014 amended the Civil Legal Aid (Remuneration) Regulations 2013, and equivalent amendments to the Community Legal Service (Funding) Order 2007, through the Community Legal Service (Funding) (Amendment) Order 2014, to cover cases continuing under the Access to Justice Act 1999.

19.49 An advocate taking on a case part-way through must satisfy themself as to whether the advocate's bundle payment(s) have already been claimed or are intended to be claimed by an advocate at an earlier hearing.[32]

19.50 There is some additional guidance in the Costs Assessment Guidance in relation to court bundles (see above for change in definition from 31 July 2014). Also note that although the 2024 Contract Specification continues to refer to 'court bundles', the Costs Assessment Guidance refers – correctly – to 'advocate's bundles'.[33]

> 14.46 The advocate's bundle will consist of those served documents relevant and necessary to the case, including a paginated index of the contents. The advocate's bundle may include the documents listed in paragraphs 4.2 and 4.3 of PD27A (and which may be included in the court bundle) and other documents relevant to the case which have been served by the parties to the proceedings to which the hearing relates. Notes of contact visits will only be included in the advocate's bundle for the purposes of the FAS if they have been included in the court bundle.
>
> 14.47 Verification of the size of the advocate's bundle will be carried out by the judge or person before whom the case is heard by way of a paginated index of documents served in the case that the advocate would be expected to have agreed with the other parties, as appropriate. Additionally, the advocate will need to provide an explanation of why any documents included in the paginated index which do not fall within paragraphs 4.2 and 4.3 of PD27A are relevant and necessary to the case.
>
> ...
>
> 14.51 An advocate must obtain certification of the relevant number of pages of the advocate's bundle on the Advocates Attendance Form in order to claim this payment. The Agency may request copies of both the agreed paginated list and the explanation of why additional documents not referred to in paragraphs 4.2 and 4.3 of PD27A are included either before or after payment is made.

Exceptional travel

19.51 Advocates may claim payments for exceptional travel on each day of the hearing (more than 25 miles each way), as long as it was reasonable for them to be instructed in all the circumstances, rather than someone more local to the court.[34]

---

32 Costs Assessment Guidance appendix 2 para 14.52.
33 Costs Assessment Guidance appendix 2 – paras as set out at para 19.50 above.
34 Standard Civil Contract 2024 Specification para 7.154.

Advocacy in family cases 541

19.52 All advocates will need to justify the payment, and documents or explanations may need to be uploaded via Client and Cost Management System (CCMS). Counsel should also supply a copy of their brief or instructions with the claim.

Payments for counsel only

19.53 Counsel's fees may be claimed under the FAS:
- for conferences, up to a maximum of two per set of proceedings;[35] and
- for opinions, up to a maximum of two per set of proceedings, unless the opinion relates to a proposed appeal against a final order:[36]
  – in private law, counsel may claim two opinions for both the children and finance aspects of a case; and
  – no opinion fee may be claimed in domestic abuse proceedings.

19.54 The Costs Assessment Guidance says this about what constitutes a single set of proceedings:

> 13.1 For particular Advocacy Services only two fees can be claimed per case. In order to determine what is or is not a 'case' for the purposes of determining appropriate claiming, applications to the court constitute a single set of proceedings, irrespective of whether they are made separately or together, where they are heard together or consecutively or are treated by the court as a single set of proceedings. In private law proceedings each aspect of the case (eg children and finance), counts as a separate case for the purposes of claiming opinions and conferences.[37]

Conference fees

19.55 There is some additional guidance in relation to conference fees in the Costs Assessment Guidance:

> 14.25 A conference fee is paid for all work carried out in connection with a conference. This can include conferences by telephone or video link or webcam where this is appropriate in the circumstances. Conference fees may only be claimed by Counsel. No bolt-ons may be claimed for conferences.
>
> 14.26 Up to two conference fees may be claimed in each single set of proceedings. As for opinions in private law proceedings, if there are separate children and finance proceedings these will be considered

---

35 Standard Civil Contract 2024 Specification para 7.141.
36 Standard Civil Contract 2024 Specification para 7.138.
37 Costs Assessment Guidance appendix 2.

separately for these purposes. However, no conference fee may be claimed under FAS in domestic abuse proceedings.

14.27 As only two conference fees may be claimed Counsel will need to designate the conferences for which he or she seeks payment under the FAS.

14.28 No conference fee may be claimed for any conference held on the same day as a Final hearing. Any discussions or negotiations taking place on any day of a final hearing will be covered by the fee for advocacy at that hearing.

14.29 A conference fee may be claimed for a conference that takes place on the same day as an interim hearing, only if the conference takes place outside of any time period that is taken into account in calculating the fee for the interim hearing. Therefore, no conference fee may be claimed for a conference that takes place between the time that the hearing is listed to start and the time that hearing actually starts as this will be claimed as part of the hearing unit.

14.30 Where different Counsel is subsequently instructed and the allowable conference fees have already been claimed, no further claims for conference fees can be made. This is so even in circumstances where the later conference was more substantial. Where one Counsel has replaced another, Counsel must make enquiries as to whether the conference fees payments have already been claimed from either the outgoing Counsel, or instructing solicitors.[38]

Opinion fees

19.56 Only counsel (see definition in para 20.10 above) may claim opinion fees.[39] The Costs Assessment Guidance has some additional guidance in relation to opinion fees:

14.22 Up to two opinion fees may be claimed in each single set of proceedings. If there are separate children and finance proceedings these will be considered separately for these purposes. No opinion fee may claimed under the FAS in domestic abuse proceedings.

14.23 In addition to the two opinions claimed per set of proceedings a further opinion may be claimed in relation to any a proposed appeal against a final order.

14.24 An opinion may include providing advice or drafting pleadings / affidavits after the issue of proceedings.[40]

---

38 Costs Assessment Guidance appendix 2.
39 Standard Civil Contract 2024 Specification para 7.137.
40 Costs Assessment Guidance appendix 2.

Assessment

19.57 The LAA assesses all fees due to counsel under the FAS. Solicitors' profit costs (including for advocacy) and disbursements are assessed in the usual way, through assessment either by the LAA or the court. See chapter 15 for more information.

CCMS and forms

19.58 Different forms are submitted depending on whether the claim falls under the FGS (cases started pre-9 May 2011) or the FAS (cases started after 9 May 2011). The forms, and accompanying guidance on how to fill them out, can be downloaded at: www.gov.uk/government/publications/family-graduated-fee-and-family-advocacy-claim-forms.

19.59 See para 19.61 below regarding CCMS, which will apply in most cases.

19.60 For older FAS claims, counsel claim on form CIVCLAIM5A and solicitors claim on form CIVCLAIM1A. Claims for advocacy under the FAS must now use the court order to evidence the claim. Note that if you are claiming a case with hearings before March 2020, you will be expected to provide the AAF to evidence the court times (form EX506).

19.61 Cases started since April 2016 (February 2016 for most public law cases and earlier for some firms) are managed through CCMS. Counsel can claim FAS payments through CCMS at the conclusion of each hearing and they will be recorded against the file, assisting the solicitor with the management of the costs of the case. In-house advocates will claim their costs as part of the solicitors' bill. No additional claims can be made for FAS hearings of in-house advocates, but they should be included in payments on account claims made during the life of the case (increased in June 2020 to 80 per cent of profit costs, four times in a 12-month period once the certificate is three months old[41]). See chapter 15 for details on claiming payments on account.

FAS in High Cost cases

19.62 Family cases where the costs are anticipated to, or actually do, exceed £25,000 (including all profit costs with enhancement, disbursements

---

41 Standard Civil Contract 2024 Specification para 6.21.

and any counsel's fees but excluding VAT) fall under the Special Case Work provisions of Part 6 of the Civil Legal Aid (Procedure) Regulations 2012 (see chapter 4 for more information on Special Case Work).

- There are two teams managing High Cost Family cases: High Cost Family (HCF) Team – deals with all single and KC/two-counsel/advocate cases in private and public law family matters (South Tyneside based).
- Exceptional and Complex Case Team (ECCT) family section – deals with all prior authority requests for KC/two-counsel cases in private and public law family matters and all Court of Protection cases. ECCT provides all technical oversight and support to the HCF (London-based) team.

19.63 There are different payment schemes depending on whether it is a care case or private law case and the number of counsel. Refer to chapter 4 for further details.

CHAPTER 20
Advocacy in criminal cases

By Itpal Dhillon

20.1	Introduction
20.7	Funding
20.9	Advocacy assistance – investigations stage
20.9	Clients detained in custody
20.15	Police bail
20.20	Advocacy assistance – court duty solicitor
20.27	Advocacy under a representation order
20.27	Overview
20.30	Magistrates' court
	Counsel in the magistrates' court • Assigned counsel
20.45	Crown Court
20.53	Appeals
20.56	Advocacy assistance – prison law

> ### Key resources
>
> **Contract**
>
> - Draft Standard Crime Contract 2025
> - Draft Standard Crime Specification 2025
> - Standard Crime Contract 2022
> - Standard Crime Specification 2022
>
> **Regulations**
>
> - Criminal Legal Aid (Remuneration) Regulations 2013
> - Criminal Legal Aid (General) Regulations 2013
> - Criminal Legal Aid (Determinations by a Court and Choice of Representative) Regulations 2013
>
> **Fees and costs**
>
> - Criminal Bills Assessment Manual
> - Criminal Legal Aid (Remuneration) Regulations 2013
> - Criminal Legal Aid (General) Regulations 2013

> ### Key points to note
> - Several upper costs limits have been increased and the Regulations should be checked as to each amount where relevant.
> - The draft 2025 Contract requires duty solicitors, where requested by the court, to provide duty solicitor services in any courtroom during the duty period at a specified magistrates' court and not only at a specific room listed on any rota.
> - The draft 2025 Contract allows duty solicitors to undertake own client contract work during a magistrates' court duty period only where this does not prevent or delay the provision of duty solicitor services.

Introduction

20.1 This chapter deals with the conduct of and payment for advocacy in criminal cases. See appendix D for a summary of the Legal Aid Agency's

(LAA's) Criminal Bills Assessment Manual,[1] in respect of the most common queries raised by caseworkers.

20.2 In criminal proceedings, advocacy can be conducted under:
- advocacy assistance; and
- representation order.

Advocacy may arise at all stages of criminal proceedings, including the investigations stage, where advocacy may arise due to an application for a warrant of further detention or where a client wishes to apply to vary police bail conditions or oppose a bail time-limit extension.

20.3 In general, we use the term 'advocate' to refer to anyone who has a right of audience to appear in the relevant court or whom the court is willing to hear where the scheme makes no distinction between solicitor and counsel. Where there is a difference according to whether advocacy is conducted by solicitor or by counsel, we will use the terms 'solicitor' and 'counsel' as appropriate.

20.4 Who is entitled to conduct advocacy, and the payment arrangements, will depend on the type of hearing and the stage of the case.

20.5 All qualified solicitors may represent a client at a hearing in the magistrates' court, as may counsel. However, whether or not counsel may be instructed will depend on the type of hearing and whether it is funded by advocacy assistance or a representation order.

20.6 In general, advocacy at Crown Court hearings and above may only be provided by counsel or a solicitor who has higher rights of audience.

Funding

20.7 In general, advocacy in a criminal case is funded by a representation order, which will cover all the hearings from the first appearance in the magistrates' court up to the final sentencing hearing. A representation order will also generally be required for advocacy in appeals.

20.8 The main stage at which advocacy is not covered by a representation order is the investigations stage. At this stage, funding is provided by advocacy assistance. Advocacy assistance is also available to fund representation by the duty solicitor and representation at prison disciplinary and Parole Board hearings.

1 V19, April 2024, available at: www.gov.uk/guidance/funding-and-costs-assessment-for-civil-and-crime-matters.

Advocacy assistance – investigations stage

Clients detained in custody

20.9 A client who is detained in police (or military) custody may require representation at court if there is an application to extend the custody time limit under Police and Criminal Evidence Act 1984 (PACE) s43 or 44, Terrorism Act 2000 Sch 8 para 29 or 36, or the relevant military legislation.[2]

20.10 The funding for such hearings is subject to the 'sufficient benefit' test; however, the test is automatically deemed satisfied by the circumstances.[3]

20.11 There is no means test[4] and the client is not required to sign any application form.[5] However, you are required to record on the file:[6]

- the client's name and address;
- the unique file number (UFN);
- the date, time and venue of the court appearance; and
- details of the relevant unit of work (as defined by the contract) and how the work falls within the scope of that unit.

These details should be recorded either before the advocacy assistance is provided or as soon as practicable after, if the advocacy is required at short notice.[7]

20.12 Reasonable preparation and follow-up work will be included within the scope of advocacy assistance, as will travel and waiting costs. However, there is an extendable costs limit of £1,574.06.[8]

20.13 There are no fixed fees for this type of work so, subject to the costs limit above, work will be claimed at the hourly rates set out in the Criminal Legal Aid (Remuneration) Regulations 2013. These vary

---

2 Standard Crime Contract 2022 Specification paras 9.166–9.191 and Standard Crime Contract 2025 Specification paras 9.161–9.173, available at: www.gov.uk/government/publications/standard-crime-contract-2022 and www.gov.uk/government/publications/standard-crime-contract-2025.
3 Standard Crime Contract 2022 Specification paras 9.167 and 9.181 and Standard Crime Contract 2025 Specification para 9.162.
4 Standard Crime Contract 2022 Specification paras 9.168 and 9.182 and Standard Crime Contract 2025 Specification para 9.163.
5 Standard Crime Contract 2022 Specification paras 9.169 and 9.182 and Standard Crime Contract 2025 Specification para 9.164.
6 Standard Crime Contract 2022 Specification paras 9.171 and 9.184 and Standard Crime Contract 2025 Specification para 9.166.
7 Standard Crime Contract 2022 Specification paras 9.169 and 9.183 and Standard Crime Contract 2025 Specification para 9.164.
8 Criminal Legal Aid (Remuneration) Regulations 2013 Sch 4, as amended.

depending on whether the hearing is before a magistrates' court or judicial authority, or before a High Court or senior judge. There are also different rates for own and duty solicitors, and for unsociable hours.

20.14 Counsel may be instructed, but if you do so, you will be responsible for paying them out of your fee.[9]

Police bail

20.15 A client who is not detained in custody may also require representation at court if there is an application to vary police bail conditions (including 'street bail' conditions), or to oppose an application to extend a bail time limit.[10]

20.16 In this situation there are no qualifying criteria to be met and there is no means test.[11] As above, the client is not required to sign an application form, but you must record the same required information on the file.[12]

20.17 Advocacy assistance in this situation includes reasonable preparation, travel, waiting and advocacy at the hearing, and the provision of advice on appeal.[13]

20.18 The same extendable costs limit applies, and the rules on claiming are the same. The applicable fees are set out in the Criminal Legal Aid (Remuneration) Regulations 2013.

20.19 You may instruct counsel in this case but if you do so, you are responsible for paying them out of your fee,[14] and you may not claim under this unit of work if you are acting as duty solicitor.[15] However, you can claim under advocacy assistance if you represented the client as duty solicitor at the police station and you are subsequently instructed in the bail proceedings.

---

9 Standard Crime Contract 2022 Specification para 9.186 and Standard Crime Contract 2025 Specification para 9.169.
10 Standard Crime Contract 2022 Specification paras 9.192–9.212 and Standard Crime Contract 2025 Specification para 9.161.
11 Standard Crime Contract 2022 Specification paras 9.193 and 9.204 and Standard Crime Contract 2025 Specification para 9.163.
12 Standard Crime Contract 2022 Specification paras 9.195 and 9.206 and Standard Crime Contract 2025 Specification para 9.166.
13 Standard Crime Contract 2022 Specification paras 9.196 and 9.207 and Standard Crime Contract 2025 Specification para 9.167.
14 Standard Crime Contract 2022 Specification paras 9.197 and 9.208 and Standard Crime Contract 2025 Specification para 9.168.
15 Standard Crime Contract 2022 Specification paras 9.167, 9.202 and 9.212 and Standard Crime Contract 2025 Specification para 9.173.

Advocacy assistance – court duty solicitor

20.20 Advocacy assistance is available to cover the representation of clients by the court duty solicitor at the magistrates' court. In practice, it will be claimed together with advice and assistance, which covers the provision of advice to such clients outside court. The two forms of assistance will be claimed together in a single claim at the end of the duty day.[16]

20.21 Advocacy assistance under this unit of work may only be provided by a qualified duty solicitor (ie one who has previously been a member of a scheme under a previous contract or is a current member of the Law Society's Criminal Litigation Accreditation Scheme and has undertaken the police station qualification[17]).

20.22 To qualify for advocacy assistance under this scheme, the client's case must come within the scope of the scheme:
- The duty solicitor must:[18]
  - advise any client who requests it who is in custody;
  - make a bail application where a client in custody requires a bail application and such an application has not previously been made by a duty solicitor;
  - advise a client before the court in connection with 'prescribed proceedings' that is civil orders deemed to be criminal for legal aid purposes (the full list appears in chapter 14 at para 14.86)[19] such as:
    - football banning orders;[20]
    - closure orders;[21]
    - sexual offences notification orders;[22]
    - sexual risk orders;[23]
    - restraining orders under Protection from Harassment Act 1997 s5A in relation to a restraining order on acquittal;

---

16 Standard Crime Contracts 2022 and 2025 Specification para 10.18.
17 Standard Crime Contract 2022 and Standard Terms para 1.1.
18 Standard Crime Contracts 2022 and 2025 Specification para 10.7. Note that the provision makes distinctions between advice, and representation.
19 Criminal Legal Aid (General) Regulations 2013 reg 9.
20 Football Spectators Act 1989 ss14B, 14D, 14G, 14H, 21B and 21D.
21 Anti-social Behaviour, Crime and Policing Act 2014 ss80, 82, 83 and 84 where a person has engaged or is likely to engage in behaviour that constitutes a criminal offence on the premises.
22 Sexual Offences Act 2003 ss97, 100 and 101.
23 Sexual Offences Act 2003 ss122A, 122D, 122E and 122G.

- domestic violence protection orders;[24]
- knife crime prevention orders;[25] and
- proceedings in any youth court in relation to the breach of a provision in an injunction under Anti-social Behaviour, Crime and Policing Act 2014 Part 1 where the person subject to the injunction is under 14; and
- a duty solicitor must also cross-examine under Youth Justice and Criminal Evidence Act 1999 s38 if appointed by the court. Payment will in this case be from central funds.[26]
- The duty solicitor must also, but subject to the exceptions below:[27]
  - advise and represent any client who is in custody on a plea of guilty and wishes the case to be concluded that day;
  - advise and represent any client before the court for failure to pay a fine or other sum or to obey an order of the court, and such failure may lead to the client being at risk of imprisonment;
  - advise and represent a client not in custody in connection with an imprisonable offence;
  - help a client in making an application for a representation order, whether the nominated solicitor is the duty solicitor or another solicitor;
  - advise and represent a client seeking to vary police-imposed bail conditions pre-charge;
  - advise and represent a client subject to an application by the police to extend police bail under section 47ZF or 47ZG of PACE.
- The exceptions are that a duty solicitor must **not**:
  - represent at a not guilty trial or in relation to a non-imprisonable offence unless with the provisions above;[28] or
  - advise or represent a client who has had the services of a duty solicitor at a previous hearing in the proceedings (except where they

---

24 Crime and Security Act 2010 ss24–33.
25 Offensive Weapons Act 2019 Part 2.
26 Standard Crime Contracts 2022 and 2025 Specification para 10.15. The Law Society has issued guidance on when exceptional circumstances may apply so that the appointment should be declined – see Practice Note *Rejecting un-remunerative publicly funded criminal work*, November 2023, at: www.lawsociety.org.uk/topics/criminal-justice/rejecting-un-remunerative-publicly-funded-criminal-work.
27 Standard Crime Contract 2022 Specification para 10.8 and Standard Crime Contract 2025 Specification paras 10.7–10.8.
28 Standard Crime Contract 2022 Specification para 10.9 and Standard Crime Contract 2025 Specification para 10.6.

are before the court this time as a result of failure to pay a fine or other sum or comply with an order imposed previously).[29]

20.23 The sufficient benefit test applies to representation by the duty solicitor (both under advocacy assistance and advice and assistance),[30] but there is no means test and clients are not required to complete an application form.[31] However, you are required to record on the file:[32]

- the client's name and address;
- details of the relevant unit of work;
- whether the client is in custody or charged with an imprisonable offence; and
- the date, time and venue of the court appearance.

These details should be recorded either before the advocacy assistance is provided or as soon as practicable after, if the advocacy is required at short notice.[33]

20.24 The scope of the scheme is limited in terms of the work covered. In addition to the advocacy, you may only claim for reasonable advice and preparation provided during the duty session. This can include advice on the consequences of the outcome and the giving of any notice of appeal or making an application for a case to be stated.[34]

20.25 Claiming for duty solicitor advocacy is done as part of a single claim submitted for the duty session. Hourly rates are set out in the Criminal Legal Aid (Remuneration) Regulations 2013 and there is a standard hourly rate for both attendance and waiting. An enhanced rate applies to sessions on non-business days.

20.26 Under the duty solicitor scheme, you cannot claim for travel time other than on a non-business day, unless you are called out having not been on the rota or having been released but then asked to return.

---

29 Standard Crime Contract 2022 Specification para 10.10 and Standard Crime Contract 2025 Specification para 10.9.
30 Standard Crime Contracts 2022 and 2025 Specification para 10.2.
31 Standard Crime Contracts 2022 and 2025 Specification para 10.4.
32 Standard Crime Contract 2022 Specification para 10.6 and Standard Crime Contract 2025 Specification para 10.5.
33 Standard Crime Contracts 2022 and 2025 Specification para 10.4.
34 Standard Crime Contracts 2022 and 2025 Specification para 10.17.

Advocacy under a representation order

Overview

20.27 All representation orders granted for criminal cases in the magistrates' court and the Crown Court will include the provision of advocacy services. This will include representation at all hearings in the case, including bail proceedings in the Crown Court.

20.28 Representation orders in both the magistrates' court and the Crown Court are granted subject to a means test. There is a merits test unless the case is tried in the Crown Court on indictment. For a full discussion of these tests, see chapter 14.

20.29 Advocacy under a representation order may be carried out either by a solicitor or by counsel, subject to the requirement for higher rights for advocacy in the Crown Court and above.

Magistrates' court

20.30 A representation order for a magistrates' court case will generally only cover advocacy provided by a solicitor.[35] Payment for advocacy services provided by a solicitor will be claimed within the magistrates' court standard fee regime.

20.31 Advocacy is claimed at the hourly rate prescribed in the Criminal Legal Aid (Remuneration) Regulations 2013, in the same way as all other types of work provided under the representation order.

20.32 Travelling and waiting time can only be claimed if neither the court nor your office is in a 'designated area'. The designated areas[36] are:

- Greater Manchester, London, West Midlands and Merseyside Criminal Justice Areas; and
- the local authority areas of:
  - Brighton and Hove;
  - Bristol;
  - Cardiff;
  - Derby and Erewash;
  - Kingston upon Hull;
  - Leeds and Bradford;

---

35 See Criminal Legal Aid (Determinations by a Court and Choice of Representative) Regulations 2013 reg 16.
36 Standard Crime Contracts 2022 and 2025 Specification para 1.2.

- Leicester;
- Nottingham;
- Portsmouth;
- Newcastle-upon-Tyne and Sunderland (including Gateshead, North and South Tyneside);
- Sheffield; and
- Southampton.

Note that you are still required to record the waiting time (but not travel), even if you cannot claim for it.[37]

20.33 The total core costs will then be compared against fee limits for the particular category of case, and this will determine whether the standard fee or a non-standard fee is payable.

20.34 In relation to matters that are committed to or sent to the Crown Court for trial under Crime and Disorder Act 1998 s51, a fixed fee for the preparation and advocacy of the hearing is payable.

20.35 For details of the fee structure under representation orders in the magistrates' court, see chapter 16.

Counsel in the magistrates' court

20.36 Although the representation order will usually only provide for advocacy by a solicitor,[38] this does not mean that counsel cannot be instructed in the magistrates' court. It simply means that counsel is usually unassigned and cannot claim their costs from the court or the LAA. Therefore, solicitors are responsible for agreeing a fee with counsel and paying that fee promptly out of their costs. If they fail to pay within 30 days, counsel can apply to the LAA for payment and that payment will be deducted from their monthly payment.[39]

20.37 Unassigned counsel are treated like solicitor agents. From the point of view of the LAA, their work is treated as solicitor's work. Their time should be recorded on the bill as if a solicitor had done the work and counts towards the calculation of the appropriate fee.[40]

---

37 Standard Crime Contract 2022 Specification para 10.87 and Standard Crime Contract 2025 Specification para 10.73.
38 See Criminal Legal Aid (Determinations by a Court and Choice of Representative) Regulations 2013 reg 16.
39 Standard Crime Contract 2022 Specification paras 10.50, 10.54 and 10.55 and Standard Crime Contract 2025 Specification paras 10.38, 10.42 and 10.43.
40 Standard Crime Contract 2022 Specification para 10.48 and Standard Crime Contract 2025 Specification para 10.36.

As for solicitors, counsel's travel and waiting time can only be claimed for cases in 'undesignated areas'.[41]

20.38 You must provide counsel with the UFN and a copy of the representation order when briefing them.[42]

Assigned counsel

20.39 In more serious cases, you can apply to the court for counsel (or an independent solicitor advocate) to be assigned.

20.40 The regulations say that counsel may be assigned in any case where the charge is an indictable offence (that is, an offence capable of being tried on indictment, including either way offences, not just indictable only offences) or where the case is an extradition matter.[43]

20.41 Indictable only cases involving adults will be sent directly to the Crown Court, so in practice counsel can be assigned in adult either way cases, youth cases where the charge, whether either way or indictable, has not been sent, and extraditions.

20.42 In order to have counsel assigned, you must persuade the court that, because of circumstances that make the case unusually grave or difficult, representation by solicitor and advocate would be desirable.

20.43 In extradition proceedings, you can apply for more than one advocate, or for a King's Counsel (KC), to be assigned where you can persuade the court that the defendant cannot be adequately represented except by a KC or more than one advocate.[44]

20.44 Where counsel is assigned, they are entitled to be paid directly by the LAA at the rates prescribed in the Criminal Legal Aid (Remuneration) Regulations 2013, though you should submit their bill with your own – see chapter 16 at para 16.58.

Crown Court

20.45 Advocacy in the Crown Court must generally be conducted by counsel or a solicitor with higher rights of audience. You must consult the

---

41 Standard Crime Contract 2022 Specification para 10.83 and Standard Crime Contract 2025 Specification para 10.70.
42 Standard Crime Contracts 2017 and 2022 Specification para 10.43 and Standard Crime Contract 2025 Specification para 10.31.
43 Criminal Legal Aid (Determinations by a Court and Choice of Representative) Regulations 2013 reg 16.
44 Criminal Legal Aid (Determinations by a Court and Choice of Representative) Regulations 2013 regs 16 and 17.

client about the choice of advocate and the alternatives available,[45] and keep a record of the discussion.[46]

20.46 Crown Court representation orders automatically allow the instruction of a single junior advocate. Even if counsel was not assigned under the order in the magistrates' court, once the case goes to the Crown Court the order is deemed to include representation by one junior advocate (that is, any advocate other than a KC).[47]

20.47 In more serious and complex cases, an application may be made to the court to amend the order to allow for the instruction of a KC or more than one advocate. The court can order representation by:

- KC alone;
- two advocates:
  – KC with junior;
  – KC with noting junior;
  – two juniors; or
  – junior and noting junior; or
- where three advocates are justified, any of the above plus an additional junior or noting junior.[48]

20.48 In order to persuade the court to make an order for senior or more than one advocate, you must demonstrate that the relevant test is met:

- For KC alone:[49]
  – the case involves substantial novel or complex issues of law or fact which could not be adequately presented except by a KC; and
  – either:
    – the prosecution has instructed a KC or senior Treasury counsel; or
    – the case for the defence is exceptional compared with the generality of cases involving similar offences.

---

45 Standard Crime Contracts 2022 and 2025 Standard Terms para 7.3.
46 Standard Crime Contract 2022 Standard Terms para 7.5 and Standard Crime Contract 2025 Specification para 7.6.
47 Criminal Legal Aid (Determinations by a Court and Choice of Representative) Regulations 2013 reg 18.
48 Criminal Legal Aid (Determinations by a Court and Choice of Representative) Regulations 2013 reg 18.
49 Criminal Legal Aid (Determinations by a Court and Choice of Representative) Regulations 2013 reg 18(2).

- For two junior advocates:[50]
  - the case involves substantial novel or complex issues of law or fact which could not be adequately presented by a single advocate; and
  - either:
    - the prosecution has instructed two or more advocates;
    - the case for the defence is exceptional compared with the generality of cases involving similar offences;
    - the number of prosecution witnesses exceeds 80; or
    - the number of pages of prosecution evidence exceeds 1,000.
- For KC plus junior or noting junior:[51]
  - the case involves substantial novel or complex issues of law or fact which could not be adequately presented except by a KC assisted by a junior advocate; and
  - either:
    - the prosecution has instructed a KC or senior Treasury counsel and two or more advocates have been instructed by the prosecution; the number of prosecution witnesses exceeds 80; the number of pages of prosecution evidence exceeds 1,000; or
    - the case for the defence is exceptional compared with the generality of cases involving similar offences.
- For three advocates:[52]
  - the case is being prosecuted by the Serious Fraud Office;
  - the court considers three advocates are required; and
  - the conditions for two juniors or KC plus junior are satisfied (as appropriate).

Only defined judges may make the relevant decisions.[53]

20.49 The payment of advocates' fees in the Crown Court is governed by the Advocates' Graduated Fee Scheme (AGFS). The rules and fees applicable to the AGFS are set out in Criminal Legal Aid (Remuneration) Regulations 2013 Sch 1, as amended. This scheme

---

50 Criminal Legal Aid (Determinations by a Court and Choice of Representative) Regulations 2013 reg 18(3).
51 Criminal Legal Aid (Determinations by a Court and Choice of Representative) Regulations 2013 reg 18(4).
52 Criminal Legal Aid (Determinations by a Court and Choice of Representative) Regulations 2013 reg 18(5) and (6).
53 Criminal Legal Aid (Determinations by a Court and Choice of Representative) Regulations 2013 reg 19.

20.50 applies to all advocates in the Crown Court, whether they are counsel or solicitor advocates.

20.50 Each case will have a trial advocate, who is the advocate responsible for claiming fees on behalf of all advocates instructed in the case.

20.51 The scheme provides for a basic fee based on the classification of the offence, to which is added an uplift for length of trial. Additional fees are paid for identified hearings and work. There is a higher basic fee for a trial and some cracked trials, and a lower fee for a guilty plea case.

20.52 For the full details, see Criminal Legal Aid (Remuneration) Regulations 2013 Sch 1.

Appeals

20.53 Advice on appeals can, in some circumstances, be provided under the Advice and Assistance scheme. Advocacy in appeal proceedings can be provided either as advocacy assistance in prescribed proceedings or under a representation order.

20.54 Representation in the Crown Court in prescribed proceedings[54] is provided for by the Standard Crime Contract[55] and is claimed as part of the normal monthly submission. A representation order must be obtained and there is an extendable fee limit of £1,574.06.[56] Counsel may not be assigned and if instructed a fee must be agreed; the underlying rate must not exceed that payable under the Regulations.[57] The litigator may be paid for preparing counsel's instructions but not for attending them at court.[58]

20.55 Representation in criminal appeal proceedings will require a representation order to be granted for the court in which the appeal is to be heard, be that the Crown Court (granted by the LAA), High Court (for appeals by way of case stated) or Court of Appeal (which both grant their own orders) It is usual for representation orders granted by the Court of Appeal to be granted to an advocate alone.[59]

---

54 Defined by Criminal Legal Aid (General) Regulations 2013 reg 9, as amended.
55 Standard Crime Contract 2022 Specification paras 11.62–11.73 and Standard Crime Contract 2025 Specification paras 11.56–11.67.
56 Criminal Legal Aid (Remuneration) Regulations 2013 Sch 4 para 10.
57 Standard Crime Contract 2022 Specification para 11.65 and Standard Crime Contract 2025 Specification para 11.59.
58 Standard Crime Contract 2022 Specification para 11.68 and Standard Crime Contract 2025 Specification para 11.62.
59 Criminal Legal Aid (Determinations by a Court and Choice of Representative) Regulations 2013 reg 8.

Advocacy assistance – prison law

20.56 Advocacy in prison law cases may be provided under the advocacy assistance scheme. Representation may be provided in disciplinary cases and in parole board cases, but see chapter 14 for scope.

20.57 You may only represent a client at hearings in these matters if the sufficient benefit test is satisfied, and the contract notes specifically that the LAA would not expect to fund a matter which did not raise a significant legal or human rights issue.[60] In addition, advocacy assistance must not be provided in disciplinary cases where:

- it appears unreasonable to grant in the particular circumstances of the case; or
- (where required) permission to be legally represented has not been granted.[61]

In all cases, you should record on the file how the merits test has been and continues to be met.[62]

20.58 In addition, there is a financial eligibility test for both advice and assistance and advocacy assistance in prison law cases. The client must complete the relevant forms (CRM1 and CRM2 or CRM3) and must pass the means test. Means are limited by both capital and disposable income, and the eligibility levels can be found on the legal aid website at: www.gov.uk/criminal-legal-aid-means-testing. The completed application forms must be retained on your file.[63]

20.59 Advocacy under this scheme is paid under a system of standard fees.[64] There are two standard fees for each type of case, and two corresponding standard fee limits. If your costs do not exceed either limit, you will be paid the respective standard fee. If your costs fall above the higher limit, you will be paid a non-standard fee for which your costs will be assessed by the LAA. See the Criminal Legal Aid (Remuneration) Regulations 2013 for details of the fees and limits.

---

60 Standard Crime Contract 2022 Specification para 12.10 and Standard Crime Contract 2025 Specification para 12.3.
61 Standard Crime Contract 2022 Specification para 12.84 and Standard Crime Contract 2025 Specification para 12.79.
62 Standard Crime Contracts 2022 and 2025 Specification para 12.6.
63 Standard Crime Contract 2022 Specification para 12.15 and Standard Crime Contract 2025 Specification para 12.10.
64 Standard Crime Contract 2022 Specification para 12.65 and Standard Crime Contract 2025 Specification para 12.62.

20.60 Under this form of advocacy assistance, advocacy may be provided by either a solicitor or counsel. However, counsel is effectively 'unassigned' in that they are not able to claim payment directly from the LAA. Counsel's fees must be agreed and paid by the instructing solicitor from the standard fee.[65]

---

65 Standard Crime Contract 2022 Specification paras 12.45 and 12.48 and Standard Crime Contract 2025 Specification paras 12.38 and 12.42.

PART C

Managing legal aid work

CHAPTER 21

Legal aid contracts

Edited by Vicky Ling

21.1	Introduction
21.4	**Standard Civil Contract**
21.5	**Standard Crime Contract**
21.9	**Elements of the contracts**
21.9	Overview
21.11	Contract for signature
	Overview • Withdrawing from contracts and giving notice to the LAA
21.15	Office schedule
21.20	Supplementary matter starts
21.21	Standard Civil Contract 2024 Standard Terms
21.22	Standard Crime Contract 2022 Standard Terms
21.23	Standard Crime Contract 2025
21.25	Civil and Crime Contract Specifications
21.28	**Applying for civil or family contracts**
21.32	How long contracts last
	Standard Civil Contract 2024 • Standard Crime Contract 2022
21.38	**Tenders**
21.42	**Applying for crime contracts**
21.44	**The Public Defender Service**
21.45	**Crime – Very High Cost Case accreditation**
21.47	**Community Legal Advice services**
21.48	**Other kinds of contract with the LAA**

Key points to note
- It is essential to read the contract.
- Do not expect the Legal Aid Agency (LAA) to notify your organisation when you need to tender for a new contract. It expects you to subscribe to its regular updates.
- In a significant change of policy, the Standard Crime Contract 2025 is expected to last for 10 years. New providers will be able to apply for a contract at any time from the start of the contract to the final year.

Summary of changes to the Civil Standard Terms 2024

- **14.7** – the LAA will give 28 days' notice of any amendments to the Costs Assessment Guidance (previously 14 days).
- **14.8** – Payments for controlled work will be made as variable monthly payments unless the provider opts to receive standard monthly payments (previously the default was payment by standard monthly payments).
- **26.4** – the contract has been clarified in relation to the LAA being able to make payments for remainder work after a contract ceases. This has been done in practice, but the wording was ambiguous.

Summary of changes to the Civil Specification 2024

Supervisor standards

- **2.10** The LAA has removed some text to make the 'full time equivalent' requirement for supervisors more flexible. They still have to work 35 hours a week, but the text referring to five days a week and seven hours a day has been removed.
- **2.19** The LAA has removed the requirement for all civil supervisors to be able to give an example of a case engaging human rights issues. It has also removed the option of demonstrating experience/knowledge of supervision through having an NVQ. This was scarcely ever used.
- **2.19** Supervisors not supervising anyone else need to do a supervisor course every 24 months (increased from every 12 months).
- **2.26** The LAA has removed the restriction on the number of offices a supervisor can supervise, as long as the one supervisor to four other caseworkers ratio is met.

Permanent presence

- **2.33** The LAA has clarified the contract so that it states explicitly that residential property is not acceptable. Further points of clarification have also been added concerning shared and serviced offices.

Summary of changes to the Crime Standard Terms 2025

- There have been numerous small amendments to clarify meaning or to ensure consistency with the Civil Contract, which are unlikely to have a significant impact on most practitioners.
- **3.3** The LAA has clarified that you may not instruct a third party if any of your personnel has an interest in it.
- **3.7** The LAA has included a clause that you must ensure that accredited representatives must maintain their status.
- **Clause 7** Previous requirements concerning the instruction of counsel have been deleted on the basis that they are professional obligations.
- **Clause 7** Reference to the LAA conducting 'mystery shopping' has been deleted.
- **Clause 11** The previous reference to key performance indicator (KPI) performance being used as a selection criterion for future contracts has been removed.
- **Clause 13** Variable monthly payments for crime lower work have become the default option, in line with the Civil Contract.
- **Clause 16** Providers are required to hold Cyber Essentials accreditation.
- **Clause 18** Has been simplified to reflect the change allowing new providers to apply for contracts at any point between the start date and the final year of the contract.
- **Clause 21** Has been amended to clarify that providers must notify the LAA at least 15 business days in advance of any material constitutional change.
- **Clause 24** The previous number-based definition of 'persistent breach' has been removed, allowing the LAA more flexibility in applying sanctions for persistent breach.

Summary of changes to the Crime Specification 2025

Section 2 – Service standards

- Removal of the supervisor to caseworker/designated fee earner ratios.

- An amendment that providers must designate fee earners not employed by them but whom they regularly instruct.
- Complete removal of the requirement that supervisors attend the office(s) of the staff they supervise.
- Allowing supervisors to supervise a maximum of two providers across all classes of work.
- Allowing appropriately qualified CILEX members to act as supervisors.
- Offices only required to be open five hours (previously seven hours), between 8 am and 8 pm each business day.
- Reduced, specific requirements for prison law only offices.
- Allowing new offices to be opened during the 2025 Standard Crime Contract and for those offices to be able to join their eligible duty scheme (this also applies to office moves).

Section 6 – Duty solicitor contract work

- Changes made to the case involvement requirements for duty solicitors so that they match supervisor requirements.
- Duty solicitors required to undertake at least one police station duty solicitor attendance allocated to them in each three-month period.
- Duty solicitors ceasing to be a member of a scheme will immediately be removed from the panel list for that scheme.

Section 9 – Criminal investigations

- **9.23 onwards** New provisions added on the work and supervision of police station accredited representatives.

Section 10 – Criminal proceedings

- Duty solicitors must cover alternative courtrooms if requested by the court.
- Clarification that that duty solicitors may conduct own client work when on duty unless that work prevents or delays the provision of duty solicitor advice.

Section 12 – Prison law

- Clarification to postal rules.
- Instructing counsel in advocacy assistance cases has been amended and expanded.

Introduction

21.1 This chapter explains the contract documentation, standard terms and obligations imposed by the Standard Civil and Crime Contracts and their respective Specifications. It also covers how to get additional work under an existing contract, and how to get a new contract with the LAA.

21.2 It also refers to some of the other contracts offered by the LAA, such as those for telephone triage and advice (Civil Legal Advice (CLA) contracts).

21.3 It is extremely important to become familiar with what your contract allows you to do and prohibits you from doing, since if you overlook something you could find yourself served with a contract notice. Clause 24 of the Standard Civil and Criminal Contracts allows for termination in relation to 'persistent breaches' – that is, three breaches of the same term in a 24-month period (or six different breaches) – so it is very important to be aware of what you must and must not do.

Standard Civil Contract

21.4 The Standard Civil Contract 2024[1] came into force from September 2024.

Standard Crime Contract

21.5 The Standard Crime Contract 2022[2] applied from 1 October 2022 and is due to be replaced by the Standard Crime Contract 2025[3] from 1 October 2025.

21.6 The Standard Crime Contract 2025 contains some key changes from the 2022 Contract in respect of offices, minimum hours of criminal defence work and supervision (see changes summary above).

---

1 Available at: www.gov.uk/government/publications/standard-civil-contract-2024.
2 Available at: www.gov.uk/government/publications/standard-crime-contract-2022.
3 Available at: www.gov.uk/government/publications/standard-crime-contract-2025.

21.7 The 2025 Contract will run for 10 years, with a six-month termination provision.

21.8 A significant change is that new providers will be able to apply for a contract at any point between the contract start date and the final year of the contract. Similarly, providers may expand their office and duty scheme network at any time during the life of the contract.

Elements of the contracts

Overview

21.9 The contracts are divided into the following sections:
- Contract for Signature, Key Information, Tables and Annexes;
- Office Schedule;
- Standard Terms;
- Specification, split into:
  - in the Civil Contract – general rules and category-specific rules; and
  - in the Crime Contract – sections 1–8 apply to all Classes of Work; sections 9–13 set out the specific rules which apply to each Unit of Work.

21.10 All of the above documents form part of the contract, and you are bound by each and every part of them.

Contract for signature

Overview

21.11 As the name suggests, this is the part of the contract that is signed by the organisation and counter-signed by the LAA.

21.12 The contract covers the whole organisation (although it specifies the work that can be done at each office through an office schedule). This means that a breach at any office can jeopardise the whole contract. The contract for signature also includes any conditions that the LAA has imposed, the office schedules which have been issued, the applicable quality standard you must hold (the SQM (Specialist Quality Mark) or Lexcel) and contact details which the LAA will use to deal with you.

21.13 The Crime Contract sets out the types of criminal defence work the organisation is allowed to do – for example, criminal investigations and criminal proceedings, appeals and reviews, prison law.

Holders of all types of contract are also authorised to undertake associated civil work.

Withdrawing from contracts and giving notice to the LAA

21.14 It is only possible for the provider to serve notice on the LAA for the whole contract. If a provider wishes to withdraw from an office or category of law, that can be done with the LAA's agreement.

Office schedule

21.15 In civil and family, the office schedule sets out the details of the work you are allowed to do, including the number of matter starts in each category of work and the monthly controlled work payment.

21.16 The schedule will set out the number of new matter starts allowed, by category.

21.17 Civil schedules contain the following tables:
- Table 1 gives the start and end dates.
- Table 2 gives the number of matter starts you are allowed by category and categories in which you may do licensed work and have delegated functions.
- Table 3 sets out the maximum amount of money the LAA will pay you for controlled work[4] while the schedule is in force and the amount of your monthly payment. Sometimes this is shown as £0.00, but for ease of LAA administration only.
- Table 4 sets out exactly what type of service and where you must provide services, and the type of office presence you are required to have, by procurement area.
- Table 5 shows whether you have been authorised to carry out work under alternative arrangements in mental health work.
- Table 6 shows any outreaches that have been authorised.
- Table 7 shows any special provisions or restrictions.
- Tables 8 and 9 show rota weeks under the detained duty scheme and slots under the fast track scheme, respectively.
- Table 10 is completed if you have a contract to deliver the Housing Loss Prevention Service, showing the court, allocated number of early advice matter starts and court duty acts of assistance.

21.18 The Crime Schedule lists the classes of work you are authorised to do and your authorised duty schemes. Numbers of cases are not specified and depend on the interests of justice test being met, as

---

4 Standard Civil Contract Specification 2024 para 1.5, Interpretation.

defined in the contract (see chapter 14 for more information about conducting criminal cases).

21.19 If you do work outside that authorised under your schedule, you will not be paid for it.

Supplementary matter starts

21.20 Under the 2024 Contract, you can self-grant up to an additional 50 per cent of matter starts per year – but you must notify your contract manager first.[5] You can apply for further matter starts to the LAA if you need to. You will need to satisfy the LAA that:[6]

1) you are unable to meet an urgent demand from clients for your services from your current matter start allocation;
2) an urgent need for services arises as a result of another provider in your procurement area ceasing to provide or reducing the provision of such services for any reason; or
3) there is a general increase in demand for services of that type within your procurement area.

If you are granted additional matter starts, the additional matter starts will be reflected in your allocation in the next schedule.[7]

Standard Civil Contract 2024 Standard Terms

21.21 The Civil Standard Terms 2024 apply to civil and family categories. Key clauses are summarised below:

- **Clause 1: Interpretation.** This clause contains the definitions of expressions which have particular meanings under the contract. These are denoted by the use of capital letters. There are further definitions in the Specification.
  - 'Good Industry Practice':
  ... means that degree of skill, care, diligence, prudence, timeliness, efficiency and foresight which could reasonably and ordinarily be expected from a skilled, experienced and professionally managed provider of legal services similar to those required to be provided under this Contract;
  - 'Qualifying event': This requires you to provide the LAA with information about significant changes to your organisation so

---

5 Standard Civil Contract 2024 Specification paras 1.21 and 1.22.
6 Standard Civil Contract 2024 Specification para 1.23.
7 Standard Civil Contract 2024 Specification para 1.24.

that it can make decisions about whether the changes impact on whether a contract should continue/be novated. See Clause 2: '"Qualifying Event" means those matters specified in this Contract as being a Qualifying Event.'
- **Clause 2: Relationship and communication.** You must appoint a contract liaison manager and notify the LAA within five business days if the person is changed. You must monitor the email address which you have given to the LAA 'frequently each business day' and communicate with the LAA electronically where stipulated.
  – Suitability to hold a contract: If there is any change to your answers to rejection criteria questions provided in a tender, you must notify the LAA and it can review whether you are still suitable to hold a contract. This ties in with qualifying events.
  – The LAA includes a controversial 'embarrassment clause', but it was re-worded following representations by the representative bodies:
  2.2 You shall ensure that neither you nor any of your Affiliates brings the legal aid scheme into disrepute by engaging in any unprofessional or unlawful conduct which is likely to substantially diminish the trust the public places in the legal aid scheme, regardless of whether or not such conduct is related to your obligations under this Contract. Any operation of this Clause is subject to our obligation to act as a responsible public body and any sanction must be proportionate. For the avoidance of doubt, the engaging by you or any of your Affiliates in any lawful challenge to or criticism or complaint of us or any of our decisions, when acting in clients' best interests or otherwise acting in your professional capacity, is not within the scope of the words 'unprofessional or unlawful conduct' under this Clause 2.2.
  – Responsibility for personnel: You are responsible for the acts and omissions of all personnel, whether employees or consultants:
  2.16 You shall be responsible for the acts and omissions of all personnel who you engage or employ in relation to the fulfilment of your obligations under this Contract.
- **Clause 3: Working with third parties.** You cannot subcontract, novate or otherwise delegate any of your obligations under the contract without the LAA's prior written consent. However, you can appoint agents to work for you as long as their work is properly supervised.
  – If an approved third party, agent, counsel or a subcontractor ceases providing services to you, you are responsible for

ensuring that you continue to fulfil the obligations under the contract.
– Payment within 30 days: This was introduced due to Public Contracts Regulations 2015 reg 113:
3.3 . . .
(b) any person pursuant to this Clause 3 you are responsible for ensuring that:
(i) all payments are made to them for their work within 30 days from receipt of a valid invoice;
– Clause 3.7 states that if the fees payable by you exceed £250 per matter or case, you must require agents, counsel or subcontractors in connection with contract work, to keep accurate records of the time they spend on the work you have appointed them to do and of the work done. They must also permit the LAA to audit the records.
- **Clause 4: Financial disclosure and risk.** Accounts must be audited or examined as required by law or professional regulation. You must notify the LAA within 14 days if your accounts are qualified.
    – Clause 4.6: Notify the LAA of changes to directors/members so that it can require indemnities from new ones during the life of the contract.
- **Clause 5: Equality and diversity.** You must comply with the equality and diversity requirements, and you must have an equality and diversity training plan.
- **Clause 6: Logos and marketing.** Restrictions on marketing your services. It is clear that you can neither pay nor receive referral fees nor any other benefit, to any third party for the referral or introduction (directly or indirectly) of any client or potential client.
- **Clause 7: Your obligations, looking after Clients, compliance and self-monitoring.** You must monitor your performance and compliance with the contract and take corrective action if there are problems.
    – Clarification that failure to look after clients (and potential clients) best interests is a fundamental breach of contract.
    – Consulting clients and providing information about the use of in-house counsel:
7.3 Where you instruct Counsel or an in-house advocate holding higher rights of audience to conduct advocacy services, before giving such instructions you must, save where the circumstances of the case mean that it is not practicable or appropriate to do so, consult the Client about the use and the selection of Counsel or in-house advocate and advise the Client of:

(a) the name;
(b) status;
(c) experience; and
(d) suitability,

of this Counsel or in-house advocate to conduct advocacy in each such case having regard to the nature of that case and its complexity and the existence of alternative Counsel or in-house advocate whom the Client may choose to be instructed (subject to availability). In circumstances where you have determined through your reasonable enquiries that there is no alternative Counsel or in-house advocate actually available, you must also advise the Client of that fact.

7.4 Where Counsel or an in-house advocate is instructed pursuant to Clause 7.3; if the chosen Counsel or in-house advocate becomes unavailable you must take all reasonable steps to instruct another Counsel or in-house advocate of equivalent standing and, so far as is practicable, advise the Client of the merits and suitability of the proposed replacement.

7.5 You must keep a Record (in accordance with the provisions of Clauses 8.3 and 8.4) to demonstrate your compliance with Clause 7.3.

- Clause 7.6: An obligation to notify a client that they should take independent advice if you become aware of a potentially justified claim against you by a client. A record must be kept on file.
- Clause 7.13: You must have access to the LAA online manual: www.gov.uk/guidance/civil-legal-aid-civil-regulations-civil-contracts-and-guidance.
- Clause 7.18: Except where the contract or legal aid legislation so provides, you must not claim or seek to claim any payment from any client or former client for any contract work or for any work that was performed in your or your client's or former client's reasonable belief that it was contract work.
- Clause 7.19 – IT systems: You must be able to use government secure email, use video conferencing, etc.

- **Clause 8: Keeping records and completing and returning forms.** Requires you to record all the information required by the contract. You are required to keep closed client files (or copies of them) for six years. If you keep electronic files, they must contain all the information that they would have if they were paper files. Documents must be in PDF format.
  - Use of in-house counsel: As clause 7.5 above.
- **Clause 9: Provision of information and access to your premises.** Concerns access to your premises and information you must provide. Note that you must inform the LAA of the outcome of

third-party audits and provide it with a copy of the report within seven days of receipt. This clause would apply, for example, to Recognising Excellence carrying out an SQM audit.
  – Time limit to provide information: If the LAA asks for records you have to provide them within 10 business days.
  – Access to third party premises and records: You have to require subcontractors to allow the LAA access to their systems (see clause 9.4).
  – You must allow access to your premises within two business days (immediately if you are subject to an official investigation). You must provide the LAA with access and facilities during any audit by it. Breach would be considered to be a fundamental breach justifying contract termination.
  – The LAA can carry out mystery shopping exercises and client satisfaction surveys of your clients. They can also obtain reports in connection with any professional misconduct.
- **Clause 10: Standard of Contract Work.** Sets out standards of work you must meet, including peer review.
  – All work must be performed with reasonable care and skill: You must achieve at least Threshold Competence (3) at peer review in order to hold a contract. If you fail a peer review, the LAA may re-charge the cost to you.
  – You must authorise the LAA to carry out status enquiries in relation to your personnel, if required.
- **Clause 11: KPIs.** Requires you to meet KPIs. If you fail to do so, the LAA will first meet with you to agree an action plan to improve performance. The LAA says it may use KPI performance as entry or selection criteria for future contracts (clause 11.6), but it has not done so to date due to the difficulty in treating previous contractors and new applicants fairly in the tender process.
- **Clause 12: Contract Documents and precedence.**
- **Clause 13: Amendments to the Contract Documents.** The LAA may amend the contract to take account of legislation or the justice system. Minor or technical amendments may be made to individual organisations' contracts. If the LAA wants to make material changes, it has to terminate the contract and issue a new one.
  – The clause lists the changes you can request, for example, closure or relocation of an office/outreach, temporary or permanent reduction or cessation of contract work; a change to your quality standard; the temporary or permanent reduc-

tion or cessation of the provision of duty solicitor services; or a change in membership of any consortium.
   – The clause gives examples of circumstances where the LAA would be justified in refusing your request.
- **Clause 14: Your account with us, Claims, payments and Assessments.** This clause creates a single account for all work done by the organisation, which is treated globally. Claims made by you are treated as credits to your account, and any payments made by the LAA as debits. You may be required to reimburse the LAA's reasonable audit costs if you have mis-claimed costs under the contract.
   – Payment within 30 days of determination of a valid and undisputed claim: This requirement is due to Public Contracts Regulations 2015 reg 113. It does not prevent the LAA from subsequently recouping a payment on assessment.
   – If you omit VAT due to an occasional clerical error in a claim to the LAA, you can submit a further claim for the VAT; but this must be within two years of the date when you should have charged VAT.
   – You have to notify the LAA within five days if tax non-compliance takes place.
- **Clause 15: Confidentiality.** Sets out confidentiality arrangements. Clarification of Freedom of Information Act (FOIA) 2000 disclosure by the LAA. Provisions allowing the LAA to share information on contract performance with other government departments (which must keep it confidential). See clause 15.10.
- **Clause 16: Data protection.** Data protection requirements. The LAA requires you to comply with applicable legislation.
   – It requires you to notify it within five business days if you receive a request for the following, within the LAA or shared data:
      – a data subject request;
      – a request to rectify, block or erase personal data;
      – a complaint or other communication about your or the LAA's handling of data; or
      – a communication from the Information Commissioner.
   – You must also indemnify the LAA if it is fined because you fail to comply with data protection legislation.
- **Clause 17: FOIA.** FOIA obligations: The LAA may release information about your organisation either following consultation with you or not, in certain circumstances.

- **Clause 18: Warranties.** Warranties that the information provided by you and the LAA is true and accurate. Breach of warranties in clause 18.1 shall be a fundamental breach.
- **Clause 19: Indemnity.** Indemnity you give the LAA against reasonable losses.
- **Clause 20: Giving notices.** How notices can be given under the contract.
- **Clause 21: Things you must tell us about.** You must notify the LAA as soon as reasonably practicable of any anticipated material constitutional change (within 14 days as a minimum) and any other change that might impact on your ability to do contract work.
  - You must provide the LAA with information about significant changes to your organisation so that it can make decisions about whether the changes impact on whether a contract should continue.
  - Clause 21.18 states that failing to inform the LAA of the matters listed in clause 21 shall be a fundamental breach.
- **Clause 22: Novations and Qualifying Events.** The LAA may novate the contract if a practice merges with another. Clarification of previous powers in relation to novations and when a novation will be refused. There was a policy paper on the legal aid website which provided more information, but this has now been withdrawn. You need to contact your contract manager with any queries. See: www.gov.uk/government/publications/novation-policy.
- **Clause 23: Bribery, collusion, false tenders, fraud and unethical behaviour.** Any breaches of these clauses are fundamental breaches.
- **Clause 24: Sanctions.** Contract sanctions may include: suspension of a contract category or delegated functions, refusal to pay for specified contract work, suspension of payments, prohibition of taking on any new matters or cases, exclusion of individuals from being supervisors or performing contract work, suspending or removing your rota allocation (if any) of holding yourself out as a provider, and termination. If you breach the contract, the LAA may serve a contract notice under clause 24.2, requiring you not to repeat the breach. If you do so, you risk contract termination.
- **Clause 25: How this Contract can be ended.** You may terminate the contract at any time on three months' notice (subject to clause

13, which gives you rights to propose amendments). The LAA can terminate the contract at any time on six months' notice.
- Clause 25.7 allows the LAA to terminate for breach of the Public Contracts Regulations 2015.
- **Clause 26: Consequences of termination.** Unless the LAA terminates the contract due to your breach, it will authorise you to continue work on existing cases (usually for up to two years). The LAA considers that the Transfer of Undertakings (Protection of Employment) Regulations 2006 (TUPE) do not apply when contracts expire or are terminated. However, if the LAA considers in future that TUPE does apply, you must co-operate, for example, by giving details of affected staff when requested. You will be liable for any claims by staff.
- **Clause 27: Reconsidering decisions and the review procedure.** Reconsidering decisions and reviews of decisions: There is an informal procedure and a formal procedure. Formal reviews may be carried out by the LAA's Chief Executive or the Contract Review Body.
- **Clause 28: Dispute resolution.**
- **Clause 29: Governing law and jurisdiction.**
- **Clause 30: General.** General provisions.

Standard Crime Contract 2022 Standard Terms

21.22 The numbering and subject matter of clauses are the same in the 2022 Crime Contract as in the 2024 Civil Contract. The slight differences are as follows:
- **Clause 7.3:** The requirements in relation to consulting the client before instructing an advocate apply to Crown Court cases (whether in-house or external counsel) and advising the client of their name; status; experience; and suitability. Where an advocate becomes unavailable, there is a duty to repeat the above and take all reasonable steps to secure an equivalent advocate. A record of the above must be kept on file. This was regarded as controversial, as it could disadvantage in-house solicitor advocates compared with independent counsel.
- **Clause 7.19(k):** You must have a system that is capable of being used to work electronically within the criminal justice system and with other criminal justice agencies, including the prosecution and police.

Standard Crime Contract 2025

21.23 The LAA has made a number of minor changes, incorporating standard Cabinet Office wording and/or improving consistency with the Civil Contract/simplifying clauses.

21.24 See summary in the Key Points to Note section at the beginning of this chapter for changes to the standard terms.

Civil and Crime Contract Specifications

21.25 The Civil and Crime Specifications contain the detailed rules that apply to the way in which cases are carried out on a day-to-day basis. We cover them in the relevant chapters – see:
- taking on civil and family cases (chapter 2);
- conducting a civil/family case (chapter 4);
- conducting a private family law case (chapter 6);
- conducting a public family law case (chapter 7);
- conducting an immigration case (chapter 9);
- conducting a mental health case (chapter 10);
- conducting a housing case (chapter 11);
- conducting a community care case (chapter 12);
- conducting a public law case (chapter 13);
- conducting a criminal case (chapter 14); and
- quality standards and performance monitoring (chapter 22).

21.26 The supervisor standards are in the relevant legal Category Specifications, but we cover them together in chapter 22, 'Quality standards and performance monitoring'.

21.27 Note that prior to 2013, civil payment rates were set out in an annex to the Contract Specification. This was removed, and payment rates are only to be found in the Civil Legal Aid (Remuneration) Regulations 2013 or Criminal Legal Aid (Remuneration) Regulations 2013, as amended.

Applying for civil or family contracts

21.28 In civil and family, the LAA allocates funds to geographical areas using a formula that attempts to estimate the number of potential legal aid clients who might experience legal problems and remain within scope. This is called 'indicative spend'.

Legal aid contracts 579

21.29 The LAA uses the formula as a starting point when considering where to direct available funding – though only in terms of Legal Help matter starts made available.

21.30 You should note that although bidding opportunities are expressed in terms of the numbers of matter starts available, where you provide services under a schedule, it will also authorise you to undertake an unlimited number of certificated cases (licensed work).

21.31 If you are an existing provider wanting to add a category, or open a new office, or if you are an organisation wishing to contract with the LAA for the first time, you will need to submit a bid in a tender process. Tender opportunities are advertised on the LAA's current tenders page: 'Procurement at LAA' at: www.gov.uk/government/organisations/legal-aid-agency/about/procurement.

How long contracts last

21.32 Historically, LAA contracts have lasted for three years, with a power for the LAA to extend for up to a further two years. The LAA generally exercised its option to extend contracts and did not run additional tenders, so if you missed a tender opportunity you had to wait a long time for another.

21.33 Usually bids for contracts need to be submitted 12 months before the contract start date. However, in April 2024, the LAA opened an additional opportunity to bid for civil contracts to start on 1 September 2024.

21.34 Then in May 2024, the LAA announced a significant change in relation to the Crime Contract 2025. New providers will be able to apply for a contract at any point between the contract start date and the final year of the contract. Similarly, providers may expand their office and duty scheme network at any time during the life of the contract.

21.35 At present it is unclear how this will affect the Standard Civil Contract 2024, if at all. However, it is a good indication that the LAA will also allow more opportunities to bid for civil and family contracts in future.

Standard Civil Contract 2024

21.36 The Standard Civil Contract 2024 started on 1 September 2024 and covers family law; family mediation; housing, debt and welfare benefits; immigration and asylum; mental health; community care; claims against public authorities (previously known as actions against the police, etc); clinical negligence; public law; education; and discrimination. It is expected to expire on 31 August 2025.[8] It can be extended to last up to up to three years.

Standard Crime Contract 2022

21.37 The Standard Crime Contract 2022 started on 1 October 2022, initially for one year. It was extended to 30 September 2025. In September 2024, the LAA started a tender process for contracts to start on 1 October 2025. See para 21.34, 'How long contracts last', above for information on how long that contract will last and the intended process for new bids during the life of the contract.

Tenders

21.38 The LAA uses an online tendering process through an online eTendering portal: https://legalaid.bravosolution.co.uk/web/technical-support.shtml – hosted by a commercial company, JaggaerOne.

21.39 Bidders have to complete a questionnaire (called a selection questionnaire) covering basic information about the organisation and its history of compliance with legal and regulatory requirements and an award questionnaire which covers the category(ies) of law and location of services.

21.40 Bidders have to satisfy the LAA that they meet essential criteria in the selection questionnaire. There may be a competitive element to tenders, including criteria based on previous experience of delivering legal services. However, where the LAA perceives there may be a lack of supply, there may be a simple registration process instead. Some tenders (eg the CLA telephone service) may include price competition.

21.41 Face-to-face contracts for crime and civil face-to-face legal work starting in 2022, 2024 and 2025, respectively, were guaranteed to those submitting technically correct bids and meeting minimum requirements. Larger numbers of matter starts for civil providers were allocated to those meeting defined requirements.

---

8 At: www.gov.uk/government/publications/civil-2024-contract-procurement-process, Award further Tender ITT para 1.4.

Applying for crime contracts

21.42 Under the pressure of a considerable number of legal challenges, the LAA did not go ahead with the two-tier contracting arrangements in 2016 that would have seen only a small number of firms eligible to do police duty solicitor work, which is the life-blood of many criminal defence firms. In the event, the tender for 2017 contracts was mainly a simple registration process, with only firms bidding for larger contracts needing to supply business plan and financial information. A similar process was adopted in October 2021 for new contracts which started on 1 October 2021.

21.43 See para 21.34, 'How long contracts last', above for information on how long the 2025 Contract will last and the intended process for new bids during the life of the contract.

The Public Defender Service

21.44 As well as contracting with private practice to deliver criminal defence work, the LAA also employs a small number of salaried lawyers in the Public Defender Service (PDS). This service was set up to benchmark the cost and quality of services provided by private practice and was never intended to be a nationwide scheme. At the time of writing, there are four PDS offices: Cheltenham, Darlington, Merthyr Tydfil and Swansea, as well as an advocacy unit which acts in PDS cases and is able to accept advocacy instructions from private practice.

Crime – Very High Cost Case accreditation

21.45 The LAA's Criminal Cases Unit (CCU) manages membership of the Very High Cost Case (VHCC) scheme. Only firms that are accredited under this scheme can represent clients in VHCC cases – any case where the trial is expected to last for more than 40 days.

21.46 From 14 July 2010, organisations and self-employed advocates wishing to work on cases classified as VHCC have had to obtain VHCC accreditation. This can be done when you become aware that you have a potential VHCC case and can be submitted at any time. There is information about the VHCC arrangements and how to apply at: www.gov.uk/high-cost-cases-crime.

Community Legal Advice services

21.47 The Community Legal Service was a concept embodied in the Access to Justice Act 1999. In some areas, the then Legal Services Commission (LSC) contracted with a single provider to deliver a face-to-face legal advice and representation service concentrating on welfare benefits, debt, employment, housing, education and community care (often referred to as social welfare law (SWL) categories), sometimes with family law services. These were known as Community Legal Advice Centres (CLACs) in urban areas, and in rural areas Community Legal Advice Networks (CLANs). The Legal Aid, Sentencing and Punishment of Offenders Act 2012 proved fatal to these developments and all those contracts were terminated at the end of March 2013.

Other kinds of contract with the LAA

21.48 The LAA has contracts with organisations for other kinds of service, for example:
- the CLA telephone service – triage and signposting to the nearest three face-to-face civil or family legal aid providers; and
- telephone advice to people in police stations (Criminal Defence Service Direct).

21.49 Opportunities are publicised on the LAA's tenders page: www.gov.uk/legal-aid-for-providers/tenders.

CHAPTER 22

Quality standards and performance monitoring

Edited by Vicky Ling

22.1	Introduction
22.3	Practice management and quality of advice standards
22.6	**Specialist Quality Mark**
22.6	Introduction
22.8	Quality Mark assessment process
	Desktop audit • Pre-Quality Mark audit
22.15	Quality Mark requirements
22.16	**Lexcel**
22.19	**Supervisors**
22.19	Supervisors – technical legal competence
22.24	Supervisor standards in the Standard Civil Contract 2024
	Common rules • Category-specific standards
22.56	Supervisor standards in the Standard Crime Contract 2022
22.62	Supervisor standards in the Standard Crime Contract 2025
22.72	Supervisors – file reviews
22.73	**Peer review**
22.73	Overview
22.78	The peer review process

continued

22.85	Tips for passing peer review
	Overview • Standard letters and documentation • Peer review representations
22.92	LAA online portal
22.96	**Key performance indicators**
22.96	Overview
22.99	KPIs: Standard Civil Contract 2024
22.110	KPIs: Standard Crime Contracts 2022 and 2025
22.111	**Service standards**
22.111	Service standards: civil and family
	Overview • Additional/variations to service and monitoring requirements • Housing Loss Prevention Advice Service (HLPAS)
22.135	Service standards: Standard Crime Contracts 2022 and 2025
22.148	**Covid-19 arrangements – civil and crime**

> Key points to note
> - From 1 August 2023, the Housing Loss Prevention Advice Service (HLPAS) scheme replaced the Housing Possession Court Duty Scheme (HPCDS).
> - From August 2023 (Crime) and November 2023 (Civil) it was decided that requiring supervisors to provide face-to-face supervision once a month was too onerous and impractical, and the contracts were changed so that a supervisor only had to be in the office they supervise and provide face-to-face supervision 'where you determine this is required'.[1] Under the Crime Contract 2025, all detailed references to how supervision should be delivered in practice are removed.
> - Under the 2024 Standard Civil Contract 'full time equivalent' means the equivalent of one individual working 35 hours a week (excluding breaks).[2] This gives an element of flexibility to accommodate, for example, a full-time equivalent (FTE) supervisor working 35 hours compressed over four days.
> - Under the 2018 Standard Civil Contract supervisors were restricted to a maximum of two offices or across two providers with one office each. However, this was removed in the 2024 Contract.
> - The 2025 Standard Crime Contract no longer contains ratios of supervisors to caseworkers.
> - The 2025 Standard Crime Contract has relaxed office opening and telephone contact arrangements for practices offering prison law only.

Introduction

22.1 This chapter deals with quality standards and performance monitoring under contracts with the Legal Aid Agency (LAA), from a management perspective. We will cover the **Standard Civil Contract 2024**,[3] which deals with the main face-to-face categories:
- family (both law and mediation);
- housing and debt;

---

1 Standard Civil Contract Specification 2024 para 2.21b and Standard Crime Contract Specification 2022 paras 2.7, 2.17b and 2.19.
2 Standard Civil Contract 2024 Specification para 2.10.
3 Available at: www.gov.uk/government/publications/standard-civil-contract-2024.

- welfare benefits;
- immigration and asylum;
- mental health;
- community care;
- claims against public authorities;
- clinical negligence;
- public law;
- discrimination; and
- education.

This chapter will also cover the Standard Crime Contracts 2022[4] and 2025.[5] There are also others – see chapter 21.

22.2 Whatever kind of contract you have with the LAA, there is no substitute for reading it! The worst-case scenario is that you overlook something fundamental – for example, your supervisor may not meet the supervisor standards, the LAA discovers this and your contract is terminated – because there is nothing you can do to remedy the historic breach.

Practice management and quality of advice standards

22.3 The LAA's practice management standards are known as the Specialist Quality Mark (SQM).[6] The LAA also accepts the Law Society's Lexcel standard[7] in place of the SQM. Until 2018, there was a separate family mediation quality mark; but this was replaced with standards set out in the Family Mediation Specification. An organisation delivering legal services must be accredited to one of the acceptable standards in order to hold a contract.

22.4 The LAA intended to introduce a Quality Assurance Scheme for Advocates (QASA) for all advocates in criminal courts. This was a controversial scheme from the start and, after several attempts to get it going, was abandoned in 2017.

---

4 Available at: www.gov.uk/government/publications/standard-crime-contract-2022.
5 Available at: www.gov.uk/government/publications/standard-crime-contract-2025.
6 The SQM standard can be downloaded from the LAA's website: www.gov.uk/guidance/legal-aid-agency-quality-standards#specialist-quality-mark.
7 See: www.lawsociety.org.uk/topics/firm-accreditations/lexcel.

22.5 The LAA worked with the Institute of Advanced Legal Studies to create a peer review scheme that assesses the quality of legal advice – see 'Legal Aid Agency audits' at: www.gov.uk/guidance/legal-aid-agency-audits. If selected for peer review, organisations with face-to-face contracts must reach at least threshold competence in order to demonstrate that they meet contractual requirements.

Specialist Quality Mark

Introduction

22.6 Organisations wanting a contract with the LAA must hold the SQM (or Lexcel – see below) by the date for verification (which is before the contract start date), set in the tender documentation. At the time of writing, the current version of the SQM is v3, dated October 2022.

22.7 Recognising Excellence[8] is appointed to deliver auditing services for the SQM. See: www.recognisingexcellence.co.uk.

Quality Mark assessment process

Desktop audit

22.8 The first stage of assessment is a desktop audit. The documentation submitted will be reviewed against the requirements of the Quality Mark. If the documentation is incomplete or so deficient that it is clear the organisation cannot meet the standard, the application will be refused. The documentation will be returned within 28 days with comments so that the organisation knows the issues it needs to address.

22.9 If the organisation passes the desktop audit, and its application for a contract is also successful (see chapter 21 for more information), it will qualify for a contract. The organisation must have evidence that it has passed the desktop audit before the end of the verification period.

Pre-Quality Mark audit

22.10 Before the SQM is confirmed, an on-site audit will be carried out, usually four to six months after the desktop audit, to make sure that the SQM requirements are in effective operation.

---

8 See: www.recognisingexcellence.co.uk.

Opening meeting

22.11 The audit will start with an opening meeting at which the auditor will explain its scope and purpose. It is useful to have a copy of the Self-Assessment Audit Checklist (SAAC)[9] to hand, as the auditor is likely to check their understanding of procedures and check any queries.

Discussions with the auditor

22.12 If it appears that an auditor is requiring procedures to operate in a certain way, which does not coincide with the organisation's interpretation of SQM requirements (and particularly if it appears that implementing such a system could cause difficulty), it is advisable to ask the auditor to refer you to the requirement in the standard. It may be that the organisation has not understood the requirement. On the other hand, as auditors are human too, they can make mistakes. Many SQM requirements are so detailed that there is a limited number of ways in which they can be met. Auditors can become so used to seeing something being implemented in a certain way that they fail to recognise that an unusual system may still comply. Some auditors conduct assessments against both Lexcel and the SQM – it is not unknown for them to assess against, for example, a Lexcel requirement that is not in the SQM by mistake. If you both consider the system against the actual wording of the requirement, and any mandatory definition, you are most likely to reach a consensus.

SQM audit procedure and outcomes

22.13 The result will be one of:
- pass;
- pass with acceptable corrective action (usually relating to general quality concerns in non-critical management areas) – this is the most common result; or
- fail (recommendation not to award or to terminate the SQM) – this would relate to critical quality concerns which cannot be addressed.

22.14 There is a representation process which can be invoked if the organisation considers that the audit was not correctly carried out, a critical quality concern should have been disregarded, or any other reasonable grounds.

---

9 See: www.recognisingexcellence.co.uk/sqm/how-to-apply-for-an-audit.

Quality Mark requirements

22.15 First, the standard itself is set out. It is split into 'Requirements', which are mandatory, and 'Definitions'. The definitions are only mandatory where the word 'must' is used. See the following table for a summary compliance aide-memoire, to assist you in maintaining compliance with SQM and contract requirements.

SQM
A: Access to service
Business plan – in detail for one year and outline for two further years. It must include an internal communications plan/regular cycle of team meetings. Safeguarding policy.
Non-discrimination in the provision of services.
Six-monthly review of plan.
Providing information about service provision.
B: Seamless service
Signposting – providing the legal adviser and family mediator finder details: https://find-legal-advice.justice.gov.uk.
Referral – records kept when a client is referred elsewhere on an existing matter.
C: Running the organisation
Staff structure.
Key roles and decision-making structure.
Demonstrate independence.
Steps to identify whether action is needed to comply with modern slavery legislation.
Financial control.
Prevention of tax evasion by associated persons if covered by Part 3 of the Criminal Finances Act 2017.
Anti-money laundering policy if required to comply with the Money Laundering, Terrorist Financing and Transfer of Funds (Information on the Payer) Regulations 2017.
D: People management
Job descriptions, responsibilities and objectives.
Equality and diversity.
Open recruitment process.
Induction procedure.

Annual performance review and feedback.
Training plans, training and records.
Named supervisors – meeting very detailed technical requirements.
Supervisory skills and conditions for supervision.
Limits of individual competence.
Legal qualifications or 12 hours' casework per week.
E: Running the service
File management – file lists, conflict of interest, locating files and tracing documents, key dates, solicitor undertakings, monitoring files for inactivity, identifying all matters for one client, logical and orderly files.
File reviews for all conducting cases – including legal and procedural issues – by supervisor with corrective action taken where required.
File review records monitored annually.
F: Meeting clients' needs
Procedures for recording and confirming information and advice at the outset, during and at the end of the case.
Keeping clients informed; case plans in complex cases; costs and cost/benefit advice; considering legal aid issues including the statutory charge.
Confidentiality and privacy.
Use of approved suppliers (eg counsel, experts, interpreters) – selected on the basis of objective assessment, evaluation, consultation with the client, clear instructions.
Data protection.
G: Commitment to quality
Complaints procedure.
Quality management – *responsibility for, review of all quality procedures annually, Quality Manual*.
Client satisfaction feedback.

Lexcel

22.16 The requirements of the Law Society's Lexcel scheme are more demanding than the SQM and more closely aligned with the Solicitors Regulation Authority (SRA) Standards and Regulations.[10] The current version at the time of writing is 6.1. There are two versions for England

---

10 Available at: www.sra.org.uk/solicitors/standards-regulations.

and Wales, legal practices (private practice) and in-house (not-for-profits). It is broken down into the following sections:

1) Structure and strategy;
2) Financial management;
3) Information management;
4) People management;
5) Risk management;
6) Client care; and
7) File and case management.

22.17 Lexcel is the preferred standard for members of the Law Centres Network.

22.18 Accrediting to Lexcel makes sense for firms that do non-contentious work or undertake work with a higher risk profile than legal aid. However, firms that have a low risk profile – for example, those specialising in criminal defence work only – may find that the simpler SQM standard suits them best.

Supervisors

Supervisors – technical legal competence

22.19 Supervisors in family and civil categories must demonstrate that they have experience in their category of 1,050 casework hours over the preceding three years if full time (in most categories but there are exceptions, see below), or five years if part time (supervisors who have been on maternity or long-term sick leave in the last three years can demonstrate the five-year requirement even if they work full time[11]).

22.20 Civil categories where less than 1,050 hours experience are acceptable are:

- Education (168 hours if full time, 280 hours if part time, over five years);
- Discrimination (168 hours if full time, 280 hours if part time over five years); and
- Welfare benefits (168 hours if full time, 280 hours if part time over five years).

---

11 *Guidance on Civil Supervisor Requirements For the 2024 Standard Civil Contract*, September 2023, para 31. Available at: www.gov.uk/government/publications/standard-civil-contract-2024.

22.21 In crime, from April 2017, full-time supervisors only need to demonstrate that they have 350 hours' experience over the past 12 months, 1,050 hours for part-time supervisors over five years.

22.22 In some categories, supervisors must be members of a specialist panel, for example, family, mental health. In immigration, supervisors must be accredited to that level under the Immigration and Asylum Accreditation Scheme (IAAS).

22.23 In categories where there is no panel, supervisors must demonstrate that they have closely defined experience of case types. In crime, supervisors have to be members of the Law Society Criminal Litigation Accreditation Scheme (CLAS) and be able to provide case examples.

Supervisor standards in the Standard Civil Contract 2024

Common rules

22.24 The common rules are to be found in the Standard Civil Contract 2024 Specification paras 2.10–2.28.

22.25 **Full-time equivalent (FTE) supervisors:** Under the contract you must (unless category-specific rules specify otherwise – see below for more information) employ at least one FTE supervisor in that category. An FTE can be made up of more than one individual. You could have, for example, two people working 17.5 hours per week each.

22.26 You need at least one FTE in categories where one is required (and you may need more if there are more than four people to supervise or multiple office arrangements mean that is the only practical way to ensure cover). For this purpose, 'full time equivalent' means the equivalent of one individual working 35 hours a week (excluding breaks).[12] This gives an element of flexibility to accommodate, for example, an FTE supervisor working 35 hours compressed over four days.

22.27 The contract goes on to say that a supervisor must at all times during their working hours (except as required for the proper performance of their role, such as attending court and/or clients) 'be accessible to those they supervise'.[13] This allows a degree of flexibility.

---

12 Standard Civil Contract 2024 Specification para 2.10
13 Standard Civil Contract 2024 Specification para 2.10b.

Quality standards and performance monitoring 593

22.28 The contract is flexible as to the way supervision is provided, but supervisors must designate time to conduct supervision of each caseworker and must ensure that the level of supervision provided reflects the skills, knowledge and experience of the caseworker.[14]

22.29 Following representations from the practitioner representative bodies, from November 2023 (Civil) it was decided that requiring supervisors to provide face-to-face supervision once a month was too onerous and impractical, and the contracts were changed so that a supervisor only had to be in the office they supervise 'where you determine this is required'.[15] However, supervisors must ensure that caseworkers perform a minimum of 12 hours casework a week in the relevant category of law.[16] Practices are advised to consider the guidance from the Law Society[17] and the SRA[18] on effective supervision when designing their own arrangements.

22.30 Supervisors must be a sole principal, an employee, or a director of or partner in or member of your organisation if your practice is a company, partnership (other than a limited liability partnership (LLP)) or an LLP.[19] Consultants are therefore not permitted to be supervisors.

22.31 Under the 2024 Civil Contract, a supervisor must not supervise more than four caseworkers. Under the 2018 Civil Contract, supervisors were restricted to a maximum of two offices or across two providers with one office each. However, this was removed in the 2024 Contract.

22.32 The LAA will only authorise external supervisors at its discretion and for temporary periods, for example, if your supervisor becomes unwell and is unable to discharge their duties for no more than six weeks.[20]

22.33 **Part-time equivalent (PTE) supervisors:** You only need a PTE supervisor in the following categories of law: welfare benefits, clinical negligence, claims against public authorities, public law, discrimination and education.

---

14 Standard Civil Contract Specification 2024 para 2.217.
15 Standard Civil Contract Specification 2024 para 2.21b.
16 Standard Civil Contract Specification 2024 para 2.20.
17 At: www.lawsociety.org.uk/topics/hr-and-people-management/supervision.
18 At: www.sra.org.uk/solicitors/guidance/effective-supervision-guidance.
19 Standard Civil Contract 2024 Specification para 2.10.
20 Standard Civil Contract 2024 Specification para 2.24.

Category-specific standards

22.34 These are to be found in the relevant category-specific section of the Specification.

22.35 **Family:** See the Family Specification (Standard Civil Contract 2024 Specification section 7).

22.36 Supervisors must be either:
1) a member of the Law Society's Family Law Accreditation Scheme; or a member of the Law Society's Advanced Accreditation Scheme;
2) a member of the Law Society's Children Law Accreditation Scheme; or
3) a Resolution Accredited Specialist or have successfully completed Part I (core assignment) of the Resolution Specialist Accreditation Scheme.[21]

22.37 **Family mediation:** See the Family Mediation Specification.

22.38 Family mediation supervisors must have:
1) at least three years' experience as a mediator;
2) been registered as a supervisor with a member body of the Family Mediation Council;
3) conducted at least 45 hours of mediation sessions (at least 15 of which have been conducted in the year prior to registration as a supervisor) in each category of work; and
4) successfully completed a mediation supervision training course recognised by a member organisation of the Family Mediation Council,

and must conduct at least 15 hours of mediation sessions per year.[22]

22.39 **Immigration/asylum:** See the Immigration/Asylum Specification (Standard Civil Contract 2024 Specification section 8).

22.40 Immigration and asylum supervisors must be accredited as an IAAS senior caseworker or advanced caseworker and have achieved the IAAS Supervising Senior Caseworker level of accreditation.[23]

22.41 **Mental health:** See the Mental Health Specification (Standard Civil Contract 2024 Specification section 9).

22.42 There are two legal competence standards for supervisors in this category:[24]

---

21 Standard Civil Contract Specification 2024 para 7.159.
22 Standard Civil Contract Family Mediation Specification 2024 paras 18.34 and 18.25.
23 Standard Civil Contract 2024 Immigration/Asylum Specification para 8.16.
24 Standard Civil Contract 2024 Mental Health Specification para 9.15.

1) the Mental Health Tribunal (MHT) Legal Competence Standard for those who predominately supervise in relation to the Mental Health Act 1983; and
2) the Mental Health and Mental Capacity Legal Competence Standard for supervisors who supervise a mixture of contract work under the Mental Health Act 1983 and Mental Capacity Act 2005.

22.43 MHT supervisors must hold current membership of either:
- the Law Society Mental Health Accreditation Scheme; or
- (for non-solicitor supervisors only) be assessed by the Law Society as meeting the Mental Health Accreditation Scheme criteria.

22.44 Supervisors must have provided representation on five MHT case files in the previous 12 months.

22.45 Mental Health and Mental Capacity Act supervisors must have evidence of having undertaken at least five Mental Capacity Act 2005 cases, two of which must have involved an application to the Court of Protection in the 12 months.

22.46 **Housing and debt** supervisors must maintain a portfolio of specified case types. (See the Housing and Debt Specification (Standard Civil Contract 2024 Specification section 10).)[25]

22.47 **Community care** supervisors must maintain a portfolio of specified case types. (See the Community Care Specification (Standard Civil Contract 2024 Specification section 11).)[26]

22.48 **Welfare benefits** supervisors must maintain a portfolio of specified case types.[27] A part-time equivalent (17.5 hours a week) is acceptable.[28] (See the Welfare Benefits Specification (Standard Civil Contract 2024 Specification section 12).)

22.49 **Claims against public authorities (CAPA):** See the Claims Against Public Authorities Specification (Standard Civil Contract 2024 Specification section 13). A PTE (17.5 hours a week) is acceptable.[29] There are two supervisor standards in this category:
1) the General Standard; and
2) the Abuse in Care Standard.

22.50 Supervisors must maintain a portfolio of specified case types.[30]

---

25 Standard Civil Contract 2024 Housing and Debt Specification paras 10.1–10.2.
26 Standard Civil Contract 2024 Community Care Specification paras 11.1–11.2.
27 Standard Civil Contract 2024 Welfare Benefits Specification paras 12.1–12.2.
28 Standard Civil Contract 2024 Welfare Benefits Specification para 12.24.
29 Standard Civil Contract 2024 CAPA Specification para 13.12.
30 Standard Civil Contract 2024 CAPA Specification paras 13.7 and 13.8, respectively.

22.51 **Public law:** See the Public Law Specification (Standard Civil Contract 2024 Specification section 14). A PTE (17.5 hours a week) is acceptable.[31] Supervisors must maintain a portfolio of specified case types.[32]

22.52 **Clinical negligence:** See the Clinical Negligence Specification (Standard Civil Contract 2024 Specification section 15). A PTE (17.5 hours a week) is acceptable.[33] Supervisors must hold current membership of one of the following:
- the Law Society's Clinical Negligence Accreditation Scheme;
- the Action against Medical Accidents (AvMA) Clinical Negligence Panel; or
- the Association of Personal Injury Lawyers (APIL) Clinical Negligence Accredited Specialist Panel.[34]

22.53 The supervisor must, during any preceding 24-month period, have worked on a minimum of five cases significantly concerned with claims for damages in respect infant neurological injury.[35]

22.54 **Education:** See the Education Specification (Standard Civil Contract 2024 Specification section 16). A PTE (17.5 hours a week) is acceptable.[36] Supervisors must maintain a portfolio of specified case types.[37]

22.55 **Discrimination:** See the Discrimination Specification (Standard Civil Contract 2024 Specification section 17). A PTE (17.5 hours a week) is acceptable.[38] Supervisors must maintain a portfolio of specified case types[39]

Supervisor standards in the Standard Crime Contract 2022

22.56 The general requirements are very similar to the 2024 Standard Civil Contract. See 'Standard Civil Contract Common Rules' at para 22.24 above regarding: FTE, being accessible, and ensuring that the level of supervision provided reflects the skills, knowledge and experience

---

31 Standard Civil Contract 2024 Public Law Specification para 14.6.
32 Standard Civil Contract 2024 Public Law Specification paras 14.1–14.2.
33 Standard Civil Contract 2024 Clinical Negligence Specification para 15.6.
34 Standard Civil Contract 2024 Clinical Negligence Specification para 15.1.
35 Standard Civil Contract 2024 Clinical Negligence Specification para 15.5.
36 Standard Civil Contract 2024 Education Specification para 16.1.
37 Standard Civil Contract 2024 Education Specification para 16.9.
38 Standard Civil Contract 2024 Discrimination Specification para 17.1.
39 Standard Civil Contract 2024 Discrimination Specification paras 17.9–17.10.

of the caseworker. In crime, supervisors must ensure that caseworkers perform a minimum of 12 hours work per week in the relevant class of work.[40]

22.57 The relevant paragraphs were also changed from 3 August 2023 to allow more flexibility and allowing practitioners to decide who needs face-to-face supervision.[41] The particular issues relating to the Standard Crime Contract are set out below.

22.58 The Crime Standard Terms clause 1, Interpretation, states that supervisors must be 'employees' of your organisation. Employee is defined as: 'an individual who undertakes Contract Work on your behalf and who: (a) is a director, member or partner of your organisation; or (b) holds a contract of employment with you.' Freelance consultants therefore cannot act as supervisors (except for temporary periods[42]). Under the 2022 Contract a supervisor can only supervise up to two offices[43] and up to four people (six for prison law[44]). Except in prison law (where it is limited to two), someone can only be a supervisor for one organisation.[45] Supervisors can supervise more than one class of work (eg investigations, proceedings, etc[46]).

22.59 **Crime** supervisors must be accredited to the Law Society's CLAS (either via the Police Station Qualification (PSQ) route or the passporting route for those who qualified under previous schemes); and have held a current non-conditional practising certificate for the previous three years. In the previous 12 months, supervisors must have:

- have undertaken a minimum of six police station advice and assistance cases (of which no more than two can be police station telephone advice where there is no subsequent police station attendance); and
- have undertaken a minimum of 20 magistrates' court representations and advocacy; or
- 10 magistrates' court representations and advocacy and five in the Crown Court.

22.60 **Prison law** supervisors must have, in the previous 12 months, undertaken a minimum of four representations for four clients before the

---

40 Standard Crime Contract 2022 Specification para 2.16.
41 Standard Crime Contract 2022 Specification paras 2.7, 2.17 and 2.19.
42 Standard Crime Contract 2022 Specification para 2.27.
43 Standard Crime Contract 2022 Specification para 2.8.
44 Standard Crime Contract 2022 Specification paras 2.29–2.30.
45 Standard Crime Contract 2022 Specification paras 2.9–2.10.
46 Standard Crime Contract 2022 Specification para 2.6.

Parole Board or the independent adjudicator/prison governor. They do not have to be legally qualified.

22.61 **Appeals and reviews** supervisors do have to be legally qualified.[47]

Supervisor standards in the Standard Crime Contract 2025

22.62 The general requirements are very similar to the 2024 Standard Civil Contract. See 'Standard Civil Contract Common Rules' at para 22.24 above regarding: FTE, being accessible, and ensuring that the level of supervision provided reflects the skills, knowledge and experience of the caseworker.

22.63 In crime and prison law, supervisors must have undertaken a minimum of 350 hours casework in the past 12 months if full time or 1,050 hours over the past five years if part time. Crime supervisors who have taken maternity leave or time off due to maternity, sickness or compassionate reasons may draw on experience for up to 24 months prior to when the forms are completed. Prison law supervisors who have taken maternity leave or time off due to maternity, sickness or compassionate reasons can complete the form over five years as if part-time supervisors.[48]

22.64 The Crime Standard Terms clause 1, Interpretation, states that supervisors must be 'employees' of your organisation. Employee is defined as: 'an individual who undertakes Contract Work on your behalf and who: (a) is a director, member or partner of your organisation; or (b) holds a contract of employment with you.' Freelance consultants therefore cannot act as supervisors (except for temporary periods[49]).

22.65 Under the 2025 Contract a supervisor can only supervise up to two offices.[50] A supervisor can supervise for more than one organisation, but if they do they can only supervise one office for each organisation.[51] Supervisors can supervise more than one class of work (eg investigations, proceedings, etc[52]).

---

47 Standard Crime Contract 2022 Specification para 2.26.
48 2025 Standard Crime Contract: Guidance on Crime Supervisor requirements, September 2024, p5. Available at: www.gov.uk/government/publications/crime-contract-2025-tender.
49 Standard Crime Contract 2025 Specification para 2.25.
50 Standard Crime Contract 2025 Specification para 2.9.
51 Standard Crime Contract 2025 Specification para 2.10.
52 Standard Crime Contract 2025 Specification para 2.6.

Quality standards and performance monitoring 599

22.66 In crime, supervisors must ensure that caseworkers perform a minimum of 12 hours work per week in the relevant class of work.[53]

22.67 The 2025 Contract removed any reference to where supervision must be carried out, so supervision can be in the same location or remote.

22.68 The 2025 Contract also removed the ratios of supervisors to other staff. However, supervision must be effective. Practices are advised to consider the guidance from the Law Society[54] and the SRA[55] on effective supervision when designing their arrangements.

22.69 **Crime** investigations and proceedings supervisors must be accredited to the Law Society's CLAS (either via the PSQ route or the passporting route for those who qualified under previous schemes) and have held a current non-conditional practising certificate for the previous three years. In the previous 12 months, supervisors must have:[56]

- undertaken a minimum of six police station advice and assistance cases (of which no more than two can be police station telephone advice where there is no subsequent police station attendance); and
- undertaken a minimum of 20 magistrates' court representations and advocacy; or
- 10 magistrates' court representations and advocacy and five in the Crown Court.

22.70 **Prison law** supervisors must have, in the previous 12 months, undertaken a minimum of four representations for four clients before the Parole Board or the independent adjudicator/prison governor. They do not have to be legally qualified.[57]

22.71 **Appeals and reviews:** Supervisors have to be legally qualified and have three years' practising certificates.[58]

Supervisors – file reviews

22.72 File reviews under the SQM must cover legal and procedural points (Lexcel allows for file reviews limited to procedural points, but that would be risky from the point of view of peer review under the contract). This can cause problems when considering who should review the supervisor's files. If there is another experienced practitioner in the

---

53 Standard Crime Contract 2025 Specification para 2.16.
54 At: www.lawsociety.org.uk/topics/hr-and-people-management/supervision.
55 At: www.sra.org.uk/solicitors/guidance/effective-supervision-guidance.
56 Standard Crime Contract 2025 Specification paras 2.19–2.20.
57 Standard Crime Contract 2025 Specification paras 2.21–2.23.
58 Standard Crime Contract 2025 Specification para 2.26.

same area of law, they can review each other's files. Where there is no one else who practises in that specialism, the supervisor will have to review their own files (as objectively as possible!) for legal issues, and someone else will review it for procedural points. The LAA does not expect an organisation to incur the expense of an external supervisor in these circumstances.

Key supervision issues from recent audits
• Have file reviews been carried out by the named supervisor (or delegated to a deputy with a training and development plan to meet full supervisor status)?
• Do the management/organisation structure and individual job descriptions agree? *It is amazing how disorganised you can look to an outsider if they do not!*
• If the supervisor has to demonstrate compliance through the portfolio route (as opposed to panel membership), can they do so over the last 12 months? *Consider the numbers of hours required and the range of cases.*
• Were independent file reviews undertaken by an appropriate person? *If you are developing a member of staff as a deputy supervisor and delegating aspects of some file reviews to them, make sure this is all properly documented.*
• Are the independent file review records completely up to date? *If there are gaps, for example, someone was on maternity leave or on the holiday of a lifetime, are the reasons for them clear?*
• *If you have not been able to do file reviews for a period due to pressures such as sickness absence or additional work demands, catch up later and put a note onto your central record explaining why some file reviews were done late.*
• Is corrective action required recorded on the file review forms, with appropriate dates? Do they also show what action was taken and by when?
• Did file reviews identify any non-compliances with SQM or contract requirements? *If the supervisor is lenient, the LAA cannot be confident that the organisation meets its requirements.*

Peer review

Overview

22.73 Peer review is the measure that the LAA uses to assess quality of advice. It has been developed over many years under the auspices of the Institute of Advanced Legal Studies (IALS). Peer reviewers have carried out thousands of assessments since 2000 and have refined the process over the years. There is information about the process at 'Legal Aid Agency audits' at: www.gov.uk/guidance/legal-aid-agency-audits.

22.74 The LAA does not have peer reviewers in all contract categories, but aims to peer review at least one category of law for every provider during the lifetime of a contract.

22.75 There are five possible scores:

- excellence (1);
- competence plus (2);
- threshold competence (3);
- below competence (4); and
- failure in performance (5).

22.76 The LAA has defined the level of skill required under the contract as at least threshold competence. At below competence level, the provider will be given at least six months to improve; if it does not achieve at least threshold competence at its next assessment, its contract will be terminated. An organisation assessed at failure in performance may have its contract terminated quickly, because of the risk to clients.

22.77 The LAA publishes guidance which you can use to benchmark your files and ensure they achieve good peer review scores. These are called *Improving Your Quality Guides*. There are updated guides in crime, family, housing, mental health and immigration/asylum. They have been developed by the peer reviewers and can be downloaded from 'Legal Aid Agency audits' at: www.gov.uk/guidance/legal-aid-agency-audits.

The peer review process

22.78 All peer reviewers are experienced practitioners, trained by the IALS to carry out peer review using its framework. A sample of its own files has to be assessed at competence plus or above. Peer reviewers are consistency-checked against each other and receive regular training. There are various reasons why a review might be carried out – for example, random selection or concern about quality raised by a contract manager – but the reviewer is not told what the reason for the review is. This ensures that they can approach all peer reviews with an open mind.

22.79 More files are requested than are eventually peer reviewed, but at least 12 are assessed.[59] The files are selected to cover the different types of work carried out by the organisation within a category of law

---

59 'Independent peer review process document 2017' para 2.9.

and are cases closed during the preceding 12 months. Peer reviewers carry out the assessment away from the practice's office. They do not meet the staff of the organisation being reviewed. Organisations do not know the identity of their reviewer, although they are sent a list of all the reviewers and asked to identify any possible conflict of interest. It usually takes one to two days to do an assessment and write a report.

22.80 The reviewers evaluate issues that relate to quality of advice and service. They do not look at how long was spent on the file and they do not carry out a transaction criteria[60] audit. They apply the 'pick up test', which is the basic question: 'If I, as another fee-earner, picked up this file, could I understand what had been done and why, and what remained to be done?'

22.81 They assess individual files and then consider the sample as a whole and form a conclusion about its overall quality. In many cases, this involves a balancing act as some files may be good, others less so. Organisations scoring competence plus tend to have a higher level of consistency. For example, if there is a change of caseworker part-way through the case the peer reviewer would look at the whole case and, in order to score competence plus or excellence, both caseworkers would need to achieve that level.

22.82 The reviewers also apply the 'friend and family test', which is simply: 'Would I refer a friend or family member to this organisation?' If the answer is 'no', the sample will be assessed below threshold competence or worse.

22.83 Peer reviewers use checklists of criteria, which they score individually, but the overall score is not simply an average of the scores on individual files. Peer reviewers take account of any trends and patterns identified, including evidence of supervision. Having assessed the files, the reviewer compiles a report identifying:

- positive findings;
- major areas of concern (if any);
- areas for development;
- suggested areas for improvement; and
- any other comments.

---

60 Transaction criteria may be remembered by some legal aid practitioners from the early days of 'franchising'. They enabled the Legal Aid Board (LAB), and later the Legal Services Commission (LSC), to assess the extent to which a lawyer had obtained appropriate information and followed steps associated with best practice. They did not allow any assessment to be made of the quality of legal advice. They were superseded by peer review.

22.84 Reports are checked by IALS to ensure that the score reflects the comments the reviewer has made about the files. So, for example, it would pick up a contradiction if the sample scored competence plus but the reviewer had identified major areas of concern, and ask the reviewer to look at the report again. IALS does not double-check the assessment. The provider should receive the final report within 28 days.

Tips for passing peer review

Overview

22.85 The peer reviewers emphasise that good practice helps to improve peer review scores, for example:
- file review and supervision support;
- ensuring workload is appropriate;
- training;
- providing appropriate advice on legal and procedural issues on every file; and
- confirming the client's initial instructions and your advice in writing.

Standard letters and documentation

22.86 Peer reviewers accept that standard letters have their place – but that it is important to take an individual approach to them. This means ensuring that standard letters should not be 'catch-alls' that try to cover all eventualities, but should be specific to a client's circumstances. So, for example, a letter setting out the different possession proceedings in relation to both owner-occupiers and tenants would not impress a peer reviewer, who would expect the client to be given only the information that applied to their case.

22.87 As in all kinds of file-based assessment, it is vital that the file is complete. Some organisations send information leaflets to clients, but do not put a copy of standard information on the file. Peer reviewers advise that if that is the way you work, it is important to include copies of all standard information leaflets with the file sample.

22.88 The LAA prefers digital files submitted via its Galaxkey secure portal.[61] It is important that the file structure is clear, to make the peer reviewer's job as easy as possible.

---

61 See: www.gov.uk/guidance/secure-file-exchange.

Peer review representations

22.89 Representations can only be made if the assessment is category 4 or 5. The LAA's rationale is that since a category 3 is acceptable for a contract, there is no point in allowing representations when only the organisation's professional pride is at stake.

22.90 Possible grounds are that: you dispute the overall peer review rating; the sample does not appear to be sufficiently representative; and any other reasonable grounds.

22.91 Representations must be made on the appropriate form and reach the LAA within 28 days following receipt of the report and the file sample. The representations will be considered by the original peer reviewer and a senior panel member. They may uphold the original rating, revise the original rating, request a new review or not reach agreement. Where the latter occurs, an external expert who is not a peer reviewer will be asked to help the peer reviewers reach a consensus. Note that, if an appeal is unsuccessful, you may have to pay the costs of the peer review under both the Civil and Crime Contracts.

LAA online portal

22.92 The LAA is moving to digital working, which you access through its online portal (not to be confused with the online tendering portal hosted by Jaggaer or the Galaxkey secure file exchange). You can download a useful guide to the online portal, 'LAA online portal help and information', at: www.gov.uk/government/publications/laa-online-portal-help-and-information.

22.93 There are several significant online applications:
- **Apply – Civil applications:** Can be used for domestic abuse cases instead of CCMS. It is designed to be more straightforward.
- **Apply – Crime applications:** To be used for criminal applications previously on CRM 14/15. Compulsory from 6 August 2024.
- **Contracted Work and Administration (CWA):** Through this you submit your monthly claims for crime lower work, controlled work and mediation, and notify the LAA of new matters started.
- **eforms:** This service for electronic payment on account claims and crime forms (CRM4/5/7/14) was withdrawn on 20 August 2024.

- **Crown Court Defence (CCD).**[62]
- **Management information (MI):**[63] Financial information about your organisation:
  - **Civil financial statement:** This shows the current financial position of a civil office account, ie monthly submissions against payments made (monthly contract payments, adjustments and repayments).
  - **Family mediation financial statement:** This shows the current financial position of a family mediation office account, ie monthly submissions against payments made (monthly contract payments, adjustments/repayments).
  - **Criminal financial statement:** This shows the current financial position of a crime office account, ie monthly submissions (CRM6 and CRM7) against payments made (monthly contract payments, adjustments/repayments).
  - **Financial statement summary:** This provides a summary of the financial position of the entire organisation and includes individual office entries across crime, civil and mediation offices.
- **Client and Cost Management System (CCMS):** Application through which you apply for, and manage, civil certificated work, including amendments, prior authorities, payments on account and billing. (See chapter 5.)

You can also view your contract for signature and schedule through CWA.

22.94 **Provider Activity Report (PAR):** You should receive PARs on a quarterly basis. They provide some key information about contract performance:

- contract status;
- civil and crime fund take; and
- claim 1 rejects.

22.95 If you are not receiving PARs, ask you contract manager to send them to you as they will help you to monitor your performance against contract key performance indicators (KPIs) (see below).

---

62 See: https://legalaidlearning.justice.gov.uk/litigator-fee-scheme-guide-for-litigators.
63 See: www.gov.uk/guidance/legal-aid-management-information-online.

Key performance indicators

Overview

22.96 Both the Civil and Crime versions of the Standard Contracts have mandatory KPIs.

22.97 Someone should be monitoring KPIs, usually a head of department or partner. Some can be monitored at individual file level; others will require the collection of data by department/work type. Contract managers monitor KPI reports, which are flagged as 'red', 'amber' or 'green'. Failing to meet KPIs will not in itself result in sanctions being taken against you or contract notices being raised. However, your contract manager may contact you to ask you to explain the reasons that your organisation is 'out of profile'. If it is an issue that the contract manager thinks should be corrected, you will be asked to formulate an action plan for doing so. Being 'out of profile' may also trigger an on-site or other type of audit.

22.98 The LAA monitors KPIs on a three-month rolling basis rather than on individual files, with minimum numbers where volumes are low.

KPIs: Standard Civil Contract 2024[64]

KPI 1 – Controlled work escape fee cases – assessment reduction 10 per cent max

22.99 When your 'escape cases' are assessed (these are the cases where the costs on a time and item basis are three times the fixed fee), the costs claimed must not be reduced by more than 10 per cent. This includes disbursements, but not VAT.

KPI 2 – Licensed work – assessment reduction 15 per cent max

22.100 This sets a similar target in relation to licensed work cases that are claimed on a time and item basis.

KPI 3A and B – Fixed fee margin – 20 per cent max

22.101 The LAA is concerned that some organisations will select clients with straightforward cases that do not require much work in order to retain a high surplus under each fixed fee case. This KPI can only be met if the total cost of cases under fixed fees when calculated on a

---

64 Standard Civil Contract 2024 Specification paras 2.52–2.72.

time and item basis is at least 80 per cent of the appropriate fixed fees.

22.102 This KPI applies to controlled work cases, and Family Private and Public Law Representation Scheme cases that are paid by way of fixed fees.

KPI 4A and B – Rejection rates for licensed work – five per cent max in the schedule period

22.103 Rejections are when applications for legal aid or claims are refused because of technical errors in submission, lack of attachments, etc. This applies to applications for legal aid (known as applications for determinations that an individual qualifies for legal aid) and claims for payment. If you think the LAA has made a mistake in rejecting an application, there are fixer services you can use to ask the LAA to correct its mistake, rather than having to go through the appeals process.

22.104 The LAA provides an 'Application Fixer' service which aims to correct errors it has made at the earliest possible opportunity. If you believe the LAA has made an error, you can email 'application fixer' detailing the case reference and why you believe an error has been made: applicationfixer@justice.gov.uk. The LAA will only review the decision based on the information submitted originally – if you wish to include additional information you will need to use the appeal route. Examples of issues the fixer process can be used for include:

- an application incorrectly rejected/refused;
- you believe information provided has not been considered in the decision;
- you have been asked for documents or information that have already been provided;
- you have not been granted the cost limit requested when delegating; and
- where Covid-19 contingency arrangements have not been followed.

This list is not exhaustive – the LAA will look at anything where it has made a mistake based on the original information – it is not an appeal or review route.

22.105 For bills, and 'secondary requests', where you have already provided documents or documents are not necessary, you can use the 'claim-fix' email: laacivilclaimfix@justice.gov.uk.

22.106 Both services ensure that LAA mistakes do not affect your KPI.

KPI 5 – Refusal rates for licensed work – 15 per cent max in the schedule period

22.107 This applies to applications for legal aid that are refused because the LAA considers that the practitioner has failed to show that they meet the applicable merits test.

KPI 6 – Legal representation outcomes – 30 per cent minimum

22.108 You must achieve a substantive benefit for the client in 30 per cent of cases. This applies to clinical negligence and claims against public authorities work only.

KPI 7 – Post investigation success

22.109 This KPI applies to licensed work in clinical negligence and claims against public authorities, in cases which proceed beyond investigation. You must achieve a substantive benefit for the client in 50 per cent of claims against public authorities cases; 60 per cent in clinical negligence cases.

KPIs: Standard Crime Contracts 2022 and 2025

22.110 The following crime KPIs[65] must be met in any three-month rolling period:

- **Claims for costs must not be reduced on assessment by more than 15 per cent:** police station advice and assistance (escape fee cases); free-standing advice and assistance claims; advocacy assistance claims; magistrates' court non-standard fees; prison law escape fee cases; prison law non-standard fees.
- **You must accept 90 per cent of communications from the Defence Solicitor Call Centre (DSCC)** (and deal with them appropriately) when you are on the rota.
- **You must accept 90 per cent of calls to attend a virtual court hearing** when you are on the rota.
- **95 per cent or more** of your cases must conclude before any change of provider under the contract.

---

65 Standard Crime Contract 2022 Specification para 2.65 and Standard Crime Contract 2025 Specification para 2.59.

Service standards

Service standards: civil and family

Overview

22.111 Service standards are to be found in the applicable contract specification.

22.112 The general rules under the 2024 Civil Contract are set out in the Specification paras 2.1–2.72.

22.113 **Use of agents and third parties:** You may use agents, counsel and third parties where it is in your client's best interests. The Specification allows independent consultants to carry out work under the contract as long as the supervision conditions are met. However, it is important to note that you cannot refer a case to a separate organisation unless the conditions in para 2.5 are met, nor can you use an agent to meet the service standards. So, for example, you cannot use an agent to meet the supervisor standards.

22.114 You must ensure that, for example:

- they comply with data protection and equality and diversity processes; and
- they are covered by your insurance and integrated into your supervision processes.

22.115 **Supervisor standards:** See above for supervisor standards.

22.116 **Authorised litigators:** You must employ an authorised litigator (see glossary for definition), at least on a PTE basis (17.5 hours a week[66]) unless the category specification requires an FTE (35 hours a week). See below for more information.

22.117 **Minimum numbers of matter starts:** Although the specification allows minimum numbers to be specified, usually they are not.

22.118 **Presence in the procurement area:** You must comply with the presence requirements set out in your schedule; that is, your office must comply with the requirements for a permanent or part-time presence.[67] You may be allowed to deliver outreach services. If so, these must be noted on your schedule.

22.119 **Referral and signposting arrangements.** You must have referral and signposting arrangements in place. As a minimum, if you hold the SQM, you must signpost clients who you are unable to assist to

---

66 Standard Civil Contract 2024 Specification para 2.8.
67 Standard Civil Contract 2024 Specification para 2.32.

the legal adviser and family mediation finder: https://find-legal-advice.justice.gov.uk.

22.120 You may wish to signpost clients to the Civil Legal Advice telephone service: 0345 345 4 345. Eligible clients with in scope cases will be signposted to their nearest legal aid providers.

Additional/variations to service and monitoring requirements

22.121 There are additional service standards for family; immigration/asylum; housing/debt; welfare benefits; and mental health – see below. Organisations with contracts to deliver the Housing Loss Prevention Advice Service (HLPAS) also need additional monitoring systems, also shown below.

Family

22.122 In order to provide services for applicants in child abduction proceedings, your organisation must remain on the Referral List of Specialist Solicitors maintained by the International Child Abduction and Contact Unit.[68]

22.123 You must have appropriate arrangements in operation to enable you, in appropriate cases, to refer clients to local family support services. You should have access to details of such services as are locally available, including: local authority family support services; any providers of family mediation services; any relevant counselling and relationship guidance services; and any support services for victims of domestic abuse.[69]

22.124 There are appointment service standards in the family category. When you are contacted by a client for whom you intend to provide services (and have sufficient matter starts) you must offer a first appointment to the client within 48 hours of the initial contact in emergency cases, or within 10 working days of the initial contact in all other cases.[70]

Immigration and asylum

22.125 The Immigration Specification (paras 8.13–8.20) sets down requirements for caseworkers and supervisors to be accredited under the Immigration and Asylum Accreditation Scheme. It also limits the type of work that can be done by reference to the level of accreditation. For example, only level 2 caseworkers can conduct cases or use deleg-

---

68 Standard Civil Contract 2024 Specification para 7.161.
69 Standard Civil Contract 2024 Specification para 7.162.
70 Standard Civil Contract 2024 Specification para 7.163.

Mental health

22.126 There are particular presence requirements, which are set out in the 2024 Mental Health Specification paras 9.4–9.5. The requirements you have to meet will be recorded in your contract schedule.

22.127 You must employ an authorised litigator; but they do not have to work on a PTE basis.[71]

22.128 All advocates before the MHT (except self-employed counsel) must be members of the Law Society Mental Health Accreditation Scheme.[72]

22.129 In this category, 70 per cent of clients must be physically located in the procurement area in which you have been granted matter starts.[73] Thirty per cent of your matter starts may be used for clients who are not physically located in the procurement area in which you have been granted matter starts. See chapter 10 for more information.

Housing/Debt

22.130 You need to employ a PTE authorised litigator who will be available to each of your offices to deliver licensed work. This will be specified in your schedule.

Welfare benefits

22.131 You only need 'access' to an authorised litigator[74] at all times.

Education

22.132 You must provide clients with a choice of advice in person or by remote means (email, telephone, webcam, post or other method as agreed). You must keep a record on the file.[75]

Housing Loss Prevention Advice Service (HLPAS)

22.133 From 1 August 2023, the HLPAS scheme replaced the Housing Possession Court Duty Scheme (HPCDS). Contracts were tendered

---

71 Standard Civil Contract 2024 Mental Health Specification para 9.6.
72 Standard Civil Contract 2024 Mental Health Specification para 9.8.
73 Standard Civil Contract 2024 Mental Health Specification para 9.13.
74 Standard Civil Contract 2024 Welfare Benefits Specification para 12.29.
75 Standard Civil Contract 2024 Education Specification paras 16.19 and 16.21.

competitively and 101 contracts were awarded. The new service enables providers to give early legal advice (Legal Help) on housing, debt and welfare benefits issues to those at risk of possession proceedings and loss of their home, as well as providing a court duty scheme. The service is not means tested, but applicants need to be able to show they are at risk of losing their home.

22.134 Provider guidance including a work report form can be found at: www.gov.uk/government/publications/housing-loss-prevention-advice-service-hlpas.

Service standards: Standard Crime Contracts 2022 and 2025

22.135 The service standards for criminal defence work are contained in the Crime Specifications 2022 and 2025 section 2.

22.136 **Supervisors:** You must have at least one person who meets the LAA's standard for supervisors, and they must carry out their duties in accordance with the contract – which contains standards for supervision and file review.

22.137 See 'Supervisors' at para 22.31 above for ratios of supervisors to other staff (2022 Crime Contract only; there are no ratios in the 2025 Contract).

22.138 You must designate the staff who work under the crime contract and the work they can do.[76] Designating staff means naming the people who do work under the criminal contract, ensuring they meet the standards required by the contract, quality standard and duty solicitor requirements set out in the contract,[77] and keeping records as shown below.

22.139 Note that the duty solicitor requirements from the 2022 Contract onwards are designed to eliminate the phenomenon of 'ghosts', so expect qualifying criteria to be checked.[78] Duty solicitors do not have to be 'employees';[79] but under the 2022 and 2025 Contracts they do have to do 50 hours work for you per month from the office relevant

---

76 Standard Crime Contract 2022 Specification para 2.32 and Standard Crime Contract 2025 Specification para 2.27.
77 Standard Crime Contract 2022 Specification paras 6.15–6.69 and Standard Crime Contract 2025 Specification paras 6.15–6.68.
78 Standard Crime Contracts 2022 and 2025 Specification paras 6.22 and 6.23.
79 Standard Crime Contract 2022 Specification para 6.21 and Standard Crime Contract 2025 Specification para 6.20.

Quality standards and performance monitoring 613

to their slots.[80] The 50 hours requirement in para 6.23 will be measured on a rolling three-monthly basis to accommodate different working patterns.[81] The contract allows for flexibility in the case of maternity or sickness.[82] There is guidance on the work that may be counted against the requirement in the LAA's Duty Solicitor Guidance 2022 para 2.11 onwards.[83]

22.140 Fee earners should be 'designated', unless they do less than three hours' contract work a month.[84] Those who regularly undertake fee earning criminal work under the contract – crime supervisors, CILEx supervisors, duty solicitors, accredited and probationary representatives – must be designated.

22.141 The Contract Specification sets out percentages of crime contract work that must be performed by designated fee earners:

- Advocacy in the magistrates' court: 50 per cent must be done by designated staff.
- Police station advice and assistance: 80 per cent must be done by designated staff.[85]

In addition you must make reasonable endeavours to make the first contact with a client in the police station within 45 mins in 80 per cent of cases for both duty and own client work.[86]

22.142 **Location:** You must have an office(s) as specified in your schedule.[87] Shared and serviced offices are acceptable, but you must have a constant right of access. Offices must be physically accessible for clients and others for at least seven hours (2022 Contract) or five hours (2025 Contract) between 8 am and 8 pm from Monday to

---

80 Standard Crime Contract 2022 Specification para 6.23 and Standard Crime Contract 2025 Specification para 6.22.
81 Standard Crime Contract 2022 Specification para 6.24 and Standard Crime Contract 2025 Specification para 6.23.
82 Standard Crime Contract 2022 Specification para 6.25 and Standard Crime Contract 2025 Specification para 6.24.
83 *Duty Solicitor Guidance 2022*, LAA: https://assets.publishing.service.gov.uk/media/6332ce0e8fa8f51d2491ae4e/3_Duty_solicitor_guidance_-_version_2__current_version___effective_from_1_October_2022_.pdf. *Duty Solicitor Guidance 2025*, LAA.
84 Standard Crime Contract 2022 Specification para 2.36 and Standard Crime Contract 2025 Specification para 2.31.
85 Standard Crime Contract 2022 Specification para 2.39 and Standard Crime Contract 2025 Specification para 2.34.
86 Standard Crime Contract 2022 Specification para 9.24 and Standard Crime Contract 2025 Specification para 9.18.
87 Standard Crime Contract 2022 Specification paras 2.41–2.52 and Standard Crime Contract 2025 Specification paras 2.36–2.48.

Friday. They must satisfy any requirements of your professional body, have adequate facilities for contract work, have confidential storage, meet health and safety requirements, provide a private interview room, and be staffed by a representative of your organisation (who need not be employed by you) to arrange appointments and to contact you about emergency matters.

22.143 Under the 2025 Contract, if your office has a contract for prison law only, there are no requirements for opening hours or staffing. They do have to meet any standards set by your regulator, health and safety, and have a private interview room where that is required.[88]

22.144 If you move your office out of your original postcode area, you must ask the LAA's permission. Even if the LAA consents you will not be able undertake work on additional duty schemes that are accessible only by virtue of your new office address.[89]

22.145 **Contacting your office:** Whenever the office is open, clients or prospective clients must be able to telephone to arrange appointments and other meetings, and where appropriate arrange advice in emergency cases. When the office is not open, people who telephone must be able to access information about opening hours and who to contact in an emergency (which can be by voicemail message). You must be contactable by the DSCC.[90]

22.146 Under the 2025 Contract, if you offer prison law only, clients must be able to telephone you during a minimum five-hour period between the hours of 8 am and 8 pm to arrange appointments, etc.[91]

22.147 **Referral and signposting arrangements:** You must have appropriate arrangements in operation to refer clients or potential clients to another provider if you do not provide the services that the client requires or for some other reason are unable to take on their case.[92]

Covid-19 arrangements – civil and crime

22.148 The LAA amended a number of its rules and procedures to accommodate the difficulties of practice during the Covid-19 pandemic, for example, delivering services remotely, obtaining clients' signatures

---

88 Standard Crime Contract 2025 Specification paras 2.38–2.39.
89 Standard Crime Contract 2022 Specification paras 2.47–2.51 and Standard Crime Contract 2025 Specification paras 2.42–2.47.
90 Standard Crime Contract 2022 Specification paras 2.47–2.51 and Standard Crime Contract 2025 Specification paras 2.42–2.47.
91 Standard Crime Contract 2025 Specification para 2.44.
92 Standard Crime Contracts 2022 and 2025 Specification paras 2.55–2.58.

on legal aid forms, meeting requirements for supervisor qualification and supervision, and the then duty solicitor '14 hour rule'. The LAA extended flexibility in line with applicable government restrictions and withdrew a number of them as restrictions were withdrawn.

22.149 The following changes have been adopted permanently:
- Civil cost appeals to be made electronically for paper claims.
- 80 per cent payment on account (POA) claims on civil and family certificates.
- Four POA claims for profit costs can be made on civil and family certificates per year.[93]
- Family Advocacy Scheme (FAS) forms not required where the hearing is held by video or telephone conference. Attendance notes are sufficient evidence.[94]
- Controlled work escape case claims to be submitted electronically.
- Costs can be claimed for setting up video links with clients in prison.

22.150 A full list of arrangements and applicable dates can be found at the 'Schedule of processes restarting after COVID-19 contingency' at: www.gov.uk/guidance/schedule-of-processes-restarting-after-covid-19-contingency.

---

93 Standard Civil Contract 2024 Specification para 6.21(b).
94 *Civil Finance Electronic Handbook* para 6.5, www.gov.uk/guidance/funding-and-costs-assessment-for-civil-and-crime-matters.

CHAPTER 23

Financial and contract management

Edited by Vicky Ling

23.1	Introduction
23.4	**Payment for civil controlled work and crime lower**
23.4	Overview
23.8	SMP or PAYG, which is best?
23.11	**Reconciliation of contracts**
23.11	Overview
23.12	The reconciliation protocol
23.14	**Payments on account**
23.18	Unrecouped payments on account
23.19	Payment on account limits
23.22	**Key performance indicators**
23.24	**Service standards**
23.25	**Costs audits**
23.25	Overview
23.31	Evidence of means
23.32	Family level 1 and 2 fees
	Private family law – conditions for level 2
23.35	Crime

continued

617

23.37	**Contract notices**
23.37	Overview
23.40	Appeals
23.43	Contract compliance audits
23.46	Contract compliance audit outcomes
23.48	Extrapolation
23.49	Contract compliance audit – appeal process
23.50	Costs appeals
23.54	Points of principle

Financial and contract management 619

> **Key points to note**
> - You should always keep your own figures for the value of your monthly submissions and monitor them against your payments. You can obtain more information and check the Legal Aid Agency's (LAA's) figures at 'Legal aid: management information online'.[1]
> - To aid cashflow you can claim up to four payments on account (POAs) on civil certificated cases in a 12-month period. These will be recouped when you submit the final bill, and you will be paid the balance. Some organisations with good cashflow choose not to claim POAs as this simplifies book-keeping.
> - The LAA needs to reconcile its own accounts and that means it needs to find out what is happening on certificates where there has been no movement for some time. Are they ready to be billed to the LAA? Expect your contract manager to ask you about the status of cases with historic POAs.
> - See 'Costs Audits' at para 23.25 onwards below for hints and tips for both crime and civil work.

Introduction

23.1 This chapter deals with issues that affect an organisation's financial and contractual position: reconciliation; POAs; key performance indicators (KPIs); contract compliance audits (CCAs); contract manager visits; and audits.

23.2 Controlled work in civil and crime 'lower' work (police station and magistrates' court work), is paid by way of a monthly payment under either the Civil or the Crime Contract.[2]

23.3 Each contract has a schedule, which sets out what the LAA will pay you each month if you have opted for the standard monthly payment option (see below). At the end of each month, you submit bills for concluded cases via the LAA's online claim portal: https://portal.legalservices.gov.uk.

---

1 At: www.gov.uk/legal-aid-management-information-online.
2 Standard Civil Contract 2024, available at: www.gov.uk/government/publications/standard-civil-contract-2024; Standard Crime Contract 2022, available at: www.gov.uk/government/publications/standard-crime-contract-2022; Standard Crime Contract 2025, available at: www.gov.uk/government/publications/standard-crime-contract-2025.

Payment for civil controlled work and crime lower

Overview

23.4 There are two options for payment of this work. You can opt for variable monthly payments (VMPs), reflecting each month's claim plus the value of any escape fee cases credited to you by the LAA during the month (sometimes referred to as 'pay as you go' (PAYG)); or you can be paid standard monthly payments (SMPs). The default under the Civil Contract is VMPs. If you want to be paid by way of SMPs, you have to elect to be paid this way.[3] The default under the Crime Contract is SMPs. You can elect to be paid by VMPs.

23.5 In 2023 the LAA consulted on simplifying the payment scheme so that all contracts are paid as VMPs for the relevant work types; but has not yet published its response to consultation. It is possible that the practice of allowing providers to choose their payment method could change.[4]

23.6 The advantage of PAYG is that reconciliation of claims against payments should be fairly straightforward.

23.7 An SMP is the amount the LAA expects to pay you over the lifetime of the schedule, divided by that number of months. The advantage is that you get a regular amount, which can help with budgeting; but since it is rare to hit contract targets exactly, it can involve you in complex reconciliation calculations. If you opt for an SMP, you will also have to keep your eye on the reconciliation protocol (see below).

SMP or PAYG, which is best?

23.8 In many civil categories of law, post the Legal Aid, Sentencing and Punishment of Offenders Act 2012 (LASPO), there is less controlled work than there used to be, and it makes less of a contribution to income, so peaks and troughs are easier to manage. If this is the case for your organisation, you may want to be paid by VMPs, as this does away with the chore of reconciliation.

23.9 If you want to change from SMP to VMP, this means reconciling the contract to give the new arrangement a fresh start. If you have a strong cash position, or the LAA owes you money, you may want to opt for VMPs. However, if you have been paid more money than you have claimed and do not wish to make repayments at once, then you

---

3 Standard Civil Contract 2024 Specification para 4.33, Standard Crime Contract 2022 Specification para 5.20 and Standard Crime Contract 2025 Specification para 5.18.
4 See: www.gov.uk/guidance/legal-aid-agency-payments-to-providers.

Financial and contract management 621

may prefer to stick with the SMP (subject to the reconciliation protocol below). If you are owed money by the LAA, assuming that this figure is less than £20,000, a single ad hoc payment will be made to you. If you owe money to the LAA, then you can choose to make a single payment or spread the payments over a six-month period.

23.10 If you have a Crime Contract and have taken advantage of the one month's 'pull forward' option, that cannot be combined with VMPs. There is more information about choosing between VMPs and SMPs in the LAA guidance: *Variable Monthly Payments Guidance (Civil Legal Help, Crime Lower and Mediation contracts)*.[5]

Reconciliation of contracts

Overview

23.11 You should always keep your own figures for the value of your monthly submissions and monitor them against your payments. You can obtain more information and check the LAA's figures at 'Legal aid: management information online'.[6] The LAA will do the same, and periodically will seek to adjust the payments to ensure that your contract remains on course. As a result of the adjustment, your payments may go up or down. The purpose is to ensure that at the end of the contract, claims equal payments, or at least that the difference between them is within an agreed band. This process is known as reconciliation, and where parity has been achieved the contract has been successfully reconciled. Where it has not, arrangements will need to be made to resolve the outstanding balance, either by payment of a lump sum or recovering the balance during the schedule. The LAA is usually reluctant to allow recovery over more than one schedule or six months, but it can be done.

The reconciliation protocol

23.12 The LAA's reconciliation protocol – *Contract Payments (Legal Help and Crime Lower work)* – sets out the approach the LAA will take.[7] The key is that the target is always reconciliation to 100 per cent – that is, for

---

5 V3, 29 June 2016: www.gov.uk/government/uploads/system/uploads/attachment_data/file/318538/LAA-variable-monthly-payments-guidance.pdf.
6 At: www.gov.uk/legal-aid-management-information-online.
7 March 2014: www.gov.uk/government/uploads/system/uploads/attachment_data/file/340267/LAA-monthly-payments-protocol.pdf (or see appendix E).

claims to equal payments over the course of the schedule. It is recognised that in practice it will often work out that 100 per cent is not exactly achieved. Therefore, the LAA will look at the position twice a year – April and September – and determine whether the contract is within the acceptable margin of 90 to 110 per cent (calculated over the shorter of the life of the contract or the last 12 months). Where it is, no action will be taken. Where the contract is outside the acceptable margin, the monthly payment will be revised with a view to paying off any balance within six months.

23.13 It is important to remember that each month you claim less than your SMP, the closer to the 90 per cent trigger point you will be. You need to try to avoid any cumulative decline in performance that takes you below 90 per cent. Once you go below the trigger point, the reduction happens automatically and the LAA does not warn you about this in advance. The new payment would remain in place for three months to monitor whether it would achieve the desired effect. You would have to ensure that claims stayed at or around the level of the previous SMP, otherwise it could trigger a further reduction at the three-month review stage.

> **Case study**
>
> My firm has Criminal and Civil Contracts on the SMP basis. The Civil Contract is currently paid at £10,000 per month. After 12 months, we have claimed £102,000. The Criminal Contract is paid at £5,000 per month and after 12 months we have claimed £64,000. Are we in band? Is the LAA likely to change our payments?
>
> **Civil:** Total claims = £102,000 over the life of the contract. Payments are £120,000, so the balance on the account is £18,000 owed to the LAA. This is a margin of 82 per cent, so outside the acceptable band (ie below 90 per cent). The payment will be amended. The target is 100 per cent. Average monthly claim is £8,500 (£102,000/12) and you owe the LAA £18,000, which must be repaid over the next six months. The new payment will be £8,500 – (£18,000/6) = £5,500 per month.
>
> **Crime:** Total claims = £64,000, and payments are £60,000. Ten per cent of claims = £6,400, so the acceptable band is £60,000 ± £6,400 – between £53,600 and £66,400. Therefore you are within band and the LAA will not automatically amend your contract payment. However, you are entitled to ask the LAA to amend your payments at any time and may want to ask for an increase. The LAA does not have to agree, but if you can demonstrate that you are likely to continue to claim more than you are paid, it should do so.

Payments on account

23.14 You are entitled to be paid your costs on civil certificates at the end of the case following assessment by the LAA or court – see chapter 15 for details. In recognition of the fact that such cases often last a considerable time and costs can be substantial, there is provision for you to claim POAs during the life of the case.

23.15 The Standard Civil Contract 2024 entitles you to claim a POA of profit costs at any time, provided that (a) you may not apply for the first until three months have elapsed since the certificate was issued; and (b) you may not apply more than four times in any 12-month period.[8] Also, cumulatively, you are not entitled to be paid more than 80 per cent of your profit costs to date[9] (or standard fee in applicable family cases[10]). These were increased from three POAs a year and 75 per cent of profit costs as part of the LAA's efforts to improve cash-flow for its providers during the Covid-19 pandemic and adopted permanently. You can make a POA for disbursements incurred, or about to be incurred, at any time.[11]

> **Case study**
>
> *It is 1 May 2024. I have two certificate files. On the first, the certificate was issued on 1 February 2024 and I have spent £1,000. On the second, the certificate was issued on 1 April 2023. I have spent £5,000 in total, and I received a POA of £2,000 in January. Am I entitled to any POAs? If so, how much?*
>
> The first certificate was issued exactly three months ago, so you are entitled to a POA. The second was issued more than three months ago and you have only made one application in the 12 months leading up to today, so you are entitled to a POA. POAs have to be submitted using the Client and Cost Management System (CCMS). You should complete a separate POA claim for each certificate. Once you have done so, CCMS will send you a notification asking you to upload your running record of costs. This must match your claim exactly. You should upload a copy of the record and mark the notification as 'documents sent' so it is picked up by a caseworker. The LAA will not assess your claim but will check that it matches the

---

8 Standard Civil Contract 2024 Specification para 6.21(b).
9 Standard Civil Contract 2024 Specification para 6.21.
10 Standard Civil Contract 2024 Specification para 7.25(b).
11 Standard Civil Contract 2024 Specification para 6.20.

running record. Provided it does in each case, you will be paid £800 on the first case and £2,000 on the second (80 per cent of £5,000, less the £2,000 already paid).

To claim a POA for a legacy, paper-based certificate, before CCMS became mandatory (February 2016 for care cases and April 2016 for all other cases) you should complete a CIV POA1 form and email it to the LAA with the relevant supporting documentation to CIS-SFE@justice.gov.uk.

23.16 POAs should be paid into your office account (Specification para 6.25).

23.17 POAs are repayable at the end of the case. When each case concludes and the bill is assessed, the LAA will pay the value of the bill and then recoup the POAs, so that the net effect is that you are paid only the outstanding balance. Where you receive costs from the other side in part or in full, you should notify the LAA even where you are making no claim for legal aid costs so that POAs can be recouped.

Unrecouped payments on account

23.18 It is really important to claim or notify the LAA at the end of a case, as the amounts to be recovered can mount up. Repaying historic unrecouped POAs has caused practitioners serious financial problems and additional work for both themselves and the LAA. From February 2018, the LAA started to send a list of all outstanding certificates every two months, in an effort to make it easier to check your records against its own and take action promptly where required. One benefit of CCMS is that once all certificates are on the system, it should be much easier to reconcile cases.

Payment on account limits

23.19 Paragraph 6.23 of the Specification entitles the LAA to impose a maximum POA limit. This would be set in each individual contract schedule and could vary from category of law to category of law, and indeed from firm to firm.

23.20 The limit would be calculated by comparing the value of debits (payments to you) as against credits (claims received) on your account with the LAA. The maximum amount by which debits would be allowed to exceed credits is the maximum POA limit, and once the limit was reached the LAA would refuse to make any further POAs and would require repayment of the excess.

23.21 However, although this clause is in the contract, no schedules currently specify a limit and the then Legal Services Commission (LSC) undertook not to introduce one without further consultation when the unified contract was introduced in 2007. The power in the 2024 Contract is discretionary, and the LAA has, at the time of writing, given no indication of whether or in what circumstances it intends to introduce the limit. The power has not been used in over 10 years since it has been in successive contracts.

Key performance indicators

23.22 The LAA monitors organisations remotely, using the data you supply as a matter of course when applying for funding or claiming at the end of the case. You need to be able to monitor your own performance against these.

23.23 The Standard Contracts include KPIs. See chapter 22 for more information about KPIs.

Service standards

23.24 The Standard Contracts include service standards. You need to comply with them. See chapter 22 for more information about service standards.

Costs audits

Overview

23.25 Historically, cost auditing of controlled work has always been a bone of contention between the LAA and practitioners. Practitioners tend to feel that LAA staff do not understand the work that has been done, and the LAA tends to feel that practitioners are not sufficiently stringent in applying the contract requirements. The LAA has published a list of five different types of audit and validation process: the two main types of LAA audit, ie (a) peer review and (b) CCAs; and also

(c) contract management activities, (d) core testing programme and (e) targeted file review (TFR).[12]

23.26 The LAA's approach is that if, from the management information evidence that it has, it appears that you are complying with contractual requirements, it is likely that you will only have one contract manager meeting a year and will not be audited further. The LAA distinguishes between a contract manager meeting (which it does not count as a formal audit) and formal audits, carried out by members of the Operational Assurance team. The distinction is lost on many practitioners, who often emerge from whichever process the LAA has used having to repay money. The way to avoid this is by robust supervision and monitoring, especially before final claims for payment are submitted. To ensure all your claims are made correctly, the LAA's Costs Assessment Guidance is helpful for civil and family claims; the Criminal Bills Assessment Manual is the equivalent for crime. They can be found here: www.gov.uk/funding-and-costs-assessment-for-civil-and-crime-matters.

23.27 The LAA's audits are undertaken to provide the Ministry of Justice with assurance that the legal aid fund has been spent correctly and to eliminate the cause of irregularities and errors identified in the past by the National Audit Office (NAO), which led to the LSC's annual accounts being qualified towards the end of its life. The LAA needs to achieve an overall level of 'materiality of error' of less than one per cent in order to meet NAO targets.

23.28 This means that in the small samples taken by contract managers when they come to visit, you are aiming for a zero per cent error rate. This is not easy!

23.29 The main problem areas are in controlled work (Legal Help, Controlled Legal Representation and Family Help Lower) cases:
- assessing the eligibility of clients incorrectly or retaining insufficient evidence on file;
- incorrect claims for payment (often caused by using the wrong claim codes) for:
  – private law family cases; and
  – immigration and asylum cases; and
- travel distances (the LAA prefers a copy of a route planner showing postcodes travelled to/from to be retained on the file).

Therefore, these tend to be the main focus of visits/audits in civil and family categories (see below for crime). For immigration and asylum

12 See: www.gov.uk/legal-aid-agency-audits.

practitioners there is guidance which aims to help practitioners avoid the most common types of error.[13]

23.30 If you disagree with an LAA decision about costs, see 'Costs appeals' at para 23.49 below and chapter 17.

Evidence of means

23.31 The contract manager will select at least five Legal Help forms. If even one of them fails (eg due to no or invalid evidence of means), a further sample will be selected. This is then audited by the organisation itself and two files are checked by the contract manager. If three or more of the aggregated samples fail, the organisation may be asked to self-assess all the files that could possibly exhibit the same failing. In larger organisations this can mean that you are expected to self-audit hundreds of files in a short period of time.

Family level 1 and 2 fees

23.32 The contract manager will be checking that level 2 fees have been claimed correctly, see below.

Private family law – conditions for level 2

23.33 Up to and including 8 May 2011, para 10.55 of the Family Contract Specification required two meetings with the client in order to justify a level 2 fee. Following certification of Point of Principle (POP) CLA 54 – definition of 'meeting' – was broadened from 20 December 2010 to include phone calls.

23.34 The LSC removed the requirement for a second meeting from 9 May 2011 and instead practitioners had to show that 'substantive negotiations' had taken place. This remains the position under the 2024 Standard Contract Specification:

> 7.58 You may only make a determination that a Client qualifies for Family Help (Lower) where all relevant criteria in the Merits Regulations, Financial Regulations and Procedure Regulations are satisfied including the criteria in Paragraph 35 of the Merits Regulations. In addition, the fee for Family Help (Lower) may only be claimed for those Family Disputes:
>
> (a) which involve more than simply taking instructions from and advising the Client, and providing any follow up written or telephone advice; and

---

13 See: www.gov.uk/legal-aid-agency-audits (scroll down the page).

(b) where you are involved in substantive negotiations with a third party (either by conducting the negotiations yourself or by advice and assistance in support of mediation); and
(c) where the dispute, if unresolved, would be likely to lead to family proceedings; and
(d) which do not primarily concern processing a divorce, nullity, judicial separation or dissolution of a civil partnership; and
(e) which do not primarily concern advice relating to child support.

Crime

23.35 There is useful guidance to help crime practitioners avoid the most common claiming errors:[14]

- Travel:
  - distances (the LAA prefers a copy of a route planner showing postcodes travelled to/from to be retained on the file);
  - increased claims due to the use of agents (you cannot claim more than if you had done the work); and
  - incorrect claiming of travel for court duty work (eg other than at a weekend or bank holiday).
- Incorrect police station codes, leading to incorrect fees being paid.
- Magistrates' court incorrect category 1 or 2 claims.
- Incorrect claims for travel for magistrates' court duty cases.
- Incorrect hourly rates for court duty work following the 15 per cent fee increase in October 2022.
- 'Duplicate' claims, for example, where two different unique file numbers (UFNs) may have been allocated to the same case, or court duty claims:
  - claiming under a subsequent representation order as well as court duty for the same case; and
  - claiming under a representation order when the case concluded on the same day as a court duty session.
- More than one police station case fee has been claimed, where the contract manager considers that there was a 'series of offences' and only one fee was payable.
- Claiming 'designated magistrates' court' fees where either the provider is based in a designated area, or the case is dealt with in a magistrates' court based in a designated area.
- Claiming Crown Court sending fees incorrectly.

---

14 See: www.gov.uk/legal-aid-agency-audits (scroll down the page).

23.36 If you disagree with an LAA decision about costs, see 'Costs appeals' at para 23.49 below and chapter 16.

Contract notices

Overview

23.37 Up to early 2018, the LAA operated a 'zero tolerance' policy in relation to errors and would issue a contract notice for a single error, even before any review or appeal process had been invoked. In January 2018, the LAA informed the Civil Contract Consultative Group (a regular meeting between the LAA and practitioner representative bodies) that since performance had improved, it would be able to take a more risk-based approach. Henceforth, contract notices would be issued when:

- the errors found pose anything other than a low-level risk to the LAA's accounts being qualified by the NAO (to be decided by the area contract manager);
- the provider does not agree that remedial action is needed;
- the contract manager has doubt as to the effectiveness of the provider to make the required changes and a follow-up visit is needed; and
- multiple breaches of different aspects are found on a sample of files, indicating poor reporting practices in the organisation.

23.38 A contract notice requires a significant improvement in performance in relation to the relevant issue within six months, when the contract manager will come back to see whether improvements have been achieved. Clause 24 of the Standard Contract (all versions, both Civil and Crime) allows the LAA to suspend or even terminate contracts for 'persistent breaches', that is, three breaches of the same term in a 24-month period (or six different breaches). It is very rare indeed for the LAA to invoke this clause, but it undoubtedly gives practitioners cause for concern.

23.39 The contract manager will also recoup money against any overpayments or ineligible payments.

Appeals

23.40 If you disagree with your contract manager, see 'Contract compliance appeals' at para 23.49 below.

23.41 You cannot appeal against a contract notice as such. It is not an appealable decision under clause 27 of the Standard Contract Terms. What you can do is appeal against any wrong decision that has led to a contract notice, and therefore undermines the basis on which it was issued.

23.42 If you disagree that a contract notice was proportionate in the circumstances, you should write to your contract manager and ask that the issue is considered by the regional contract manager. It may be useful to have evidence that you did not agree to a breach in the long term if the LAA wishes to suspend or terminate your contract under the 'totting up' provisions in clause 24. If all else fails, you can use the LAA's complaints procedure.[15]

Contract compliance audits

23.43 If it has concerns, the LAA may choose to carry out a CCA. However, no CCAs have been carried out since 2018.

23.44 A minimum of 30 and maximum of 50 files are assessed, depending on the level of claims you have made across the 12-month sample period. The LAA employs a formula devised by the NAO to select samples to test the accuracy of assessments.

23.45 CCAs are carried out off-site on the LAA's premises. The LAA checks compliance with the Civil/Crime Contracts, guidance, the Criminal Bills Assessment Manual and the Civil Costs Assessment Guidance. It assesses whether there is appropriate evidence of eligibility, work done and disbursements on the file, costs incurred are reasonable and the bill is in line with the appropriate guidance.

Contract compliance audit outcomes

23.46 Files are either nil assessed, because the file should not have been funded at all (eg the client was not financially eligible or the matter was out of scope), or reduced by a percentage because a higher fee was claimed than was appropriate (eg a family level 2 fee was claimed when the LAA says it should have been level 1).

23.47 Firms used to be given a categorisation, depending on the outcome of a CCA. The LSC stopped doing that, and would simply apply reductions in fees and take action as shown in the table below. However, the LAA has not conducted CCAs for several years.

---

15 See: www.gov.uk/government/organisations/legal-aid-agency/about/complaints-procedure.

Financial and contract management 631

Final % value assessed down	Action and sanctions	Old rating name
0.00%–10.00%	Recoup or credit value of incorrectly claimed files within audit sample.	Category 1
10.01%–20.00%	Extrapolation of % reduction. Re-audit to be scheduled. Contract notice(s).	Category 2
20.01% and over	Extrapolation of % reduction. Re-audit to be scheduled. Contract notice(s) (further action, including possible termination, to be taken on an individual basis if result of re-audit not improved).	Category 3

Extrapolation

23.48 Extrapolation is one of the reasons that CCAs were dreaded by practitioners, as an audit of a relatively small sample can result in significant sums having to be repaid. The Standard Contract[16] allows the LAA to apply the findings of a controlled work costs audit back to the date when the file sample was requested for the previous CCA, or 12 months prior to the date the sample was requested in the current CCA, whichever is the most recent. For example, suppose the file sample of 20 files was requested on 1 July 2021 and the eventual reduction was 25 per cent. If the value of claims from 1 July 2021 to 30 June 2022 were £146,000, the recoupment would be 25 per cent of £146,000, ie £36,500.

Contract compliance audit – appeal process

23.49 The appeal process is the same as other types of costs appeal, see below.

Costs appeals

23.50 For the first stages of the appeal process, see the Standard Civil Contract 2024 Specification para 6.71 onwards; and the Standard

---

16 Standard Civil Contract 2024 Specification para 4.47 onwards, Standard Crime Contract 2022 Specification para 8.15 onwards and Standard Crime Contract 2025 Specification para 8.16 onwards.

Crime Contract 2022 para 8.19 onwards and 2025 Specification para 8.20 onwards. The substantive provisions in relation to the initial stages are the same in the different contracts (only the paragraph numbers differ).

23.51 The first stage is an internal review by another member of the LAA's audit team. You must set out the reasons for the appeal in writing within 28 days and send the file(s) back with the appeal. The LAA suggests that it may be more effective to send only relevant documentation, as this will save time; but whether that would be the best course of action depends on the nature of the appeal. If you need an extension of time, you must have a 'good reason' and request the extension within 21 days. It is likely to be granted, but for only up to a further 14 days.

23.52 If the initial stage is not successful, you move to independent costs assessment. Independent Costs Assessors (ICAs) are solicitors, barristers, FCILEx or cost lawyers who are members of the LAA's Review Panel. They are contracted on a sessional basis and are not LAA employees.

23.53 ICA appeals are generally considered on the papers only, although in exceptional circumstances either party can apply to the assessor for an oral hearing – although these are rarely granted. The ICA reviews the assessment and may confirm, increase or decrease the amount assessed. However, in contracts issued after 2013, the process ends here. Any further challenge would need to be brought by way of judicial review. For more information on ICA appeals, see chapter 17.

Points of principle

23.54 Under contracts issued up to 2013, it was possible to apply for a 'point of principle of general importance' (POP) to be certified if raised by an issue in the costs appeal and overlooked by the ICA. The Civil 2024 and Crime 2022 and 2025 Contracts have no further costs appeal process after the ICA process described above. The only recourse would be by way of judicial review. POPs in respect of regulations or contract provisions still applicable or replicated in current rules should, however, be persuasive authority in LAA and ICA decision-making.

APPENDICES

A Legal Aid, Sentencing and Punishment of Offenders Act 2021 Sch 1   635

B Standard Civil Contract 2024 Category Definitions   669

C Civil costs: what you can claim for   683

D Criminal costs: what you can claim for   691

E Standard monthly payment reconciliation process   697

APPENDIX A

Legal Aid, Sentencing and Punishment of Offenders Act 2021 Sch 1[1]

SCHEDULE 1: CIVIL LEGAL SERVICES

Section 9

PART 1: SERVICES

Care, supervision and protection of children

1 (1) Civil legal services provided in relation to–
   (a) orders under section 25 of the Children Act 1989 ('the 1989 Act') (secure accommodation);
   (b) orders under Part 4 of the 1989 Act (care and supervision);
   (c) orders under Part 5 of the 1989 Act (protection of children);
   (d) approval by a court under paragraph 19 of Schedule 2 to the 1989 Act (arrangements to assist children to live abroad);
   (e) parenting orders under section 8 of the Crime and Disorder Act 1998 ('the 1998 Act') or section 366 or 369 of the Sentencing Code;
   (f) child safety orders under section 11 of the 1998 Act;
   (g) orders for contact under section 26 of the Adoption and Children Act 2002 ('the 2002 Act');
   (h) applications for leave of the court to remove a child from a person's custody under section 36 of the 2002 Act;
   (i) placement orders, recovery orders or adoption orders under Chapter 3 of Part 1 of the 2002 Act (see sections 21, 41 and 46 of that Act);
   (j) orders under section 84 of the 2002 Act (parental responsibility prior to adoption abroad);
   (k) orders under section 119 of the Social Services and Well-being (Wales) Act 2014 ('the 2014 Act') (secure accommodation);
   (l) approval by a court under section 124 of the 2014 Act (arrangements to assist children to live abroad).

(2) Civil legal services provided in relation to an order under an enactment made–
   (a) as an alternative to an order mentioned in sub-paragraph (1), or
   (b) in proceedings heard together with proceedings relating to such an order.

Exclusions

(3) Sub-paragraphs (1) and (2) are subject to the exclusions in Parts 2 and 3 of this Schedule.

1 © Crown Copyright. Reproduced as amended up to date to 5 December 2024.

Definitions
(4) In this paragraph 'children' means persons under the age of 18.

Special Guardianship
1A (1) Civil legal services provided in relation to special guardianship orders as defined in section 14A of the Children Act 1989.

Exclusions
(2) Sub-paragraph (1) is subject to the exclusions in Parts 2 and 3 of this Schedule.

Special educational needs
2(1) Civil legal services provided in relation to–
   (a) matters arising under Part 4 of the Education Act 1996 Part 2 of the Additional Learning Needs and Education Tribunal (Wales) Act 2018 or Part 3 of the Children and Families Act 2014 (special educational needs);
   (b) assessments relating to learning difficulties under section 140 of the Learning and Skills Act 2000.

Exclusions
(2) Sub-paragraph (1) is subject to the exclusions in Parts 2 and 3 of this Schedule.

Abuse of child or vulnerable adult
3(1) Civil legal services provided in relation to abuse of an individual that took place at a time when the individual was a child or vulnerable adult, but only where–
   (a) the services are provided to the individual, or
   (b) the individual has died and the services are provided–
      (i) to the individual's personal representative, or
      (ii) for the purposes of a claim under the Fatal Accidents Act 1976 for the benefit of the individual's dependants.

General exclusions
(2) Sub-paragraph (1) is subject to–
   (a) the exclusions in Part 2 of this Schedule, with the exception of paragraphs 1, 2, 3, 8 and 12 of that Part, and
   (b) the exclusion in Part 3 of this Schedule.

Specific exclusions
(3) The services described in sub-paragraph (1) do not include services provided in relation to clinical negligence.
(4) The services described in sub-paragraph (1) do not include services provided in relation to a matter arising under a family enactment.

Definitions
(5) In this paragraph–
'abuse' means physical or mental abuse, including–
   (a) sexual abuse, and
   (b) abuse in the form of violence, neglect, maltreatment and exploitation;
'child' means a person under the age of 18;
'clinical negligence' means breach of a duty of care or trespass to the person committed in the course of the provision of clinical or medical services (including dental or nursing services);
'family enactment' has the meaning given in paragraph 12;
'personal representative', in relation to an individual who has died, means–

(a) a person responsible for administering the individual's estate under the law of England and Wales, Scotland or Northern Ireland, or
(b) a person who, under the law of another country or territory, has functions equivalent to those of administering the individual's estate;
'vulnerable adult' means a person aged 18 or over whose ability to protect himself or herself from abuse is significantly impaired through physical or mental disability or illness, through old age or otherwise.

Working with children and vulnerable adults

4(1) Civil legal services provided in relation to–
(a) the inclusion of a person in a barred list or the removal of a person from a barred list;
(b) a disqualification order under section 28, 29 or 29A of the Criminal Justice and Court Services Act 2000 (disqualification from working with children);
(c) a direction under section 142 of the Education Act 2002 (prohibition from teaching etc).

Exclusions
(2) Sub-paragraph (1) is subject to the exclusions in Parts 2 and 3 of this Schedule.

Definitions
(3) In this paragraph 'barred list' means a list maintained under–
(a) section 2 of the Safeguarding Vulnerable Groups Act 2006 (persons barred from regulated activities relating to children or vulnerable adults);
(b) section 81 of the Care Standards Act 2000;
(c) section 1 of the Protection of Children Act 1999.

Mental health and mental capacity

5(1) Civil legal services provided in relation to matters arising under–
(a) the Mental Health Act 1983;
(b) paragraph 5(2) of the Schedule to the Repatriation of Prisoners Act 1984;
(c) the Mental Capacity Act 2005.

General exclusions
(2) Sub-paragraph (1) is subject to the exclusions in Parts 2 and 3 of this Schedule.

Specific exclusion
(3) The services described in sub-paragraph (1) do not include services provided in relation to–
(a) the creation of lasting powers of attorney under the Mental Capacity Act 2005, or
(b) the making of advance decisions under that Act.
(4) Sub-paragraph (3) does not exclude services provided in relation to determinations and declarations by a court under the Mental Capacity Act 2005 as to the validity, meaning, effect or applicability of–
(a) a lasting power of attorney that has been created, or
an advance decision that has been made.

Community care

6(1) Civil legal services provided in relation to community care services.

Exclusions
(2) Sub-paragraph (1) is subject to the exclusions in Parts 2 and 3 of this Schedule.

Definitions
(3) In this paragraph–
'community care services' means services which a relevant person may provide or arrange to be provided under–
(a) . . .
(b) . . .
(c) . . .
(d) . . .
(e) section 117 of the Mental Health Act 1983 (after-care);
(f) section 17 of the Children Act 1989 ('the 1989 Act') (provision of services for children in need);
(g) section 20 of the 1989 Act (provision of accommodation for children);
(h) sections 22A, 22B and 22C of the 1989 Act (accommodation and maintenance for children in care and looked after children);
(i) sections 23B and 23C of the 1989 Act (local authority functions in respect of relevant children);
(j) sections 24, 24A and 24B of the 1989 Act (provision of services for persons qualifying for advice and assistance);
(k) . . .
(l) . . .
(m). . .
(n) Part 1 of the Care Act 2014 (local authority's functions of meeting adult's needs for care and support);
(o) section 15 of the Social Services and Well-being (Wales) Act 2014 ('the 2014 Act') (preventative services);
(p) Part 4 of the 2014 Act (local authority's functions of meeting a person's needs for care and support);
(q) section 76 of the 2014 Act (provision of accommodation for children);
(r) sections 79, 80 and 81 of the 2014 Act (accommodation and maintenance for children in care and looked after children);
(s) sections 105 to 116 of the 2014 Act (local authority support for certain children);
'relevant person' means–
(a) a district council;
(b) a county council;
(c) a county borough council;
(d) a London borough council;
(e) the Common Council of the City of London;
(f) a Primary Care Trust established under section 18 of the National Health Service Act 2006;
(g) a Local Health Board established under section 11 of the National Health Service (Wales) Act 2006;
(h) any other person prescribed for the purposes of this paragraph.

Facilities for disabled persons
7(1) Civil legal services provided in relation to grants under Part 1 of the Housing Grants, Construction and Regeneration Act 1996 for the provision of facilities for disabled persons.

Exclusions

(2) Sub-paragraph (1) is subject to the exclusions in Parts 2 and 3 of this Schedule.

Definitions

(3) In this paragraph 'disabled person' has the meaning given in section 100 of the Housing Grants, Construction and Regeneration Act 1996.

Appeals relating to welfare benefits

8(1) Civil legal services provided in relation to an appeal on a point of law to the Upper Tribunal, the Court of Appeal or the Supreme Court relating to a benefit, allowance, payment, credit or pension under–
(a) a social security enactment,
(b) the Vaccine Damage Payments Act 1979, or
(c) Part 4 of the Child Maintenance and Other Payments Act 2008.

Exclusions

(2) Sub-paragraph (1) is subject to–
(a) the exclusions in Part 2 of this Schedule, with the exception of paragraphs 1 and 15 of that Part, and
(b) the exclusion in Part 3 of this Schedule.

Definitions

(3) In this paragraph 'social security enactment' means–
(a) the Social Security Contributions and Benefits Act 1992,
(b) the Jobseekers Act 1995,
(c) the State Pension Credit Act 2002,
(d) the Tax Credits Act 2002,
(e) the Welfare Reform Act 2007,
(f) the Welfare Reform Act 2012, or
(g) any other enactment relating to social security.

Appeals relating to council tax reduction schemes

8A (1) Civil legal services provided in relation to an appeal on a point of law to the High Court, the Court of Appeal or the Supreme Court relating to a council tax reduction scheme.

General exclusions

(2) Sub-paragraph (1) is subject to the exclusions in Parts 2 and 3 of this Schedule.

Specific exclusion

(3) The services described in sub-paragraph (1) do not include advocacy in proceedings in the High Court.

Definitions

(4) In this paragraph 'council tax reduction scheme' has the same meaning as in Part 1 of the Local Government Finance Act 1992 (council tax: England and Wales) (see section 13A(9) of that Act).

Inherent jurisdiction of High Court in relation to children and vulnerable adults

9(1) Civil legal services provided in relation to the inherent jurisdiction of the High Court in relation to children and vulnerable adults.

Exclusions
(2) Sub-paragraph (1) is subject to the exclusions in Parts 2 and 3 of this Schedule.

Definitions
(3) In this paragraph–
'adults' means persons aged 18 or over;
''children' means persons under the age of 18.

Unlawful removal of children
10(1) Civil legal services provided to an individual in relation to the following orders and requirements where the individual is seeking to prevent the unlawful removal of a related child from the United Kingdom or to secure the return of a related child who has been unlawfully removed from the United Kingdom–
(a) a prohibited steps order or specific issue order (as defined in section 8(1) of the Children Act 1989);
(b) an order under section 33 of the Family Law Act 1986 for disclosure of the child's whereabouts;
(c) an order under section 34 of that Act for the child's return;
(d) a requirement under section 37 of that Act to surrender a passport issued to, or containing particulars of, the child.
(2) Civil legal services provided to an individual in relation to the following orders and applications where the individual is seeking to secure the return of a related child who has been unlawfully removed to a place in the United Kingdom–
(a) a prohibited steps order or specific issue order (as defined in section 8(1) of the Children Act 1989);
(b) an application under section 27 of the Family Law Act 1986 for registration of an order relating to the child;
(c) an order under section 33 of that Act for disclosure of the child's whereabouts;
(d) an order under section 34 of that Act for the child's return.

Exclusions
(3) Sub-paragraphs (1) and (2) are subject to the exclusions in Parts 2 and 3 of this Schedule.

Definitions
(4) For the purposes of this paragraph, a child is related to an individual if the individual is the child's parent or has parental responsibility for the child.
(5) In this paragraph 'child' means a person under the age of 18.

Family homes and domestic violence
11(1) Civil legal services provided in relation to home rights, occupation orders and non- molestation orders under Part 4 of the Family Law Act 1996.
(2) Civil legal services provided in relation to the following in circumstances arising out of a family relationship–
(a) an injunction following assault, battery or false imprisonment;
(b) the inherent jurisdiction of the High Court to protect an adult.

Exclusions
(3) Sub-paragraphs (1) and (2) are subject to–

Legal Aid, Sentencing and Punishment of Offenders Act 2021 Sch 1 641

(a) the exclusions in Part 2 of this Schedule, with the exception of paragraphs 3 and 11 of that Part, and
(b) the exclusion in Part 3 of this Schedule.

Definitions
(4) For the purposes of this paragraph–
  (a) there is a family relationship between two people if they are associated with each other, and
  (b) 'associated' has the same meaning as in Part 4 of the Family Law Act 1996 (see section 62 of that Act).
(5) For the purposes of this paragraph, the Lord Chancellor may by regulations make provision about when circumstances arise out of a family relationship.

Victims of domestic violence and family matters
12(1) Civil legal services provided to an adult ('A') in relation to a matter arising out of a family relationship between A and another individual ('B') where–
there has been, or is a risk of, domestic violence between A and B, and
A was, or is at risk of being, the victim of that domestic violence.

General exclusions
(2) Sub-paragraph (1) is subject to the exclusions in Part 2 of this Schedule, with the exception of paragraph 11 of that Part.
(3) But the exclusions described in sub-paragraph (2) are subject to the exception in sub-paragraph (4).
(4) The services described in sub-paragraph (1) include services provided in relation to conveyancing, but only where–
  (a) the services in relation to conveyancing are provided in the course of giving effect to a court order made in proceedings, and
  (b) services described in that sub-paragraph (other than services in relation to conveyancing) are being or have been provided in relation to those proceedings under arrangements made for the purposes of this Part of this Act.
(5) Sub-paragraph (1) is subject to the exclusion in Part 3 of this Schedule.

Specific exclusion
(6) The services described in sub-paragraph (1) do not include services provided in relation to a claim in tort in respect of the domestic violence.

Definitions
(7) For the purposes of this paragraph–
  (a) there is a family relationship between two people if they are associated with each other, and
  (b) 'associated' has the same meaning as in Part 4 of the Family Law Act 1996 (see section 62 of that Act).
(8) For the purposes of this paragraph–
  (a) matters arising out of a family relationship include matters arising under a family enactment, and
  (b) (subject to paragraph (a)) the Lord Chancellor may by regulations make provision about when matters arise out of a family relationship.
(9) In this paragraph–

'adult' means a person aged 18 or over;
'domestic violence' means any incident, or pattern of incidents, of controlling, coercive or threatening behaviour, violence or abuse (whether psychological, physical, sexual, financial or emotional) between individuals who are associated with each other;
'family enactment' means–
- (a) section 17 of the Married Women's Property Act 1882 (questions between husband and wife as to property);
- (b) the Maintenance Orders (Facilities for Enforcement) Act 1920;
- (c) the Maintenance Orders Act 1950;
- (d) the Maintenance Orders Act 1958;
- (e) the Maintenance Orders (Reciprocal Enforcement) Act 1972;
- (f) Schedule 1 to the Domicile and Matrimonial Proceedings Act 1973 (staying of matrimonial proceedings) and corresponding provision in relation to civil partnerships made by rules of court under section 223 of the Civil Partnership Act 2004;
- (g) the Matrimonial Causes Act 1973;
- (h) the Inheritance (Provision for Family Dependants) Act 1975;
- (i) the Domestic Proceedings and Magistrates' Courts Act 1978;
- (j) Part 3 of the Matrimonial and Family Proceedings Act 1984 (financial relief after overseas divorce etc);
- (k) Parts 1 and 3 of the Family Law Act 1986 (child custody and declarations of status);
- (l) Parts 1 and 2 of the Children Act 1989 (orders with respect to children in family proceedings);
- (m) section 53 of, and Schedule 7 to, the Family Law Act 1996 (transfer of tenancies on divorce etc or separation of cohabitants);
- (n) Chapters 2 and 3 of Part 2 of the Civil Partnership Act 2004 (dissolution, nullity and other proceedings and property and financial arrangements);
- (o) sections 54 and 54A of the Human Fertilisation and Embryology Act 2008 (applications for parental orders).
- (xvi) section 51A of the Adoption and Children Act 2002 (post-adoption contact orders).

Protection of children and family matters

13(1) Civil legal services provided to an adult ('A') in relation to the following orders and procedures where the child who is or would be the subject of the order is at risk of abuse from an individual other than A–
- (a) orders under section 4(2A) of the Children Act 1989 ('the 1989 Act') (removal of father's parental responsibility);
- (b) orders under section 6(7) of the 1989 Act (termination of appointment of guardian);
- (c) orders mentioned in section 8(1) of the 1989 Act (child arrangements orders and other orders);
- (d) special guardianship orders under Part 2 of the 1989 Act;
- (e) orders under section 33 of the Family Law Act 1986 ('the 1986 Act') (disclosure of child's whereabouts);
- (f) orders under section 34 of the 1986 Act (return of child).

(g) orders under section 51A of the Adoption and Children Act 2002 (post-adoption contact).

Exclusions
(2) Sub-paragraph (1) is subject to the exclusions in Parts 2 and 3 of this Schedule.

Definitions
(3) In this paragraph–
'abuse' means physical or mental abuse, including–
  (a) sexual abuse, and
  (b) abuse in the form of violence, neglect, maltreatment and exploitation;
'adult' means a person aged 18 or over;
'child' means a person under the age of 18.

Mediation in family disputes
14(1) Mediation provided in relation to family disputes.
(2) Civil legal services provided in connection with the mediation of family disputes.

Exclusions
(3) Sub-paragraphs (1) and (2) are subject to the exclusions in Part 2 of this Schedule, with the exception of paragraph 11 of that Part.
(4) But the exclusions described in sub-paragraph (3) are subject to the exception in sub-paragraph (5).
(5) The services described in sub-paragraph (2) include services provided in relation to conveyancing, but only where–
  (a) the services in relation to conveyancing are provided in the course of giving effect to arrangements for the resolution of a family dispute, and
  (b) services described in that sub-paragraph or sub-paragraph (1) (other than services in relation to conveyancing) are being or have been provided in relation to the dispute under arrangements made for the purposes of this Part of this Act.
(6) Sub-paragraphs (1) and (2) are subject to the exclusion in Part 3 of this Schedule.

Definitions
(7) For the purposes of this paragraph–
  (a) a dispute is a family dispute if it is a dispute between individuals about a matter arising out of a family relationship between the individuals,
  (b) there is a family relationship between two individuals if they are associated with each other, and
  (c) 'associated' has the same meaning as in Part 4 of the Family Law Act 1996 (see section 62 of that Act).
(8) For the purposes of this paragraph–
  (a) matters arising out of a family relationship include matters arising under a family enactment, and
  (b) (subject to paragraph (a)) the Lord Chancellor may by regulations make provision about when matters arise out of a family relationship.
(9) In this paragraph–
'child' means a person under the age of 18;
'family enactment' has the meaning given in paragraph 12.

Children who are parties to family proceedings

15(1) Civil legal services provided to a child in relation to family proceedings–
  (a) where the child is, or proposes to be, the applicant or respondent;
  (b) where the child is made a party to the proceedings by a court under rule 16.2 of the Family Procedure Rules;
  (c) where the child is a party to the proceedings and is conducting, or proposes to conduct, the proceedings without a children's guardian or litigation friend in accordance with rule 16.6 of the Family Procedure Rules.

Exclusions
(2) Sub-paragraph (1) is subject to the exclusions in Parts 2 and 3 of this Schedule.

Definitions
(3) For the purposes of this paragraph–
  (a) proceedings are family proceedings if they relate to a matter arising out of a family relationship,
  (b) there is a family relationship between two individuals if they are associated with each other, and
  (c) 'associated' has the same meaning as in Part 4 of the Family Law Act 1996 (see section 62 of that Act).
(4) For the purposes of this paragraph–
  (a) matters arising out of a family relationship include matters arising under a family enactment, and
  (b) (subject to paragraph (a)) the Lord Chancellor may by regulations make provision about when matters arise out of a family relationship.
(5) In this paragraph–
'child' means a person under the age of 18;
'family enactment' has the meaning given in paragraph 12.

Female genital mutilation protection orders

15A (1) Civil legal services provided in relation to female genital mutilation protection orders under paragraph 1 of Schedule 2 to the Female Genital Mutilation Act 2003.

Exclusions
(2) Sub-paragraph (1) is subject to the exclusions in Parts 2 and 3 of this Schedule.

Forced marriage

16(1) Civil legal services provided in relation to forced marriage protection orders under Part 4A of the Family Law Act 1996.

Exclusions
(2) Sub-paragraph (1) is subject to the exclusions in Parts 2 and 3 of this Schedule.

Transitional EU arrangements and international agreements concerning children

17(1) Civil legal services provided in relation to–
  (a) an application made to the Lord Chancellor under the 1980 European Convention on Child Custody for the recognition or enforcement in England and Wales of a decision relating to the custody of a child;
  (b) an application made to the Lord Chancellor under the 1980 Hague

Legal Aid, Sentencing and Punishment of Offenders Act 2021 Sch 1 645

Convention in respect of a child who is, or is believed to be, in England and Wales;
(c) the recognition or enforcement of a judgment in England and Wales in accordance with Article 21, 28, 41, 42 or 48 of the 2003 Brussels Regulation.

Exclusions

(2) Sub-paragraph (1) is subject to the exclusions in Parts 2 and 3 of this Schedule.

Definitions

(3) In this paragraph–
'the 1980 European Convention on Child Custody' means the European Convention on Recognition and Enforcement of Decisions concerning Custody of Children and on the Restoration of Custody of Children which was signed in Luxembourg on 20 May 1980;
'the 1980 Hague Convention' means the Convention on the Civil Aspects of International Child Abduction which was signed at The Hague on 25 October 1980;
'the 2003 Brussels Regulation' means Council Regulation (EC) No. 2201/2003 of 27 November 2003 concerning jurisdiction and the recognition and enforcement of judgments in matrimonial matters and the matters of parental responsibility.

(4) For the purposes of this paragraph, an application is made to the Lord Chancellor if it is addressed to the Lord Chancellor or transmitted to the Lord Chancellor in accordance with section 3 or 14 of the Child Abduction and Custody Act 1985.

Transitional EU arrangements and international agreements concerning maintenance

18(1) Civil legal services provided in relation to an application under the following for the recognition or enforcement in England and Wales of a maintenance order–
(a) the 1968 Brussels Convention;
(b) the 1973 Hague Convention;
(c) the 1989 Lugano Convention;
(d) the 2000 Brussels Regulation;
(e) the 2007 Lugano Convention.

(2) Civil legal services provided in relation to an application under Article 56 of the EU Maintenance Regulation (applications relating to maintenance decisions).

(3) Civil legal services provided to an individual in relation to proceedings in England and Wales relating to the recognition, enforceability or enforcement of a maintenance decision in circumstances in which the individual falls within Article 47(2) or (3) of the EU Maintenance Regulation (parties who benefited from free legal aid etc in Member State of origin).

(3A) Civil legal services provided in relation to an application under Article 10 of the 2007 Hague Convention (applications relating to maintenance decisions).

(3B) Civil legal services provided to an individual in relation to proceedings in England and Wales relating to the recognition or enforcement of a maintenance decision in circumstances in which–
(a) Article 17(b) of the 2007 Hague Convention (free legal assistance for persons who benefited from such assistance in State of origin) applies to

the proceedings by virtue of Article 37(2) of that Convention (direct request to competent authority of Contracting State), and
(b) the individual falls within Article 17(b) as so applied.

Exclusions
(4) Sub-paragraphs (1) to (3B) are subject to–
(a) the exclusions in Part 2 of this Schedule, with the exception of paragraph 11 of that Part, and
(b) the exclusion in Part 3 of this Schedule.

Definitions
(5) In this paragraph–
'the 1968 Brussels Convention' means the Convention on jurisdiction and the enforcement of judgments in civil and commercial matters (including the Protocol annexed to that Convention) signed at Brussels on 27 September 1968;
'the 1973 Hague Convention' means the Convention on the recognition and enforcement of decisions relating to maintenance obligations concluded at The Hague on 2 October 1973;
'the 1989 Lugano Convention' means the Convention on jurisdiction and the enforcement of judgments in civil and commercial matters (including the Protocols annexed to that Convention) opened for signature at Lugano on 16 September 1988 and signed by the United Kingdom on 18 September 1989;
'the 2000 Brussels Regulation' means Council Regulation (EC) No. 44/2001 of 22 December 2000 on jurisdiction and the recognition and enforcement of judgments in civil and commercial matters;
'the 2007 Hague Convention' means the Convention on the international recovery of child support and other forms of family maintenance concluded at The Hague on 23 November 2007;
'the 2007 Lugano Convention' means the Convention on jurisdiction and enforcement of judgments in civil and commercial matters, between the European Community and the Republic of Iceland, the Kingdom of Norway, the Swiss Confederation and the Kingdom of Denmark signed on behalf of the European Community on 30 October 2007;
'the EU Maintenance Regulation' means Council Regulation (EC) No. 4/2009 of 18 December 2008 on jurisdiction, applicable law, recognition and enforcement of decisions and co-operation in matters relating to maintenance obligations;
'maintenance order', in relation to a convention or regulation listed in this paragraph, means a maintenance judgment within the meaning of that convention or regulation.

Judicial review
19(1) Civil legal services provided in relation to judicial review of an enactment, decision, act or omission.

General exclusions
(2) Sub-paragraph (1) is subject to–
(a) the exclusions in Part 2 of this Schedule, with the exception of paragraphs 1, 2, 3, 4, 5, 6, 8, 12, 15, 16 and 18 of that Part, and
(b) the exclusion in Part 3 of this Schedule.

Specific exclusion: benefit to individual

(3) The services described in sub-paragraph (1) do not include services provided to an individual in relation to judicial review that does not have the potential to produce a benefit for the individual, a member of the individual's family or the environment.

(4) Sub-paragraph (3) does not exclude services provided in relation to a judicial review where the judicial review ceases to have the potential to produce such a benefit after civil legal services have been provided in relation to the judicial review under arrangements made for the purposes of this Part of this Act.

Specific exclusions: immigration cases

(5) The services described in sub-paragraph (1) do not include services provided in relation to judicial review in respect of an issue relating to immigration where—
   (a) the same issue, or substantially the same issue, was the subject of a previous judicial review or an appeal to a court or tribunal,
   (b) on the determination of the previous judicial review or appeal (or, if there was more than one, the latest one), the court, tribunal or other person hearing the case found against the applicant or appellant on that issue, and
   (c) the services in relation to the new judicial review are provided before the end of the period of 1 year beginning with the day of that determination.

(6) The services described in sub-paragraph (1) do not include services provided in relation to judicial review of removal directions in respect of an individual where the directions were given not more than 1 year after the latest of the following—
   (a) the making of the decision (or, if there was more than one, the latest decision) to remove the individual from the United Kingdom by way of removal directions;
   (b) the refusal of leave to appeal against that decision;
   (c) the determination or withdrawal of an appeal against that decision.

(7) Sub-paragraphs (5) and (6) do not exclude services provided to an individual in relation to—
   (a) judicial review of a negative decision in relation to an asylum application (within the meaning of the EU Procedures Directive) where there is no right of appeal to the First-tier Tribunal against the decision;
   (b) judicial review of certification under section 94 or 96 of the Nationality, Immigration and Asylum Act 2002 (certificate preventing or restricting appeal of immigration decision).

(8) Sub-paragraphs (5) and (6) do not exclude services provided in relation to judicial review of removal directions in respect of an individual where prescribed conditions relating to either or both of the following are met—
   (a) the period between the individual being given notice of the removal directions and the proposed time for his or her removal;
   (b) the reasons for proposing that period.

Definitions

(9) For the purposes of this paragraph an individual is a member of another individual's family if—
   (a) they are relatives (whether of the full blood or half blood or by marriage or civil partnership),

(b) they are cohabitants (as defined in Part 4 of the Family Law Act 1996), or
(c) one has parental responsibility for the other.

(10) In this paragraph–

'EU Procedures Directive' means Council Directive 2005/85/EC of 1 December 2005 on minimum standards on procedures in Member States for granting and withdrawing refugee status;

'an issue relating to immigration' includes an issue relating to rights described in paragraph 30 of this Part of this Schedule;

'judicial review' means–
(a) the procedure on an application for judicial review (see section 31 of the Senior Courts Act 1981), but not including the procedure after the application is treated under rules of court as if it were not such an application, and
(b) any procedure in which a court, tribunal or other person mentioned in Part 3 of this Schedule is required by an enactment to make a decision applying the principles that are applied by the court on an application for judicial review;

'removal directions' means directions under–
(a) paragraphs 8 to 10A of Schedule 2 to the Immigration Act 1971 (removal of persons refused leave to enter and illegal entrants);
(b) paragraphs 12 to 14 of Schedule 2 to that Act (removal of seamen and aircrew);
(c) paragraph 1 of Schedule 3 to that Act (removal of persons liable to deportation);
(d) section 10 of the Immigration and Asylum Act 1999 (removal of certain persons unlawfully in the United Kingdom);
(e) ...

Habeas corpus

20(1) Civil legal services provided in relation to a writ of habeas corpus ad subjiciendum.

Exclusions

(2) Sub-paragraph (1) is subject to the exclusions in Parts 2 and 3 of this Schedule.

Abuse of position or powers by public authority

21 (1) Civil legal services provided in relation to abuse by a public authority of its position or powers.

General exclusions

(2) Sub-paragraph (1) is subject to–
(a) the exclusions in Part 2 of this Schedule, with the exception of paragraphs 1, 2, 3, 4, 5, 6, 8 and 12 of that Part, and
(b) the exclusion in Part 3 of this Schedule.

Specific exclusion

(3) The services described in sub-paragraph (1) do not include services provided in relation to clinical negligence.

Definitions

(4) For the purposes of this paragraph, an act or omission by a public authority does not constitute an abuse of its position or powers unless the act or omission–

(a) is deliberate or dishonest, and
(b) results in harm to a person or property that was reasonably foreseeable.
(5) In this paragraph–
'clinical negligence' means breach of a duty of care or trespass to the person committed in the course of the provision of clinical or medical services (including dental or nursing services);
'public authority' has the same meaning as in section 6 of the Human Rights Act 1998.

Breach of Convention rights by public authority
22(1) Civil legal services provided in relation to–
(a) a claim in tort, or
(b) a claim for damages (other than a claim in tort),
in respect of an act or omission by a public authority that involves a significant breach of Convention rights by the authority.

General exclusions
(2) Sub-paragraph (1) is subject to–
(a) the exclusions in Part 2 of this Schedule, with the exception of paragraphs 1, 2, 3, 4, 5, 6, 8 and 12 of that Part, and
(b) the exclusion in Part 3 of this Schedule.

Specific exclusion
(3) The services described in sub-paragraph (1) do not include services provided in relation to clinical negligence.

Definitions
(4) In this paragraph–
'clinical negligence' means breach of a duty of care or trespass to the person committed in the course of the provision of clinical or medical services (including dental or nursing services);
'Convention rights' has the same meaning as in the Human Rights Act 1998;
'public authority' has the same meaning as in section 6 of that Act.

Clinical negligence and severely disabled infants
23(1) Civil legal services provided in relation to a claim for damages in respect of clinical negligence which caused a neurological injury to an individual ('V') as a result of which V is severely disabled, but only where the first and second conditions are met.
(2) The first condition is that the clinical negligence occurred–
(a) while V was in his or her mother's womb, or
(b) during or after V's birth but before the end of the following period–
(i) if V was born before the beginning of the 37th week of pregnancy, the period of 8 weeks beginning with the first day of what would have been that week;
(ii) if V was born during or after the 37th week of pregnancy, the period of 8 weeks beginning with the day of V's birth.
(3) The second condition is that–
(a) the services are provided to V, or
(b) V has died and the services are provided to V's personal representative.

General exclusions
(4) Sub-paragraph (1) is subject to–

(a) the exclusions in Part 2 of this Schedule, with the exception of paragraphs 1, 2, 3 and 8 of that Part, and
(b) the exclusion in Part 3 of this Schedule.

Definitions
(5) In this paragraph–
'birth' means the moment when an individual first has a life separate from his or her mother and references to an individual being born are to be interpreted accordingly;
'clinical negligence' means breach of a duty of care or trespass to the person committed in the course of the provision of clinical or medical services (including dental or nursing services);
'disabled' means physically or mentally disabled;
'personal representative', in relation to an individual who has died, means–
(a) a person responsible for administering the individual's estate under the law of England and Wales, Scotland or Northern Ireland, or
(b) a person who, under the law of another country or territory, has functions equivalent to those of administering the individual's estate.

Special Immigration Appeals Commission
24(1) Civil legal services provided in relation to proceedings before the Special Immigration Appeals Commission.

Exclusions
(2) Sub-paragraph (1) is subject to the exclusions in Parts 2 and 3 of this Schedule.

Immigration: detention
25(1) Civil legal services provided in relation to–
(a) detention under the authority of an immigration officer;
(b) detention under Schedule 3 to the Immigration Act 1971;
(c) detention under section 62 of the Nationality, Immigration and Asylum Act 2002;
(d) detention under section 36 of the UK Borders Act 2007.

Exclusions
(2) Sub-paragraph (1) is subject to the exclusions in Parts 2 and 3 of this Schedule.

Immigration: temporary admission
26 (1) Civil legal services provided in relation to temporary admission to the United Kingdom under–
(a) paragraph 21 of Schedule 2 to the Immigration Act 1971;
(b) section 62 of the Nationality, Immigration and Asylum Act 2002.

Exclusions
(2) Sub-paragraph (1) is subject to the exclusions in Parts 2 and 3 of this Schedule.

Immigration: residence etc restrictions
27 (1) Civil legal services provided in relation to restrictions imposed under–
(a) paragraph 2(5) or 4 of Schedule 3 to the Immigration Act 1971 (residence etc restrictions pending deportation);
(b) section 71 of the Nationality, Immigration and Asylum Act 2002 (residence etc restrictions on asylum-seekers).

Legal Aid, Sentencing and Punishment of Offenders Act 2021 Sch 1 651

Exclusions

(2) Sub-paragraph (1) is subject to the exclusions in Parts 2 and 3 of this Schedule.

Immigration: victims of domestic violence and indefinite leave to remain

28(1) Civil legal services provided to an individual ('V') in relation to an application by V for indefinite leave to remain in the United Kingdom on the grounds that–
 (a) V was given leave to enter or remain in the United Kingdom for a limited period as the partner of another individual present and settled in the United Kingdom, and
 (b) V's relationship with the other individual broke down permanently because V was the victim of domestic violence.

General exclusions

(2) Sub-paragraph (1) is subject to the exclusions in Parts 2 and 3 of this Schedule.

Specific exclusion

(3) The services described in sub-paragraph (1) do not include attendance at an interview conducted on behalf of the Secretary of State with a view to reaching a decision on an application.

Definitions

(4) For the purposes of this paragraph, one individual is a partner of another if–
 (a) they are married to each other,
 (b) they are civil partners of each other, or
 (c) they are cohabitants.

(5) In this paragraph–
 'cohabitant' has the same meaning as in Part 4 of the Family Law Act 1996 (see section 62 of that Act);
 'domestic violence' means any incident, or pattern of incidents, of controlling, coercive or threatening behaviour, violence or abuse (whether psychological, physical, sexual, financial or emotional) between individuals who are associated with each other (within the meaning of section 62 of the Family Law Act 1996);
 'indefinite leave to remain in the United Kingdom' means leave to remain in the United Kingdom under the Immigration Act 1971 which is not limited as to duration;
 'present and settled in the United Kingdom' has the same meaning as in the rules made under section 3(2) of the Immigration Act 1971.

Immigration: victims of domestic violence and residence cards

29(1) Civil legal services provided to an individual ('V') in relation to a residence card application where V–
 (a) has ceased to be a family member of a qualified person on the termination of the marriage or civil partnership of the qualified person,
 (b) is a family member who has retained the right of residence by virtue of satisfying the conditions in regulation 10(5) of the Immigration (European Economic Area) Regulations 2006 (S.I. 2006/1003) ('the 2006 Regulations'), and
 (c) has satisfied the condition in regulation 10(5)(d)(iv) of the 2006 Regulations on the ground that V or a family member of V was the victim

of domestic violence while the marriage or civil partnership of the qualified person was subsisting.

General exclusions
(2) Sub-paragraph (1) is subject to the exclusions in Parts 2 and 3 of this Schedule.

Specific exclusion
(3) The services described in sub-paragraph (1) do not include attendance at an interview conducted on behalf of the Secretary of State with a view to reaching a decision on an application.

Definitions
(4) In this paragraph–
'domestic violence' means any incident, or pattern of incidents, of controlling, coercive or threatening behaviour, violence or abuse (whether psychological, physical, sexual, financial or emotional) between individuals who are associated with each other (within the meaning of section 62 of the Family Law Act 1996);
'family member' has the same meaning as in the 2006 Regulations (see regulations 7 and 9);
'family member who has retained the right of residence' has the same meaning as in the 2006 Regulations (see regulation 10);
'qualified person' has the same meaning as in the 2006 Regulations (see regulation 6);
'residence card application' means–
(a) an application for a residence card under regulation 17 of the 2006 Regulations, or
(b) an application for a permanent residence card under regulation 18(2) of the 2006 Regulations.

Immigration: rights to enter and remain
30(1) Civil legal services provided in relation to rights to enter, and to remain in, the United Kingdom which–
(a) arise from–
(i) the Refugee Convention; or
(ii) Article 2 or 3 of the Human Rights Convention; or
(b) are conferred by–
(i) immigration rules, insofar as they implemented the Qualification Directive; or
(ii) any other provision of assimilated law which implemented the Qualification Directive.

General exclusions
(2) Sub-paragraph (1) is subject to the exclusions in Parts 2 and 3 of this Schedule.

Specific exclusion
(3) The services described in sub-paragraph (1) do not include attendance at an interview conducted on behalf of the Secretary of State with a view to reaching a decision on a claim in respect of the rights mentioned in that sub-paragraph, except where regulations provide otherwise.

Definitions

(4) In this paragraph–
'the Human Rights Convention' means the Convention for the Protection of Human Rights and Fundamental Freedoms, agreed by the Council of Europe at Rome on 4 November 1950 as it has effect for the time being in relation to the United Kingdom;
'immigration rules' has the meaning given by section 33(1) of the Immigration Act 1971;
'the Qualification Directive' means Council Directive 2004/83/EC of 29 April 2004 on minimum standards for the qualification and status of third country nationals or stateless persons as refugees or as persons who otherwise need international protection and the content of the protection granted;
'the Refugee Convention' means the Convention relating to the Status of Refugees done at Geneva on 28 July 1951 and the Protocol to the Convention;

. . .

Immigration: accommodation for asylum-seekers etc

31(1) Civil legal services provided in relation to the Secretary of State's powers to provide, or arrange for the provision of, accommodation under–
  (a) section 4 or 95 of the Immigration and Asylum Act 1999 (accommodation for persons temporarily admitted and asylum-seekers);
  (b) section 17 of the Nationality, Immigration and Asylum Act 2002 (support for destitute asylum-seekers).

Exclusions

(2) Sub-paragraph (1) is subject to the exclusions in Parts 2 and 3 of this Schedule.

Immigration, citizenship and nationality: separated children

31A (1) Civil legal services provided in relation to a relevant application where the services are provided to an individual who, at the time of applying for those services, is a separated child.

(2) A relevant application is–
  (a) an application made by the separated child or another person under the immigration rules for the grant of entry clearance, leave to enter or leave to remain in the United Kingdom (whether under or outside of the immigration rules),
  (b) an application made by the separated child outside of the immigration rules for the grant of leave to remain in the United Kingdom, or
  (c) an application made by the separated child for registration under the British Nationality Act 1981 as–
    (i) a British citizen,
    (ii) a British overseas territories citizen,
    (iii) a British Overseas citizen, or
    (iv) a British subject.

Exclusions

(3) Sub-paragraph (1) is subject to the exclusions in Parts 2 and 3 of this Schedule.

Definitions

(4) In this paragraph–
  'child' means an individual–
  (a) who is under the age of 18, or
  (b) whose age is uncertain, but who is treated by the Director as being under the age of 18;
  'entry clearance' has the same meaning as in the Immigration Act 1971;
  'immigration rules' has the same meaning as in the Immigration Act 1971;
  'leave to enter' and 'leave to remain' are to be construed in accordance with the Immigration Act 1971;
  'separated', in relation to a child, means–
  (a) not being cared for by a parent,
  (b) not being cared for by a person with parental responsibility for the child (within the meaning of section 3 of the Children Act 1989), or
  (c) looked after by a local authority (within the meaning of section 107(6)).

Victims of trafficking in human beings

32(1) Civil legal services provided to an individual in relation to an application by the individual for leave to enter, or to remain in, the United Kingdom where–
  (a) there has been a conclusive determination that the individual is a victim of trafficking in human beings, or
  (b) there are reasonable grounds to believe that the individual is such a victim and there has not been a conclusive determination that the individual is not such a victim.

(2) Civil legal services provided in relation to a claim under employment law arising in connection with the exploitation of an individual who is a victim of trafficking in human beings, but only where–
  (a) the services are provided to the individual, or
  (b) the individual has died and the services are provided to the individual's personal representative.

(3) Civil legal services provided in relation to a claim for damages arising in connection with the trafficking or exploitation of an individual who is a victim of trafficking in human beings, but only where–
  (a) the services are provided to the individual, or
  (b) the individual has died and the services are provided to the individual's personal representative.

Exclusions

(4) Sub-paragraph (1) is subject to the exclusions in Parts 2 and 3 of this Schedule.
(5) Sub-paragraphs (2) and (3) are subject to–
  (a) the exclusions in Part 2 of this Schedule, with the exception of paragraphs 1, 2, 3, 4, 5, 6 and 8 of that Part, and
  (b) the exclusion in Part 3 of this Schedule.

Definitions

(6) For the purposes of sub-paragraph (1)(b) there are reasonable grounds to believe that an individual is a victim of trafficking in human beings if a competent authority has determined for the purposes of Article 10 of the Trafficking Convention (identification of victims) that there are such grounds.
(7) For the purposes of sub-paragraph (1) there is a conclusive determination

Legal Aid, Sentencing and Punishment of Offenders Act 2021 Sch 1 655

that an individual is or is not a victim of trafficking in human beings when, on completion of the identification process required by Article 10 of the Trafficking Convention, a competent authority concludes that the individual is or is not such a victim.

(8) In this paragraph–

'competent authority' means a person who is a competent authority of the United Kingdom for the purposes of the Trafficking Convention;

'employment' means employment under a contract of employment or a contract personally to do work and references to 'employers' and 'employees' are to be interpreted accordingly;

'employment law' means an enactment or rule of law relating to employment, including in particular an enactment or rule of law conferring powers or imposing duties on employers, conferring rights on employees or otherwise regulating the relations between employers and employees;

'exploitation' means a form of exploitation described in section 3 of the Modern Slavery Act 2015 (meaning of exploitation for purposes of human trafficking offence in section 2 of that Act);

'personal representative', in relation to an individual who has died, means–
(a) a person responsible for administering the individual's estate under the law of England and Wales, Scotland or Northern Ireland, or
(b) a person who, under the law of another country or territory, has functions equivalent to those of administering the individual's estate;

'the Trafficking Convention' means the Council of Europe Convention on Action against Trafficking in Human Beings (done at Warsaw on 16 May 2005);

'trafficking in human beings' has the same meaning as in the Trafficking Convention.

Victims of slavery, servitude or forced or compulsory labour

32A (1) Civil legal services provided to an individual in relation to an application by the individual for leave to enter, or to remain in, the United Kingdom where–
(a) there has been a conclusive determination that the individual is a victim of slavery, servitude or forced or compulsory labour, or
(b) there are reasonable grounds to believe that the individual is such a victim and there has not been a conclusive determination that the individual is not such a victim.

(2) Civil legal services provided in relation to a claim under employment law arising in connection with the conduct by virtue of which an individual who is a victim of slavery, servitude or forced or compulsory labour is such a victim, but only where–
(a) the services are provided to the individual, or
(b) the individual has died and the services are provided to the individual's personal representative.

(3) Civil legal services provided in relation to a claim for damages arising in connection with the conduct by virtue of which an individual who is a victim of slavery, servitude or forced or compulsory labour is such a victim, but only where–
(a) the services are provided to the individual, or
(b) the individual has died and the services are provided to the individual's personal representative.

Exclusions

(4) Sub-paragraph (1) is subject to the exclusions in Parts 2 and 3 of this Schedule.
(5) Sub-paragraphs (2) and (3) are subject to–
   (a) the exclusions in Part 2 of this Schedule, with the exception of paragraphs 1, 2, 3, 4, 5, 6 and 8 of that Part, and
   (b) the exclusion in Part 3 of this Schedule.

Definitions

(6) For the purposes of sub-paragraph (1)(b) there are reasonable grounds to believe that an individual is a victim of slavery, servitude or forced or compulsory labour if a competent authority has determined that there are such grounds.
(7) For the purposes of sub-paragraph (1) there is a conclusive determination that an individual is or is not a victim of slavery, servitude or forced or compulsory labour when a competent authority concludes that the individual is or is not such a victim.
(8) For the purposes of this paragraph 'slavery', 'servitude' and 'forced or compulsory labour' have the same meaning as they have for the purposes of article 4 of the Human Rights Convention.
(9) The 'Human Rights Convention' means the Convention for the Protection of Human Rights and Fundamental Freedoms, agreed by the Council of Europe at Rome on 4 November 1950, as it has effect for the time being in relation to the United Kingdom.
(10) The definitions of 'competent authority', 'employment', 'employment law' and 'personal representative' in paragraph 32(8) also apply for the purposes of this paragraph.

Loss of home

33 (1) Civil legal services provided to an individual in relation to–
court orders for sale or possession of the individual's home, or
the eviction from the individual's home of the individual or others.
(1A) Civil legal services provided to an individual, where the Director has determined the individual qualifies for any services described in sub-paragraph (1) (and has not withdrawn the determination), in relation to–
   (a) housing matters;
   (b) debt;
   (c) a benefit, allowance, payment, credit or pension under–
      (i) a social security enactment;
      (ii) the Vaccine Damage Payments Act 1979;
      (iii) Part 4 of the Child Maintenance and Other Payments Act 2008;
   (d) a council tax reduction scheme.
(2) Civil legal services provided to an individual in relation to a bankruptcy order against the individual under Part 9 of the Insolvency Act 1986 where–
   (a) the individual's estate includes the individual's home, and
   (b) the petition for the bankruptcy order is or was presented by a person other than the individual,
   including services provided in relation to a statutory demand under that Part of that Act.

General exclusions
(3) Sub-paragraphs (1) and (2) are subject to the exclusions in Part 2 of this Schedule, with the exception of paragraph 14 of that Part.
(4) But the exclusions described in sub-paragraph (3) are subject to the exceptions in sub-paragraphs (5) and (6).
(5) The services described in sub-paragraph (1) include services provided in relation to proceedings on an application under the Trusts of Land and Appointment of Trustees Act 1996 to which section 335A of the Insolvency Act 1986 applies (application by trustee of bankrupt's estate).
(6) The services described in sub-paragraph (1) include services described in any of paragraphs 3 to 6 or 8 of Part 2 of this Schedule to the extent that they are–
  (a) services provided to an individual in relation to a counterclaim in proceedings for a court order for sale or possession of the individual's home, or
  (b) services provided to an individual in relation to the unlawful eviction from the individual's home of the individual or others.
(7) Sub-paragraphs (1) and (2) are subject to the exclusion in Part 3 of this Schedule.
(7A) Sub-paragraph (1A) is subject to the exclusions in Part 2 of this Schedule, with the exception of paragraphs 14 and 15 of that Part.

Specific exclusion
(8) The services described in sub-paragraph (1) do not include services provided in relation to–
  (a) proceedings under the Matrimonial Causes Act 1973;
  (b) proceedings under Chapters 2 and 3 of Part 2 of the Civil Partnership Act 2004 (dissolution, nullity and other proceedings and property and financial arrangements).
(8A) The services described in sub-paragraph (1A) do not include advocacy.

Definitions
(9) In this paragraph–
'council tax reduction scheme' has the meaning given in paragraph 8A(4);
'home', in relation to an individual, means the house, caravan, houseboat or other vehicle or structure that is the individual's only or main residence, subject to sub-paragraph (10);
'housing matters' means matters which concern–
  (i) the possession of, status of, terms of occupation, repair of, improvement of, quiet enjoyment of, or payment of rent or other charges for, an individual's home;
  (ii) the rights of leaseholders under the terms of their lease or under any statutory provision;
  (iii) the allocation and transfer of housing and the provision of sites for occupation,
but does not include disputes relating to any boundary of a property; 'social security enactment' has the meaning given in paragraph 8(3).
(10) References in this paragraph to an individual's home do not include a vehicle or structure occupied by the individual if–
  (a) there are no grounds on which it can be argued that the individual is occupying the vehicle or structure otherwise than as a trespasser, and
  (b) there are no grounds on which it can be argued that the individual's

occupation of the vehicle or structure began otherwise than as a trespasser.
(11) In sub-paragraphs (9) and (10), the references to a caravan, houseboat or other vehicle include the land on which it is located or to which it is moored.
(12) For the purposes of sub-paragraph (10) individuals occupying, or beginning occupation, of a vehicle or structure as a trespasser include individuals who do so by virtue of–
   (a) title derived from a trespasser, or
   (b) a licence or consent given by a trespasser or a person deriving title from a trespasser.
(13) For the purposes of sub-paragraph (10) an individual who is occupying a vehicle or structure as a trespasser does not cease to be a trespasser by virtue of being allowed time to leave the vehicle or structure.

Homelessness
34(1) Civil legal services provided to an individual who is homeless, or threatened with homelessness, in relation to the provision of accommodation and assistance for the individual under–
   (a) Part 6 of the Housing Act 1996 (allocation of housing accommodation);
   (b) Part 7 of that Act (homelessness).

Exclusions
(2) Sub-paragraph (1) is subject to the exclusions in Parts 2 and 3 of this Schedule.

Definitions
(3) In this paragraph 'homeless' and 'threatened with homelessness' have the same meaning as in section 175 of the Housing Act 1996.

Risk to health or safety in rented home
35(1) Civil legal services provided to an individual in relation to the removal or reduction of a serious risk of harm to the health or safety of the individual or a relevant member of the individual's family where–
   (a) the risk arises from a deficiency in the individual's home,
   (b) the individual's home is rented or leased from another person, and
   (c) the services are provided with a view to securing that the other person makes arrangements to remove or reduce the risk.

Exclusions
(2) Sub-paragraph (1) is subject to–
   (a) the exclusions in Part 2 of this Schedule, with the exception of paragraphs 6 and 8 of that Part, and
   (b) the exclusion in Part 3 of this Schedule.

Definitions
(3) For the purposes of this paragraph–
   (a) a child is a relevant member of an individual's family if the individual is the child's parent or has parental responsibility for the child;
   (b) an adult ('A') is a relevant member of an individual's family if–
      (i) they are relatives (whether of the full blood or half blood or by marriage or civil partnership) or cohabitants, and
      (ii) the individual's home is also A's home.

Legal Aid, Sentencing and Punishment of Offenders Act 2021 Sch 1 659

(4) In this paragraph–
'adult' means a person aged 18 or over; 'building' includes part of a building; 'child' means a person under the age of 18;
'cohabitant' has the same meaning as in Part 4 of the Family Law Act 1996 (see section 62(1) of that Act);
'deficiency' means any deficiency, whether arising as a result of the construction of a building, an absence of maintenance or repair, or otherwise;
'harm' includes temporary harm; 'health' includes mental health;
'home', in relation to an individual, means the house, caravan, houseboat or other vehicle or structure that is the individual's only or main residence, together with any garden or ground usually occupied with it.

Anti-social behaviour
36(1) Civil legal services provided to an individual in relation to an application for, or proceedings in respect of, an injunction against the individual under section 1 of the Anti-social Behaviour, Crime and Policing Act 2014.

Exclusions

(2) Sub-paragraph (1) is subject to the exclusions in Parts 2 and 3 of this Schedule.

Protection from harassment
37(1) Civil legal services provided in relation to–
(a) an injunction under section 3 or 3A of the Protection from Harassment Act 1997;
(b) the variation or discharge of a restraining order under section 5 or 5A of that Act.

Exclusions

(2) Sub-paragraph (1) is subject to the exclusions in Parts 2 and 3 of this Schedule.

Gang-related violence and drug-dealing activity
38(1) Civil legal services provided in relation to injunctions under Part 4 of the Policing and Crime Act 2009 (injunctions to prevent gang-related violence and drug-dealing activity).

Exclusions

(2) Sub-paragraph (1) is subject to the exclusions in Parts 2 and 3 of this Schedule.

Sexual offences
39(1) Civil legal services provided in relation to a sexual offence, but only where–
(a) the services are provided to the victim of the offence, or
(b) the victim of the offence has died and the services are provided to the victim's personal representative.

Exclusions

(2) Sub-paragraph (1) is subject to–
(a) the exclusions in Part 2 of this Schedule, with the exception of paragraphs 1, 2, 3, 8 and 12 of that Part, and
(b) the exclusion in Part 3 of this Schedule.

Definitions

(3) In this paragraph–
'personal representative', in relation to an individual who has died, means–

(a) a person responsible for administering the individual's estate under the law of England and Wales, Scotland or Northern Ireland, or
(b) a person who, under the law of another country or territory, has functions equivalent to those of administering the individual's estate;
'sexual offence' means–
(a) an offence under a provision of the Sexual Offences Act 2003 ('the 2003 Act'), . . .
(b) an offence under section 1 of the Protection of Children Act 1978 ('the 1978 Act') (indecent photographs of children), and
(c) an offence under section 2 of the Modern Slavery Act 2015 (human trafficking) committed with a view to exploitation that consists of or includes behaviour within section 3(3) of that Act (sexual exploitation).
(4) The references in sub-paragraph (1) to a sexual offence include–
 (a) incitement to commit a sexual offence,
 (b) an offence committed by a person under Part 2 of the Serious Crime Act 2007 (encouraging or assisting crime) in relation to which a sexual offence is the offence which the person intended or believed would be committed,
 (c) conspiracy to commit a sexual offence, and
 (d) an attempt to commit a sexual offence.
(5) In this paragraph references to a sexual offence include conduct which would be an offence under a provision of the 2003 Act or section 1 of the 1978 Act but for the fact that it took place before that provision or section came into force.
(6) Conduct falls within the definition of a sexual offence for the purposes of this paragraph whether or not there have been criminal proceedings in relation to the conduct and whatever the outcome of any such proceedings.

Proceeds of crime

40(1) Civil legal services provided in relation to–
 (a) restraint orders under section 41 of the Proceeds of Crime Act 2002 ('the 2002 Act') including orders under section 41(7) of that Act (orders for ensuring that restraint order is effective);
 (b) orders under section 47M of the 2002 Act (detention of property);
 (c) directions under section 54(3) of the 2002 Act (distribution of funds in the hands of a receiver);
 (d) directions under section 62 of the 2002 Act (action to be taken by receiver);
 (e) orders under section 67A of the 2002 Act (realising property), including directions under section 67D of that Act (distribution of proceeds of realisation);
 (f) orders under section 72 or 73 of the 2002 Act (compensation);
 (g) applications under section 351 of the 2002 Act (discharge or variation of a production order or order to grant entry);
 (h) applications under section 362 of the 2002 Act (discharge or variation of disclosure order);
 (i) applications under section 369 of the 2002 Act (discharge or variation of customer information order);
 (j) applications under section 375 of the 2002 Act (discharge or variation of account monitoring orders).

General exclusions
(2) Sub-paragraph (1) is subject to–
  (a) the exclusions in Part 2 of this Schedule, with the exception of paragraph 14 of that Part, and
  (b) the exclusion in Part 3 of this Schedule.

Specific exclusions
(3) Where a confiscation order has been made under Part 2 of the 2002 Act against a defendant, the services described in sub-paragraph (1) do not include services provided to the defendant in relation to–
  (a) directions under section 54(3) of that Act (distribution of funds in the hands of a receiver), or
  (b) directions under section 67D of that Act (distribution of proceeds of realisation),
  that relate to property recovered pursuant to the order.
(4) Where a confiscation order has been made under Part 2 of the 2002 Act against a defendant and varied under section 29 of that Act, the services described in sub-paragraph (1) do not include services provided in relation to an application by the defendant under section 73 of that Act (compensation).

Inquests
41(1) Civil legal services provided to an individual in relation to an inquest under the Coroners Act 1988 into the death of a member of the individual's family.

Exclusions
(2) Sub-paragraph (1) is subject to–
  (a) the exclusions in Part 2 of this Schedule, with the exception of paragraph 1 of that Part, and
  (b) the exclusion in Part 3 of this Schedule.

Definitions
(3) For the purposes of this paragraph an individual is a member of another individual's family if–
  (a) they are relatives (whether of the full blood or half blood or by marriage or civil partnership),
  (b) they are cohabitants (as defined in Part 4 of the Family Law Act 1996), or
  (c) one has parental responsibility for the other.

Environmental pollution
42(1) Civil legal services provided in relation to injunctions in respect of nuisance arising from prescribed types of pollution of the environment.

Exclusions
(2) Sub-paragraph (1) is subject to the exclusions in Parts 2 and 3 of this Schedule.

Equality
43(1) Civil legal services provided in relation to contravention of the Equality Act 2010 or a previous discrimination enactment.

Exclusions
(2) Sub-paragraph (1) is subject to–

(a) the exclusions in Part 2 of this Schedule, with the exception of paragraph 15 of that Part, and
(b) the exclusion in Part 3 of this Schedule.

Definitions

(3) In this paragraph 'previous discrimination enactment' means–
   (a) the Equal Pay Act 1970;
   (b) the Sex Discrimination Act 1975;
   (c) the Race Relations Act 1976;
   (d) the Disability Discrimination Act 1995;
   (e) the Employment Equality (Religion or Belief) Regulations 2003 (S.I. 2003/1660);
   (f) the Employment Equality (Sexual Orientation) Regulations 2003 (S.I. 2003/1661);
   (g) the Equality Act 2006;
   (h) the Employment Equality (Age) Regulations 2006 (S.I. 2006/1031);
   (i) the Equality Act (Sexual Orientation) Regulations 2007 (S.I. 2007/1263).
(4) The reference in sub-paragraph (1) to contravention of the Equality Act 2010 or a previous discrimination enactment includes–
   (a) breach of a term modified by, or included by virtue of, a provision that is an equality clause or equality rule for the purposes of the Equal Pay Act 1970 or the Equality Act 2010, and
   (b) breach of a provision that is a non-discrimination rule for the purposes of the Equality Act 2010.

Cross-border disputes

44 . . .

Terrorism prevention and investigation measures etc

45(1) Civil legal services provided to an individual in relation to a TPIM notice relating to the individual.
(2) Civil legal services provided to an individual in relation to control order proceedings relating to the individual.

Exclusions

(3) Sub-paragraphs (1) and (2) are subject to the exclusions in Parts 2 and 3 of this Schedule.
(4) In this paragraph–
   'control order proceedings' means proceedings described in paragraph 3(1)(a) to (e) of Schedule 8 to the Terrorism Prevention and Investigation Measures Act 2011 ('the 2011 Act');
   'TPIM notice' means a notice under section 2(1) of the 2011 Act.

Extension of time for retention of travel documents

45A (1) Civil legal services provided in relation to proceedings under paragraph 8 of Schedule 1 to the Counter-Terrorism and Security Act 2015.

Exclusions

(2) Sub-paragraph (1) is subject to the exclusions in Parts 2 and 3 of this Schedule.

Foreign power threat activity prevention and investigation measures

45B (1) Civil legal services provided to an individual in relation to a notice under section 39(1) of the National Security Act 2023 relating to the individual.
(2) Sub-paragraph (1) is subject to–

(a) the exclusions in Part 2 of this Schedule, with the exception of paragraph 18 of that Part, and
(b) the exclusion in Part 3 of this Schedule.

Connected matters

46(1) Prescribed civil legal services provided, in prescribed circumstances, in connection with the provision of services described in a preceding paragraph of this Part of this Schedule.

Exclusions

(2) Sub-paragraph (1) is subject to—
(a) the exclusions in Parts 2 and 3 of this Schedule, except to the extent that regulations under this paragraph provide otherwise, and
(b) any other prescribed exclusions.

PART 2: EXCLUDED SERVICES

The services described in Part 1 of this Schedule do not include the services listed in this Part of this Schedule, except to the extent that Part 1 of this Schedule provides otherwise.

1. Civil legal services provided in relation to personal injury or death.
2. Civil legal services provided in relation to a claim in tort in respect of negligence.
3. Civil legal services provided in relation to a claim in tort in respect of assault, battery or false imprisonment.
4. Civil legal services provided in relation to a claim in tort in respect of trespass to goods.
5. Civil legal services provided in relation to a claim in tort in respect of trespass to land.
6. Civil legal services provided in relation to damage to property.
7. Civil legal services provided in relation to defamation or malicious falsehood.
8. Civil legal services provided in relation to a claim in tort in respect of breach of statutory duty.
9. Civil legal services provided in relation to conveyancing.
10. Civil legal services provided in relation to the making of wills.
11. Civil legal services provided in relation to matters of trust law.
12 (1) Civil legal services provided in relation to a claim for damages in respect of a breach of Convention rights by a public authority to the extent that the claim is made in reliance on section 7 of the Human Rights Act 1998.

(2) In this paragraph—
'Convention rights' has the same meaning as in the Human Rights Act 1998;
'public authority' has the same meaning as in section 6 of that Act.

13. Civil legal services provided in relation to matters of company or partnership law.
14. Civil legal services provided to an individual in relation to matters arising out of or in connection with—
(a) a proposal by that individual to establish a business,

(b) the carrying on of a business by that individual (whether or not the business is being carried on at the time the services are provided), or
(c) the termination or transfer of a business that was being carried on by that individual.

15 (1) Civil legal services provided in relation to a benefit, allowance, payment, credit or pension under–
   (a) a social security enactment,
   (b) the Vaccine Damage Payments Act 1979, or
   (c) Part 4 of the Child Maintenance and Other Payments Act 2008.
   (2) In this paragraph 'social security enactment' means–
   (a) the Social Security Contributions and Benefits Act 1992,
   (b) the Jobseekers Act 1995,
   (c) the State Pension Credit Act 2002,
   (d) the Tax Credits Act 2002,
   (e) the Welfare Reform Act 2007,
   (f) the Welfare Reform Act 2012, or
   (g) any other enactment relating to social security.

16 Civil legal services provided in relation to compensation under the Criminal Injuries Compensation Scheme.

17 Civil legal services provided in relation to changing an individual's name.

18 (1) Civil legal services provided in relation to judicial review of an enactment, decision, act or omission.
   (2) In this paragraph ' judicial review ' means–
   (a) the procedure on an application for judicial review (see section 31 of the Senior Courts Act 1981), but not including the procedure after the application is treated under rules of court as if it were not such an application, and
   (b) any procedure in which a court, tribunal or other person mentioned in Part 3 of this Schedule is required by an enactment to make a decision applying the principles that are applied by the court on an application for judicial review.

PART 3: ADVOCACY: EXCLUSION AND EXCEPTIONS

The services described in Part 1 of this Schedule do not include advocacy, except as follows–
(a) those services include the types of advocacy listed in this Part of this Schedule, except to the extent that Part 1 of this Schedule provides otherwise;
(b) those services include other types of advocacy to the extent that Part 1 of this Schedule so provides.

Exceptions: courts

1 Advocacy in proceedings in the Supreme Court.
2 Advocacy in proceedings in the Court of Appeal.
3 Advocacy in proceedings in the High Court.
4 Advocacy in proceedings in the Court of Protection to the extent that they concern–
   (a) a person's right to life,
   (b) a person's liberty or physical safety,
   (c) a person's medical treatment (within the meaning of the Mental Health Act 1983),

(d) a person's capacity to marry, to enter into a civil partnership or to enter into sexual relations, or
(e) a person's right to family life.
5 Advocacy in proceedings in the county court.
5A Advocacy in proceedings in the family court.
6 Advocacy in the following proceedings in the Crown Court–
(a) proceedings for the variation or discharge of an order under section 360 of the Sentencing Code or section 5A of the Protection from Harassment Act 1997, . . .
(aa) proceedings on an appeal under section 10(1)(b) of the Crime and Disorder Act 1998(1) against the making of a parenting order where an injunction is granted under section 1 of the Anti-social Behaviour, Crime and Policing Act 2014,
(b) proceedings under the Proceeds of Crime Act 2002 in relation to matters listed in paragraph 40 of Part 1 of this Schedule.
(c) proceedings on an appeal under section 46B of the Policing and Crime Act 2009, . . .
(d) proceedings on an appeal under section 15 of the Anti-social Behaviour, Crime and Policing Act 2014 . . .
(e) proceedings for the variation or discharge of an order under paragraph 1 of Schedule 2 to the Female Genital Mutilation Act 2003, and
(f) proceedings on an appeal under section 46(1) or (5) of the Domestic Abuse Act 2021.
7 Advocacy in a magistrates' court that falls within the description of civil legal services in any of the following provisions of Part 1 of this Schedule–
(a) paragraph 1(1)(e)
(b) paragraph 1(2) so far as relating to paragraph (1)(1)(e),
(ba) paragraph 11(1A)(a) and, in so far as it relates to a domestic abuse protection order made under section 28 of the Domestic Abuse Act 2021, paragraph 11(1A)(c), and
(c) paragraphs 11(2), 12, 13(1)(e), 15, 17 (1)(a) and (b), 36 and 38.
8 Advocacy in the following proceedings in a magistrates' court–
(a) . . .
(b) proceedings in relation to–
(i) bail under Schedule 2 to the Immigration Act 1971, or
(ii) arrest under Schedule 2 or 3 to that Act,
(c) proceedings for the variation or discharge of an order under section 360 of the Sentencing Code or section 5A of the Protection from Harassment Act 1997, . . .
(d) proceedings under the Proceeds of Crime Act 2002 in relation to matters listed in paragraph 40 of Part 1 of this Schedule; and
(e) proceedings for the variation or discharge of an order under paragraph 1 of Schedule 2 to the Female Genital Mutilation Act 2003.

Exceptions: tribunals
9 Advocacy in proceedings in the First-tier Tribunal under–
(a) the Mental Health Act 1983, or
(b) paragraph 5(2) of the Schedule to the Repatriation of Prisoners Act 1984.
10 Advocacy in proceedings in the Mental Health Review Tribunal for Wales.

11 Advocacy in proceedings in the First-tier Tribunal under–
    (a) Schedule 2 to the Immigration Act 1971, or
    (b) Part 5 of the Nationality, Immigration and Asylum Act 2002.
12 Advocacy in proceedings in the First-tier Tribunal under–
    (a) section 40A of the British Nationality Act 1981, or
    (b) regulation 26 of the Immigration (European Economic Area) Regulations 2006 (S.I. 2006/1003),
    but only to the extent that the proceedings concern contravention of the Equality Act 2010.
13 Advocacy in the First-tier Tribunal that falls within the description of civil legal services in paragraph 28, 29, 31A, or, 32(1) or 32A(1) of Part 1 of this Schedule.
14 Advocacy in proceedings in the First-tier Tribunal under–
    (a) section 4 or 4A of the Protection of Children Act 1999 (appeals and applications relating to list of barred from regulated activities with children or vulnerable adults),
    (b) section 86 or 87 of the Care Standards Act 2000 (appeals and applications relating to list of persons unsuitable to work with vulnerable adults),
    (c) section 32 of the Criminal Justice and Court Services Act 2000 (applications relating to disqualification orders), or
    (d) section 144 of the Education Act 2002 (appeals and reviews relating to direction prohibiting person from teaching etc).
15 Advocacy in proceedings in the Upper Tribunal arising out of proceedings within any of paragraphs 9 to 14 of this Part of this Schedule.
16 Advocacy in proceedings in the Upper Tribunal under section 4 of the Safeguarding Vulnerable Groups Act 2006.
17 Advocacy in proceedings in the Upper Tribunal under section 11 of the Tribunals, Courts and Enforcement Act 2007 (appeals on a point of law) from decisions made by the First-tier Tribunal or the Education Tribunal for Wales in proceedings under–
    (a) Part 2 of the Additional Learning Needs and Education Tribunal (Wales) Act 2018,
    (b) the Equality Act 2010, or
    (c) Part 3 of the Children and Families Act 2014(6) (children and young people in England with special educational needs or disabilities).
18 Advocacy in proceedings which are brought before the Upper Tribunal (wholly or primarily) to exercise its judicial review jurisdiction under section 15 of the Tribunals, Courts and Enforcement Act 2007.
19 Advocacy where judicial review applications are transferred to the Upper Tribunal from the High Court under section 31A of the Senior Courts Act 1981.
20 Advocacy in proceedings in the Employment Appeal Tribunal, but only to the extent that the proceedings concern contravention of the Equality Act 2010.

Other exceptions
21 Advocacy in proceedings in the Special Immigration Appeals Commission.
22 Advocacy in proceedings in the Proscribed Organisations Appeal Commission.

22A   Advocacy in proceedings before a District Judge (Magistrates' Courts) under paragraph 8 of Schedule 1 to the Counter-Terrorism and Security Act 2015.
23   Advocacy in legal proceedings before any person to whom a case is referred (in whole or in part) in any proceedings within any other paragraph of this Part of this Schedule.
24   Advocacy in bail proceedings before any court which are related to proceedings within any other paragraph of this Part of this Schedule.
25   Advocacy in proceedings before any person for the enforcement of a decision in proceedings within any other paragraph of this Part of this Schedule.

PART 4: INTERPRETATION

1   For the purposes of this Part of this Act, civil legal services are described in Part 1 of this Schedule if they are described in one of the paragraphs of that Part (other than in an exclusion), even if they are (expressly or impliedly) excluded from another paragraph of that Part.
2   References in this Schedule to an Act or instrument, or a provision of an Act or instrument—
   (a) are references to the Act, instrument or provision as amended from time to time, and
   (b) include the Act, instrument or provision as applied by another Act or instrument (with or without modifications).
3   References in this Schedule to services provided in relation to an act, omission or other matter of a particular description (however expressed) include services provided in relation to an act, omission or other matter alleged to be of that description.
4   References in this Schedule to services provided in relation to proceedings, orders and other matters include services provided when such proceedings, orders and matters are contemplated.
5 (1) Where a paragraph of Part 1 or 2 of this Schedule describes services that consist of or include services provided in relation to proceedings, the description is to be treated as including, in particular—
   (a) services provided in relation to related bail proceedings,
   (b) services provided in relation to preliminary or incidental proceedings,
   (c) services provided in relation to a related appeal or reference to a court, tribunal or other person, and
   (d) services provided in relation to the enforcement of decisions in the proceedings.
  (2) Where a paragraph of Part 3 of this Schedule describes advocacy provided in relation to particular proceedings in or before a court, tribunal or other person, the description is to be treated as including services provided in relation to preliminary or incidental proceedings in or before the same court, tribunal or other person.
  (3) Regulations may make provision specifying whether proceedings are or are not to be regarded as preliminary or incidental for the purposes of this paragraph.
6   For the purposes of this Schedule, regulations may make provision about—
   (a) when services are provided in relation to a matter;
   (b) when matters arise under a particular enactment;
   (c) when proceedings are proceedings under a particular enactment;

(d) when proceedings are related to other proceedings.
7   In this Schedule 'enactment' includes–
    (a) an enactment contained in subordinate legislation (within the meaning of the Interpretation Act 1978), and
    (b) an enactment contained in, or in an instrument made under, an Act or Measure of the National Assembly for Wales.

APPENDIX B

Standard Civil Contract 2024 Category Definitions

CATEGORY DEFINITIONS 2024

Introduction

1. These are the Category Definitions 2024 as referred to in the 2024 Standard Civil Contract. Definitions of terms set out in those Contracts also apply to these Category Definitions.
2. In these Category Definitions:
   (a) References to 'Legal Help' include Help at Court and in the Family Category only, Family Help (Lower) and Help with Family Mediation;
   (b) References to 'proceedings in a Category' cover the provision of Legal Representation (including Controlled Legal Representation) in that Category and, in the Family Category only, Family Help (Higher).
3. Services within the Crime Category are automatically excluded from all Civil Categories, except for the specific overlaps between Categories specified at paragraph 18 of this document.

Legal Aid, Sentencing and Punishment of Offenders Act 2012

4. The Legal Aid, Sentencing and Punishment of Offenders Act 2012 (hereafter referred to as 'the Act' in this document) sets out the matters for which civil and criminal legal services may be provided.
5. The Category Definitions show into which Category cases will fall but providers will need to satisfy themselves before undertaking work for any individual client that it is within the scope of the Act or that an application for exceptional funding has been approved.
6. Descriptions in this document of matters within scope of Part 1 of Schedule 1 to the Act should be read subject to the full provisions in that Part. For example, services referred to in Part 1 of Schedule 1 to the Act may be subject to exclusions in Parts 2 and 3 of Schedule 1 to the Act.

   Where a specific paragraph of Part 1 of Schedule 1 to the Act is referred to in a Category Definition then the services covered by that Category are at most only as wide as described in the given paragraph. For example, paragraph 39(a) of Immigration Category Definition allows the detention matters listed in paragraph 25 of Part 1 of Schedule 1 to fall within Immigration but not damages claims arising from such detention.

Exceptional Funding

7. Civil legal services that do not fall within the scope of Part 1 of Schedule 1 to the Act will fall to be funded under section 10 if the Director makes either: (i) an exceptional case determination (under section 10(2)(a) of the Act), or (ii) a wider public interest determination (under section 10(4)(b) of the Act).
8. Matters that are funded by virtue of a determination of the Director under section 10 of the Act will fall within the Category to which the primary problem or issue relates or, in the case of matters that are wholly unrelated to in-scope categories will be classed as Miscellaneous Work. The extent to which a Category of Law encompasses services made available under section 10 of the Act is set out within each individual Category Definition.

Overlaps between Categories

9. The Categories are drafted to ensure that the majority of cases clearly fall within one Category or another. However, there will be some cases which genuinely fall within more than one Category. For example, certain work under the Mental Capacity Act 2005 falls under both the Mental Health Category of Law and Community Care.
10. Some cases will arise as the result of a number of different underlying issues, which may either be in scope or the subject of an exceptional funding application, and in those instances classification to a Category will depend upon the overall substance or predominant issue of the case when taken as a whole.
11. The following civil legal services fall into the Category of Law that relates to the underlying substance of the case as referenced by the widest Category Definition:
    (a) Public law challenges to the acts, omissions or decisions of public bodies by way of judicial review (as described in paragraph 19 of Part 1 of Schedule 1 to the Act). These cases are also covered by the Public Law Category
    (b) Civil legal services provided in relation to a writ of habeas corpus ad subjiciendum (as described in paragraph 20 of Part 1 of Schedule 1 to the Act). These cases are also covered by the Public Law Category
    (c) Cases involving a contravention of the Equality Act 2010 or previous discrimination enactment (as described in paragraph 43 of Part 1 of Schedule 1 to the Act). These cases are also covered by the Discrimination category.
12. For the purposes of paragraph 11, the widest Category Definition includes those services that can only be made available via exceptional funding. For example, a judicial review would fall into the Housing Category of Law where the challenge was related to issues described in either paragraph 37 or 38 of the Housing Category Definition.

Damages under the Human Rights Act 1998

13. There are special provisions for claims for damages under the Human Rights Act 1998 (to the extent these are in scope by virtue of paragraphs 21 or 22 of Part 1 of Schedule 1 to the Act). A claim for damages made in reliance on section 7(1)(b) of the 1998 Act within existing proceedings described in Part 1 of Schedule 1 to the Act falls exclusively within the Category of Law that includes the primary proceedings being heard.

14. Except as specified at paragraph 15 below, other claims for damages under the Human Rights Act 1998 fall exclusively within either the Claims Against Public Authorities Category of Law or the Public Law Category (depending on the facts of the claim). This includes damages claims made within proceedings that are not otherwise described in Part 1 of Schedule 1 to the Act except under paragraph 21 or 22, and all freestanding claims for damages under section 7(1)(a) of the 1998 Act.
15. Finally, some cases are included within both the Family Category of Law and the Public Law Category. These are claims for damages brought under the Human Rights Act 1998 where the breach, or alleged breach, of a Convention right relates to an act, decision or omission of a local authority in relation to the care, supervision or protection of a child. Such claims may also fall into the Claims Against Public Authorities Category where the proceedings are described by paragraph 20 to 21 below.

Inquests

16. Civil legal services in relation to an inquest under the Coroners Act 1988 will fall into the Category of Law which relates most closely to the underlying subject matter of the inquest, taking into the specific legal issues that will be raised in the inquiry, the place and manner of the individual's death, and the classification of any separate proceedings that are dependent on the outcome of the inquest.
17. As with paragraphs 10-11 above, the widest definition of each Category should be used to determine classification of the case, including services that can only be provided via exceptional funding. For example, Legal Help for an inquest where the client died in prison will be funded in the Claims Against Public Authorities Category of Law given that this Category includes all matters relating to 'death in custody' (see paragraphs 20 to 21 below). Where an inquest does not fall within one of the Categories, it will be classified as Miscellaneous Work.

Minor Civil/Criminal Overlaps

18. Work falling within the Crime Category is generally excluded from any civil Category, but there are some minor exceptions:
    (a) Enforcement proceedings in the magistrates court arising out of the breach of an order of that court made in family proceedings where there is a risk of imprisonment also fall within the Family Category;
    (b) Civil proceedings in the magistrates' court arising out of the breach of a financial order of that court where there is a risk of imprisonment also fall within the Debt Category;
    (c) Proceedings against a child for a Sexual Harm Prevention Order and any associated Parenting Order, and for a Parenting Order made on the conviction of a child where the parent cannot be reasonably represented by the child's solicitor also fall within the Family Category; and,
    (d) Committal applications for civil contempt of court arising out of proceedings described in Part 1 of Schedule 1 also fall under the civil Category of Law covering the underlying proceedings, or where the underlying proceedings do not fall within a Category of Law, are classified as Miscellaneous Work.
19. The exceptions in paragraph 18 can be carried out under the 2024 Standard Civil Contract as well as by criminal practitioners under the 2022 Standard Crime Contract.

Claims Against Public Authorities

20. Legal Help and all proceedings in relation to:
    (a) abuse of a child or a vulnerable adult (as described in paragraph 3 of Part 1 of Schedule 1 to the Act
    (b) abuse of position or power by a public authority (as described in paragraph 21 of Part 1 of Schedule 1 to the Act
    (c) significant breach of convention rights by a public authority (as described in paragraph 22 of Part 1 of Schedule 1 to the Act)
    (d) sexual offences (as described in paragraph 39 of Part 1 of Schedule 1 to the Act) to the extent specified in paragraph 21.
21. A case listed in paragraph 20 will only fall within the Claims Against Public Authorities Category where at least one of the following conditions apply:
    (a) The defendant is a public authority with the power to prosecute, detain or imprison and the claim arises out of, or is closely related to, the exercise of such a power; or,
    (b) The claim is for personal injury based on allegations of deliberate abuse of a person while in the care of a public authority or other institution, or the failure of such a body to take a person into care.
22. To the extent that any relevant grant of exceptional funding is made (in accordance with section 10 of the Act) this Category also includes all other Legal Help and related proceedings concerning assault, trespass, false imprisonment, wrongful arrest, interference with goods, malicious prosecution, personal injury, wrongful conviction or death in custody, misfeasance in public office or other abuse of authority or neglect of duty against any body or person, private or public, with the power to detain, imprison or prosecute and the claim arises out of, or is closely related, to the exercise of such a power.

Clinical Negligence Category

23. Legal Help and all proceedings in relation to a claim for damages in respect of clinical negligence which caused a neurological injury to an infant as a result of which they are now severely disabled (as described in paragraph 23(1) of Part 1 of Schedule 1 to the Act).
24. To the extent that any relevant grant of exceptional funding is made (in accordance with section 10 of the Act) this Category also includes Legal Help and all proceedings in relation to a claim for damages or a complaint to a relevant professional body in respect of an alleged breach of duty of care or trespass to the person committed in the course of the provision of clinical or medical services (including dental or nursing services); or a claim for damages in respect of alleged professional negligence in the conduct of such a claim.

Community Care

25. Legal Help and related proceedings in relation to:
    (a) the provision of community care services (as described in paragraph 6 of Part 1 of Schedule 1 to the Act);
    (b) the provision of facilities for disabled persons (as described in paragraph 7 of Part 1 of Schedule 1 to the Act); and,
    (c) the inherent jurisdiction of the High Court in relation to vulnerable adults (as described in paragraph 9 of Part 1 of Schedule 1 to the Act);

Standard Civil Contract 2024 Category Definitions 673

(d) the inherent jurisdiction of the High Court in relation to children (as described in paragraph 9 of Part 1 of Schedule 1 to the Act) where the case relates to a decision on medical treatment; and

(e) a person's capacity, their best interests (health and welfare), and deprivation of liberty issues under the Mental Capacity Act 2005 (as described in subparagraph 5(1)(c) of Part 1 of Schedule 1 to the Act).

26. To the extent that any relevant grant of exceptional funding is made (in accordance with section 10 of the Act), this category also includes all other Legal Help and related proceedings concerning the provision of services or facilities in the community, nursing accommodation or hospital arranged by social services or a public health authority, excluding services falling within the Welfare Benefits or Clinical Negligence Categories. It also covers advocacy in the Court of Protection for matters arising under the Mental Capacity Act 2005 listed at paragraph 25(e) above that are not described by paragraph 4 of Part 3 of Schedule1.

Debt

27. Legal Help and all proceedings in relation to:
    (a) Court orders for sale of an individual's home (as described in 33(1)(a) of Part 1 of Schedule 1 to the Act);
    (b) Court orders for possession of an individual's home arising out of failure to make payment due under a mortgage (as described in paragraph 33(1)(a) of Part 1 of Schedule 1 to the Act)[1]; and,
    (c) A bankruptcy order against the individual under Part 9 of the Insolvency Act 1986 where the estate includes the individual's home and where the petition for bankruptcy was not presented by the client, including in relation to a statutory demand under Part 9 of that Act (as described in paragraph 33(2) of Part 1 to Schedule 1 to the Act).

28. To the extent that any relevant grant of exceptional funding is made (in accordance with section 10 of the Act), this category includes Legal Help and all proceedings:
    (a) For the payment of monies due or the enforcement of orders in such proceedings (excluding any matter which falls within the Housing Category); and,
    (b) Arising out of personal insolvency, including bankruptcy, administration, Debt Relief representation or IVA proceedings, but excluding representation in proceedings against parties in default of a fine or other order in criminal proceedings in the magistrates' court who are at risk of imprisonment.

Discrimination

29. Legal Help and proceedings in relation to:
    (a) Contravention of the Equality Act 2010 (as described in paragraph 43(1) of Part 1 of Schedule 1 to the Act);
    (b) Contravention of a previous discrimination enactment (as described in paragraph 43(3) of Part 1 of Schedule 1 to the Act), namely;
        i. The Equal Pay Act 1970;

---

1 Possession of the home arising out of any matter other than failure to make payments on a mortgage fall within the Housing Category.

ii. The Sex Discrimination Act 1976;
  iii. The Race Relations Act 1976;
  iv. The Disability Discrimination Act 1995;
  v. The Employment Equality (Religion or Belief) Regulations 2003 (S.I. 2003/1660);

Education

30. Legal Help and all proceedings in relation to:
    (a) matters arising under Part 4 of the Education Act 1996 (Special Educational Needs) (as described in subparagraph 2(1)(a) of Part 1 of Schedule 1 to the Act);
    (b) matters arising under Part 3 of the Children and Families Act 2014 (as described in subparagraph 2(1)(a) of Part 1 of Schedule 1 to the Act);
    (c) assessments relating to learning difficulties under sections 140 of the Learning and Skills Act 2000 (as described in subparagraph 2(1)(b) of Part 1 of Schedule 1 to the Act); and,
    (d) any other matter within the scope of Part 1 of Schedule 1 to the Act where the primary problem or issue relates to the provision of, or failure to provide, education or funding for education.
31. For the avoidance of doubt, the Education Category includes brief advice and assistance on the social care provision and health care provision that have been included, or ought to be included, in an Education, Health and Care plan prepared under section 37 of the Children and Families Act 2014. However, where substantive advice is required to resolve any dispute concerning such provision this work falls under Community Care.
32. To the extent that exceptional funding is granted (in accordance with section 10 of the Act) this category includes all other Legal Help and proceedings in relation to any matter where the primary problem or issue relates to the provision of or failure to provide education or funding for education.

Family

33. Legal Help and all proceedings in relation to:
    (a) orders under section 25 of the Children Act 1989 (as described in subparagraph 1(1)(a) of Part 1 of Schedule 1 to the Act);
    (b) orders under Part 4 and Part 5 of the Children Act 1989 Act (as described in subparagraphs 1(1)(b) and 1(1)(c) of Part 1 of Schedule 1 to the Act);
    (c) approval by a court under paragraph 19 of Schedule 2 to the Children Act 1989 Act (as described in subparagraphs 1(1)(d) of Part 1 of Schedule 1 to the Act);
    (d) parenting orders under sections 8 of the Crime and Disorder Act 1998 (as described in subparagraphs 1(1)(e) of Part 1 of Schedule 1 to the Act);
    (e) child safety orders under section 11 of the Crime and Disorder Act 1998 (as described in subparagraphs 1(1)(f) of Part 1 of Schedule 1 to the Act);
    (f) applications under the Adoption and Children Act 2002 (as described in subparagraphs 1(1)(g) to 1(1)(j) of Part 1 of Schedule 1 to the Act);
    (g) orders under an enactment made as an alternative to an order mentioned in subparagraphs (a) to (f) above (as described in subparagraph 1(2) of Part 1 of Schedule 1 to the Act);
    (h) orders under an enactment made in proceedings heard together with proceedings relating to an order mentioned in subparagraphs (a) to (f)

above (as described in subparagraph 1(2) of Part 1 of Schedule 1 to the Act);
(i) the inherent jurisdiction of the High Court in relation to children (as described in paragraph 9 of Part 1 of Schedule 1 to the Act);
(j) the orders and requirements listed in subparagraph 10(1) of Part 1 of Schedule 1 to the Act in relation to unlawful removal or potential unlawful removal of children from the United Kingdom;
(k) the orders and applications listed in subparagraph 10(2) of Part 1 of Schedule 1 to the Act in relation to the return of children unlawfully removed to a place in the United Kingdom;
(l) home rights, occupation orders and non-molestation orders under Part 4 of the Family Law Act 1996 (as described in paragraph 11(1) of Part 1 of Schedule 1 to the Act);
(m) injunctions following assault, battery and false imprisonment in circumstances arising out of a family relationship (as described in paragraph 11(2)(a) of Part 1 of Schedule 1 to the Act);
(n) the protection of an adult in proceedings under the inherent jurisdiction of the High Court in circumstances arising out of a family relationship (as described in paragraph 11(2)(b) of Part 1 of Schedule 1 to the Act);
(o) the mediation of family disputes (as described in subparagraph 14(2) of Part 1 of Schedule 1 to the Act);
(p) services provided to a child under paragraph 15 of Part 1 of Schedule 1 to the Act in relation to family proceedings where the child:
  i. is, or proposes to be, the applicant or respondent;
  ii. is made a party to the proceedings by a court under rule 16.2 of the Family Procedure Rules; or
  iii. is a party to the proceedings and is conducting, or proposing to conduct, the proceedings themselves in accordance with rule 16.6 of the Family Procedure Rules;
(q) female genital mutilation protection orders under paragraph 1 of Schedule 2 to the Female Genital Mutilation Act 2003 (as described in paragraph 15A of Part 1 of Schedule 1 to the Act);
(r) forced marriage protection orders under Part 4A of the Family Law Act 1996 (as described in paragraph 16 of Part 1 of Schedule 1 to the Act);
(s) the following EU and international agreements concerning children (as described in paragraph 17 of Part 1 of Schedule 1 to the Act):
  i. an application made to the Lord Chancellor under the 1980 European Convention on Child Custody for the recognition or enforcement in England and Wales of a decision relating to the custody of a child;
  ii. an application made to the Lord Chancellor under the 1980 Hague Convention in respect of a child who is, or is believed to be, in England and Wales;
  iii. the recognition or enforcement of a judgment in England and Wales in accordance with Article 21, 28, 41, 42 or 48 of the 2003 Brussels Regulation.
(t) the following EU and international agreements in relation to an application for the recognition or enforcement in England and Wales of a maintenance order (as described in paragraph 18 of Part 1 of Schedule 1 to the Act):

i. the 1968 Brussels Convention;
ii. the 1973 Hague Convention;
iii. the 1989 Lugano Convention;
iv. the 2000 Brussels Regulation;
v. the 2007 Lugano Convention;
vi. the EU Maintenance Regulation;
vii. the 2007 Hague Convention;
(u) Proceedings under section 3, 3A, 5 or 5A of the Protection from Harassment Act 1997 (as described in paragraph 37 of Part 1 of Schedule 1 to the Act) arising out of a family relationship.
34. Legal Help and all proceedings in relation to matters arising out of a family relationship where the client has been, or is at risk of being, a victim domestic violence (as described by paragraph 12 of Part 1 of Schedule 1 of Part 1 to the Act), including matters under the following enactments:
(a) section 17 of the Married Women's Property Act 1882;
(b) the Maintenance Orders (Facilities for Enforcement) Act 1920;
(c) the Maintenance Orders Act 1950;
(d) the Maintenance Orders Act 1958;
(e) the Maintenance Orders (Reciprocal Enforcement) Act 1972;
(f) Schedule 1 to the Domicile and Matrimonial Proceedings Act 1973 (staying of matrimonial proceedings) and corresponding provision in relation to civil partnerships made by rules of court under section 223 of the Civil Partnership Act 2004;
(g) the Matrimonial Causes Act 1973;
(h) the Inheritance (Provision for Family Dependants) Act 1975;
(i) the Domestic Proceedings and Magistrates' Courts Act 1978;
(j) Part 3 of the Matrimonial and Family Proceedings Act 1984;
(k) Parts 1 and 3 of the Family Law Act 1986;
(l) Parts 1 and 2 of the Children Act 1989;
(m) section 53 of, and Schedule 7 to, the Family Law Act 1996;
(n) Chapters 2 and 3 of Part 2 of the Civil Partnership Act 2004;
(o) section 54 of the Human Fertilisation and Embryology Act 2008
(p) section 51A of the Adoption and Children Act 2002
(q) applications for an order under section 14 of the Trusts of Land and Appointment of Trustees Act 1996 arising out of a family relationship
35. Legal Help and all proceedings in relation to the following orders and procedures where the child involved is at risk of abuse (as described in paragraph 13 of Part of Schedule 1 to the Act):
(a) orders under section 4(2A) of the Children Act 1989 (removal of father's parental responsibility);
(b) orders under section 6(7) of the Children Act 1989 (termination of appointment of guardian);
(c) orders mentioned in section 8(1) of the Children Act 1989 (child arrangement orders and other orders);
(d) special guardianship orders under Part 2 of the Children Act 1989;
(e) orders under section 33 of the Family Law Act 1986 (disclosure of child's whereabouts);
(f) orders under section 34 of the Family Law Act 1986 (return of child)

(g) orders under section 51A of the Adoption and Children Act 2002 (post-adoption contact)
36. To the extent that any relevant grant of exceptional funding is made (in accordance with section 10 of the Act) this Category also includes all other Legal Help and related proceedings arising out of family relationships, including proceedings in which the welfare of children is to be determined

Housing

37. Legal Help and proceedings in relation to:
    (a) Possession of an individual's home (other than mortgage possession) (as described in subparagraph 33(1)(a) of Part 1 of Schedule 1 to the Act)[2];
    (b) Eviction from an individual's home of the individual or others, including unlawful eviction and planning eviction matters and closure orders not arising out of criminal conduct (as described in subparagraph 33(1)(b) of Part 1 of Schedule 1);
    (c) The provision of accommodation and assistance under Parts 6 and 7 of the Housing Act 1996 for an individual who is homeless or threatened with homelessness (as described in paragraph 34 of Part 1 of Schedule 1 to the Act)[3];
    (d) The provision of accommodation by way of community care services as specified in paragraph 6 of Part 1 of Schedule 1 to the Act, in relation to an individual who is homeless or threatened with homelessness;
    (e) Housing disrepair matters described in paragraph 35 of Part 1 of Schedule 1 to the Act, namely removing or reducing a serious risk of harm to the health or safety of the individual or relevant family member where the risk arises from a deficiency in the individual's rented or leased home and the legal services are provided with a view to securing that the landlord makes arrangements to remove or reduce the risk. This includes Legal Help for applications under section 82 of the Environmental Protection Act 1990 for a statutory nuisance, where the application falls within the terms of paragraph 35 of Part 1 of Schedule 1;
    (f) Applications to vary or discharge an injunction under section 153A of the Housing Act 1996;
    (g) Injunctions under the Protection from Harassment Act 1997 arising from matters within paragraphs 37 and 38 of these Category Definitions (paragraph 37 of Part 1 of Schedule 1 to the Act); and,
    (h) The powers of the Secretary of State to provide or arrange to provide accommodation under section 4 or 95 of the Immigration and Asylum Act 1999 and section 17 of the Nationality, Immigration and Asylum Act 2002 (as described by paragraph 31 of Part of Schedule 1 to the Act).
38. To the extent that any relevant grant of exceptional funding is made (in accordance with section 10 of the Act) this category also includes all other Legal Help and related proceedings in relation to matters which concern the possession, status, terms of occupation, repair, improvement, eviction from,

---

2 Possession arising from mortgage arrears and court orders for sale of the home fall within the Debt Category.
3 References to Part 7 of the Housing Act 1996 (or to provisions within Part 7 of the Housing Act 1996) include reference to Part 2 of the Housing (Wales) Act 2014 (or equivalent provisions within Part 2 of the Housing (Wales) Act 2014.

quiet enjoyment of, or payment of rent or other charges for premises (including vehicles and sites they occupy) which are occupied as a residence, including the rights of leaseholders under the terms of their lease or under any statutory provision (including enfranchisement). Cases including allocation, transfers and the provision of sites for occupation are also included.

Immigration and Asylum
39. Legal Help on matters and all proceedings in relation to:
    (a) Immigration-related detention powers referred to in paragraph 25(1) of Part 1 of Schedule 1 to the Act;
    (b) Conditions of immigration bail under provisions referred to in paragraph 26(1) or 27(1) of Part 1 of Schedule 1 to the Act;
    (c) Conditions imposed on an individual under the provisions referred to in paragraph 27A(1) of Part 1 of Schedule 1 to the Act;
    (d) An application for indefinite leave by a victim of domestic violence (as described in paragraph 28 of Part 1 of Schedule 1 to the Act);
    (e) A residence card application by a victim of domestic violence (as described in paragraph 29 of Part 1 of Schedule 1 to the Act);
    (f) Rights to enter and to remain in the United Kingdom under the provisions referred to in paragraph 30(1) of Part 1 of Schedule 1 to the Act;
    (g) An application by a victim of human trafficking for leave to enter or remain in the United Kingdom (as described in subparagraph 32(1) of Part 1 of Schedule 1 to the Act);
    (h) A Terrorism Prevention and Investigation Measure notice (as described in paragraph 19 or paragraph 45 of Part 1 of Schedule 1 to the Act:
    (i) An application by a victim of slavery, servitude or forced or compulsory labour for leave to enter or remain in the United Kingdom (as described in subparagraph 32A(1) of Part 1 of Schedule 1 to the Act);
    (j) A claim for damages arising from any of the powers listed in (a)-(c) of this paragraph 39 (as described in paragraphs 3, 21, 22, of 39) of Part 1 of Schedule 1 to the Act);
    (k) All new services introduced by the Nationality and Borders Act 2022; and
    (l) All new services introduced by the Illegal Migration Act 2023.
40. Legal help and all proceedings before the Special Immigration Appeals Commission (as described in paragraph 24 of Part 1 of Schedule 1 to the Act).
41. To the extent that any relevant grant of exceptional funding is made (in accordance with section 10 of the Act) this category includes all other Legal Help and proceedings in relation to any matter where the primary problem or issue is an immigration or asylum matter.

Mental Health Category
42. Legal Help and all proceedings in relation to:
    (a) cases under the Mental Health Act 1983, the Mental Capacity Act 2005, and paragraph 5(2) of the Schedule to the Repatriation of Prisoners Act 1984 (as described in paragraph 5 of Part 1 of Schedule 1 to the Act);
    (b) the inherent jurisdiction of the High Court in relation to vulnerable adults (as described in paragraph 9 of Part 1 of Schedule 1 to the Act);
    (c) the inherent jurisdiction of the High Court in relation to children (as described in paragraph 9 of Part 1 of Schedule 1 to the Act) where the case relates to a decision on medical treatment; and

Standard Civil Contract 2024 Category Definitions 679

43. For the avoidance of doubt, except as permitted by paragraph 13 above the Mental Health Category does not include any civil legal services made available under paragraphs 21 or 22 of Part 1 of Schedule 1 to the Act, including, but not limited to, matters arising from an individual's detention under the Mental Health Act 1983 or the Mental Capacity Act 2005. Nor does it included services under the Mental Health Act 1983 that are required to be made available under sections 13, 15 and 16 of the Act (criminal legal aid).
44. To the extent that any relevant grant of exceptional funding is made (in accordance with section 10 of the Act), this category also includes advocacy for matters arising under the Mental Capacity Act 2005 (as described in paragraph 5 of Part 1 of Schedule 1 to the Act) that are not listed in paragraph 4 of Part 3 of Schedule 1 to the Act.

Public Law Category
45. Legal Help and related proceedings in relation to:
    (a) public law challenges to the acts, omissions or decisions of public bodies by way of judicial review or habeas corpus (as described in paragraphs 19 and 20 of Part 1 of Schedule 1);
    (b) any claim described in paragraph 21 or 22 of Part 1 of Schedule 1 to the Act concerning the human rights of the client or a dependant of the client other than matters that fall within the definition of another Category[4]; or
    (c) A Terrorism Prevention and Investigation Measure notice (as described by paragraph 45 of Part 1 of Schedule 1 to LASPO).

Welfare Benefits
46. Legal Help in relation to appeals on a point of law in the Upper Tribunal, Court of Appeal and Supreme Court for all welfare benefits (including housing benefit, war pensions, state pensions and other similar benefits under a social security enactment, the Vaccine Damage Payments Act 1979 or Part 4 of the Child Maintenance and Other Payments Act 2008) (as described in paragraph 8 of Part 1 of Schedule 1 to the Act).
47. Legal Help in relation to appeal on a point of law relating to a council tax reduction scheme from the Valuation Tribunal England and the Valuation Tribunal Wales to the High Court, Court of Appeal and Supreme Court (as described in paragraph 8A of Part 1 of Schedule 1 to the Act).
48. Legal representation for appeals to the Court of Appeal and the Supreme Court on a point of law in relation to all welfare benefits (including housing benefit, war pensions, state pensions and other similar benefits under a social security enactment, the Vaccine Damage Payments Act 1979 and Part 4 of the Child Maintenance and Other Payments Act 2008) and appeals on a point of law relating to a council tax reduction scheme to the Court of Appeal and Supreme Court (as described in paragraphs 8 and 8A of Part 1 of Schedule 1 to the Act).
49. To the extent that any grant of exceptional funding is made this category includes Legal Help in relation to all welfare benefits (including council tax reduction scheme appeals, housing benefit, war pensions, state pensions and

---

4 However, see paragraph 15 above for services under the Human Rights Act 1998 in relation to damages claims that fall within Public Law notwithstanding the overlap with the Family and Claims Against Public Authorities Categories.

vaccine damage payments or similar payments), and in relation to proceedings before any welfare benefit review or appeal body any subsequent or related proceedings before a court.

Miscellaneous Work
50. Civil legal services that are not included within any Category of Law are classified as 'Miscellaneous Work'. For ease of reference, the following matters or proceedings that are described in Part 1 of Schedule 1 to the Act are likely to fall outside all Civil Categories and thus be classified as Miscellaneous Work.

Working with children and vulnerable adults
51. Legal Help and all proceedings in relation to:
    (a) The inclusion of a person in a barred list or the removal of a person from a barred list (as described in paragraph 4(1)(a) of Part 1 of Schedule 1 to the Act);
    (b) A disqualification order under section 28, 29, or 29A of the Criminal Justice and Court Services Act 2000 (disqualification from working with children) (as described in paragraph 4(1)(b) of Part 1 of Schedule 1 to the Act);
    (c) A direction under section 142 of the Education Act 2002 (prohibition from teaching etc) (as described in paragraph 4(1)(c) of Part 1 of Schedule 1 to the Act).

Protection from Harassment
52. Legal Help and all proceedings in relation to:
    (a) An injunction under section 3 or 3A of the Protection from Harassment Act 1997 (as described in paragraph 37(1)(a) of Part 1 of Schedule 1 to the Act);
    (b) The variation or discharge of a restraining order under section 5 or 5A of that Act (as described in paragraph 37(1)(b) of Part 1 of Schedule 1 to the Act),
    (other than where they are included in the Family or Housing Categories of Law by virtue of paragraphs 33(u) and 37(g) of the Category Definitions respectively).

Proceeds of Crime
53. Legal Help and proceedings in relation to:
    (a) Restraint orders under section 41 of the Proceeds of Crime Act 2002 (POCA) including orders under section 41(7) of POCA (orders for ensuring that restraint order is effective) (as described in paragraph 40(1)(a) of Part 1 of Schedule 1 to the Act);
    (b) Orders under section 47M of POCA (detention of property) (as described in paragraph 40(1)(b) of Part 1 of Schedule 1 to the Act);
    (c) Directions under section 54(3) of POCA (distribution of funds in the hands of a receiver) (as described in paragraph 40(1)(c) of Part 1 of Schedule 1 to the Act);
    (d) Directions under section 62 of POCA (action to be taken by receiver) (as described in paragraph 40(1)(d) of Part 1 of Schedule 1 to the Act);
    (e) Orders under section 67A of POCA (realising property), including directions under section 67D of POCA (distribution of proceeds of realisation) (as described in paragraph 40(1)(e) of Part 1 of Schedule 1 to the Act);

Standard Civil Contract 2024 Category Definitions 681

- (f) Orders under section 72 or 73 of POCA (compensation) (as described in paragraph 40(1)(f) of Part 1 of Schedule 1 to the Act);
- (g) Applications under section 351 of POCA (discharge or variation of a production order or order to grant entry) (as described in paragraph 40(1)(g) of Part 1 of Schedule 1 to the Act);
- (h) Applications under section 362 of POCA (discharge or variation of disclosure order) (as described in paragraph 40(1)(h) of Part 1 of Schedule 1 to the Act);
- (i) Applications under section 369 of POCA (discharge or variation of customer information order) (as described in paragraph 40(1)(i) of Part 1 of Schedule 1 to the Act);
- (j) Applications under section 375 of POCA (discharge or variation of account monitoring orders) (as described in paragraph 40(1)(j) of Part 1 of Schedule 1 to the Act).

54. Note that where a confiscation order has been made against a defendant under Part 2 of POCA, civil legal services provided to the defendant in relation to directions under section 54(3) or section 67D of POCA that relate to property recovered pursuant to the order are not within scope of Part 1 of Schedule 1 to the Act.

55. Note that where a confiscation order has been made under Part 2 of POCA against a defendant and varied under section 29 of POCA, civil legal services provided in relation to an application by the defendant under section 73 of POCA are not within scope of Part 1 of Schedule 1 to the Act.

Environmental Pollution

56. Legal Help and all proceedings in relation to injunctions in respect of nuisance arising from pollution of the environment (as described in paragraph 42(1) of Part 1 of Schedule 1 to the Act).

Sexual offences

57. Legal help and all proceedings in relation to a sexual offence where the client is the victim of the offence, including incitement to commit a sexual offence, encouraging or assisting a sexual offence which the person intended or believed would be committed, conspiracy to commit a sexual offence, and an attempt to commit a sexual offence (as described in paragraph 39 of Part 1 of Schedule 1 to the Act) other than where these matters are included in the Claims Against Public Authorities Category.

Victims of trafficking in human beings or modern slavery

58. Legal Help and all proceedings in connection with:
    - (a) a claim for damages arising in connection with the trafficking or exploitation of an individual who is a victim of human trafficking (as described in subparagraph 32(3) of Part 1 of Schedule 1 to the Act);
    - (b) claims under employment law arising in connection with the exploitation of an individual who is a victim of human trafficking (as described in subparagraph 32(2) of Part 1 of Schedule 1 to the Act);
    - (c) a claim under employment law arising in connection with the conduct by virtue of which an individual who is a victim of slavery, servitude or forced or compulsory labour is such a victim (as described in subparagraph 32A(2) of Part 1 of Schedule 1 to the Act); and,

(d) a claim for damages arising in connection with the conduct by virtue of which an individual who is a victim of slavery, servitude or forced or compulsory labour is such a victim (as described in subparagraph 32A(2) of Part 1 of Schedule 1 to the Act)

Injunctions to prevent gang-related violence

59. Legal Help and all proceedings in relation to injunctions to prevent gang-related violence under Part 4 of the Policing and Crime Act 2009 (as described in subparagraph 38(1) of Part 1 of Schedule 1 to the Act).

Abuse of child or vulnerable adult

60. Legal Help and all proceedings in relation to abuse of an individual that took place at a time when the individual was a child or vulnerable adult (as described in paragraph 3(1) of Part 1 of Schedule 1 to the Act other than where these matters are included in the Claims Against Public Authorities Category.

Anti-social behaviour injunctions

61. Legal Help and proceedings in relation to an injunction in respect of anti-social behaviour or alleged anti-social behaviour under Part 1 of the Anti-social Behaviour, Crime and Policing Act 2014 and related parenting orders (as described in paragraph 36(1) of Part 1 of Schedule 1 and paragraph 1(1)(e) of Part 1 of Schedule 1).

APPENDIX C

Civil costs: what you can claim for

A quick reference guide
This is a summary of the Legal Aid Agency's (LAA's) Costs Assessment Guidance for use with the 2018 Standard Civil Contracts, v10, December 2023, current at the time of writing. If is updated after publication of this Handbook, amendments are briefly described in the document control log of the guidance. Paragraph numbers are from the guidance. The most up-to-date version can be found on the website at: www.gov.uk/guidance/funding-and-costs-assessment-for-civil-and-crime-matters.

Admin work
Opening and setting up files, maintaining time costing records and other time spent in complying with the requirements of the Standard Contract are not chargeable (para 2.1). Letters confirming appointments, etc with no legal content are administrative if sent by a non-fee-earner. They may be allowable if considered by a fee-earner to be appropriate in the particular circumstances of a client (para 2.18a).

Advocacy
Normally (and where claimable), this is time on your feet before a court or tribunal; but note that in the Family Advocacy Scheme advocacy also includes travel to court, waiting time and attendance at advocates' meetings. The Costs Assessment Guidance states that where you do your own advocacy, it is reasonable to claim for preparing a brief to yourself (para 2.39).

Agents
They stand in your shoes and their costs are part of your profit costs. You cannot claim their fees as a disbursement. A London rate will only apply if the agent is based in London (paras 2.48–2.51).

Attendance
This is the conventional legal costing term for interviewing someone face to face, or speaking to them on the telephone (see below for more details on telephone calls).

All claims for attendance must be justified in an attendance note. The longer the time claimed, the more detail is expected.

You may be able to justify more than one caseworker being present, but this would be exceptional – for example, in a complex case where different aspects of it have been split between different people (para 2.36). In a complex case you may be able to justify the time of two caseworkers in the same category of law where you would be able to justify claiming legal research (see 'Legal research' for more details). You may be able to justify the time of two caseworkers in different categories of law if a difficult or unusual point arises and it would be reasonable. Supervision is a generally considered to be an overhead and not chargeable (para 2.37).

You can claim for attendance on the client or conference during the lunchtime adjournment if at court (para 2.55). A lower rate applies if you are attending with counsel.

Bundles

Fee earners must prepare master bundles for court, and often for counsel. Identifying the documents for the master bundle and drafting the index is fee earner work. Making up or copying of additional bundles is not chargeable. Where the bundles are above average size it is reasonable for fee earners to check that copies have been properly collated and reproduced (para 2.16). See also chapters 15 and 19 for bundle payments under the Family Advocacy Scheme.

Client and Cost Management System (CCMS)

Prior to the issue of updated guidance below in September 2018, the only way to claim additional fees due to CCMS was to cost the extra time and submit a claim through the LAA's complaint and compensation scheme.[1]

The LAA has confirmed that the updated guidance was clarification of the existing position rather than substantive change. As such, these principles apply to all assessments that take place after the revised guidance was issued on 3 September 2018, regardless of when the certificate was granted.

Guideline times are shown below with the previous guidelines they replaced, but do not forget that additional time may be justified on a case-by-case basis.

It worth noting how much longer they are in every case where they replace previous guidance. There are also new allowances for processes introduced by CCMS that simply did not exist before.

Where a provider sends a message on CCMS (and by implication receives one where allowable), this is treated as equivalent to sending an email or letter to the LAA and may be claimed as such (para 2.31).

Non-merits tested application (previously – no specific time) new guideline – 30 min (para 2.61).

Merits tested application (previously – no specific time) new guideline – 48 min (para 2.61).

The guidance goes on to say that for CCMS claims additional time may be claimed for inputting the means information into CCMS.

Where this is done in the client's presence it will form part of the costs of the attendance on the client. Where the information is input into CCMS by the fee earner without the client being present 30 minutes will generally be considered reasonable (para 2.61).

---

1 At: www.gov.uk/government/organisations/legal-aid-agency/about/complaints-procedure.

For allocation of costs to counsel, 12–18 minutes will usually be considered reasonable (para 2.63).

Amendments (previously – 6 min) new guideline – 24–30 min (para 2.63); Disbursement payment on account (POA) (previously – 6 min) new guideline – 12 min (para 2.63); Profit costs POA (previously – 6 min) new guideline – 12 min (para 2.63).

CCMS outcome codes with no costs recovery/statutory charge – new guideline – 12 min (para 2.63).

CCMS outcome codes with costs recovery/statutory charge – (previously – 12–18 min) new guideline – 24 min (para 2.63).

Hourly rate bill claims – (previously – 30–60 min up to £2,500; more than 60 min over £2,500) new guideline – 48 min per page of 10 items (para 2.63).

Court assessed bills with FAS – (previously – 12–18 min) new guideline – 54–60 min (para 2.63).

Court assessed bills without FAS – (previously – 12–18 min) new guideline – 30–36 min (para 2.63).

Congestion charge
This is claimable where incurred exclusively in relation to the case, but not where your journey to work would have meant you incurred the charge anyway (para 3.20).

Consideration of documents
See 'Perusal'.

Disbursements
This means counsel's fees, experts' fees, court fees, travelling and witness expenses and other out-of-pocket expenses properly incurred by a fee earner which would be properly chargeable to a client. They must be reasonably and proportionately incurred and reasonable in amount (para 3.1). Some are explicitly excluded under the Contract Specification, where they are listed (see para 4.28 of the Specification in relation to controlled work and para 6.61 in relation to licensed work (2024 Specification)). Most communication support professionals' fees are regarded as a reasonable adjustment under the Equality Act 2010 and therefore an overhead which cannot be charged for; but sign language interpreters' costs can be claimed. They must be accounted for separately as they are excluded from the statutory charge (para 3.7). See also chapter 15 for information about guideline rates and amounts for experts' fees.

Distant clients
No extra costs can be claimed that arise because you are in a location that is distant from your client, where it would be reasonable for the client to instruct someone closer (para 2.46) (see also 'Travel time'). However, vulnerable clients are not expected to make exhaustive searches for closer providers. If you are within 10 miles of the relevant court or tribunal, it will be considered reasonable to instruct you, even though the client may be distant from you.

Drafting documents
As a guideline, 6–12 minutes' preparation time would be expected per page of a straightforward document, but more complex documents will take longer

(para 2.15). It is reasonable to re-examine the core documents to consider their effect on the case. However, the degree to which this will be justified depends entirely on the complexity of the issues (para 2.9).

Emails
See 'Letters'.

Enhancements
It is up to you to justify any enhancement of your costs on certificated cases. You cannot apply an enhancement in order to escape any fixed fee (Standard Contract Specification 2024 para 6.12). You may be able to argue for an enhancement of 50 or 100 per cent in High Court, Upper Tribunal, Court of Appeal and Supreme Court cases.

First you must be able to demonstrate one of the following features:

1) the work was done with exceptional competence, skill or expertise;
2) the work was done with exceptional speed; or
3) the case involved exceptional circumstances or complexity (para 12.4).

If accepted, the caseworker will go on to consider the percentage enhancement to apply.

The LAA caseworker will consider:

1) the degree of responsibility accepted by the fee earner;
2) the care, speed and economy with which the case was prepared; and
3) the novelty, weight and complexity of the case. (para 12.5).

A guaranteed minimum enhancement of 15 per cent is available in respect of work carried out by a fee-earner on the Resolution Accredited Specialist Panel, the Law Society's Children Panel or the Law Society Family Law Panel Advanced. This is not paid in addition to any other enhancement that may be justified (para 12.23).

Where the fee earner is a member of the accredited specialist panel of Resolution, the Law Society Children Panel or the Law Society Panel Advanced, the enhancement is applied to all work done in any family case (para 12.21).

Faxes
These are treated as letters; but you cannot claim for sending a copy by post as well as the fax. See 'Letters' for more detail.

Form completion – see also CCMS
- Generally not claimable; but there are exceptions (paras 2.58–2.65):
- CW1 where the client is eligible;
- CLR in immigration cases;
- application forms for certificates (30 min is standard but may be exceeded where justifiable);
- applications for amendments to certificates;
- POA claims;
- applications to increase financial limitations on certificates; Claim 1, Claim 1A and Claim 2 (12–18 minutes);
- POA 1 (6 min).
- Completion of forms on behalf of clients is only claimable where legal assistance is justified.

See also 'CCMS' for time which may be claimed for time spent when using CCMS.

Legal research
Not claimable unless on a novel, developing or unusual point of law or the impact of new legislation to the particular case (para 2.5). However, it may still be reasonable for time for checking on the application of established law or procedural rules to individual circumstances to be claimed, provided the reasons are recorded (para 2.6).

Letters in
You can only claim for reading routine letters received in family licensed work cases paid at family rates, otherwise CPR 47 PD 5.22(1) applies. Payment for reading the letter is deemed to be included in the charge for a routine letter out (para 2.22). You can charge for reading non-routine letters received in all categories.

Letters out
These are either 'routine' and claimed at the item rate, because they are standard letters or take up to six minutes to write, or they are preparation rate letters, because they take longer than six minutes to write and the letter is justifiable (para 2.17).

You cannot charge for administrative letters, for example, confirming an appointment sent by a non-fee earner. You may be able to charge if the fee earner has considered the letter appropriate in the circumstances of a particular client. You cannot charge for multiple letters sent to the same client or party on the same day unless there is a good reason that justifies it. You cannot charge for a letter correcting your own mistake (para 2.18).

Office overheads
The following are office overheads and not claimable: costs of postage, stationery, faxes, scanning, typing, the actual cost of telephone calls and most photocopying, but see 'Photocopying' for exceptional photocopying costs (para 3.39). Supervision is generally considered to be an overhead (para 2.37).

Overnight expenses
Overnight expenses can only be claimed in exceptional circumstances, where it would be unreasonable to travel the distance there and back and carry out whatever was required in one day (para 3.18). It should be noted that the rate allowed in specified major cities is £111.25, and £81.25 elsewhere (para 3.19).

Perusal
Perusal is also known as consideration of documents. An initial brief perusal of all the documents to identify which documents are relevant is reasonable. Later, detailed consideration of documents may also be reasonable (para 2.8). As a very rough guide it takes approximately two minutes per A4 page to read the most simple document. Time taken will depend on the quality and layout of the document, for example, whether handwritten or typed, single- or double-spaced, large or small font, etc. More complex documents may take a longer (para 2.12).

Photocopying
Photocopying in-house is generally an overhead expense, but if there are 'unusual circumstances', or documents are unusually numerous (as a rule of thumb, 500 pages), you may claim the lowest commercial photocopying rate as a disbursement, even when carried out in-house (para 3.39).

Preparation
Includes drafting of documents; consideration of documents and evidence provided by the client or other parties; general consideration of strategy, evidence needed and evidence to be put forward; whether to make or accept offers to settle a case; and 'thinking time' (para 2.7).

Reviewing files
You are expected to be familiar with your own files, so you would need to justify any claim for reading a file, for example, prior to seeing a client when you had not dealt with the file for some time (para 2.40). You cannot charge for reviewing a file when it is reallocated from one caseworker to another, unless this is due to unforeseeable circumstances, for example, the client needs to give urgent instructions and the first caseworker is not available (para 2.41).

Telephone calls
These are either 'routine' and claimed at the item rate, because they take up to six minutes, or they are attendance rate calls, because they take longer than six minutes (para 2.23). You can claim for an unsuccessful call; but if you make repeated calls to the same number, you would have to justify it. You can claim a routine call for leaving a message on an answering machine. If you are put 'on hold', after the first six minutes on the call you can charge the waiting time at the waiting rate (para 2.26). However, bear in mind that it may be more efficient to write a letter or send an email.

Texts
These are treated as telephone calls. See 'Telephone calls' for more detail.

Transferring files between fee earners
See 'Reviewing files'.

Travel time
The general rule is that if the round trip travel time is five hours or more, it is usually more reasonable to instruct an agent than to go yourself. However, in some circumstances it may be reasonable to go (para 2.44):
1) court applications, other than those that are straightforward;
2) conference with counsel;
3) interviewing a witness where the fee earner wishes to test the witness's credibility for themself;
4) because of the specialised nature of the case, the fee earner's close personal understanding of the matter or the nature of the client; and
5) there is a lack of suitably qualified agents in the area concerned.

The reason for making the journey must be recorded on the file.

Travel time to clients
Usually, the client should come to you; but if, for example, the client is housebound, in hospital or in detention, it may be reasonable for you to travel to

the client (para 2.47). See also the Standard Civil Contract Specification 2018 para 2.38c, which says you may provide contract work at the client's location for 'good reason', although this is not defined further. If you need to travel to a client before a CW1 Legal Help Form is signed, where this is justified and the client subsequently signs the form and is eligible, you can claim the outward travel (para 2.47). The reason must always be recorded on the file.

Travelling expenses (caseworkers)
Caseworkers' travelling expenses can be claimed where the journey was necessary and the most appropriate form of transport was used (para 3.11). The LAA considers that public transport should normally be used; but time saved will be considered as well as travel fares or mileage. Taxis may be justified, for example, when transporting heavy bundles. You will need to give justifiable reasons for using other than public transport. Local travelling expenses to court cannot be claimed (eg within a 10-mile radius) unless public transport is known to be poor. Documentary evidence must support claims over £20 (except mileage) (para 3.17). Note that the LAA expects mileage details to include the postcodes of the start and end location. If you had to use a different route from that indicated on a standard route planner (eg Google Maps), it is recommended to download the route you took and explain why (eg roadworks, accident, etc).

Travelling expenses (clients)
You can pay clients' expenses to attend court and claim them back from the LAA as a disbursement (documentary evidence is required as for caseworkers). The client's presence must be 'necessary'. The Family Procedure Rules 2010 (r27.3) require that parties to proceedings attend any hearing or directions appointment of which they have notice, unless the court has directed otherwise (para 3.31).

Prior authority can be sought for a clients' travelling expenses to an expert where the client cannot afford them and a report is essential for the proper conduct of proceedings, as the request would be considered 'unusual in nature' (para 3.27). Client's travel to their lawyer can be claimed in asylum cases (Standard Civil Contract 2024 Specification para 8.64).

Travelling expenses (experts)
Note that the LAA expects mileage details of experts' journeys, including the postcodes of the start and end location, as they do for fee-earners (see above).

Waiting
You should not normally arrive at court more than 30 minutes before a hearing. If you have to, perhaps due to transport timetables, you should record the reason on file (para 2.53). You cannot claim waiting time during the lunchtime adjournment; but you can claim for attendance or conference undertaken during that time (para 2.55).

Waiting on the telephone
If you are put 'on hold', after the first six minutes on the call you can charge the waiting time at the waiting rate (para 2.26).

APPENDIX D

Criminal costs: what you can claim for

A quick reference guide
This is a summary based on the Legal Aid Agency's (LAA's) Costs Assessment Guidance for criminal defence work. Paragraph numbers are from the Criminal Bills Assessment Manual, v19, April 2024 edition. If is updated after publication of this book, amendments are briefly described in the document control log of the guidance. Paragraph numbers are from the guidance. The most up-to-date version be found at: www.gov.uk/guidance/funding-and-costs-assessment-for-civil-and-crime-matters.

Admin work
Opening and setting up files, taxes, postage, stationery, typing, faxing and telephone bills are not chargeable (para 3.1.1). Letters written by a non-fee earner that are not fee earner work are administrative (para 3.8.14).

Advocacy
Normally (and where claimable), this is time on your feet before a court (para 6.2).

Agents
They stand in your shoes and their costs are part of your profit costs. You cannot claim their fees as a disbursement (para 3.6.3).

Attendance
All claims for attendance must be justified in an attendance note. The longer the time claimed, the more detail is expected. Time spent dictating an attendance note may be allowed as long as it is reasonable (or typing it up if the fee earner is self-servicing) (para 3.3.3).

You may be able to justify more than one caseworker being present, but this would be exceptional; for example, in a complex case where different aspects of it have been split between different people (para 3.5.1) or appropriate delegation or supervision (paras 3.5.4 and 3.5.5).

Congestion charge/toll roads
This is claimable where incurred exclusively in relation to the case, but not where your journey to work would have meant you incurred the charge anyway (paras 3.9.33–3.9.34).

Consideration of documents
See 'Perusal'.

Disbursements
Must be reasonably incurred and reasonable in amount. See section 7 of the Criminal Bills Assessment Manual for disbursements generally.

Distant clients
No extra costs that arise because you are in a location that is distant from your client can normally be claimed, where it would be reasonable for the client to instruct someone closer.

It is unlikely to be reasonable for a provider to claim for travel for more than one hour each way (para 3.9.7). A useful rule of thumb is that if the round-trip travel time is more than two hours, it would not be reasonable, and you should instruct a local agent or the client should instruct someone more local to them.

However, it may be reasonable to accept instructions from a more distant client where:
1) there is no other more local contractor available;
2) the client's problem is so specialised that, in the solicitor's reasonable view, there is no more local contractor with the expertise to deal with the case;
3) the solicitor has significant previous knowledge of the case or dealings with the client in relation to the issues raised by the case so as to justify renewed involvement even though the client is at a distance; or
4) the local court or the remand centre where the client is located is more than one hour's travelling time away.

It may be reasonable to travel to counsel, experts, witnesses and site inspections (para 3.9.7).

Drafting documents
As a guideline, 6–12 minutes' preparation time would be expected per page of a straightforward document, but more complex documents will take longer (para 3.3.2). You charge for the time actually taken, but test reasonableness against that standard. The longer you take, the greater the explanation that is needed.

Emails
See 'Letters'.

Faxes
These are treated as letters, but you cannot claim for sending a copy by post as well as the fax (para 3.8.24). See 'Letters' for more detail.

Legal research
Not claimable unless on a novel, developing or unusual point of law or the impact of new legislation to the particular case (paras 3.4.2–3.4.3). However, you should be paid for the application of established law or procedural rules to individual circumstances.

Letters in
You cannot normally claim for reading routine letters received (para 3.8.10), but it becomes an item of preparation when time is reasonably taken on a more detailed letter.

Letters out
Letters sent will not automatically allowed. It has to be reasonable to send them (para 3.8.2). Letters are either 'routine' and claimed at the item rate because they are standard letters or are the equivalent of the item rate (para 3.8.1), or you can charge for non-routine items at the preparation rate (para 3.8.8). The LAA describes such letters as a preparation item because they take longer than six minutes, although confusingly the guidance suggests that timed letters should take more than 12 minutes (para 3.8.8). You should consider preparation rates at around the 12-minute point if substantive issues were considered.

You cannot charge for multiple letters sent to the same recipient on the same day, unless there is a good reason that justifies it (para 3.8.12). You cannot charge for a letter correcting your own mistake (para 3.8.3).

Office overheads
The following are office overheads and not claimable: costs of postage; stationery; faxes; scanning; typing; the actual cost of telephone calls; and most photocopying (para 3.1), but see below for exceptional costs. Supervision is an overhead unless required by the needs of a particular case (para 3.5.5).

Overnight expenses
Overnight expenses can only be claimed in exceptional circumstances, where it would be unreasonable to travel the distance there and back and carry out whatever was required in one day (paras 3.9.31–3.9.32). Rates were updated on 1 September 2023: up to £100.00 per night in major cities and up to £65.00 per night elsewhere, plus subsistence (para 3.9.33).

Perusal
Perusal is also known as consideration of documents. An initial perusal of all the documents to identify which documents are relevant is reasonable. Later, detailed consideration of relevant documents will be reasonable. As a very rough guide the LAA allows approximately one to two minutes per A4 page to read the simplest document. Time taken will depend on the quality and layout of the document, for example, whether handwritten or typed, single- or double-spaced, large or small font, etc. The time to be claimed is the amount actually taken, but the reasonableness will be tested against this time. If longer is taken an explanation should be recorded. More complex documents may take a longer time to consider (para 3.3.10).

Photocopying
Photocopying in-house is generally an overhead expense, but if there 'unusual circumstances' or documents are unusually numerous (usually over 500 pages), you may claim the lowest commercial photocopying rate as a disbursement, even when carried out in-house (para 7.14.1).

Preparation
Includes drafting of documents; consideration of documents and evidence provided by the client or other parties; general consideration of strategy, evidence needed and evidence to be put forward; and 'thinking time' (see para 3.3, which is headed 'Preparation of Documents' but includes other case preparation activities).

Reviewing files
You are expected to be familiar with your own files, so you would need to justify any claim for reading a file, for example, prior to seeing a client when you had not dealt with the file for some time (para 6.9).

Telephone calls
These are either 'routine' and claimed at the item rate, because they take up to six minutes, or they are attendance rate calls, because they take longer than the item charge (again, as for letters, the Criminal Bills Assessment Manual says more than 12 minutes) (para 3.8.16). Consider claiming preparation when the call progresses the case and is around 12 minutes in length. You cannot claim for an unsuccessful call, ie where it is not answered and no message is left. You can claim a routine call for leaving a message on an answering machine provided it was an attempt to progress the case (para 3.8.19).

Texts
These are treated as telephone calls. See 'Telephone calls' for more detail.

Transferring files between fee earners
See 'Reviewing files', but the LAA will not pay for duplicated work caused by changes within the organisation.

Travel time
A useful rule of thumb is that if the round-trip travel time is more than two hours it would not be reasonable, and you should instruct a local agent or the client should instruct someone more local to them. In some circumstances you may be able to justify greater travelling times (para 3.9.8), for example:
1) there is no other more local contractor available;
2) the client's problem is so specialised that, in the solicitor's reasonable view, there is no more local contractor with the expertise to deal with the case;
3) the solicitor has significant previous knowledge of the case or dealings with the client in relation to the issues raised by the case so as to justify renewed involvement even though the client is at a distance; or
4) the local court or the remand centre where the client is located is more than one hour's travelling time away.

The reason for making the journey must be recorded on the file.

Travel time to clients
Usually, the client should come to you; but if the client is housebound, in hospital or detention, it may be reasonable for you to travel to the client if, for instance, a telephone call or video link will not enable you to take proper instructions (para 3.9.14).

Note that the Standard Crime Contract limits travel time to 45 minutes each way on a police station exceptional claim (para 3.9.15) and to one hour each way on a prison law escape fee case. The only exception to this is when a client is moved prison and the case has already reached the escape fee threshold. If so, you may claim up to three hours travel either way (Standard Crime Contract 2022 Specification paras 12.36–12.37).

Travelling expenses (caseworkers)

Caseworkers' travelling expenses can be claimed where the journey was reasonable and the most appropriate form of transport was used (see para 3.9 generally). The LAA takes as a starting point that public transport should normally be used, but you should consider the time saved as well as travel fares or mileage (para 3.9.5). The Standard Crime Contracts 2022 and 2025 set a contractual mileage rate of £0.45 (Standard Crime Contract Specification 2022 para 5.48 and Standard Crime Contract Specification 2025 para 5.43) for cases other than in the Crown Court. Travel expenses will not normally accepted if the court is within walking distance, although issues such as the need to transport bulky files or sensitivity of documentation may be taken into consideration. Taxis may be justified, for example, for an out of hours attendance at a police station. Documentary evidence must support claims over £20.00, for example, ticket or print out from the internet (except mileage) (para 3.9.22).

Travelling expenses (clients)

You can in exceptional circumstances pay clients' expenses to attend court and claim them back from the LAA as a disbursement using eform CRM4, submitted electronically (documentary evidence is required as for caseworkers) (para 7.3). Prior authority can be sought for a client's travelling expenses to an expert where the client cannot afford them, and a report is essential for the proper conduct of proceedings (para 7.3.2).

Waiting

If at court, you cannot claim waiting time whilst taking lunch. However, you can claim for preparation or attendance on your client or counsel during the lunch break (paras 3.9.28–3.9.29).

APPENDIX E

Standard monthly payment reconciliation process[1]

1. Introduction
The Legal Aid Agency (LAA) offers providers a choice as to how they are paid for Civil (Legal Help), Crime (Lower) and Mediation work. Providers can be paid a Standard Monthly Payment (SMP) or can opt for a Variable Monthly Payment (VMP).

2. Standard Monthly Payments
The Standard Monthly Payment reconciliation process implements the Protocol set out in the Deed of Settlement as agreed between the Legal Aid Agency (formerly Legal Services Commission) and the Law Society in 2008. The information in this section provides a guide on how the LAA applies the process.

The aim is to reconcile accounts (claims versus payments) to a 100% balanced position. The contract position percentage is calculated using the following formula:

$$\frac{\text{Claims in last 12 months}}{\text{Total payments aligned to last claim} - (\text{Total Claims} - \text{Claims in last 12 months})} \times 100\%$$

Where an account is within the 90%–110% band no action will be taken to change the SMP. Where an account is below 90% (meaning payments exceed claims by a variance of more than 10%) we will take action to adjust the SMP with the aim of recovering the balance over a period of 6 months to return the contract position to 100%. Likewise where an account is in excess of 110% we will adjust the payment upwards with the aim of bringing the account back to 100% in 6 months.

The new SMP is calculated by taking the average claim value over the preceding 6 months and adding or subtracting 1/6th of the current balance (whether overpaid or underpaid at the time of the review).

---

1 Monthly Contract Payments (Legal Help, Crime Lower and Mediation contracts) June 2016. Available at: https://assets.publishing.service.gov.uk/media/5a80097d40f0b62302691215/laa-payment-reconciliation-process.pdf.

Although this initial action is intended to return the account to 100% balanced, it may not have the desired effect due to fluctuations in claims. Prior to the setting of the 6th payment following the initial review, if the account is still outside of the 90%–110% band further action will be taken to clear the remaining balance over a 3 month period. This is achieved by setting the SMP to the 6 month average claim figure with a series of 3 credits or debits (depending on whether the account is underpaid or overpaid).

If at any time the contract position is less than 50% or in excess of 150% action will be taken to clear the balance over a 3 month period (as above).

Any proposed change to your SMP will be communicated one month in advance of the date of the first SMP at the revised amount.

Every account will be reconciled in accordance with this process, but there may be exceptional circumstances where it is appropriate to vary the action required to reconcile an account. Any exceptions are subject to agreement with the Assurance Reconciliation team.

3. Variable Monthly Payments

If you elect to receive a Variable Monthly Payment (VMP) this is calculated using the amount of the latest monthly submission plus or minus any changes to claims since the previous payment, for example, claim amendments and escape fee case assessments.

All other aspects of the contract payments process including the payment dates and submissions deadlines will remain the same.

The intention of VMP is to make a balancing payment each month so there may be a period of transition required in order to achieve a zero account balance.

On transition if an account is underpaid the balanced will be cleared in a single payment and VMPs will commence from the following month.

If an account is overpaid on transition the balance will generally be recovered over a period of six months by reducing the variable payments by 1/6th of the balance. Providers have the opportunity to discharge the balance by making a single payment or by requesting payments are stopped until the account moves into a position of credit, or by a combination of these options. Providers should contact the Assurance Reconciliation team to discuss transitional arrangements.

4. Mediation

Previously Mediation contracts had been paid by SMP although not strictly to the Protocol agreed with the Law Society in 2008 as that only covered solicitor contracts.

From 2015 the LAA was able to offer VMP to Mediation providers and from August 2016 will implement the Protocol to those accounts remaining on SMP.

Contact Details

Telephone: 0191 4962052
Email: reconciliation@legalaid.gsi.gov.uk
DX: Reconciliation Team, Legal Aid Agency, DX 742350, Jarrow 2
Post: Reconciliation Team, Legal Aid Agency, South Tyneside Office, Berkley Way, Viking Business Park, Jarrow, NE31 1SF.

Index

abroad, clients based 12.37–12.39
  accommodation and support 12.37–12.38
  EU, people resident outside the 4.18–4.19
  immigration and asylum cases 12.37
  local authorities 12.37–12.38
  means test, evidence of 12.39
  nationality 12.37
  no recourse to public funds 4.90
  representation certificates 4.88–4.90
accreditation
  Advocacy Assistance 20.21
  clinical negligence 22.52
  immigration and asylum cases, conducting 9.59–9.63, 22.22, 22.40, 22.125
  Law Society's Criminal Litigation Accreditation Scheme 14.79, 20.21, 22.23, 22.59, 22.69
  mental health cases, conducting 10.14–10.15, 22.43, 22.128
  police station work 14.33–14.35, 22.59
    Police Station Qualification (PSQ) 14.33
    Police Station Representative Accreditation Scheme (PSRAS) 14.34
    probationary representatives 14.34
  practice management standards 22.3
  probationary representatives 14.34

  supervisor standards 22.36, 22.40, 22.43, 22.52, 22.59, 22.69
accommodation *see* **accommodation for children; homelessness and allocations**
accommodation for children
  age assessment cases 12.28
  community care cases for children, conducting 12.18, 12.22–12.25, 12.28–12.29
  homelessness cases 12.23, 12.25
  suitability 12.24–12.25
adjournments 10.22, 10.41, 11.13
advice and assistance 14.49–14.76
  Advocacy Assistance 14.81, 16.37, 20.7–20.8, 20.20
  appeals 14.182–14.187, 16.69, 20.53
  application process 14.69–14.71
  attend at office, where clients cannot 14.70
  audits 14.66
  capital 14.61–14.63, 14.65
  change of solicitors 14.71
  children 14.70
  costs limits 14.74
  counsel, use of 14.194
  CRM1 form 14.69
  CRM2 form 14.69
  definition 1.10
  duty solicitors 14.81, 20.20
  evidence 14.66
  forms 14.69–14.70
  freestanding 14.60–14.76
  hourly rates 14.196, 16.29
  income 14.61–14.62, 14.64–14.65
  interviews with non-police agencies 14.60

699

advice and assistance *continued*
   investigations class work (criminal) 16.16–16.19, 16.21, 16.29, 14.60
   means test 14.60, 14.61–14.66, 14.193
   Mental Capacity Act 2005 14.70
   merits test 14.60, 14.67–14.68, 14.193
   Parole Board 14.194, 14.203–14.204
   passported benefits 14.62
   police station work, alongside 14.74
   postal applications 14.70
   pre-charge engagement *see* **pre-charge engagement, advice and assistance for (criminal cases)**
   previous advice and assistance, where clients have received 14.71
   prison law work 14.191–14.196, 14.198, 14.203–14.205, 16.69
   separate matters 14.75–14.76
   signing, exceptions to 14.70
   telephone advice 14.70
   travel and waiting time 14.70
   websites 14.65
advocacy *see* **Advocacy Assistance; advocacy in civil cases; advocacy in criminal cases; advocacy in family cases**
Advocacy Assistance 20.2, 20.5, 20.8, 20.9–20.26
   accreditation 20.21
   advice and assistance 14.81, 16.37, 20.7–20.8, 20.20
   appeals 20.24, 20.53
   bail 1.9
   billing and payment 16.69
   counsel, use of 14.202, 20.60
   court duty solicitors 20.8, 20.20–20.26
   custody, clients detained in 1.9, 20.9–20.14
   hourly rates 16.37, 20.25
   information to be put on file 20.23
   investigations class work 16.37, 20.2, 20.9–20.19
   magistrates' courts 20.20–20.26
   means test 14.200, 20.58
   merits test 20.57
   Parole Board 14.197, 20.56
   police bail 20.8, 20.15–20.19
   police station work 14.44–14.46, 14.48, 16.37
   prison law work 14.191–14.192, 14.197–14.202, 20.56–20.60
     billing and payment 16.69
     CRM1/CRM2/CRM3 forms 20.58
     disciplinary proceedings 14.197, 14.200, 20.8, 20.56–20.57
     means test 14.200, 20.58
     merits test 20.57
   qualified duty solicitors 20.21
   reasonable advice and preparation 20.24
   scope 20.22–20.24
   solicitors 1.9
   standard fees 20.59
   sufficient benefit test 20.23, 20.57
   travel and waiting time 20.25
   warrants of further detention 14.44–14.46
advocacy in civil cases 18.1–18.54
   advocate, definition of 18.2
   CCMS 18.49
   Controlled Legal Representation (CLR) 18.5, 18.23
   counsel, use of 18,2, 18.25–18.27, 18.45
     2013, 2 December, work started before 18.30–18.31
     2013, 2 December, work started on or after 18.32–18.37
     payments on account (POAs) 18.38–18.42
     unpaid fees 18.47–18.49
   exceptional case funding (ECF) 3.38, 3.62, 3.68, 3.71
   general principles 18.5–18.7
   guidance 18.31, 18.37
   Help at Court *see* **Help at Court**

Index 701

High Cost civil cases 18.43–18.46
hourly rates 18.29
informal advocacy 4.67
inquest exceptional case funding (ECF) 3.38, 3.62, 3.71
inter partes costs 18.50
legal aid only costs 18.51–18.54
mental health cases, conducting 10.14–10.15
payment 18.29–18.54
payments on account (POAs) of counsel's fees 18.38–18.42, 18.48
preparation 18.29
representation certificates 4.83, 18.24–18.28
rights of audience 18.2, 18.6
solicitors 18.2, 18.28–18.29
Standard Civil Contract 2024 18.49, 18.50
statutory charge 18.26
travel and waiting time 18.29
unpaid fees 18.47–18.49
who can provide advocacy 18.21
advocacy in criminal cases 20.1–20.57
Advocacy Assistance 20.2, 20.5, 20.8, 20.9–20.26
advocate, definition of 20.3
Advocates' Graduated Fee Scheme (AGFS) 20.49
appeals 20.53–20.55
bail time-limit extension 20.2
billing and payment 16.100–16.103
classification of offences 20.51
committal or sending to the Crown Court 20.34
counsel, use of 20.3, 20.45–20.49
  Crown Court hearings 20.6, 20.36–20.44
  magistrates' courts 20.5, 20.36–20.44
Crown Court hearings 20.6, 20.27–20.29, 20.34, 20.44–20.52
designated areas 20.32
fixed fees 20.34
funding 20.7–20.8

hourly rates 20.31
investigations stage 20.2, 20.8–20.19
magistrates' courts cases 20.7, 20.27–20.44, 20.141
police bail conditions, variation of 20.2
Public Defender Service (PDS) 21.44
representation orders *see* **representation orders**
solicitors 20.3, 20.5–20.6, 20.30, 20.36–20.37, 20.42, 20.45, 20.49
standard fees 20.30, 20.33
supervisor standards 22.141
total core costs 20.33
travel and waiting time 20.32, 20.37
trial advocates 20.50
trials on indictment 20.28
unpaid fees 20.36
advocacy in family cases 19.1–19.63
2011, 9 May, cases started prior to 19.7–19.9
2011, 9 May, cases started prior on or after 19.10–19.63
advocate, definition of 19.3, 19.11
Advocates' Attendance Form 19.5, 19.60
assessment 19.57
bolt-on payments 19.21, 19.34–19.56
cancelled hearings 19.33, 19.34
care orders during which there are DoL orders, cases for 19.19
categories of case 19.16, 19.18
CCMS 19.59–19.61
CIVCLAIM1A form 19.60
CIVCLAIM5A form 19.60
Controlled Legal Representation (CLR) 19.2
counsel, use of 19.3, 19.9, 19.11–19.12, 19.61–19.63
Covid-19, remote hearings during 19.5
escape fee cases 15.172, 19.17

advocacy in family cases *continued*
  Exceptional and Complex Case Team (ECCT) family section 19.62
  exclusions 19.15
  Family Advocacy Scheme (FAS) *see* **Family Advocacy Scheme (FAS)**
  Family Graduated Fees Scheme (FGFS) 19.7–19.9, 19.58
  family private law cases (certificates) 6.77
  final hearings 19.20–19.21, 19.28–19.32
  fixed fees 19.9
  forms 19.58–19.61
  guidance 19.5, 19.30–19.31, 19.58
  hearing fees 19.20–19.21
  Help at Court 19.2
  High Cost cases, Family Advocacy Scheme (FAS) in 19.62–19.63
  hourly rates 19.8, 19.14
  interim hearing units 19.22–19.27
  legal representation certificates 19.2
  merits test 19.6
  preparation 19.13, 19.33
  private law proceedings 19.63
  remote hearings 19.5, 19.27
  representation certificates 4.83
  scope 19.32
  solicitors 19.3, 19.8, 19.12–19.13
  Standard Civil Contract 2024 19.10, 19.14, 19.20
  standard fee payments 19.9
  travel and waiting time 19.13
aftercare services under MHA 1983 12.4, 12.16–12.17
after the event (ATE) insurance 4.100, 11.38–11.39, 13.35
aggregation of means 2.38–23.9, 2.47, 2.58, 4.92, 12.19, 12.21
alternative means of funding
  after the event (ATE) insurance 4.100, 11.38–11.39, 13.35
  Conditional Fee Agreements (CFAs) *see* **Conditional Fee Agreements (CFAs)**
  legal expenses insurance 4.7, 4.96, 4.100
  Legal Help 4.7
  public law cases, conducting 13.32–13.34
  representation certificates 4.96, 4.99–5.100
  trade union membership 4.7, 4.96
anti-social behaviour (ASB) injunctions 11.5, 11.15, 11.64–11.70
  'Apply' online portal 11.69
  billing and payment 16.73, 16.76
  breach as a crime 11.67–11.70
  closure orders 11.70
  committal proceedings following breach of injunctions 11.15
  counsel, use of 11.68
  CRMCLAIM11 form 15.65
  emergency delegated functions 11.62
  housing cases 11.62–11.70
  individual case contracts (ICCs) 11.67, 11.69
  Legal Help 11.62
  possession proceedings 11.15, 11.63, 11.65–11.67, 11.70
  representation certificates 15.65–15.66
  representation orders 11.67, 15.65
  scope 11.62
  website 15.66
  youth court 11.62, 14.206
appeals
  advice and assistance 20.53
  advocacy in criminal cases 20.53–20.55
  assessment of inter partes costs by the courts 15.133
  asylum seekers 11.32
  authorised costs officers, appeals from 15.133
  bail 16.53, 20.17
  CCMS 14.102
  contract compliance audits (CCAs) 23.49
  contract notices 23.40–23.42, 23.49, 23.50–23.53, 23.54

controlled work 9.45, 9.100–9.101, 9.110, 15.42, 17.35–17.45
costs *see* **costs appeals**
counsel, use of 4.135, 20.54
criminal appeals *see* **criminal appeals, conducting**
emergency delegated functions 4.209, 11.26
escape fee cases 10.48
exceptional case funding (ECF) 3.17, 3.19
family cases 6.95, 7.4
First-tier Tribunal (FTT) 9.46–9.47, 9.71, 9.95, 9.120
homelessness 11.23, 11.25–11.27
housing cases 5.18
human trafficking, modern slavery, servitude or forced labour, victims of 9.46
immigration and asylum cases, conducting 9.37, 9.45–9.48, 9.55, 9.74–9.75
  Controlled Legal Representation (CLR) 9.45, 9.99–9.101, 9.110
  First-tier Tribunal (FTT) 9.46–9.47, 9.71, 9.95, 9.120
  licensed works 9.48, 9.119
  post-appeal work 9.74, 9.117–9.119
Independent Costs Assessors (ICAs) *see* **Independent Costs Assessors (ICAs)**
Independent Funding Adjudicators (IFAs) *see* **Independent Funding Adjudicators (IFAs)**
judicial review 13.15
Legal Representation 9.45, 9.117
licensed work 9.48, 9.119, 15.168
mental health cases, conducting 10.18, 10.41, 10.48
nil assessment appeals 17.35–17.45
police bail 20.17
representation certificates 4.125–4.126
representation orders 14.88, 14.108, 20.7, 20.54–20.55
Standard Crime Contracts 20.54, 22.61, 22.71
supervisor standards 22.61, 22.71
Supreme Court *see* **Supreme Court**
Upper Tribunal (UT) *see* **Upper Tribunal (UT)**
Application Fixer services 22.103–22.106
'Apply' online portal 5.7–5.14
addresses, inconsistencies with 5.10
anti-social behaviour (ASB) injunctions 11.69
CCMS, replacement of 1.66, 4.118, 5.7–5.14
criminal cases, extension to 5.11
domestic abuse cases 5.7, 5.13, 22.93
emergency delegated functions 5.13
evidence 5.8–5.9
exclusions 5.13
guidance 5.14
means test 5.9
online banking, applicants as having to use 5.9
partners who need to be means-tested, exclusion of 5.13
peer review 22.93
problems within CCMS 5.8
self-employed clients, exclusion of 5.13
simplification of applications 5.8
website 5.14
when civil Apply can be used 5.13–5.14
armed forces custody hearings 14.46
assessment of costs
Costs Assessment Guidance 1.50–1.51, 4.54, 6.4
courts, by **assessment of costs by the courts (civil and family cases); assessment of inter partes costs by the courts (civil and family)**
detailed assessment 15.107–15.118, 15.123–15.143, 15.153

assessment of costs *continued*
  inter partes costs *see* **assessment of inter partes costs by the courts (civil and family)**
  LAA, by *see* **assessment of costs by the LAA (civil cases)**
  nil assessment appeals in controlled work cases 17.35–17.45
  summary assessment 15.124, 15.130, 15.152
  terms of assessment 15.9–15.14
assessment of costs by the courts (civil and family cases) 15.107–15.118
  appropriate office, bills and requests lodged at 15.112
  CCMS 15.84, 15.87–15.97, 15.114, 15.116
  CIVCLAIM1, CIVCLAIM1A and CIVCLAIM2 forms 15.115
  counsel, use of 15.115–15.117
  Designated Family Courts 15.112
  detailed assessment 15.107–15.118
  exceed the costs limit, where costs 15.118
  Family Graduated Fees Scheme (FGFS) 15.57
  FAS Unit Entry Screen 15.114
  final bills 15.56–15.59
  guidance 15.114
  inter partes costs *see* **assessment of inter partes costs by the courts (civil and family)**
  LAA, submission of claims for payment to 15.114
  legal aid only 15.107–15.118
  licensed work in family cases, billing and payment for 15.163
  prescribed form, bills in 15.108
  profit costs 15.108, 15.110, 15.118
  provisional assessment on papers 15.109
  removal of courts as an assessing body 15.58–15.59, 15.62
  representation certificates 15.107–15.118, 15.123–15.143
  requesting court assessments 15.83
  Senior Courts Costs Office (SCCO) 15.112
assessment of inter partes costs by the courts (civil and family) 15.123–15.143
  appeals 15.133
  apportionment 15.138–15.143
  authorised costs officers, appeals from 15.133
  case management steps 15.125
  CCMS 15.136–15.137, 15.143
  CIVCLAIM1 and CIVCLAIM1A forms 15.137
  CIVCLAIM2 form 15.136–15.137, 15.143
  controlled work 15.126
  costs-only proceedings 15.126, 15.136
  detailed assessment 15.123–15.143
  disclosure 15.125
  enforcement of costs certificates 15.137
  evidence 15.125
  guidance 15.123
  interest 15.127, 15.135
  interim or final costs certificates, applications for 15.131
  LAA 15.134–15.137
  legal aid only costs 15.138–15.143
  licensed work 15.124, 15.134
  misconduct 15.127
  multiple recoveries 15.136
  N258 form 15.132
  negotiations, costs of 15.130
  Points of Dispute (PoDs), service of 15.128–15.129
  procedure 15.123–15.133
  provisional assessments 15.132
  quantum, disagreement on 15.126
  replies 15.129–15.130
  sanctions for delay 15.127
  Senior Courts Costs Office (SCCO) 15.132–15.133

Index 705

service of notice, bills and other specified enclosures 15.127
set off of debts against the client 15.130
settlements, reaching 15.127
Standard Civil Contract 2024 15.138–15.139
summary assessment 15.124, 15.130
Supreme Court 15.123
timetable 15.127–15.129, 15.132–15.133, 15.136
VHCC cases 15.138
written submissions 15.132

assessment of costs by the LAA (civil cases) 15.83–15.97
adjustment bills 15.90
amendments 15.88
CCMS 15.84, 15.87–15.97
checklists 15.85
CIVCLAIM1 and CIVCLAIM2 forms 15.84
claims 15.83–15.86
court assessments, requesting 15.83
counsel, use of 15.94–15.95
final bills 15.56, 15.58, 15.62–15.63
financial interests, clients with 15.86, 15.91
guidance 15.84–15.85
licensed work in family cases, billing and payment for 15.162–15.164
representation certificates 15.83–15.97

asylum seekers and refugees *see also* **immigration and asylum cases, conducting**
advice work 9.32
appeals 11.32
asylum matter, definition of 9.57–9.58
Asylum Screening Unit (ASU), applications at 9.128
attendance at interviews 9.19
billing and payment *see* **immigration and asylum cases, billing and payment for**
children 9.81, 9.105, 13.50
community care cases 12.38
costs, managing 9.128
destitute failed asylum-seekers 11.32
Detained Fast Track Scheme/Detained Asylum Casework Scheme 9.68, 9.122
Differentiation Policy 9.31–9.34
  Group 1 refugees 9.31, 9.33–9.34
  Group 2 refugees 9.31, 9.33
  suspension 9.33–9.34
disbursements 9.128
Dublin III Regulation 9.133
emergency delegated functions 11.34
enter and remain, right to 9.16, 9.17
exceptional case funding (ECF) 9.18
family reunion 9.18
habeas corpus 13.50
homelessness 11.32–11.34
human trafficking, modern slavery, servitude or forced labour, victims of 9.24
indefinite leave to remain (ILR) under Refugee Settlement Protection policy 9.17
inhuman or degrading treatment 9.16, 9.17
interviews, attendance at 9.105
judicial review 9.52, 9.133
leave to remain 9.16, 9.17, 9.31
Legal Help 11.32–11.33
life, right to 9.16
means test 9.89
merits test 9.133
National Referral Mechanism (NRM) 9.25–9.27
private and family life, right to respect for 9.18
Procedures Directive 9.52
Public Law category 11.33
Qualification Directive 9.16
Refugee Convention 1951 9.16
serious medical conditions, applications for leave to remain on basis of 9.17

asylum seekers and refugees see also immigration and asylum cases, conducting *continued*
  Special Immigration Appeals Commission (SIAC) proceedings 9.17
  subsistence-only support 11.33
  Temporary Protection Directive 9.16
  temporary refugee permission 9.31
  unaccompanied asylum seeker children (UASC) 9.81
audits
  contract compliance audits (CCAs) see **contract compliance audits (CCAs)**
  costs audits see **costs audits**
  desktop audit 22.8–22.9
  means test 14.66
  on-site 22.10–22.14
  outcomes 22.13–22.14
  peer review see **peer review**
  pre-Quality Mark audits 22.10–22.14
  Recognising Excellence 22.7
  Self-Assessment Audit Checklist (SAAC) 22.11
  Specialist Quality Mark (SQM) 22.7–22.14

backdating 2.27, 3.70–3.71, 5.48–5.50, 14.110
bail
  Advocacy Assistance 14.48, 20.15–20.19
  appeals 16.53
  conditions 14.47, 20.2
  Crown Court 14.88
  damages 9.36
  extension of time 14.47, 20.2
  High Court 14.88
  immigration and asylum cases 9.6–9.9, 9.109–9.111, 15.232
  merits test 9.110
  police bail 14.47–14.48, 20.2, 20.15–20.19

police station work 14.31, 14.41, 14.43, 14.47–14.48, 16.20, 16.22
pre-charge 14.43, 16.37
representation orders (magistrates' courts) 14.88
street bail 14.47
Bar Standards Board (BSB) 1.18
barristers see **counsel, use of; King's Counsel, use of**
benefits see **welfare benefits**
billing and payment see **civil cases, billing and payment for; criminal cases, billing and payment for; family cases, billing and payment for**
bolt-on payments (children, cases involving) 19.34–19.56
  advocates' meetings 19.40–19.41
  bundles 19.44–19.50
    advocates' bundle payments (ABPs) 19.44, 19.49–19.50
    content and format 19.45–19.46
    court bundle payments (CBPs) 19.45–19.48
    indexes 19.47
    Standard Civil Contract 2024 19.48, 19.50
  cancelled hearings 19.34
  CCMS 19.58–19.61
  complex work 19.34–19.56
  counsel, use of 19.53–19.57
  cumulative, payments as 19.36
  disbursements 19.57
  domestic abuse cases 19.34
  early resolution fees 19.43
  experts, cross-examination of 19.35, 19.39, 19.42
  Family Advocacy Scheme (FAS) 19.53
  final hearings 19.21
  finance cases 19.34
  forms 19.58–19.61
  guidance 19.41, 19.47, 19.50, 19.54
  interim hearings 19.21
  judges, magistrates or legal advisers, verification by 19.34

private law proceedings 19.34,
  19.42–19.43
public law proceedings 19.34,
  19.35–19.41
serious harm, allegations of
  19.35, 19.37
significant harm, allegations of
  19.42
Standard Civil Contract 2024
  19.37, 19.48, 19.50
travel and waiting time 19.51–
  19.52
understanding, lack of 19.35,
  19.38
bundles
  advocates' bundle payments
    (ABPs) 19.44, 19.49–19.50
  bolt-on payments (children cases)
    19.44–19.50
  CCMS 5.82–5.85
  content and format 19.45–19.46
  court bundle payments (CBPs)
    19.45–19.48
  guidance 19.47, 19.50
  indexes 19.47
  Standard Civil Contract 2024
    19.48, 19.50

cancelled hearings 19.33, 19.34
capital *see* **capital (civil and family);**
  capital (criminal cases)
capital (civil and family) 1.11, 2.30,
  2.40, 2.43, 2.44–2.52
  60, disregard for clients over
    2.50–2.51
  aggregation of means 2.47
  assessment 2.44–2.56
  businesses, exclusion of money
    clients could realise on
    sale or borrowing on 2.45
  cars, exclusion of 2.45
  case study 2.49
  clothing, exclusion of 2.45
  contributions from capital 2.52,
    4.152
  definition 2.44
  domestic violence injunctions,
    exclusion for applications
    for 2.49

evidence 2.43
exclusions 2.45
furniture and effects, exclusion
  of 2.45
jointly owned property 2.47–2.48
Legal Help 4.22, 4.26
Legal Representation 2.43
life insurance and endowments
  2.44
lower limit 2.52, 4.152
marriage protection proceedings,
  exclusion for 2.49
money owed to clients 2.44
mortgage possession proceedings
  11.20
online calculator 2.51
passported benefits 2.40, 2.43
real property, ownership of
  2.46–2.49, 2.52
refunds 2.52
tools of trade, exclusion of 2.45
upper limit 2.52, 4.152
capital (criminal cases)
  advice and assistance 14.61–
    14.63, 14.65
  Advocacy Assistance 20.58
  billing and payment 16.70
  contributions 14.145–14.148,
    14.152
  Crown Court 14.134, 14.137,
    14.145–14.148, 14.152,
    14.154
  definition 14.63
  disbursements 14.145
  family home 14.63
  means test 14.61–14.63, 14.65
  partners 14.63
  prison law work 14.199, 20.58
  representation orders (magis-
    trates' courts) 14.92
  thresholds 14.65
  uprating 14.65
care and care proceedings
  Abuse in Care Standard 22.49
  advocacy 19.19
  Care Case Fee Scheme (CCFS)
    7.57, 7.58–7.62
  care leavers 12.29
  counsel, use of 19.63

care and care proceedings *continued*
    deprivation of liberty (DoL) orders 19.19
    means test 6.14
    Very High Cost Cases (VHCC) – family 15.194
Care Case Fee Scheme (CCFS) 4.220–4.222, 7.57, 7.58–7.62
case management
    assessment of inter partes costs by the courts 15.125
    Case Management Supervisors 1.68, 5.24, 5.44
    CCMS 5.24–5.26
    Common Platform digital case management system 14.78
    notifications 1.79–1.81
    roles, allocation of 1.68, 5.24
case stated, appeals to High Court by way of 14.178, 14.179–14.181, 16.75
caseworker hours 22.19–22.21
    Standard Civil Contract 2024 22.25-22.26, 22.29, 22.48–22.51, 22.54–22.55
    Standard Crime Contract 2022 22.56, 22.139, 22.141
CCAs *see* **contract compliance audits (CCAs)**
CCMS *see* **Client and Cost Management System (CCMS) (civil and family)**
certificates *see* **family private law cases (certificates); investigative representation certificates; licensed work; representation certificates (civil and family)**
change of solicitors
    advice and assistance 14.58–14.59, 14.71
    court, agreement of the 14.126
    criminal cases 14.40, 14.58–14.59, 14.71, 14.126–14.128, 16.55
    licensed work in family cases, billing and payment for 15.187–15.190

    magistrates' court cases, billing and payment for 16.55
    police station work 14.40
    pre-charge engagement, advice and assistance for 14.58–14.59
    previous advice, restrictions where clients have received 2.75
    public family law fee scheme 15.187–15.190
children and young people 6.53, 6.96–6.98, 8.7
    abduction
        Exceptional and Complex Case Team (ECCT) 4.215
        Hague Convention 1980, returns under 6.39
        return orders 6.8, 6.19, 6.39
        service standards 22.122
        unlawful removal 6.8
        whereabouts, orders for disclosure of child's 6.8, 6.19
    abuse, risk of 6.6
    adoption orders 6.13, 7.6
    advice and assistance 14.70
    age of child 9.105–9.106, 13.50
    aggregation of means 4.92
    anti-social behaviour injunctions 14.206
    'Apply' online portal 5.13
    asylum seekers and refugees 9.81, 9.105, 13.50
    bolt-on payments *see* **bolt-on payments (children cases)**
    CAFCASS, litigation friend or official solicitor, role of 3.26
    care leavers 12.29
    care proceedings *see* **care and care proceedings**
    CCMS 4.92, 5.1, 5.51
    Children Act 1989
        care orders or supervision orders 15.159
        section 8 proceedings 5.13
        Special cases 2.60, 5.1, 5.51, 7.4–7.5

community care cases *see* **community care cases for children, conducting**
contributions 4.92
Crown Court 14.150
custody cases 2.60
domestic abuse 6.16, 6.19–6.20
EU agreements 6.12
exceptional case funding (ECF) 3.26
habeas corpus 13.50
homelessness 12.29
Housing Loss Prevention Advice Service (HLPAS) 2.60
immigration and asylum cases 9.105–9.106
international agreements 6.12
interviews, attendance at 9.105–9.106
Legal Help 2.57–2.59, 2.60, 4.11, 4.14–4.16
litigation friends 4.91
maturity and intelligence 3.26
means test 2.57–2.59, 2.60, 9.89
   aggregation of means 4.92, 2.58
   parents 2.57, 2.60
   representation certificates 4.91–4.92
   representation orders (magistrates' courts) 14.94, 14.97, 14.101
merits test 6.96–6.98
placement orders 6.13
public law children cases 7.4–7.6, 7.10, 15.174–15.175
representation certificates 4.91–4.92
representation orders (magistrates' courts) 14.94, 14.97, 14.101
Standard Civil Contract 2024 22.122
unaccompanied asylum seeker children (UASC) 9.81
Very High Cost Cases (VHCC) – family 15.194
wardship 6.7

young offenders' institutions, review of classification in 14.203
youth court 11.62, 14.206, 16.73
civil and family cases, conducting 1.6, 1.37–1.53, 4.1–4.235
Access to Justice Act scheme 2.2
advice and assistance 1.22–1.23
advocacy *see* **advocacy in civil cases**
applications 21.28–21.37
billing and payment *see* **civil cases, billing and payment for; family cases, billing and payment for**
category definitions 2.9–2.10
CCMS *see* **Client and Cost Management System (CCMS) (civil and family)**
Civil Legal Advice (CLA) contracts 21.2
community care cases *see* **community care cases, conducting**
contracts 21.28–21.37
Costs Assessment Guidance 4.4
Covid-19 22.148–22.150
criminal cases 1.8, 14.206–14.209
cuts 1.91
disbursements *see* **disbursements (civil and family)**
duration of contracts 21.32–21.37
emergency delegated functions 4.202–4.212
ending a case 4.71–4.82
exceptional case funding (ECF) 1.15, 1.25
exclusions 2.6–2.8
face-to-face debt work 2.11
factors to take into account, list of 2.1
fixed fees 4.74, 4.77
forms 4.117–4.4.124
geographical areas 21.28–21.29
guidance 1.44–1.51
Help at Court *see* **Help at Court**
Help with Family Mediation 4.70
homelessness *see* **homelessness and allocations**

civil and family cases, conducting *continued*
  housing *see* **housing cases, conducting**
  human rights 1.14
  Independent Funding Adjudicators (IFAs) 17.1, 17.4–17.45
  indicative spend 21.28–21.29
  judicial review 2.8
  key documentation 1.37–1.53
  key performance indicators (KPIs) 4.80–4.82
  Legal Help *see* **Legal Help**
  Legal Representation *see* **Legal Representation**
  licensed work *see* **licensed work**
  means test *see* **means test (civil and family)**
  mediation *see* **family mediation**
  mental health *see* **mental health cases, conducting**
  merits test 1.11, 2.29, 2.66
  monitoring 4.79–4.82
  new organisations contracting for the first time 21.31
  offices, opening new 21.32
  permitted work 2.76–2.84
  possession proceedings 2.7–2.8
  prescribed proceedings 14.164–14.167
  previous advice, restrictions where clients have received 2.68–2.75
  private family law *see* **family private law cases, conducting**
  public law *see* **family public law cases, conducting**
  referral fees, prohibition on 2.67
  representation certificates *see* **representation certificates (civil and family)**
  scope 1.13–1.16, 1.21–1.25, 2.13–2.28
  Standard Civil Contract 2024 *see* **Standard Civil Contract 2024**
  supervisor standards 22.35–22.38
  taking on cases 2.1–2.84
  tender processes 21.31
  time limits 4.78
  up to date, keeping 1.35
  urgent work 4.189–4.212
  very expensive cases/special case work 4.213–4.235, 15.193–15.206
  welfare benefits appeals 2.7–2.8
civil cases, billing and payment for 15.1–15.236
  advocacy 18.29–18.54
  appeals 15.42
  appropriate office, bills and requests lodged at 15.112
  assessment of costs 15.107–15.118
    courts, by the 15.107–15.118, 15.123–15.143
    inter partes 15.123–15.143
  audits 15.43–15.44
  backdating 3.70
  CCMS 5.77–5.89, 15.115
  Civil Legal Advice (CLA) contract 15.38–15.40
  Contracted Work and Administration (CWA) 15.37
  controlled work 15.8, 15.10–15.11, 15.37–15.45
  counsel, use of 5.87–5.88, 15.40, 15.115–15.117
  criminal cases 16.73–16.74
  disbursements 15.10, 15.17–15.36, 15.57
  escape fee cases 15.39–15.41, 23.4
  exceptional case funding (ECF) 3.69–3.72, 15.15–15.17
  Family Graduated Fees Scheme (FGFS) 15.57
  final bills 15.56–15.64
  financial and contract management 23.2–23.10
  forms 15.115
  guidance 15.11–15.14, 15.37
  hourly rates 15.39
  immigration and asylum cases *see* **immigration and asylum cases, billing and payment for**
  investigative representation 15.17

Legal Help 15.17, 15.40
Legal Representation 1.19
licensed work 15.10–15.11. 15.14
mental health cases 15.45
mis-claiming 15.43–15.44
online portals 23.2
over-claiming 15.43–15.44
PAYG (pay as you go) 23.4, 23.6, 23.8–23.10
payments on account *see* **payments on account (POAs) (civil cases)**
pro bono costs orders 15.148–15.155
rates
    legislation, list of 15.6–15.7
    London boroughs 15.8
    prescribed rates 15.6–15.8
reconciliation 15.37, 23.7, 23.8–23.9
recoupment and limitation 15.144–15.147
representation certificates *see* **representation certificates in civil cases, billing and payment for**
Senior Courts Costs Office (SCCO) 15.112
software, use of billing 5.78
standard basis, costs assessed on the 15.13
Standard Civil Contract 2024 15.43
standard monthly payments (SMPs) 23.4, 23.7–23.10
terms of assessment 15.9–15.14
time limits 15.38, 15.41, 15.144–15.147
transitional provisions 15.10
variable monthly payments (VMPs) 15.37, 23.4–23.5, 23.9–23.10
VHCC contracts 15.60
Claimfix service 15.47, 22.105
Client and Cost Management System (CCMS) (civil and family) 1.65, 4.117–4.124, 5.1–5.96
access CCMS, inability to 1.87, 4.120, 5.90–5.93

adjustment bills 15.90
administration support, advantages of 5.32–5.33
advocacy 18.49, 19.59–19.61
aftercare services under MHA 1983 12.17
amendments 5.52–5.55, 15.88
appeals 15.102
applications, making 1.71–1.77, 1.80, 5.6, 5.24, 5.32–5.76
'Apply', replacement with 1.66, 4.118, 5.7–5.14
assessment of costs by LAA 15.84, 15.87–15.97, 15.114, 15.116
backdating 5.52
billing and payment 5.77–5.89
    Bill of Costs if bills created but not assessed 5.79
    Bill Preparation 1.69, 5.27, 5.33
    Bill Supervisor 1.69, 5.27, 5.33
    licensed work 15.169–15.170
    software, recommendation to use billing 5.78
    supporting papers, uploading 5.82–5.85
bolt-on payments (children cases) 19.58–19.61
bundles, uploading billing 5.82–5.85
case management 5.24–5.26
    Case management 1.68, 5.24, 5.33
    Case Management Supervisors 1.68, 1.73, 5.24, 5.44
    notifications 1.79–1.81
    roles 1.68, 5.24
children 5.51, 19.58–19.61
communication 1.73–1.74
community care cases 12.17
Conditional Fee Agreements (CFAs) 4.99
contingency plans if CCMS is unavailable 5.90–5.93
contingency reference numbers 4.120
control, effects on costs 5.77
counsel, use of 1.83, 4.131, 5.87–5.88, 15.94–15.95, 15.115–15.117

Client and Cost Management System (CCMS) (civil and family) *continued*
  Covid-19 arrangements 1.78, 5.57–5.64, 5.66
  Cross Office Access role 5.28, 5.31
  declarations
    Declarations against Instructions (CCMS) 5.72–5.75
    payment, validation for 1.78
    promissory 1.78
    signed 1.78
  delays 5.82, 5.84–5.85, 5.87
  DWP, direct links with 1.77
  efficiency 5.33
  emergency certificates 5.89
  emergency delegated functions 4.207, 5.35–5.45, 5.53, 5.55–5.56, 5.72–5.73, 5.92
  emergency non-delegated function applications 5.46–5.50, 5.55
  enhanced rates 15.71
  errors and technical difficulties 1.86–1.88, 4.120, 5.78, 5.90–5.96
  evidence requirements 1.80, 5.21, 5.82
  exceptional case funding (ECF) applications 3.56–3.65, 4.123, 5.76
  experts 4.143
  expiry dates 1.82
  external costs draftsmen 1.69
  family cases 5.51, 5.87, 6.99–6.103, 6.105, 6.109
  Firm Administrator role 5.28, 5.30
  guidance 5.2–5.3, 5.34. 5.83, 15.89–15.90, 15.97
  homelessness 11.22, 11.26, 11.31
  hourly rates 5.79
  Housing Act statutory appeals cases 5.18
  how to use CCMS in practices 5.15–5.20
  immigration and asylum cases 9.120, 9.124
  inactivity, consequences of 15.93
  inquests 3.62–3.65
  instructions, declarations against 5.72–5.75
  judicial review 13.41, 15.80
  key performance indicators (KPIs) 4.124
  knowledge, importance of sharing 5.20
  LAA Customer Service Team by telephone, contacting 5.53
  licensed work in family cases, billing and payment for 15.169–15.170
  limitations, amendments to cost 4.133–4.134
  logic of CCMS 5.4–5.14
  maintenance updates 5.3
  mandatory, as 1.66, 5.1, 6.99
  means test 4.122, 5.6, 5.22–5.24
  merits test 5.6, 5.23–5.24
  notifications 1.79–1.81, 1.84, 1.86, 5.29
  Office Manager role 1.70, 5.28–5.30, 5.33
  online calculators 5.22–5.23
  online support team, contacting the 5.53, 5.90
  outcome codes commission, processing the 5.86
  paper-based system 5.4–5.5, 5.17, 5.24
  paralegal/trainee solicitors, role of 5.24
  payments on account (POAs) 1.84–1.85, 15.50, 18.38, 23.18
  peer review 22.93
  preparation of work offline 5.21, 5.24
  present, where clients cannot be 5.56–5.75
  problems with system 5.16–5.18, 5.34
  promissory declarations 5.65–5.71, 6.103
  Quick Guides 5.3
  record-keeping 1.76
  reference numbers 1.74, 1.83, 5.90
  rejects 15.88

representation certificates 4.117–4.124, 4.131, 4.133–4.134, 15.71, 15.82, 15.87–15.97
roles and responsibilities 1.69, 5.15–5.33
scope limitations, amendments to 4.133–4.134
screenshots 1.76
secure online message boards 1.73
signing applications 5.56–5.75, 6.103
special characters, copying and pasting 5.96
Specialist Quality Mark/Lexcel 5.24
statements of case, drafting 5.24
statutory charge 4.172, 4.178
super users 5.32–5.33
supervision 1.71–1.77, 5.24, 5.26–5.27, 5.33
support staff 1.75
supporting papers, uploading 5.82–5.85
technical difficulties and errors 1.86–1.88, 4.210, 5.78, 5.90–5.96
time ledgers, uploading 15.50
time taken for applications 5.32
training and support 1.44, 5.2–5.3, 5.16, 5.19, 5.34, 5.76, 5.95, 15.90
travel and waiting time 5.85, 19.52
trouble-shooting 1.86–1.87
unavailability of CCMS 1.87, 4.120, 5.90–5.93
unpaid fees 18.49
up to date, keeping 5.3, 5.20, 5.33
urgent applications 4.120, 4.198, 5.5, 5.24, 5.35–5.55
very expensive cases/special case work 4.227–4.228, 15.202–15.204
website 5.2
who does what within CCMS 5.21–5.33
work-arounds 5.20
XML reports, use of 5.78
workflow 5.80

Client and Cost Management System (CCMS) (civil and family cases), assessment of costs by
clinical negligence 2.14, 3.48, 22.33, 22.52–22.53
closure orders 11.5, 11.70
co-defendants and conflicts of interest 14.123–14.125
Common Platform digital case management system 14.78
community care cases, conducting 12.1–12.42, 13.7
abroad, people from 12.37–12.39
adults 12.3–12.4, 12.34–12.36
aftercare services under MHA 1983 12.4, 12.16–12.17
assessment of needs 12.13–12.14
asylum support, challenges to 12.38
care plans, formulation and implementation of 12.13–12.14
CCMS 12.17
children *see* **community care cases for children, conducting**
community care law, definition of 12.3–12.5
damages claims 12.11, 12.42
emergency delegated functions 12.15, 12.36
European Convention on Human Rights (ECHR), breach of 12.10
examples 12.7
guidance 12.2
homelessness 11.29–11.31
investigative representation certificates 12.11–12.12, 12.15, 12.17
judicial review 12.10, 12.12, 12.17, 13.30
Legal Help 12.10, 12.15, 12.17
levels of funding 12.10–12.12
litigation friends, use of 12.40–12.41
local authorities 12.3–12.4, 12.10, 12.13, 12.16, 12.35
means test 12.39

Client and Cost Management System (CCMS) (civil and family cases), assessment of costs by *continued*
merits test 12.10–12.11
NHS 12.3
notification of defendants 12.11
procurement areas 12.9
supervisor standards 22.47
who can do community care work 12.9
community care cases for children, conducting 12.3–12.4, 12.17–12.33
accommodation 12.18, 12.22–12.25
age assessment cases 12.27–12.28
assessment of needs 12.22
care, children in 12.29–12.33
Children Act 1989 12.17–12.33
children in need 12.22
emergency delegated functions 12.23, 12.26, 12.31, 12.33
examples of common challenges 12.30
guidance 12.22
judicial review 12.23, 12.25
Legal Help 12.18, 12.21, 12.23
Legal Representation 12.18, 12.20, 12.23
litigation friends 12.20, 12.40
local authorities 12.22–12.25, 12.29–12.31
looked after children 12.32–12.33
means test 12.19–12.21, 12.23
out of area placements 12.22
statutory framework 12.13
support 12.18, 12.22, 12.28–12.29
withdrawal of support 12.22
Community Legal Advice (CLA) services 21.47, 21.48
complaints 18.48, 23.42
Conditional Fee Agreements (CFAs)
CCMS 4.99
damages 11.38, 11.50, 11.52–11.53
eviction 11.38
guidance 4.99
housing conditions and disrepair 11.50, 11.52–11.53

merits test 11.38
public law cases, conducting 13.32, 13.35
representation certificates 4.87, 4.99–4.100
confiscation orders 14.207–14.208
conflicts of interest 1.18, 12.21, 14.123–14.125, 22.79
consolidated claims 14.5, 14.81
contempt of court 14.87, 15.65–15.66
contract compliance audits (CCAs) 23.1, 23.25, 23.43–23.49
disbursements 23.45
guidance 23.45
number of files checked 23.44
off-site, as carried on 23.45
outcomes 23.46–23.47
repayments 23.48
contract notices 23.37–23.54
6 month period, requirement for significant improvement in 23.38
appeals 23.40–23.42, 23.49, 23.50–23.53, 23.54
complaints procedure (LAA) 23.42
contract compliance audits (CCAs) 23.43–23.49
extrapolation 23.44–23.48
errors, zero tolerance policy for 23.37
ineligible payments 23.39
overpayments 23.39
recoupment 23.39
Standard Civil Contract 2024 23.38, 23.45, 23.48
Standard Crime Contract 23.38, 23.45
suspension for persistent breaches 23.38, 23.42
termination for persistent breaches 23.38, 23.42
Contracted Work and Administration (CWA) 11.96, 15.37, 15.49, 22.93
contracts *see* **legal aid contracts**
contributions *see* **contributions (civil and family); contributions (criminal)**

contributions (civil and family) 4.151–4.156
  amount 4.152–4.153
  capital 4.152
  children 4.92
  costs estimates 4.151
  domestic abuse 2.49, 6.87–6.88
  exclusion 4.151
  failure to pay 4.155
  fixed sum 4.153
  income 4.153
  Legal Help 4.22
  means test 2.35
  online calculators 2.35, 4.154
  passported benefits 4.151
  property or money, recovery of 4.151
  real property, ownership of 2.52
  refunds 4.156
  statutory charge *see* **statutory charge**
contributions (criminal) 14.138–14.144
  appeals 14.169–14.170
  apportionment orders 14.148
  cap on income contributions 14.140, 14.157
  capital 14.145–14.148, 14.152
  convictions, after 14.135
  Crown Court 14.135, 14.138–14.144
  income 14.138–14.144, 14.146, 14.148, 14.152, 14.157–14.158
  maximum 14.140
  notices or orders 14.154
  sanctions 14.152, 14.154
  shortfalls 14.147
  without, orders 14.135
Controlled Legal Representation (CLR) 18.5, 18.23
  advocacy in family work 19.2
  appeals 9.45, 9.75, 9.100–9.101, 9.110
  audits 23.29
  bail applications 9.110
  case study 10.23
  counsel, use of 15.220
  disbursements 15.222, 15.224
  fee exemption and remission scheme 1.52
  hourly rates 15.232–15.233
  immigration and asylum cases 9.42–9.45, 9.62, 9.72, 9.74, 9.81, 15.207–15.210, 15.232, 18.23
  appeals 9.45, 9.75, 9.100–9.101, 9.110
  attendance at hearings 9.112
  granting CLR 9.92–9.96
  licensed work 9.131–9.132
  means test 9.92
  merits test 9.93–9.101, 9.117
  permitted work 2.79
  post-appeal work 9.74, 9.117–9.118
  refusal 9.97–9.101
  separate matters 9.82
  Upper Tribunal (UT) 9.131
  withdrawal 9.97–9.101
  Independent Funding Adjudicators (IFAs) 17.5, 17.18–17.23, 17.35–17.45
  Legal Help 15.214
  licensed work 9.131–9.132
  means test 9.92, 10.32
  mental health cases, conducting 2/79, 10.18, 10.19–10.23, 10.31–10.33, 18.23
  merits test 9.93–9.101, 9.117, 10.33
  signatures 10.31
  Standard Civil Contract 2024 2.19
  standard fees 10.19–10.23
controlled work (civil and family work)
  appeals 17.35–17.45
  asylum seekers and refugees 9.17
  audits 23.25, 23.29
  billing and payment 15.8, 15.10–15.11, 15.37–15.45, 15.157, 15.158–15.160, 23.2–23.10
  Civil Legal Advice (CLA) contract 15.38–15.40
  contract notices 6.32
  Controlled Legal Representation (CLR) *see* **Controlled Legal Representation (CLR)**

controlled work (civil and family work) *continued*
  definition 2.19
  errors 6.32
  escape fee cases 15.39–15.41, 22.99, 23.4
  exceptional case funding (ECF) 3.70
  exclusions 4.49–4.53
  family private law work 6.30, 6.32–6.76
    Family Help (Lower) 6.30, 6.51–6.67, 7.13, 7.25–7.33, 23.29
    Help with Family Mediation 6.68–6.76
    Legal Help 6.30, 6.33–6.50, 7.13, 7.15–7.24, 23.29
  Help at Court 2.19
  immigration and asylum cases 15.207–15.210, 15.214–15.215, 15.218, 15.222, 15.224–15.226
  Independent Funding Adjudicators (IFAs) 17.35–17.45
  key performance indicators (KPIs) 4.82
  Legal Help 2.19, 6.30, 6.33–6.50, 23.29
  means test 2.32
  mis-claiming 15.43–15.44
  nil assessment appeals 17.35–17.45
  online portals 23.2
  over-claiming 15.43–15.44
  PAYG (pay as you go) 23.4, 23.6, 23.8–23.10
  previous advice, restrictions where clients have received 2.70
  problem areas 23.29
  public law cases, conducting 7.13, 7.15–7.23, 13.51
  reconciliation 23.7, 23.8–23.9
  Standard Civil Contract 2024 2.19–2.20, 6.30, 7.13, 22.99, 23.2
  Standard Crime Contracts 23.2
  standard fee matters 4.76
  standard monthly payments (SMPs) 23.4, 23.7–23.10
  variable monthly payments (VMPs) 23.4–23.5, 23.9
costs
  advice and assistance 14.74
  advocacy 15.172, 20.33
  appeals *see* **costs appeals**
  assessment *see* **assessment of costs; assessment of costs by the courts (civil and family cases)**
  audits *see* **costs audits**
  CCMS on costs control, effect of 5.77
  central funds, from 1.61
  children 5.51
  Costs Assessment Guidance 1.50–1.51
  courts, assessment by the 15.107–15.118 *see also* **assessment of inter partes costs by the courts (civil and family)**
  estimates 4.151, 4.195, 6.114
  experts 11.46–11.48, 14.16
  external costs draftsmen 1.69
  High Costs Contracts 4.222, 7.60
  immigration and asylum 9.125–9.130
  Independent Costs Assessors (ICAs) *see* **Independent Costs Assessors (ICAs)**
  inter partes costs *see* **inter partes costs**
  judicial review 13.48–13.49
  LAA, assessment by 15.83–15.97
  legal aid only costs 18.51–18.54
  limitations 4.129–4.130, 4.133–4.134, 5.51, 11.3, 14.42, 14.74, 16.19
  only proceedings 15.126, 15.136
  opponents' costs after revocation, responsibility for 4.195
  payments on account (PoA) 1.84
  police station work 14.42
  pre-order costs 14.109–14.110
  pro bono costs orders 15.148–15.155

Index 717

profit costs 1.7, 1.84–1.85, 14.145, 15.49–15.50, 15.55, 23.15
protection 1.26, 4.59, 4.84, 4.138, 11.17, 13.48–13.49
recovery of defence costs orders (RDCO) 14.172–14.177, 14.180
representation orders (magistrates' courts) 14.109–14.110, 14.112
Requested Cost Limitation box 5.51
sanctions 4.73, 22.91
statutory charge 4.163
costs appeals 23.50–23.53
  APP10 form 15.101
  audits 23.30, 23.36
  CCMS appeals 15.102
  court, seeking assessment by the 15.99
  electronic appeals 15.101
  guidance 15.99, 15.101
  Independent Costs Assessors (ICAs) 15.100, 15.104, 23.52–23.53
  internal reviews 15.100, 23.51
  key performance indicators (KPIs) 15.98
  licensed work 15.101
  payments on account (POAs) 15.99
  points of principle (POP) of general importance 15.106
  proformas 15.102
  reasons for the appeal 23.51
  reduction on assessment 15.98–15.106
  representation certificates 15.98–15.106
  Standard Civil Contract 2024 15.105, 23.50
  Standard Crime Contracts 2022/2025 23.50
  time limits, extension of 23.51
  written representations 15.103
costs audits 23.1, 23.25–23.36
  advice and assistance 14.66
  appeals 23.30, 23.36
  common claiming errors 23.35
  contract compliance audits (CCAs) 23.25
  contract manager meetings 23.36
  controlled work 15.43–15.44, 23.25, 23.29
  criminal cases 14.66, 16.2, 16.9, 16.11, 23.35, 23.36
  core testing programme 23.25
  evidence of means 23.31
  formal audits 23.36
  guidance 23.36, 23.29
  Independent Costs Assessors (ICAs) 17.46
  materiality of error targets 23.27–23.28
  means test 23.31
  monitoring 23.36
  National Audit Office (NAO) 23.27
  Operational Assurance team 23.36
  peer reviews 23.25
  problem areas 23.29
  purpose 23.27
  repayments 23.36
  targeted file review (TFR) 23.25
  types 23.25
counsel, use of
  Advocacy Assistance 20.60
  Advocates' Graduated Fee Scheme (AGFS) 20.49
  anti-social behaviour (ASB) injunctions 11.68
  appeals 18.33, 20.54
  assigned counsel 14.116–14.118, 20.39–20.44, 20.46, 20.54
  authority, failure to obtain 4.136
  bail 20.19
  bolt-on payments (children cases) 19.53–19.57
  Care Case Fee Scheme (CCFS) 7.60
  case stated 14.181
  CCMS 1.83, 5.87–5.88, 15.94–15.95, 15.116
  civil cases 18.2, 18.25–18.27, 18.45
    2013, 2 December, work started before 18.30–18.31

counsel, use of *continued*
   2013, 2 December, work started on or after 18.32–18.37
   disbursements 15.31
   payments on account (POAs) 18.38–18.42
   unpaid fees 18.47–18.49
 complex cases 10.17
 conferences 9.115, 19.53, 19.55
 controlled work cases, billing and payment for 15.40
 Counsel Cost Ceiling Remaining line 5.87
 criminal cases 20.3, 20.5–20.6
   Advocates' Graduated Fee Scheme (AGFS) 20.49
   Crown Court 1.20, 14.132–14.133, 14.158, 20.6, 20.45–20.49
   magistrates' courts 20.5
   police station work 14.48
   prison law work 14.195, 14.202
 custody, clients detained in 20.14
 disbursements 10.16, 15.31, 19.57
 enhanced rates, criteria for 18.34–18.37
 exceptional complexity or importance, cases of 4.135
 extradition 20.40, 20.43
 family cases 19.3, 19.9, 19.11–19.12, 19.61–19.63
   billing and payment 15.40
   bolt-on payments (children cases) 19.53
   certificates 6.109
   Family Advocacy Scheme (FAS) 5.87, 19.53
   hourly rates 15.40
   Very High Cost Cases (VHCC) 15.195, 15.197–15.203
 guidance 4.135, 18.31, 18.37, 19.54
 Help at Court 4.55
 High Court 18.34, 18.36, 18.45
 higher rates in County Court, payment at 18.31
 homelessness 11.26
 hourly rates 15.40
 immigration and asylum cases, billing and payment for 15.220–15.221
 indictable offences 20.40–20.41
 in-house (not-for-profits) 18.25, 19.61
 judicial review 13.41
 King's Counsel, use of *see* **King's Counsel, use of**
 Legal Help 15.40, 15.161
 London or non-London rates 18.30, 18.32
 magistrates' courts 14.116–14.118, 16.57–16.58, 20.5, 20.36–20.44
 means test 14.158
 mental health cases, conducting 10.16–10.17
 more than one counsel
   Care Case Fee Scheme (CCFS) 7.60
   CCMS 5.88
   civil cases 18.26
   Crown Court 20.47–20.48
   family cases 19.62–19.63
   magistrates' court cases 20.43
   representation certificates 4.135
   very expensive cases/special case work 4.215, 4.222–4.223, 15.195, 15.198, 15.200
 opinions 19.53, 19.56
 payments on account (POAs) 15.49, 15.203, 18.38–18.42
 police station work 14.48, 20.19
 prescribed rates 18.33–18.36, 20.44
 prior authority, copies of 18.27
 prison law work 14.195, 14.202
 reduction in rates 18.32–18.37
 representation certificates 4.135–4.136, 15.65, 18.25–18.26
 representation orders 1.10, 14.116–14.119, 14.132–14.133, 20.29
 service standards 22.113
 solicitors out of contract payment, payment by 1.20

Index 719

Standard Civil Contract 2024
  22.113
Supreme Court 18.33
time limits 5.88
unassigned counsel 20.37, 20.60
unique file numbers (UFNs)
  14.118, 20.38
unpaid fees 18.47–18.49, 20.36
Upper Tribunal (UT) 18.32–
  18.33, 18.36
very expensive cases/special case
  work 4.215, 4.222–4.223
County Court 18.31
court duty solicitor cases 14.77,
  14.79–14.84
  advice and assistance 14.81
  Advocacy Assistance 14.81
  bills and payment 11.95–11.96,
    11.98–11.99
  consolidated claims 14.81
  Contract Report form 11.96
  disbursements 11.99
  file notes 14.82
  Housing Loss Prevention Advice
    Service (HLPAS) 11.73,
    11.75, 11.87–11.92,
    11.95–11.96
  Law Society's Criminal Litigation
    Accreditation Scheme
    14.79, 20.21
  means test 14.82
  police station qualification 14.79
  procurement areas 14.80
  representation orders 14.84
  scope 14.83
  Stage Two 11.73, 11.75, 11.87–
    11.92, 11.95–11.96,
    11.98–11.99
Court of Appeal
  counsel, use of 18.33
  criminal appeals 14.184, 14.188–
    14.190, 20.55
  notice to appeal 14.188
  immigration and asylum cases
    9.48, 9.75, 9.123
  recovery of defence costs orders
    (RDCO) 14.176
  representation orders 14.188–
    14.190

Court of Protection (CoP) 2.60,
  4.215, 10.5–10.6, 10.18,
  10.59–10.60, 15.32, 22.45
Covid-19 arrangements 1.98–1.100
  Advocates Attendance Forms
    (AAFs) 19.5
  CCMS 1.78, 5.57–5.64, 5.66
  civil cases 22.148–22.150
  criminal cases 22.148–22.150
  duty solicitor 14 hour work 22.148
  emails, exchange of 5.62
  Family Advocacy Scheme (FAS)
    19.5
  family mediation 8.15–8.17
  guidance 4.23, 5.57–5.58, 5.64,
    11.2, 11.85, 19.5
  hardship 16.99
  housing cases 11.2, 11.83–11.86
  Housing Loss Prevention Advice
    Service (HLPAS) 11.83–
    11.86
  LAA responses 1.98–1.100,
    2.23–2.24
  Law Society's Practice Note
    5.59–5.61
  Legal Help 4.9, 4.12, 4.23
  local arrangements 11.84
  means test 11.86
  mental health cases, conducting
    10.3, 10.26
  payments on account (POAs) 23.15
  permanent changes, list of 22.149
  promissory declarations 5.66
  quality standards and perfor-
    mance monitoring 22.148–
    22.150
  remote hearings 15.199, 19.5
  schedule of processes restarting
    after Covid-19 contingency
    1.100, 2.24
  scope 2.23–2.24
  signatures
    digital signatures 5.57–5.64
    mental health cases 10.26
    present, where clients cannot
      be 5.57–5.64
    promissory declarations 5.66
  Standard Civil Contract 2024
    2.23–2.24

Covid-19 arrangements *continued*
  text messages 5.61
  Very High Cost Cases (VHCC) 15.199
  websites 1.99, 2.23, 11.2, 22.150
criminal appeals, conducting 1.9, 14.178, 14.179–14.181
  advice and assistance 14.182–14.187
  Advocacy Assistance (court duty solicitors) 20.24
  billing and payment 16.83
  case stated, appeals to High Court by way of 14.178, 14.179–14.181, 16.75
  conviction, against 1.6, 14.182
  Court of Appeal 14.184, 14.188–14.190
  Criminal Cases Review Commission (CCRC) 14.182, 14.185–14.187
  Crown Court 14.168–14.171, 16.83
  disbursements *see* **disbursements (criminal cases)**
  means test 14.180, 14.186
  merits test 14.180, 14.186, 14.190
  notice 20.24
  representation orders 14.183–14.190
  scope 14.178
  sentence, against 14.182
criminal cases, billing and payment for 16.1–16.108
  advice and assistance 16.69
  Advocacy Assistance 16.69
  advocates' fees 16.100–16.103
  anti-social behaviour injunctions, breach of 16.73, 16.76
  appeals 16.75, 16.80–16.81
  audits 16.2, 16.9, 16.11, 23.35, 23.36
  case stated, appeals by way of 16.75
  civil proceedings 16.73–16.74
  claiming process 16.77–16.81
  court duty solicitor claims 16.39–16.41
  crime lower 23.2–23.10
  Criminal Bills Assessment Manual (CBAM) 1.46, 1.63–1.64, 16.1, 16.61
  CRM6 form 16.78
  CRM7 form 16.79
  Crown Court *see* **Crown Court, billing and payment of litigator fees in the**
  escape fee cases 23.4
  financial and contract management 23.2–23.10
  habeas corpus 16.73
  Independent Costs Assessor (ICA) 16.80
  investigations class work *see* **investigations class work (criminal), billing and payment for**
  judicial review 16.73
  magistrates' courts *see* **magistrates' courts, billing and payment for standard fees in the**
  means test 16.70
  merits test 16.69
  monthly contract payments 16.6–16.7
  non-standard fees 16.79
  online portals 16.78, 23.2
  other contract work 16.69–16.76
  PAYG (pay as you go) 23.4, 23.6, 23.8–23.10
  police station work 14.43
  pre-charge engagement 16.33–16.36
  prison law work 16.69–16.71
  proceedings class work 16.38–16.45
  Proceeds of Crime Act 2002, civil proceedings under 16.73
  rates 16.24–16.37
  reconciliation 16.7, 16.78, 23.7, 23.8–23.9
  record-keeping 16.3–16.5
  regulations 16.10–16.11
  representation orders 16.7, 16.11, 16.42–16.45, 16.74

Senior Courts Costs Office (SCCO) 15.112
sentencing cases 16.72
Standard Crime Contract 16.73–16.76
standard fees 16.46–16.69
standard monthly payments 16.78, 23.4, 23.7–23.10
time limits 16.80
topping up fees 16.106–16.108
unique file numbers (UFNs) 16.11
variable monthly payments (VMPs) 23.4–23.5, 23.9
VHCCs 16.104–16.105
youth court, proceedings in the 16.73
criminal cases, conducting 1.54–1.64, 14.1–14.211
advice and assistance *see* **advice and assistance**
advice and representation 1.6, 1.9–1.10
advocacy *see* **advocacy assistance; advocacy in criminal cases**
anti-social behaviour injunctions in youth court 14.206
appeals *see* **criminal appeals, conducting**
'Apply' online portal 5.11
associated civil cases 14.206–14.209
billing and payment *see* **criminal cases, billing and payment for**
case stated 14.178, 14.179–14.181
Central Funds after acquittal, reclaiming costs from 1.61
classes of work 14.2–14.5
confiscation orders 14.207–14.208
consolidated claims 14.5
contracts 21.42–21.43
coverage 1.9
Covid-19 22.148–22.150
Criminal Bills Assessment Guidance (CBAM) 1.63–1.64
Crown Court *see* **Crown Court cases**
cuts 1.91
defences, investigation of 1.9
disbursements 14.9–14.17
duty solicitors 1.9, 14.77, 14.79–14.84
expert witness evidence, commissioning 1.9
general rules 14.5–14.17
guidance 1.46, 1.60–1.62
habeas corpus 14.206
interviews under caution 1.9
investigations class, work in the 14.18–14.76
judicial review 14.206
key documentation 1.54–1.64
law and evidence, advice on the 1.9
means testing 1.60
merits test 1.11
police station work *see* **police station cases**
prison law work 14.191–14.205
proceedings class work 14.77–14.177
Proceeds of Crime Act 2002, cases under the 14.206–14.208
representation orders *see* **representation orders**
reviews 14.178
Standard Crime Contract 2022 1.54–1.59, 14.1, 14.4
Standard Crime Contract 2025 1.54–1.59, 14.1, 14.4, 14.206
supervisors 22.21, 22.23
types of funding 1.10
unique file numbers (UFNs) 14.5–14.8
up to date, keeping 1.35
Very High Cost Cases (VHCC) 14.2, 14.210–14.213
witnesses, interviewing 1.9
Criminal Cases Review Commission (CCRC) 14.182, 14.185–14.187
Criminal Defence Direct (CDD) 14.19, 14.24, 16.29–16.30, 21.48
crowdfunding 13.34

Crown Court *see* Crown Court, billing and payment of litigator fees in the; Crown Court cases; Crown Court, means-testing of representation orders in the
Crown Court, billing and payment of litigator fees in the 16.82–16.99
  appeals 16.83
  breaches 16.83
  categories 16.84
  committal or sending to the Crown Court 16.83, 20.34
  fixed fees 16.83, 16.89
  graduated fees 16.83–16.87
  hardship 16.98, 16.99
  hourly rates 16.89
  payments on account (POAs) 16.95–16.99
  peer review 22.93
  redetermination of an assessment, right to 16.92
  representation orders 16.7
  time limits 16.92–16.93
  trials on indictment 16.83
  unused material 16.88
  variables 16.86
  written reasons, application for 16.93
Crown Court cases
  advocacy 20.3, 20.6, 20.27–20.29, 20.44–20.52
  bail proceedings 14.88
  billing and payment *see* Crown Court, billing and payment of litigator fees in the
  Central Funds after acquittal, reclaiming costs from 1.62
  committal or sending to the Crown Court 20.34
  counsel, use of 14.132–14.133, 20.6, 20.45–20.49
  Crown Court Digital Case System 14.78
  forms 1.62
  litigator fees, billing and payment of 16.82–16.99

magistrates' courts representation orders, continuance of 14.132–14.133
merits test 14.131–14.133
recovery of defence costs orders (RDCO) 14.173
representation orders 1.19, 14.77, 14.130–14.177, 20.27–20.29, 20.44–20.52 *see also* Crown Court, means-testing of representation orders in the
solicitors 20.6
Crown Court, means-testing of representation orders in the 1.62, 14.134–14.177, 20.28
  acquittals 14.143, 14.148
  appeals to the Crown Court 14.159, 14.168–14.171
  applications 14.149–14.155
  apportionment orders 14.148
  capital 14.134, 14.137, 14.145–14.148, 14.152, 14.154
  charges to property 14.147
  children 14.150
  contributions 14.135, 14.138–14.148
    appeals 14.169–14.170
    apportionment orders 14.148
    cap on income contributions 14.140, 14.157
    convictions, after 14.135
    income 14.138–14.144, 14.146, 14.148, 14.152, 14.157–14.158
    maximum 14.140
    notices or orders 14.154
    sanctions 14.152, 14.154
    shortfalls 14.147
    without, orders 14.135
  counsel, use of 14.158
  costs
    assessment of case costs 14.156–14.158
    effects of means testing 14.159–14.160
    evidence 14.156
    prescribed proceedings 14.167

disbursements and prior authority 14.162–14.163
effects of means testing 14.159–14.160
evidence 14.152–14.153, 14.156, 14.158–14.159
experts 14.156, 14.158, 14.159
hardship, reviews on the grounds of 14.155, 14.160
high cost disbursements 14.145
income 14.134, 14.137–14.144
   capital 14.144, 14.146, 14.152
   contributions 14.138–14.144, 14.146, 14.148, 14.157–14.158
   disposable 14.137–14.138
   overpayments, refund of 14.144, 14.158
   sanctions 14.152, 14.154
magistrates' courts 14.149–14.151. 14.153, 14.161–14.162
   appeals to the Crown Court 14.168–14.171
   disbursements 14.162
   stage 14.149–14.151. 14.153, 14.161–14.162
merits test 14.171
online portal, applications using the 14.149
orders for sale 14.147
overpayments, refund of 14.144, 14.158
passported benefits 14.136
prescribed proceedings (civil) 14.164–14.167
profit costs 14.145
recovery of defence costs orders (RDCO) 14.172–14.177
refusal of legal aid 14.135
sanctions 14.152
self-declaration of means 14.151–14.152
shortfalls 14.147
vulnerable adults 14.150
custody, clients detained in 20.9–20.14
armed forces custody hearings 14.46
counsel, use of 20.14
fixed fees 20.13
hourly rates 20.13
information to be recorded 20.11
means test 20.11
military custody 20.9
preparation and follow-up work 20.12
statements of truth 14.102
sufficient benefit test 20.10
time limits, extension of custody 20.9
travel and waiting time 20.12
warrants of further detention 14.44–14.46, 20.2
cuts to legal aid 1.90–1.91

damages claims
bail 9.36
community care cases 12.11, 12.42
Conditional Fee Agreements (CFAs) 11.38, 11.50, 11.52–11.53
damages-based agreements (DBAs) 4.87
eviction 11.35, 11.38–11.40
false imprisonment 4.107
housing conditions and disrepair 4.181, 11.45, 11.50–11.53, 11.59
Human Rights Act 1998 12.42, 13.21
immigration and asylum cases 9.36
public authorities, claims against (CAPA) 12.42
public law cases, conducting 13.21
representation certificates 4.103, 4.105, 4.107, 4.110
statutory charge 3.65
data protection 13.5, 15.27
declarations *see* **Declarations against Instructions (CCMS)**; **promissory declarations**
Declarations against Instructions (CCMS) 5.72–5.75

Defence Solicitor Call Centre (DSCC) 16.23, 22.110
delegated functions *see* **emergency delegated function applications**
deportation/expulsion/removals 9.9, 9.50–9.53
 exclusive immigration removal centre contracts, organisations with 9.67–9.68
 inhuman or degrading treatment 9.56
 judicial review 9.50–9.53, 9.56
 life, right to 9.56
 Priority Removal Notices (PRN) 9.28–9.30, 9.56
 removal notices 9.50–9.53, 9.56
deprivation of liberty (DoL) orders 2.60, 19.19
detailed assessment of costs 15.107–15.118, 15.123–15.143, 15.153
disbursements *see* **disbursements (civil and family); disbursements (criminal)**
disbursements (civil and family) 1.7, 4.48–4.54, 4.137–4.139
 asylum seekers and refugees 9.128
 best interests test 4.48
 billing and payment 15.18–15.36, 15.40, 15.57
 bolt-on payments (children cases) 19.57
 certificates 6.109
 CCMS 4.138, 15.53
 CIVAPP8A form 15.53
 Civil Legal Advice (CLA) contract 2018 15.30–15.31
 codified rates 15.18–15.20, 15.29–15.30
 contract compliance audits (CCAs) 23.45
 costs protection 4.138
 counsel, use of 10.16, 15.31, 19.57
 data protection 15.27
 destitute clients, travel expenses of 15.28
 electronic CIVPOA1 form 15.55
 enhanced costs 4.54

 escape fee cases 15.40
 exceptional case funding (ECF) 15.17
 exclusions 4.49–4.53, 15.10
 experts 4.50, 4.138, 4.149, 15.18–15.23, 15.26–15.28, 15.32–15.34, 15.53–15.54
 failure to apply for prior authority 4.139
 fee exemption and remission scheme 1.52
 guidance 15.29
 hourly rates 15.223
 Housing Loss Prevention Advice Service (HLPAS) 11.99
 immigration and asylum cases 9.86, 9.107, 9.121, 9.126–9.128, 15.222–15.225
 interpreters 15.18, 15.22–15.23
 judicial review 15.73
 King's Counsel or more than one Counsel, instructing 4.139
 Legal Help 4.48–4.54
 licensed work 4.49, 4.53, 15.163
 London boroughs 15.20
 mental health cases, conducting 10.16, 10.21, 10.55–10.57
 normal orders, departure from 15.35
 payments on account (POA) 1.84–1.86, 15.53–15.55, 23.15
 prior authority 4.137–4.139, 15.18–15.19, 15.36, 15.53–15.55
 profit costs 15.55
 quotes 4.138, 15.24
 reasonableness 4.48
 representation certificates 4.131, 4.137–4.139
 Standard Civil Contract 2024 4.49, 4.51–4.52, 10.57
 substantial disbursements 15.17
 third-party suppliers 15.18
 travel and waiting time 15.21, 15.23, 15.28
 vouchers 4.149
 witness intermediaries, exclusion of 15.25

Index 725

disbursements (criminal) 14.9–14.17, 14.145
  advice or representation, purposes of giving 14.9–14.10, 14.12
  amount 14.9
  best interests test 14.9–14.11
  case stated 14.181
  central funds, out of 14.114
  experts, reports of 14.11–14.12, 14.16
  medical reports 14.12
  Mental Health Act (MHA) 1983 reports 14.114
  mileage expenses 14.15
  payment from clients or third parties following refusal 14.115
  payments on account (POAs) 16.94
  prior authority 14.112–14.115, 14.162–14.163, 14.195
  prison law work 14.195
  reasonableness 14.9–14.11, 14.13
  receipts or invoices 14.14
  refusal 14.112–14.115
  representation orders (magistrates' courts) 14.112–14.115
  three-stage test 14.9
  travel and waiting time 14.11–14.12, 14.15
  witness expenses 14.17
discrimination 1.93, 2.15, 15.39, 22.33, 22.55 *see also* **Equality Act 2010**
disrepair *see* **housing conditions and disrepair**
domestic abuse 6.9–6.13, 6.16–6.29
  'Apply' online portal 5.7, 5.13, 22.93
  assault, injunctions following 6.9
  battery, injunctions following 6.9
  bolt-on payments (children cases) 19.34
  case study 2.49
  child arrangement orders (CAOs) 6.19
  children 6.16, 6.19–6.20, 6.29
  contributions 2.49, 6.87–6.89
  Destitution Domestic Violence Concession (DDVC) 9.12
  domestic violence and abuse, definition of 6.18, 6.20, 9.10
  emergency delegated functions 5.41
  evidence of abuse 1.92, 6.10, 6.21–6.29
  false imprisonment, injunctions following 6.9
  family private law cases (certificates) 6.82–6.84, 6.87–6.89, 6.110–6.111
  father's parental responsibility, removal of 6.19
  financial abuse 6.27
  guardians, termination of appointment of 6.19
  guidance 6.11, 6.24, 6.27, 6.112
  home rights 6.9
  immigration and asylum cases 9.10–9.15
  inherent jurisdiction of the High Court 6.9
  injunctions 2.49, 2.61, 6.110
  Legal Help 6.10, 6.22, 6.25, 6.37–6.38, 6.49, 6.87
  licensed work in family cases, billing and payment for 15.178, 15.181, 15.183
  means test 2.61
  mediation 6.82–6.84
  merits test 6.111
  National Centre for Domestic Violence (NCDV) 15.183
  non-molestation orders 6.9
  occupation orders 6.9
  other private law matters arising out of family relationships 6.17–6.18
  private law cases, conducting 6.9–6.13
  private law funding, domestic violence gateway to 1.92
  prohibited steps orders (PSOs) 6.19
  referral fees, exclusion of 15.183

domestic abuse *continued*
  respondents 6.11
  return of a child, orders for 6.19
  scope of the scheme 6.11–6.13, 6.16–6.20, 6.32
  special guardianship orders (SGOs) 6.19
  specific issue orders (SIOs) 6.19
  time limits 1.92
  urgent cases 6.89
  warning letters prior to injunctions 6.10
  whereabouts, orders for disclosure of child's 6.19
duration of contracts 21.32–21.37
duty solicitors 1.9, 1.54
  Advocacy Assistance 20.8, 20.20–20.26
  bail 20.19
  court duty solicitor work *see* **court duty solicitor cases**
  Covid-19 22.148
  Defence Solicitor Call Centre (DSCC) 16.23
  location 22.144
  police station work 14.23–14.24, 14.32, 14.34–14.35, 14.79, 20.19, 21.34, 21.42
  service standards 22.144
  Standard Crime Contract 2025 21.34
  supervisor standards 22.139

early resolution fees 19.43
ECF *see* **exceptional case funding (ECF)**
education 15.39, 22.33, 22.54, 22.132
email advice 4.11, 4.21
emergencies *see* **emergency delegated function applications; urgent cases (civil and family)**
emergency delegated function applications 4.202–4.212, 5.35–5.45
  amendments 4.208, 5.39, 5.41, 5.45
  anti-social behaviour (ASB) injunctions 11.62
  appeals 4.209
  'Apply' online portal 5.13
  CCMS 4.207, 5.35–5.45, 5.53, 5.55–5.56, 5.72–5.73, 5.92
  change of circumstances 4.204
  children 12.23, 12.26, 12.31, 12.33
  civil cases 4.202–4.212
  community care cases 12.15, 12.23, 12.26, 12.31, 12.33, 12.36
  Declarations against Instructions (CCMS) 5.72–5.73
  domestic violence gateway 5.41
  dual stage application 5.38–5.39, 5.45
  eviction 11.35–11.36
  exceptional case funding (ECF) 3.51, 4.205
  guidance 4.206, 4.208
  homelessness 11.26, 11.28, 11.31, 11.34, 12.23, 13.30–13.31
  housing cases 5.42–5.43
  Housing Loss Prevention Advice Service (HLPAS) 11.90
  immigration and asylum cases 9.124
  judicial review 5.40–5.41, 9.124, 13.30–13.31
  licensed work 6.31
  means test 4.210, 5.38
  merits test 4.211, 5.38
  methods 5.38
  monitoring 4.203
  non-molestation orders 5.40–5.41
  out-of-hours 9.124
  possession of the home cases 11.11
  promissory declarations 5.65–5.71
  public law cases, conducting 13.37–13.38
  purpose 5.36
  scope 4.202–4.209
  sign, where clients are not available to 5.55
  single stage application 4.208, 5.38, 5.45
  suspension 4.203
  Table of Delegated Authorities 4.202

termination 4.203
timetable 5.40, 5.42–5.43
training resources 5.39
type of applications 5.35–5.36
websites 4.206, 4.208
emergency non-delegated function applications (CCMS)
5.46–5.50
amendments to certificates 5.50
backdating 5.48–5.50
delays 5.46
dual stage applications 5.50
entry into force of changes 5.47
out of hour applications 5.47
sign, where clients are not available to 5.55
ending cases
civil and family cases 4.71–4.82, 4.185–4.188, 7.33
peer review 22.76
proceedings class (criminal cases) work 14.129
representation certificates 4.185–4.188
enhanced rates
CCMS 15.71
counsel, use of 18.34–18.37
disbursements 4.54
experts 4.142–4.145
factors stage 4.54
hourly rates 15.67, 15.70, 16.62–16.65, 18.29
magistrates' court cases, billing and payment for 16.62–16.65
public family law fee scheme 15.184–15.186
representation certificates 15.67–15.71
threshold stage 4.54, 15.68–15.70
two-stage criteria 15.68
Equality Act 2010 3.66, 4.168, 9.47, 10.27, 11.9, 11.16, 11.18, 13.5
Equality and Human Rights Commission (EHRC)
13.36
errors and technical difficulties
access CCMS, inability to 1.87

Application Fixer services 22.103–22.106
audits 23.27–23.28, 23.35
browser caches, clearing 5.95
CCMS 1.87–1.88, 5.78, 5.87, 5.90–5.96
common claiming errors 23.35
contingency plans if CCMS is unavailable 5.90–5.93
contract compliance audits (CCAs) 23.37
controlled work 6.32
corrective actions, requirement for 22.13
counsel fees 5.87
delay 5.87
document requests 15.46–15.48
key performance indicators (KPIs) 22.103–22.106
materiality of error targets 23.27–23.28
notification of 1.86
special characters, copying and pasting 5.96
Standard Civil Contract 2024 22.103–22.106
training and support 5.96
website 1.86
escape fee cases
advocacy in family cases 15.172, 19.17
civil cases, payment for 23.4
controlled work cases 15.39–15.41, 22.99, 23.4
criminal cases, payment for 23.4
definition 15.39
Discrimination Contract 15.39
EC-Claim 1 IMM form 15.228
Education Contract 15.39
electronic we-based EC Claim 1 form 15.41
exceptional case funding (ECF) 1.25
family cases, billing and payment for 15.40, 15.157, 15.160–15.161, 15.172
Family Help (Lower) 6.57
fixed fees 4.74, 4.77
Help at Court 18.22

escape fee cases *continued*
  hourly rates 15.39, 15.226
  immigration and asylum cases 9.86, 9.113, 9.126, 15.226–15.228
  investigations class work (criminal) 16.21, 16.24, 16.30–16.32
  Legal Help 1.25, 6.50, 15.160–15.161
  police station work 16.24, 16.30–16.32
  public family law fee scheme 15.172
  Standard Civil Contract 2024 15.39, 22.99
  standard monthly payments (SMPs) 16.32
  statutory charge 6.64
  timetable 15.41
European Convention on Human Rights (ECHR)
  community care cases 12.10
  exceptional case funding (ECF) 3.2, 3.7–3.15, 3.24–3.30
  experts 15.32–15.33
  fair hearing, right to a 3.7–3.8, 3.11, 3.13, 3.23–3.28, 3.30, 3.33, 14.205
  homelessness 11.25
  inhuman or degrading treatment 9.16, 9.17, 9.56
  judicial review 13.36
  life, right to 3.39–3.49, 9.16, 9.56
  possession of the home cases 11.9, 11.16
  private and family life, right to respect for 9.18
  procedural obligations 3.9
  slavery, forced or compulsory labour and servitude 3.28–3.30
  very expensive cases/special case work 4.226
European Union
  assimilated/retained EU law 3.2, 3.12, 13.5
  Brexit transition period 3.12
  people resident outside the EU 4.18–4.19

eviction 11.5, 11.35–11.40
  after the event (ATE) insurance 11.38–11.39
  closure orders not arising from criminal conduct 11.5
  Conditional Fee Agreements (CFAs) 11.38
  damages claims 11.35, 11.38–11.40
  emergency delegated functions 11.35–11.36
  exceptional case funding (ECF) 11.5
  guidance 11.38
  injunctions 11.36
  Legal Representation 11.36–11.37
  merits test 11.37–11.38
  planned 11.5
  scope 11.35
  statutory charge 11.40
  threats 11.35–11.36
  unlawful eviction 11.5, 11.35–11.40
  warning letters 11.35
  withdrawal of services 11.35
evidence
  advice and assistance 14.66
  'Apply' online portal 5.8–5.9
  assessment of inter partes costs by the courts 15.125
  CCMS 1.80, 5.21, 5.82
  children 6.29
  controlled work cases, nil assessment appeals in 17.37
  Crown Court 14.152–14.153, 14.156, 14.158–14.159
  domestic abuse 1.92, 6.10, 6.21–6.29
  exceptional case funding (ECF) 3.13, 3.26
  experts *see* **experts**
  Help with Family Mediation 6.72
  housing conditions and disrepair 11.48
  Legal Help 4.23–4.28
  means test
    'Apply' online portal 5.9
    attendance notes 4.25
    costs audits 23.31

Crown Court 14.152–14.153, 14.156, 14.158–14.159
representation certificates 4.93
self-employed clients 14.153
preparation work 5.21
promissory declarations 5.68, 5.71
public law cases, conducting 13.37, 13.51
representation certificates 4.93
representation orders (magistrates' courts) 14.102, 14.105
Exceptional and Complex Case Team (ECCT) family section 19.62
exceptional case funding (ECF) *see* **non-inquest exceptional case funding (ECF)**
experts 4.140–4.150
apportionment 15.32–15.36
bolt-on payments (children cases) 19.35, 19.39, 19.42
CCMS 4.143
codified rates 4.140–4.150
Court of Protection (CoP) 15.32
criminal cases 1.9. 14.11–14.12, 14.16
cross-examination 19.35, 19.39, 19.42
Crown Court 14.156, 14.158, 14.159
data protection 15.27
disbursements 4.149, 15.18–15.23, 15.26–15.28, 15.32–15.36, 15.53–15.55
enhanced rates 4.142–4.145
European Convention on Human Rights (ECHR) 15.32–15.33
fixed fees 4.140
guidance 4.140, 11.47, 15.19
hourly rates 4.50, 4.140, 4.147, 4.149–4.150, 15.55
housing conditions and disrepair 11.46–11.48
joint experts 4.146–4.148, 11.48, 15.32
justification for exceeding rate 4.143

Legal Help 4.50, 4.143
Legal Representation 1.16
London and non-London rates 4.141
peer review, external help with 22.91
prior authority 4.142–4.146, 11.47
pro rata approach where legally aided and non-legally aided parties 4.147–4.148
quotes 4.145
rates 4.140–4.150
reduction in fees 4.140
reports 14.11–14.12, 14.16
representation certificates 4.140–4.150
travel and waiting time 15.21, 15.23

face-to-face debt work 2.11
fair hearing, right to a 3.7–3.8, 3.11, 3.13, 3.23–3.28, 3.30, 3.33, 14.205
Family Advocacy Scheme (FAS) 19.5, 19.10–19.19
bolt-on payments (children cases) 19.53
cancelled hearings 19.33
certificates 6.79, 6.106, 6.109
CCMS 5.87, 15.114
counsel, use of 5.87, 19.11–19.12, 19.61–19.62
Exceptional and Complex Case Team (ECCT) family section 19.62
High Cost cases 19.62–19.63
interim hearing units 19.24–19.25
licensed work 15.165, 15.191–15.192
mixed categories 19.18
payments on account (POAs) 15.50, 18.42
public family law fee scheme 15.191–15.192
scope 19.11–19.19
Special Case Work 19.62
Unit Entry Screen 15.115
uplifts 19.17
Very High Cost Cases (VHCC) 15.195, 15.199

family cases *see* **advocacy in family cases; children and young persons; civil and family cases, conducting; family cases, billing and payment for**
family cases, billing and payment for 15.156–15.206
  appropriate office, bills and requests lodged at 15.112
  assessment of costs
    courts, by the 15.107–15.118, 15.123–15.143
    inter partes 15.123–15.143
  CCMS 5.77–5.89
  Children Act 1989, care orders or supervision orders under 15.159
  controlled work 15.157, 15.158–15.160
  counsel, use of 15.40
  court, assessment of costs by the 15.107–15.118, 15.123–15.143
  Designated Family Courts 15.112
  destitute clients, travel expenses of 15.28
  disbursements 15.40
  escape fee cases 15.40, 15.157, 15.160–15.161
  Family Help (Lower) 15.40, 15.158, 15.160–15.161
  FAS Unit Entry Screen 15.114
  fixed fees 15.157
  Help with Family Mediation 15.158, 15.160
  hourly rates 15.40
  inter partes costs, assessment of 15.123–15.143
  Legal Help 15.158, 15.160–15.161
  licensed work *see* **licensed work in family cases, billing and payment for**
  non-advocacy fees 15.157
  private family law 15.156
  public family law 15.156–15.159
  settlement fees 15.160
  Standard Civil Contract 2024 15.157

Family Graduated Fees Scheme (FGFS) 15.57, 19.7–19.9, 19.58
Family Help (Lower) (family private law cases) 6.30, 6.51–6.67
  audits 23.29
  billing and payment 15.40, 15.158, 15.160–15.161
  children 6.53
  client's point of view, funding from the 6.57–6.67
  conditions for level 2 6.52
  consent orders 6.53–6.54, 6.58
  counsel, use of 15.40, 15.161
  CW1 form 6.56
  escape fee cases 6.57, 15.160–15.161
  finance 6.54
  forms 6.56
  funding 6.57–6.67
  guidance 6.52
  scope 6.51–6.55
  settlement fees 6.58–6.61
  significant family dispute, definition of 6.52
  Standard Civil Contract 2024 6.52, 6.58
  statutory charge 6.57–6.67
  substantive negotiations, existence of 6.52
Family Help (Lower) – level 2 (public family law cases) 7.13, 7.25–7.33
  audits 23.32–23.34
  closing controlled work matters 7.33
  CWiPL form 7.30
  exceptional cases 7.32
  forms 7.30
  funding 7.31
  means test 7.29
  local authorities
    negotiations with 7.25–7.26
    notice to issue proceedings 7.25–7.26, 7.30–7.31
  merits test 7.28
  permitted work 2.80
  President's Public Law Outline 7.25

scope 7.25–7.26
Standard Civil Contract 2024 7.27
family homes *see* **possession of the home cases; real property/ family home**
family mediation 8.1–8.24
all issues mediation 8.7
CCMS 6.105
certificates 6.81–6.84, 6.101, 6.105
child mediation 8.7
contributions 8.16
Covid-19, voucher scheme for 8.15–8.17
CW5 form 8.19
domestic abuse 6.82–6.84
examples 8.6
family dispute, definition of 8.5
forms 8.19–8.20
free taster sessions 8.14
funding 8.21–8.24
guidance 8.5, 8.10, 8.15, 8.18
Help with Family Mediation 6.68–6.72, 8.2
Independent Funding Adjudicators (IFAs) 17.55
internal reviews 17.55
Legal Help 8.3, 8.11
means test 6.81, 8.11–8.14
Mediation Information and Assessment Meetings (MIAM) 6.81, 6.101, 8.7–8.8, 8.12
merits test 6.81, 8.6, 8.18
minor disputes 8.6
non-family mediation 8.3–8.4, 8.11, 8.20
permitted work 2.80
practice management standards 22.3
private law family disputes 6.12, 8.2
property and financial mediation 8.7
representation certificates 8.4, 8.11
scope 8.4–8.8
Standard Civil Contract 2024 8.3, 8.9–8.10, 22.37–22.38
supervisor standards 22.37–22.38
voucher scheme 8.15–8.17

family private law cases (certificates) 6.77–6.117
advocacy 6.77, 6.79
appealing refusals 6.95
avoid proceedings, steps to 6.77
change of circumstances 6.95
children 6.96–6.98
CCMS 6.99–6.103, 6.105, 6.109
controlled work 6.30, 6.32–6.67
counsel's fees 6.109
disbursements 6.109
domestic abuse cases 6.82–6.84, 6.87–6.89, 6.110–6.112
Family Advocacy Scheme (FAS) 6.106, 6.109
Family Help (Higher) 2.80, 6.78, 6.85
final hearings 6.85
financial matters, merits test for 6.104
forms 6.99–6.103, 6.105
funding 6.106
grant and scope of certificates 6.107–6.117
incidental steps 6.77
Legal Representation 6.78, 6.85
limitations 6.107–6.109, 6.114
litigation, conduct of 6.77
means test 6.81, 6.86, 6.114
mediation 6.81–6.84, 6.101, 6.105
merits test
  borderline or marginal cases 6.92, 6.98, 6.104, 6.111
  children 6.96–6.98
  cost-benefit/successful outcome 6.94
  domestic violence or abuse 6.111
  financial matters 6.104
  mediation 6.81
  proportionality test 6.111
  prospects of success 6.92–6.93, 6.111
  stages 6.92–6.94
  standard criteria 6.90–6.94
  urgent cases 6.114
preliminary steps 6.77
preparation 6.78

family private law cases (certificates)
continued
  Private Law Representation Scheme (PLRS) 6.78, 6.106
  representation 6.77–6.78
  scope 6.77–6.84, 6.107–6.117
  settlements 6.77, 6.102
  urgent cases 6.113–6.117
family private law cases, conducting 6.1–6.117
  abuse, without evidence of 6.6, 6.12–6.15
  adoption orders 6.13
  billing and payment 15.156
  bolt-on payments (children cases) 19.34, 19.42–19.43
  certificates *see* **family private law cases (certificates)**
  care proceedings 6.14
  change of name cases 6.50
  child abuse, risk of 6.6
  children 6.8, 6.12–6.14, 19.34, 19.42–19.43
  counsel, use of 19.63
  CW1 form 6.45
  divorce or judicial separation, uncontested proceedings for 6.34, 6.41, 6.47, 6.49
  domestic abuse *see* **domestic abuse**
  escape fee cases 6.50
  Family Help (Lower) *see* **Family Help (Lower) (family private law cases)**
  female genital mutilation (FGM) 6.12
  fixed fees 6.49
  forced marriage protection orders (FMPOs) 6.12
  Help with Family Mediation 6.68–6.76
  LAA's Costs Assessment Guidance 6.4
  Legal Help 6.14–6.15, 6.30, 6.33–6.50
  licensed work 6.31
  maintenance, EU and international agreements concerning 6.12

  means-test 6.14, 6.42–6.43, 6.45
  mediation 6.12
  merits test 6.14, 6.44
  placement orders 6.13
  representation at court, exclusion of 6.24
  scope 6.5–6.32, 6.36–6.41
  service standards 22.122–22.124
  special guardianship orders (SGOs) 6.12, 6.15
  Standard Civil Contract 2024 6.45, 22.122–22.124
  wardship 6.7
  wills 6.40
family public law cases, conducting 7.1–7.62
  adoption orders 7.6
  appeals 7.4
  billing and payment 15.156–15.159, 15.166, 15.171–15.177
  bolt-on payments (children cases) 19.34, 19.35–19.41
  Care Proceedings Graduated Fee Scheme (CPGFS) 15.171
  children 7.4–7.6, 7.10, 15.174–15.175
  controlled work 7.13, 7.15–7.33
  CW1 form 7.21
  CW1PL form 7.21, 7.30
  enhanced fees 15.184–15.186
  escape fee cases 15.172
  exceptional case funding (ECF) 3.5, 7.32
  Family Advocacy Scheme (FAS) 15.191–15.192
  Family Help (Lower) 7.13, 7.25–7.33
  forms 7.2, 7.21–7.23, 7.30
  funding 7.2, 7.24, 7.31
  hourly rates 15.171, 15.184–15.187
  inherent jurisdiction of the High Court 7.10
  joined parties 15.174–15.176
  Legal Help 7.7–7.8, 7.15–7.24
  legal representation standard fee 15.171–15.177
  letters, writing 7.15
  licensed work 7.14

local authorities
  negotiations with 7.25–7.26
  notice to issue proceedings 7.25–7.26, 7.30–7.31
means test 7.2, 7.18–7.20, 7.22, 7.29
merits test 7.2, 7.7, 7.17, 7.28
parents 15.174–15.175
parties 15.174–15.175
placement orders 7.6
public family law, definition of 7.4–7.8
regions 15.176–15.177
scope 7.2, 7.9–7.12, 7.15–7.16, 7.25–7.26
service standards 22.122–22.124
Special Children Act proceedings 7.4–7.5
Standard Civil Contract 2024 7.22, 7.27, 22.122–22.124
fee exemption and remission scheme 1.52–1.53
female genital mutilation (FGM) 6.12
final bills (civil cases), assessment of 15.56–15.64
final hearings
advocacy in family cases 19.20–19.21, 19.28–19.32
bolt-on payments (children cases) 19.21
daily rates 19.28
family private law cases (certificates) 6.85
finding of fact hearings in private and public cases 19.28
guidance 19.30–19.31
issue resolution hearings in public law cases 19.29
reading days 19.28
finance cases 6.104, 8.7, 19.34
financial and contract management 23.1–23.54
contract notices 23.37–23.54
costs audits 23.1, 23.25–23.36
key performance indicators (KPIs) 23.1, 23.22–23.23
payments for civil controlled cases and crime lower 23.2–23.10
payments on account (POAs) 23.1, 23.14–23.21
reconciliation of contacts 23.1, 23.11–23.13
financial eligibility *see* **means test; means test (civil and family); means test (criminal cases)**
First-tier Tribunal (FTT) 2.8, 9.46–9.47, 9.71, 9.95, 9.120
fixed fees
advocacy in family cases 19.9
Crown Court, litigator fees in the 16.83, 16.89
custody, clients detained in 20.13
escape fee cases 4.44, 4.74, 4.77
experts 4.140
family cases 6.76, 15.157, 15.167, 15.169
Help at Court 4.68, 18.14, 18.22
Help with Family Mediation 6.76
HLPAS Early Legal Advice, Legal Help and Legal Representation 4.47
hourly rates 1.7, 4.44
key performance indicators (KPIs) 4.82
Legal Help 4.44–4.45
magistrates' court cases, advocacy in 20.34
mental health cases, conducting 10.21
police station work 16.20, 16.31
prison law work 14.196, 16.69
representation orders 16.66–16.67
Standard Civil Contract 2024 4.45, 22.101–22.102
Very High Cost Cases (VHCC) 15.197
forced labour *see* **human trafficking, modern slavery, servitude or forced labour, victims of**
forced marriage protection orders (FMPOs) 2.61, 6.12
forms *see under* **individual entries**
full legal aid certificates *see* **representation certificates (civil and family)**

Galaxkey secure portal 22.88, 22.92
geographical areas 10.7–10.10, 21.28–21.29 *see* **London rates**
graduated fees
  Advocates' Graduated Fee Scheme (AGFS) 20.49
  Crown Court, litigator fees in the 16.83–16.87
  Family Graduated Fees Scheme (FGFS) 15.57, 19.7–19.9, 19.58
  online calculator 16.86
guidance 1.45–1.46 *see also* under individual entries

habeas corpus 4.107, 4.111, 13.20, 13.50–13.51, 14.206
harassment injunctions 11.5, 11.60–11.61
  notified of complaints, requirement that landlord has been 11.60
  Protection from Harassment Act 1997 11.5, 11.60–11.61
  warning letters 11.61
hardship 14.103, 14.155, 14.160, 16.98, 16.99
Help at Court (civil cases) 4.55–4.69, 18.5, 18.8–18.22
  definition 4.55
  costs protection 4.59
  counsel, exclusion of 4.55
  CW1 Legal Help, Help at Court and Family Help (Lower) form 4.65–4.66
  enforcement of orders 18.11
  escape fee cases 18.22
  family cases 19.2
  fixed fees 4.68, 18.14, 18.22
  forms 4.8, 4.65–4.66
  funding 4.67–4.69
  guidance 18.16
  housing cases 11.9, 11.11, 11.16, 11.19, 18.10, 18.16–18.20
  informal advocacy 4.67
  Legal Help 4.66, 18.19, 18.22
  merits test 4.62–4.64, 18.12–18.15
  mental health cases, conducting 10.18–10.19
  mortgage possession proceedings 11.19
  payment for advocacy services 18.22
  permitted work 2.78
  possession of the home cases 11.9, 11.11, 11.16, 18.10, 18.17–18.18
  preparation 18.22
  representation certificates 4.57–4.59, 18.9–18.10
  scope 4.55–4.60, 18.8–18.11
  specific areas of work 18.16–18.20
  statutory charge 6.63, 6.65
  travel and waiting time 4.69, 18.15, 18.22
  who can provide advocacy 18.21
Help with Family Mediation (private family law cases) 6.68–6.76
  billing and payment 15.158, 15.160
  consent orders 6.70, 6.76
  controlled work 4.70, 6.68–6.76
  CW5 form 6.73, 6.76
  evidence 6.72
  Family Help in relation to same dispute 6.74
  fixed fees 6.76
  forms 6.73
  funding 6.74–6.76
  means test 6.71
  merits test 6.72
  number of clients, one fee regardless of the 6.75
  permitted work 2.82
  reluctance of practitioners to take on work 6.76
  same dispute within six months, unavailability for 6.74
  scope 6.69–6.70
  signatures 6.73
High cost cases *see* **High Cost civil cases; very expensive cases/special case work (civil and family); Very High Cost Cases (VHCC) – criminal; Very High Cost Cases (VHCC) – family**

High Cost civil cases 18.43–18.46
  advocacy 18.43–18.46, 19.62–19.63
  agreement to rates 18.44
  classification of cases 18.45
  counsel 18.45
  family cases *see* **Very High Cost Cases (VHCC) – family**
  High Costs Contract and Counsel Acceptance Forms 7.60
  individual case contracts (ICCs) 18.43
  inter partes costs 18.45
  King's Counsel, use of 7.60
  payments on account (POA) 1.85
  very expensive cases *see* **very expensive cases/special case work (civil and family)**
High Court
  bail proceedings 14.88
  case stated, appeals by way of 14.178, 14.179–14.181, 16.75
  counsel, use of 18.34, 18.36, 18.45
  criminal cases 20.55
  immigration and asylum cases 9.48
  inherent jurisdiction 6.7, 6.9, 7.10, 10.4
homelessness and allocations 11.21–11.34
  accommodation, provision of 11.5
  appeals 11.23, 11.25–11.27
  assistance, provision of 11.5
  asylum-seekers 11.32–11.34
  borderline or marginal cases 11.25, 11.30
  care leavers 12.29
  CCMS 11.22, 11.26, 11.31
  children 12.23, 12.25
  Code of Guidance 11.22, 11.24
  community care services, accommodation by way of 11.29–11.31
  counsel, use of 11.26
  emergency delegated functions 11.26, 11.28, 11.31, 11.34, 12.23, 13.30–13.31
  entitlement 11.23
  European Convention on Human Rights (ECHR), breach of 11.25
  guidance 11.22, 11.24
  homeless, definition of 11.22
  Housing Act 1996 11.21–11.28
  Housing (Wales) Act 2014 11.22, 11.24, 11.27
  judicial review 11.23–11.25, 11.28, 11.30, 11.32, 12.23, 13.30–13.31
  Legal Help 11.21, 11.24, 11.29–11.33
  Legal Representation 11.21, 11.25, 11.29
  merits test 11.25, 11.30
  representation certificates 4.107, 4.111
  scope 11.22–11.23
  suitability of accommodation 11.23
  telephone advice from LAA 11.27, 11.31
  threats of homelessness 11.21
hourly rates
  Advocacy Assistance 16.37, 20.25
  advocacy in civil cases 18.29
  advocacy in family cases 19.8, 19.14
  appeals 15.168
  controlled work, billing and payment for 15.39
  counsel, use of 15.40
  Crown Court, litigator fees in the 16.89
  custody, clients detained in 20.13
  disbursements 15.223
  enhanced rates 16.62–16.65, 18.29
  escape fee cases 15.39, 15.226
  experts 4.50, 4.140, 4.147, 4.149–4.150, 15.55
  family cases, billing and payment for 15.40, 15.167–15.168
  fixed fees per case 1.7
  immigration and asylum cases
    billing and payment 15.208, 15.211, 15.216, 15.220, 15.223, 15.226, 15.229–15.235
    conducting 9.75–9.80, 9.107, 9.111, 9.113, 9.126

hourly rates *continued*
  licensed work 15.207, 15.216
  line-by-line hourly rate bills 5.79
  magistrates' court cases 16.62–16.65, 20.31
  mental health cases, conducting 10.17, 10.19, 10.43–10.46
  police station work 16.24
  prison law work 14.196
  public family law fee scheme 15.171, 15.184–15.187
  representation certificates 4.128, 15.65, 15.67, 15.70
  Upper Tribunal (UT) 15.235
  very expensive cases/special case work 4.232, 4.234–4.235
housing cases, conducting 11.1–11.102
  anti-social behaviour (ASB), injunctions against 11.5, 11.62–11.70
  appeals 5.18
  Category Definitions 11.5
  CCMS 5.18
  charges for premises 11.5
  conditions *see* **housing conditions and disrepair**
  counterclaims 11.3
  Covid-19 arrangements 11.2, 11.83–11.86
  disrepair *see* **housing conditions and disrepair**
  emergency delegated functions 5.42–5.43
  eviction *see* **eviction**
  exceptional case funding (ECF) 11.1, 11.5
  face-to-face debt work 2.11
  guidance 11.2–11.3, 18.16
  harassment injunctions 11.5, 11.60–11.61
  Help at Court 18.10, 18.16–18.20
  home rights 6.9
  homelessness *see* **homelessness and allocations**
  housing work, definition of 11.5
  immigration and asylum cases 11.5
  legal representation certificates 18.17–18.18
  possession cases *see* **possession of the home cases**
  quiet enjoyment 11.5
  rent, payment of 11.5
  representation certificates 11.3
  scope 2.14, 11.1, 11.5–11.71
  service standards 22.130
  Standard Civil Contract 2024 11.5, 22.46, 22.130
  supervisor standards 22.46
housing conditions and disrepair 11.5, 11.41–11.59
  Conditional Fee Agreements (CFAs) 4.182, 11.50, 11.52–11.53
  counterclaims 11.41–11.42, 11.55–11.59
  damages claims 4.181, 11.45, 11.50–11.53, 11.59
  exceptional case funding (ECF) 11.5
  exclusions 11.43, 11.54–11.57
  experts' reports, costs of 11.46–11.48
  fitness for human habitation 11.42, 11.45
  freestanding claims 11.41–11.55
  guidance 11.47, 11.49
  judicial review 11.48
  Legal Help 11.46, 11.53, 11.54
  medical evidence 11.48
  merits test 11.44
  notified of complaints, requirement that landlord has been 11.44
  personal injury claims 11.55
  possession proceedings 11.55–11.59
  rent, withholding 11.56–11.59
  review, right to request a 11.48
  scope 11.42–11.43, 11.50–11.51, 11.57–11.59
  serious risk of harm 11.45–11.46, 11.48–11.49
  specific performance 4.181
  statutory charge 4.180–4.182, 11.51
  statutory nuisance 11.54

Index   737

Housing Loss Prevention Advice Service (HLPAS) 11.13, 11.72–11.102
10% buffer 11.82
adjournments 11.89
agents, qualifications of 11.91
amount of fee 11.88
commencement of scheme 11.81
Contract Report form 11.96, 11.100
Contracted Work and Administration (CWA) system, claims for payment via 11.96
Covid-19 arrangements 11.83–11.86
disbursements 11.99
Early Legal Advice – Stage One 11.13, 11.74–11.75, 11.89, 11.93–11.102
emergency delegated functions 11.90
face-to-face Housing and Debt contracts, requirement to hold 11.81
forms 11.92
guidance 11.76, 11.85, 11.93, 11.96–11.102, 22.134
In Court duty scheme – Stage Two 11.73, 11.75, 11.87–11.92, 11.95–11.96
  Contract Report form 11.96
  disbursements 11.99
  making a claim for payment 11.95–11.96, 11.98–11.99
Legal Help 11.74–11.75, 11.86, 11.93–11.102, 22.133
list of providers 11.79–11.80
making a claim for payment 11.95–11.102
means test 11.86, 11.87, 11.94
monitoring forms 11.92
more than one client 11.97–11.98
more than one hearing 11.89
operation of the scheme 11.87–11.92
Secure File Exchange 11.100
service standards 22.133–22.34
Standard Civil Contract 2024 1.38, 2.15, 11.76, 22.133–22.134
supervision and file review procedures 11.92
tenders 22.133
timetables 11.100–11.102
travel and waiting time 11.99
website 11.77, 11.79–11.80, 22.134
Housing Possession Court Duty Scheme (HPCDS), quashing of LAA's tender for 1.93
human rights *see also* **European Convention on Human Rights (ECHR)**
care and wardship proceedings 4.180, 4.183–4.184
Charter of Fundamental Rights of the EU (CFREU) 9.39
damages 4.184, 12.42, 13.21
Equality and Human Rights Commission (EHRC) 13.36
Human Rights Act 1998 4.180, 4.183–4.184, 13.5, 13.21–13.22
public law cases, conducting 13.5, 13.21–13.22
scope 1.14
human trafficking, modern slavery, servitude or forced labour, victims of
appeals 9.46
asylum claims 9.24
conclusive grounds decisions 9.22–9.23
Council of Europe Convention on Action against Trafficking in Human Beings 2005 9.21
exceptional case funding (ECF) 3.28–3.30, 3.36–3.37
guidance 9.20
identification of victims 9.22, 9.27
leave to enter or remain, applications for 9.20–9.24
National Referral Mechanism (NRM) 3.36–3.37, 9.21–9.22, 9.27
reasonable grounds decisions 9.21–9.22

human trafficking, modern slavery, servitude or forced labour, victims of *continued*
  Single Competent Authority (SCA) 9.21–9.23
  time restrictions, lack of 9.23

ICAs *see* **Independent Costs Assessors (ICAs)**
IFAs *see* **Independent Funding Adjudicators (IFAs)**
immigration and asylum cases *see* **immigration and asylum cases, billing and payment for; immigration and asylum cases, conducting**
immigration and asylum cases, billing and payment for 15.45, 15.207–15.236
  additional payments 15.219
  audits 23.29
  bail applications 15.232
  Controlled Legal Representation (CLR) 15.207–15.210, 18.23
    counsel, use of 15.220
    disbursements 15.222, 15.224
    hourly rates 15.232–15.233
    Legal Help 15.214
    Online Procedure 15.215
  controlled work 15.207–15.210, 15.214–15.215, 15.218, 15.222, 15.224–15.226
  counsel, use of 15.220–15.221
  Detained Fast Track Scheme 15.236
  disbursements 15.222–15.225
  escape fee cases 15.226–15.228
  EU, people resident outside the 4.19
  exceptional fee cases 15.212
  fee stages 15.213–15.218
  hourly rates 15.208, 15.211, 15.216, 15.220, 15.223, 15.226, 15.229–15.235
  Legal Help 15.207, 15.209, 15.214, 15.222–15.223, 15.226, 15.231, 15.233
  licensed work 15.207, 15.215

Online Procedure 15.208, 15.209, 15.215, 15.219
Standard Civil Contract 2024 15.217, 22.39–22.40
Standard Fee Stage 15.208–15.212, 15.219–15.220, 15.226–15.233
travel and waiting time 15.220, 15.224
Upper Tribunal (UT) cases 15.234–15.236

immigration and asylum cases, conducting 9.1–9.131
  accreditation 9.59–9.63, 22.22, 22.40, 22.125
  appeals 9.37, 9.45–9.48, 9.55, 9.74–9.75, 9.99
  Controlled Legal Representation (CLR) 9.45, 9.100–9.101, 9.110
  Court of Appeal cases 9.48, 9.75, 9.123
  First-tier Tribunal (FTT) 9.46–9.47, 9.71, 9.95, 9.120
  Independent Funding Adjudicators (IFAs) 9.100–9.101
  Legal Representation 9.45, 9.117
  licensed works 9.48, 9.119
  post-appeal work 9.74, 9.117–9.119
  Special Immigration Appeals Commission (SIAC) proceedings 9.37
  Upper Tribunal (UT) 9.46–9.47, 9.71, 9.80, 9.95, 9.119, 9.120–9.122, 9.128
asylum seekers *see* **asylum seekers and refugees**
attendance at hearings 9.112–9.115
bail 9.6–9.9, 9.36, 9.109–9.111
billing and payment *see* **immigration and asylum cases, billing and payment for**
caseworkers, role of 9.59–9.66
Category Definitions 9.3–9.4, 9.57
CCMS 9.120, 9.124
children 9.5, 9.61, 9.89, 9.105–9.106, 22.125

conducting the case 9.102–9.104
Controlled Legal Representation (CLR) 2.79, 9.42–9.45, 9.62, 9.72, 9.74–9.75, 9.81
  appeals 9.45, 9.75, 9.100–9.101, 9.110
  attendance at hearings 9.112
  bail applications 9.110
  granting 9.92–9.96
  Independent Funding Adjudicators (IFAs) 17.18–17.23
  licensed work 9.131–9.132
  means test 9.92
  merits test 9.93–9.101, 9.117
  passported benefits 2.42
  post-appeal work 9.74, 9.117–9.118
  refusal 9.97–9.101
  senior caseworkers 9.62
  separate matters 9.82
  supplier, change of 9.100–9.101
  Upper Tribunal (UT) 9.131
  withdrawal 9.97–9.101
costs, managing 9.125–9.130
Court of Appeal cases 9.48, 9.75, 9.123
CW1 form 9.29
CW2 form 9.101
damages claims 9.36
deportation/expulsion/removals 9.9
  exclusive immigration removal centre contracts, organisations with 9.67–9.68
  inhuman or degrading treatment 9.56
  judicial review 9.50–9.53, 9.56
  life, right to 9.56
  Priority Removal Notices (PRN) 9.28–9.30, 9.56
  removal notices 9.50–9.53, 9.56, 13.19
detention 9.6–9.9
  bail 9.6–9.9, 9.36, 9.109–9.111
  damages 9.36
  Detained Duty Advice Scheme 9.68
  Detained Fast Track Scheme/ Detained Asylum Casework Scheme 9.68, 9.122
  exclusive immigration removal centre contracts, organisations with 9.67–9.68
  interviews, attendance at 9.105
  otherwise than in an IRC, clients detained 9.69
  travel to detained clients 9.108
  waiting times 9.108
disbursements 9.86, 9.107, 9.121, 9.126–9.128
domestic violence victims 9.10–9.15
emergency delegated functions 9.124
entry clearance 9.71, 9.74
Equality Act 2010 9.47
escape fee claims 9.86, 9.113, 9.126
EU, persons from outside the 4.18–4.19
exceptional case funding (ECF) 3.33–3.37, 9.3, 9.38–9.41, 9.90
  Charter of Fundamental Rights of the EU (CFREU) 9.39
  Customer Services Team, contact from 3.61
  grant rate 3.5
  list of organisations to assist individuals, creation of a 3.61
  relevant issues 3.14
exclusions 9.4, 9.49–9.53
  exclusive immigration removal centre contracts, organisations with 9.67–9.68
fee types 9.76–9.81
First-tier Tribunal (FTT) 9.46–9.47, 9.71, 9.95, 9.120
High Court appeals 9.48
higher courts litigation 9.120, 9.123–9.124
hourly rates 9.75–9.80, 9.107, 9.111, 9.113, 9.126
housing cases 11.5
Illegal Migration Act 2023 9.56, 9.127
Immigration and Asylum Accreditation Scheme (IAAS) 9.59

immigration and asylum cases, conducting *continued*
immigration and asylum work, definition of 9.3
immigration matter, definition of 9.57–9.58
indefinite leave to remain (ILR) 9.46
Independent Funding Adjudicators (IFAs) 17.18–17.23
inhuman or degrading treatment 9.56
instructing advocates and in conference, time spent 9.115
interviews, attendance at 9.105–9.107
judicial review 1.94, 9.49–9.56, 9.124, 13.19
leave to remain (LTR) 9.71, 9.74
licensed work 9.48, 9.119, 9.131–9.133
Legal Help 9.37, 9.42–9.44, 9.72, 9.74–9.75, 9.88–9.91
 appeals 9.99, 9.128
 attendance at hearings 9.112
 passported support 2.42, 9.88
 post-appeal work 9.117
 senior caseworkers 9.62
 separate matters 9.82
Legal Representation for appeal work 9.45
licensed work 9.120–9.122
low remuneration, judicial review of 1.94
matter starts 9.82–9.87
means test 9.88–9.89, 9.92
merits test 9.91, 9.93–9.99, 9.101–9.102, 9.110
 borderline or marginal cases 9.93–9.94, 9.96
 Controlled Legal Representation (CLR) 9.93–9.101, 9.117
 licensed work 9.132
 refusal or withdrawal 9.97–9.99
 sufficient benefit test 9.91
 unclear cases 9.94, 9.96

Office of the Immigration Services Commissioner (OISC) 1.18, 9.59
online procedure advocacy services, additional payments for 9.116
passported benefits 2.42
Priority Removal Notices (PRN) 9.28–9.30
private and family life, right to respect for 3.9
proportionality test 9.94
public interest 9.93–9.94, 9.114
refugees *see* **asylum seekers and refugees**
removal directions 9.50–9.53, 9.56, 13.19
representation certificates 9.123–9.124
residence, right of 9.47
revived cases 9.87
scope 2.14, 9.70
separate matters 9.82–9.87
separated children 9.5
service standards 22.125
Special Immigration Appeals Commission (SIAC) proceedings 9.37
Standard Civil Contract 2024 9.3, 9.57–9.58, 9.61–9.63, 9.66, 9.73, 9.76–9.79, 9.83
 online procedure advocacy services, additional payments for 9.116
 service standards 22.125
Standard Fee Scheme rates 9.42–9.44, 9.76, 9.79–9.80, 9.107, 9.113
 managing costs 9.125–9.127
 online procedure advocacy services, additional payments for 9.116
structure of immigration work 9.71–9.101
supervisor standards 22.39–22.40
supplier, change of 9.100–9.101
Supreme Court appeals 9.48
suspensive claims 9.56

Terrorism Prevention and Immigration Measures (TPIMs) 9.35
travel to detained clients 9.108, 9.116
Upper Tribunal (UT) 9.46–9.47, 9.71, 9.80, 9.95, 9.119, 9.120–9.122, 9.128
  licensed work 9.120–9.122, 9.131
  permission to appeal 9.120–9.122
waiting times 9.108, 9.116
who can carry out the work 9.59–9.70
income 1.11, 2.30, 2.40–2.42, 2.53–2.56
  assessment 2.53–2.56
  contributions 4.153
  criminal cases *see* **income (criminal cases)**
  disposable income 2.30, 2.53, 2.55, 2.64, 4.153
  expenses, deduction of 2.55
  gross income 2.30, 2.53–2.55
  Legal Help 4.22, 4.26
  online calculators 2.56
  passported benefits 2.40–2.41
  thresholds 2.53, 4.153
  welfare benefits 2.54
income (criminal cases)
  advice and assistance 14.61–14.62, 14.64–14.65
  Advocacy Assistance 20.58
  billing and payment 16.70
  case study 14.98
  contributions 14.138–14.144, 14.146, 14.148, 14.157–14.158
  Crown Court 14.134, 14.137–14.144
  definition 14.64
  dependants 14.64
  disposable income 14.92, 14.95, 14.99–14.100, 14.137–14.138, 14.199
  gross income 14.92, 14.95–14.99
  exceptions 14.64
  living expenses allowance 14.100–14.101
  means test 14.61–14.62, 14.64–14.65
  overpayments, refund of 14.144, 14.158
  partners 14.64
  prison law work 14.199, 20.58
  representation orders (magistrates' courts) 14.92, 14.95–14.99
  sanctions 14.152, 14.154
  thresholds 14.65
  uprating 14.65
  weighting 14.97–14.99
indemnity principle 15.119–15.122, 15.148, 15.152
Independent Costs Assessors (ICAs) 17.46–17.53
  appeals 15.100, 15.104, 16.80, 23.52–23.53
  audits 17.46
  criminal cases 16.80
  guidance 17.51, 17.53
  judicial review 23.53
  oral hearings, exceptional circumstances for 17.52, 23.53
  papers only, on 23.53
  procedure 17.47–17.52
  reasonable remuneration 17.51
  reduction of remuneration 17.1, 17.46–17.53
  time limits 17.48–17.49
  tips for appeals 17.53
  when you might need to appeal 17.3
  written representations 17.49
Independent Funding Adjudicators (IFAs) 17.1, 17.4–17.45
  appeals 17.1, 17.3–17.45
  civil cases 17.1, 17.4–17.45
  controlled work 17.5, 17.18–17.23, 17.35–17.45
  CW4 form 17.19–17.20
  emergency representation, refusal of 17.25
  exceptional case funding (ECF) 17.18
  family mediation 17.55

Independent Funding Adjudicators (IFAs) *continued*
further information, submission of 17.29
guidance 17.29
immigration and asylum cases 17.18–17.23
interim, work done in the 17.33–17.34
internal review, right of 17.7–17.17
licensed work 17.3, 17.24–17.25, 17.33–17.34
merits test 17.5–17.6
new applications 17.6
nil assessment appeals in controlled work cases 17.35–17.45
oral hearings 17.30
panels 17.31
powers of the IFA 17.26–17.28
refusal of legal aid 17.1, 17.3, 17.4–17.5, 17.18–17.34
special casework decisions 17.54
upheld, where decisions of LAA are 17.32
when you might need to appeal 17.3
withdrawal of funding 17.5, 17.18–17.34
written reasons, provision of 17.28
individual case contracts (ICCs)
anti-social behaviour (ASB) injunctions 11.67, 11.69
exceptional case funding (ECF) 3.54–3.55, 3.72
High Cost civil cases 18.43
very expensive cases/special case work 4.215, 14.211–14.212, 15.193, 15.196, 16.104
inhuman or degrading treatment 9.16, 9.17, 9.56
Initial Details of Prosecution Case (IDPC) 14.104
injunctions *see* **anti-social behaviour (ASB) injunctions**
inquest exceptional case funding (ECF) 3.38–3.78
advocacy 3.38, 3.62, 3.68, 3.71
associated legal help 3.62
backdating 3.71
categories 3.52–3.54
CCMS 3.56–3.65, 3.73
CIV ECF1 form 3.56–3.57, 3.67
CIV ECF2 (INQ) 3.64
CIVAPP1 3.70
CIVAPP 3 3.70
delegated functions 3.51
direct applicants 3.60
effective administration of justice test 3.52–3.54
Equality Act 2010 3.66
forms 3.56–3.65, 3.73
fresh applications 3.76
grant rate 3.5
grounds 3.39
guidance 3.39–3.49, 3.77
help and support for practitioners 3.77–3.78
immigration and asylum cases 3.61
individual case contracts 3.54–3.55, 3.72
INQUEST charity 3.78
Inquest Funding Provider Packs 3.51
Inquest Lawyer's Group 3.78
judicial review 3.75–3.76
Legal Help 3.38, 3.62
Lexcel 3.55
life, right to 3.39–3.49
means test 2.62, 3.57, 3.62
merits test 3.57
payment 3.69–3.72
Provider Pack 3.39, 3.62
public interest 3.38–3.39, 3.50
review process 3.73–3.76
Specialist Quality Mark (SQM) 3.55
Standard Civil Contract 2024 3.54
statutory charge 3.65
timetable 3.66–3.68
urgent applications 3.67–3.69
websites 3.39, 3.58–3.59, 3.73, 3.78
inter partes costs
advocacy in civil cases 18.50

assessment *see* **assessment of inter partes costs by the courts (civil and family)**
High Cost civil cases 18.45
indemnity principle 15.119–15.122
interim orders 15.122
market rates 15.119
set off 15.120–15.121
struck out claims 15.122
interest on costs 15.127, 15.135
interim hearings 19.21–19.27
internal reviews 17.7–17.17
APP9E form 17.10
costs appeals 15.100, 23.51
exceptional case funding (ECF) 17.9–17.13
family mediation 17.55
Independent Funding Adjudicators (IFAs) 17.7–17.17
judicial review 17.13
licensed work 17.14–17.17
right to reviews 17.2, 17.7–17.17
time limits 17.8, 17.10, 17.16
website 17.11
withdrawal takes effect, date when 17.17
written representations 17.10, 17.14, 17.17
interpreters 15.18, 15.22–15.23
investigations *see* **investigations class work; investigative representation certificates**
investigations class work 14.18–14.76, 20.8–20.19
advice and assistance 14.60
Advocacy Assistance 20.2, 20.9–20.19
billing and payment *see* **investigations class work, billing and payment for**
custody, clients detained in 20.9–20.14
Investigative Representation scheme 13.39, 13.41
police bail 20.15–20.19
representation orders 20.8
investigations class work, billing and payment for 16.12–16.23

Advocacy Assistance 16.37
bail 16.37
case study 16.23
costs limit 16.19
Criminal Defence Direct acceptance fee 16.29–16.30
Defence Solicitor Call Centre (DSCC) reference number 16.23
escape fee cases 16.21, 16.24, 16.30–16.32
exceptional cases 16.24, 16.29
free-standing advice and assistance 16.16–16.19, 16.21, 16.29, 16.34, 16.37
hourly rates 16.16, 16.19, 16.29–16.30, 16.37
more than one client, acting for 16.18
police station attendance 16.20–16.34, 16.37
police station telephone advice only 16.13–16.16, 16.21
rates 16.24–16.32
standard monthly payments 16.32
unique file numbers (UFNs) 16.34, 16.37
when bills should be submitted 16.12, 16.17
investigative representation certificates
community care cases 12.11–12.12, 12.15, 12.17
exceptional case funding (ECF) 15.17
guidance 4.86
Legal Help escape fee claims 4.85
merits test 4.85–4.86, 12.11
permitted work 2.83–2.84
public law cases, conducting 13.28, 13.29

jointly owned property 2.47–2.48
judicial review 2.8, 13.2–13.6
Administrative Court 13.47–13.49
after the event (ATE) insurance 13.35
appeals 13.15

jointly owned property *continued*
  asylum seekers and refugees 9.52, 9.133
  benefiting the individual and/or the family or environment 13.12, 13.15–13.16
  CCMS 13.41, 15.80
  community care cases 12.12, 12.23, 12.25, 12.30
  conditional payments 15.72–15.81
  costs orders 13.48
  costs protection 13.48–13.49
  counsel, use of 13.41
  criminal cases 14.206, 16.73
  disbursements 15.73
  discretionary payments 15.72, 15.79–15.81
  emergency delegated functions 5.40–5.41, 11.28, 13.30–13.31
  Equality and Human Rights Commission (EHRC) 13.36
  exceptional case funding (ECF) 3.75–3.76
  European Convention on Human Rights (ECHR), breach of 13.36
  examples 13.23
  exclusions 13.10, 13.19
  exhaustion of internal reviews and appeals 9.55
  guidance 13.47–13.49
  habeas corpus 13.50
  homelessness 11.23–11.25, 11.28, 12.23, 13.30–13.31
  housing conditions and disrepair 11.48
  immigration and asylum cases 9.49–9.56, 9.124, 13.19
  Independent Costs Assessors (ICAs) 23.53
  internal reviews 17.13
  Investigative Representation scheme 13.39, 13.41
  judicial review, definition of 13.11, 13.17
  Legal Help 13.39
  Legal Representation 11.25
  lodging claims 13.41–13.42
  merits test 13.29
  number of applications 13.6
  payment for judicial review work 13.44–13.46
  permission applications 13.42–13.43, 15.72–15.77
  points of principle of general public importance (PoP) 23.54
  possession of the home cases 11.14
  Pre-Action Protocol 11.30, 11.32, 12.10, 12.17, 12.25, 13.26, 13.39
  principles, list of 13.3
  public spaces protection orders (PSPOs) 13.13–13.17
  R (Liberty) v Director of Legal Aid Casework 13.13–13.17
  refusal of legal aid, reasons for 13.35–13.36
  refusal of permission 13.45
  removal directions 9.50–9.53, 9.56
  representation certificates 4.111, 15.72–15.81
  scope 13.10–13.19
  steps in a judicial review case 13.39–13.43
  standing 13.14
  substantive hearings 13.43
  time limits 13.40

key performance indicators (KPIs) 22.96–22.110, 23.1, 23.22–23.23
  assessment reductions 22.99–22.100
  costs appeals 15.98
  controlled work 4.82, 22.99
  escape fee cases 22.99
  fixed fee margin 4.82, 22.101–22.102
  legal representation outcomes 4.82, 22.108
  licensed work 4.82, 22.100, 22.103–22.106
  mandatory KPIs 22.96
  monitoring 22.97–22.98, 23.22
  out of profile, being 22.97

Provider Activity Report (PAR) 22.95
quality standards and performance monitoring 22.96–22.110
refusal rates 22.107
rejection rates 1.3, 4.82, 15.46, 15.48, 22.103–22.106
reports 22.97
Standard Civil Contract 2024 4.71, 4.80–4.82, 22.99–22.110, 23.23
Standard Crime Contract 2022/2025 22.96, 22.110, 23.23
technical errors 22.103–22.106
timetable 22.98
King's Counsel, use of
appeals 4.135
Care Case Fee Scheme (CCFS) 7.60
civil cases 18.26, 18.30, 18.33
Crown Court 20.46–20.48
Exceptional and Complex Case Team (ECCT) 4.215
High Costs Contract and Counsel Acceptance Forms 4.222, 7.60
family cases 4.222–4.223, 19.9, 19.62
magistrates' court cases 20.43
representation certificates 4.135–4.136
very expensive cases/special case work 4.215, 4.222–4.223, 15.195
KPIs *see* **key performance indicators (KPIs)**

Law Centres Network (LCN) 22.17
Law Society *see* **Lexcel standard (Law Society)**
legal aid contracts 21.1–21.49
applications 21.28–21.37, 21.42–21.43
Civil and Crime Specifications 21.25–21.27
elements of the contracts 21.9–21.27
office schedules 21.12, 21.15–21.19
other kinds of contract 21.48–21.49
signatures 21.11–21.14
Standard Civil Contract 2024 *see* **Standard Civil Contract 2024**
Standard Crime Contract 2022 *see* **Standard Crime Contract 2022**
Standard Crime Contract 2025 *see* **Standard Crime Contract 2025**
tenders 21.38–21.41, 21.49
legal aid only costs 15.107–15.118, 15.138–15.143, 18.51–18.54
Legal Aid Practitioners Group (LAPG), online course of 1.3
legal aid representation certificates *see* **representation certificates (civil and family)**
legal challenges 1.88–1.95
Legal Help 4.5–4.54, 21.29
aftercare services under MHA 1983 12.17
anti-social behaviour (ASB) injunctions 11.62
applications 21.29
attendance notes 4.13
audits 23.29, 23.31
billing and payment 15.17, 15.40, 15.158, 15.160–15.161
case study 4.9
children 4.11, 4.14–4.16, 6.39
clients' details 4.9
community care cases 12.10, 12.15, 12.17–12.18, 12.20, 12.23
controlled work 10.25
counsel, use of 15.40
CW1 form 4.8, 6.45, 7.21
definition 1.16
disbursements 4.48–4.54
divorce or judicial separation, uncontested proceedings for 6.34, 6.41, 6.47, 6.49

Legal Help *continued*
  domestic abuse 6.10, 6.22, 6.25, 6.37–6.38, 6.49
  escape fee cases 1.25, 6.50, 15.160–15.161
  EU, people resident outside the 4.18–4.19
  evidence 6.22, 6.25, 6.27
  exceptional case funding (ECF) 3.4, 3.31, 3.38, 3.62, 3.70, 15.17
  exclusions 4.6
  experts 4.143
  family cases
    billing and payment for 15.158, 15.160–15.161
    change of name cases 6.40
    Family Help (Lower) form 4.8, 7.21
    private law cases – level 1 6.30, 6.33–6.50
    means test 6.14–6.15
    mediation 8.3, 8.11
    public law cases – level 1 7.7–7.8, 7.15–7.24
  fax, applications by 4.20
  fee exemption and remission scheme 1.52
  fixed fees 4.44–4.47, 6.49
  forms 4.8–4.21, 6.45–6.46, 7.21–7.23, 23.31
  funding 4.44–4.47, 6.47–6.50, 7.24
  harassment injunctions 11.61
  Help at Court 4.8, 4.66, 7.21, 18.19, 18.22
  housing
    conditions and disrepair 11.46, 11.53, 11.54
    homelessness 11.21, 11.24, 11.29–11.33
    Housing Loss Prevention Advice Service (HLPAS) 11.74–11.75, 11.86, 11.93–11.102, 22.133
    mortgage possession proceedings 11.19–11.20
    possession of the home cases 11.6, 11.10–11.11
  immigration and asylum cases
    billing and payment 15.207, 15.209, 15.214, 15.222–15.223, 15.226, 15.231, 15.233
    conducting 9.37, 9.42–9.44, 9.72, 9.74–9.75, 9.88–9.91, 9.99, 9.112, 9.128–9.129
  inquest exceptional case funding (ECF) 3.38, 3.62
  judicial review 13.39
  letters, writing 7.15, 18.19
  litigation friends 10.25
  means test 4.9, 4.22–4.28, 6.14–6.15, 9.88, 23.31
    evidence 4.23–4.28, 6.45
    family public law cases 7.18–7.20
    family private law cases 6.42–6.43, 6.45
    mental health cases, conducting 10.28–10.29
    Standard Civil Contract 2024 7.22
  mental health cases, conducting 10.4, 10.18, 10.24–10.30, 12.17
  merits test 4.29–4.35, 6.44, 7.17, 10.30
  more than one matter, opening 4.36–4.43, 4.45
  mortgage possession proceedings 11.19
  other sources of funding 4.7
  permitted work 2.78
  possession of the home cases 11.6, 11.10–11.11
  post, applications by 4.17–4.19
  previous advice, restrictions where clients have received 2.68
  protected parties 4.11, 4.14–4.16
  public law cases, conducting 13.8, 13.22, 13.26, 13.29, 13.31
  reopening closed matters 4.35
  scope 4.5–4.6, 7.15–7.16
  signatures 4.11–4.13, 4.66
  Standard Civil Contract 2024 4.11, 4.21, 4.23, 4.31–4.34, 7.22

statutory charge 4.159–4.160, 6.62, 6.65
telephone, webcam and email advice 4.11, 4.21
wills 6.40
Legal Representation
appeals 9.45, 11.25
certified work 1.16
community care cases for children, conducting 12.18, 12.20, 12.23
definition 1.16
eviction 11.36–11.37
experts 1.16
family private law cases (certificates) 6.78, 6.85
homelessness 11.21, 11.25, 11.29
immigration and asylum cases 9.45
judicial review 11.25
key performance indicators (KPIs) 4.82
mental health cases, conducting 10.18
merits test 11.37
payment 1.19
permitted work 2.78, 2.80
solicitors 1.16
Lexcel standard (Law Society) 22.3, 22.16–22.18
CCMS 5.24
current version 22.16
exceptional case funding (ECF) 3.55
in-house (not-for-profits) 22.16
Law Centres Network (LCN) 22.17
legal practices (private practice) 22.16
Solicitors Regulation Authority (SRA) Standards and Regulations 22.16
Specialist Quality Mark (SQM) 22.12, 22.16, 22.18
licensed work
appeals 9.48, 9.119
applications 21.30
backdated work 17.33–17.34

billing and payment 15.10–15.11, 15.14 *see also* **licensed work in family cases, billing and payment for**
contributions 2.64
disbursements 4.49, 4.53
emergency delegated functions 7.14
family public law cases, conducting 7.14
hourly rates 15.207, 15.216
immigration and asylum cases 9.48, 9.119–9.122, 9.131–9.133, 15.207, 15.216
Independent Funding Adjudicators (IFAs) 17.3, 17.24–17.25, 17.33–17.34
internal reviews 17.14–17.17
key performance indicators (KPIs) 4.82, 22.100, 22.103–22.106
means test 2.63–2.64
mental health cases, conducting 10.58–10.60
refusal rates 22.107
rejection rates 22.103–22.106
representation certificates *see* **representation certificates (civil and family)**
Standard Civil Contract 2024 2.19, 2.21, 22.100, 22.103–22.106
Upper Tribunal (UT) 15.216, 15.234
licensed work in family cases, billing and payment for
£2,500, costs exceeding 15.163
appeals 15.101, 15.168
assessment of fees by the LAA 15.124, 15.134, 15.162–15.164
CCMS 15.169–15.170
change of solicitors 15.187–15.190
CIVCLAIM1A form 15.169
court, assessment by the 15.163
disbursements 15.163
domestic abuse 15.178, 15.181, 15.183
escape fee cases 15.172

licensed work in family cases, billing and payment for *continued*
  Family Advocacy Scheme (FAS) 15.165, 15.191–15.192
  fixed fees 15.157, 15.164, 15.167, 15.169
  hourly rates 15.167–15.168
  multiple clients 15.170
  Private Family Law Representation Scheme (PFLRS)/ Higher Standard Fee Scheme 15.166, 15.178–15.192
  private law cases 6.31
  public family law fee scheme 15.166, 15.171–15.177
  related proceedings 15.166
  VHCC claims 15.193–15.206
life, right to 3.39–3.49, 9.16, 9.56
limitation periods *see under individual entries*
litigants in person 3.13, 3.26, 3.30
litigation friends 3.26, 4.91, 12.20, 12.40–12.41
Lockley orders 15.120, 15.130
logos 1.96
London rates 4.141, 15.8, 15.20, 18.30, 18.32
Lord Chancellor, challenges to 1.89
magistrates' court cases
  advocacy 20.7, 20.20–20.44
  billing and payment *see* **magistrates' courts, billing and payment for standard fees in the**
  committal or sending to the Crown Court 20.34
  counsel, use of 20.5
  Crown Court 14.149–14.151. 14.153, 14.161–14.162
    appeals to the Crown Court 14.168–14.171
    disbursements 14.162
    means test 14.149–14.151. 14.153, 14.161–14.162, 14.168–14.171
    stage 14.149–14.151. 14.153, 14.161–14.162

  means test 14.149–14.151. 14.153, 14.161–14.162, 14.168–14.171
  recovery of defence costs orders (RDCO) 14.172
  representation orders *see* **representation orders (magistrates' courts)**
  solicitors 20.30, 20.36, 20.37, 20.42
  travel and waiting time 20.32, 20.37
  unpaid fees 20.36
magistrates' courts, billing and payment for standard fees in the 16.46–16.68
  arrest warrants, issue of 16.52
  bail applications 16.53
  case study 16.56
  categories 16.46, 16.51–16.56
  change of solicitors 16.55
  counsel, use of 16.57–16.58
  Criminal Bills Assessment Manual (LAA) 16.61
  CRM7 form 16.79
  designated area standard fees 16.47–16.49
  district judges 15.164
  enhanced rates 16.62–16.65
  higher standard fees 16.46, 16.49–16.50, 16.54
  hourly rates 16.62–16.65
  licensed work in family cases, billing and payment for 15.164
  lower standard fees 16.46, 16.50
  representation orders for matters sent to the Crown Court 16.66–16.68
  separate matters 16.59–16.61
  structure of fees 16.50
  travel and waiting time 16.49, 16.62
  types of fee 16.47
  undesignated area standard fees 16.47, 16.49
management *see* **financial and contract management**

matrimonial homes *see* real property/family home
means test 1.11–1.12, 1.26, 5.9, 5.13
  see also means test (civil and family); means test (criminal cases)
means test (civil and family) 2.29–2.65
  aggregation 12.19, 12.21
  audits 23.31
  capital *see* capital (civil and family)
  case study 2.37
  CCMS 5.6, 5.22–5.24
  certificates 6.81, 6.86, 6.114
  change of circumstances 2.63–2.65, 4.127, 4.157
  children 2.57–2.59, 2.60, 12.19–12.21
  community care cases 12.19–12.21, 12.39
  conflicts of interest 12.19, 12.21
  contributions 2.35, 4.22
  controlled work 2.32, 2.63–2.64, 17.35, 17.37–17.45
  Court of Protection cases where client is deprived of liberty 2.60
  criteria 2.30
  cross-border disputes 2.62
  decision-making 2.32
  domestic violence, injunctions for 2.61
  definition 1.11
  emergency delegated functions 4.210, 5.38
  evidence 4.23–4.28, 4.93, 6.45, 12.23, 17.37, 17.44–17.45, 23.31
  exceptional case funding (ECF) 3.3, 3.17, 3.57, 3.62
  Family Help (Lower) 7.29
  forced marriage proceedings 2.61
  forms 4.9
  Help with Family Mediation 6.71
  immigration and asylum cases 9.88–9.89, 9.92
  income 1.11, 2.30, 2.40–2.42, 2.53–2.56, 4.22, 4.26
  inquests 2.62, 3.62

  Housing Loss Prevention Advice Service (HLPAS) 11.86, 11.87, 11.94
  Legal Help 4.22–4.28, 6.42–6.43, 6.45, 7.18–7.20
  licensed work 2.32, 2.63–2.64
  limits 2.31
  manifestly unreasonable decisions 17.38–17.39
  mediation 8.11–8.14
  Mental Capacity Act 2005 10.4–10.5, 10.11–10.13, 10.54, 10.58
  mental health cases, conducting 2.60, 10.4, 10.29
  multi-party actions 2.62
  non means tested, legal aid which is not 2.60–2.62
  online calculators 2.33–2.37, 5.22–5.23
  partners living together, aggregation of means of 2.38–2.39
  passported benefits 2.40–2.43
  private law cases 6.14
  promissory declarations 5.65, 5.68
  public law cases 7.2
  reassessment of means 2.63–2.65
  representation certificates 4.93, 4.127
  self-employed clients 2.34
  Standard Civil Contract 2024 4.23, 7.22
  urgent cases 4.192–4.195
means test (criminal cases) 1.60, 14.61–14.66
  advice and assistance 14.60, 14.61–14.66
  Advocacy Assistance 20.58
  appeals 14.180, 14.186
  audits 14.66
  billing and payment 16.70
  capital 14.61–14.63, 14.65, 16.70
  case stated 14.180
  court duty solicitor work 14.82
  Crown Court *see* Crown Court, means-testing of representation orders in the
  custody, clients detained in 20.11
  evidence 14.66

means test (criminal cases)
continued
  income 14.61–14.62, 14.64–14.65, 16.70
  partners 14.63, 14.64
  passporting benefits 14.62
  police station work 1.60, 14.19, 14.36, 14.45, 14.48
  pre-charge engagement, advice and assistance for 14.55
  prison law work 14.193, 14.199, 16.70, 20.58
  representation orders *see* **representation orders (magistrates' courts), means testing for**
  websites 14.65
mediation 1.23, 2.80, 4.158, 6.82–6.84 *see also* **family mediation**
Mental Capacity Act 2005 10.4–10.5, 10.11–10.13, 10.54, 10.58
  advice and assistance 14.70
  supervisor standards 22.42–22.45
mental health cases, conducting 10.1–10.61
  accreditation 10.14–10.15, 22.43, 22.128
  adjournments, fees for 10.22, 10.41
  advocacy 10.14–10.15
  aftercare services under MHA 1983 12.4, 12.16–12.17
  appeals 10.18, 10.41, 10.48
  billing and payment 10.47, 15.45
  Category Definitions 10.6
  Controlled Legal Representation (CLR) 2.79, 10.18, 10.19–10.23, 10.31–10.33, 10.39, 18.23
  counsel, use of 10.16–10.17
  Court of Protection work 10.5–10.6, 10.18, 10.59–10.60, 22.45
  Covid-19, flexible working arrangements during 10.3
  disbursements 10.16, 10.21, 10.55–10.57, 14.114
  EC1 claim forms 10.47
  Equality Act 2010 10.27
  escape fee cases 10.43–10.48
  exceptional case funding (ECF) 10.4–10.5
  fixed fees 10.21
  geographical procurement areas 10.7–10.10
  guidance 10.2, 10.28
  Help at Court 10.18–10.19
  hourly rates 10.17, 10.19, 10.43–10.46
  inherent jurisdiction of the High Court 10.4
  LAA, contact with the 10.61
  Law Society's practice note 10.2
  Legal Help 10.4, 10.18, 10.24–10.30, 10.34, 10.37
  Legal Representation (certificates) 10.18
  levels of funding 10.18–10.33
  licensed work 10.58–10.60
  lot boundaries 10.9
  major concerns 10.2
  means test 2.60, 10.10, 10.28–10.29, 10.60
  Mental Capacity Act 2005 10.4–10.5, 10.11–10.13, 10.54, 10.58
  Mental Health Act patients 10.4, 10.29, 12.4, 12.16–12.17
  mental health, definition of 10.4–10.6
  Mental Health Contract Specification 10.49
  Mental Health Tribunal (MHT) 2.60, 10.15, 10.31, 10.36–10.42, 10.50–10.54
  Standard Civil Contract 2024 10.37–10.38
  standard fees 10.20, 10.36–10.42, 10.46, 22.42–22.43
  supervisor standards 22.42–22.43
  merits test 10.10, 10.30, 10.59
  nearest relatives 10.33
  new matter starts 10.49–10.52
  non-Mental Health Tribunal (MHT) cases 10.34–10.35, 10.45, 10.50

peer review process 10.2
physical location 22.129
separate matters 10.49–10.54
service standards 22.126–22.129
signatures 10.26–10.27, 10.31
Standard Civil Contract 2024 10.1, 10.7, 10.9–10.12, 10.27, 10.57
    Mental Health Tribunal (MHT) cases 10.37–10.38
    service standards 22.126–22.129
    supervisors 10.11–10.13, 22.41–22.45
standard fees 10.19–10.23, 10.34–10.42, 10.44–10.46
supervisor requirements 10.8, 10.11–10.13, 10.25, 22.41–22.45
travel to hospital, fees for 10.23
Upper Tribunal (UT), appeals to 10.18, 10.41
merits test (civil and family cases) 1.26, 2.29, 2.66
advocacy in family cases 19.6
bail 9.110
borderline or marginal cases 6.92, 6.98, 6.104, 6.111
    eviction 11.37
    exceptional case funding (ECF) 3.16
    harassment injunctions 11.60
    homelessness 11.25, 11.30
    housing conditions and disrepair 11.44
    immigration and asylum cases 9.93–9.94, 9.96
    possession of the home cases 11.12
    representation certificates 7.41
CCMS 5.6, 5.23–5.24
certificates 6.81, 6.90–6.94, 6.96–6.98, 6.104, 6.111, 6.114
children 6.96–6.98
community care cases 11.30, 12.10–12.11
Conditional Fee Agreements (CFAs) 11.38
controlled work 9.93–9.101, 9.117, 17.35, 17.37, 17.38–17.39
cost-benefit/successful outcome 6.94
definition 1.11
domestic abuse 6.111
emergency delegated functions 4.211, 5.38
eviction 11.37–11.38
exceptional case funding (ECF) 3.3, 3.16, 3.18, 3.57
exceptions 1.12
Family Help (Lower) 7.28
financial matters 6.104
harassment injunctions 11.60
Help at Court 4.62–4.64, 18.12–18.15
housing 11.12, 11.25, 11.30, 11.44
immigration and asylum cases 9.91, 9.93–9.99, 9.101–9.102
importance of case 1.11
Independent Funding Adjudicators (IFAs) 17.5–17.6
judicial review 13.29
Legal Help 4.29–4.35
Legal Representation 11.37
licensed work 9.132
manifestly unreasonable decisions 17.38–17.39
mediation 6.81, 8.6, 8.18
mental health cases, conducting 10.10, 10.30, 10.59
nil assessment appeals 17.35, 17.37, 17.38–17.39
overwhelming importance to the individual, cases of 9.94
possession of the home cases 11.12
proportionality test 6.111, 9.94, 11.25, 11.37, 11.44, 11.60, 12.10
public law cases, conducting 7.2, 7.7, 13.28–13.29, 13.32
public interest 9.93–9.94
reasonable private paying individual test 9.94
representation certificates *see* **representation certificates (civil and family), merits test for**

merits test (civil and family cases)
continued
  stages 6.92–6.94
  standard criteria 6.90–6.94, 13.29
  unclear cases 9.94, 9.96
  urgent cases 4.196–4.197, 6.114
  very expensive cases/special case work 4.225–4.226
merits test (criminal cases)
  advice and assistance 14.60, 14.67–14.68
  Advocacy Assistance 20.57
  appeals 14.180, 14.186, 14.190
  case stated 14.180
  Crown Court 14.131–14.133, 14.171
  guidance 14.104
  interests of justice test 14.104, 14.131–14.132
  prison law work 14.193, 14.200–14.201, 20.57
  representation orders 14.104–14.108, 20.28
  sentence, seriousness of 1.11
  seriousness of cases 1.11
  sufficient benefit test *see* **sufficient benefit test**
military custody 20.9
modern slavery *see* **human trafficking, modern slavery, servitude or forced labour, victims of**
monitoring *see also* **quality standards and performance monitoring**
  audits 23.36
  civil and family cases, ending 4.79–4.82
  emergency delegated functions 4.203
  key performance indicators (KPIs) 22.97–22.98, 23.22
  service standards 22.122–22.132
mortgage possession proceedings 2.11, 11.19–11.20
multi-party actions 2.62, 4.106, 4.109, 4.217, 4.224, 4.226

nearest relatives 10.33
nil assessment appeals in controlled work cases 17.35–17.45
non-inquest exceptional case funding (ECF) 3.1–3.37, 3.51–3.78
  advocacy cases 3.68
  appeals 3.17, 3.19
  applications 2.26–2.28, 3.51–3.78
  assimilated EU law 3.2, 3.12
  asylum seekers and refugees 9.18
  availability 3.7–3.15
  backdating 2.27, 3.70–3.71
  blended applications 5.76
  borderline prospects of success 3.16
  cases, examples of 3.33–3.35
  categories 3.52–3.54
  CCMS 3.56–3.65, 3.73, 5.76
  Charter of Fundamental Rights of the EU (CFREU) 9.39
  children 3.26
  CIV ECF1 form 3.56–3.57, 3.67
  CIV ECF2 (INQ) 3.64
  CIVAPP1 3.70
  CIVAPP 3 3.70
  civil cases, billing and payment for 15.15–15.17
  complexity of procedural, legal and evidential issues 3.13, 3.26
  controlled work cases 3.70, 17.37
  definition 1.15
  direct applicants 3.60
  disbursements 15.17
  effective administration of justice test 3.52–3.54
  emergency delegated functions 3.51, 4.205
  Equality Act 2010 3.66
  escape fee cases 1.25
  European Convention on Human Rights (ECHR) 3.2, 3.7–3.15, 3.24–3.30
  evidence 14.66
  eviction 11.5
  Exceptional and Complex Case Team (ECCT) 4.215, 4.219

extent of services provided 3.31–3.32
fair hearing, right to a 3.7–3.8, 3.11, 3.13, 3.23–3.30, 3.33, 9.39
family cases 3.5, 7.32
forms 3.56–3.65, 3.73
Gudanaviciene case 3.7–3.17, 3.27–3.28, 9.39–9.41
guidance 2.26, 2.28, 3.6, 3.10, 3.16, 3.22–3.32, 3.77, 9.39, 9.41
help and support for practitioners 3.77–3.78
housing cases 11.1, 11.5
immigration and asylum cases 3.33–3.37, 3.61, 9.3, 9.38–9.41, 9.90
importance of issues 3.13, 3.26
Independent Funding Adjudicators (IFAs) 17.18
individual case contracts 3.54–3.55, 3.72
inquests *see* **inquest exceptional case funding (ECF)**
internal reviews 17.9–17.13
IS v Director of Legal Aid Casework and Lord Chancellor 3.16–3.21
judicial review 3.17, 3.33–3.35, 3.75–3.76, 9.40
lawfulness of tests 3.6, 3.16–3.21
Legal Help 3.4, 3.31, 3.70, 15.17
Lexcel Practice Management Standard 3.55
litigants in person 3.13, 3.26, 3.30
means test 3.3, 3.17, 3.57
mental health cases, conducting 10.4–10.5
merits test 3.57
minimum services required 3.32
National Referral Mechanism (NRM) 3.36–3.37
number of applications 3.4–3.5
operation of scheme 3.16–3.21
payment 3.69–3.72
personal injury claims 11.18
possession of the home cases 11.5, 11.14, 11.18

private and family life, right to respect for 3.7, 3.9, 3.11, 3.28, 9.39, 9.41
problems with scheme, list of 3.17
review process 3.73–3.76
right to civil legal aid 3.7
scope 2.25–2.28
self-represent, ability to 3.13, 3.26
slavery, forced or compulsory labour and servitude 3.28–3.30, 3.36–3.37
Specialist Quality Mark (SQM) 3.55
Standard Civil Contract 3.54
success rate 3.17
timescales 3.66–3.68, 3.73
training and support 5.76
urgent applications 3.67–3.69
Very High Cost Cases (VHCC) 15.194
websites 2.28, 3.22, 3.58–3.59, 3.73, 3.78
non-molestation orders (NMOs) 5.40–5.41, 6.9

occupation orders 6.9
office managers, role of 1.70
online calculators
60, disregard of capital for clients over 2.51
capital 2.51
CCMS 5.22–5.23
contributions 2.35, 4.154
example of outcomes 2.36
income 2.56
means test 2.33–2.37, 5.22–5.23
print-outs or PDFs 2.37
representation orders (magistrates' courts) 14.90
self-employed clients 2.34
websites 2.33–2.34
online portals
'Apply' *see* **'Apply' online portal**
CCMS *see* **Client and Cost Management System (CCMS) (civil and family)**
civil controlled work, payment for 23.2

online portals *continued*
  criminal cases 14.149, 16.78, 23.2
  Galaxkey secure portal 22.88, 22.92
  peer review 22.92–22.93
  representation orders (magistrates' courts) 14.105
  tenders 21.38
  website 22.92
overview of legal aid 1.1–1.100
  civil and family 1.6, 1.37–1.53
  Covid-19 arrangements 1.98–1.100
  criminal defence cases 1.6, 1.54–1.64
  how legal aid works 1.5–1.27
  LAA documentation 1.28–1.29, 1.37–1.64
  legal challenges 1.88–1.95
  training and support 1.67–1.87
  up to date, keeping 1.30–1.36

Parole Board 14.194, 14.203–14.204
  Advocacy Assistance 14.197, 20.8, 20.56
  supervisor standards 22.60, 22.70
partners and spouses
  aggregation of means 2.38–2.39
  income 14.64
  means test 2.38–2.39, 5.13, 14.63, 14.64
  partner, definition of 2.38
  representation orders (magistrates' courts) 14.93, 14.97, 14.101
  signing forms 2.38
passported benefits 2.40–2.43
  advice and assistance 14.62
  capital 2.40, 2.43
  CCMS' links with DWP 1.77
  change of circumstances 2.64
  contributions 4.151
  Crown Court 14.136
  immigration and asylum 2.42
  income 2.40–2.41
  means test 2.40–2.43, 14.62
  representation orders (magistrates' courts) 14.92, 14.94

PAYG (pay as you go) 23.4, 23.6, 23.8–23.10
payments *see* civil cases, billing and payment for; criminal cases, billing and payment for; family cases, billing and payment for
payments on account *see* payments on account (POAs) (civil cases); payments on account (POAs) (criminal cases)
payments on account (POAs) (civil cases) 15.49–15.52, 23.1, 23.14–23.21
  advocacy 18.38–18.42
  appeals 15.99
  case studies 18.41, 23.15
  CCMS 1.84–1.85, 15.50, 18.38, 23.18
  Contracted Work and Administration (CWA) 15.49
  counsel, use of 15.49, 18.38–18.42
  Covid-19 arrangements 23.15
  disbursements 1.84–1.86, 23.15
  electronic CIVPOA1 form 15.49
  disputes with LAA 15.51
  eforms 22.93
  Family Advocacy Scheme (FAS) 15.50, 18.42
  financial and contract management 23.1, 23.14–23.21
  further POAs 15.49
  high cost cases 1.85
  Legal Services Commission (LSC) 23.21
  limits 23.19–23.21
  maximum POA limit 23.20
  office account, paid into 23.16
  profit costs 1.84–1.85, 15.49–15.50, 23.15
  recoupment 15.144–15.147, 23.17
  representation certificates 15.49–15.55
  Standard Civil Contract 2024 15.49, 23.15
  timetable 15.49, 15.144–15.147, 18.39–18.40, 23.15
  unpaid fees 18.48

unrecouped payments 23.18
very expensive cases/special case work 4.221, 15.203
payments on account (POAs) (criminal cases) 16.95–16.99
   cracked trial rate 16.96
   Crown Court, litigator fees in the 16.95–16.99
   disbursements 16.94
   hardship, evidence of 16.98
   pre-trial preparation hearings (PTPH) 16.96
   stages 16.96–16.97
peer review 22.5, 22.73–22.95
   'Apply' 22.93
   audits 23.25
   categories of law 22.74
   CCMS 22.93
   change of caseworkers 22.81
   checklist of criteria 22.83
   conflicts of interest 22.79
   consistency, checking 22.78, 22.81
   Contracted Work and Administration (CWA) 22.93
   costs sanctions 22.91
   Crown Court Litigator Fee (CCLF) 22.93
   eforms 22.93
   external experts, assistance from 22.91
   failure in performance 22.76
   friend and family test 22.82
   guidance 22.77
   IALS 22.5, 22.73, 22.78, 22.84
   identity of reviewers, not knowing the 22.79
   Management information (MI) 22.93
   mental health cases, conducting 10.2
   number of files assessed 22.79
   online portal 22.92–22.93
   pick-up test 22.80
   process 22.78–22.84
   Provider Activity Report (PAR) 22.94–22.95
   quality of advice 22.5, 22.73–22.95
   random selection 22.78
   reasons for review 22.78
   reports 22.83–22.84
   representations 22.89–22.91
   scores 22.75, 22.77, 22.81–22.84, 22.89–22.91
   standard letters and documentation 22.86–22.88
   termination of contracts 22.76
   threshold competence 22.76
   timetable 22.84, 22.91
   tips for passing peer review 22.86–22.91
   training 22.78
   transaction criteria audits, exclusion of 22.80
   websites 22.73, 22.77
performance *see* **key performance indicators (KPIs); quality standards and performance monitoring**
permitted work (children and family) 2.76–2.84, 14.26–14.31
personal injury claims 11.18
POAs *see* **payments on account (POAs) (civil cases)**
Points of Dispute (PoDs), service of 15.128–15.129
points of principle of general public importance (PoP) 15.106, 23.34, 23.54
police station work 1.9, 1.10, 14.19–14.48
   accreditation 14.33–14.35, 22.59
   advice and assistance 14.74
   Advocacy Assistance 14.44–14.46, 14.48, 16.37
   armed forces custody hearings 14.46
   arrest 14.38
   attendance in person at the police station 14.19, 14.24, 14.26–14.31
   bail 14.31, 14.41, 14.43, 16.20, 16.22
      attendance 14.41
      conditions 14.47
      extension of bail time limits 14.47

police station work *continued*
  police bail, applications in relation to 14.47–14.48
  pre-charge 14.43
  street bail 14.47
 bills, submitting 14.43
 case studies 14.21, 14.25, 16.31
 categories 16.25
 change of solicitors 14.40
 conducting work 14.41–14.43
 costs limitation 14.42
 counsel, use of 14.48
 Criminal Defence Direct (CDD) Scheme 14.19, 14.24, 16.14, 21.48
 Defence Solicitor Call Centre (DSCC) 14.22–14.23, 14.32, 14.37
 duty solicitors 14.23–14.24, 14.32, 14.34–14.35, 14.79, 16.28, 21.34, 21.42
 escape fee cases 16.24, 16.30–16.32
 exclusions 14.27
 first contact, target time for 14.38, 22.141
 fixed fees 16.20, 16.31
 investigations class work (criminal) 16.20–16.28, 16.30–16.34, 16.41
 means test 1.60, 14.19, 14.36, 14.45, 14.48
 merits test 14.29–14.31
 own client work 14.32, 14.35
 permitted work 14.26–14.31
 police station, definition of 14.21
 Police Station Qualification (PSQ) 14.33
 post charge work 14.20, 14.31
 pre-charge engagement 16.34
 previous advice, where client has received 14.39–14.40
 probationary representatives 14.34–14.35
 qualification 14.79
 scope 2.14, 14.19–14.21
 separate matters, claims for 16.22
 serious offence rates 16.27–16.28
 social hours 16.26
 sources of work 14.22–14.25
 Standard Civil Contract 2024 16.20
 starting a case 14.36–14.40
 supervisor standards 22.59, 22.69, 22.141
 surrender to police 14.25
 telephone advice 14.19, 14.23, 14.25, 16.13–16.16, 16.21, 21.48
 third parties, contact from 14.25
 travel and waiting time 16.25
 volunteers at the police station 14.30
 warrants of further detention 14.44–14.46
 who may carry out the work 14.32–14.33
 witnesses, advice and assistance to 14.19
possession of the home cases 11.6–11.20
 adjournments 11.13
 anti-social behaviour (ASB), allegations of 11.15, 11.63, 11.65–11.67, 11.70
 caravans 11.7
 CCMS 11.15
 committal proceedings following breach of injunction 11.15
 costs protection 11.17
 counterclaims 11.18
 emergency delegated functions 11.11
 Equality Act 2010 grounds 11.9, 11.16, 11.18
 eviction *see* **eviction**
 European Convention on Human Rights (ECHR) 11.9, 11.16
 exceptional case funding (ECF) 11.5, 11.14, 11.18
 general advice 11.10–11.11
 guidance 11.14, 11.16
 Help at Court 11.9, 11.11, 11.16, 18.22
 home, definition of 11.7
 houseboats 11.7
 Housing and Debt category 11.6
 housing conditions and disrepair 11.55–11.59

Index 757

housing benefit 11.13–11.14
Housing Loss Prevention Advice Service (HLPAS) *see* **Housing Loss Prevention Advice Service (HLPAS)**
Housing Possession Court Duty Scheme (HPCDS), quashing of LAA's tender for 1.93
Investigative Help 11.6, 11.9, 11.11
judicial review 11.14
Legal Help 11.6, 11.10–11.11
merits test 11.12
mortgage possession proceedings 2.11, 11.19–11.20
notification of intent to take proceedings 11.10–11.11
only or main residence 11.7
personal injury claims 11.18
postponement 11.16
public law defences 11.9, 11.16
reasonableness 11.9, 11.16
rent arrears 11.13–11.14, 11.56–11.59
representation certificates 11.6, 11.10, 11.16, 11.17
scope 1.14, 2.7–2.8
squatters 11.8
suspension 11.16–11.17
trespassers 11.8
vehicles 11.7
welfare benefits 11.13–11.14
pre-charge engagement, advice and assistance for (criminal cases) 14.49–14.59, 16.34
agreements between clients and prosecutors or investigators 14.50, 14.54
application process 14.56–14.59
Attorney General's Guidelines on Disclosure 14.49, 14.51
change of solicitor 14.58–14.59
extendable upper limit 14.53
first PACE interview, after 14.49
further PACE interviews as not covered 14.52
information to be recorded on file 14.56–14.57
list of work covered 14.51
means test 14.55
merits test 14.54
preparatory work 14.49
previous advice and assistance, receipt of 14.58–14.59
qualifying criteria 14.54–14.55
reasons for undertaking work, records of 14.54
scope of work 14.50–14.53
preparation
advocacy in civil cases 18.29
advocacy in family cases 19.13, 19.33
Bill Preparation 1.69, 5.27, 5.33, 10.47
CCMS 5.21, 5.24, 15.87
custody, clients detained in 20.12
evidence 5.21
family private law cases (certificates) 6.78
Help at Court 18.22
pre-charge engagement, advice and assistance for 14.49
prescribed proceedings (civil) 14.164–14.167
present, where clients cannot be 5.56–5.75
CCMS 5.56–5.75
Covid-19 arrangements 5.57–5.64
Declarations against Instructions (CCMS) 5.72–5.75
digital signatures 5.57–5.64
emergency delegated function applications 5.56
emergency non-delegated function applications 5.56
Legal Help 4.11–4.13
promissory declarations 5.65–5.71
representation orders (magistrates' courts) 14.105
preservation cases 4.158, 4.161–4.163, 4.173
previous advice, restrictions where clients have received 2.68–2.75
6th months, within the last 2.68, 4.33
advice and assistance 14.71

previous advice, restrictions where clients have received *continued*
 case studies 4.34, 4.35
 certificated work 2.75
 change of solicitors 2.75
 circumstances, change in 2.70, 2.72, 4.33
 controlled work 2.70
 exceptions 2.68–2.69, 4.33
 Legal Help 2.68, 4.30–4.35
 new matter starts 4.30–4.34
 original providers 2.70, 2.72, 2.74–2.75
 police station work 14.39–14.40
 pre-charge engagement, advice and assistance for 14.58–14.59
 reasonable enquiries, making 2.73
 reopening a closed matter 4.35
 second matter starts 2.70
 second providers 2.69, 2.72, 2.74–2.75
 Standard Civil Contract 2024 4.31–4.34
 Specification 2.71
 termination of previous retainer, reasons for 4.34
 urgent work 2.74
previous convictions 14.104
prison law work 1.6, 14.191–14.205
 advice and assistance 14.191–14.196, 14.198, 14.203–14.205, 16.69
 Advocacy Assistance 16.69, 20.56–20.60
 agents, use of 14.195
 billing and payment 16.69–16.71
 classification, reviews of prisoners' 14.203
 counsel, use of 14.195, 14.202
 CRM1, CRM2 and CRM3 forms 14.199
 disbursements and prior authority 14.195
 disciplinary cases 14.197, 14.200, 14.205, 16.71, 20.8
 fair hearing, right to a 14.205
 fixed fees 14.196, 16.69
 forms 14.199
 hourly rates 14.196
 means test 14.193, 14.199, 16.70
 merits test 14.193, 14.200–14.201
 number of matters that may be opened 14.194
 Parole Board *see* **Parole Board**
 release 1.9
 scope 14.203–14.205, 16.71
 service standards 22.143, 22.146
 supervisor standards 22.58, 22.60, 22.63, 22.70
 telephone contact, availability of 22.146
 travel and waiting time 14.195, 14.196
 types of cases 14.192
 young offenders' institutions, review of classification in 14.203
private and family life, right to respect for 3.7, 3.9, 3.11, 3.23, 3.27, 3.28, 3.33, 9.18
Private Family Law Representation Scheme (PFLRS)/Higher Standard Fee Scheme 15.166, 15.178–15.192
 CCMS 15.179
 certificates 6.78, 6.106
 change of solicitors 15.187–15.190
 children 15.178, 15.181
 domestic abuse 15.178, 15.181, 15.183
 enhancement of hourly rates 15.184–15.186
 escape fee cases 15.181
 exclusions 15.182
 Family Advocacy Scheme (FAS) 15.191–15.192
 Family Help (Higher) 15.179
 finance 15.178, 15.181
 hourly rates 15.182, 15.184–15.187
 Legal Representation 15.179
 London boroughs 15.180
 multiple clients 15.189–15.190
private law cases *see* **family private law cases, conducting**

Index 759

pro bono costs orders 15.148–15.155
  Access to Justice Foundation, payment of costs to 15.149, 15.152–15.154
  indemnity principle 15.148, 15.152
probationary representatives 14.34–14.35
proceedings class (criminal) work 14.77–14.177
  billing and payment 16.38–16.45
  change of solicitors 14.126–14.128
  Common Platform digital case management system 14.78
  court duty solicitor cases 16.39–16.41, 14.77, 14.79–14.84
  Crown Court, representation in the 14.77, 14.130–14.177
  Crown Court Digital Case System 14.78
  matter ends 14.129
  representation orders (magistrates' courts) 14.77, 14.85–14.119, 14.123–14.125
  separate matters 14.120–14.122
  travel and waiting time 16.40–16.41
  types of funding 14.77
  virtual court claims 16.38
Proceeds of Crime Act 2002 14.206–14.208, 16.73
professional misconduct 4.84
profit costs 1.7, 14.145
  assessment of costs by the courts 15.108, 15.110, 15.118
  Crown Court 14.145
  guidance 15.110
  payments on account (POA) 1.84–1.85, 15.49–15.50, 23.15
promissory declarations (CCMS) 5.65–5.71
  emergency delegated function certificates 5.65–5.71
  office protocol, use of an 5.65
  signatures 5.69–5.71
  training and support 5.65, 5.68

property
  charges to property 14.147
  contributions 4.151
  family mediation 8.7
  money *see* **recovery of money (civil and family)**
  jointly owned property 2.47–2.48
  real property *see* **real property/family home**
  recovery of property 4.158, 4.161–4.163, 4.173
  representation certificates 4.173
protected parties 4.11, 4.14–4.16
Provider Activity Report (PAR) 22.94–22.95
public authorities, claims against
  judicial review *see* **judicial review**
  police station work *see* **police station work**
  representation certificates 4.113
  supervisor standards 22.33, 22.49–22.50
Public Defender Service (PDS) 21.44
public interest 3.38–3.39, 3.50, 9.93–9.94, 9.114
public law cases, conducting 1.88–1.95, 13.1–13.51
  alternative sources of funding 13.32–13.34
  'Apply' online portal 5.12
  Category Definitions 13.22
  community care cases 13.7
  Conditional Fee Agreements (CFAs) 13.32, 13.35
  Controlled Work Guidance 13.51
  crowdfunding 13.34
  CW1 form 13.51
  damages claims 13.21
  Data Protection Act 1998 13.5
  decisions, ways of challenging 13.4
  defences 11.9, 11.16
  emergency delegated functions 13.37–13.38
  Equality Act 2010 13.5
  evidence 13.37, 13.51
  examples 13.23
  exhaust all reasonable alternatives, failure to 13.38

public law cases, conducting *continued*
   family law cases *see* **family public law cases, conducting**
   guidance 4.112, 13.34
   habeas corpus, writs for 13.20, 13.50–13.51
   Human Rights Act 1998 claims 13.5, 13.21–13.22
   investigative representation certificates 13.28, 13.29
   judicial review *see* **judicial review**
   Legal Help 13.8, 13.22, 13.26, 13.29, 13.51
   legal representation certificates 13.27
   levels of funding 13.26–13.31
   merits test 13.28–13.29, 13.32
   overlap between categories 13.7–13.8
   possession of the home cases 11.9, 11.16
   premature applications 13.38
   procurement areas 13.25
   refusal of legal aid, common reasons for 13.32–13.38
   representation certificates 4.111–4.112
   retained EU law 13.5
   scope 13.9–13.24
   Standard Civil Contract 2024 13.25, 13.51, 22.33, 22.51, 22.55
   supervisor standards 22.33, 22.51, 22.55
   who can do public law 13.25
public spaces protection orders (PSPOs) 13.13–13.17

quality standards and performance monitoring 22.1–22.150
   Covid-19 arrangements 22.148–22.150
   key performance indicators (KPIs) 22.96–22.110
   Lexcel standard (Law Society) 22.3, 22.16–22.18
   peer review 22.5, 22.73–22.95
   practice management standards 22.3–22.15
   quality of legal advice standards 22.5
   service standards 22.111–22.147
   Specialist Quality Mark (SQM) *see* **Specialist Quality Mark (SQM)**
   Standard Civil Contract 2024 22.1–22.2
   Standard Crime Contract 2022 22.1–22.2
   Standard Crime Contract 2025 22.1–22.2
   supervisors 22.19–22.73

real property/family home 2.46–2.49
   contributions 2.52
   domestic violence injunctions, exclusion for applications for 2.49
   jointly owned property 2.47
   mortgage possession proceedings 2.11, 11.19–11.20
   orders for sale 14.147
   ownership 2.46–2.49
   possession *see* **possession of the home cases**
   sale, deduction of costs of 2.46
   statutory charge 4.176, 6.63
   subject matter of the dispute (SMOD) disregard 2.48
reassessment of means 2.63–2.65
reconciliation 23.1, 23.11–23.13
   adjustments 23.11
   case study 23.13
   controlled work, billing and payment for 15.37, 23.7, 23.8–23.9
   criminal cases, billing and payment for 16.7, 16.78, 23.7, 23.8–23.9
   definition 23.11
   Legal aid: management information online 23.11
   PAYG (pay as you go) 23.6
   reconciliation protocol (LAA) 23.12
   settlement fees 6.59

standard monthly payments
    (SMPs) 23.7–23.9, 23.13
variable monthly payments
    (VMPs) 23.8–23.9
recoupment
  civil cases, billing and payment
    for 15.144–15.147
  contract compliance audits
    (CCAs) 23.39
  payments on account (POAs)
    15.144–15.147, 23.17
  statutory charge *see* **statutory charge**
**recovery of defence costs orders
    (RDCO)** 14.172–14.177,
    14.180
  acquittals 14.172–14.177
  Court of Appeal 14.176
  limits on recovery 14.174
  magistrates' courts 14.172
  refusal of legal aid in Crown
    Court 14.173
  Supreme Court 14.176
recovery of money (civil and family)
    4.169–4.172
  Admin 1 form 4.172
  contributions 4.151
  exempt property 4.170
  refunds 4.170–4.171
  representation certificates
    4.169–4.172
  solicitor, all monies owed to be
    paid to a 4.169–4.171
  statutory charge 4.169–4.172
recovery of property 4.158, 4.161–
    4.163, 4.173
referrals
  fees, prohibition on 2.67
  signposting and referral arrange-
    ments 22.119–22.120,
    22.122–22.123, 22.147
refugees *see* **asylum seekers and
    refugees**
remote hearings during Covid-19
    19.5, 15.199
rent arrears 11.13–11.14
  adjournments 11.13
  housing benefit 11.13–11.14
  Housing Loss Prevention Advice
    Service (HLPAS) 11.13
  universal credit 11.13
  welfare benefits exclusion 11.13
**representation certificates (civil and
    family)** 4.83–4.188, 7.14
  abroad, clients based 4.88–4.90
  advocacy 4.83, 7.34, 7.52–7.54,
    18.24–18.28, 19.2
  anti-social behaviour (ASB) in-
    junctions 11.62–11.67
  appeals 7.49
  before applying 4.87
  billing and payment *see* **represen-
    tation certificates (civil),
    billing and payment for**
  Care Case Fee Scheme (CCFS)
    7.57, 7.58–7.62
  CCMS 4.117–4.124, 4.131–4.134,
    7.42–7.44
  change of circumstances 4.58,
    7.37
  children 4.91–4.92, 7.50
    aggregation of means 4.92
    Special Children Act cases
      7.35–7.36, 7.38, 7.40, 7.44,
      7.48–7.49, 7.55
  CIVAPP3 form 7.43
  CIVAPP5 form 7.43, 7.55
  client's point of view, funding
    from the 4.151–4.188
  contributions 4.151–5.156
  costs limitations 4.133–4.134
  costs protection 4.84
  counsel, use of 4.135–4.136,
    18.25–18.26
  disbursements 4.131, 4.137–4.139
  discharge of certificates 4.186
  emergency delegated functions
    7.34, 7.55–7.56
  ending a case 4.185–4.188
  experts' fees 4.140–4.150
  family mediation 8.4, 8.11
  family public law cases 7.34–7.62
  fee exemption and remission
    scheme 1.52
  final bills, submission of 4.188
  forms 4.117–4.124, 7.42–7.44
  funding 4.128–4.188, 7.46–7.56
  Help at Court 4.57–4.59, 18.9–
    18.10

representation certificates (civil and family) *continued*
  hourly rates 4.128, 7.51
  housing cases 11.6, 11.10, 11.16, 11.17, 18.17–18.18
  immigration and asylum cases 9.123–9.124
  interim care orders 7.38
  investigative representation 4.85–4.86
  licensed work *see* **licensed work**
  limitations 4.129–4.134
  litigation, conduct of 4.83, 4.87
  local authorities, issue of proceedings by 7.34
  location of solicitors' offices 7.46–7.47
  means test 4.93, 4.127, 7.38–7.39
  merits test *see* **representation certificates (civil and family), merits test for**
  professional misconduct, failure to inform clients of ability to seek funding as 4.84
  property, and preservation cases, recovery of 4.173
  revocation of certificates 4.187
  recovery of money 4.169–4.172
  refusal of representation 7.41
  scope 4.83–4.84, 4.133–4.134, 7.34, 18.24
  solicitors 18.24–18.25
  Standard Civil Contract 2024 18.25
  standard costs limits, categories of 4.130
  standard criteria 4.87
  standard fees 4.128, 7.46–7.48, 7.52–7.54
  statutory charge 4.151, 4.158–4.184
  urgent work 4.117
  Very High Cost Cases (VHCC) 7.57, 7.58–7.62
representation certificates (civil and family), merits test for 4.94–4.116
  allocation to track 4.101
  alternative means of funding 4.96, 4.99–4.100
  appeals 4.125–4.126
  borderline or marginal cases 4.102–4.103, 4.110, 4.112–4.113
  change of circumstances 4.157
  Conditional Fee Agreements (CFAs), suitability for 4.99–4.100
  cost-benefit criteria 4.105, 4.109, 4.115–4.116
  damages claims 4.103, 4.105, 4.107, 4.110
  declarations as to means 4.97–4.98
  delegated functions 4.202–4.212
  family public law cases 7.40–7.41
  general merits test for full representation 4.109–4.110
  guidance 4.116
  habeas corpus 4.107, 4.111
  homelessness 4.107, 4.111
  judicial review 4.111
  limitations, amendments to 4.133
  multi-party action criteria 4.106, 4.109
  need for representation 4.101
  overwhelming importance to the individual test 4.107–4.108
  particular criteria 4.94
  proportionality test 4.104, 4.113
  prospects of success test 4.102–4.104, 4.109, 4.113, 4.115–4.116
  public authorities, claims against 4.113
  public law claims 4.111–4.112
  reasonable private paying individual test 4.104
  refusals 4.125–4.126
  scope limitations, amendments to 4.133
  significant wider public interest test 4.104–4.106, 4.110, 14.113
  standard criteria 4.94, 4.95–4.101, 4.112
  types of test 4.102–4.104
  urgent cases 4.189–4.201
  value of outcome 4.103

Index 763

representation certificates (civil), billing and payment for 15.46–15.143
  Anti-social Behaviour, Crime and Policing Act 2014, injunctions under 15.65–15.66
  appeals 15.98–15.106
  assessment of costs by the courts 15.107–15.118, 15.123–15.143
  assessment of costs by the LAA 15.83–15.97
  CCMS 15.71, 15.87–15.97
  contempt proceedings 15.65–15.66
  costs appeals 15.98–15.106
  counsel, use of 15.65
  disbursements, prior authority for 15.53–15.55
  enhanced rates 15.67–15.71
  erroneous document requests 15.46–15.48
  final bills, assessment of 15.56–15.64
  hourly rates 15.65, 15.67, 15.70
  inter partes costs and the indemnity principle 15.119–15.122
  judicial review, conditional payments for 15.72–15.81
  payment on account 15.49–15.55
  rejected claims 15.46–15.48
representation orders 1.61–1.62, 20.2, 20.5, 20.7, 20.27–20.52
  appeals 14.183–14.190, 20.54–20.55
  billing and payment 16.7, 16.11, 16.74
  case stated 16.75
  Central Funds after acquittal, reclaiming costs from 1.62
  counsel, use of 1.10, 14.132–14.133, 20.29
  court duty solicitor work 14.84
  Crown Court 1.19, 14.77, 14.130–14.177, 16.7, 16.66–16.68, 20.27–20.29, 20.44–20.52
  investigations stage 20.8
  magistrates' courts *see* **representation orders (magistrates' courts)**
  means test *see* **Crown Court, means-testing of representation orders in the**
  merits test 14.131–14.133, 20.28
  solicitors 1.10, 20.29
  trials on indictment 20.28
representation orders (magistrates' courts) 1.61, 14.77, 14.85–14.119, 20.27–20.44
  Advocacy Assistance 20.7–20.8, 20.20
  appeals 14.88, 14.108, 20.7
  applications 14.105–14.106
  backdating 14.110
  bail proceedings 14.88
  case studies 14.87
  co-defendants and conflicts of interest 14.123–14.125
  contempt of court 14.87
  costs 14.109–14.110, 14.112
  counsel, use of 14.116–14.119
  CRM forms, replacement of 14.105
  Crown Court 14.132–14.133, 20.46
  disbursements and prior authority 14.112–14.115
  early cover 14.111
  electronic applications 14.105–14.106
  funding in the absence of an order 14.109–14.111
  guidance 14.104
  interests of justice test 14.104
  investigations work 20.8
  LAA portal 14.105
  means test *see* **representation orders (magistrates' courts), means testing for**
  merits test 14.104–14.108
  Pre-Order Cover claims 14.111
  previous convictions 14.104
  scope 14.85–14.88
  signatures 14.105
  website 14.105

representation orders (magistrates' courts), means testing for 14.89–14.103, 20.28
  capital, disregard of 14.92
  children/dependants 14.94, 14.97, 14.101
  evidence 14.102, 14.105
  guidance 14.91
  hardship funding 14.103
  income 14.92, 14.95–14.101
  living expenses allowance 14.100–14.101
  online calculator 14.90
  partners 14.93, 14.97, 14.101
  passported benefits 14.92, 14.94
  proof of means 14.102
  refusal 14.108
  statements of truth from clients in custody 14.102
  website 14.91, 14.103
  welfare benefits 14.92, 14.94, 14.102
reviews *see* **contract compliance audits (CCAs); costs audits; internal review of LAA decisions, right to; peer review**

scope of civil and family contracts 2.13–2.28
self-employed clients 2.34, 5.13
Senior Courts Costs Office (SCCO) 15.112, 15.132–15.133
service standards *see* service standards in Standard Civil Contract 2024; service standards in Standard Crime Contracts 2022/2025
service standards in Standard Civil Contract 2024 22.111–22.134, 23.24
  agents, use of 22.113–22.114
  authorised litigators 22.116
  child abduction 22.122
  counsel, use of 22.113
  education 22.132
  family cases 22.122–22.124
  housing/debt 22.130
  Housing Loss Prevention Advice Service (HLPAS) 22.133–22.134
  immigration and asylum cases 22.125
  independent consultants, work by 22.113–22.114
  mental health 22.126–22.129
  minimum number of matter starts 22.117
  monitoring requirements, additions/variations to 22.122–22.132
  procurement area, presence in the 22.118
  referral and signposting arrangements 22.119–22.120, 22.122–22.123
  service requirements, additions/variations to 22.122–22.132
  supervision 22.113, 22.115
  third parties, use of 22.113–22.114
  welfare benefits 22.131
service standards in Standard Crime Contracts 2022/2025 22.135–22.147, 23.24
  accessibility of offices 22.142
  contacting your office 22.145–22.146
  duty solicitor schemes 22.144
  emergency work 22.142, 22.145
  facilities at offices 22.142
  location 22.142–22.144
  opening hours 22.142–22.143
  prison work only 22.143, 22.146
  referral and signposting arrangements 22.147
  supervisors 22.135–22.141
  telephone contact, availability of 22.145–22.146
signatures 21.11–21.14
  advice and assistance 14.70
  capacity 4.11
  CCMS 5.56–5.75
  checklist 10.31
  children 4.11

Controlled Legal Representation (CLR) 10.31
Covid-19 4.12, 5.57–5.64, 10.26
digital signatures 5.57–5.64, 10.26
Declarations against Instructions (CCMS) 5.74
exceptions 14.70
Help with Family Mediation 6.73
Legal Help 4.11–4.13, 7.22
mental health cases, conducting 10.26–10.27, 10.31
present, where client cannot be 5.55–5.75
  Covid-19 5.57–5.64
  digital signatures 5.57–5.64
  Legal Help 4.11–4.13
  representation orders (magistrates' courts) 14.105
  promissory declarations 5.69–5.71
  representation orders (magistrates' courts) 14.105
  Standard Civil Contract 2024 4.11, 4.21
supervisors 10.25–10.26
slavery *see* **human trafficking, modern slavery, servitude or forced labour, victims of**
social security *see* **welfare benefits**
solicitors
Advocacy Assistance 1.10, 20.60
advocacy cases in civil cases 18.2, 18.28–18.29
advocacy cases in criminal cases 20.3, 20.5–20.6, 20.28, 20.30, 20.36–20.37, 20.42
advocacy in family cases 19.3, 19.8, 19.12–19.13
change of solicitors *see* **change of solicitors**
Crown Court hearings, advocacy in 20.6, 20.45, 20.49
Legal Representation 1.16
List of Defaulting Solicitors 18.48
magistrates' court hearings, advocacy in 20.6, 20.30, 20.36–20.37, 20.42
paralegal/trainee solicitors, role of 5.24
recovery of money 4.169–4.171

representation certificates 18.24–18.25
representation orders 20.28
Solicitors Regulation Authority (SRA) 18.48, 22.16
statutory charge 4.164
unpaid fees 18.48
special case work (civil and family) *see* **very expensive cases/ special case work (civil and family**
Specialist Quality Mark (SQM) 22.3, 22.6–22.15
assessment process 22.8–22.14
auditing services 22.7–22.14
CCMS 5.24
corrective actions, requirement for 22.13
current version 22.6
definitions 22.15
desktop audit 22.8–22.9
discussions with the auditor 22.12
evidence 22.9
exceptional case funding (ECF) 3.55
failure 22.13
file reviews 22.72
Lexcel requirements 22.12, 22.16, 22.18
on-site audits 22.10–22.14
opening meetings 22.11
outcomes 22.13–22.14
passing 22.13
pre-Quality Mark audits 22.10–22.14
procedure 22.13–22.14
Recognising Excellence 22.7
referral and signposting arrangements 22.119
refusal of applications 22.8
requirements 22.15
representation process 22.14
Self-Assessment Audit Checklist (SAAC) 22.11
supervisors 22.72
timetable 22.8
verification, date for 22.6, 22.9
website 22.7

spouses *see* **partners and spouses**
squatters 11.8
Standard Civil Contracts 1.41–1.43
　category-specific rules 1.41, 1.43
　general rules 1.41
　sections 1.42–1.43
　Standard Civil Contract 2013 2.14
　Standard Civil Contract 2014 2.14
　Standard Civil Contract 2015 2.14
　Standard Civil Contract 2018 15.43
　Standard Civil Contract 2024 *see* **Standard Civil Contract 2024**
　website 1.41
　welfare benefits 2.14
Standard Civil Contract 2024 1.37–1.43, 2.3, 2.15–2.22, 4.3
　accreditation 10.15
　advocacy 18.49, 18.50, 19.10, 19.14, 19.20
　applications 21.36
　assessment of inter partes costs by the courts 15.138–15.139
　audits 23.34
　bolt-on payments (children cases) 19.37, 19.48, 19.50
　bundles 19.48, 19.50
　categories 2.16–2.17
　Category Definitions 2.9–2.10, 9.3–9.4, 10.6, 11.5, 13.22
　commencement 2.12, 2.15
　community care cases 12.9
　contract compliance audits (CCAs) 23.38, 23.45, 23.48
　controlled work 2.19–2.20, 4.82, 6.30
　costs appeals 15.105, 23.50
　Covid-19 arrangements 2.23–2.24
　cuts to number of contracts 1.91
　disbursements 4.49, 4.51–4.52, 10.57
　duration of contracts 21.35, 21.36
　ending cases 4.71, 4.80–4.82
　entry into force 21.4
　escape fee cases 15.39, 22.99
　exceptional case funding (ECF) 3.54

　expiry 21.36
　extension 21.36
　face-to-face work 2.15
　family cases
　　billing and payment for 15.157
　　Family Help (Lower) 6.52, 6.58, 7.27
　　mediation 8.3, 8.9–8.10
　fixed fees 4.45, 4.82, 22.101–22.102
　general rules 2.17
　Housing Loss Prevention Advice Service (HLPAS) 1.38, 2.15, 11.76
　immigration and asylum cases 9.3, 9.57–9.58, 9.61–9.63, 9.66, 9.73, 9.76–9.79, 9.83, 9.116, 15.217
　key performance indicators (KPIs) 4.71, 4.80–4.82, 22.99–22.110, 23.23
　legal aid only costs 15.138–15.139
　Legal Help 4.11, 4.21, 4.23, 7.22, 10.27
　licensed work 2.19, 2.21, 4.82, 22.100, 22.103–22.106
　means test 7.22
　mental health cases, conducting 10.1, 10.7, 10.9–10.13, 10.15, 10.27, 10.57
　Mental Health and Mental Capacity Legal Competence Standard 10.11–10.12
　Mental Health Tribunal (MHT) cases 10.37–10.38
　MHT Legal Competence Standard 10.11–10.12
　payments on account (POAs) 15.49, 23.15
　police station work 16.20
　previous advice, provision of 4.31–4.34
　public law cases, conducting 13.25, 13.51
　quality standards and performance monitoring 22.1–22.2
　referral fees, prohibition on 2.67
　relationship with LAA 1.39

representation certificates 18.25
schedules 2.19
scope 2.15–2.22, 21.36, 22.1
service standards *see* **service standards in Standard Civil Contract 2024**
signatures 4.11
specific rules 2.16, 2.19
Standard Civil Contract Specification 1.41–1.43, 21.25–21.27
standard monthly payments (SMPs) 23.13
standard terms 21.21
supervisor standards *see* **supervisor standards in the Standard Civil Contract 2024**
supplementary matter states 2.22
technical errors 22.103–22.106
telephone, webcam and email advice 4.11, 4.21
tenders 21.35, 21.41
unpaid fees 18.49
variable monthly payments (VMPs) 23.4
website 1.39
Standard Crime Contract 2022 1.54–1.59, 14.1, 14.4 *see also* **Standard Crime Contracts**
applications 21.37
costs appeals 23.50
Defence Solicitor Call Centre (DSCC) 22.110
duration of contract 21.37
entry into force 1.54
extension 21.37
key performance indicators (KPIs) 22.96, 22.110, 23.23
quality standards and performance monitoring 22.1–22.2
replacement of 21.5–21.6
service standards *see* **service standards in Standard Crime Contracts 2022/2025**
standard terms 21.22

supervisor standards *see* **supervisor standards in the Standard Crime Contract 2022**
tender process 21.37
termination 1.54
website 1.57
Standard Crime Contract 2025 1.54–1.59, 14.1, 14.4, 14.206 *see also* **Standard Crime Contracts**
applications 21.34
costs appeals 23.50
Defence Solicitor Call Centre (DSCC) 22.110
duration 1.55, 21.34, 21.43
key changes 21.6
key performance indicators (KPIs) 22.96, 22.110, 23.23
new providers 21.8
offices, expansion of 21.34
police duty scheme 21.34
quality standards and performance monitoring 22.1–22.2
service standards *see* **service standards in Standard Crime Contracts 2022/2025**
signatures 21.13
Specifications 21.25–21.27
standard terms 21.23–21.24
supervisor standards 21.26
tenders 1.55, 21.41
website 157
Standard Crime Contracts 1.54–1.59
2022 *see* **Standard Crime Contract 2022**
2025 *see* **Standard Crime Contract 2025**
appeals 20.54
applications 21.42–21.43
billing and payment 16.73–16.76
contract compliance audits (CCAs) 23.38, 23.45
cuts to number of contracts 1.91
duty solicitor work 1.54
fees 1.59
own client work 1.54
police duty solicitor work 21.42

Standard Crime Contracts *continued*
   registration process 21.42
   regulations 1.57, 1.59
   Specification 1.57–1.58
   standard monthly payments (SMPs) 23.13
   tenders 21.42
   topping up fees 16.107
   variable monthly payments (VMPs) 23.10
standard fees
   Advocacy Assistance 20.59
   advocacy in family cases 19.9
   change of solicitor 10.42
   controlled work 10.19–10.23, 15.38
   criminal cases, billing and payment for 16.46–16.69
   immigration and asylum cases 9.42–9.44, 9.76, 9.79–9.80, 9.107, 9.113, 9.116, 9.125–9.127
   magistrates' court cases 20.30, 20.33 *see also* **magistrates' courts, billing and payment for standard fees in the**
   mental health cases, conducting 10.19–10.23, 10.34–10.42, 10.44–10.46
   representation certificates 4.128
standard monthly payments (SMPs) 15.37, 16.32, 16.78, 23.4, 23.7–23.10, 23.13
standards *see* **quality standards and performance monitoring; service standards in Standard Civil Contract 2024; service standards in Standard Crime Contracts 2022/2025; supervisor standards in the Standard Civil Contract 2024**
statements of case, drafting 5.24
statutory charge 1.26, 4.151, 4.158–4.184
   ADMIN form, reporting using the appropriate 4.178
   advocacy in civil cases 18.26
   amount 4.167
   bills of costs 4.168
   CCMS 4.172, 4.178
   damages 3.65, 4.166
   costs, repayment of 4.163
   enforcement 4.174–4.178
   Equality Act 2010 obligations to clients with disabilities 4.168
   escape fee cases 6.64
   eviction 11.40
   exempt property, list of 4.165
   Family Help (Lower) 6.57–6.67
   guidance 4.178
   Help at Court 6.63, 6.65
   housing conditions and disrepair 4.180–4.182, 11.51
   Human Rights Act 1998 claims in care and wardship proceedings 4.180, 4.183–4.184
   inquest exceptional case funding (ECF) 3.65
   instalments 4.177
   Land Registry, registration at the 4.176
   Legal Help 4.159–4.160, 6.62, 6.65
   mediation 4.158
   money, recovery of 4.169–4.172
   payment, method of 4.172
   preservation of property 4.158, 4.161–4.163, 4.173
   real property, exemption of 6.63
   recovery of property 4.158, 4.161–4.163, 4.173
   related proceedings 4.179–4.184
   representation certificates 4.151, 4.158–4.184
   settlement deeds in family cases 4.168
   solicitors, payment of all monies due to clients to 4.164
   third parties, recovery or preservation of property for 4.162
   waiver 4.174
statutory foundation 1.21–1.27
sufficient benefit test
   advice and assistance 14.67–14.68
   Advocacy Assistance 20.23, 20.57

criminal cases 14.67–14.68,
  14.186, 16.69
custody, clients detained in 20.10
Help with Family Mediation 6.72
Legal Help 4.29, 6.44, 7.17
police station work 14.29–14.31
pre-charge engagement, advice
  and assistance for 14.54
summary assessment of costs
  15.124, 15.130, 15.152
**supervisor standards in the
  Standard Civil Contract
  2024** 22.24–22.55
accreditation 22.36, 22.40, 22.43,
  22.52
caseworker hours 22.25-22.26,
  22.29, 22.48–22.51,
  22.54–22.55
category-specific standards
  22.34–22.55
clinical negligence 22.33,
  22.52–22.53
common rules 22.24–22.33
community care supervisors
  22.47
discrimination 22.33, 22.55
education 22.33, 22.54
external supervisors, authorising
  22.32
family cases 22.35–22.38
full-time equivalent (FTE) supervisors 22.25–22.32
guidance 22.29
housing and debt 22.46
immigration and asylum cases
  22.39–22.40
mental health 22.41–22.45
number of caseworkers supervised 22.31
part-time equivalent (PTE) supervisors 22.33, 22.49
portfolio of specified case types
  22.50–22.55
public authorities, claims against
  (CAPA) 22.33, 22.49–
  22.50
public law 22.33, 22.51, 22.55
Standard Crime Contract 2022
  22.56

Standard Crime Contract 2025
  22.62
welfare benefits 22.33, 22.48
who can be supervisors 22.30
**supervisor standards in the
  Standard Crime Contract
  2022** 22.56–22.61
accreditation 22.59
advocacy in the magistrates'
  courts, amount of work on
  22.141
appeals and reviews 22.61
caseworker hours 22.56, 22.139,
  22.141
designation of staff and work
  22.138, 22.140–22.141
duty solicitors 22.139
employees, supervisors as 22.58,
  22.139
full-time equivalent (FTE) supervisors 22.56
Law Society Criminal Litigation
  Accreditation Scheme
  (CLAS) 22.59
minimum amount of work 22.56
number of people supervised
  22.58, 22.60
Parole Board 22.60
police station work 22.59, 22.141
prison law work 22.58, 22.60
ratio of supervisors to other staff
  22.137
Standard Civil Contract 2024
  22.56
who can be supervisors 22.58
**supervisor standards in the
  Standard Crime Contract
  2025** 21.26, 22.62–22.71
advocacy in the magistrates'
  courts, amount of work on
  22.141
appeals and reviews 22.71
casework hours 22.63, 22.66,
  22.139, 22.141
designation of staff and work
  22.138, 22.140–22.141
duty solicitors 22.139
employees, supervisors as 22.64,
  22.139

supervisor standards in the Standard Crime Contract 2025 *continued*
full-time equivalent (FTE) supervisors 22.62
guidance 22.68, 22.139
Law Society Criminal Litigation Accreditation Scheme (CLAS) 22.69
magistrates' court representations and advocacy 22.69
maternity, sickness or compassionate leave 22.63, 22.139
number of offices supervised 22.65
Parole Board 22.70
part-time equivalent (PTE) supervisors 22.63
police station advice and assistance 22.69, 22.141
prison law work 22.63, 22.70
ratio of supervisors to other staff 22.68, 22.137
Standard Civil Contract 2024 22.62
standard terms 22.64
where supervision can be carried out 22.67
supervisors 1.71–1.77, 22.19–22.73
audits 23.36
Bill Supervisor 1.69, 5.27, 5.33
Case Management Supervisors 1.68, 1.73, 5.24, 5.44
casework hours 22.19–22.21
CCMS 1.71–1.77, 5.24, 5.26–5.27, 5.33
civil categories 22.20
criminal categories 22.21, 22.23
experience of case types, demonstration of 22.23
file reviews 22.72
Housing Loss Prevention Advice Service (HLPAS) 11.92
Immigration and Asylum Accreditation Scheme (IIAS) 22.22
key issues from recent audits 22.72

Law Society Criminal Litigation Accreditation Scheme (CLAS) 22.23
mental health cases, conducting 10.8, 10.11–10.13, 10.25
quality standards and performance monitoring 22.19–22.73
service standards 22.113, 22.115, 22.135–22.141
signatures 10.25
specialist panels, as members of 22.22
Standard Civil Contract 2024 10.11–10.13, 22.113, 22.115
Standard Crime Contract 2022 *see* **supervisor standards in the Standard Crime Contract 2022**
Standard Crime Contract 2025 *see* **supervisor standards in the Standard Crime Contract 2025**
technical legal competence 22.19–22.23
Supreme Court
assessment of inter partes costs 15.123
counsel, use of 18.33
immigration and asylum cases 9.48
recovery of defence costs orders (RDCO) 14.176
very expensive cases/special case work 4.226, 15.193

targeted file review (TFR) 23.25
technical difficulties *see* **errors and technical difficulties**
telephone services
advice and assistance 14.70
CCMS 5.53
Civil Legal Advice contracts 1.37, 21.2, 22.120
Criminal Defence Direct (CDD) 21.48
Defence Solicitor Call Centre (DSCC) 16.23, 22.110

homelessness 11.27, 11.31
LAA Customer Service Team by telephone, contacting 5.53
Legal Help 4.11, 4.21
police station work 14.19, 14.23, 14.25, 16.13–16.16, 16.21, 21.48
prison law work 22.146
service standards 22.145–22.146
tenders 21.38–21.42
award questionnaire 21.39
competitive element 21.40
eTendering portal 21.38
extension of existing contracts 21.32
face-to-face contracts 21.41
Housing Possession Court Duty Scheme (HPCDS), quashing of LAA's tender for 1.93
minimum requirements 21.41
processes 21.31
selection questionnaire 21.39–21.40
Standard Civil Contract 2024 21.35, 21.41
Standard Crime Contract 2022 21.37
Standard Crime Contract 2025 21.41
websites 21.31, 21.38, 21.49
Terrorism Prevention and Immigration Measures (TPIMs) 9.35
timetable/time limits *see under individual entries*
trafficking *see* **human trafficking, modern slavery, servitude or forced labour, victims of**
training and support (LAA) 1.67–1.87
CCMS 5.2–5.3, 5.16, 5.19, 5.34, 5.39, 5.96, 15.90
exceptional case funding (ECF) applications 5.76
peer review 22.78
promissory declarations 5.65, 5.68
Twitter/X, on 1.97
Very High Cost Cases (VHCC) 15.204
website 1.44, 1.47, 1.67

transfer cases *see* **change of solicitors**
travel and waiting time
advice and assistance 14.70
Advocacy Assistance 20.25
advocacy in civil cases 18.29
advocacy in family cases 19.13
bail 20.17
bolt-on payments (children cases) 19.51–19.52
CCMS 5.85, 19.52
counsel, use of 20.37
custody, clients detained in 20.12
destitute clients 15.28
detained clients, t0 9.108, 9.116
disbursements 14.11–14.12, 14.15, 15.21, 15.23, 15.28
duty solicitors 16.40–16.41
exceptional travel 19.51–19.52
experts 15.21, 15.23
Help at Court 4.69, 18.15, 18.22
Housing Loss Prevention Advice Service (HLPAS) 11.99
immigration and asylum cases, billing and payment for 15.220, 15.224
magistrates' court cases 16.49, 16.62, 20.32, 20.37
mental health cases, conducting 10.23
police station work 16.25
prison law work 14.195, 14.196
trespassers 11.8
Twitter/X 1.34, 1.97

unique file numbers (UFNs) 14.5–14.8, 14.118, 16.11, 16.34, 16.37, 20.38
unpaid fees
advocacy in civil cases 18.47–18.49
counsel, use of 18.47–18.49, 20.36
List of Defaulting Solicitors 18.48
magistrates' court cases, advocacy in 20.36
payments on account (POAs) 18.48
sanctions 18.49

unpaid fees *continued*
  Solicitors Regulation Authority (SRA), complaints to 18.48
  time limits 18.47, 18.49
up to date, keeping 1.30–1.36
Upper Tribunal (UT)
  counsel, use of 18.32–18.33, 18.36
  hourly rates 15.235
  immigration and asylum cases 9.46–9.47, 9.71, 9.80, 9.95, 9.119, 9.120–9.122, 9.128, 9.131, 15.234–15.236
  Legal Representation 10.18
  licensed work 15.216, 15.234
  mental health cases, conducting 10.18, 10.41
  permission to appeal 15.216, 15.234–15.236
  standard fees 10.41
urgent cases *see* **emergency delegated function applications; urgent cases (civil and family)**
urgent cases (civil and family) 4.189–4.201
  amendments 5.52–5.55
  backdating 4.190
  CCMS 4.120, 4.198, 5.24, 5.35–5.50, 5.55, 5.89
  certificates 6.113–6.117
  contributions 6.114
  costs
    estimates 4.195, 6.114
    opponents' costs after revocation, responsibility for 4.195
    protection 4.195
  duration of certificates 4.201
  emergency delegated functions *see* **emergency delegated function applications**
  emergency non-delegated function applications 5.46–5.50, 5.55
  exceptional case funding (ECF) 3.67–3.69
  forms 4.198–4.199
  funding 4.200–4.201

Independent Funding Adjudicators (IFAs) 17.25
  means test 4.192–4.195, 6.114
  merits test 4.196–4.197, 6.114
  previous advice, restrictions where clients have received 2.74
  representation certificates 4.117, 4.189–4.201
  revocation of certificates 4.193, 4.194–4.195
  scope 4.189–4.191
  service standards 22.142, 22.145
  time for processing ordinary applications 4.189
  time limits for receipt of substantive applications 4.199
  urgent, definition of 4.189
variable monthly payments (VMPs) 1.19, 15.37, 23.4–23.5, 23.8–23.10
very expensive cases/special case work (civil and family) 4.213–4.235
  assessment of inter partes costs by the courts 15.138
  Care Case Fee Scheme (CCFS) 4.220–4.221, 4.222
  CCMS 4.227–4.229
  community actions 4.226
  European Convention on Human Rights (ECHR), breach of 4.226
  Exceptional and Complex Case Team (ECCT) 4.215, 4.219
  family high cost cases *see* **Very High Cost Cases (VHCC) – family**
  final bills 15.60
  forms 4.227–4.229
  fully costed case plans, contents of 4.228–4.229
  funding 4.230–4.235
  guidance 4.223, 4.230
  hourly rates 4.232, 4.234–4.235
  individual case contracts 4.216
  King's Counsel and two-counsel cases 4.215, 4.222–4.223

means test 4.224
merits test 4.225–4.226
more than one set of proceedings or certificates as a single case, treatment of 4.218
multi-party actions (MPAs) 4.217, 4.224, 4.226
payments on account 4.221
registration of cases 4.227
scope 4.215–4.219
single counsel/advocate cases 4.215
special controls, cases subject to 4.226
Supreme Court, appeals to 4.226
types of cases 4.217–4.219
webinars 4.214
websites 4.227, 4.229, 4.230
very high cost cases *see* **very expensive cases/special case work (civil and family); Very High Cost Cases (VHCC) – criminal; Very High Cost Cases (VHCC) – family**
Very High Cost Cases (VHCC) – criminal 14.2, 14.210–14.213
billing and payment 16.104–16.105
Criminal Cases Unit (CCU) (LAA) 21.45
guidance 14.213
individual case contracts (ICCs) 14.211–14.212, 16.104
LAA National Courts Team, notification of the 14.211
websites 14.213, 16.105, 21.46
Very High Cost Cases (VHCC) – family 15.193–15.206
£25,000 threshold 15.193
assessment by LAA 15.206
billing and payment 15.193–15.206
Care Case Fee Scheme (CCFS) 4.220–4.221, 7.57, 15.193–15.195, 15.197, 15.201–15.205

case plans 15.194, 15.200–15.202, 15.205
CCMS 15.202–15.204
Children Act 1989 care cases 15.194
counsel, use of 15.195, 15.197–15.203
Covid-19, remote hearings during 15.199
event fees 15.194, 15.197–15.199
exceptional cases 15.194
Family Advocacy Scheme (FAS) 15.195, 15.199
fixed fees 15.197
guidance 15.196, 15.206
hourly rates 15.194
individual case contracts (ICCs) 15.193, 15.196
Information Packs 15.196, 15.200
licensed work 15.193–15.206
more than one party, representing 15.193
payments on account (POA) 15.203
pre-contract costs 15.193
Special Case Work requiring ICCs 15.193
Supreme Court, appeals to 15.193
training and support 15.204
Very High Cost case (VHCC) Family Team (South Tyneside) 4.215, 4.219
website 15.206

waiting time *see* **travel and waiting time**
wardship 6.7
warning letters 6.10, 6.84, 11.35, 11.61
webcam advice 4.11, 4.21
welfare benefits
appeals 2.7, 2.8
DWP, computer link with 14.102
exceptional case funding (ECF) 11.14
exclusions 2.7–2.8
housing benefit 2.7, 11.13–11.14
income 2.54

welfare benefits *continued*
  judicial review 11.14
  passported benefits *see* **passported benefits**
  possession of the home cases 11.13–11.14
  representation orders (magistrates' courts) 14.92, 14.94, 14.102
  service standards 22.131
  Social Entitlement Chamber of the FTT 2.8
  Standard Civil Contracts 2.14, 22.33, 22.48, 22.131
  supervisor standards 22.33, 22.48
  universal credit, exclusion of 2.7
witnesses 1.9, 14.17, 14.19, 15.25 *see also* **experts**

X/Twitter 1.34, 1.97

young people *see* **children and young people**